# The Complete Dead Sea Scrolls in English

GEZA VERMES

# The Complete Dead Sea Scrolls in English

ALLEN LANE
THE PENGUIN PRESS

ALLEN LANE
THE PENGUIN PRESS
Published by the Penguin Group
Penguin Putnam Inc., 375 Hudson Street,
New York, New York 10014, U.S.A.
Penguin Books Ltd, 27 Wrights Lane,
London W8 5TZ, England
Penguin Books Australia Ltd, Ringwood,
Victoria, Australia
Penguin Books Canada Ltd, 10 Alcorn Avenue,
Toronto, Ontario, Canada M4V 3B2
Penguin Books (N.Z.) Ltd, 182–190 Wairau Road,
Auckland 10, New Zealand

Penguin Books Ltd, Registered Offices:
Harmondsworth, Middlesex, England

This edition first published in the United States of America in 1997 by
Allen Lane The Penguin Press, a member of Penguin Putnam Inc.

1 3 5 7 9 10 8 6 4 2



The extracts on pages 95 and 241 are reproduced by kind permission of the Israel Museum, Jerusalem; the extracts on pages 333, 385, 393, 427, and 505 are reproduced by kind permission of the Israel Antiquities Authority; page 581: a cut segment from *The Copper Scroll* from *The Dead Sea Scrolls: A Reappraisal* by John Allegro (Penguin Books 1956, second edition 1990), copyright © John Allegro, 1956, 1964. Reproduced by permission of Penguin Books Ltd.

Maps drawn by Nigel Andrews

LIBRARY OF CONGRESS CATALOGING IN PUBLICATION DATA
Dead Sea scrolls. English
The complete Dead Sea scrolls in English /
[translated from the Hebrew and Aramaic and edited by] Géza Vermès.
p. cm.
Includes bibliographical references and index.
ISBN 0-7139-9131-3 (alk. paper)
I. Vermès, Géza, 1924– . II. Title.
BM487.A3V4 1997
296.1′55—dc21 97-3722

This book is printed on acid-free paper.
∞

Printed in the United States of America
Set in Adobe Janson

*For M and I with love*
*and in loving memory of P*

# *Contents*



## A. THE RULES

## B. HYMNS AND POEMS



## C. CALENDARS, LITURGIES AND PRAYERS

## D. APOCALYPTIC WORKS



## E. WISDOM LITERATURE

## F. BIBLE INTERPRETATION



## G. BIBLICALLY BASED APOCRYPHAL WORKS

## H. MISCELLANEA



## I. APPENDIX

# *Preface*

Fifty years ago a young Arab shepherd climbed into a cave in the Judaean desert and stumbled on the first Dead Sea Scrolls. For those of us who lived through the Qumran story from the beginning, the realization that all this happened half a century ago brings with it a melancholy feeling. The Scrolls are no longer a *recent* discovery as we used to refer to them, but over the years they have grown in significance and now the golden jubilee of the first manuscript find calls for celebration with joy and satisfaction. Following the 'revolution' which 'liberated' all the manuscripts in 1991 – until that moment a large portion of them was kept away from the public gaze – every interested person gained free access to the entire Qumran library. I eagerly seized the chance and set out to explore the whole collection. Today, after four and a half years of intense study, I feel confident that I can present the complete canvas of the Dead Sea Scrolls and disclose to the many interested readers the message of these ancient manuscripts about ancient Judaism and to a more limited extent about early Christianity.

In its successive editions this book has endeavoured to serve a dual audience of scholars and educated lay people. Over the years it has grown in size – it contained only 255 pages in 1962 – and I trust also in its grasp of the subject. While this translation does not claim to cover every fragment retrieved from the caves, it is complete in one sense: it offers in a readable form all the texts sufficiently well preserved to be understandable in English. In plain words, meaningless scraps or badly damaged manuscript sections are not inflicted on the reader. Those who wish to survey texts consisting only of broken lines, or of single letters and half-letters, should turn to the official series *Discoveries in the Judaean Desert*, in which every surviving detail is put on record.

In addition to the English rendering of the Hebrew and Aramaic texts found in the eleven Qumran caves, two inscribed potsherds (ostraca)

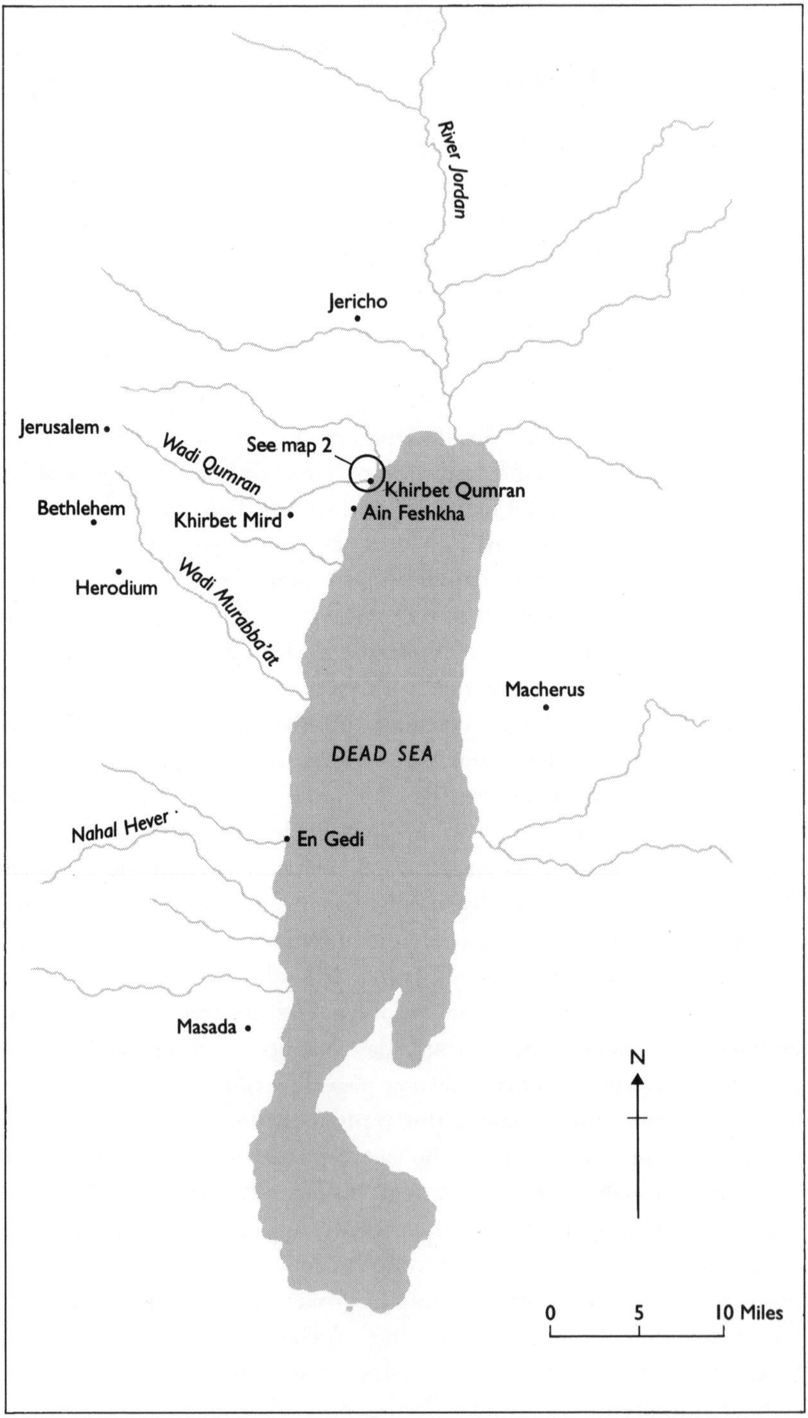


Map 1: The area surrounding the Dead Sea, showing Qumran

retrieved from the Qumran site and two Qumran-type documents discovered in the fortress of Masada, and brief introductory notes to each text, this volume also provides an up-to-date general introduction, outlining the history of fifty years of Scroll research and sketching the organization, history and religious message of the Qumran Community. A Scroll catalogue, an essential bibliography and an index of Qumran texts are appended to facilitate further study and research.

Has the greatly increased source material substantially altered our perception of the writings found at Qumran? I do not think so. Nuances and emphases have changed, but additional information has mainly helped to fill in gaps and clarify obscurities; it has not undermined our earlier conceptions regarding the Community and its ideas. We had the exceptionally good fortune that all but one of the major non-biblical Scrolls were published at the start, between 1950 and 1956: the Habakkuk Commentary (1950), the Community Rule (1951), the War Scroll and the Thanksgiving Hymns (1954/5) and the best-preserved columns of the Genesis Apocryphon (1956). Even the Temple Scroll, which had remained concealed until 1967 in a Bata shoebox by an antique dealer, was edited ten years later. The large Scrolls have served as foundation and pillars, and the thousands of fragments as building stones, with which the unique shrine of Jewish religion and culture that is Qumran is progressively restored to its ancient splendour.

Finally, it is a most pleasant duty to express my warmest thanks to friends and colleagues who helped to make this book less imperfect than it might otherwise have been. First and foremost, I wish publicly to convey my gratitude to Professor Emanuel Tov, editor-in-chief of the Dead Sea Scrolls Publication Project, for his generosity in answering queries and assisting in every possible way. My very special thanks are due also to Professor Joseph M. Baumgarten, who allowed me to consult his edition of the Damascus Document fragments from Cave 4 prior to their publication in *DJD*, and to my former pupil, Dr Jonathan G. Campbell, who did not shirk the onerous task of reading through and commenting on the rather bulky printout of this volume.

G.V.

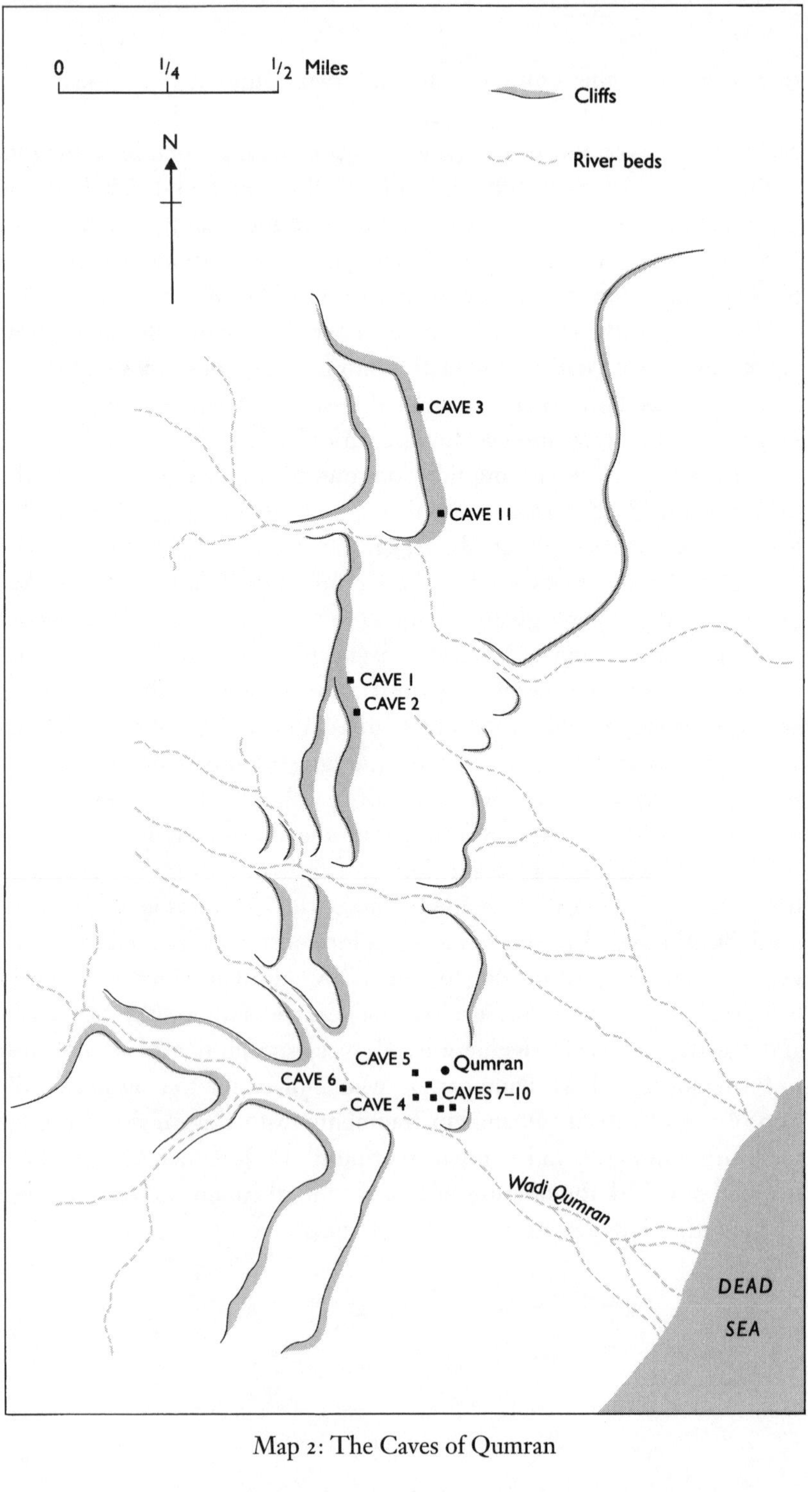


Map 2: The Caves of Qumran

# *Chronology*

| | |
|---|---|
| BCE 197 | Judaea became a province of the Seleucid Empire ruled by the Syrian successors of ALEXANDER THE GREAT. |
| 187–175 | SELEUCUS IV. Beginning of Hellenistic infiltration, resisted by the Zadokite High Priest ONIAS III. |
| 175–164 | ANTIOCHUS IV (EPIPHANES). ONIAS deposed and replaced by his Hellenophile brother JASON. |
| 172 | JASON expelled from office in favour of MENELAUS, Hellenizing High Priest from 172 to 162 BCE. |
| 171 | ONIAS III murdered at the instigation of MENELAUS. Forced Hellenization. |
| 169 | ANTIOCHUS led by MENELAUS profaned and plundered the Temple of Jerusalem. |
| 168 | ANTIOCHUS thwarted by the Romans in his second campaign against Egypt. |
| 167 | Persecution of those Jews who opposed the unification of the Seleucid Empire on the basis of Greek culture and religion. Official abolition of Jewish religion and practice under threat of death. The Temple transformed into a sanctuary of Olympian Zeus. |
| 166 | Rising of the Maccabees supported by all the traditional parties under the leadership of JUDAS MACCABEE. |
| 164 | Truce. Cleansing of the Temple, still held by MENELAUS. |
| 162–150 | DEMETRIUS I. MENELAUS executed by the Syrians. ALCIMUS appointed High Priest by the king. |
| 161 | JUDAS killed in battle. JONATHAN assumed leadership of the rebels (161–152 BCE). |

| | |
|---|---|
| 160 | ALCIMUS, the last Hellenizing High Priest, died of a stroke. End of Syrian military intervention. |
| 152–145 | ALEXANDER BALAS usurped the Seleucid throne and appointed JONATHAN High Priest (152–143/2 BCE). |
| 145–142 | ANTIOCHUS VI, son of ALEXANDER, raised to the throne by TRYPHON, his father's general. JONATHAN named governor of Syria. SIMON, his brother, made military governor of the Palestinian littoral. |
| 143 | JONATHAN arrested by TRYPHON. |
| 143/2–135/4 | SIMON High Priest and ethnarch. |
| 142 | JONATHAN executed in prison. |
| 140 | SIMON's titles confirmed as hereditary. Foundation of the Maccabaean, or Hasmonaean, dynasty. |
| 135/4 | SIMON murdered by his son-in-law. |
| 135/4–104 | JOHN HYRCANUS I High Priest and ethnarch. Opposed by the Pharisees. |
| 104–103 | ARISTOBULUS I High Priest and king. |
| 103–76 | ALEXANDER JANNAEUS High Priest, king, and conqueror. Resisted by the Pharisees. |
| 76–67 | ALEXANDRA, widow of JANNAEUS, queen. Friend of the Pharisees. HYRCANUS II High Priest. |
| 67 | HYRCANUS II king and High Priest. Deposed by his brother ARISTOBULUS. |
| 67–63 | ARISTOBULUS II king and High Priest. Taken prisoner by POMPEY in 63 BCE after the fall of Jerusalem. Judaea became a Roman province. |
| 63–40 | HYRCANUS II reinstated as High Priest without the royal title. |
| 40–37 | ANTIGONUS, son of ARISTOBULUS II, occupied the throne and pontificate with Parthian support. HYRCANUS maimed and exiled. |
| 37–4 | HEROD THE GREAT. End of Hasmonaean dynasty. HYRCANUS executed in 30 BCE. |
| 27–14 CE | AUGUSTUS emperor. |
| 6 BCE (?) | Birth of JESUS OF NAZARETH. |
| 4 BCE–6 CE | ARCHELAUS ethnarch of Judaea and Samaria. |
| 14–37 CE | TIBERIUS emperor. |
| 26–36 | PONTIUS PILATE prefect of Judaea. |
| 30 (?) | Crucifixion of JESUS. |

| | |
|---|---|
| 66–70 | First Jewish War ending with the capture of Jerusalem and the destruction of the Temple by TITUS. |
| 73/74 | Fall of Masada. |

# The Complete
# Dead Sea Scrolls
# in English

# *I. Introduction*

On the western shore of the Dead Sea, about eight miles south of Jericho, lies a complex of ruins known as Khirbet Qumran. It occupies one of the lowest parts of the earth, on the fringe of the hot and arid wastes of the Wilderness of Judaea, and is today, apart from occasional invasions by coachloads of tourists, lifeless, silent and empty. But from that place, members of an ancient Jewish religious community, whose centre it was, hurried out one day and in secrecy climbed the nearby cliffs in order to hide away in eleven caves their precious scrolls. No one came back to retrieve them, and there they remained undisturbed for almost 2,000 years.

The account of the discovery of the Dead Sea Scrolls, as the manuscripts are inaccurately designated, and of the half a century of intense research that followed, is in itself a fascinating as well as an exasperating story. It has been told many a time, but this fiftieth anniversary of the first Scroll find excuses, and even demands, yet another rehearsal.

## A BIRD'S-EYE VIEW OF FIFTY YEARS OF DEAD SEA SCROLLS RESEARCH

### *1. 1947–1967*

News of an extraordinary discovery of seven ancient Hebrew and Aramaic manuscripts began to spread in 1948 from Israeli and American sources.[1] The original chance find by a young Bedouin shepherd, Muhammad edh-Dhib, occurred during the last months of the British

1. E. L. Sukenik, *Megillot genuzot*, I, Jerusalem, 1948; W. F. Albright, *Bulletin of the American Schools for Oriental Research* 110 (April 1948), 1–3; G. E. Wright, 'A Sensational Discovery', *Biblical Archaeologist* (May 1948), 21–3.

mandate in Palestine in the spring or summer of 1947, unless it was slightly earlier, in the winter of 1946.[2] In 1949, the cave where the scrolls lay hidden was identified, thanks to the efforts of a bored Belgian army officer of the United Nations Armistice Observer Corps, Captain Philippe Lippens, assisted by a unit of Jordan's Arab Legion, commanded by Major-General Lash. It was investigated by G. Lankester Harding, the English Director of the Department of Antiquities of Jordan, and the French Dominican archaeologist and biblical scholar, Father Roland de Vaux. They retrieved hundreds of leather fragments, some large but most of them minute, in addition to the seven scrolls found in the same cave.

Three of the rolls, an incomplete Isaiah manuscript, a scroll of Hymns and one describing the War of the Sons of Light against the Sons of Darkness, were purchased in 1947 by the Hebrew University's Professor of Jewish Archaeology, E. L. Sukenik, who proceeded at full speed towards their publication. The other four were entrusted for study and eventual publication by their owner, the Arab metropolitan archbishop Mar Athanasius, head of the Syrian Orthodox monastery of St Mark in Jerusalem, to the resident staff of the American School for Oriental Research in Jerusalem, Millar Burrows, W. H. Brownlee and J. C. Trever. These three took charge of a complete Isaiah manuscript, the Commentary on Habakkuk and the Manual of Discipline, later renamed the Community Rule. Finally, after the splitting of British mandatary Palestine into Israel and Jordan, at the École Biblique et Archéologique Française in Jordanian Jerusalem two young researchers, the Frenchman Dominique Barthélemy and the Pole Józef Tadeusz Milik, were commissioned by de Vaux and Harding in late 1951 to edit the fragments collected in Cave 1.

Between 1951 and 1956, ten further caves were discovered, most of them by Bedouin in the first instance. Two yielded substantial quantities of material. Thousands and thousands of fragments were found in Cave 4 and several scrolls, including the longest, the Temple Scroll, were retrieved from Cave 11. The previously neglected ruins of a settlement in the proximity of the caves were also excavated by Harding and de Vaux, and the view soon prevailed that the texts, the caves and the Qumran site were interconnected, and that consequently the study of

2. Cf. the interview with the discoverer reported by John C. Trever, *The Dead Sea Scrolls: A Personal Account*, Grand Rapids, 1979, 191–4.

the script and contents of the manuscripts should be accompanied by archaeological research.

Progress was surprisingly quick despite the fact that in those halcyon days, apart from the small Nash papyrus, containing the Ten Commandments, found in Egypt and now in the Cambridge University Library, no Hebrew documents dating to Late Antiquity were extant to provide terms of comparison. In 1948 and 1949, Sukenik published in Hebrew two preliminary surveys entitled *Hidden Scrolls from the Judaean Desert* (1948, 1949), and concluded that the religious community involved was the ascetic sect of the Essenes, well known from the first-century CE writings of Philo, Josephus and Pliny the Elder, a thesis worked out in great detail from 1951 onwards by André Dupont-Sommer in Paris.[3] The first Qumran scrolls to reach the public, and the archaeological setting in which they were discovered, echoed three striking Essene characteristics. The Community Rule, a basic code of sectarian existence, reflects Essene common ownership and celibate life, while the geographical location of Qumran tallies with Pliny's Essene settlement on the north-western shore of the Dead Sea, south of Jericho. The principal novelty provided by the manuscripts consists of cryptic allusions to the historical origins of the Community, launched by a priest called the Teacher of Righteousness, who was persecuted by a Jewish ruler, designated as the Wicked Priest. The Teacher and his followers were compelled to withdraw into the desert, where they awaited the impending manifestation of God's triumph over evil and darkness in the end of days, which had already begun.

An almost unanimous agreement soon emerged, dating the discovery, on the basis of palaeography and archaeology, to the last centuries of the Second Temple, i.e. second century BCE to first century CE. For a short while there was controversy between de Vaux, who decreed that the pottery and all the finds belonged to the Hellenistic era (i.e. pre-63 BCE), and Dupont-Sommer, who argued for an early Roman (post-63) date. But the finding of further caves and the excavation of the ruins of Qumran brought about, on 4 April 1952, de Vaux's dramatic retraction before the French Académie des Inscriptions et Belles-Lettres. His

3. Cf. *Observations sur le Manuel de discipline découvert près de la Mer Morte*, Paris, 1951. His major synthesis in English is *The Essene Writings from Qumran*, Oxford, 1961. For the latest survey, see G. Vermes and Martin Goodman, *The Essenes According to the Classical Sources*, Sheffield, 1989.

revised archaeological synthesis, presented in the 1959 Schweich Lectures of the British Academy, while admittedly incomplete, is still the best comprehensive statement available today.[4]

A third point of early consensus concerns the chronology of the events alluded to in the Qumran writings, especially the biblical commentaries published in the 1950s and the Damascus Document. The so-called Maccabaean theory, placing the conflict between the Teacher of Righteousness and the politico-religious Jewish leadership of the day, in the time of the Maccabaean high priest or high priests, Jonathan and/or Simon, was first formulated in my 1952 doctoral dissertation, published in 1953,[5] and was soon to be adopted with variations in detail by such leading specialists as J. T. Milik, F. M. Cross and R. de Vaux.[6]

As long as the editorial task consisted only of publishing the seven scrolls from Cave 1, work was advancing remarkably fast. Millar Burrows and his colleagues published their three manuscripts in 1950 and 1951.[7] Sukenik's three texts appeared in a posthumous volume in 1954–5.[8] In the interest of speed, these editors generously abstained from translating and interpreting the texts, and were content with releasing the photographs and their transcription. The best-preserved sections of the Aramaic Genesis Apocryphon followed closely in 1956.[9] Even the fragments from Cave 1, handled with alacrity and loving care by Barthélemy and Milik, appeared in 1955.[10] The secrecy rule of later years, restricting access to unpublished texts to a small team of editors appointed by de Vaux, had not yet been applied. On my first visit to Jerusalem in 1952, I was allowed to examine the fragments of the Rule of the Congregation (1QSa), as may be seen from the inclusion in the final edition of a reading suggested by me to the editors.

4. *Archaeology and the Dead Sea Scrolls*, Oxford, 1973.

5. *Les Manuscrits du désert de Juda*, Tournai and Paris, 1953; *Discovery in the Judean Desert*, New York, 1956.

6. J. T. Milik, *Dix ans de découvertes dans le désert de Juda*, Paris, 1957 (English translation: *Ten Years of Discovery in the Wilderness of Judaea*, London, 1959); F. M. Cross, *The Ancient Library of Qumran and Modern Biblical Studies*, New York, 1958; R. de Vaux, op. cit. (in note 4 above).

7. *The Dead Sea Scrolls of St Mark's Monastery*, I, New Haven, 1950; II/2, New Haven, 1951.

8. *The Dead Sea Scrolls of the Hebrew University*, Jerusalem, 1954–5.

9. N. Avigad and Y. Yadin, *A Genesis Apocryphon*, Jerusalem, 1956. See now J. C. Greenfield and E. Qimron, 'The Genesis Apocryphon Col. XII', in *Studies in Qumran Aramaic*, edited by T. Muraoka (*Abr-Nahrain* Suppl. I), Louvain, 1992, 70–77.

10. *Discoveries in the Judaean Desert*, I: *Qumran Cave 1*, Oxford, 1955.

The scroll fragments, partly found by the archaeologists, but mostly purchased from the Arabs, who nine times out of ten outwitted their professional rivals, were cleaned, sorted out and displayed in the so-called Scrollery in the Rockefeller Museum, later renamed the Palestine Archaeological Museum, to become after 1967 once more the Rockefeller Museum. If the mass of material disgorged by Cave 4 had not upset the original arrangements, the scandalous delays in publishing in later years need never have happened.

To deal with Cave 4, Father de Vaux improvised, in 1953 and 1954, a team of seven on the whole young and untried scholars. Barthélemy opted out, and the brilliant but unpredictable Abbé J. T. Milik, who later left the Roman Catholic priesthood, became the pillar of the new group. He was joined by the French Abbé Jean Starcky, and two Americans, Monsignor Patrick Skehan and Frank Moore Cross. John Marco Allegro and John Strugnell were recruited from Britain, and from Germany, Claus-Hunno Hunzinger, who soon resigned and was replaced later by the French Abbé Maurice Baillet.

It should have been evident to anyone with a modicum of good sense that a group of seven editors, of whom only two, Starcky and Skehan, had already established a scholarly reputation, was insufficient to perform such an enormous task on any level, let alone to produce the kind of 'last word' edition de Vaux appears to have contemplated. The second serious error committed by de Vaux was that he wholly relied on his personal, quasi-patriarchal authority, instead of setting up from the start a supervisory body empowered, if necessary, to sack those members of the team who might fail to fulfil their obligations promptly and to everyone's satisfaction.

Yet before depicting the chaos characterizing the publishing process in the 1970s and 1980s, in fairness it should be stressed that, during the first decade or so, the industry of the group could not seriously be faulted. Judging from the completion around 1960 of a primitive Concordance, recorded on handwritten index cards, of all the words appearing in the fragments found in Caves 2 to 10, it is clear that at an early date most of the texts had been identified and deciphered. The many criticisms advanced in subsequent years, focusing on these scholars' refusal to put their valuable findings into the public domain, should not prevent one from acknowledging that this original achievement, in which J. T. Milik had the lion's share, deserves unrestricted admiration.

After the publication of the Cave 1 fragments in 1955, the contents of the eight minor caves (2–3, 5–10) were released in a single volume in 1963.[11] In 1965, J. A. Sanders, an American scholar who was not part of the original team, edited the Psalms Scroll, found in Cave 11 in 1956.[12] Finally, with its typescript completed and dispatched to the printers a year before the fatal date of 1967, the first poorly edited volume of Cave 4 fragments saw the light of day in 1968.[13]

## 2. *1967–1990*

With the occupation of East Jerusalem in the Six Day War, all the scroll fragments housed in the Palestine Archaeological Museum came under the control of the Israel Department of Antiquities. Only the Copper Scroll and a few other fragments exhibited in Amman remained in Jordanian hands. The Temple Scroll, which until then had been held by a dealer in Bethlehem,[14] was quickly retrieved with the help of army intelligence and acquired by the State of Israel. Yigael Yadin, deputy prime minister of Israel in the 1970s, mixing politics with scholarship, managed to complete a magisterial three-volume publication by 1977.[15] A gentlemanly gesture on the part of the Israelis, who decided not to interfere with de Vaux, left him and his scattered troup in charge of the Cave 4 texts.[16] As for the unpublished manuscripts from Cave 11, they were handled by Dutch and American academics.[17]

Father de Vaux, whose anti-Israeli sentiments were no secret, quietly

11. M. Baillet, J. T. Milik and R. de Vaux, *Discoveries in the Judaean Desert of Jordan*, III: *Les petites grottes de Qumrân*, Oxford, 1963.

12. J. A. Sanders, *Discoveries in the Judaean Desert of Jordan*, IV: *The Psalms Scroll from Qumran Cave 11 (11QPs^a)*, Oxford, 1965.

13. J. M. Allegro and A. A. Anderson, *Discoveries in the Judaean Desert of Jordan*, V: *I (4Q158–186)*, Oxford, 1968. A re-edition of this volume by George J. Brooke is planned.

14. Khalil Iskandar Sahin, familiarly known as Kando, a cobbler cum antique dealer, had been the principal middle man between the Bedouin discoverers of thousands of fragments and Roland de Vaux in the 1950s.

15. *Megillat ha-Miqdash I–III*, Jerusalem, 1977 (English translation: *The Temple Scroll I–III*, Jerusalem, 1983). See also E. Qimron, *The Temple Scroll: A Critical Edition with Extensive Reconstructions*, Beer-Sheva/Jerusalem, 1996.

16. Members of the original editorial team spent a great deal of time working in Jerusalem in the 1950s, but were subsequently disbanded, most of them occupying full-time teaching posts in Britain, France and the United States.

17. J. P. M. van der Ploeg, A. S. van der Woude and B. Jongeling, *Le Targum de Job de la grotte XI de Qumrân*, Leiden, 1971; D. N. Freedman and K. A. Matthews, *The Paleo-Hebrew Leviticus Scroll (11QpaleoLev)*, Winona Lake, 1985.

withdrew to his tent and remained inactive until his death in 1971. Another French Dominican, Pierre Benoit, succeeded him as it were by natural selection in the editorial chair in 1972. The Israeli archaeological establishment, still aloof, conferred its blessing on him. By then, at my instigation, C. H. Roberts, Secretary to the Delegates, i.e. chief executive of Oxford University Press, decided to demand speedier publication, but Benoit's ineffectual rallying call either elicited no response from his men, or produced promises which were never honoured.[18] In a lecture delivered in 1977, I coined the phrase which was thereafter often repeated that the greatest Hebrew manuscript discovery was fast becoming 'the academic scandal *par excellence* of the twentieth century'.[19]

One may ask how and why, after such an apparently propitious beginning, a group of scholars, most of whom were gifted, had turned the editorial work on the Scrolls into such a lamentable story? In my opinion, the 'academic scandal of the century' resulted from a concatenation of causes. Lack of organization and unfortunate choice of collaborators can be blamed on de Vaux. For the majority of the team members who had other jobs to cope with, the overlong part-time effort caused their original enthusiasm to fade and vanish. J. T. Milik, the most productive of them until the mid-seventies, appears to have been disenchanted by the cool reception of his highly speculative thesis contained in his edition of *The Books of Enoch: Aramaic Fragments of Qumran Cave 4* (1976). 'Academic imperialism' was also a factor. It was easier to hold that 'These texts belong to us, not to you!' than to admit that the procrastinating editors had undertaken more than they could deliver. Add to this the initial unwillingness of the Israelis to shoulder their responsibilities, and, as will be shown, their lack of foresight and repeated misjudgements before, finally, in the late 1980s, they began to take an active part in matters of editorial policy. Need I say more?

The inevitable began to happen: in 1980 Patrick Skehan died, followed by Jean Starcky in 1986, both without publishing their assignments. Eugene Ulrich and Emile Puech became their heirs, while F. M. Cross and J. Strugnell distributed portions of their texts to serve as dissertation

**18.** In the 1970s, only J. T. Milik remained productive – *The Books of Enoch: Aramaic Fragments of Qumran Cave 4*, Oxford, 1976; *Discoveries in the Judaean Desert*, VI: (*4Q128–57*), Oxford, 1977 – before he, too, entered a state of hibernation. By 1991, he was persuaded to relinquish all his unpublished documents, which were re-assigned to new editors.

**19.** *The Dead Sea Scrolls: Qumran in Perspective*, London, 1977, 24 (originally the 1977 Margaret Harris Lectures delivered at the University of Dundee).

topics for doctoral students at Harvard University. Though responsible for some good, and occasionally excellent, monographs, this unfortunate practice further delayed progress as thesis writers like to keep their cards close to their chests until their PhDs are in the bag.

In 1986, a year before his death, Pierre Benoit resigned as editor-in-chief and the depleted international team elected as his successor the talented but tardy John Strugnell, who in thirty-three years failed to produce a single volume of text. In 1987, at a public session of a Scrolls Symposium held in London, I urged him to publish at once the photographic plates, while he and his acolytes carried on with their work at their customary snail pace. This request was met with a one-syllable negative answer. To the surprise of many, the Israel Antiquities Authority (or IAA) acquiesced in Strugnell's appointment. His grandiose schemes never bore fruit. In 1990, after a compromising interview given by him to an Israeli newspaper, in which he was reported as having made disparaging remarks not only about Israelis, but also about the Jewish religion – he called it horrible – his fellow editors persuaded him to tender his resignation. It was accepted by the IAA on health grounds. Belatedly even the Israelis saw the light, and *de facto* terminated the thirty-seven-year-old and ultimately disastrous reign of the international team.

## *3. 1990–1996*

After John Strugnell's withdrawal, the very capable Emanuel Tov, Professor of Biblical Studies at the Hebrew University, was appointed chief editor, the first Jew and the first Israeli to head the Qumran publication project. He began his activities auspiciously by redistributing the unpublished texts among freshly recruited collaborators. The new editorial team, of which I became a member in 1991, consists of some sixty scholars compared to the original seven! Unfortunately, Tov did not feel free to cancel the 'secrecy rule', introduced and strictly enforced by de Vaux and his successors, prohibiting access to unpublished texts to all but a few chosen editors. However, the protective dam erected around the fragments by the international team collapsed in the autumn of 1991 under the growing pressure of public opinion, mobilized in particular by Hershel Shanks, in the columns of the widely read *Biblical Archaeology Review* (*BAR*). The first landmark event leading towards full freedom was the publication in early September by *BAR*'s parent body, the Biblical Archaeology Society, of seventeen Cave 4 manuscripts reconstructed with the help of a computer by Ben Zion Wacholder and Martin Abegg[20] from the Preliminary Concordance, alluded to earlier, which was privately issued in twenty-five copies (in theory only for the use of the official editors) by John Strugnell in 1988.[21] Later in the same month out of the blue came the announcement by William A. Moffett that the Huntington Library of San Marino, California, a renowned research institution, would bring to an end the forty-year-old closed shop by opening its complete photographic archive of the Qumran Scrolls to all qualified scholars.[22]

The IAA and the official editors attempted to resist but, by the end of October, under pressure from the Knesset, Israel's parliament, they were all forced to recognize that the battle was lost and all restrictions had to be lifted. Almost at once, the Scroll photograph archives at the Oxford Centre for Postgraduate Hebrew Studies and at the Ancient Biblical Manuscript Center at Claremont, previously legally compelled to restrict access only to persons approved by Jerusalem, were also thrown open to all competent research scholars. Moreover, in November 1991 the Biblical Archaeology Society published a two-volume photographic edition of the bulk of the Qumran fragments compiled by Robert Eisenman and

20. *A Preliminary Edition of the Unpublished Dead Sea Scrolls: The Hebrew and Aramaic Texts from Cave 4*, Biblical Archaeology Society, Washington, 1991. Two further volumes appeared in 1992 and 1995.

21. *A Preliminary Concordance to the Hebrew and Aramaic Fragments from Qumran Caves II to X* (distributed by H. Stegemann, Göttingen, 1988).

22. The following brief account of the Huntington Library's involvement with the Dead Sea Scrolls is based on documentary evidence kindly provided by its President, Robert A. Skotheim. In 1982, Elizabeth Hay Bechtel, a renowned Californian philanthropist and Scroll Maecenas, deposited at the Huntington a set of negatives of Qumran manuscripts. These had been taken in 1980 by Robert Schlosser, the chief photographer of the library, for whom Mrs Bechtel obtained permission from the Jerusalem Department of Antiquities to photograph all the Dead Sea Scrolls. Two series of pictures were produced, one for the Ancient Biblical Manuscript Center founded by Mrs Bechtel in Claremont, California, and another for herself. The latter ended up in a 'climatized' vault specially constructed at the Huntington with the help of a Bechtel grant of $50,000. In 1986, a year before her death, Mrs Bechtel donated her Scroll photographs to the Huntington. Paragraph 9 of the agreement made in April 1982 specifies that materials on which no restrictive policy is applied by Mrs Bechtel 'will be made available to use by scholars in accordance with the Huntington's general policies for its own materials'. No such restriction was ever conveyed by her to the trustees of the library. Bill Moffett became director of the Library in 1990. It was on the basis of clause 9 of the agreement that he proposed to the trustees the opening of the Huntington's Qumran photographs to all qualified users of the library.

Bill Moffett, the 'liberator of the Scrolls', died on 20 February 1995 at the age of sixty-two.

James Robinson.[23] How the two Californian professors obtained the material remains unclear. This new policy has had an essentially beneficial effect on Qumran studies. Since vested interests are no longer protected, the rate of publication has noticeably accelerated and from 1992 learned periodicals have been flooded with short or not so short papers by scholars claiming fresh insights. Free competition has expedited the official edition itself. The first Cave 4 volume of biblical texts, announced as imminent by Father Benoit in 1983, actually appeared – *pace* the 1992 date on the cover page – on 4 March 1993.[24] Scholarship and the general public were to become the beneficiaries of the new era of liberty. Only the procrastinators and the selfish stood to lose. By 1996, thanks to the highly efficient stewardship of the editor-in-chief, Emanuel Tov, four further volumes have been published and another four are in the pipeline. Compared with the output of the previous regime, this is an admirable change indeed.

## THE PRESENT STATE OF DEAD SEA SCROLLS STUDIES

Between 1947 and 1956, the eleven Qumran caves yielded a dozen scrolls written on leather and one embossed on copper. To these we have to add fragments on papyrus or leather, the precise number of which is unknown but probably in the order of six figures. About 800 original documents are fully or partly represented. The Cave 4 list alone contains 575 titles,[25] though it seems that some twenty documents (4Q**342–61**) probably originating from non-Qumran Judaean desert locations were mistakenly catalogued as 4Q material. Most scrolls are written in Hebrew, a smaller portion in Aramaic and only a few attest the ancient Greek or Septuagint version of the Bible.[26]

Among the texts previously known, all the books of the Hebrew

**23**. Robert H. Eisenman and James M. Robinson, *A Facsimile Edition of the Dead Sea Scrolls*, I–II, Washington, 1991. The quality of many of these pictures leaves much to be desired, but others are serviceable.

**24**. Patrick W. Skehan, Eugene Ulrich and Judith E. Sanderson, *Discoveries in the Judaean Desert*, IX: *Qumran Cave 4, IV, Palaeo-Hebrew and Greek Biblical Manuscripts*, Oxford, 1992.

**25**. Cf. Emanuel Tov, 'The Unpublished Qumran Texts from Caves 4 and 11', *JJS* 43 (1992), 101–36.

**26**. The claim that several minute Greek scraps from Cave 7 represent the New Testament is unsubstantiated. Cf. below, pp. 440–41.

Scriptures are extant at least in fragments save Esther, the absence of which may be purely accidental.[27] Even Daniel, the most recent work to enter the Palestinian canon in the mid-second century BCE, is attested to by eight manuscripts.[28] There are also remains of Aramaic and Greek scriptural translations.

Furthermore, the caves have yielded some of the Apocrypha, i.e. religious works missing from the Hebrew Scriptures but included in the Septuagint, the Bible of Greek-speaking Jews. Caves 4 and 11 revealed the Book of Tobit in Aramaic and in Hebrew, Psalm cli, described in the Greek version as a 'supernumerary' psalm, and the Wisdom of Jesus ben Sira or Ecclesiasticus in Hebrew. Part of the latter, chapters xxxix–xliv, has also survived at Masada, and hence cannot be later than 73/4 CE, the date when the stronghold was captured by the Romans, and two medieval manuscripts, discovered in the storeroom (*genizah*) of a synagogue in Cairo in 1896, have preserved about two thirds of the Greek version.

A third category of religious books, the Pseudepigrapha, though very popular in some Jewish circles, failed to attain canonical rank either in Palestine or in the Diaspora. Some of them, previously known in Greek, Latin or Syriac translations, have turned up in their original Hebrew (e.g. the Book of Jubilees) or Aramaic (e.g. the Book of Enoch). A good many further compositions pertaining to this class have also come to light, such as fictional accounts relating among others to Joseph, Amram, Moses, Joshua or Jeremiah, as well as apocryphal psalms, five of which have survived also in Syriac translation, others being revealed for the first time at Qumran.

The sectarian Dead Sea Scrolls, thought to have been composed or revised by the Qumran Community, constitute, with one exception,[29] a complete novelty. This literature comprises rule books, Bible interpretation of various kinds, religious poetry, Wisdom compositions in prose and in verse, sectarian calendars and liturgical texts, one of them purporting to echo the angelic worship in the heavenly temple. To these are

**27.** It is suggested that the Aramaic fragments of 4Q550 derive from a proto-Esther.

**28.** 4Q242–6 testify to the existence of a non-canonical Daniel cycle.

**29.** The exception is the Damascus Document, well attested in Caves 4, 5 and 6, but previously known from two incomplete medieval manuscripts found in the Cairo Genizah, and first published by S. Schechter as *Documents of Jewish Sectaries*, I: *Fragments of a Zadokite Work*, Cambridge, 1910; repr. with a Prolegomenon by J. A. Fitzmyer (Ktav, 1970). For a better edition see Magen Broshi, *The Damascus Document Reconsidered*, Jerusalem, 1992.

to be added several 'horoscopes' or, more precisely, documents of astrological physiognomy, a literary genre based on the belief that the temper, physical features and fate of an individual depend on the configuration of the heavens at the time of the person's birth, and a text (*brontologion*) predicting prodigies if thunder is heard on certain days, with the moon passing through given signs of the Zodiac. Finally, the Copper Scroll alludes in cryptic language to sixty-four caches of precious metals and scrolls, including another copy of this same inventory written without riddles.

After a first few gaffes committed before the excavation of the site, the palaeographical, archaeological and literary-historical study of the evidence produced a general consensus among scholars concerning (*a*) the age, (*b*) the provenance and (*c*) the significance of the discoveries. Holders of fringe opinions have recently tended to explain this consensus as tyrannically imposed from above by Roland de Vaux and his henchmen. The truth, however, is that the *opinio communis* has resulted from a natural evolutionary process – from arguments which others found persuasive even when advanced by single individuals often unconnected with the international team – and not from an almighty establishment forcing an official view down the throats of weaklings.

## (*a*) *The Dating of the Manuscripts*

Palaeography was the first method employed to establish the age of the texts. Despite the paucity of comparative material, experts independently arrived at dates ranging between the second century BCE and the first century CE. By the 1960s, in addition to the Qumran texts, they could make use also of manuscripts from Masada (first century CE), as well as from the Murabba'at and other Judaean desert caves yielding first- and second-century CE Jewish writings. A rather too rigid, but useful, comprehensive system was quickly devised by F. M. Cross.[30] While admittedly controversial if unsupported either by actual dates in the manuscripts themselves (a phenomenon, alas, unknown at Qumran) or by external criteria, these palaeographical conclusions were to receive a twofold boost from archaeology and radiocarbon dating. The archaeological thesis, based *inter alia* on the study of pottery and coins, was formulated by

30. 'The Development of the Jewish Scripts', in *The Bible and the Ancient Near East: Essays in Honor of W. F. Albright*, Garden City, NY, 1961, 133–202.

R. de Vaux (cf. note 4 on p. 4). He assigned the occupation of Qumran to the period between the second half of the second century BCE and the first war between Jews and Romans (66–70 CE).

Radiocarbon tests were first applied to the cloth wrapping of one of the scrolls as early as 1951. The date suggested was 33 CE, but one had to reckon with a 10 per cent margin of error each way.[31] However, with the improved techniques of the 1990s, eight Qumran manuscripts were subjected to Accelerator Mass Spectrometry or AMS. Six of them were found to be definitely pre-Christian, and only two straddled over the first century BCE/first century CE dividing line.[32] Most importantly, with a single exception – the Testament of Qahat being shown to be about 300 years earlier than expected – the radiocarbon dates confirm in substance those proposed by the palaeographers. Unfortunately, the manuscripts tested in 1990 did not include historically sensitive texts. But in 1994 the IAA invited the Arizona AMS Laboratory at the University of Arizona, Tucson to analyse eighteen texts and two linen fragments. Thirteen of the manuscripts came definitely from Qumran and one of these had already been carbon-dated in Zurich. Three texts were 'date-bearing'. The general conclusion is as follows: 'Measurements on samples of known ages are in good agreement with those known ages. Ages determined from $^{14}C$ measurements on the remainder of the Dead Sea Scroll samples are in reasonable agreement with paleographic estimates of such ages, in the case where those estimates are available.'[33] On the whole, the results of this second radiocarbon analysis are somewhat disappointing in that, while the dates arrived at accommodate the palaeographic proposals, the margin of error is considerably greater than that appearing in the 1990 Zurich tests. Nevertheless, Arizona has scored on one highly significant point: the Habakkuk Commentary, chief source of the history of the Qumran sect, is definitely put in the pre-Christian era between 120 and 5 BCE. In consequence, fringe scholars who see in this writing allusions to events described in the New Testament will find they have a problem on their hands. In sum, the general scholarly view today places the Qumran Scrolls roughly between 200 BCE and 70 CE, with a small portion of the texts

31. Cf. O. R. Sellers, 'Radiocarbon Dating of Cloth from the 'Ain Feshkha Cave', *BASOR* 123 (1951), 22–4.

32. G. Bonani et al., 'Radiocarbon Dating of the Dead Sea Scrolls', *'Atiqot* 20 (1991), 25–32.

33. A. J. T. Jull et al., 'Radiocarbon Dating of Scrolls and Linen Fragments from the Judean Desert', *Radiocarbon* 37 (1995), 11–19. The quotation appears on p. 17.

possibly stretching back to the third century BCE, and the bulk of the extant material dating to the first century BCE, i.e. late Hasmonaean or early Herodian in the jargon of the palaeographers.

### (b) *The Provenance of the Manuscripts*

With negligible exceptions, scholarly opinion recognized already in the 1950s that the Scrolls found in the caves and the nearby ruined settlement were related. To take the obvious example, Cave 4 with its 575 (or perhaps 555) documents lies literally within a stone's throw from the buildings. At the same time, the Essene identity of the ancient inhabitants of Qumran gained general acceptance. Today the Essene theory is questioned by some, but usually for unsound reasons. They adopt a simplistic attitude in comparing the two sets of evidence, namely the classical sources (Philo, Josephus and Pliny the Elder) and Qumran, and any disagreement or contradiction between them is hailed as final proof against the Essene thesis. Yet, if its intricacies are handled with sophistication, it is still the best hypothesis today.[34] Indeed, it accounts best for such striking peculiarities as common ownership of property and the lack of reference to women in the Community Rule, the probable co-existence of celibate and married sectaries (in accordance with Flavius Josephus' account of two kinds of Essenes), and the remarkable coincidence between the geographical setting of Qumran and Pliny the Elder's description of an Essene establishment near the Dead Sea between Jericho and Engedi. I admit of course that the Scrolls and the archaeological data surrounding them do not always fully agree with the Greek and Latin notices, and that both the Qumran and the classical accounts need to be interpreted and adjusted, bearing in mind that the Scrolls represent the views of initiates against those of more or less complete outsiders.[35] But since none of the competing theories associating the Qumran group with Pharisees, Sadducees, Zealots, or Jewish-Christians

34. Cf. most recently in *The Essenes According to the Classical Sources*, Sheffield, 1989, 12–23. The co-author of this volume, Martin Goodman, has recently questioned the use of the evidence by Josephus to prove the Essene identity of the sect, arguing that Josephus never presents a full picture of the Jewish scene of his time and that consequently he may have referred to a group merely similar to the Essenes. Cf. 'A Note on the Qumran Sectarians, the Essenes and Josephus', *JJS* 46 (1995), 161–6. Despite my admiration for his learning, I exceptionally beg to differ.

35. For a fuller argument, see below, pp. 46–8.

can withstand critical scrutiny, I remain unrepentant in upholding my statement formulated in 1977 as still valid today: 'The final verdict must . . . be that of the proposed solutions the Essene theory is relatively the soundest. It is even safe to say that it possesses a high degree of intrinsic probability.'[36]

### *(c) The Significance of the Qumran Scrolls*

The uniqueness of the Qumran discovery was due to the fact that with the possible exception of the Nash papyrus referred to earlier (p. 3), no Jewish text in Hebrew or Aramaic written on perishable material could previously be traced to the pre-Christian period. Before 1947, the oldest Hebrew text of the whole of Isaiah was the Ben Asher codex from Cairo dated to 895 CE, as against the complete Isaiah Scroll from Cave 1, which is about a millennium older. The Apocrypha and Pseudepigrapha, save the Hebrew Ben Sira and the Aramaic fragments of the Testament of Levi from the Cairo Genizah, had survived only in translation. The sectarian writings found in the caves, apart from the already mentioned Damascus Document (p. 11), count as a total novelty.

To begin with, the Qumran Scrolls and the other Judaean Desert finds have created a new discipline: ancient, i.e. pre-medieval, Hebrew *codicology*. We now possess concrete evidence that scribes carefully prepared the leather or papyrus on which they were to write, often ruling them, with vegetable ink, kept in ink-wells. Paragraphs and larger unit openings were indicated by symbols in the margins. Longer compositions were written on scrolls, on one side of the sheets only, some of them numbered, which were subsequently sewn together. Papyrus documents were often reused, with a different text inscribed on the verso. Short works such as letters were recorded on small pieces of writing material: leather, papyrus, wood or potsherd. By contrast, no book or codex, with pages covered with script on both sides and bound together, has come to light at Qumran, or in any other Judaean Desert site.

The Qumran finds have also substantially altered our views concerning the *text* and *canon of the Bible*. The many medieval Hebrew scriptural manuscripts, representing the traditional or Masoretic text, are remarkable for their almost general uniformity. Compared to the often meaningful divergences between the traditional Hebrew text and its ancient

**36**. G. Vermes, *The Dead Sea Scrolls: Qumran in Perspective*, London, 1994, 117.

Greek, Latin or Syriac translations, the few variant readings of the Masoretic Bible manuscripts, ignoring obvious scribal errors, mainly concern spelling. By contrast, the Qumran scriptural scrolls, and especially the fragments, are characterized by extreme fluidity: they often differ not just from the customary wording but also, when the same book is attested by several manuscripts, among themselves. In fact, some of the fragments echo what later became the Masoretic text; others resemble the Hebrew underlying the Greek Septuagint; yet others recall the Samaritan Torah or Pentateuch, the only part of the Bible which the Jews of Samaria accepted as Scripture. Some Qumran fragments represent a mixture of these, or something altogether different. It should be noted, however, that none of these variations affects the scriptural message itself. In short, while largely echoing the contents of biblical books, Qumran has opened an entirely new era in the textual history of the Hebrew Scriptures.[37]

The Community's attitude to the biblical canon, i.e. the list of books considered as Holy Writ, is less easy to define, as no such list of titles has survived. Canonical status may be presumed indirectly either from authoritative quotations or from theological commentary. As regards the latter, the caves have yielded various interpretative works on the Pentateuch (the Temple Scroll, reworked Pentateuch manuscripts, the Genesis Apocryphon and other commentaries on Genesis) and the Prophets (e.g. Isaiah, Habakkuk, Nahum, etc.), but only on the Psalms among the Writings, the third traditional division of the Jewish Bible. From the texts available in 1988, I collected over fifty examples of Bible citations which were used as proof in doctrinal expositions, thus indicating that they were thought to possess special religious or doctrinal importance.[38]

On the other hand, the Psalms Scroll from Cave 11 contains seven apocryphal poems, including chapter LI of the Wisdom of Jesus ben Sira, not annexed to, but interspersed among, the canonical hymns. This may be explained as a liturgical phenomenon, a collection of songs chanted during worship; but it may, and in my view probably does, mean that at Qumran the concept 'Bible' was still hazy, and the 'canon' open-ended, which would account for the remarkable freedom in the treatment of the

37. For a major restatement of the whole subject, see Emanuel Tov, *Textual Criticism of the Hebrew Bible*, Minneapolis–Assen/Maastricht, 1992.

38. Cf. 'Biblical Proof-texts in Qumran Literature', *JSS* 34 (1989), 493–508. It should be noted, however, that the Damascus Document quotes also the Book of Jubilees and a work attributed to the Patriarch Levi. It is unclear what their status was.

text of Scripture by a community whose life was nevertheless wholly centred on the Bible.

There are two Apocrypha attested at Qumran. In connection with Tobit one can note that four out of the five Cave 4 manuscripts are in Aramaic and only one in Hebrew, but they all reflect the longer version of the Greek Tobit. So the long-debated original language of this book is still uncertain, but Aramaic has become the likeliest candidate. On the other hand, the Hebrew poem from Ben Sira LI has a patently better chance of reflecting the original than either the Greek translation by the author's grandson, preserved in the Septuagint, or the Hebrew of the medieval Cairo Genizah manuscripts, because the Qumran version alone faithfully reflects the acrostic character of the composition with the lines starting with the successive letters of the Hebrew alphabet, *aleph*, *bet*, *gimel*, etc.

Qumran has also added to the Pseudepigrapha several new works dealing with biblical figures such as Joseph, Qahat, Amram, Moses, Joshua, Samuel. Among the works in this category which were previously known, the Aramaic fragments of Enoch deserve special mention because they appear to attest only four out of the five books of the Ethiopic Enoch.[39] Book 2 (i.e. chapters XXXVII–LXXII), which describes the heavenly apocalyptic figure called *son of man*, a subject on which New Testament scholars have wasted a considerable amount of ink without approaching even the vaguest consensus, is missing at Qumran. Thus the Aramaic Enoch does not support their speculations any more than do the Greek manuscripts, which are also without chapters XXXVII–LXXII of the Ethiopic Enoch.[40]

The contribution of the Scrolls to general *Jewish history* is negligible, and even to the *history of the Community* is fairly limited. The chief reason for this is that none of the non-biblical compositions found at Qumran belongs to the historical genre. The sectarian persons and events mentioned in the manuscripts are depicted in cryptic language as fulfilment of ancient prophecies relating to the last age. The chief sources of sectarian history, the Damascus Document and the Bible commentaries or *pesharim*, identify the Community's principal enemies as the kings of Yavan (Greece) and the rulers of the Kittim (Romans). Also, the Nahum

39. Cf. J. T. Milik, *The Books of Enoch: Aramaic Fragments of Qumran Cave 4*, Oxford, 1976.
40. Cf. E. Schürer, G. Vermes, F. Millar and M. Goodman, *The History of the Jewish People in the Age of Jesus Christ*, III, Edinburgh, 1986, 250–68.

Commentary's historical perspective extends from Antiochus (no doubt Epiphanes, *c.* 170 BCE) to the conquest by the Kittim (probably 63 BCE). Names familiar from Jewish or Graeco-Roman history appear here and there. The Nahum Commentary alludes to Antiochus, and to another Syrian Greek king, Demetrius (most likely Demetrius III at the beginning of the first century BCE). A very fragmentary historical calendar from Cave 4 contains the phrase 'Aemilius killed', meaning no doubt Aemilius Scaurus, governor of Syria at the time of Pompey's conquest of Jerusalem in 63. The same document mentions also Jewish rulers of the Maccabaean–Hasmonaean era (second–first centuries BCE), Shelamzion or Salome-Alexandra, widow and successor of Alexander Jannaeus (76–67 BCE); Hyrcanus and John (Yohanan), either John Hyrcanus I (135/4–104 BCE) or more likely II (63–40 BCE), and King Jonathan, Alexander Jannaeus or, in my opinion, more likely Jonathan Maccabaeus (161–143/2 BCE).[41] In one respect, despite the absence of detail, the evidence is telling: all these characters belong to the second or the first half of the first century BCE. So also do most of the coins discovered at Qumran.

The mainstream hypothesis, built on archaeology and literary analysis, sketches the history of the Scrolls Community (or *Essene* sect) as follows.[42] Its prehistory starts in Palestine – some claim also Babylonian antecedents – with the rise of the Hasidic movement, at the beginning of the second century BCE as described in the first book of the Maccabees (1 Mac. ii, 42–44; vii, 13–17). Sectarian (Essene) history itself originated in a clash between the Wicked Priest or Priests (Jonathan and/or possibly Simon Maccabaeus) and the Teacher of Righteousness, the anonymous priest who was the spiritual leader of the Community. The sect consisted of the survivors of the Hasidim, linked with a group of dissident priests who, by the mid-second century, came under the leadership of the sons of Zadok, associates of the Zadokite high priests. This history continues at Qumran, and no doubt in many other Palestinian localities, until the years of the first Jewish rebellion against Rome, when possibly in 68 CE the settlement is believed to have been occupied by Vespasian's soldiers. Whether the legionaries encountered sectarian resistance – such a theory would be consonant with Josephus' reference to an Essene general

**41**. Cf. 'Qumran Forum Miscellanea II: The so-called King Jonathan Fragment (4Q**448**)', *JJS* 44 (1993), 294–300.

**42**. For a more detailed exposition, see Chapter III below.

among the revolutionaries[43] and to a massacre of the Essenes by the Romans[44] – or whether the threatening presence of the contingents of Zealot Sicarii, who had already expelled the Essenes from Qumran, provoked a Roman intervention, are purely speculative matters. One fact is certain, however. No one of the original occupants of Qumran returned to the caves to reclaim their valuable manuscripts.

A variation on this theme, called the Groningen hypothesis, postulates a whole series of six Wicked Priests, and identifies the Community not with the main Essene sect but with one of its splinter groups.[45] The Zealot theory, elaborated in the 1950s in Oxford by Sir Godfrey Driver and Cecil Roth,[46] is hard to reconcile with the totality of the available evidence, as most of the Qumran documents predate the Zealot period.

More recently Norman Golb of Chicago has launched a forceful attack on the common opinion. His objections, reiterated in a series of papers,[47] culminated in 1995 in a hefty tome.[48] The target of his criticism is the provenance of the scrolls found at Qumran. According to him, the manuscripts originated in a Jerusalem library (or libraries), the contents of which were concealed in desert caves when the capital was besieged between 67 and 70 CE. The chief corollary of the hypothesis is that the

43. Cf. *War* II, 567; III, 11, 19.

44. Cf. *War* II, 152–3.

45. Cf. F. García Martínez, 'Qumran Origins and Early History: A Groningen Hypothesis', *Folia Orientalia* 25 (1988), 113–36; F. García Martínez and A. S. van der Woude, 'A Groningen Hypothesis of Qumran Origins and Early History', *RQ* 14 (1989–90), 521–42.

46. G. R. Driver, *The Judaean Scrolls: The Problem and a Solution*, Oxford, 1965; C. Roth, *The Historical Background of the Dead Sea Scrolls*, Oxford, 1958.

47. 'The Problem of Origin and Identification of the Dead Sea Scrolls', *Proceedings of the American Philosophical Society* 124/1 (1980), 1–24; 'Who Hid the Dead Sea Scrolls?', *BA* 48 (1982), 68–82; 'Khirbet Qumran and the Manuscripts of the Judaean Wilderness: Observations on the Logic of their Investigation', *JNES* 49 (1990), 103–14. For a criticism of the Golb thesis, see Timothy H. Lim, 'The Qumran Scrolls: Two Hypotheses', *Studies in Religion* 21/4 (1992), 455–66.

48. *Who Wrote the Dead Sea Scrolls? – The Search for the Meaning of the Qumran Manuscripts*, Scribner, New York/London, 1995. This volume repeats a completely misconceived attack on the Oxford Centre for Hebrew and Jewish Studies and on myself as director of the Centre's Forum for Qumran Research, although the facts misinterpreted by Professor Golb (first in *The Qumran Chronicle* 2/1, 1992, 3–25) have been set out correctly by G. Vermes and P. Alexander, 'Norman Golb and Modern History' (ibid., 2/2, 1993, 153–6, with a correction in the same periodical 4/1–2, 1994, 74).

Essenes had nothing to do either with the Qumran settlement – a fortress in Golb's opinion[49] – or with the manuscripts.

The early assumption of Scroll scholars that every non-biblical Dead Sea text was an Essene writing[50] might have justified to some extent Norman Golb's scepticism. But nowadays specialists distinguish between Qumran manuscripts written by members of the Essene sect, and others either predating the Community, or simply brought there from outside. Emanuel Tov, for instance, has drawn a dividing line on scribal grounds between scrolls produced at Qumran and the rest.[51] However, in my view the soft underbelly of the Jerusalem hypothesis is revealed – apart from the patent weakness of the archaeological interpretation, for Qumran is not a fortress – by the composition of the manuscript collection itself, definitely pointing towards a *sectarian* library. If Cave 4 is taken as representative, whereas several biblical books (Kings, Lamentations, Ezra and Chronicles) are attested only in *single* copies; and others, as important as Numbers, Joshua, Judges, Proverbs, Ruth and Ecclesiastes, in *two* copies, we find *ten* copies of the Community Rule and *nine* of the Damascus Document. Over a *dozen* manuscripts contain sectarian calendars, yet not one mainstream calendar figures among the 575 (or 555) compositions found in that cave! So, if the texts discovered at Qumran came from the capital, can their source have been an *Essene* library in Jerusalem?[52]

**49.** At the Scrolls Symposium held at the Library of Congress in Washington on 21–2 April 1993, Magen Broshi, Director of the Shrine of the Book at the Israel Museum in Jerusalem, delivered a powerful rebuttal of the Golb conjecture as well as the speculative theory advanced at another conference, held in New York in December 1992, by Pauline Donceel-Voûte, in whose view Qumran was a winter villa built for wealthy inhabitants of Jerusalem and the room which de Vaux identified as a *scriptorium* a dining hall. Against the latter theory, see R. Reich, 'A Note on the Function of Room 30 (the "Scriptorium") at Khirbet Qumran', *JJS* 46 (1995), 157–60.

**50.** Cf. e.g. John Strugnell, 'Moses Pseudepigrapha at Qumran', in *Archaeology and History in the Dead Sea Scrolls*, ed. Lawrence H. Schiffman (*Journal for the Study of the Pseudepigrapha*, Supplement, Series 8, Sheffield, 1990, 221).

**51.** 'Hebrew Biblical Manuscripts from the Judaean Desert: Their Contribution to Textual Criticism', *JJS* 39 (1988), 10–19.

**52.** It may also be wondered why the librarians of Jerusalem should have chosen such a distant place to hide their manuscripts when equally inaccessible caves could have been found closer to home?

### *Postscript*

In January 1996, two Israeli archaeologists, H. Eshel and M. Broshi, investigated man-made caves close to the settlement which, in their opinion, were used as sleeping quarters by the members of the sect.

Another search, organized in early 1996 by James Strange of the University of South Florida, discovered two ostraca, or inscribed potsherds, on the Qumran site itself. They include a document attesting the transfer of a servant, by the name of Hisday, of a house and the produce of an orchard to an Eleazar son of Nahmani by a certain Honi in fulfilment of an oath to the 'Community' (*Yahad*). This ostracon connects for the first time a sectarian text with the Qumran site itself. This document is due to be published by F. M. Cross and Esti Eshel (cf. below, pp. 596–7).

## QUMRAN AND THE NEW TESTAMENT

Since Qumran and early Christianity partly overlap, it is not surprising that from the very beginning of Dead Sea Scrolls research some scholars endeavoured to identify the two. The first attempt came from England in the early 1950s, with Jacob Teicher of Cambridge modestly advancing the thesis that Jesus was the Teacher of Righteousness and Saint Paul the Wicked Priest.[53] This trend was continued with loud media support by J. M. Allegro's speculation about the role of *ammanita muscaria*, a hallucinogenic fungus, in the genesis of the Christian Church.[54] It reached its climax with Barbara Thiering's discovery that John the Baptist was the Teacher of Righteousness and the married, divorced and remarried Jesus, father of four children, the Wicked Priest.[55] As for Robert Eisenman, he ignores Jesus, and casts instead his brother, James, in the role of the Teacher of Righteousness, with Paul playing the Wicked Priest.[56] In my

53. See his numerous articles in *JJS* between 1951 and 1955.

54. *The Sacred Mushroom and the Cross*, London, 1970.

55. *Jesus the Man: A New Interpretation from the Dead Sea Scrolls*, Doubleday, London and New York, 1992; *Jesus and the Riddle of the Dead Sea Scrolls*, Harper, San Francisco and New York, 1992.

56. Robert Eisenman and Michael Wise, *The Dead Sea Scrolls Uncovered*, London and New York, 1992.

opinion all these theories fail the basic credibility test: they do not spring from, but are foisted on, the texts.[57]

These – to say the least – improbable speculations as well as the no less fantastic claim that Qumran Cave 7 yielded remains of the Gospel of Mark and other New Testament writings in Greek[58] need not detain us any longer.

Turning to the real relationship between the Scrolls and the New Testament, this can be presented under a threefold heading. (1) We note *(a)* fundamental similarities of language (both in the Scrolls and in the New Testament the faithful are called 'sons of light'); *(b)* ideology (both communities considered themselves as the true Israel, governed by twelve leaders, and expected the imminent arrival of the Kingdom of God); *(c)* attitude to the Bible (both considered their own history as a fulfilment of the words of the Prophets). However, all correspondences such as these may be due to the Palestinian religious atmosphere of the epoch, without entailing any direct influence. (2) More specific features, such as monarchic administration (i.e. single leaders, overseers at Qumran, bishops in Christian communities) and the practice of religious communism in the strict discipline of the sect and at least in the early days in the Jerusalem church (cf. Acts ii, 44–5), would suggest a direct causal connection. If so, it is likely that the young and inexperienced church modelled itself on the by then well-tried Essene society.

(3) In the study of the historical Jesus, the charismatic–eschatological aspects of the Scrolls have provided the richest gleanings for comparison. For example, the Prayer of Nabonidus, known since the mid-1950s,[59] and concerned with the story of Nabonidus' cure by a Jewish exorcist who forgave his sins, provides the most telling parallel to the Gospel account of the healing of a paralytic in Capernaum whose sins Jesus declared forgiven.[60]

The second example is the so-called Resurrection fragment (4Q**521**,

57. See my review of *The Dead Sea Scrolls Uncovered* in the *TLS* of 4 December 1992 and 'The War over the Dead Sea Scrolls', *The New York Review of Books*, 11 August, 1994, 10–13.

58. Cf. below, pp. 440–41.

59. Cf. below, p. 573.

60. Cf. G. Vermes, *Jesus the Jew*, London, 1973, 67–9; *The Religion of Jesus the Jew*, London, 1993, 192–3.

cf. below, pp. 391–2).[61] In this poem, the age of the eschatological kingdom is characterized, with the help of Psalm cxlvi, 7–8 and Isaiah lxi, 1, by the liberation of captives, the curing of the blind, the straightening of the bent, the healing of the wounded, the raising of the dead and the proclamation of the good news to the poor. Likewise, in the Gospels, victory over disease and the devil is viewed as the sure sign of the initial manifestation of God's reign. Jesus is reported to have announced:

If it is by the finger of God that I cast out demons, the Kingdom of God has come upon you. (Lk. xi, 20)

Similarly, to John the Baptist's inquiry whether Jesus was the final messenger the following reply is sent:

Go and tell John what you hear and see: the blind receive their sight, and the lame walk, lepers are cleansed and the deaf hear, and the dead are raised up, and the poor have good news preached to them. (Matth. xi, 4–5)

Note furthermore that Community Rule 4:6 lists healing as the chief eschatological reward and that according to the Palestinian Aramaic paraphrases of Genesis iii, 15, the days of the Messiah will bring an ultimate cure to the children of Eve wounded by the serpent in the garden of Eden.[62]

## QUMRAN'S GREATEST NOVELTY

If one had to single out the most revolutionary novelty furnished by Qumran, its contribution to our understanding of the genesis of Jewish literary compositions could justifiably be our primary choice. Comparative study of biblical manuscripts, where no two copies display the same text, and of sectarian works, attested in a number of sometimes startlingly different redactions, has revealed in one leading scholar's words 'insufficiently controlled copying'.[63] In my view, however, the phenomenon would better be described as scribal creative freedom.

**61**. Robert Eisenman and Michael Wise, op. cit. (in note 56 on p. 21), 19–23; G. Vermes, 'Qumran Forum Miscellanea I', *JJS* 43 (1992), 303–4; Michael O. Wise and James D. Tabor, 'The Messiah at Qumran', *BAR* 18 (Nov.–Dec. 1992), 60–65; Emile Puech, 'Une apocalypse messianique', *RQ* 15 (1991–2), 475–522.

**62**. Cf. Targum Neofiti, Fragmentary Targum and Pseudo-Jonathan on Gen. iii, 15.

**63**. S. Talmon in F. M. Cross and S. Talmon, *Qumran and the Origin of the Biblical Text*, Cambridge, Mass., 1975, 380.

Qumran manuscripts of Scripture, and even more of the Community Rule and the War Scroll, indicate that diversity, not uniformity, reigned there and then, and that redactor–copyists felt free to improve the composition which they were reproducing. Or, to quote myself,

> The Dead Sea Scrolls have afforded for the first time direct insight into the creative literary-religious process at work within that variegated Judaism which flourished during the last two centuries of quasi-national independence, before the catastrophe of 70 CE forced the rabbinic successors of the Pharisees to attempt to create an 'orthodoxy' by reducing dangerous multiplicity to a simple, tidy and easily controllable unity.[64]

Looking at the Qumran discoveries from an overall perspective, it is – I believe – the student of the history of Palestinian Judaism in the inter-Testamental era (150 BCE–70 CE) who is their principal beneficiary. For such an expert, the formerly quite unknown sectarian writings of the Dead Sea literature have opened new avenues of exploration in the shadowy era of the life of Jesus, the rise of Christianity and the emergence of rabbinic Judaism. From the Jewish side, it was previously poorly documented. The rabbis of the first and second centuries CE had not permitted religious writings of that epoch to go down to posterity unless they conformed fully to their ideas, and although some of these texts were preserved by Christians (viz. the Apocrypha and many of the Pseudepigrapha), the fact that they had served as a vehicle for Church apologetics caused their textual reliability to be suspect. But the Scrolls are unaffected by either Christian or rabbinic censorship, and now that their evidence is complete, historians will be thoroughly acquainted, not with just another aspect of Jewish beliefs or customs, but with the whole organization, teaching and aspirations of a religious community flourishing during the last centuries of the Second Temple.

The Scrolls have understandably awakened intense interest in the academic world, but why have they appealed so strongly to the imagination of the non-specialist? I would say, the outstanding characteristic of our age appears to be a desire to reach back to the greatest attainable purity, to the basic truth free of jargon. Affecting the whole of our outlook, it has necessarily included the domain of religious thought and behaviour, and with it, in the Western world, the whole subject of Judaeo-Christian culture and spirituality. A search is being made for the

64. *The Dead Sea Scrolls Forty Years On*, Oxford, 1987, 15–16.

original meaning of issues with which we have become almost too familiar and which with the passing of the centuries have tended to become choked with inessentials, and it has led not only to a renewed preoccupation with the primitive but fully developed expression of these issues in the Scriptures, but also to a desire for knowledge and understanding of their prehistory.

The laws and rules, hymns and other liturgical works as well as the Bible commentaries of the Qumran Community respond to this need in that they add substance and depth to the historical period in which Jewish Christianity and rabbinic Judaism originated. They reveal one facet of the spiritual ferment at work among the various Palestinian religious parties at that time, a ferment which culminated in a thorough re-examination and reinterpretation of the fundamentals of the Jewish faith. By dwelling in such detail on the intimate organization of their society, on the role attributed to their Teacher and on their ultimate hopes and expectations, the sect of the Scrolls has exposed its own resulting synthesis. This in its turn has thrown into relief and added a new dimension to its dissenting contemporaries. Thus, compared with the ultra-conservative rigidity of the Essene Rule, rabbinic Judaism reveals itself as progressive and flexible, while the religion preached and practised by Jesus of Nazareth stands out invested with religious individuality and actuality. Also, by comparison to all three, the ideology of the Gentile Church sounds a definitely alien note.[65] Yet at the same time, the common ground from which they all sprang, and their affinities and borrowings, show themselves more clearly than ever before. It is no exaggeration to state that none of these religious movements can properly be understood independently of the others.

Essenism is dead. The brittle structure of its stiff and exclusive brotherhood was unable to withstand the national catastrophe which struck Palestinian Judaism in 70 CE. Animated by the loftiest of ideals and devoted to the observance of 'perfect holiness', it yet lacked the pliant strength and the elasticity of thought and depth of spiritual vision which enabled rabbinic Judaism to survive and flourish. And although the Teacher of Righteousness clearly sensed the deeper obligations implicit in the Mosaic Law, he was without the genius of Jesus the Jew who succeeded in uncovering the essence of religion as an existential relationship between man and man and man and God.

65. On this, see G. Vermes, *The Religion of Jesus the Jew*, London and Minneapolis, 1993.

# *II. The Community*

Since the early 1950s, the information garnered from the Scrolls and from Qumran's archaeological remains has been combined by experts to form a persuasive portrait of the people to which they allude. Yet for all the advances made in knowledge and understanding, the enigma of the sect is by no means definitely solved. After all this time, we are still not certain that we have collated the whole evidence correctly or interpreted it properly. Questions continue to arise in the mind and there is still no way to be sure of the answers.

Our perplexity is mainly due to an absence in the documents, singly or together, of any systematic exposition of the sect's constitution and laws. The Community Rule legislates for a group of ascetics living in a kind of 'monastic' society, the statutes of the Damascus Document for an ordinary lay existence; MMT (*Miqsat Ma'ase ha-Torah*, or Some Observances of the Law) probably echoes the prehistory or early history of the sect; and the War Rule and Messianic Rule in their turn, while associated with the Community Rule and the Damascus Document, and no doubt reflecting to some extent a contemporary state of affairs, first and foremost plan for a future age.

Taken together, however, it is clear from this literature that the sectaries regarded themselves as the true Israel, the repository of the authentic traditions of the religious body, from which they had seceded. Accordingly, they organized their movement so that it corresponded faithfully to that of the Jewish people, dividing it into priests and laity (or Aaron and Israel), and the laity grouped after the biblical model into twelve tribes. This structure is described in the War Scroll's account of reconstituted Temple worship as it was expected to be at the end of time:

> The twelve chief Priests shall minister at the daily sacrifice before God ... Below them ... shall be the chiefs of the Levites to the number of twelve, one for each tribe ... Below them shall be the chiefs of the tribes. (1QM II, 1–3)

Still following the biblical pattern, sectarian society (apart from the tribe of Levi) was further distinguished into units of Thousands, Hundreds, Fifties and Tens (1QS II, 21; CD XIII, 1–2). To what extent these figures are symbolical, we do not know, but it is improbable that 'Thousands' amounted to anything more than a figure of speech. It is not irrelevant, in this connection, to note that the archaeologists have deduced from the fact that the cemetery contained 1,100 graves, dug over the course of roughly 200 years, that the population of Qumran, an establishment of undoubted importance, can never have numbered more than 150 to 200 souls at a time. Also, it should be borne in mind that the total membership of the Essene sect in the first century CE only slightly exceeded 'four thousand' (Josephus, *Antiquities* XVIII, 21).

To consider now the two types separately, the 'monastic' brotherhood at Qumran alludes to itself in the Community Rule as 'the men of holiness' and 'the men of perfect holiness', and to the sect as 'the Community' and 'Council of the Community' or 'the men of the Law' (4Q S$^{d}$=4Q**258**). The establishment was devoted exclusively to religion. Work must have formed a necessary part of their existence; it is obvious from the remains discovered at Qumran that they farmed, made pots, cured hides and reproduced manuscripts. But no indication of this appears in the documents. It is said only that they were to 'eat in common and bless in common and deliberate in common' (1QS VI, 2–3), living in such a way as to 'seek God with a whole heart and soul' (1QS I, 1–2). Perfectly obedient to each and every one of the laws of Moses and to all that was commanded by the Prophets, they were to love one another and to share with one another their 'knowledge, powers and possessions' (1QS I, 11). They were to be scrupulous in their observance of the times appointed for prayer, and for every other aspect of a liturgical existence conducted apart from the Temple of Jerusalem and its official cult. 'Separate from the habitation of unjust men' (1QS VIII, 13), they were to study the Torah in the wilderness and thereby 'atone for the Land' (1QS VIII, 6, 10) and its wicked men, for whom they were to nourish an 'everlasting hatred' (1QS IX, 21), though this went together with a firm conviction that their fate was in God's hands alone. And the poet proclaims in the Hymn with which the Community Rule ends:

> I will pay to no man the reward of evil;
> I will pursue him with goodness.
> For judgement of all the living is with God
> And it is He who will render to man his reward. (1QS X, 17–18)

They were to be truthful, humble, just, upright, charitable and modest. They were to

watch in community for a third of every night of the year, to read the Book and to study the Law and to bless together. (1QS VI, 7–8)

These are, as may be seen, mostly the sort of recommendations to be expected of men devoting themselves to contemplation. A point to bear in mind, however, is that the contemplative life is not a regular feature of Judaism. An additional distinctive trait of these sectaries is that another qualification was required of them besides holiness: they were expected to become proficient in the knowledge of the 'two spirits' in which all men 'walk', the spirits of truth and falsehood, and to learn how to discriminate between them. They were taught in the so-called 'instruction concerning the Two Spirits', the earliest Jewish theological tractate incorporated into the Community Rule, how to recognize a 'son of Light' or potential 'son of Light', and how to distinguish a 'son of Darkness' belonging to the lot of Belial (1QS III, 13–IV, 25; cf. below pp. 73–4).

The hierarchy at Qumran was strict and formal, from the highest level to the lowest. Every sectary was inscribed in 'the order of his rank' (1QS VI, 22) – the term 'order' recurs constantly – and was obliged to keep to it in all the Community meetings and at table, an order that was subject to an annual review on the Feast of the Renewal of the Covenant. But after democratic beginnings, with the 'Congregation' (literally, 'the Many') as such forming the supreme authority, testified to by what seems to be the earliest formulation of the communal constitution (cf. 4QS$^{b,d}$=4Q**256**, **258**), see below, pp. 118–19), the 'sons of Zadok, the priests', members of the 'Zadokite' high-priestly family, took over the leadership of the sect. Although nothing to this effect is mentioned specifically in the Community Rule, the superior, the so-called *mebaqqer* or Guardian, was undoubtedly one of their number, as was the Bursar of the Congregation entrusted with handling the material affairs of the Community. In their hands lay the ultimate responsibility for decisions on matters of doctrine, discipline, purity and impurity, and in particular everything pertaining to 'justice and property' (1QS IX, 7). It was also a basic rule of the order that a priest was required to be present at any gathering of ten or more members who were meeting for debate, Bible study or prayer. A priest was to recite the grace before the common meals and to pronounce blessings (1QS VI, 3–8). He was no doubt the man whose duty it was to study the Law continually (1QS VI, 7; VIII, 11–12). One interesting feature of the priesthood at Qumran is that their precedence was absolute. In Judaism as represented by the Mishnah, the priest is superior to the Levite, the Levite to the Israelite, and the Israelite to the 'bastard' (Horayot III, 8). But the priestly precedence is conditional. If the 'bastard' is a man of learning, we are told, and the High Priest an uneducated 'boor', 'the bastard . . . precedes the High Priest'.

The highest office was vested in the person of the Guardian, known also, it would seem, as the 'Master' (*maskil*). The Community was to be taught by him how to live in conformity with the 'Book of the Community Rule' (1QS I, 1; 4QS[a]=4Q**255**), and to be instructed by him in the doctrine of the 'two spirits'. He was to preside over assemblies, giving leave to speak to those wishing to do so (1QS VI, 11–13). He was to assess, in concert with the brethren, the spiritual progress of the men in his charge and rank them accordingly (1QS VI, 21–2). And negatively, he was not to dispute with 'the men of the Pit (or Dawn)' and not to transmit to them the sect's teachings (1QS IX, 16–17). Of the sect's institutions, the most significant appears to have been the Council of the Community, or assembly of the Congregation. From a passage ordering all the members to sit in their correct places – 'The Priests shall sit first, and the elders second, and all the rest of the people according to their rank' (1QS VI, 8–9) – the Council seems to have been a gathering of the whole community, under the priests and men of importance, marshalled by the Levites, and with the Guardian at the head. But in another text, generally held to be an early section, the rule is as follows:

> In the Council of the Community there shall be twelve men and three Priests, perfectly versed in all that is revealed of the Law, whose works shall be truth, righteousness, justice, loving-kindness and humility. They shall preserve the faith in the Land with steadfastness and meekness and shall atone for sin by the practice of justice and by suffering the sorrows of affliction. They shall walk with all men according to the standard of truth and the rule of the time.
>
> (1QS VIII, 1–4)

These three priests and twelve men are referred to also as 'fifteen men' in a hybrid version of the Community Rule and the Damascus Document (4Q**265** fr. 7 ii). Their presence was obviously essential: both documents state that when they 'are in Israel, the Council of the Community shall be established in truth' (1QS VIII, 4–5; 4Q**265** fr. 7 ii, 7–8). But whether they formed the nucleus of the sect as a whole, or the minimum quorum of the leadership of the Community, symbolically portrayed as consisting of the twelve tribes and the three Levitical clans, or a special elite within the Council designated elsewhere 'the Foundations of the Community', must be left open to question. The purpose of the meetings is in any case clear. It was to debate the Law, to discuss their current business, to select or reject newcomers under the guidance of the Guardian, to hear charges against offenders and to conduct a yearly inquiry into the progress of every sectary, promoting or demoting them in rank, again under the Guardian's supervision (1QS V, 23–4; VI, 13–23). During their sessions, order and quiet were to prevail: a person wishing to offer his opinion or ask a question was to crave permission in a prescribed way. He was to rise and tell the Guardian and the Congregation, 'I have something to say to the Congregation' and then wait for their consent before going ahead (1QS VI, 8–13).

The procedure followed in inquiries into infringements of the Law and the sect's Rule has been preserved, and the list of faults with their corresponding sentences tells us more about the mentality of the Dead Sea ascetics than any isolated exposition of their doctrine and principles can do.

Beginning with the blackest sins: any transgression, by commission or omission, of 'one word of the Law of Moses, on any point whatever' earned outright expulsion. No former companion might from then on associate with the sinner in any way at all (1QS VIII, 21–4). Expulsion followed, secondly, the pronouncement for any reason whatever of the divine Name:

> If any man has uttered the [Most] Venerable Name, even though frivolously, or as a result of shock, or for any other reason whatever, while reading the Book or blessing, he shall be dismissed and shall return ... no more. (1QS VI, 27–VII, 2)

Thirdly, a sectary was expelled for slandering the Congregation (1QS VII, 16). Fourthly, he was sent away for rebelling against the 'Foundations' of the Community:

> Whoever has murmured against the authority of the Community shall be expelled and shall not return. (1QS VII, 17)

Lastly, where a man had been a member of the Council for at least ten years and had then defected to 'walk in the stubbornness of his heart', not only was he to be expelled, but the same judgement was extended to any of his former colleagues who might take pity on him and share with him their food or money (1QS VII, 22–3).

The remaining offences are of a kind that might be confessed and censured in any Christian religious order of today, though one cannot perhaps say the same of the penances imposed for them.

In a descending order of gravity: a man who 'betrayed the truth and walked in the stubbornness of his heart' (1QS VII, 18–21), or transgressed the Mosaic Law inadvertently (1QS VIII, 24–IX, 1), was visited with two years of penance. He was to lose his rank and during the first year be separated from the 'purity' of the Congregation, and during the second year, from its 'drink'. Both notions will be developed presently. He was then to be re-examined by the Congregation and subsequently returned to his place in the order.

Lying in matters of property, in all probability, the partial concealment of personal possessions, earned exclusion from 'purity' for a year and a cut by one quarter in the food ration (1QS VI, 25–7). The penal code of 4Q**265**, which closely resembles that of 1QS, prescribes for deceiving a companion an exclusion for six months and a halving of the guilty person's food portion. Disrespect to a companion of higher rank, rudeness and anger towards a priest, slander and deliberate insult, all earned one year of penance and exclusion from 'purity' (1QS VI, 25–7; VII, 2–5). After this, the sentences decrease to six months, three months, thirty days and ten days of penance.

For lying deliberately and similarly deceiving by word or deed, for bearing malice unjustly, for taking revenge, for murmuring against a companion unjustly and also for going 'naked before his companion, without having been obliged to do so' – a curious proviso – the sectary was to atone for six months. For failing to care for a companion and for speaking foolishly: three months. For falling asleep during a meeting of the Council, for leaving the Council while members were standing (in prayer?), for spitting in Council, for 'guffawing foolishly', for being 'so poorly dressed that when drawing his hand from beneath his garment his nakedness has been seen': thirty days. The penal code contained in another of the Cave 4 manuscripts of the Damascus Document (4Q**266**) mentions also ten days' penance, in addition to the thirty days' expulsion inflicted on someone who has fallen asleep during a meeting! And for leaving an assembly three times without reason, for interrupting another while speaking, for gesticulating with the left hand: ten days (1QS VII, 15). A fascinating fragment (4Q**477**) has preserved in writing cases of misbehaviour by *named* sectaries: 'Yohanan son of . . . ' was 'short-tempered'; 'Hananiah Notos' led astray 'the spirit of the Community' and either pampered himself or showed favouritism to his near kin(?); and another 'Hananiah son of Sim[on]' 'loved' something no doubt prohibited.

That the common table was of high importance to Qumran daily life is evident from the fact that only the fully professed and the faultless, that is to say those who were 'inscribed ... for purity' and not subsequently disqualified, were allowed to sit at it. There is no explicit mention of a ritual bath preceding the meals, but from various references to purification by water, as well as the presence of bathing installations at Qumran, it is likely that the sectaries immersed themselves before eating as did the Essenes according to Josephus (*War* II, 129). But little more is learnt of the meal itself from the Community Rule than that when the table had been 'prepared for eating, and the new wine for drinking', the priest was to be the first to bless the food and drink (1QS VI, 4–5). The implication would be that after him the others did the same, an inference supported by the Messianic Rule, where a similar meal is described attended by two Messiahs (1QSa II, 17–21). Some uncertainty surrounds the meaning of 'new wine', but it would seem from the use in the Scrolls (with the exception of the Temple Scroll), of the alternative Hebrew words for wine – *tirosh* and *yayin* – that the latter often has pejorative connotations. More likely than not, the 'wine' drunk by the sectaries, 'the drink of the Congregation', was unfermented grape-juice.

Another topic to be considered under the heading of communal life and institutions is the crucial one of induction into the sect. And if it should seem strange to place it towards the end rather than at the beginning, the explanation is that with an idea, however sketchy, of what was entailed by adherence to the movement, the process by which it admitted a Jew into its company becomes easier to follow. According to the regime adopted at Qumran, a person desiring to join the sect remained on probation, certainly for two years and possibly for three or more. His first move was to appear before the Guardian 'at the head of the Congregation', meaning no doubt during a session of the Congregation, who inquired into his principles to discover if he was a suitable postulant. If they were satisfied, he 'entered the Covenant' (1QS VI, 13–15). That is to say, he solemnly swore there and then to adhere to the Torah as the sect interpreted it, vowing

> by a binding oath to return with all his heart and soul to every commandment of the Law of Moses in accordance with all that has been revealed of it to the sons of Zadok ... the Keepers of the Covenant. (1QS V, 7–11)

After a further period of unspecified length, during which he received instruction from the Guardian 'in all the rules of the Community', he appeared once more before the Congregation, who confirmed him as a novice or dismissed him. But although he was now accepted into the Council of the Community, he was nevertheless still not admitted to 'purity' for another full year. The same rule applied also in the group represented by 4Q265 fr. 1.

This concept of pure things (*tohorah*, *taharah* or *tohorot*, literally 'purity' or 'purities') needs some comment. It seems to designate here as in rabbinic literature ritually pure food (cf. also 4Q264 1), as well as the vessels and utensils in which it is contained or cooked. It includes also garments. The *tohorot*, moreover, are distinguished by the rabbis from *mashqin*, liquids, the latter being considered much more susceptible to contract impurity than solid comestibles. Hence, in ordering the novice not to touch the pure things of the Congregation, the Community forbade him all contact with its pots, plates, bowls and necessarily the food that they held. He was not, in effect, to attend the common table and had to eat elsewhere. Although the context is very different, a parallel rule figures in the Temple Scroll (LXIII, 13–14), prohibiting a Gentile woman married to her Jewish captor to touch his *tohorah* for seven years.

During this first year of the novitiate, the newcomer could not share the sect's property. At a third Community inquiry, he was examined for 'his understanding and observance of the Law' and, if his progress was judged to be adequate, he handed over his money and belongings to the 'Bursar of the Congregation', but they were set aside and not yet absorbed into Community ownership. During this second year, furthermore, the ban on touching the pure things was relaxed, but he could still not touch liquids, the 'Drink [*mashqeh*] of the Congregation' (1QS VI, 20–21; VII, 20; cf. also 4Q284 1). Finally, with the second year over, the novice had once more to undergo an examination, after which, 'according to the judgement of the Congregation', he was at last inscribed among the brethren in the order of his rank 'for the Law, and for justice, and for purity'. Also, his property was amalgamated with theirs and he possessed the right from then on to speak his mind in the Council of the Community (1QS VI, 13–23).

In sum, this strict and extended curriculum falls into two stages. The postulant is first brought into the Covenant, swearing total fidelity to the Mosaic Law as interpreted by the sect's priestly teachers, and to 'separate from all the men of injustice who walk in the way of wickedness'

(1QS v, 10–11). He then secondly embarks on a course of training as a preliminary to joining the 'holy Congregation' (1QS v, 20). In other words, entering the Covenant and entering the Community was not one act, but two.

It has long been debated whether the Qumran sectaries were married or celibate. From the image of their life projected so far on the basis of the Community Rule, few will probably disagree that the idea of the presence of women among them appears incongruous. The impression received is that of a wholly masculine society: indeed, they were actually enjoined 'to not follow a sinful heart and lustful eyes, committing all manner of evil' (1QS I, 6). In further support of the argument for celibacy, the word *ishah*, woman, occurs nowhere in the Community Rule. Or rather, to be more exact, it is encountered once in the final Hymn, in the cliché, 'one born of woman' (1QS XI, 21). Moreover, against the Cave 4 Damascus Document regulation (4Q**270** fr. 7), which envisages a membership of married people and imposes the penalty of expulsion on anyone murmuring against 'the Fathers' but only a ten-day penance for murmuring against 'the Mothers', the Community Rule speaks only of the crime of murmuring against 'the authority of the Community' (1QS VII, 17). Silence concerning the presence of women seems therefore deliberate. Yet the fact cannot be overlooked that although in the main graveyard itself the twenty-six tombs so far opened at random (out of 1,100) have all contained adult male skeletons, the archaeologists have uncovered on the peripheries of the cemetery the bones of six women and three children too (R. de Vaux, *Archaeology*, 47–8; J.-P. Humbert, *Fouilles de Kh. Qumrân*, 346–52). A more extensive exploration of the cemetery would eliminate most of these uncertainties.

The Damascus Document, the hybrid Community Rule–Damascus Document text (4Q**265**) and the Temple Scroll, as well as the Messianic Rule and occasionally the War Rule and MMT, are concerned with a style of religious existence quite at variance with that at Qumran. In the 'towns' or 'camps', as the Damascus Document terms them (CD XII, 19, 23), adherents of the sect lived an urban or village life side by side, yet apart from, their fellow Jewish and Gentile neighbours. They had wives and reared children, but clearly their sexual morality followed particularly strict rules. A Cave 4 Damascus Document manuscript lays down that 'whoever has approached his wife, not according to the rules, (thus) fornicating, he shall leave and will not return again' (4Q**270** fr. 7 i). The married sectaries employed servants, engaged in commerce and trade (even with Gentiles), tended cattle, grew vines and corn in the surrounding fields, discharged their duties to the Temple by way of offerings, but in doing so they were obliged like their brothers in the desert to show absolute obedience to the Law and to observe the sect's 'appointed times'. There is no indication, however, that the continual and intensive study of the Torah played any part in their lives. Nor in their regard is there any mention of instruction in the doctrine of the two spirits, as membership of the group was a birthright and not the outcome of a process of selection and training.

How many of these people, if any, lived in Jerusalem is not known, but they must at least have visited the city from time to time, since a statute forbids them to enter the 'house of worship' (possibly the Temple) in a state of ritual uncleanness, or to 'lie with a woman in the city of the Sanctuary to defile the city of the Sanctuary with their uncleanness' (CD I, 22; XII, 1; TS XLV, 11–12).

Little is revealed in the Damascus Document of how the life span of the individual progressed in the 'towns', and for this we have to turn to the Messianic Rule in the hope that it reflects contemporary actuality as well as the ideal life of an age to come.

According to the latter Rule, members of the Covenant were permitted to marry at the age of twenty, when they were estimated to have reached adulthood and to 'know [good] and evil' (1QSa I, 9–11). For the subsequent five years they were then allowed to 'assist' (as opposed to taking an active part) at hearings and judgements. At twenty-five, they advanced one grade further and qualified to 'work in the service of the Congregation' (1QSa I, 12–13). At thirty, they were regarded as at last fully mature and could 'participate' in the affairs of the tribunals and assemblies, taking their place among the higher ranks of the sect, the 'chiefs of the thousands of Israel, the Hundreds, the chiefs of the Fifties and Tens, the judges and the officers of their tribes, in all their families [under the authority] of the sons of [Aar]on the Priests' (1QSa I, 8–16). As office-holders, they were expected to perform their duties to the best of their ability and were accorded more honour or less in conformity with their 'understanding' and the 'perfection' of their 'way'. As they grew older, so their burdens became lighter (1QSa I, 19).

As at Qumran, supreme authority rested in the hands of the priests, and every group of ten or more was to include a priest 'learned in the Book of Meditation' and to be 'ruled by him' (CD XIII, 2–3). His precedence, on the other hand, is not represented as absolute in the 'towns'.

It is explicitly stated that in the absence of a properly qualified priest, he was to be replaced by a Levite who would perform all the functions of a superior except those specially reserved in the Bible to the priesthood such as applying the laws of leprosy (CD XIII, 3–7). The Cave 4 manuscripts of the Damascus Document (4Q**266**, **269**, **272–3**) describe at length the diagnosis of the onset and eventual cure of skin disease. Priests with speech defects, those who had been prisoners of war or had settled and been active among Gentiles were disqualified from performing priestly duties or eating 'sacred food' (4Q**266** fr. 5). The Cave 4 version of the Damascus Document legislates also on agricultural priestly dues (4Q**266** fr. 6; **271** fr. 2).

As in the Community Rule, the head of the 'camp' is designated in the Damascus Document, as well as in 4QD[a] (4Q**266** fr. 5 i) and in the hybrid 4Q**265** fr. 1 ii, as the *mebaqqer* or Guardian. He appears, however, not to be supported by a council. In fact, the words 'Council of the Community' are absent from this document apart from the transitional 4Q**265** frs. 1 ii and 7 ii, where the use of the term is more general in the first case and represents the ideal nucleus of the sect in the second. There is reference to the 'company of Israel', on the advice of which it would be licit to attack Gentiles (CD XII, 8), but this type of war council, mentioned also in the Messianic Rule (1QSa I, 26), can surely have had nothing to do with the assemblies described in the Community Rule. (The only possible parallel is the 'council of Holiness' in CD XX, 24, in which a not strictly observant member was to be judged.) The Guardian of the 'camps', in any case, stands on his own as teacher and helper of his people. He shall love them, writes the author,

> as a father loves his children, and shall carry them in all their distress like a shepherd his sheep. He shall loosen all the fetters which bind them that in his Congregation there may be none that are oppressed or broken. (CD XIII, 9–10)

The Guardian was to examine newcomers to his congregation, though not, it should be noted, to determine their 'spirit', and was to serve as the deciding authority on the question of their admission (cf. also 4Q**265** fr. 1 ii). These offices are of course already familiar to us from the Community Rule. But an additional task of the *mebaqqer* in the towns was to ensure that no friendly contact occurred between his congregation and everyone outside the sect. Whatever exchanges took place had to be paid for; and even these transactions were to be subject to his consent (CD XIII, 14–16).

Instead of dealing with offenders in Community courts of inquiry, the towns had their tribunals for hearing cases, equipped moreover with 'judges'. These were to be ten in number, elected for a specific term and drawn from the tribes of Levi, Aaron and Israel: four priests and Levites, and six laymen (CD x, 4–7). They were to be not younger than twenty-five and not older than sixty – in the Messianic Rule, which also speaks of judges, the age-limits are thirty and sixty years (1QSa I, 13–15) – and were to be expert in biblical law and the 'constitutions of the Covenant'. The arrangement would seem, in fact, to be fairly straightforward. Yet it is not entirely so. For example, it is evident that the Guardian was also implicated in legal matters; he had to determine whether a proper case had been made out against a sectary and whether it should be brought before the court (CD IX, 16–20), and in certain cases he appears to have imposed penalties on his own (CD XV, 13–14). The 'Priest overseeing the Congregation' of one of the Cave 4 fragments of the Damascus Document (4Q**270** fr. 7 i–ii) appears to perform the same single judicial function as the Guardian in the case of an inadvertent sin. We are not told whether the ten judges sat together, whether they were all drawn from the locality in which they lived, or whether they travelled as it were on circuit as nowadays. The code of law they were expected to administer, as laid down in the Damascus Document, differs in content from that of the Community Rule. Furthermore, although, unlike the Qumran code, a sentence is prescribed only rarely, sometimes it is the death penalty. We have here, in addition to matters relating primarily to communal discipline to a large extent identical with the Community Rule, a more detailed sectarian reformulation of scriptural laws regulating Jewish life as such.

The first group of statutes, concerned with vows, opens with the injunction that in order to avoid being put to death for the capital sin of uttering the names of God, the sectary must swear by the Covenant alone. Such an oath would be fully obligatory and might not be cancelled (CD XVI, 7–8). If he subsequently violated his oath, he would then have only to confess to the priest and make restitution (CD XV, 1–5). The sectary is also ordered not to vow to the altar articles acquired unlawfully, or the food of his own house (CD XVI, 13–15), and not to make any vow 'in the fields' but always before the judges (CD IX, 9–10). He is threatened with death if he 'vow another to destruction by the laws of the Gentiles' (CD IX, 1). As for the right conferred by the Bible on fathers and husbands to annul vows made by their daughters or wives, the Damascus Document limits it to the cancellation of oaths which should have never been made in the first place (CD XVI, 10–12; for a somewhat different rule, see TS LIII, 16–LIV, 5). It is clearly stated that no accusation is valid without prior warnings before witnesses (CD IX, 2–3). A record of reported moral failings (4Q477) has already been quoted (cf. above, pp. 31–2).

A few ordinances are concerned with witnesses. No one under the age of twenty was to testify before the judges in a capital charge (CD IX, 23–X, 2). Also, whereas the normal biblical custom is that two or three witnesses are needed before any sentence can be pronounced (Deut. xix, 15; cf. also 11QTS LXI, 6–12), a single witness being quite unacceptable, *unus testis nullus testis*, sectarian law allowed the indictment of a man guilty of repeating the same capital offence on the testimony of single witnesses to the separate occasions on which it was committed, providing they reported it to the Guardian at once and that the Guardian recorded it at once in writing (CD IX, 17–20). With regard to capital cases, to which should be added apostasy in a state of demonic possession (CD XII, 2–3), the adultery of a betrothed girl (4Q159, fr. 224, 10–11), slandering the people of Israel and treason (TS LXIV, 6–13), it is highly unlikely that either the Jewish or the Roman authorities would have granted any rights of execution to the sect. So this is probably part of the sect's vision of the future age, when it as Israel *de jure* would constitute *de facto* the government of the chosen people.

The penal code of the Damascus Document (4Q270) stipulates irrevocable expulsion in the case of a man 'fornicating' with his wife. This may refer to illicit sexual relations with a menstruating woman or, perhaps more likely, with a pregnant or post-menopausal woman since, as Josephus clearly states in connection with married Essenes, sex between spouses was licit only if it could result in conception (*War* II, 161).

A section devoted to Sabbath laws displays a marked bias towards severity. In time, rabbinic law developed the Sabbath rules in still greater detail than appears here, but the tendency is already manifest.

The sectary was not only to abstain from labour 'on the sixth day from the moment when the sun's orb is distant by its own fullness from the gate (wherein it sinks)' (CD X, 15–16), he was not even to speak about work. Nothing associated with money or gain was to interrupt his Sabbath of rest (CD X, 18–19). No member of the Covenant of God was to go out of his house on business on the Sabbath. In fact, he was not to go out, for any reason, further than 1,000 cubits (about 500 yards), though he could pasture his beast at a distance of 2,000 cubits from his town (CD x, 21; xi, 5–6). He could not cook. He could not pick and eat fruit and other edible things 'lying in the fields'. He could not draw water and carry it away, but must drink where he found it (CD x, 22–3). He could not strike his beast or reprimand his servant (CD xi, 6, 12). He could not carry a child, wear perfume or sweep up the dust in his house (CD xi, 10–11). He could not assist his animals to give birth or help them if they fell into a pit; he could, however, pull a man out of water or fire without the help of a ladder or rope (CD xi, 13–14, 16–17). Interpreting the Bible restrictively (Lev. xxiii, 38), the sect's lawmaker (or makers) commanded him to offer no sacrifice on the Sabbath save the Sabbath burnt-offering, and never to send a gift to the Temple by the hand of one 'smitten with any uncleanness permitting him thus to defile the altar' (CD xi, 19–20). He was also never to have intercourse while in the 'city of the Sanctuary' (CD xii, 1–2; 11QTS xlv, 1–12).

The punishment imposed for profaning the Sabbath and the feasts in any of these ways was not death as in the Bible (Num. xv, 35), nor even expulsion as in the Community Rule. It was seven years' imprisonment.

> It shall fall to men to keep him in custody. And if he is healed of his error, they shall keep him in custody for seven years and he shall afterwards approach the Assembly. (CD xii, 4–6)

In the last group, the ordinances appear to be only loosely connected, though some of them involve relations with the larger Jewish–Gentile world. One such forbids killing or stealing from a non-Jew, 'unless so advised by the company of Israel' (CD xii, 6–8). Another proscribes the sale to Gentiles of ritually pure beasts and birds, as well as the produce of granary and wine-press, in case they should blaspheme by offering them in heathen sacrifice. MMT further prohibits acceptance of offerings (wheat or meat) by Gentiles (4Q**394** frs. 3–7). A ban is similarly laid on selling to Gentiles foreign servants converted to the Jewish faith (CD xii, 11). But in addition to these regulations affecting contacts with non-Jews, a few are concerned with dietary restrictions. Thus:

> No man shall defile himself by eating any live creature or creeping thing, from the larvae of bees to all creatures which creep in water. (CD xii, 12–13)

Others deal with the laws of purity (CD xii, 16–18) and purification (CD x, 10–13) and with uncleanness resulting from various sexual discharges and childbirth (4Q**266** fr. 6 i–ii). Outside the Damascus

Document, the B section of MMT (4Q**394–5**), 4QPurities (4Q**274**, **276–7**, **284**) and the Temple Scroll (11QTS XLV–LI) provide ample information on purity matters, including the law relative to the burning of the 'red heifer' whose ashes were a necessary ingredient for the making of the 'water for (removing) uncleanness' (MMT 4Q**394** 3–7 i, **395**; 4Q**276–7**).

Two types of meeting are provided for, with equal laconism: the 'assembly of the camp' presided over by a priest or a Levite and the 'assembly of all the camps' (CD XIV, 3–6). Presumably the latter was the general convention of the whole sect held on the Feast of the Renewal of the Covenant, the annual great festival alluded to in 4QD (**266**, **270**), when both the 'men of holiness' and the 'men of the Covenant' confessed their former errors and committed themselves once more to perfect obedience to the Law and the sect's teachings. According to the available texts, the sectaries were to be mustered and inscribed in their rank by name, the priests first, the Levites second, the Israelites third. A fourth group of proselytes is unique to the 'towns', but as has been observed these were Gentile slaves converted to Judaism. A further remark that in this order the sect's members were to 'be questioned on all matters' leads one to suppose that the allusion must be to the yearly inquiry into their spiritual progress mentioned in the Community Rule (CD XIV, 3–6).

Two Cave 4 manuscripts of the Damascus Document describe the expulsion ceremony of an unfaithful member. He was cursed and dismissed by the Priest overseeing the Congregation and cursed also by all the inhabitants of the camps. Should the latter maintain contact with the renegade, they would forfeit their own membership of the sect (4Q**266** fr. 11 ii; **270** fr. 7 i–ii).

Apart from these familiar directions, we learn only that the priest who mustered the gathering was to be between thirty and sixty years old and, needless to say, 'learned in the Book of Meditation'. The 'Guardian of all the camps', in his turn, was to be between thirty and fifty, and to have 'mastered all the secrets of men and the language of all their clans'. He was to decide who was to be admitted, and anything connected with a 'suit or judgement' was to be brought to him (CD XIV, 7–12).

As for the initiation of new members, the Statutes appear to legislate for young men reaching their majority within the brotherhood and for recruits from outside. This is not entirely clear, but the instruction that an aspirant was not to be informed of the sect's rules until he had stood before the Guardian can hardly have applied to a person brought up within its close circle (CD xv, 5–6, 10–11).

Of the sect's own young men the Damascus Document writes merely:

> And all those who have entered the Covenant, granted to all Israel for ever, shall make their children who have reached the age of enrolment, swear with the oath of the Covenant. (CD xv, 5–6)

The Messianic Rule is more discursive. There, enrolment into the sect is represented as the climax of a childhood and youth spent in study. Teaching of the Bible and in the 'precepts of the Covenant' began long before the age of ten, at which age a boy embarked on a further ten years of instruction in the statutes. It was not until after all this that he was finally ready.

> From [his] youth they shall instruct him in the Book of Meditation and shall teach him, according to his age, the precepts of the Covenant. They [shall be edu]cated in their statutes for ten years ... At the age of twenty years [he shall be] enrolled, that he may enter upon his allotted duties in the midst of his family (and) be joined to the holy congregation. (1QSa I, 6–9)

The newcomer from outside who repented of his 'corrupted way' was to be enrolled 'with the oath of the Covenant' on the day that he spoke to the Guardian, but no sectarian statute was to be divulged to him 'lest when examining him the Guardian be deceived by him' (CD xv, 7–11). Nevertheless, if he broke that oath, 'retribution' would be exacted of him. The text subsequently becomes fragmentary and unreliable, but he is told where to find the liturgical calendar which his oath obliges him to follow.

> As for the exact determination of their times to which Israel turns a blind eye, behold it is strictly defined in the *Book of the Divisions of the Times into their Jubilees and Weeks.* (CD xvi, 2–4)

It should be added here that one big difference between the organization of the brethren in the towns and those of the 'monastic' settlement is that new members were not required to surrender their property. There was none of the voluntary communism found at Qumran. On the other hand, where the desert sectaries practised common ownership, those of the towns contributed to the assistance of their fellows in need. Every man able to do so was ordered to hand over a minimum of two days' wages a month to a charitable fund, and from it the Guardian and the judges distributed help to the orphans, the poor, the old and sick, to unmarried women without support and to prisoners held in foreign hands and in need of redemption (CD xiv, 12–16).

When the two varieties of sectarian life are compared, we find many similarities, especially since the fragments of 4QD and 4Q265 have become accessible, but some of the differences still remain striking. In the desert of Qumran men lived together in seclusion; in the towns they were grouped in families, surrounded by non-members with whom they were in inevitable though exiguous contact. The desert brotherhood was to keep apart from the Temple in Jerusalem until the restoration of the true cult in the seventh year of the eschatological war; the town sectaries participated in worship there. The judges of the towns had no counterparts at Qumran. The Qumran Guardian was supported by a Council; the town Guardians acted independently. Unfaithful desert sectaries were sentenced to irrevocable excommunication, or to temporary exclusion from the common life, or to suffer lighter penances; the penal code concerned with the towns envisages also the death penalty (whether actually executed or not) as well as corrective custody. The common table and the 'purity' associated with it played an essential role at Qumran; in connection with the towns the common meal, but not the pure food, goes unmentioned. Furthermore, at Qumran all the new recruits came from outside; in the towns, some were converts but others were the sons of sectaries. The desert novices underwent two years of training and were instructed in the doctrine of the 'two spirits'; the towns' converts were subjected to neither experience. In the desert, property was owned in common; in the towns, it was not. And last but not least, the desert community appears to have practised celibacy, whereas the town sectaries patently did not.

Yet despite the dissimilarities, at the basic level of doctrine, aims and principles, a perceptible bond links the brethren of the desert with those of the towns. They both claim to represent the true Israel. They both are led by priests, Zadokite priests according to 1QS, the Damascus Document and the Messianic Rule, but not 4QS$^{b}$(=4Q256), 4QS$^{d}$ (=4Q258) and MMT.[1] Both form units of Thousands, Hundreds, Fifties

1. The absence of any mention of the 'sons of Zadok, the Priests' in MMT deals a serious blow to the hypothesis that a proto-Sadducaean priestly group lurks behind this document. The basis of this theory is that three legal doctrines (out of a list of more than twenty) voiced in MMT are attributed to the Sadducees in rabbinic literature. But the soundest position is to consider these teachings as priestly halakhot, held by the forerunners of the Qumran Community and the later Sadducees.

and Tens, both insist on a wholehearted return to the Mosaic Law in accordance with their own particular interpretation of it. They are both governed by priests (or Levites). The principal superior, teacher and administrator of both is known by the unusual title of *mebaqqer*. In both cases, initiation into the sect is preceded by entry into the Covenant, sworn by oath. Both groups convene yearly to review the order of precedence of their members after an inquiry into the conduct of each man during the previous twelve months. Above all, both embrace the same 'unorthodox' liturgical calendar that sets them apart from the rest of Jewry.

There can be only one logical conclusion: this was a single religious movement with two branches. It does not, however, answer all our questions. It does not tell us in particular whether the differentiation resulted from a relaxation or from a hardening of the original ascetic rules. Neither are we told whether the sectaries of desert and towns maintained regular contact among themselves. After all, the history of religions furnishes scores of examples of sister sects which turned into mortal enemies. Did the Qumran and towns fellowships profess and practise unity? A few vital clues suggest that they did.

One indication of a living relationship between the two groups derives from the Qumran library itself. In it were discovered no less than ten copies of the Damascus Document and other writings reflecting the same form of life. It seems hardly likely that they would have figured so prominently among the Qumran literary treasures if they had been the rule books of some rival institution. Besides, there was no trace of any other book in the caves relating to an opposing religious faction except perhaps in the shape of rebuttal in MMT. Another pointer towards unity appears in the passage of the Damascus Document outlining the procedure for the 'assembly of all the camps' and prescribing that the members were to be 'inscribed by name' in hierarchical rank. This clause corresponds exactly to the statute in the Community Rule ordaining a yearly ranking of the sectaries (1QS II, 19–23), with a solemn ritual for the Renewal of the Covenant (for an analysis of the rite, see pp. 80–81). This leads us to suppose that the Feast of the Covenant, when the desert brethren held their annual spiritual survey, was also the occasion for that of the towns. Can we go further still and establish that the two ceremonies took place, not only at the same time, but at the same place? In effect, the literary and archaeological evidence tends to support the theory that the 'assembly of all the camps', identical with the yearly assembly of the Qumran branch, gathered at Qumran.

The first clue turns on the qualifications of the *mebaqqer* of the Community Rule and the Damascus Document respectively. As may be remembered, the superior at Qumran was required to be expert in recognizing 'the nature of all the children of men according to the kind of spirit which they possess' (1QS III, 13–14), while the *mebaqqer* of the towns was to be concerned rather more with a man's 'deeds', 'possessions', 'ability', etc., than with his inner spirit. When, however, the Damascus Document describes the attributes needed of the 'Guardian of all the camps', what do we find but a reformulation of those accredited to the superior of the desert community, that he should know 'all the secrets of men and all the languages of their clans'? It would emerge from this, therefore, that the Guardian of all the camps and the Guardian at Qumran were one and the same person. The next hint comes from the fact that the Damascus Document is directed to both desert and town sectaries. As an example, the passage from the Exhortation advising men to choose whatever is pleasing to God and to reject whatever he hates, 'that you may walk perfectly in all his ways and not follow after thoughts of the guilty inclination and after eyes of lust' (CD II, 14–16), seems to be addressed to celibates. Yet in this very same document we later come upon injunctions aimed explicitly at non-celibates:

> And if they live in camps according to the rule of the Land, marrying and begetting children, they shall walk according to the Law and according to the statute concerning binding vows, according to the rule of the Law which says, *Between a man and his wife and between a father and his son* (Num. xxx, 17).
>
> (CD VII, 6–9)

The Exhortation would seem in short to be a sermon intended for delivery on a certain occasion to married and unmarried members of the sect; and as its theme is perseverance in the Covenant, the appropriate setting would be the Feast of the Renewal of the Covenant in the third month (4Q**266** fr. 11; **270** fr. 7 i–ii), i.e. the Feast of Weeks or Pentecost (see below, pp. 79–80), and the venue, Qumran.

These literary pointers are supported by two archaeological finds. Firstly, the twenty-six deposits of animal bones buried on the Qumran site – goats, sheep, lambs, calves, cows or oxen – have for long intrigued scholars. Can J. T. Milik be correct in identifying them as the remains of meals served to large groups of pilgrims in the Qumran mother-house of the sect (*Ten Years of Discovery in the Wilderness of Judaea*, p. 117)? Naturally, he too connects the gathering with the Covenant festival.

The second archaeological clue also is concerned with bones. The skeletons of four women and one child, and possibly of two further female bodies and those of two children, were found in the extension of the Qumran cemetery. Now, if the Renewal of the Covenant was attended by sectaries from the towns and their families, this may well account for the presence of dead women and children among the otherwise male skeletons of the graveyard proper.

Drawing the threads of these various arguments together, there would seem to be little doubt not only that the desert and town sectaries were united in doctrine and organization, but that they remained in actual and regular touch with each other, under the ultimate administrative and spiritual authority of the shadowy figure of the Priest, of whom we hear so little, and his dominant partner, the Qumran Guardian, Guardian of all the camps. Qumran, it seems, was the seat of the sect's hierarchy and also the centre to which all those turned who professed allegiance to the Council of the Covenant.

# APPENDIX: THE ESSENES AND THE QUMRAN COMMUNITY

## *The Essenes*

Prior to Qumran, the primary sources concerning the Essenes, a Jewish religious community flourishing during the last two centuries of the Second Temple era (*c.* 150 BCE–70 CE), were furnished by the Greek writings of two Jewish authors, Philo of Alexandria (*That Every Good Man Should be Free*, 75–91; *Apology for the Jews*, quoted in Eusebius, *Praeparatio evangelica* VIII, 6–7) and Flavius Josephus (*War* II, 119–61; *Antiquities* XVIII, 18–22) and by the Roman geographer and naturalist, Pliny the Elder, who left a short but very important notice in Latin (*Natural History* V, 17, 4 [73]). For a more detailed account, see Geza Vermes and Martin Goodman, *The Essenes According to the Classical Sources* (Sheffield, 1989). Despite the apparent importance attributed to it by Philo, Josephus and Pliny, the sect is not explicitly mentioned either in the New Testament or in rabbinic literature. There is no general agreement regarding the meaning of the group's name: *Essaioi* or *Essenoi* in Greek, and *Esseni* in Latin. The designation may signify 'the Pious', or 'the Healers', devoted to the cure of body and soul. If the latter interpretation is adopted, it provides a parallel to the Greek *therapeutai*, the title given by Philo to an Egyptian–Jewish ascetic society akin to the Essenes (cf. HJP II, 593–7; Vermes–Goodman, *The Essenes* . . . , 15–17). There are a number of other, less well-established, explanations.

The membership of the Palestinian group exceeded four thousand. Josephus and Philo locate them in Judaean towns; Pliny refers only to a single Essene settlement in the wilderness between Jericho and Engedi.

Individual congregations, directed by superiors, resided in commonly occupied houses. Initiation consisted of one year of probation, and two years of further training, leading to full table-fellowship on swearing an oath of loyalty to the sect. Only adult men qualified according to Philo and Pliny, but Josephus reports that boys were also trained by them. Serious disobedience resulted in expulsion from the order.

One of the principal characteristics of the Essenes was common ownership of property. New members handed over their belongings to the superiors, who collected also the wages earned by every sectary. Agriculture was the main Essene occupation. Having renounced private possessions, the members received all that they needed: food, clothes, care. Further peculiarities included the wearing of white garments; ritual bathing before meals which were given only to initiates, and cooked and blessed by priests; the rejection of animal sacrifice and of oaths to support their statements, and, above all, of marriage. Josephus, however, admits that one Essene branch adopted the married state as long as sex was used only for the purpose of procreation.

Theologically, they showed extreme reverence for the Law and were famous for their strictest observance of the Sabbath. Their esoteric teachings were recorded in secret books. Experts in the healing of body and soul, they also excelled in prophecy. They preferred belief in Fate to freedom of the will and, rejecting the notion of bodily resurrection, envisaged a purely spiritual afterlife.

## *Essenes and Qumran*

The common opinion identifying or closely associating the Qumran sectaries with the Essenes is based on three principal considerations.

1. There is no better site than Qumran to correspond to Pliny's settlement between Jericho and Engedi.

2. Chronologically, Essene activity placed by Josephus in the period between Jonathan Maccabaeus (*c.* 150 BCE) and the first Jewish war (66–70 CE) and the sectarian occupation of the Qumran site coincide perfectly.

3. The similarities of common life, organization and customs are so fundamental as to render the identification of the two bodies extremely probable as long as some obvious differences can be explained.

A good many contradictions appear in the diverse sources and are not simply due to a lack of harmony between the Scrolls and the Graeco-Latin documents. Thus Qumran attests both communism and private property; married and unmarried states. Likewise, Josephus speaks of celibate and married Essenes and, as has been noted (p. 38 above), the prohibition to 'fornicate' with one's wife remarkably echoes the married Essenes' ban on marital sex when the woman was not in a state to conceive.[2] Furthermore, the Qumran movement incorporated two separate branches and the manuscripts reflect an organizational and doctrinal development of some two centuries. It would be unreasonable to expect complete agreement among the sources. It must finally be borne in mind that the sectarian compositions were written by initiates for insiders, whereas Pliny and Philo, and to some extent even Josephus (although he claims to have undergone a partial Essene education), are bound to have reproduced hearsay evidence, unlikely to echo fully the views and beliefs prevalent among members. Hence the identification of Essenism and the Qumran sect remains in my view the likeliest of all proposed solutions.

2. The *therapeutai* or Egyptian ascetics of Philo adopted celibacy, but formed separate male and female communities (mature men having left behind family and property, and women being mostly aged virgins; cf. Philo, *Contemplative Life*, 13, 68) whose members met for worship. A badly damaged manuscript from Cave 4 (4Q502), repeatedly mentioning old men and women, is interpreted by J. M. Baumgarten as probably alluding to a similar institution ('4Q502, Marriage or Golden Age Ritual?', *JJS* 34 (1983), 125–35). 4Q502 consists of 344 papyrus fragments. Its editor, M. Baillet (*DJD* VII, 81–105), gave it the title 'Marriage Ritual', which is almost certainly a misnomer (see Baumgarten above). Not a single coherent section of this liturgical composition has survived; hence no meaningful translation can be supplied. However, it is worth noting that fr. 2 contains the phrase 'daughter of truth' and an allusion to the examination of women concerning their 'intelligence and understanding'. Josephus states in connection with the marrying Essenes that they trained their women – like their men – for three years (*War* II, 161; cf. G. Vermes, *Discovery in the Judean Desert*, New York, 1956, 57, note 176; J. M. Baumgarten, *DJD* XVIII, 143).

# *III. The History of the Community*

The absence from the Dead Sea Scrolls of historical texts proper should not surprise us. Neither in the inter-Testamental period, nor in earlier biblical times, was the recording of history as we understand it a strong point among the Jews. Chroniclers are concerned not with factual information about bygone events, but with their religious significance. In Scripture, the 'secular' past is viewed and interpreted by the prophets as revealing God's pleasure or displeasure. Victory or defeat in war, peace or social unrest, abundance of harvest or famine, serve to demonstrate the virtue or sinfulness of the nation and to forecast its future destiny. And when prophecy declined in the fifth century BCE, it was still not succeeded by a growth of historiography: only the memoirs of Ezra and Nehemiah and the retelling of the age-old stories of the kings of Israel and Judah in the Books of Chronicles belong to the historical *genre*. It was followed instead by eschatological speculation, by apocalyptic visions of the end of time, with their awe-inspiring beasts and battles, and by announcements of the ultimate triumph of truth and justice in a future Kingdom of God.

In the Scrolls, the apocalyptic compositions form part of this later tradition. On the other hand, apart from occasional snippets in a liturgical calendar (4Q322, 324), an odd poem alluding to 'King' Jonathan (4Q448), and deductive conclusions made from the comparative study of rules, most of the knowledge we possess of the sect's history originates from works of Bible interpretation. The Qumran writers, while meditating on the words of the Old Testament prophets, sought to discover in them allusions to their own past, present and future. Convinced that they were living in the last days, they read the happenings of their times as the fulfilment of biblical predictions.

Yet all that these non-historical sources provide are fragments. Even with the help of the archaeological data from Qumran they cannot be made into a consistent and continuous narrative. For an understanding of the sect's past as it developed within the larger framework of late Second Temple Jewish history, we have to rely principally on Flavius Josephus, the Palestinian Jew who became a Greek man of letters, and on other Jewish Hellenists, such as the authors of the Books of the Maccabees, and Philo of Alexandria, all of whom inherited the Greek predilection for recording and interpreting the past and set out to depict the life of the Jews of Palestine in itself, and as part of the Graeco-Roman world, from the early second century BCE to the first anti-Roman war in 66–70 CE. It is only with the help of the wider canvas painted by these ancient writers that places can be found for the often cryptic historical allusions contained in the Scrolls.

## 1 INTER-TESTAMENTAL JEWISH HISTORY: 200 BCE–70 CE

At the beginning of the second century BCE, Palestinian Jewry passed through a state of crisis. Alexander the Great had conquered the Holy Land in 332 BCE and, after the early uncertainties which followed his death, it became part of the empire of the Greeks of Egypt, known as the Ptolemies. During the third century, the Ptolemies avoided, as much as possible, interfering with the internal life of the Jewish nation and, while taxes were required to be paid, it remained under the rule of the High Priest and his council. Important changes in the patterns of population nevertheless took place during this time. Hellenistic cities were built along the Mediterranean coast, such as Gaza, Ascalon (Ashkelon), Joppa (Jaffa), Dor and Acco, re-named Ptolemais. Inland also, to the south of the Lake of Tiberias, the ancient town of Beth Shean was reborn as the Greek city of Scythopolis; Samaria, the capital city of the Samaritans, was Hellenized as Sebaste; and in Transjordan, Rabbath-Ammon (Amman) was re-founded as Philadelphia. In other words, Greeks, Macedonians and Hellenized Phoenicians took up permanent residence on Palestinian soil and the further spread of Greek civilization and culture was merely a matter of time.

With the conquest of the Holy Land by the Seleucids, or Syrian Greeks, in 200 BCE, the first signs appeared of Jews succumbing to a foreign cultural influence. In the apocryphal Book of Ecclesiasticus, dated to the beginning of the second century BCE, its author, Jesus ben Sira, a sage from Jerusalem, rages against those 'ungodly men' who have 'forsaken the Law of the Most High God' (xli, 8). But the real trouble started when Antiochus IV Epiphanes (175–164 BCE) officially promoted a Hellenizing programme in Judaea that was embraced with eagerness by the Jewish elite. The leader of the modernist faction was the brother of the High Priest Onias III. Known as Jesus among his compatriots, he adopted the Greek name of Jason, and set about transforming Jerusalem into a Hellenistic city, by building a gymnasium there and persuading the Jewish youth to participate in athletic games. As 2 Maccabees describes the situation:

> So Hellenism reached a high point with the introduction of foreign customs through the boundless wickedness of the impious Jason, no true High Priest. As a result, the priests no longer had any enthusiasm for their duties at the altar, but despised the temple and neglected the sacrifices; and in defiance of the law they eagerly contributed to the expenses of the wrestling-school whenever the opening gong called them. They placed no value on their hereditary dignities, but cared above everything for Hellenic honours. (2 Mac. iv, 13–15)

Jason was succeeded by two other High Priests with the same Greek sympathies, Menelaus and Alcimus. In 169 BCE Antiochus IV visited Jerusalem and looted the Temple. But when in 167 he actually prohibited the practice of Judaism under pain of death and rededicated the Jerusalem Sanctuary to Olympian Zeus, the 'abomination of desolation', the opponents of the Hellenizers finally rose up in violent resistance. An armed revolt was instigated by the priest Mattathias and his sons the Maccabee brothers, supported by all the traditionalist Jews, and in particular by the company of the Pious, the Asidaeans or Hasidim, 'stalwarts of Israel, every one of them a volunteer in the cause of the Law' (1 Mac. ii, 42–3). Led by Judas Maccabaeus and, after his death on the battlefield, by his brothers Jonathan and Simon, the fierce defenders of Judaism were able not only to restore Jewish worship in Jerusalem, but against all expectations even managed to eject the ruling Seleucids and to liberate Judaea.

The Maccabaean triumph was, however, not simply a straightforward victory of godliness and justice over idolatry and tyranny; it was accompanied by serious social and religious upheavals. There was firstly a change in the pontifical succession. With the murder in 171 BCE of Onias III and the deposition of the usurper, his brother Jason, the Zadokite family, from which the incumbents of the High Priest's office traditionally came, lost the monopoly which it had held for centuries. Furthermore, when

Onias IV, the son of Onias III, was prevented from taking over the High Priesthood from Menelaus, he emigrated to Egypt and in direct breach of biblical law, which authorizes only a single sanctuary in Jerusalem, erected a Jewish temple in Leontopolis with the blessing of King Ptolemy Philometor (182–146 BCE). His inauguration of Israelite worship outside Zion, with the connivance of some priests and Levites, must have scandalized every Palestinian conservative, especially other priests who belonged, or were allied, to the Zadokite dynasty.

There was trouble also within the ranks of the Maccabees themselves. The Hasidim – or part of their group – defected when Alcimus, whom they trusted, was appointed High Priest in 162 BCE. This move on their part turned out to be naïve; Alcimus' Syrian allies massacred sixty of them in one day (1 Mac. vii, 2–20).

Lastly, a major political change came about when Jonathan Maccabaeus, himself a priest but not a Zadokite, accepted in 153–152 BCE pontifical office from Alexander Balas, a usurper of the Seleucid throne. Alexander was anxious for Jewish support and was not mistaken in thinking that an offer of the High Priesthood would be irresistible. For the conservatives this was an illegal seizure of power. But they were even more scandalized by the appointment in 140 BCE, following Jonathan's execution in 143–142 by the Syrian general Tryphon, of Simon Maccabee as High Priest and hereditary leader of the people by means of a decree passed by a Jewish national assembly.

From then on, until Pompey's transformation of the independent Jewish state into a Roman province in 63 BCE, Judaea was ruled by a new dynasty of High Priests, later Priest-Kings, known as the Hasmonaeans after the grandfather of the Maccabees, Hasmon, or Asamonaeus according to Josephus (*War* I, 36). During the intervening years, all Simon's successors, but especially John Hyrcanus I (134–104 BCE) and Alexander Jannaeus (103–76 BCE), for whom their political role took precedence over their office of High Priest, occupied one by one the Hellenistic cities of Palestine and conquered the neighbouring territories of Idumaea in the south, Samaria in the centre and Ituraea in the north.

Throughout this period of territorial expansion, the Hasmonaean rulers enjoyed the support of the Sadducees, one of the three religious parties first mentioned under Jonathan Maccabaeus (cf. Josephus, *Antiquities* XIII, 171) and regular allies of the government. They were opposed by the Pharisees, an essentially lay group formed from one of the branches of the Hasidim of the Maccabaean age. Already in the days of John Hyrcanus I there was Pharisaic objection to his usurpation of the High Priesthood, though they were willing to recognize him as national leader (*Antiquities* XIII, 288–98), but on one other occasion, at least, their opposition was overcome by force. Accused of plotting against Alexander Jannaeus in 88 BCE in collusion with the Syrian Seleucid king Demetrius III Eucaerus, 800 Pharisees were condemned by Jannaeus to die on the cross (*Antiquities* XIII, 380–83; *War* I, 96–8).

After Pompey's seizure of Jerusalem, the Hasmonaean High Priesthood continued for another three decades, but the political power formerly belonging to them passed to the Judaized Idumaean, Herod the Great, when he was promoted to the throne of Jerusalem by Rome in 37 BCE. It is to the last year or two of his reign – he died in 4 BCE – that the Gospels of Matthew and Luke date the birth of Jesus of Nazareth (Matth. ii, 1; Lk. i, 5).

After the ephemeral rule of the successor to Herod the Great, Herod Archelaus (4 BCE–6 CE), who was deposed by Augustus for his misgovernment of Jews and Samaritans alike, Galilee continued in semi-autonomy under the Herodian princes Antipas (4 BCE–39 CE) and Agrippa (39–41 CE), but Judaea was placed under the direct administration of Roman authority. In 6 CE, Coponius, the first Roman prefect of Judaea, arrived to take up his duties there. This prefectorial regime, whose most notorious representative was Pontius Pilate (26–36 CE), lasted for thirty-five years until 41, when the emperor Claudius appointed Agrippa I as king. He died, however, three years later, and in 44 CE the government of the province once more reverted to Roman officials, this time with the title of procurator. Their corrupt and unwise handling of Jewish affairs was one of the chief causes of the war of 66 which led to the destruction of Jerusalem in 70 CE, and to the subsequent decline of the Sadducees, the extinction of the Zealots in Masada in 74, the disappearance of the Essenes, and the survival and uncontested domination of the Pharisees and their rabbinic successors.

It is into this general course of events that the history of Qumran has to be inserted. Document by document the Scrolls will be scrutinized and the literary information combined, both with the findings of Qumran archaeology and with the incidental reports provided by Josephus. In the end it is hoped that the history of the Essene sect will begin to fall reliably into place.

## 2 THE HISTORY OF THE ESSENES

### *(a) Concealed References in the Scrolls*

The search for clues to the origins and story of the movement begins with the Damascus Document because it is a writing particularly rich in such hints. Here, the birth of the Community is said to have occurred in the 'age of wrath', 390 years after the destruction of Jerusalem by Nebuchadnezzar, king of Babylon. At that time, a 'root' sprung 'from Israel and Aaron', i.e. a group of pious Jews, laymen and priests, and came into being in a situation of general ungodliness. These people 'groped for the way' for twenty years, and then God sent them a 'Teacher of Righteousness' to guide them 'in the way of His heart' (I, 5–11). The Teacher did not meet with unanimous approval within the congregation, and a faction described as 'seekers of smooth things', 'removers of the bounds' and 'builders of the wall', all metaphors seeming to point to religious laxity and infidelity, turned against him and his followers. The leader of the breakaway party, though accorded a number of unflattering sobriquets, such as 'Scoffer', 'Liar' or 'Spouter of Lies', seems to be one and the same person. His associates erred in matters of ritual cleanness, justice, chastity, the dates of festivals and Temple worship; they were lovers of money and enemies of peace. In the ensuing fratricidal struggle, the Teacher and those who remained faithful to him went into exile in the 'land of Damascus' where they entered into a 'new Covenant'. There, the Teacher of Righteousness was 'gathered in', meaning that he died. In the meantime, the wicked dominated over Jerusalem and the Temple, though not without experiencing God's vengeance at the hands of the 'Chief of the Kings of Greece'.

A similar picture emerges from the Habakkuk Commentary with its explicit mention of desertion by disciples of the Teacher of Righteousness to the Liar, but also by members unfaithful to the 'new Covenant'. The allusions to the protagonists of the conflict are sharper in this work than in the Damascus Document. We learn that the villain, known in this Scroll as the 'Wicked Priest' as well as the 'Liar' and 'Spouter of Lies', was 'called by the name of truth' before he became Israel's ruler and was corrupted by wealth and power (VIII, 8–11) – the implication being that for a time he had met with the sect's approval. Subsequently, however, he defiled Jerusalem and the Temple. He also sinned against the Teacher of Righteousness and his disciples, chastising him while the 'House of

Absalom' looked silently on (v, 9–12), and confronting him in his place of exile on the sect's Day of Atonement (xi, 6–8). He 'vilified and outraged the elect of God', 'plotted to destroy the Poor', i.e. the Community, and stole their riches. As a punishment, God delivered him 'into the hand of his enemies', who 'took vengeance on his body of flesh' (ix, 2). At the last judgement, predicts the Commentary, the Wicked Priest will empty 'the cup of wrath of God'. His successors, the 'last Priests of Jerusalem', are also charged with amassing 'money and wealth by plundering the peoples', i.e. foreigners. But, so the commentator asserts, all their riches and booty will be snatched from them by the Kittim, the conquerors of the world commissioned by God to pay them their just deserts.

Because of lacunae, one cannot be quite sure from the Habakkuk Commentary that the Teacher was a priest. The Commentary on Psalms (Ps. xxxvii, 4Q**171**, **173**), by contrast, makes this plain. Interpreting verses 23–4, it reads: 'this concerns the Priest, the Teacher of [Righteousness]'. It further supplies a significant detail by assigning to 'the violent of the nations', that is to say to the Gentiles as opposed to the Jews, the execution of judgement on the Wicked Priest. Another point of interest is that the enemies of the sect are alluded to as 'the wicked of Ephraim and Manasseh', i.e. as of two distinct factions. They appear also in the Commentary on Nahum.

In the Messianic Anthology or Testimonia (4Q**175**), references appear in the final section, borrowed from a Joshua Apocryphon or Psalms of Joshua (4Q**379** fr. 22 ii), to two 'instruments of violence' who ruled Jerusalem. They are cursed for making the city a 'stronghold of ungodliness' and for committing 'an abomination' in the land. They are also said to have shed blood 'like water on the ramparts of the daughter of Zion'. The relationship of the two tyrants to one another cannot be established with certainty because of the fragmentary nature of the manuscript. They could be father and son. On the other hand, the expression, 'instruments of violence', depends on Genesis xlix, 5 where it describes the brother murderers, Simeon and Levi, the destroyers of Shechem.

The Nahum Commentary moves on to an age following that of the Teacher of Righteousness and the Wicked Priest, as neither of them is mentioned. The principal character here is the 'furious young lion', a Jewish ruler of Jerusalem. He is said to have taken revenge on the 'seekers of smooth things', whom he reproached for having invited 'Demetrius' the king of Greece to Jerusalem. The attempt failed; no foreigner entered the city 'from the time of Antiochus until the coming of the rulers of the

Kittim'. The enemies of the 'furious young lion' were 'hanged alive on the tree', a familiar Hebrew circumlocution for crucifixion. As in the Commentary on Psalm xxxvii, the sobriquets 'Ephraim' and 'Manasseh' are attached to the Community's opponents. 'Ephraim' is said to 'walk in lies and falsehood', but because of gaps in the manuscript, the description of 'Manasseh' is less clear. It seems nevertheless that this party included 'great men', 'mighty men' and 'men of dignity'.

The Nahum Commentary was the first of the Qumran Scrolls to disclose historical names: those of two Seleucid kings, Antiochus and Demetrius. But their identity has still to be determined because nine monarchs in all bore the first name, and three the second. Additional names figure in various Cave 4 manuscripts of a liturgical calendar (4Q**322**, **324a–b**): 'Shelamzion', the Hebrew name of Queen Salome-Alexandra, widow of Alexander Jannaeus, who reigned from 76 to 67 BCE; 'Hyrcanus' and 'John', probably John Hyrcanus II, son of Alexandra and High Priest from 76 to 67 and again from 63 to 40; and 'Emilius', no doubt M. Aemilius Scaurus, the first Roman governor of Syria from 65 to 62 BCE, who is charged with killing people. Note also that the Balakros of 4Q**243** may be the Seleucid usurper Alexander Balas.

A remarkable piece of prayer-poetry (4Q**448**) refers to 'King Jonathan' in connection with Jerusalem and diaspora Jewry. A good case has been made out by E. and H. Eshel (*IEJ* 42, 1992, 199–229) for identifying him with Alexander Jannaeus, but in my opinion an even stronger argument points towards Jonathan Maccabaeus as 'King Jonathan' (cf. *JJS* 44, 1993, 294–300). Also, one of the proposed readings of line 9 of the List of False Prophets (4Q**339**), '[John son of Sim]on', would provide an allusion to John Hyrcanus I.

In the Commentaries on Habakkuk and Nahum, the Kittim are represented as instruments appointed by God to punish the ungodly priests of Jerusalem. The War Rule, however, testifies to a changed attitude towards them on the part of the sect by making the Kittim appear as the chief allies of Belial or Satan and the final foe to be subjugated by the hosts of the sons of Light. The Rule of War (4Q**285**), although very fragmentary, appears to point in the same direction.

Several Qumran Hymns reflect the career and sentiments of a teacher, possibly of the Teacher of Righteousness himself. According to them, he was opposed by 'interpreters of error', 'traitors', 'deceivers', by 'those who seek smooth things', all of whom were formerly his 'friends' and 'members of [his] Covenant', bearers of the 'yoke of [his] testimony'. In one of them, the reference to a 'devilish scheme' is reminiscent of the allusion in the Habakkuk Commentary to the visit of the Wicked Priest to the Community's place of exile in order to cause them 'to stumble':

> Teachers of lies [have smoothed] Thy people [with words],
> and [false prophets] have led them astray . . .
> They have banished me from my land like a bird from its nest . . .
> And they, teachers of lies and seers of falsehood,
> have schemed against me a devilish scheme,
> to exchange the Law engraved on my heart by Thee
> for the smooth things (which they speak) to Thy people.
> And they withhold from the thirsty the drink of Knowledge,
> and assuage their thirst with vinegar,
> that they may gaze on their straying,
> on their folly concerning their feast-days,
> on their fall into the snares. (1QH XII [formerly IV], 7–12)

Another Hymn appears to hint at the Teacher's withdrawal from society and to announce with confidence his eventual glorious justification:

> For Thou, O God, hast sheltered me
> from the children of men,
> and hast hidden Thy Law [within me]
> against the time when Thou shouldst reveal
> Thy salvation to me. (1QH XIII [formerly V], 11–12)

Some scholars consider these poems autobiographical, i.e. written by the Teacher, but this is mere speculation.

It would be unrealistic, taking into account the vagueness of all these statements, the cryptic nature of the symbolism and the entire lack of any systematic exposition of the sect's history, to expect every detail to be identified. We can, however, attempt to define the chronological framework of the historical references and thus be in a position to place at least some of the key events and principal personalities within the context of Jewish history as we know it.

## *(b) The Chronological Framework*

The chronological setting of Qumran history may be reconstructed from archaeological and literary evidence. The excavations of 1951–6 date the beginning, the *terminus a quo*, of the sectarian establishment to 150–140 BCE and its end, the *terminus ad quem*, to the middle of the first war against Rome, 68 CE. The literary allusions, particularly the identifiable historical names, confirm this general finding. It goes without saying, however, that the initial phases of the Community's existence must have preceded by some years or decades the actual establishment of the sect at Qumran. The first task therefore is to examine the Scrolls for indications of its origins. The Nahum Commentary implies that a king by the name of Antiochus was alive at the beginning of the period with which the documents are concerned. This Antiochus, although one among several so called, can only have been Antiochus IV Epiphanes, notorious for his looting of Jerusalem and the profanation of the Temple in 169–168 BCE.

More significant as a chronological pointer is the dating, in the Damascus Document, of the sect's beginnings to the 'age of wrath', 390 years after the conquest of Jerusalem by Nebuchadnezzar in 586 BCE. This should bring us to 196 BCE but, as is well known, Jewish historians are not very reliable in their time-reckoning for the post-exilic era. They do not seem to have had a clear idea of the length of the Persian domination, and they were in addition not free of the theological influence of the Book of Daniel, where a period of seventy weeks of years, i.e. 490 years, is given as separating the epoch of Nebuchadnezzar from that of the Messiah. As it happens, if to this figure of 390 years is added, firstly twenty (during which the ancestors of the Community 'groped' for their way until the entry on the scene of the Teacher of Righteousness), then another forty (the time span between the death of the Teacher and the dawn of the messianic epoch), the total stretch of years arrived at is 450. And if to this total is added the duration of the Teacher's ministry of, say, forty years – a customary round figure – the final result is the classic seventy times seven years.

Yet even if the literal figure of 390 is rejected, there are still compelling reasons for placing the 'age of wrath' in the opening decades of the second pre-Christian century. Only the Hellenistic crisis which occurred at that time, and which is recalled in various Jewish literary sources from the last two centuries BCE, provides a fitting context for the historical allusions made in the sectarian writings (cf. Daniel ix–xi; Enoch xc, 6–7; Jubilees xxiii, 14–19; Testament of Levi xvii; Assumption of Moses iv–v). Also, it is the Hasidim of the pre-Maccabaean and early Maccabaean era who best correspond to the earlier but unorganized group as it is described there (cf. pp. 51–2).

As for the *terminus ad quem* of Qumran history, as this is linked to the appearance of the Kittim, we have to determine who these people were. In its primitive sense, the word 'Kittim' described the inhabitants of Kition, a Phoenician colony in Cyprus. Later the name tended to be applied indiscriminately to those living in 'all islands and most maritime countries' (Josephus, *Antiquities* i, 128). But from the second century BCE, Jewish writers also used 'Kittim' more precisely to denote the greatest world power of the day. In Maccabees (i, 1; viii, 5) they are Greeks; Alexander the Great and Perseus are called kings of the 'Kittim'. In Daniel xi, 30 on the other hand, the 'Kittim' are Romans; it was the ambassador of the Roman senate, Poppilius Laenas, brought to Alexandria by 'ships of Kittim', i.e. the Roman fleet, who instructed the 'king of the North', the Seleucid monarch Antiochus Epiphanes, to withdraw at once from Egypt. The term 'Romans' is substituted for 'Kittim' already in the old Greek or Septuagint version of Daniel xi, 30. None of these texts is critical of the 'Kittim'. They are seen as the ruling force of the time, but not as hostile to Israel. In fact, in Daniel they humiliate the enemy of the Jews. It is not till a later stage, especially after 70 CE, that they come to symbolize oppression and tyranny.

In the Habakkuk Commentary, the portrait of the Kittim is neutral, as in Maccabees and Daniel. (In the Damascus Document they play no part; the alien adversary there is the 'Chief of the Kings of *Greece*'.) Feared and admired by all, they are seen to be on the point of defeating the 'last Priests of Jerusalem' and confiscating their wealth, as they have done to many others before. Such a representation of a victorious and advancing might would hardly apply to the Greek Seleucids of Syria, who by the second half of the second century BCE were in grave decline. But it does correspond to the Romans, whose thrust to the east in the first century BCE resulted in their triumphs over Pontus, Armenia and Seleucid Syria, and finally, with the arrival of Pompey in Jerusalem in 63 BCE, in the transformation of the Hasmonaean state into Judaea, a province of the Roman republic.

Since the identification of the 'Kittim' as Romans is nowadays generally accepted, it will suffice to cite a single, but very striking, feature in the Habakkuk Commentary to support it. Interpreting Hab. I, 14–16 as referring to the 'Kittim', the commentator writes: 'This means that they sacrifice to their standards and worship their weapons of war' (1QpHab. VI, 3–5). Now this custom of worshipping the *signa* was a characteristic of the religion of the Roman armies both in republican and in imperial times, as Josephus testifies in his report of the capture of the Temple of Jerusalem by the legionaries of Titus in 70.

> The Romans, now that the rebels had fled to the city, and the Sanctuary itself and all around it were in flames, carried their standards into the Temple court, and setting them up opposite the eastern gate, there sacrificed to them.
>
> (*War* VI, 316)

It is also worth noting that the 'Kittim' of the War Scroll, the final opponents of the eschatological Israel, are subject to a king or emperor (*melekh*). Previously, in the Commentaries of Habakkuk and Nahum, they are said to have been governed by rulers (*moshelim*). In sum, therefore, the time-limits of the sect's history appear to be at one extreme, the beginning of the second century BCE, and at the other, some moment during the Roman imperial epoch, i.e. after 27 BCE. And this latter date is determined by Qumran archaeology as coinciding with the first Jewish war, and even more precisely, with the arrival of the armies of Vespasian and Titus in the neighbourhood of the Dead Sea in June 68 CE.

### *(c) Decipherment of Particular Allusions*

The 'age of wrath' having been identified as that of the Hellenistic crisis of the beginning of the second century BCE, the 'root' as the Hasidim of the pre-Maccabaean age, and the 'Kittim' as the Romans, the next major problem is to discover who was, or were, the principal Jewish enemy or enemies of the sect at the time of the ministry of the Teacher of Righteousness variously known as the 'Scoffer', the 'Liar', the 'Spouter of Lies' and the 'Wicked Priest' (1QpHab, 4QpPs[a], CD).

It is not unreasonable to conclude that all these insults are directed at the same individual. It would appear from the Damascus Document that the 'Scoffer' and the 'Liar' (cf. also 4QpPs[a] [XXXVII]) were one and the same ('when the Scoffer arose who shed over Israel the waters of lies', CD I, 14). And we read of the 'Wicked Priest' that he was called 'by the name of truth' (1QpHab VIII, 8–9) at the outset of his career, the inference being that later he changed into a 'Liar'.

Another basic premise must be that the person intended by the fragments of information contained in the Scrolls became the head, the national leader, of the Jewish people. For although biblical names are often used symbolically, including that of 'Israel', the actions attributed to the 'Wicked Priest' make little sense if the person in question did not exercise both pontifical and secular power. He 'ruled over Israel'. He 'robbed . . . the riches of the men of violence who rebelled against God', probably Jewish apostates, as well as 'the wealth of the peoples', i.e. the Gentiles. He built 'his city of vanity with blood', committed 'abominable deeds in Jerusalem and defiled the Temple of God' (1QpHab VIII). Taken separately, these observations might be understood allegorically, but considered together, they constitute a strong argument for recognizing the 'Wicked Priest' as a ruling High Priest in Jerusalem.

The 'Wicked Priest', then, was a Pontiff who enjoyed good repute before he assumed office. He was victorious over his adversaries at home and abroad. He rebuilt Jerusalem (cf. 1QpHab VIII, 8–11; 4Q448). And he was eventually captured and put to death by a foreign rival.

The chronological guidelines established in the preceding section locate the period in which this individual flourished between the reign of Antiochus Epiphanes (175–164 BCE) and the probable date of the foundation at Qumran (150–140 BCE). During that time, five men held the office of High Priest. Three of them were pro-Greek: Jason, Menelaus and Alcimus. The remaining two were the Maccabee brothers, Jonathan and Simon. All the Hellenizers can be eliminated as candidates for the role of 'Wicked Priest' since none can be said to have enjoyed anything like good repute at the beginning of their ministry. Jason and Alcimus fail also because neither was killed by an enemy, as implied in 1QpHab VIII–IX. Jason died in exile (2 Mac. v, 7–9) and Alcimus in office (1 Mac. ix, 54–6). The Maccabee brothers, by contrast, meet all the conditions. The careers of both men fall easily into two stages, marked, in the case of Jonathan, by his acceptance of the High Priesthood from Alexander Balas, and in the case of Simon by his willingness to become a hereditary High Priest. Both were also 'instruments of violence' and both died by violence. Jonathan is nevertheless to be chosen rather than Simon because he alone suffered the vengeance of the 'Chief of the Kings of Greece' and died at the hands of the 'violent of the nations', whereas Simon was murdered by his son-in-law (1 Mac. xvi, 14–16). A gallant defender of Jewish religion and independence, Jonathan succeeded the heroic Judas in 161 BCE when the latter fell in battle. But he qualified for the epithet 'Wicked Priest' when he accepted in 153–152 BCE from Alexander Balas, a heathen usurper of the Seleucid throne who had no right to grant them, the pontifical vestments which Jonathan was not entitled to wear. Captured later by a former general of Alexander Balas, Tryphon, he was killed by him at Bascama in Transjordan (1 Mac. xiii, 23).

Concerning the identity of the 'last Priests of Jerusalem', the passion for conquest, wealth and plunder for which they are reproached points to the Hasmonaean priestly rulers, from Simon's son, John Hyrcanus I (134–104 BCE), to Judas Aristobulus II (67–63 BCE). There can in particular be little doubt that the 'furious young lion', designated also as 'the last Priest' in a badly damaged Commentary on Hosea (4Q**167** II 2–3), was one of them, namely Alexander Jannaeus. The application to him of the words of Nahum, 'who chokes prey for its lionesses', and the report that the 'young lion' executed the 'seekers of smooth things' by 'hanging men alive', accord perfectly with the known story that Jannaeus crucified 800 Pharisees whilst feasting with his concubines (cf. above, p. 53).

From this it follows that 'Ephraim', equated in the Commentary on Nahum with the 'seekers of smooth things', symbolizes the Pharisees, and that if so, 'Manasseh' and his dignitaries must refer to the Sadducees. In other words, the political and doctrinal opponents of the Essene community, though itself with proto-Sadducaean links on account of its priestly leadership as insinuated by MMT, were the Sadducees and the Pharisees.

This division of Jewish society into three opposing groups corresponds to the conformation described by Josephus as existing from the time of Jonathan Maccabaeus (*Antiquities* XIII, 171), but the new insight provided by the Scrolls suggests that the united resistance to Hellenism first fell apart when the Maccabees, and more precisely Jonathan, refused to acknowledge the spiritual leadership of the Teacher of Righteousness, the priestly head of the Hasidim. From then on, the sect saw its defectors as 'Ephraim' and 'Manasseh', these being the names of the sons of Joseph, associated in biblical history with the apostate Northern kingdom, and referred to itself as the 'House of Judah', the faithful South.

Unfortunately, on the most vital topic of all, the question of the identity of the Teacher of Righteousness, we can be nothing like as clear. If the 'Wicked Priest' was Jonathan Maccabaeus, the Teacher would, of course, have been one of his contemporaries. Yet all we know of him is that he was a priest (1QpHab II, 8; 4QpPs [XXXVII ii, 15=4Q**171**]), no doubt of Zadokite affiliation, though obviously opposed to Onias IV since he did not follow him to Egypt and to his unlawful Temple in

Leontopolis.[1] He founded or re-founded the Community. He transmitted to them his own distinctive interpretation of the Prophets and, if we can rely at least indirectly on the Hymns, of the laws relating to the celebration of festivals. The 'Liar' and his sympathizers in the congregation of the Hasidim disagreed with him, and after a violent confrontation between the two factions in which the 'Liar' gained the upper hand, the Teacher and his remaining followers fled to a place of refuge called 'the land of Damascus': it has been suggested that this is a cryptic designation of Babylonia, the original birthplace of the group, or else that 'Damascus' is a symbolical name for Qumran. The 'House of Absalom' gave the Teacher of Righteousness no help against the 'Liar', writes the Habakkuk commentator (1QpHab v, 9–12), the implication being that this was support on which he might have relied. If 'Absalom' is also a symbol, it doubtless recalls the rebellion of Absalom against his father David, and thus points to the perfidy of a close relation or intimate friend of the Teacher. On the other hand, since the 'House of Absalom' is accused not of an actual attack but simply of remaining silent during the Teacher's 'chastisement', this allegorical solution may not be convincing. The allusion may then be a straightforward one. A certain Absalom was an ambassador of Judas Maccabaeus (2 Mac. xi, 17), and his son Mattathias was one of Jonathan's gallant officers (1 Mac. xi, 70). Another of his sons, Jonathan, commanded Simon's army which captured Joppa (1 Mac. xiii, 11).

Meanwhile, even in his 'place of exile' the Teacher continued to be harassed and persecuted by the Wicked Priest. In this connection, the

1. The Zadokite affiliation of the Teacher of Righteousness may be supported by circumstantial evidence. According to the older version of the Community Rule, represented by 4Q**258** and **256**, the democratic 'Congregation' ('the Many') constituted the supreme authority of the Community with ordinary priests (sons of Aaron) forming the top layer in doctrinal and legal administration. This position is attributed to the 'sons of Zadok', members of the high-priestly family, in the revised 1QS v. In other words, at some early stage in the history of the sect there was a Zadokite takeover. Combining this information with the account of CD I (supported by 4QD), we may reasonably surmise that the change occurred with the arrival of the Teacher of Righteousness sent by God to take care of the 'plant' of Aaron and Israel (ordinary priests and lay Jews), who had been groping, leaderless, for twenty years. The crisis in the Zadokite ranks in the 160s BCE, following the secession of Onias IV to Egypt, provides the likeliest background for these events (cf. G. Vermes, 'The Leadership of the Qumran Community' in *Geschichte-Tradition-Reflexion* [Martin Hengel Festschrift] I (Tübingen, 1996, 375–84). In this connection it may not be irrelevant to note that according to 4Q**266** fr. 5 ii priests who had emigrated among the Gentiles were disqualified.

most important and painful episode appears to have been the Priest's pursuit of the Teacher to his settlement with the purpose of pouring on him 'his venomous fury'. Appearing before the sectaries on 'their Sabbath of repose', at the 'time appointed for rest, for the Day of Atonement', his intention was to cause them 'to stumble on the Day of Fasting'. It is impossible to say, from the evidence so far available, precisely what happened on this portentous occasion, or whether it was then or later that the Wicked Priest 'laid hands' on the Teacher 'that he might put him to death'. The wording is equivocal. For example, the verb in 1QpHab XI, 5, 7, translated 'to confuse', can also mean 'to swallow up', and some scholars have chosen to understand that the Teacher was killed by the Wicked Priest at the time of the visit. On the other hand, we find recounted in the imperfect tense (which can be rendered into English as either the future or the present tense): 'The wicked of Ephraim and Manasseh ... seek/will seek to lay hands on the Priest and the men of his Council ... But God redeems/will redeem them from out of their hand' (4QpPs$^a$ [XXXVII, II, 17–19=4Q171]). In other words, we neither know who the founder of the Essenes was, nor how, nor where, nor when he died. Only writers upholding the most unlikely Christian identification of the Community claim to be better informed, but disagree among themselves. J. L. Teicher thought the Teacher was Jesus. For Barbara Thiering Jesus was the Wicked Priest, John the Baptist the Teacher; R. H. Eisenman rejects both and prefers James the Just, 'the brother of the Lord', as the Teacher of Righteousness. Only the sensation-seeking media have been taken in by their theories.

It has been suggested that this inability to identify the Teacher of Righteousness in the context of the Maccabaean period undermines the credibility of the reconstruction as a whole. Is it conceivable, it is asked, that a figure of the stature of the Teacher should have left no trace in the literature relating to that time? The answer to this objection is that such writings are to all intents and purposes restricted to the Books of the Maccabees, sources politically biased in favour of their heroes and virtually oblivious of the very existence of opposition movements. Josephus himself relies largely on 1 Maccabees and cannot therefore be regarded as an independent witness. But even were this not so, and he had additional material at his disposition, his silence *vis-à-vis* the Teacher of Righteousness would still not call for particular comment since he also makes no mention of the founder of the Pharisees. And incidentally, not a few historians hold that he has nothing to say either of Jesus of Nazareth. The so-called

Testimonium Flavianum (*Antiquities* XVIII, 63–4), they maintain, is a Christian interpolation into the genuine text of *Antiquities* (though others, myself included, think that part of the text is authentic). Be this as it may, not a word is breathed by him about Hillel, the greatest of the Pharisee masters, or about Yohanan ben Zakkai, who reorganized Judaism after the destruction of the Temple, although both of these men lived in Josephus' own century and Yohanan was definitely his contemporary.

Admittedly, the various fragments of information gleaned from the Dead Sea Scrolls result in an unavoidably patchy story, but it is fundamentally sound, and the continuing anonymity of the Teacher does nothing to impair it. For the present synthesis to be complete it remains now to turn to Josephus for his occasional historical references to individual Essenes and to Essenism.

To begin with it should be pointed out that four members of the Community are actually mentioned by the Jewish historian, three of them associated with prophecy, one of the distinctive interests of the Teacher of Righteousness himself. The first, called Judas, is encountered in Jerusalem surrounded by a group of pupils taking instruction in 'foretelling the future', which probably means how to identify prophetic pointers to future events. Josephus writes of him that he had 'never been known to speak falsely in his prophecies', and that he predicted the death of Antigonus, the brother of Aristobulus I (104–103 BCE) (*Antiquities* XIII, 311–13). A second Essene prophet, Menahem, apparently foretold that Herod would rule over the Jews (XV, 373–8). Herod showed his gratitude to him by dispensing the Essenes, who were opposed to all oaths except their own oath of the Covenant, from taking the vow of loyalty imposed on all his Jewish subjects. A third Essene named Simon interpreted a dream of Archelaus, ethnarch of Judaea (4 BCE–6 CE), in 4 BCE to mean that his rule would last for ten years (XVII, 345–8). John the Essene, the last sectary to be referred to by Josephus, was not a prophet, but the commander or *strategos* of the district of Thamna in north-western Judaea, and of the cities of Lydda (Lod), Joppa (Jaffa) and Emmaus at the beginning of the first revolution (*War* II, 567). A man of 'first-rate prowess and ability', he fell in battle at Ascalon (III, 11, 19).[2]

2. To these four outstanding Essenes we may now add possibly the name of a Bursar or Guardian, Eleazar son of Nahmani, mentioned in one of the Qumran ostraca (cf. below, p. 596), and the three imperfect members, Yohanan and two men called Hananiah mentioned in 4Q477. See above, pp. 31–2.

Finally, Josephus depicts in vivid language the bravery of the Essenes subjected to torture by the Romans.

The war with the Romans tried their souls through and through by every variety of test. Racked and twisted, burned and broken, and made to pass through every instrument of torture in order to induce them to blaspheme their lawgiver or to eat some forbidden thing, they refused to yield to either demand, nor ever once did they cringe to their persecutors or shed a tear. Smiling in their agonies and mildly deriding their tormentors, they cheerfully resigned their souls, confident that they would receive them back again. (*War* II, 152–3)

Since it would appear from this passage that the Romans were persecuting not individuals, but a group, it is tempting, bearing in mind the archaeologists' claim that the Qumran settlement was destroyed by the Romans, to associate it with the story of Essenes captured by the Dead Sea. If such a surmise is correct, the sect's disappearance from history may well have been brought about in the lethal blow suffered by its central establishment during the fateful summer of 68 CE. The fact that no attempt was made to recover nearly 800 manuscripts from the caves confirms, it would seem, such a reconstruction of the end of Qumran and, with the annihilation of its central establishment, of the whole Essene movement.

# *IV. The Religious Ideas of the Community*

The first essays in the 1950s on the religious outlook of the Qumran sect all suffered from a serious defect in that scholars in those days tended to envisage the Scrolls as self-contained and entitled to independent treatment. Today, with the hindsight of five decades of research and with the entire corpus to hand, it is easier to conceive of the theology of the Community as part of the general doctrinal evolution of ancient Judaism.

Nevertheless, it is no simple task to follow that development itself, the reason being that the systematic exposition of beliefs and customs is not a traditional Jewish discipline. In a sense, the Instruction on the Two Spirits, incorporated in the Community Rule, alluded to earlier (p. 28), is an exception, forming the one and only doctrinal treatise among ancient Hebrew writings. The theology of Judaism, biblical, inter-Testamental, medieval or modern, when written by contemporary Jewish authors, is often modelled consciously or unconsciously on Christian dogmatic structures: God, creation, human destiny, messianic redemption, judgement, resurrection, heaven and hell. Such structures may and sometimes do distort the religious concepts of Judaism. For example, the interest of the Church in the messianic role of Jesus is apt to assign a greater importance to Messianism in Jewish religion than the historical evidence justifies, and Paul's hostility to the 'legalism' of Israel obscures the Jewish recognition of the humble realities of everyday life prescribed by the Law as no mere 'works' but as a path to holiness walked in obedience to God's commandments.

## 1 THE COVENANT

Since the key to any understanding of Judaism must be the notion of the Covenant, it may safely be taken as an introduction to Essene religious thought. The history of mankind and of the Jewish people has seen a series of such covenants. God undertook never to destroy mankind again by a flood; in exchange, Noah and his descendants were required to abstain from shedding human blood and, on the ritual level, from eating animal 'flesh with the life, which is the blood, still in it' (Gen. ix, 1–17). To Abraham, who was childless and landless, God offered posterity and a country, provided he led a perfect life and marked his body and that of all his male progeny with a visible reminder of the Covenant between himself and heaven, circumcision (Gen. xvii, 1–14). Again, in the days of Moses the Israelites were declared 'a kingdom of priests, and a holy nation' (Exod. xix, 5), God's special possession, on condition that they obeyed the Torah, the divine Teaching of the religious, moral, social and ritual precepts recorded in the Pentateuch from Exodus xx and repeated in the farewell discourse addressed by Moses to his people in the Book of Deuteronomy. After the conquest of Canaan and the distribution of the land to the tribes, the fulfilment of God's promise to Abraham, the Covenant was renewed by Joshua and the Israelites reasserted their commitment to their heavenly Helper (Jos. xxiv). From then on, the biblical story is one of continuous unfaithfulness to the Covenant. But God was not to be thwarted by human unworthiness and ingratitude, and for the sake of the handful of just men appearing in every generation he allowed the validity of the Covenant to endure. Though he punished the sinful and the rebellious, he spared the 'remnant' because of their fidelity to it. From time to time, saintly leaders of the Jewish people, King David and King Josiah before the Babylonian exile (2 Sam. vii; 2 Kings xxiii, 1–3) and Ezra the Priest after the return from Mesopotamia (Neh. viii–x), persuaded them to remember their Covenant with God with solemn vows of repentance and national rededication; but the promises were usually short-lived. This would no doubt account for the development of an idea in the sixth century BCE of a 'new Covenant' founded not so much on undertakings entered into by the community as on the inner transformation of every individual Jew for whom the will of God was to become, as it were, second nature.

> The time is coming ... when I will make a new Covenant with Israel ... This is the new Covenant which I will make with Israel in those days ... I will set my law within them and write it on their hearts ... (Jer. xxxi, 31–3; Isa. liv, 13)

It was this same Covenant ideology that served as the foundation of the Qumran Community's basic beliefs. The Essenes not only considered themselves to be the 'remnant' of their time, but the 'remnant' of all time, the final 'remnant'. In the 'age of wrath', while God was making ready to annihilate the wicked, their founders had repented. They had become the 'Converts of Israel' (cf. CD IV, 2; 4Q**266** fr. 5 i). As a reward for their conversion, the Teacher of Righteousness had been sent to establish for them a 'new Covenant', which was to be the sole valid form of the eternal alliance between God and Israel. Consequently, their paramount aim was to pledge themselves to observe its precepts with absolute faithfulness. Convinced that they belonged to a Community which alone interpreted the Holy Scriptures correctly, theirs was 'the last interpretation of the Law' (4Q**266** fr. 11; **270** fr. 7 ii), and they devoted their exile in the wilderness to the study of the Bible. Their intention was to do according to all that had been 'revealed from age to age, and as the Prophets had revealed by His Holy Spirit' (1QS VIII, 14–16; cf. 4Q**365** fr. 7 ii).

Without an authentic interpretation it was not possible properly to understand the Torah. All the Jews of the inter-Testamental era, the Essenes as well as their rivals, agreed that true piety entails obedience to the Law, but although its guidance reaches into so many corners of life – into business and prayer, law court and kitchen, marriage-bed and Temple – the 613 positive and negative commandments of which it consists still do not provide for all the problems encountered, especially those which arose in the centuries following the formulation of biblical legislation. To give but one example, the diaspora situation was not envisaged by the jurists of an autonomous Jewish society.

Torah interpretation was entrusted to the priests and Levites during the first two or three centuries following the Babylonian exile. Ezra and his colleagues, the ancient scribes of Israel, 'read from the book of the Law . . . made its sense plain and gave instruction in what was read'. In this passage from the Book of Nehemiah viii, 8, Jewish tradition acknowledges the institution of a regular paraphrase of Scripture known as Targum, or translation into the vernacular of the members of the congregation. When the parties of the Pharisees, Sadducees, Essenes, etc., came into being with their different convictions, they justified them by interpretations suited to their needs.

A classic example of idiosyncratic Bible interpretation in the Scrolls concerns a law on marriage. Since no directly relevant ruling is given in the Pentateuch on whether a niece may marry her uncle, Pharisaic and rabbinic Judaism understands this scriptural silence to mean that such a union is licit. When the Bible wishes to declare a degree of kinship unlawful, it does so: thus we read apropos of marriage between nephew and aunt, 'You shall not approach your mother's sister' (Lev. xviii, 13). Thus a tradition surviving in the Babylonian Talmud is able to go so far as even to praise marriage with a 'sister's daughter' and to proclaim it as a particularly saintly and generous act comparable to the loving-kindness shown to the poor and needy (Yebamoth 62b). The Qumran Essenes did not adopt this attitude at all. On the contrary, they regarded an uncle–niece union as straightforward 'fornication'. Interpreted correctly, they maintained, the Leviticus precept signifies the very opposite of the meaning accepted by their opponents; the truth is that whatever applies to men in this respect applies also to women.

Moses said, *You shall not approach your mother's sister* (i.e. your aunt); *she is your mother's near kin* (Lev. xviii, 13). But although the laws against incest are written for men, they also apply to women. When, therefore, a brother's daughter uncovers the nakedness of her father's brother, she is (also his) near kin.
(CD v, 7–9)

The Temple Scroll proclaims clearly this prohibition in proper legal terms:

A man shall not take the daughter of his brother or the daughter of his sister for this is abominable. (11QTS LXVI, 16–17)

Again, according to the strict views of the sectaries, fidelity to the Covenant demanded not only obedience to the Law, to all that God has 'commanded by the hand of Moses', but also adherence to the teaching of 'all His servants, the Prophets' (1QS I, 2–3). Although not expressly stated, this special attention to the Prophets implies, firstly, that the Essenes subscribed to the principle incorporated into the opening paragraph of the Sayings of the Fathers in the Mishnah that the Prophets served as an essential link in the transmission of the Law from Moses to the rabbis.

Moses received the Torah from (God on) Sinai and passed it on to Joshua; Joshua to the Elders (= Judges); the Elders to the Prophets; and the Prophets passed it on to the members of the Great Assembly (= the leaders of Israel in the post-exilic age). (Aboth I, 1)

The second inference to be drawn is that the sect believed the Prophets to be not only teachers of morality, but also guides in the domain of the final eschatological realities. But as in the case of the Law, their writings were considered to contain pitfalls for the ignorant and the misinformed, and only the Community's sages knew how to expound them correctly. Properly understood, the Books of Isaiah, Hosea and the rest indicate the right path to be followed in the terrible cataclysms of the last days. A simple reading can convey only their superficial meaning, but not their profounder significance. The Book of Daniel sets the biblical example here when it announces that Jeremiah's prediction that the Babylonian domination would last for seventy years is not to be taken literally; the real and final message is that seventy times seven years would separate Nebuchadnezzar from the coming of the Messiah (Dan. ix, 21–4). But the Qumran sectaries went even further than Daniel. They argued that it is quite impossible to discover the meaning without an inspired interpreter because the Prophets themselves were ignorant of the full import of what they wrote. Habakkuk, for instance, was commanded to recount the history of the 'final generation', but he did so without having any clear idea of how far ahead the eschatological age lay. God 'did not make known to him when time would come to an end'. Knowledge of the authentic teaching of the Prophets was the supreme talent of the Teacher of Righteousness. The surviving Bible commentaries are almost all concerned with predictions concerning the ultimate destiny of the righteous and the wicked, the tribulations and final triumph of the 'House of Judah' and the concomitant annihilation of those who had rebelled against God. But in addition to this general evidence of the subject-matter, the Scrolls directly impute to the Teacher a particular God-given insight into the hidden significance of prophecy. He was 'the Teacher of Righteousness to whom God made known all the mysteries ... of His servants the Prophets' (1QpHab VII, 1–5). He was 'the Priest [in whose heart] God set [understanding] that he might interpret all the words of His servants the Prophets, through whom He foretold all that would happen to His people' (1QpHab II, 8–10). He was the Teacher who 'made known to the latter generations that which God had done to the latter generation, the congregation of traitors, to those who departed from the way' (CD I, 12–13). The Teacher's interpretation alone, propagated by his disciples, offered true enlightenment and guidance.

Supported in this way by the infallible teaching of the Community, the sectary believed himself to be living in the true city of God, the city of the Covenant built on the Law and the Prophets (cf. CD VII, 13–18). Again and again, the architectural metaphors used in the Scrolls suggest security and protection. The sect is a 'House of Holiness', a 'House of Perfection and Truth' (1QS VIII, 5, 9), a 'House of the Law' (CD XIX (B2), 10, 13); it is a 'sure House' (CD III, 19) constructed on solid foundations. Indeed the language used is reminiscent of Isaiah xxviii, 16, and of Jesus' simile about the Church built not on sand but on rock (Matth. vii, 24–7; xvi, 18):

> But I shall be as one who enters a *fortified city*,
> as one who seeks refuge behind a *high wall* . . .
> I will [lean on] Thy truth, O my God.
> For Thou wilt set the *foundation* on *rock*
> and the *framework* by the *measuring-cord* of justice;
> and the tried *stones* [Thou wilt lay]
> by the *plumb-line* [of truth],
> to [build] a mighty [wall] which shall not sway;
> and no man entering there shall stagger.
> (1QS XIV [formerly VI], 24–7)

Fortified by his membership of the brotherhood, the sectary could even carry his notions of solidity and firmness over into his own self so that he too became a 'strong tower':

> Thou hast strengthened me
> before the battles of wickedness . . .
> Thou hast made me like a *strong tower*, a *high wall*,
> and hast established my *edifice* upon rock;
> *eternal foundations*
> serve for my ground,
> and all my *ramparts* are a *tried wall*
> which shall not sway. (1QH XV [formerly VII], 7–9)

## 2 ELECTION AND HOLY LIFE IN THE COMMUNITY OF THE COVENANT

In the ideology of the Old Testament, to be a member of the chosen people is synonymous with being party to the Covenant. Israel willingly accepts the yoke of the Law given on Sinai, and God in his turn acknowledges her as His 'special possession' (Exod. xix, 5):

> For you are a people holy to the Lord your God; the Lord your God has chosen you to be a people for His own possession, out of all the peoples that are on the face of the earth . . . You shall therefore be careful to do the commandment, and the statutes, and the ordinances which I command you this day. (Deut. vii, 6, 11)

Theoretically, there is no distinction between election *de jure* and election *de facto*: every Jew is chosen. But already in biblical times a deep gulf is in fact seen to divide righteous observers of the Covenant from the wicked of Israel. Though not deprived of their birthright, the unfaithful are viewed as burdened with guilt and as such excluded, provisionally at least, from the congregation of the children of God. The fully developed concept of election is summarized in the Palestinian Talmud by the third-century CE Galilean Rabbi Lazar. Expounding the words of Deuteronomy quoted above, he comments:

When the Israelites do the will of the Holy One, blessed be He, they are called sons; but when they do not do His will, they are not called sons.

(Kiddushin 61c)

Inevitably, for the Qumran Essenes such a notion of Covenant membership was far too elastic. Consistent with their approach to legal matters, their attitude in regard to the Covenant was that only the initiates of their own 'new Covenant' were to be reckoned among God's elect and, as such, united already on earth with the angels of heaven.

God has given them to His chosen ones
   and has caused them to inherit
   the lot of the Holy Ones.
He has joined their assembly
   to the Sons of Heaven,
to be a Council of the Community,
a foundation of the Building of Holiness,
an eternal Plantation throughout all ages to come.

(1QS XI, 7–9)

They insisted, moreover, on the individual election of each sectary. The ordinary Jew envisaged entry into the congregation of the chosen primarily through birth, and secondly through the symbolical initiation of an eight-day-old male infant submitted to circumcision. An Essene became a member of either branch of his sect by virtue of the deliberate and personal adult commitment of himself. For this reason, as will be remembered, even children born to married members and brought up in their schools had to wait until their twentieth birthday before they were allowed to make their solemn vows of entry into the Covenant. Also, believing in divine foreknowledge, they considered their adherence to the 'lot of God' as the effect of grace, as having been planned for each of them in heaven from all eternity. They, the elect, were guided by the spirit of truth in the ways of light, while the unprivileged, Jew and Gentile alike, were doomed to wander along paths of darkness. The section of the Community Rule known as the Instruction on the Two Spirits gives a fascinating description of these two human groups, the chosen and the unchosen.

The Master shall instruct all the sons of light and shall teach them the nature of all the children of men according to the kind of spirit which they possess ...

From the God of Knowledge comes all that is and shall be. Before ever they existed He established their whole design, and when, as ordained for them, they come into being, it is in accord with His glorious design that they accomplish their task without change ...

He has created man to govern the world, and has appointed for him two spirits in which to walk until the time of His visitation: the spirits of truth and injustice. Those born of truth spring from a fountain of light, but those born of injustice spring from a source of darkness. All the children of righteousness are ruled by the Prince of Light and walk in the ways of light, but all the children of injustice are ruled by the Angel of Darkness and walk in the ways of darkness. The Angel of Darkness leads all the children of righteousness astray, and until his end, all their sins, iniquities, wickedness, and all their unlawful deeds are caused by his dominion in accordance with the mysteries of God ...

But the God of Israel and His Angel of Truth will succour all the sons of light. For it is He who created the spirits of Light and Darkness and founded every action upon them and established every deed [upon] their [ways]. And He loves the one everlastingly and delights in its works for ever; but the counsel of the other He loathes and for ever hates its ways. (1QS III, 13–IV, 1)

Convictions of this kind, with their theories of individual election and predestination, coupled with a precise knowledge of the boundary dividing right from wrong, can lead to self-righteousness and arrogant intolerance of the masses thought to be rejected by God. The Essenes, however, appear to have concentrated more on the blessedness of the chosen than on the damnation of the unpredestined. Besides, they could always argue that Jews who refused to repent and remained outside the new Covenant were responsible for their own doom.

But the spiritual masters of the Community were doubtless aware of the danger of the sin of pride to which their less enlightened brothers were exposed and attacked it on three fronts. The Qumran Hymns, unlike certain biblical Psalms (e.g. Psalm xxvi) which testify to an acute form of sanctimoniousness, never cease to emphasize the sectary's frailty, unworthiness and total dependence on God.

> Clay and dust that I am,
> what can I devise unless Thou wish it,
> and what contrive unless Thou desire it?
> What strength shall I have
> unless Thou keep me upright
> and how shall I understand
> unless by (the spirit) which Thou hast shaped for me?
> (1QH XVIII [formerly X], 5–7)

Not only is election itself owed to God's grace, but perseverance in the way of holiness cannot be counted on unless he offers his continuous help and support.

> When the wicked rose against Thy Covenant
> and the damned against Thy word,
> I said in my sinfulness,
> 'I am forsaken by Thy Covenant.'
> But calling to mind the might of Thy hand
> and the greatness of Thy compassion,
> I rose and stood . . .
> I lean on Thy grace
> and on the multitude of Thy mercies.
> (1QH XII [formerly IV], 34–7)

Another theme constantly stressed in Essene teaching is that not only is God's assistance necessary in order to remain faithful to his Law; the very knowledge of that Law is a gift from heaven. All their special understanding and wisdom comes from God.

> From the source of His righteousness
> is my justification,
> and from His marvellous mysteries
> is the light in my heart.
> My eyes have gazed
> on that which is eternal,
> on wisdom concealed from men,
> on knowledge and wise design
> (hidden) from the sons of men;

on a fountain of righteousness
  and on a storehouse of power,
on a spring of glory
  (hidden) from the assembly of flesh.
God has given them to His chosen ones
  as an everlasting possession,
and has caused them to inherit
  the lot of the Holy Ones. (1QS XI, 5–8)

The sentiments expressed in the Hymns, of love and gratitude and awareness of God's presence, represent a true religiousness and must have helped the sectary not to allow his life – governed as it was by laws and precepts – to slide into one of mere religious formalism.

Thou hast upheld me with certain truth;
  Thou hast delighted me with Thy Holy Spirit
  and [hast opened my heart] till this day . . .
The abundance of (Thy) forgiveness is with my steps
  and infinite mercy accompanies Thy judgement of me.
Until I am old Thou wilt care for me;
  for my father knew me not
  and my mother abandoned me to Thee.
For Thou art a father
  to all [the sons] of Thy truth,
and as a woman who tenderly loves her babe,
  so dost Thou rejoice in them;
and as a foster-father bearing a child in his lap,
  so carest Thou for all Thy creatures.
(1QH XVII [formerly IX], 32–6)

Whether the average Essene actually succeeded in fulfilling his high ideals, we cannot of course know: experience past and present has shown that paths to sanctity devised by organized religion are beset with snares. As has been noted earlier (pp. 31–2 on 4Q477), in some individual cases, moral shortcomings were actually recorded. But there can be no doubt of the sectaries' intention. The aim of a holy life lived within the Covenant was to penetrate the secrets of heaven in this world and to stand before God for ever in the next. Like Isaiah, who beheld the seraphim proclaiming 'Holy, holy, holy', and like Ezekiel, who in a trance watched the winged cherubim drawing the divine throne-chariot, and like the ancient

Jewish mystics who consecrated themselves, despite official disapproval by the rabbis, to the contemplation of the same throne-chariot and the heavenly Palaces, the Essenes, too, strove for a similar mystical knowledge, as one of their number testifies in a description of his own vision of the ministers of the 'Glorious Face'.

The [cheru]bim prostrate themselves before Him and bless. As they rise, a whispered divine voice [is heard], and there is a roar of praise. When they drop their wings, there is a [whispere]d divine voice. The cherubim bless the image of the throne-chariot above the firmament, [and] they praise [the majes]ty of the luminous firmament beneath His seat of glory. When the wheels advance, angels of holiness come and go. From between His glorious wheels there is as it were a fiery vision of most holy spirits. About them, the appearance of rivulets of fire in the likeness of gleaming brass, and a work of ... radiance in many-coloured glory, marvellous pigments, clearly mingled. The spirits of the living 'gods' move perpetually with the glory of the marvellous chariot(s). The whispered voice of blessing accompanies the roar of their advance, and they praise the Holy One on their way of return. When they ascend, they ascend marvellously, and when they settle, they stand still. The sound of joyful praise is silenced and there is a whispered blessing of the 'gods' in all the camps of God.

(4Q405 20, ii–22)

## 3 WORSHIP IN THE COMMUNITY OF THE COVENANT

In addition to the worship of God offered through a life of holiness, the Qumran sectary had more particularly to perform the ritual acts prescribed by Moses in the correct manner and at the right times. The earthly liturgy was intended to be a replica of that sung by the choirs of angels in the celestial Temple.

To judge from the many references to it, the time element both calendric and horary was crucial. The Community Rule lays down that the Community was not to 'depart from any command of God concerning their appointed times; they shall be neither early nor late for any of their appointed times, they shall stray neither to the right nor to the left of any of His true precepts' (1QS 1, 13–15). This injunction asks for exact punctuality in regard to the two daily moments of prayer meant to coincide with and replace the perpetual burnt-offering sacrificed in the Temple at sunrise and sunset (Exod. xxix, 30; Num. xxviii, 4), but it demands in addition a strict observance of the sect's own liturgical calendar.

He shall bless Him [with the offering] of the lips at the times ordained by Him: at the beginning of the dominion of light, and at its end when it retires to its appointed place; at the beginning of the watches of darkness when He unlocks their storehouse and spreads them out, and also at their end when they retire before the light; when the heavenly lights shine out from the dwelling-place of Holiness, and also when they retire to the place of Glory; at the entry of the (monthly) seasons on the days of the new moon, and also at their end when they succeed to one another ... (1QS IX, 26–X, 4)

To understand the peculiarity of Essenism in this respect, a few words need to be said about the calendar followed by non-sectarian Judaism. Essentially, this was regulated by the movements of the moon; months varied in duration from between twenty-nine and thirty days and the year consisted of twelve months of 354 days. Needless to say, such a lunar year does not correspond to the four seasons determined by the movements of the sun in terms of solstices and equinoxes. The shortfall of about ten days between the lunar and the solar years was therefore compensated for by means of 'intercalation', i.e. by inserting after Adar (February/March), the twelfth month of the year, a supplementary 'Second Adar' at the end of every thirty-six lunar months.

The Qumran sect rejected this seemingly artificial system and adopted instead a chronological reckoning, probably of priestly origin, based on the sun, a practice attested also in the Book of Jubilees and 1 Enoch, and fully laid out in the remains of a series of calendrical documents (4Q**320–30**). The outstanding feature of this solar calendar was its absolute regularity in that, instead of 354 days, not divisible by seven, it consisted of 364 days, i.e. fifty-two weeks precisely. Each of its four seasons was thirteen weeks long divided into three months of thirty days each, plus an additional 'remembrance' day (1QS X, 5) linking one season to another ($13 \times 7 = 91 = 3 \times 30 + 1$). In tune in this way with the 'laws of the Great Light of heaven' (1QH XII, 5) and not with the 'festivals of the nations' (4QpHos=4Q**171** II, 16), Qumran saw its calendar as corresponding to 'the certain law from the mouth of God' (1QH XX [formerly XII], 9). Its unbroken rhythm meant furthermore that the first day of the year and of each subsequent season always fell on the same day of the week. For the Essenes this was Wednesday, since according to Genesis i, 14–19, it was on the fourth day that the sun and the moon were created. Needless to add, the same monotonous sequence also implied that all the feasts of the year always fell on the same day of the week: Passover, the fifteenth day of the first month, was always celebrated on a Wednesday; the Feast of Weeks, the fifteenth day of the third month, always on a Sunday; the Day of Atonement, the tenth day of the seventh month, on a Friday; the Feast of Tabernacles, the fifteenth day of the seventh month, on a Wednesday, etc. This solar calendar with its eternal regularity cannot of course stand up to the astronomical calculation of 365 days 5 hours 48 minutes and 48 seconds to the year, but the Scrolls so far published give no indication of how the Essenes proposed to cope with this inconvenience, or whether indeed they were even aware of it.

One practical consequence of the sect's adherence to a calendar at variance with that of the rest of Judaism was that its feast-days were working days for other Jews and vice versa. The Wicked Priest was thus able to travel (journeys of any distance being forbidden on holy days of rest) to the 'place of exile' of the Teacher of Righteousness while he and his followers were celebrating the Day of Atonement (cf. above, p. 55). In fact, it is likely that the persecutors of the sect deliberately chose that date to oblige the sectaries to attend to them on what they considered to be their 'Day of Fasting' and 'Sabbath of repose', and thus 'confuse them and cause them to stumble'. The same sort of story is told in the Mishnah of the Patriarch Gamaliel II, who endeavoured to humiliate Rabbi Joshua ben Hananiah by sending him the following instruction: 'I charge you that you come to me with your staff and your money on the Day of Atonement according to your reckoning' (Rosh ha-Shanah II, 9).

Another peculiarity of the liturgical calendar of the Community, attested in the Temple Scroll, was the division of the year into seven fifty-day periods – hence the name pentecontad calendar – each marked by an agricultural festival, e.g. the Feast of New Wine, the Feast of Oil, etc. A similar system is mentioned by Philo in connection with the Therapeutae in his book, *On the Contemplative Life*. One of these festivals, the Feast of the New Wheat, coincided with the Feast of Weeks and was for the Essenes/Therapeutae also the principal holy day of the year, that of the Renewal of the Covenant, the importance of which is discussed above (p. 44). From the Book of Jubilees, where, as has been said, the same calendar is followed, it is clear that Pentecost (the Feast of Weeks), together with the Feast of the Renewal of the Covenant, were celebrated on the fifteenth day of the third month (Jub. VI, 17–19; cf. also 4Q**266** fr. 11 ii; **270** fr. 7 ii). An outline of the ceremony performed on this holy day, with its confession of sin and its blessings and curses, is preserved in the Community Rule (1QS I, 16–II, 25; cf. also 4Q280, 286–7). The sectaries assemble for the service in strict hierarchical order: the priests first, ranked in order of status, after them the Levites, and lastly 'all the people one after another in their Thousands, Hundreds, Fifties and Tens, that every Israelite may know his place in the Community of God according to the everlasting design' (1QS II, 22–3). Blessing God, the priests then recite his acts of loving-kindness to Israel and the Levites recall Israel's rebellions against him. This recognition of guilt is followed by an act of public repentance appropriate to a community of converts.

We have strayed! We have [disobeyed!] We and our fathers before us have sinned and acted wickedly in walking [counter to the precepts] of truth and righteousness. [And God has] judged us and our fathers also; but He has bestowed His bountiful mercy on us from everlasting to everlasting.

(1QS I, 24–II, 1)

After the confession, the priests solemnly bless the converts of Israel, calling down on them in particular the gifts of wisdom and knowledge:

May He bless you with all good and preserve you from all evil! May He lighten your heart with life-giving wisdom and grant you eternal knowledge! May He raise His merciful face towards you for everlasting bliss! (1QS II, 2–4)

This paraphrase of the blessing of Israel which God commanded Moses to transmit to Aaron and his sons in Numbers vi, 24–6, and which recalls the fourth of the daily Eighteen Benedictions of traditional Judaism, is accompanied by a Levitical curse of the party of Belial and a special malediction directed by both priests and Levites at any sectary whose conversion may be insincere:

Cursed be the man who enters this Covenant while walking among the idols of his heart, who sets up before himself his stumbling-block of sin so that he may backslide! Hearing the words of this Covenant, he blesses himself in his heart and says, 'Peace be with me, even though I walk in the stubbornness of my heart'. (1QS II, 11–12)

The Cave 4 sources of the Damascus Document depict also the ritual of dismissal from the Community. The Priest overseeing the Congregation, addressing God, declares:

Thou hast cursed those who transgress (the boundary) but we maintain it.

Thereupon 'the dismissed man shall leave and whoever eats from what is his or greets the man who has been dismissed, and agrees with him, ... his judgement shall be complete' (4Q**266** fr. 11 ii; **270** fr. 7 ii).

Each benediction and curse is approved by the whole congregation with a twice repeated 'Amen'.

The ceremony of the Renewal of the Covenant seems to be the only rite described in any detail in the Community Rule and the Damascus Document, but as the Essenes laid so much emphasis on the full and punctilious observance of the Law of Moses it may be taken for granted that they did not omit the many other basic acts of Jewish religion and worship. The fact that the Community Rule is satisfied simply to state without any specification that a single deliberate transgression of the Mosaic Law would entail irrevocable expulsion from the sect implies that the elite sectaries subject to this rule did not need detailed guidance: they were supposed to be fully versed in the Torah. Legislation addressed to less well-trained members, contained in the Damascus Document and in the Temple Scroll, is more discursive. Circumcision, for example, which was certainly practised, is mentioned in connection with female uncleanness after childbirth when Leviticus xii, 3 is cited in passing (4Q**266** fr. 6 ii). It is also referred to figuratively in the context of severing the 'foreskin of the evil inclination' (1QS v, 5), or possibly and by implication as the 'Covenant of Abraham' mentioned in connection with (Gentile) manservants (CD XII, 11; XVI, 6). The laws of purity were also assuredly essential to the sect, and some practical guidance is given in 11QTS XLVI–LI, 4Q**274–84**, and MMT. The dietary laws are dealt with in the Damascus Document, MMT and the Temple Scroll. For instance, the eating of 'live creatures' (e.g. larvae of bees, fish and locusts) is declared to be prohibited in CD XII, 11–15. MMT states that a live animal foetus must be slaughtered before becoming fit for consumption (4Q**396** frs. 1–21). Further laws appear in the Temple Scroll XLVII–XLVIII. Josephus also remarks that an Essene was forbidden to eat food prepared by people not belonging to the brotherhood (*War* II, 143).

On three other topics, the Qumran sources are less taciturn: ritual ablutions, Temple worship and the sacred meal. Discussed already as part of the life of the sect, it remains now to consider the doctrinal significance of these rites.

Josephus, as will be recalled, observes that the Essenes took a ritual bath twice daily before meals (cf. *War* II, 129, 132). **4Q414** – entitled 'Baptismal liturgy' – deals definitely with such a bathing ritual but the text is so mutilated that no readable translation is possible. As regards the bath itself, the Damascus Document adds that the minimum quantity of clean water required for a valid act of purification was to be the amount necessary to cover a man (CD X, 12–13). This is not of course an Essene invention, but typically, where the Mishnah prescribes a minimum of forty *seahs* (about 120 gallons), the sect's teaching concentrates on the practical purpose of the Mishnaic rule, namely that 'in them men may immerse themselves' (Mikwaot VII, 1), and eliminates the obligation of having carefully to measure out what that quantity should be. Of greater interest, however, is the theological aspect, with its insistence on a correlation between the inner condition of a man and the outer rite. The wicked, according to the Community Rule, 'shall not enter the water ... for they shall not be cleansed unless they turn from their wickedness' (1QS V, 13–14). True purification comes from the 'spirit of holiness' and true cleansing from the 'humble submission' of the soul to all God's precepts.

> For it is through the spirit of true counsel concerning the ways of man that all his sins shall be expiated ... He shall be cleansed from all his sins by the spirit of holiness ... and his iniquity shall be expiated by the spirit of uprightness and humility. And when his flesh is sprinkled with purifying water and sanctified by cleansing water, it shall be made clean by the humble submission of his soul to all the precepts of God. (1QS III, 6–9)

The second issue has to do with the sect's attitude towards the Temple and Temple sacrifice. While some Essenes, notwithstanding their vow of total fidelity to the Law of Moses, rejected the validity of the Sanctuary and refused to participate (temporarily) in its rites (cf. Philo, *Omnis probus* 75; Josephus, *Antiquities* XVIII, 19), they evaded the theological dilemma in which this stand might have placed them by contending that until the rededication of the Temple, the only true worship of God was to be offered in their establishment. The Council of the Community was to be the 'Most Holy Dwelling for Aaron' where, 'without the flesh of holocausts and the fat of sacrifice', a 'sweet fragrance' was to be sent up to God, and where prayer was to serve 'as an acceptable fragrance of righteousness' (1QS VIII, 8–9; IX, 4–5). The Community itself was to be the sacrifice offered to God in atonement for Israel's sins (1QS VIII, 4–5; **4Q265** fr. 7 ii).

Besides this evidence in the Community Rule, the equation of Council of the Community with the Temple also appears in the Habakkuk Commentary (XII, 3–4) in a most interesting interpretation of the word 'Lebanon'. Traditionally, 'Lebanon' is understood by ancient Jewish interpreters to symbolize 'the Temple'. For example, Deuteronomy iii, 25, 'Let me go over ... and see ... that goodly mountain and Lebanon', is rendered in Targum Onkelos as, 'Let me go over ... and see ... that goodly mountain and the Temple'. The Qumran commentator, explaining the Habakkuk text, 'For the violence done to Lebanon shall overwhelm you' (Hab. II, 17), proceeds from the belief that the Council of the Community is the one valid Temple. He then sets out to prove it by directly associating Lebanon with the Council in the conviction that the traditional exegesis will be familiar to all his readers: Lebanon = Temple. Temple = Council of the Community, *ergo* Lebanon = Council of the Community.[1]

The symbolical approach of the sect to sacrificial worship may account for Essene celibacy (where it was practised). Sexual abstinence was imposed on those participating in the Temple services, both priests and laymen; no person who had sexual intercourse (or an involuntary emission, or even any physical contact with a menstruating woman) could lawfully take part. More importantly still, bearing in mind the central place occupied by prophecy in Essene doctrine, clear indications exist in inter-Testamental and rabbinic literature that a similar renunciation was associated with the prophetic state. Thus Moses, in order always to be ready to hear the voice of God, is said by Philo to have cleansed himself of 'all calls of mortal nature, food, drink, and intercourse with women' (*Life of Moses* II, 68–9). Consequently, despite the attempt made by Philo and by Josephus to attribute the sect's celibacy to misogyny, a more reasonable explanation would be that it was thought that lives intended to be wholly consecrated to worship and wholly preoccupied with meditation on prophecy should be kept wholly, and not just intermittently, pure.

The common table of the Essenes, the third special cultic subject to be examined, has already been discussed in Chapter II (p. 32), but one remaining point needs to be mentioned, namely that since the rules relating to the daily meal and the messianic meal are the same, it is not unreasonable to infer from the New Testament parallel that the former

1. Another metaphorical use of Lebanon (= the foreign nations) is implied in the quotation of Isa. x, 34 in the Rule of War (4Q285 fr. 5).

was thought to prefigure the latter. As is well known, the evangelist Matthew portrays the Last Supper as the prototype of the great eschatological feast, quoting Jesus as saying:

I tell you, I shall not drink again of this fruit of the vine until that day when I drink it new with you in my Father's Kingdom. (Matth. xxvi, 29)

## 4 FUTURE EXPECTATIONS IN THE COMMUNITY OF THE COVENANT

The Essene sect was born into a world of eschatological ferment, of intense expectation of the end foretold by the Prophets. Using biblical models as vehicles for their own convictions, the Teacher of Righteousness and the Community's sages projected an image of the future which is elaborate and colourful, but which cannot always be fully comprehended by us, partly because some of the associations escape us, and partly because of gaps in the extant texts. They foresaw in their Community's story the fulfilment of the prophetic expectations concerning the salvation of the righteous. It was from their ranks, swollen by the re-conversion of some of the 'Simple of Ephraim' (4QpNah=4Q**169** III, 4–5) who had caused such distress by their previous apostasy, and by other Jewish recruits (1QSa I, 1–5; cf. also 4Q**471**[a]), that the sons of Light would go to battle against the sons of Darkness. The Community or the 'exiles of the desert' would move to Jerusalem after a preliminary attack on the 'army of Belial', symbolized by the 'ungodly of the Covenant' and their foreign allies from the environs of Judaea, and an assault on the Kittim occupying the Holy Land. These events were expected to cover a period of six years. The seventh, the first sabbatical year of the War, would see the restoration of Temple worship.

Of the remaining thirty-three years of its duration, four would be sabbatical years, so the War would be waged during twenty-nine: against the 'sons of Shem' for nine years, against the 'sons of Ham' for ten years, and against the 'sons of Japheth' for another ten years (1QM I–II). The final conflict would end with the total defeat of the 'King of the Kittim' and of Satan's hosts, and with the joyful celebrations of the Hero, i.e. God, by the victorious sons of Light.

[Rise up, O Hero!
Lead off Thy captives, O Glorious One!

Gather up] Thy spoils, O Author of mighty deeds!
Lay Thy hand on the neck of Thine enemies
and Thy feet [on the pile of the slain!
Smite the nations, Thine adversaries],
and devour the flesh of the sinner with Thy sword!
Fill Thy land with glory
and Thine inheritance with blessing!
[Let there be a multitude of cattle in Thy fields,
and in] Thy palaces
[silver and gold and precious stones]!

O Zion, rejoice greatly!
Rejoice all you cities of Judah!
[Keep your gates ever open
that the] host of the nations
[may be brought in]!
Their kings shall serve you
and all your oppressors shall bow down before you;
[they shall lick the dust of your feet.
Shout for joy, O daughters of] my people!
Deck yourselves with glorious jewels
[and rule over the kingdom of the nations!
Sovereignty shall be to the Lord]
and everlasting dominion to Israel. (1QM XIX, 2–8)

Such was to be the course of the War in its earthly dimensions. But it would possess in addition a cosmic quality. The hosts of the sons of Light, commanded by the 'Prince of the Congregation', were to be supported by the angelic armies led by the 'Prince of Light', also known in the Scrolls as the archangel Michael or Melchizedek. Similarly, the 'ungodly of the Covenant' and their Gentile associates were to be aided by the demonic forces of Satan, or Belial, or Melkiresha'. These two opposing camps were to be evenly matched, and God's intervention alone would bring about the destruction of evil (1QM XVIII, 1–3). Elsewhere the grand finale is represented as a judgement scene in which the heavenly prince Melchizedek recompenses 'the Holy Ones of God' and executes 'the vengeance of the judgements of God' over Belial and his lot (11QMelch II, 9, 13). Yet, if my interpretation of another non-messianic composition (4Q**246**) is correct, the symbolical opponent, usurping in this writing the title 'son of God' and 'son of the Most High', is said to be overcome by 'the people of God' ready to establish with the help of the Great God an eternal kingdom.

The role of the priests and Levites in this imaginary ultimate grappling of good with evil, as described in the War Scroll, emerges as that of non-combatants, performing various battle rituals and directing the various war activities (advance, retreat, ambush, etc.). However, it is more difficult to determine the function of the commander-in-chief, the so-called 'Prince of the Congregation'. We learn that on his shield will be inscribed his name, the names of Israel, Levi and Aaron, and those of the twelve tribes and their chiefs (1QM v, 1–2); but little room appears to be left in the War Rule for him to act as the Royal Messiah. God himself is the supreme agent of salvation and after him in importance is Michael.

In some other Scrolls, by contrast, the theme of Messianism is more prominent. Complex and *sui generis*, it envisages sometimes one messianic figure, royal, Davidic, triumphant (**4Q285**, **4Q161**, and the Damascus Document speaking of the Messiah – in the singular, cf. **4Q266** fr. 11 i, 12 – of Aaron and Israel), again and again two, and once possibly even three Messiahs. The lay King-Messiah, otherwise known as the 'Branch of David', the 'Messiah of Israel', the 'Prince of [all] the Congregation' and the 'Sceptre', was to usher in, according to the sect's book of Blessings, 'the Kingdom of his people' and 'bring death to the ungodly' and defeat '[the kings of the] nations' (1QSb v, 21, 25, 28). The recently and groundlessly advanced theory that 'the Prince of the Congregation, Branch of David' of **4Q285** is a suffering and executed Messiah is contradicted both by the immediate context and the broader exegetical framework of Isaiah x, 34–xi, 1 on which **4Q285** depends (cf. **4Q161**, frs. 8–10; 1QSb v, 20–29). As befits a priestly sect, however, the Priest-Messiah comes first in the order of precedence; he is also called the 'Messiah of Aaron', the 'Priest', the 'Interpreter of the Law' (cf. 1QSa II, 20). The King-Messiah was to defer to him and to the priestly authority in general in all legal matters: 'As they teach him, so shall he judge' (4QpIsa=**4Q161** frs. 8–11, 1.23). The 'Messiah of Aaron' was to be the final Teacher, 'he who shall teach righteousness at the end of days' (CD VI, 11). But he was also to preside over the battle liturgy (1QM XV, 4; XVI, 13; XVIII, 5) and the eschatological banquet (1QSa II, 12–21).

The third figure, 'the Prophet', is mentioned directly though briefly only once: we are told that his arrival was expected together with that of the Messiahs of Aaron and Israel (1QS IX, 11). The whole messianic phrase is absent, however, from all the extant 4Q manuscripts of the Community Rule. Viewed in the context of inter-Testamental Jewish ideas, the Prophet was to be either an Elijah returned as a precursor of the Messiah (Mal. iv, 5; 1 Enoch xc, 31, 37; Matth. xi, 13; xvii, 12), or as a divine guide sent to Israel in the final days (1 Mac. iv, 46; xiv, 41; Jn. i, 21), no doubt identical with 'the Prophet' promised by God to Moses ('I will raise up for them a prophet like you ... He shall convey all my commands to them', Deut. xviii, 15–18; cf. Acts iii, 22–3; vii, 37). An identification of 'the Prophet' with a 'new Moses' is supported by the inclusion of the Deuteronomy passage in the Messianic Anthology or Testimonia from Cave 4 (4Q**175**) as the first of three messianic proof-texts, the second being Balaam's prophecy concerning the Star to rise out of Jacob (Num. xxiv, 15–17), and the third, the blessing of Levi by Moses (Deut. xxxiii, 11), prefiguring respectively the royal Messiah and the Priest-Messiah.

If it is proper to deduce from these not too explicit data that, if ever expected by the Qumran sect, the messianic Prophet (or prophetic Messiah) was to teach the truth revealed on the eve of the establishment of the Kingdom, it would follow that his part was to all intents and purposes the same as that attributed by the Qumran Essenes to the Teacher of Righteousness. If this is correct, it would not be unreasonable to suggest that at some point of the sect's history the coming of the Prophet was no longer expected; he was believed to have already appeared in the person of the Teacher of Righteousness.

The evidence available does not permit categorical statements on the sectaries' views about what was to follow the days of the Messiahs. Some kind of metamorphosis was awaited by them, as is clear from the Community Rule – 'until the determined end, and until the Renewal' (1QS IV, 25). But one cannot be sure that it was understood as synonymous with the new creation of the Apocalypses of Ezra (vii, 75) and Baruch (xxxii, 6). Similarly, the 'new Jerusalem' described in various manuscripts (cf. 1Q**32**; 2Q**24**; 4Q**554–555**; 5Q**15**; 11Q**18**) does not match by definition the Holy City descending from above of 1 Enoch (xc, 28–9) or Revelation xxi, but could be an earthly city rebuilt according to the plans of angelic architects.

As for the afterlife proper, and the place it occupied in Essene thought, for many centuries in the biblical age Jews paid little attention to this question. They believed with most peoples in antiquity that after death the just and wicked alike would share a miserable, shadowy existence in

Sheol, the underworld, where even God is forgotten: 'Turn, O Lord, save my life,' cries the psalmist, 'for in death there is no remembrance of thee; in Sheol who can give thee praise?' (Ps. vi, 5; cf. Isa. xxxviii, 18; Ps. lxxxviii, 10–12, etc.) The general hope was for a long and prosperous life, many children, a peaceful death in the midst of one's family, and burial in the tomb of one's fathers. Needless to say, with this simple outlook went a most sensitive appreciation of the present time as being the only moment in which man can be with God.

Eventually, the innate fear of death, and the dissatisfaction of later biblical thinkers with a divine justice that allowed the wicked to flourish on earth and the just to suffer, led to attempts in the post-exilic era to solve this fundamental dilemma. The idea of resurrection, or rather of the re-unification of body and soul after death, first appears as a metaphor in Ezekiel's vision of the re-birth of the Jewish nation after the Babylonian captivity as the re-animation of dry bones (Ezek. xxxvii; cf. also 4Q385 frs. 2–3). Later, after the historical experience of martyrdom under the persecution of Antiochus Epiphanes, resurrection was expected to be the true reward of individuals who freely gave their lives for God – i.e. for their religion (Dan. xii, 2; 2 Mac. vii, 9; xii, 44; xiv, 46, etc.). At the same time, the notion of immortality also emerged, the idea that the righteous are to be vindicated and live for ever in God's presence. This view is developed fully in the Greek apocryphal Book of Wisdom (iii, 1–v, 16).

Josephus tells us that the Essenes subscribed to this second school of thought. According to him, they adopted a distinctly Hellenistic concept of immortality, holding the flesh to be a prison out of which the indestructible soul of the just escapes into limitless bliss 'in an abode beyond the ocean' after its final deliverance (*War* II, 154–8). Resurrection, implying a return of the spirit to a material body, can thus play no part in this scheme.

Until recently, the Scrolls themselves have not been particularly helpful. The Hymns include equivocal statements such as, 'Hoist a banner, O you who lie in the dust! O bodies gnawed by worms, raise up an ensign . . .!' (1QH XIV [formerly VI], 34–5; cf. XIX [formerly XI], 10–14), which may connote bodily resurrection. On the other hand, the poet's language may just be allegorical. Immortality, as distinct from resurrection, is better attested. The substance of Josephus' account is confirmed, though not surprisingly without any typically Hellenistic colouring (no doubt introduced by him to please his Greek readers). The Community Rule, discussing the reward of the righteous and the wicked, assures the just of 'eternal joy in life without end, a crown of glory and a garment of majesty in unending light' (1QS IV, 7–8), and sinners of 'eternal torment and endless disgrace together with shameful extinction in the fire of the dark regions' (1QS IV, 12–13). It is interesting to observe that immortality was not conceived of as an entirely new state, but rather as a direct continuation of the position attained on entry into the Community. From that moment, the sectary was raised to an 'everlasting height' and joined to the 'everlasting Council', the 'congregation of the Sons of Heaven' (1QH XI [formerly III], 20–22).

Shortly after the 'liberation' of the Scrolls in 1991 a previously unknown poetic text, usually designated as the 'Resurrection fragment' (4Q**521**), surfaced which, echoing Isaiah lxi, 1, describes God in the age of the Messiah as healing the wounded and *reviving the dead*. If this poem is an Essene composition and not a psalm dating to the late biblical period, it can be said that one out of many hundreds of Qumran manuscripts definitely testifies to the sect's belief in bodily resurrection.

In sum, the portrait of the sectary as it is reflected in his religious ideas and ideals bears the marks of a fastidious and deeply committed observance of the Mosaic Law, an overwhelming assurance of the correctness of his beliefs, and certainty of his own eventual salvation. But whereas these characteristics may strike readers today as far too self-confident, one would do well not to overlook other traits conspicuous in particular, in the Essenes' prayers and hymns, which testify to an absolute dependence on the Almighty and a total devotion to what was believed to be God's cause.

> For without Thee no way is perfect,
>   and without Thy will nothing is done.
> It is Thou who hast taught all knowledge
>   and all things come to pass by Thy will.
> There is none beside Thee to dispute Thy counsel
>   or to understand all Thy holy design,
> or to contemplate the depth of Thy mysteries
>   and the power of Thy might.
>
> Who can endure Thy glory,
>   and what is the son of man
>   in the midst of Thy wonderful deeds?
> What shall one born of woman
>   be accounted before Thee?
> Kneaded from the dust,

his abode is the nourishment of worms.
He is but a shape, but moulded clay,
and inclines towards dust. (1QS XI, 17–22)

# *List of Abbreviations*

| | |
|---|---|
| *BAR* | *Biblical Archaeology Review* |
| *BASOR* | *Bulletin of the American Schools of Oriental Research* |
| *CBQ* | *Catholic Biblical Quarterly* |
| CD | Cairo Damascus Document |
| *DJD* | *Discoveries in the Judaean Desert*, Oxford, 1955– |
| DSS | Dead Sea Scrolls |
| *DSSU* | R. Eisenman and M. Wise, *The Dead Sea Scrolls Uncovered*, London and New York, 1992 |
| Fr. | Fragment |
| H | *Hodayoth*=Hymns |
| *HJP* | E. Schürer, G. Vermes, F. Millar and M. Goodman, *The History of the Jewish People in the Age of Jesus Christ*, Vols. I–III, Edinburgh, 1973–87 |
| *IEJ* | *Israel Exploration Journal* |
| *JBL* | *Journal of Biblical Literature* |
| *JJS* | *Journal of Jewish Studies* |
| *JNES* | *Journal of Near Eastern Studies* |
| *JQR* | *Jewish Quarterly Review* |
| *JSJ* | *Journal for the Study of Judaism* |
| *JSS* | *Journal of Semitic Studies* |
| M | *Milḥamah*=War Rule |
| MMT | *Miqsat Ma'ase ha-Torah*=Some Observances of the Law |
| *MQC* | J. Trebolle Barrera and L. Vegas Montaner, eds., *The Madrid Qumran Congress 1991*, Vols. I–II, Leiden, 1992 |
| *NTS* | *New Testament Studies* |
| p | *pesher*=sectarian Bible commentary |
| $Ps^a$ | Psalms Scroll a=$11QPs^a$ |
| Q | Qumran cave (1Q, 2Q, etc.=Qumran cave 1, 2, etc.) |
| *RB* | *Revue biblique* |

| | |
|---|---|
| *RQ* | *Revue de Qumrân* |
| S | *Serekh*=Community Rule=1QS |
| Sa | *Serekh:* Appendix a=Messianic Rule=1QSa |
| Sb | *Serekh:* Appendix b=Blessings=1QSb |
| S–D | Hybrid Community Rule–Damascus Document (4Q265) |
| TS | Temple Scroll=11QTS |
| *UDSS* | *A Preliminary Edition of the Unpublished Dead Sea Scrolls* I–III, ed. B. Z. Wacholder and M. G. Abegg, Washington, 1991–5. |

# *Note on This Translation*

The purpose of this translation is to enable the reader to come into direct contact with the literary works found at Qumran. The English does not follow slavishly the Hebrew and Aramaic originals but aims at being faithful, intelligible and as far as possible readable. For this reason the Hebrew word order had to be altered and the numbering of the English lines, which often did not correspond to those of the manuscript, had to be sacrificed. However, as already in the 1995 fourth Penguin edition, every fifth line of the manuscript is indicated in the margin of the translation.

As stated in the preface, only meaningful texts are included in this volume, with the occasional exception of some broken lines which nevertheless reveal important information. When the same writing is extant in several manuscripts, the translation either represents a composite text, or indicates significant variants, but identical passages are not normally repeated. Experts are referred to the *DJD* volumes.

Lacunae impossible to complete with any measure of confidence are indicated by dots in the translation. Texts supplied from a different manuscript of the same document appear between { }. Hypothetical but likely reconstructions are placed between [ ] and glosses necessary for fluency between ( ). Biblical quotations appearing in the text are printed in italics, as well as the titles and headings which figure in the manuscripts. Each scroll is divided into columns. The beginning of each of these columns is indicated in the translation by bold Roman numerals: **I**, **II**, **III**, etc. The word *vacat* indicates an empty space in the manuscript.

Finally, I wish to acknowledge here the considerable benefit I have derived from the decipherment by J. T. Milik and J. Strugnell of the many Cave 4 texts which are contained in *A Preliminary Edition of the Unpublished Dead Sea Scrolls* I–III, edited by B. Z. Wacholder and M. G. Abegg (Washington, 1991–5).

# A. The Rules

'The Manual of Discipline',
*Israel Museum, Jerusalem*

# The Community Rule

## (1QS, 4Q255–64, 4Q280, 286–7, 4Q502, 5Q11, 13)

Discovered in Cave 1, the eleven relatively well-preserved columns of this manuscript (1QS) were first published in 1951 by M. Burrows under the title *The Manual of Discipline* (*The Dead Sea Scrolls of St Mark's Monastery*, II, New Haven). Important fragments of ten other manuscripts of the Rule containing a certain number of variant readings were also found in Cave 4 ($4QS^{a\text{–}j}$ = 4Q255–64), and two small fragments in Cave 5 (5Q11=1QS II, 4–7 and 13 quoting 1QS III, 4–5 and ii, 19). Other citations of the Community Rule, especially the penal code from 1QS VII, may be found in the 4Q fragments of the Damascus Document (cf. 4Q266, fr. 10 and 270, fr. 7) and in the hybrid S–D (4Q265). The latter quotes also from 1QS IV, VI and VIII. Finally, 4Q502, fr. 16 includes a quotation from 1QS IV, 4–6.

The 1Q manuscript bears the stamp of editorial modification. For instance, in column X the original 'I will *conceal* knowledge with discretion' is corrected to 'I will *impart* knowledge with discretion'. The section covered by columns VIII–IX was particularly subjected to alteration as indicated by corrections and interlinear additions in 1QS, but remarkably none of these appears in the 4QS manuscripts. The same section is considerably abridged in $4QS^e$=4Q259, where the text jumps from 1QS VIII, 15 directly to IX, 12.

The Community Rule is probably one of the oldest documents of the sect; its composition may have originated around 100 BCE, and the Cave 1 copy itself is said to have been produced during the quarter of a century following that date. It seems to have been intended for the Community's teachers, for its Masters or Guardians, and contains extracts from liturgical ceremonies, an outline of a tractate on the spirits of truth and falsehood, statutes concerned with initiation into the sect and with its common life, organization and discipline, a penal code, and finally a poetic dissertation on the fundamental religious duties of the Master and his disciples, and on the sacred seasons proper to the Community.

Literary analysis suggests that the main document begins at 1QS V, 1. This is where $4QS^d$ (=4Q258) starts. The preceding columns in 1QS I–IV prefix to the

Rule proper a liturgical text (1QS I, I–III, 11) and the probably independent tractate on the two spirits (1Q III, 12–IV, 25). Among the 4Q manuscripts only 4QS$^{b}$ (=4Q**256**) contains remains of all the sections of 1QS. The other documents represent either 1QS I–IV or 1QS V–XI. 4QS$^{e}$ (4Q**259**) substitutes, it seems, the text of 4QOtot (4Q**319**) to that of 1QS X–XI.

There are, to my knowledge, no writings in ancient Jewish sources parallel to the Community Rule, but a similar type of literature flourished among Christians between the second and fourth centuries, the so-called 'Church Orders' represented by works such as the Didache, the Didascalia, the Apostolic Constitution.

The contents of 1QS may be divided into three main sections, but further subheadings appear in the text itself:

1. Entry into the Covenant, followed by an instruction on the two spirits (I–IV).
2. Statutes relating to the Council of the Community (V–IX).
3. Directives addressed to the Master, and the Master's Hymn (IX–XI).

Some of the variant readings appearing in the Cave 4 manuscripts have been adopted in this translation, but the significantly different texts of 4QS$^{d}$ (4Q**258**) and 4QS$^{e}$ (4Q**259**) will be appended to 1QS.

For the *editio princeps* of 1QS, see M. Burrows et al., *The Dead Sea Scrolls of St Mark's Monastery Vol. II, Fasc. 2: Plates and transcription of the Manual of Discipline*, 1951. Cf. also J. H. Charlesworth et al., eds., *The Dead Sea Scrolls Vol. I: Rule of the Community and Related Documents* 1994, 1–51. S. Metso, *The Textual Development of the Qumran Community Rule* (Helsinki, 1996).

## 1QS

**I** [The Master shall teach the sai]nts to live(?) {according to the Book} (4Q**255**, **257**) of the Community [Rul]e, that they may seek God with a whole heart and soul, and do what is good and right before Him as He commanded by the hand of Moses and all His servants the Prophets; that they may love all that He has chosen and hate all that he has rejected; that they may abstain from all evil and hold fast to all good; that they may practise truth, righteousness, and justice upon earth and no longer stubbornly follow a sinful heart and lustful eyes, committing all manner of evil. He shall admit into the Covenant of Grace all those who have freely devoted themselves to the observance of God's precepts, that they may be joined to the counsel of God and may live perfectly before Him in accordance with all that has been revealed concerning their appointed times, and that they may love all the sons of light, each according to his lot in God's design, and hate all the sons of darkness, each according to his guilt in God's vengeance.

All those who freely devote themselves to His truth shall bring all their knowledge, powers and possessions into the Community of God, that they may purify their knowledge in the truth of God's precepts and order their powers according to His ways of perfection and all their possessions according to His righteous counsel. They shall not depart from any command of God concerning their times; they shall be neither early nor late for any of their appointed times, they shall stray neither to the right nor to the left of any of His true precepts. All those who embrace the Community Rule shall enter into the Covenant before God to obey all His commandments so that they may not abandon Him during the dominion of Belial because of fear or terror or affliction.

On entering the Covenant, the Priests and Levites shall bless the God of salvation and all His faithfulness, and all those entering the Covenant shall say after them, 'Amen, Amen!'

Then the Priests shall recite the favours of God manifested in His mighty deeds and shall declare all His merciful grace to Israel, and the Levites shall recite the iniquities of the children of Israel, all their guilty rebellions and sins during the dominion of Belial. And after them, all those entering the Covenant shall confess and say: 'We have strayed! We have [disobeyed!] We and our fathers before us have sinned and done wickedly in walking [counter to the precepts] of truth and righteousness. [And God has] judged us and our fathers also; **II** but He has bestowed His bountiful mercy on us from everlasting to everlasting.' And the Priests shall bless all the men of the lot of God who walk perfectly in all His ways, saying: 'May He bless you with all good and preserve you from all evil! May He lighten your heart with life-giving wisdom and grant you eternal knowledge! May He raise His merciful face towards you for everlasting bliss!'

And the Levites shall curse all the men of the lot of Belial, saying: 'Be cursed because of all your guilty wickedness! May He deliver you up for torture at the hands of the vengeful Avengers! May He visit you with destruction by the hand of all the Wreakers of Revenge! Be cursed without mercy because of (**4Q256**) the darkness of your deeds! Be damned in the shadowy place of everlasting fire! May God not heed when you call on Him, nor pardon you by blotting out your sin! May He raise His angry face towards you for vengeance! May there be no "Peace" for you in the mouth of those who hold fast to the Fathers!' And after the blessing and the cursing, all those entering the Covenant shall say, 'Amen, Amen!'

And the Priests and Levites shall continue, saying: 'Cursed be the man who enters this Covenant while walking among the idols of his heart, who sets up before himself his stumbling-block of sin so that he may backslide! Hearing the words of this Covenant, he blesses himself in his heart and says, "Peace be with me, even though I walk in the stubbornness of my heart" (Deut. xxix, 18–19), whereas his spirit, parched (for lack of truth) and watered (with lies), shall be destroyed without pardon. God's wrath and His zeal for His precepts shall consume him in everlasting destruction. All the curses of the Covenant shall cling to him and God will set him apart for evil. He shall be cut off from the midst of all the sons of light, and because he has turned aside from God on account of his idols and his stumbling-block of sin, his lot shall be among those who are cursed for ever.' And after them, all those entering the Covenant shall answer and say, 'Amen, Amen!'

Thus shall they do, year by year, for as long as the dominion of Belial endures. The Priests shall enter first, ranked one after another according to the perfection of their spirit; then the Levites; and thirdly, all the people one after another in their Thousands, Hundreds, Fifties, and Tens, that every Israelite may know his place in the Community of God according to the everlasting design. No man shall move down from his place nor move up from his allotted position. For according to the holy design, they shall all of them be in a Community of truth and virtuous humility, of loving-kindness and good intent one towards the other, and (they shall all of them be) sons of the everlasting Company.

No man [shall be in the] Community of His truth who refuses to enter [the Covenant of] God so that he may walk in the stubbornness of his heart, for **III** his soul detests the wise teaching of just laws. He shall not be counted among the upright for he has not persisted in the conversion of his life. His knowledge, powers, and possessions shall not enter the Council of the Community, for whoever ploughs the mud of wickedness returns defiled (?). He shall not be justified by that which his stubborn heart declares lawful, for seeking the ways of light he looks towards darkness. He shall not be reckoned among the perfect; he shall neither be purified by atonement, nor cleansed by purifying waters, nor sanctified by seas and rivers, nor washed clean with any ablution. Unclean,

unclean shall he be. For as long as he despises the precepts of God he shall receive no instruction in the Community of His counsel.

For it is through the spirit of true counsel concerning the ways of man that all his sins shall be expiated, that he may contemplate the light of life. He shall be cleansed from all his sins by the spirit of holiness uniting him to His truth, and his iniquity shall be expiated by the spirit of uprightness and humility. And when his flesh is sprinkled with purifying water and sanctified by cleansing water, it shall be made clean by the humble submission of his soul to all the precepts of God. Let him then order his steps {to walk} (4Q255) perfectly in all the ways commanded by God concerning the times appointed for him, straying neither to the right nor to the left and transgressing none of His words, and he shall be accepted by virtue of a pleasing atonement before God and it shall be to him a Covenant of the everlasting Community.

The Master shall instruct all the sons of light and shall teach them the nature of all the children of men according to the kind of spirit which they possess, the signs identifying their works during their lifetime, their visitation for chastisement, and the time of their reward.

From the God of Knowledge comes all that is and shall be. Before ever they existed He established their whole design, and when, as ordained for them, they come into being, it is in accord with His glorious design that they accomplish their task without change. The laws of all things are in His hand and He provides them with all their needs.

He has created man to govern the world, and has appointed for him two spirits in which to walk until the time of His visitation: the spirits of truth and injustice. Those born of truth spring from a fountain of light, but those born of injustice spring from a source of darkness. All the children of righteousness are ruled by the Prince of Light and walk in the ways of light, but all the children of injustice are ruled by the Angel of Darkness and walk in the ways of darkness. The Angel of Darkness leads all the children of righteousness astray, and until his end, all their sin, iniquities, wickedness, and all their unlawful deeds are caused by his dominion in accordance with the mysteries of God. Every one of their chastisements, and every one of the seasons of their distress, shall be brought about by the rule of his persecution; for all his allotted spirits seek the overthrow of the sons of light.

But the God of Israel and His Angel of Truth will succour all the sons of light. For it is He who created the spirits of Light and Darkness and founded every action upon them and established every deed [upon] their [ways]. And He loves the one **IV** everlastingly and delights in its works for ever; but the counsel of the other He loathes and for ever hates its ways.

These are their ways in the world for the enlightenment of the heart of man, and so that all the paths of true righteousness may be made straight before him, and so that the fear of the laws of God may be instilled in his heart: a spirit of humility, patience, abundant charity, unending goodness, understanding, and intelligence; (a spirit of) mighty wisdom which trusts in all the deeds of God and leans on His great loving-kindness; a spirit of discernment in every purpose, of zeal for just laws, of holy intent with steadfastness of heart, of great charity towards all the sons of truth, of admirable purity which detests all unclean idols, of humble conduct sprung from an understanding of all things, and of faithful concealment of the mysteries of truth. These are the counsels of the spirit to the sons of truth in this world.

And as for the visitation of all who walk in this spirit, it shall be healing, great peace in a long life, and fruitfulness, together with every everlasting blessing and eternal joy in life without end, a crown of glory and a garment of majesty in unending light.

But the ways of the spirit of falsehood are these: greed, and slackness in the search for righteousness, wickedness and lies, haughtiness and pride, falseness and deceit, cruelty and abundant evil, ill-temper and much folly and brazen insolence, abominable deeds (committed) in a spirit of lust, and ways of lewdness in the service of uncleanness, a blaspheming tongue, blindness of eye and dullness of ear, stiffness of neck and heaviness of heart, so that man walks in all the ways of darkness and guile.

And the visitation of all who walk in this spirit shall be a multitude of plagues by the hand of all the destroying angels, everlasting damnation by the avenging wrath of the fury of God, eternal torment and endless disgrace together with shameful extinction in the fire of the dark regions. The times of all their generations shall be spent in sorrowful mourning and in bitter misery and in calamities of darkness until they are destroyed without remnant or survivor.

The nature of all the children of men is ruled by these (two spirits), and during their life all the hosts of men have a portion of their divisions and walk in (both) their ways. And the whole reward for their deeds shall be, for everlasting ages, according to whether each man's portion in their two divisions is great or small. For God has established the spirits in equal measure until the final age, and has set everlasting hatred between their divisions. Truth abhors the works of injustice, and injustice hates all the ways of truth. And their struggle is fierce in all their arguments for they do not walk together. But in the mysteries of His understanding, and in His glorious wisdom, God has ordained an end for injustice, and at the time of the visitation He will destroy it for ever. Then truth, which has wallowed in the ways of wickedness during the dominion of injustice until the appointed time of judgement, shall arise in the world for ever. God will then purify every deed of man with His truth; He will refine for Himself the human frame by rooting out all spirit of injustice from the bounds of his flesh. He will cleanse him of all wicked deeds with the spirit of holiness; like purifying waters He will shed upon him the spirit of truth (to cleanse him) of all abomination and injustice. And he shall be plunged into the spirit of purification, that he may instruct the upright in the knowledge of the Most High and teach the wisdom of the sons of heaven to the perfect of way. For God has chosen them for an everlasting Covenant and all the glory of Adam shall be theirs. There shall be no more lies and all the works of injustice shall be put to shame.

Until now the spirits of truth and injustice struggle in the hearts of men and they walk in both wisdom and folly. According to his portion of truth so does a man hate injustice, and according to his inheritance in the realm of injustice so is he wicked and so hates truth. For God has established the two spirits in equal measure until the determined end, and until the Renewal, and He knows the reward of their deeds from all eternity. He has allotted them to the children of men that they may know good [and evil, and] that the destiny of all the living may be according to the spirit within [them at the time] of the visitation.

V *And this is the Rule for the men of the Community who have freely pledged themselves to be converted from all evil and to cling to all His commandments according to His will*

They shall separate from the congregation of the men of injustice and shall unite, with respect to the Law and possessions, under the authority of the sons of Zadok, the Priests who keep the Covenant, and of the multitude of the men of the Community who hold fast to the Covenant. Every decision concerning doctrine, property, and justice shall be determined by them.

They shall practise truth and humility in common, and justice and uprightness and charity and modesty in all their ways. No man shall walk in the stubbornness of his heart so that he strays after his heart and eyes and evil inclination, but he shall circumcise in the Community the foreskin of evil inclination and of stiffness of neck that they may lay a foundation of truth for Israel, for the Community of the everlasting Covenant. They shall atone for all those in Aaron who have freely pledged themselves to holiness, and for those in Israel who have freely pledged themselves to the House of Truth, and for those who join them to live in community and to take part in the trial and judgement and condemnation of all those who transgress the precepts.

On joining the Community, this shall be their code of behaviour with respect to all these precepts.

Whoever approaches the Council of the Community shall enter the Covenant of God in the presence of all who have freely pledged themselves. He shall undertake by a binding oath to return with all his heart and soul to every commandment of the Law of Moses in accordance with all that has been revealed of it to the sons of Zadok, the Priests, Keepers of the Covenant and Seekers of His will, and to the multitude of the men of their Covenant who together have freely pledged themselves to His truth and to walking in the way of His delight. And he shall undertake by the Covenant to separate from all the men of injustice who walk in the way of wickedness.

For they are not reckoned in His Covenant. They have neither inquired nor sought after Him concerning His laws that they might know the hidden things in which they have sinfully erred; and matters revealed they have treated with insolence. Therefore Wrath shall rise up to condemn, and Vengeance shall be executed by the curses of the Covenant, and great chastisements of eternal destruction shall be visited on them, leaving no remnant. They shall not enter the water to partake of the pure Meal of the men of holiness, for they shall not be cleansed unless they turn from their wickedness: for all who transgress His word are unclean. Likewise, no man shall consort with him in regard to his work or property lest he be burdened with the guilt of his sin. He shall indeed keep away from him in all things: as it is written, *Keep away from all that is false* (Exod. xxiii, 7). No member of the Community shall follow them in matters of doctrine and justice, or eat or drink anything of theirs, or take anything from them except for a price; as it is written, *Keep away from the man in whose nostrils is breath, for wherein is he counted?* (Isa. ii, 22). For all those not reckoned in His Covenant are to be set apart, together with all that is theirs. None of the men of holiness shall lean upon works of vanity: for they are all vanity who know not His Covenant, and He will blot from the world all them that despise His word. All their deeds are defilement before Him, and all their property unclean.

But when a man enters the Covenant to walk according to all these precepts that he may be joined to the holy Congregation, they shall examine his spirit in community with respect to his understanding and practice of the Law, under the authority of the sons of Aaron who have freely pledged themselves in the Community to restore His Covenant and to heed all the precepts commanded by Him, and of the multitude of Israel who have freely pledged themselves in the Community to return to His Covenant. They shall inscribe them in order, one after another, according to their understanding and their deeds, that every one may obey his companion, the man of lesser rank obeying his superior. And they shall examine their spirit and deeds yearly, so that each man may be advanced in accordance with his understanding and perfection of way, or moved down in accordance with his distortions. They shall rebuke one another in truth, humility, and charity. Let no man address his companion with anger, or ill-temper, or obdu[racy, or with envy prompted by (4Q258)] the spirit of wickedness. Let him not hate him [because of his uncircumcised] heart, but let him rebuke him on the very same day lest **VI** he incur guilt because of him. And furthermore, let no man accuse his companion before the Congregation without having admonished him in the presence of witnesses.

These are the ways in which all of them shall walk, each man with his companion, wherever they dwell. The man of lesser rank shall obey the greater in matters of work and money. They shall eat in common and bless in common and deliberate in common.

Wherever there are ten men of the Council of the Community there shall not lack a Priest among them. And they shall all sit before him according to their rank and shall be asked their counsel in all things in that order. And when the table has been prepared for eating, and the new wine for drinking, the Priest shall be the first to stretch out his hand to bless the firstfruits of the bread and new wine.

And where the ten are, there shall never lack a man among them who shall study the Law continually, day and night, concerning the right conduct of a man with his companion. And the Congregation shall watch in community for a third of every night of the year, to read the Book and to study the Law and to bless together.

*This is the Rule for an Assembly of the Congregation*

Each man shall sit in his place: the Priests shall sit first, and the elders second, and all the rest of the people according to their rank. And thus shall they be questioned concerning the Law, and concerning any counsel or matter coming before the Congregation, each man bringing his knowledge to the Council of the Community.

No man shall interrupt a companion before his speech has ended, nor speak before a man of higher rank; each man shall speak in his turn. And in an Assembly of the Congregation no man shall speak without the consent of the Congregation, nor indeed of the Guardian of the Congregation. Should any man wish to speak to the Congregation, yet not be in a position to question the Council of the Community, let him rise to his feet and say: 'I have something to say to the Congregation.' If they command him to speak, he shall speak.

Every man, born of Israel, who freely pledges himself to join the Council of the Community shall be examined by the Guardian at the head of the Congregation concerning his understanding and his deeds. If he is fitted to the discipline, he shall admit him into the Covenant that he may be converted to the truth and depart from all injustice; and he shall instruct him in all the rules of the Community. And later, when he comes to stand before the Congregation, they shall all deliberate his case, and according to the decision of the Council of the Congregation he shall either enter or depart. After he has entered the Council of the Community he shall not touch the pure Meal of the Congregation until one {full} (4Q**256**) year is completed, and until he has been examined concerning his spirit and deeds; nor shall he have any share of the property of the Congregation. Then when he has completed one year within the Community, the Congregation shall deliberate his case with regard to his understanding and observance of the Law. And if it be his destiny, according to the judgement of the Priests and the multitude of the men of their Covenant, to enter the company of the Community, his property and earnings shall be handed over to the Bursar of the Congregation who shall register it to his account and shall not spend it for the Congregation. He shall not touch the Drink of the Congregation until he has completed a second year among the men of the Community. But when the second year has passed, he shall be examined, and if it be his destiny, according to the judgement of the Congregation, to enter the Community, then he shall be inscribed among his brethren in the order of his rank for the Law, and for justice, and for the pure Meal; his property shall be merged and he shall offer his counsel and judgement to the Community.

*These are the Rules by which they shall judge at a Community (Court of) Inquiry according to the cases*

If one of them has lied deliberately in matters of property, he shall be excluded from the pure Meal of the Congregation for one year and shall do penance with respect to one quarter of his food.

Whoever has answered his companion with obstinacy, or has addressed him impatiently, going so far as to take no account of the dignity of his fellow by disobeying the order of a brother inscribed before him, he has taken the law into his own hand; therefore he shall do penance for one year [and shall be excluded].

If any man has uttered the [Most] Venerable Name **VII** even though frivolously, or as a result of shock or for any other reason whatever, while reading the Book or blessing, he shall be dismissed and shall return to the Council of the Community no more.

If he has spoken in anger against one of the Priests inscribed in the Book, he shall do penance for one year and shall be excluded for his soul's sake from the pure Meal of the Congregation. But if he has spoken unwittingly, he shall do penance for six months.

Whoever has deliberately lied shall do penance for six months.

Whoever has deliberately insulted his companion unjustly shall do penance for one year and shall be excluded.

Whoever has deliberately deceived his companion by word or by deed shall do penance for six months.

If he has failed to care for his companion, he shall do penance for three months. But if he has failed to care for the property of the Community, thereby causing its loss, he shall restore it in full. And if he be unable to restore it, he shall do penance for sixty days.

Whoever has borne malice against his companion unjustly shall do penance for six months/one year; and likewise, whoever has taken revenge in any matter whatever.

Whoever has spoken foolishly: three months.

Whoever has interrupted his companion whilst speaking: ten days.

Whoever has lain down to sleep during an Assembly of the Congregation: thirty days. And likewise, whoever has left, without reason, an

Assembly of the Congregation as many as three times during one Assembly, shall do penance for ten days. But if he has departed whilst they were standing he shall do penance for thirty days.

Whoever has gone naked before his companion, without having been obliged to do so, he shall do penance for six months.

Whoever has spat in an Assembly of the Congregation shall do penance for thirty days.

Whoever has been so poorly dressed that when drawing his hand from beneath his garment his nakedness has been seen, he shall do penance for thirty days.

Whoever has guffawed foolishly shall do penance for thirty days.

Whoever has drawn out his left hand to gesticulate with it shall do penance for ten days.

Whoever has gone about slandering his companion shall be excluded from the pure Meal of the Congregation for one year and shall do penance. But whoever has slandered the Congregation shall be expelled from among them and shall return no more.

Whoever has murmured against the authority of the Community shall be expelled and shall not return. But if he has murmured against his companion unjustly, he shall do penance for six months.

Should a man return whose spirit has so trembled before the authority of the Community that he has betrayed the truth and walked in the stubbornness of his heart, he shall do penance for two years. During the first year he shall not touch the pure Meal of the Congregation, and during the second year he shall not touch the Drink of the Congregation and shall sit below all the men of the Community. Then when his two years are completed, the Congregation shall consider his case, and if he is admitted he shall be inscribed in his rank and may then question concerning the Law.

If, after being in the Council of the Community for ten full years, the spirit of any man has failed, so that he has betrayed the Community and departed from the Congregation to walk in the stubbornness of his heart, he shall return no more to the Council of the Community. Moreover, if any member of the Community has shared with him his food or property which . . . of the Congregation, his sentence shall be the same; he shall be ex[pelled].

**VIII** In the Council of the Community there shall be twelve men and three Priests, perfectly versed in all that is revealed of the Law, whose works shall be truth, righteousness, justice, loving-kindness and humility. They shall preserve the faith in the Land with steadfastness and meekness and shall atone for sin by the practice of justice and by suffering the sorrows of affliction. They shall walk with all men according to the standard of truth and the rule of the time.

When these are in Israel, the Council of the Community shall be established in truth. It shall be an Everlasting Plantation, a House of Holiness for Israel, an Assembly of Supreme Holiness for Aaron. They shall be witnesses to the truth at the Judgement, and shall be the elect of Goodwill who shall atone for the Land and pay to the wicked their reward. It shall be that tried wall, that *precious corner-stone*, whose foundations shall neither rock nor sway in their place (Isa. xxviii, 16). It shall be a Most Holy Dwelling for Aaron, with everlasting knowledge of the Covenant of justice, and shall offer up sweet fragrance. It shall be a House of Perfection and Truth in Israel that they may establish a Covenant according to the everlasting precepts. And they shall be an agreeable offering, atoning for the Land and determining the judgement of wickedness, and there shall be no more iniquity. When they have been confirmed for two years in perfection of way in the Foundation of the Community, they shall be set apart as holy within the Council of the men of the Community. And the Interpreter shall not conceal from them, out of fear of the spirit of apostasy, any of those things hidden from Israel which have been discovered by him.

And when these become members of the Community in Israel according to all these rules, they shall separate from the habitation of unjust men and shall go into the wilderness to prepare there the way of Him; as it is written, *Prepare in the wilderness the way of . . . , make straight in the desert a path for our God* (Isa. xl, 3). This (path) is the study of the Law which He commanded by the hand of Moses, that they may do according to all that has been revealed from age to age, and as the Prophets have revealed by His Holy Spirit.

And no man among the members of the Covenant of the Community who deliberately, on any point whatever, turns aside from all that is commanded, shall touch the pure Meal of the men of holiness or know anything of their counsel until his deeds are purified from all injustice and he walks in perfection of way. And then, according to the judgement of the Congregation, he shall be admitted to the Council and shall be inscribed in his rank. This rule shall apply to whoever enters the Community.

*And these are the rules which the men of perfect holiness shall follow in their commerce with one another*

Every man who enters the Council of Holiness, (the Council of those) who walk in the way of perfection as commanded by God, and who deliberately or through negligence transgresses one word of the Law of Moses, on any point whatever, shall be expelled from the Council of the Community and shall return no more; no man of holiness shall be associated in his property or counsel in any matter at all. But if he has acted inadvertently, he shall be excluded from the pure Meal and the Council and they shall interpret the rule (as follows). For two years he shall take no part in judgement or ask for counsel; but if, during that time, his way becomes perfect, {then he shall return} (**4Q258**) to the (Court of) Inquiry and the Council, in accordance with the judgement of the Congregation, provided that he commit no further inadvertent sin during two full years.

**IX** For one sin of inadvertence (alone) he shall do penance for two years. But as for him who has sinned deliberately, he shall never return; only the man who has sinned inadvertently shall be tried for two years, that his way and counsel may be made perfect according to the judgement of the Congregation. And afterwards, he shall be inscribed in his rank in the Community of Holiness.

When these become members of the Community in Israel according to all these rules, they shall establish the spirit of holiness according to everlasting truth. They shall atone for guilty rebellion and for sins of unfaithfulness, that they may obtain loving-kindness for the Land without the flesh of holocausts and the fat of sacrifice. And prayer rightly offered shall be as an acceptable fragrance of righteousness, and perfection of way as a delectable free-will offering. At that time, the men of the Community shall set apart a House of Holiness in order that it may be united to the most holy things and a House of Community for Israel, for those who walk in perfection. The sons of Aaron alone shall command in matters of justice and property, and every rule concerning the men of the Community shall be determined according to their word.

As for the property of the men of holiness who walk in perfection, it shall not be merged with that of the men of injustice who have not purified their life by separating themselves from iniquity and walking in the way of perfection. They shall depart from none of the counsels of the Law to walk in all the stubbornness of their hearts, but shall be ruled by the primitive precepts in which the men of the Community were first instructed until there shall come the Prophet and the Messiahs of Aaron and Israel.

*These are the precepts in which the Master shall walk in His commerce with all the living, according to the rule proper to every season and according to the worth of every man*

He shall do the will of God according to all that has been revealed from age to age.

He shall measure out all knowledge discovered throughout the ages, together with the Precept of the age.

He shall separate and weigh the sons of righteousness according to their spirit.

He shall hold firmly to the elect of the time according to His will, as He has commanded.

He shall judge every man according to his spirit. He shall admit him in accordance with the cleanness of his hands and advance him in accordance with his understanding. And he shall love and hate likewise.

He shall not rebuke the men of the Pit nor dispute with them.

He shall conceal the teaching of the Law from men of injustice, but shall impart true knowledge and righteous judgement to those who have chosen the Way. He shall guide them all in knowledge according to the spirit of each and according to the rule of the age, and shall thus instruct them in the mysteries of marvellous truth, so that in the midst of the men of the Community they may walk perfectly together in all that has been revealed to them. This is the time for the preparation of the way into the wilderness, and he shall teach them to do all that is required at that time and to separate from all those who have not turned aside from all injustice.

*These are the rules of conduct for the Master in those times with respect to His loving and hating*

Everlasting hatred in a spirit of secrecy for the men of perdition! He shall leave to them wealth and earnings like a slave to his lord and like a poor man to his master.

He shall be a man zealous for the Precept whose time is for the Day of Revenge. He shall perform the will of God in all his deeds, and in all his dominion as He has commanded. He shall freely delight in all that befalls him and nothing shall please him save God's will. He shall delight in all the words of His mouth and shall desire nothing except His command. He shall watch always [for] the judgement of God, and shall bless his Maker [for all His goodness] and declare [His mercies] in all that befalls.

He shall bless Him [with the offering] of the lips **X** at the times ordained by Him: at the beginning of the dominion of light, and at its end when it retires to its appointed place; at the beginning of the watches of darkness when He unlocks their storehouse and spreads them out, and also at their end when they retire before the light; when the heavenly lights shine out from the dwelling-place of Holiness, and also when they retire to the place of Glory; at the entry of the (monthly) seasons on the days of the new moon, and also at their end when they succeed to one another. Their renewal is a great day for the Holy of Holies, and a sign for the unlocking of everlasting mercies at the beginning of seasons in all times to come.

At the beginning of the months of the (yearly) seasons
 and on the holy days appointed for remembrance,
in their seasons I will bless Him
 with the offering of the lips
 according to the Precept engraved for ever:
at the beginning of the years
 and at the end of their seasons
 when their appointed law is fulfilled,
on the day decreed by Him
 that they should pass from one to the other –
the season of early harvest to the summer time,
the season of sowing to the season of grass,
the seasons of years to their weeks (of years) –
and at the beginning of their weeks
 for the season of Jubilee.
All my life the engraved Precept shall be on my tongue
 as the fruit of praise
 and the portion of my lips.

I will sing with knowledge and all my music
 shall be for the glory of God.
(My) lyre (and) my harp shall sound
 for His holy order
and I will tune the pipe of my lips
 to His right measure.
With the coming of day and night
 I will enter the Covenant of God,
and when evening and morning depart
 I will recite His decrees.
I will place in them my bounds without return.

I will declare His judgement concerning my sins,
and my transgressions shall be before my eyes
as an engraved Precept.
I will say to God, 'My Righteousness'
and 'Author of my Goodness' to the Most High,
'Fountain of Knowledge' and 'Source of Holiness',
'Summit of Glory' and 'Almighty Eternal Majesty'.
I will choose that which He teaches me
and will delight in His judgement of me.

Before I move my hands and feet
I will bless His Name.
I will praise Him before I go out or enter,
or sit or rise,
and whilst I lie on the couch of my bed.
I will bless Him with the offering
of that which proceeds from my lips
from the midst of the ranks of men,
and before I lift my hands to eat
of the pleasant fruits of the earth.
I will bless Him for His exceeding wonderful deeds
at the beginning of fear and dread
and in the abode of distress and desolation.
I will meditate on His power
and will lean on His mercies all day long.
I know that judgement of all the living
is in His hand,
and that all His deeds are truth.
I will praise Him when distress is unleashed
and will magnify Him also because of His salvation.

I will pay to no man the reward of evil;
I will pursue him with goodness.
For judgement of all the living is with God
and it is He who will render to man his reward.
I will not envy in a spirit of wickedness,
my soul shall not desire the riches of violence.
I will not grapple with the men of perdition
until the Day of Revenge,

but my wrath shall not turn from the men of falsehood
and I will not rejoice until judgement is made.
I will bear no rancour
against them that turn from transgression,
but will have no pity
on all who depart from the way.
I will offer no comfort to the smitten
until their way becomes perfect.

I will not keep Belial within my heart,
and in my mouth shall be heard
no folly or sinful deceit,
no cunning or lies shall be found on my lips.
The fruit of holiness shall be on my tongue
and no abominations shall be found upon it.
I will open my mouth
in songs of thanksgiving,
and my tongue shall always proclaim
the goodness of God and the sin of men
until their transgression ends.
I will cause vanities
to cease from my lips,
uncleanness and crookedness
from the knowledge of my heart.

I will impart/conceal knowledge with discretion
and will prudently hedge it within a firm bound
to preserve faith and strong judgement
in accordance with the justice of God.
I will distribute the Precept
by the measuring-cord of the times,
and . . . righteousness
and loving-kindness towards the oppressed,
encouragement to the troubled heart
**XI** and discernment to the erring spirit,
teaching understanding to them that murmur
that they may answer meekly
before the haughty of spirit
and humbly before men of injustice
who point the finger and speak of iniquity
and who are zealous for wealth.

As for me,
my justification is with God.
In His hand are the perfection of my way
and the uprightness of my heart.
He will wipe out my transgression
through His righteousness.

For my light has sprung
from the source of His knowledge;
my eyes have beheld His marvellous deeds,
and the light of my heart, the mystery to come.
He that is everlasting
is the support of my right hand;
the way of my steps is over stout rock
which nothing shall shake;
for the rock of my steps is the truth of God
and His might is the support of my right hand. 5

From the source of His righteousness
is my justification,
and from His marvellous mysteries
is the light in my heart.
My eyes have gazed
on that which is eternal,
on wisdom concealed from men,
on knowledge and wise design
(hidden) from the sons of men;
on a fountain of righteousness
and on a storehouse of power,
on a spring of glory
(hidden) from the assembly of flesh.
God has given them to His chosen ones
as an everlasting possession,
and has caused them to inherit
the lot of the Holy Ones.
He has joined their assembly
to the Sons of Heaven
to be a Council of the Community,
a foundation of the Building of Holiness,
and eternal Plantation throughout all ages to come.

As for me,
I belong to wicked mankind,
to the company of unjust flesh.
My iniquities, rebellions, and sins,
together with the perversity of my heart,
belong to the company of worms
and to those who walk in darkness.
For mankind has no way,
and man is unable to establish his steps
since justification is with God
and perfection of way is out of His hand.
All things come to pass by His knowledge;
He establishes all things by His design
and without Him nothing is done.

As for me,
if I stumble, the mercies of God
shall be my eternal salvation.
If I stagger because of the sin of flesh,
my justification shall be
by the righteousness of God which endures for ever.
When my distress is unleashed
He will deliver my soul from the Pit
and will direct my steps to the way.
He will draw me near by His grace,
and by His mercy will He bring my justification.
He will judge me in the righteousness of His truth
and in the greatness of His goodness
He will pardon all my sins.
Through His righteousness he will cleanse me
of the uncleanness of man
and of the sins of the children of men,
that I may confess to God His righteousness,
and His majesty to the Most High.

Blessed art Thou, my God,
who openest the heart of Thy servant to knowledge!
Establish all his deeds in righteousness,
and as it pleases Thee to do for the elect of mankind,
grant that the son of Thy handmaid
may stand before Thee for ever.

For without Thee no way is perfect,
  and without Thy will nothing is done.
It is Thou who hast taught all knowledge
  and all things come to pass by Thy will.
There is none beside Thee to dispute Thy counsel
  or to understand all Thy holy design,
or to contemplate the depth of Thy mysteries
  and the power of Thy might.

Who can endure Thy glory,
  and what is the son of man
  in the midst of Thy wonderful deeds?
What shall one born of woman
  be accounted before Thee?
Kneaded from the dust,
  his abode is the nourishment of worms.
He is but a shape, but moulded clay,
  and inclines towards dust.
What shall hand-moulded clay reply?
  What counsel shall it understand?

# Community Rule manuscripts from Cave 4

## 4QS^d=4Q258

This is the best preserved of the ten 4QS manuscripts. Seven columns of the text have survived, five of them containing full-length lines. Column I, with a wide margin on the right, is almost certainly the beginning of the Scroll. It corresponds to 1QS v, 1. The last identifiable passage represents 1QS XI, 7. The word 'God' (*'el*) is written twice with palaeo-Hebrew letters (at 1QS IX, 25 and X, 9). Columns I and II of S^d (1QS v, 1–VI, 7) provide a shorter and smoother version of the Rule than 1QS. The more fragmentary 4QS^b (=4Q**256**) supports the present version on the essential points. The most significant peculiarities of 4QS^d (=4Q**258**) are the almost complete absence of the 'full' spelling characteristic of the Qumran sectarian manuscripts, the different opening line and a repeated failure to mention 'the Priests, the Sons of Zadok'. For both its occurrences in 1QS, 4QS^d (and 4QS^b) read 'the Congregation' (*ha-rabbim*), an alternative reading likely to possess important historical implications.

For preliminary studies, see G. Vermes, 'Preliminary Remarks on the Unpublished Fragments of the Community Rule from Qumran Cave 4', *JJS* 42 (1991), 250–55; 'Qumran Forum Miscellanea I', *JJS* 43 (1992), 300–301; 'Corrigendum to Qumran Forum Miscellanea I', *JJS* 44 (1993), 300; 'The Leadership of the Qumran Community: Sons of Zadok – Priests – Congregation', in the Martin Hengel Festschrift *Geschichte-Tradition-Reflexion*, ed. P. Schäfer (Tübingen, 1996), 375–84; Charlotte Hempel, 'Comments on the Translation of 4QS^d I, 1', *JJS* 44 (1993), 127–8. For a preliminary edition, see E. Qimron in J. H. Charlesworth et al., eds., *The DSS I, Rule of the Community* ... 1994, 72–83.

**I** (=1QS v, 1–20) Teaching for the Master concerning the men of the Law (or: the Master who is the superior of the men of the Law) who have freely pledged themselves to convert from all evil and hold fast to all that He has commanded. And they shall separate from the congregation of the men of injustice and shall unite with respect to doctrine and property, and they shall be under the authority of the Congregation concerning all matters of doctrine and property. They shall practise humility and righteousness and justice and loving-[kindness] and modesty in all their ways. And no man shall walk in the stubbornness of his heart so as to stray. He is rather to lay [a foundation] of truth for Israel for the Community, for all those who have freely pledged themselves to Holiness in Aaron and to a House of Truth in Israel and for those who jo[in th]em for a Community. Whoever enters the Council [of the Commu]nity shall undertake by binding (oath) to [return t]o the Law of Moses with all (his) heart and soul, to all that has been revealed from the L[aw].

[And whoever enters] the Council of the me[n] of the Communi[ty shall separate from all the men] of injustice ... He shall not touch the purity of the men [of holine]ss and shall not eat with (them) [in community. And no] one of the men of the Community [shall follow] their decision in any [doctrine] and judgement. And ... of work. No one from the men of holiness shall eat ... [And] they shall not lean upon [work]s of vanity, for they are all vanity who [do not know His Covenant and all who despis]e His word He will blot them out from the world. All their deeds are defileme[nt] be[fore Him and al]l [their property unclean.] ... Gentiles(?) and they pronounce oaths and execrations and vows. [But when a man enters the Covenant according to all these precepts, that he may be joined to the h]oly [Congregation,] they [shall examine their spirit in community,] am[ong themselves] con[cerning their understanding] **II** (1QS v, 21–vii, 7) and their practice of the Law under the authority of the sons of Aaron who have freely pledged themselves to restore His Covenant and heed to all the precepts commanded by Him to be practised by the multitude of Israel who have freely pledged themselves to return in common. They shall be inscribed in the order, one after another, each according to his understanding and his deeds in the Law, that all may obey one another, the man of lesser rank the greater. And they shall examine their spirit and their deeds in the Law yearly so that each man may be advanced in accordance with [his] un[derstanding] or moved down in accordance with his aberrations. They shall rebuke one another (in) loving-kindness. Let no man address his companion with anger or ill-temper or wicked envy. Also let no man accuse his companion before the Congregation without having rebuked him before witnesses. These are the ways in which all of them shall walk, each man with his companion, wherever they dwell. [The man of lesser rank] shall ob[ey] the greater in matters of work and pro[perty. And they shall e]at [in common] and bless in common and delibera[te] in common. [And wherever there are ten] **III** (1QS vi, 7–10) men of [the Council of the Community, there shall not lack] a pri[est from a]mong them. [And] they [shall sit, each m]an according to his rank, [before him and shall be asked their counsel in all things in that order.] And when [the table has been prepared for eating or the n]ew wine [for drinking, the] priest shall [be first to stretch out his hand to bless the firstfruit of the bread] and of the wine. [And where the ten are, there shall never lack a man among them who shall study the Law day and night. And the Congregation shall w]atch [for one third of every night of the year, to read the Book] **IV** ... **V** (1QS vii, 13) ... [and whoever draws] his hand from be[neath his garment] ... **VI** (1QS viii, 6–21) ... [and] to pay to the wicked [their reward. It shall be a tried wall, that precious corner-stone whose foundations shall not rock nor sway from] their [pl]ace; (it shall be) a most holy dwelling-place [for Aaron, with the knowledge of them all of a covenant of justice and of the offering of fragrance; (it shall be) a house of perfection and truth for Israe]l to establish a covenant according to the everlasting precepts.

[They shall be an acceptance to atone for the land and to determine the judgement of wickedness with no injustice (any more). When these have been confirmed in the fou]ndation of the Community for two years, [in perfection of way, they shall be separated as holy within the council of the men] of the Communi[ty. And anything hidden from Is]rael but discovered by the man [who interprets, he shall not conceal it from them for fear of the spirit of apostasy.] And when these become (part of) the Community/in Israel, they shall separate fr[om the midst of the habitation] of the men [of injustice to go into the wilderness to prepare there the way of HIM (or: {the truth} (4Q259). This is the study of the La]w which He has commanded by the ha[nd of Moses, to pra]ctise all [that has been revealed from age to age, and as the prophets have revealed by His holy spirit. And no ma]n from the men of the covenant of the [Community who turns aside from any commandment] deliberately shall touch the purity of the men of holiness, nor shall he know any of their counsel until his deeds are purified from all injustice so that he walks in perfection of way. And they shall admit him to the council by the decision of the Congregation and afterwards he shall be inscribed in his rank. And this rule (shall apply) to everyone who attaches himself] to the Community. [And these are the rules which the men of holiness shall follow, one regarding another.] Everyone who [enters the council of the Community ... **VII** (1QS vii, 24–ix, 10, 15) ... they shall exclude him from purity and from council and from judgement for tw[o year]s and he shall return to study and to council if he has not committed again a sin by inadvertence for two full years. For one sin of inadvertence he shall do penance for two years, and for a deliberately committed sin he shall return no more. But he shall be tried for two [y]ears concerning the perfection of his way and for his counsel according to the decision of the Congregation and he shall be inscribed in his rank in the Community of holiness. [When] these [become part] of the Community in Israel according to these rules, they shall [es]tablish the spirit of holiness as eternal truth. They shall atone for guilty rebellion [and the sin of unfaithful]ness and shall gain (divine) acceptance for the lan[d without the flesh] of holocausts and the fat of sacrifices and offerings. And the cor[r]ect free-will gift of the lips shall be like a fragrance [of righteousness and the perfection] of the way like the free-will offerin[g of a]greeable [tribute]. And at that time they shall separate a house of Aaron for holiness for all [ ] of God [and a house of Community for Is]rael who walk in perfe[ction. Only the sons of Aa]ron [shall comm]a[nd in matters of ju]stice and property. And the property [of the men of holiness who wa]lk in perfection, let [their property] not be mer[ged with] the property [of the men of falsehood] who have not confir[med their way to separate from all] e[vil things] so as to walk in [the way of perfection. Let them not depart from any counsel of the Law] and they shall be judged by the [primitive precepts in which the men of the Community began to be instructed. He shall perform the judgement of every man according to his spirit and he shall admit him according to the cleanness of his hands] **VIII** (1QS IX, 15–X, 3) and shall advance him according to his understanding, and so shall be his love and his hatred. Furthermore he shall not rebuke a man and shall not dispute with the men of the pit. He shall conceal his counsel among the men of injustice, but he shall impart true knowledge and righteous judgement to those who have chosen the way, to each according to his spirit and according to the rule of the age, [guiding the]m with knowledge. And thus shall he instruct them in the mysteries of marvel and truth among the men of the Community that they may walk in perfection each man with [his fellow in all that has been] revealed to them. This is the time for the preparation of the way into the wilderness. He shall instruct them in all that is to be done in that time.

[And he shall separate] from every man who has not turned away from all injustice. And these are the rules of conduct for the Master in [those] ti[mes] [with respect to his loving and] hating. Everlasting hatred for the men of the pit in a spirit of secrecy. He shall leave to them property and gain [and the earnings of toil like a slave to] his [lo]rd and the poor man to his master. Each shall be zealous for the precept and his time shall become a day [of revenge.] He shall [perform the will (of God) in all his actions and in al]l his dominion a[s He has commanded. And a]ll that befalls him, he shall enjoy as a free gift and without the will [of GOD] [he shall not enjoy (anything). He shall delight in all the words of His mouth and shall desire nothing that He has] n[ot commanded. And] he shall watch al[ways for the judgemen]t of GOD [ ] and he shall bless his Maker and in all that befalls he shall declare [ ] and with the offering of the lips he shall bless Him at [the times which He has decreed. At the beginning of the dominion of light a]nd the c[ompletion of its circuit when it ret]ires to [its] appointed dwelling at the beginning [of the watches darkness. When He opens its storehouse and spreads it out and at the completion of its circuit when it retires bef]ore the light. When [the heavenly lights] shine out [from the a]bode [of His holiness together with their withdrawal to the dwelling of glory. At the entry of seasons according to the new moon as well as their completion of their circuit when one succeeds to the other]; **IX** (1QS x, 4–12) at their renewal there is a great day for the Holy of Holies and a sign for the opening of the everlasting mercies at the beginning of the seasons for all ages to come. At the beginning of the months for their seasons and on the holy days according to their rules for remembrance in [their] seasons, I will bless Him [with the offering of the l]ips according to the precept [en]graved for ever. At the beginning of the years and at the completion of the circ[uit of their seasons, when they ful]fil their determined precept on the day decreed for one to follow another, the seas[on of early harvest the summer, and the season of so]wing the season of grass, the seasons of the ye[ar]s thei[r] weeks [and at the beginning of] their weeks the seasons of jubilee. And during all my existence the [en]graved precept shall be on [my tongue as a fruit] of praise and a po[rtion] of my lips. I will sin[g] with knowledge and all my music is for the glory of GOD. [And I will] strike my lyre to the order [of His holiness and the pipe of my lips I will] tune to [His r]ight measure. [At the coming] of the day [and the n]ight I will enter the covenant [of GOD and at the departure of evening and morning I will recite His precepts. And in them will I re-establish [my boundaries without return. I will declare His judgement correct concerning] my [trans]gression [and] my [rebel]lion shall be before my eyes [as an engraved precept. And I say to GOD, 'My righteousness' and to the Most High, 'A]uthor of my goodness', 'Foun[tain of Knowledge' and 'Source of Holiness', 'Summit of Glory' and 'Almighty Eternal Majesty'. I will choose] **X** (1QS x, 12–18) that which He teaches [me and I will delight in His judgement of me. Before I move my hands] and feet I will bless [His name and before I lift my hand to grow fat from] the pleasant pro[duce of the world. At the beginning of fear and dread and in the abode of distress] a[nd desolation, I will confess (His) marvel and I will meditate on His might and on His mercies] I will lea[n all day long. I know that in His hand is the judgement of all the living and all His deeds are truth.] When [distress] sta[rts I will praise Him and I will exalt Him for His salvation. And I will not pay] an [evil] reward [to a man; I will pursue him with goodness. For the judgement of all the living is with GOD, and He] will repay [man his reward . . . ] **XI** . . . **XII** (1QS xi, 7) . . . [and He has caused] them [to inher]it the l[ot of the Holy Ones] . . . **XIII** (1QS xi, 14–15) . . . [He will a]tone [for all] my sins. Through His righteousness He will cleanse me of the uncleanness of man and from the sins of the child[ren of m[en that I may confess to God] His righ]teousness . . .

## 4QS$^{e}$=4Q259

Three fragmentary columns of a leather scroll contain damaged sections of 1QS vii–ix. The text translated comes from columns ii and iii and represents an important doctrinal section of 1QS (viii, 4–ix, 11) in an abridged form. Not only are some of the interlinear additions to 1QS absent, suggesting their later editorial nature, but 4QS$^{e}$ (4Q259) jumps from 1QS viii, 15 to ix, 12, thus omitting among other things the mention of the 'Prophet and the Messiah of Aaron and Israel' (1QS ix, 11). It would seem that the copyist of this manuscript substituted 4Q319 (the calendric document of *Otot*) for the text corresponding to 1QS x–xi.

For a preliminary study, see Sarianna Metso, 'The Primary Results of the Reconstruction of 4QS$^{e}$', *JJS* 44 (1993), 303–8; *The Textual Development of the Qumran Community Rule* (Helsinki, 1996), 56–60. For a preliminary edition, see E. Qimron in J. H. Charlesworth et al., eds., *The DSS I, Rule of the Community* . . . 1994, 84–9.

**II** (1QS vii, 20–viii, 10) . . . And when [he has] comple[ted] [two years, the Congregation shall consider his case and he shall be inscribed in] his

[ran]k and afterwards he may question [concerning the law. And anyone who has been in the Co]uncil of the Community until he has completed [ten years, and then his spirit turned back so that he has betrayed the Community and has departed from] the Congregation to walk [in the stubbornness of his heart, he shall return no more to the Council of the Community. And any of the m]en of the Community who [has shared with him his purity or his property, his sentence shall be [like his: he shall be expelled. In the Council of the Community there shall be twelve m]en [and] three priests, perfect in all that has been revealed from the whole Law to practise] truth, righteousness and justice [loving-kindness and modesty towards one another. They shall preserve f]aith in the land with steadfastness and with humility [and a bro]ken [spirit.] And they shall atone for in[iquity by the practice of justice and the distress of te]sting. They shall walk with all men[ by the standard] of truth, by the rule [of the time. When these are in] Israel, the Council of the Community shall be established [to be an] ever[lasting plantation, a House of Holiness for Israel and an Assembly] of Supreme Holiness for Aaron. They shall be witnesses of the truth at the Judgement, and shall be the elect of good [will who atone for] the Lan[d and pay] to the wicked their reward. It shall be the tried wall, [*that precious*] *cor*[*ner-stone*. They shall] ne[ither rock, no]r sway from their place (Isa. xxviii, 16). It shall be a m[ost] Holy Dwelling for Aar[on f]or a Covenan[t of justice to offer up sweet] fragrance. It shall be a House of Perfection and Truth in [Israel that they may establish a Covenant according to the everlast]ing [precepts.] When they have been confirmed **III** (1QS viii, 11–15; ix, 12 ...) [for two years in the perfection of way in the Foundation of the Community, they shall be set apart] as holy within the Council of the men [of the Community. And] the interpreter shall not con[c]eal [from them, out of fear of the spirit of apostasy, any of those things hidden from Israel which have been discover]ed by him. [And when] these shall become the Community, they shall separate fro[m the habit]ation [of unjust men and shall] go into the wil[derness to prepare there th]e way of the Truth; a[s] it is written, [*In the wildernes*]*s pr*[*epare the way of* ... (?), *make strai*]*ght in the desert a path for our God* (Isa. xl, 3). This (path) is [the study of the Law which] He commanded by the hand of Moses. (The manuscript omits the section corresponding to 1QS viii, 15b to ix, 11, and continues with ix, 12 on the same line.) These are the pre[cepts in which] the Mas[ter shall walk] in his commerce with all the living, according to the rule proper to every season and according to the wort[h of every man].

# The Damascus Document

## (CD, 4Q265–73, 5Q12, 6Q15)

Extensive fragments of the Damascus Document have been recovered from three of the Qumran caves (4Q265–73, 5Q12=CD IX, 7–10, 6Q15=CD IV, 19–21, V, 13–14, V, 18–VI, 2, VI, 20–VII, 1, plus a text unparalleled in CD), but two incomplete medieval copies of this document had been found already many years earlier, in 1896–7, amongst a mass of discarded manuscripts in a store-room (*genizah*) of an old Cairo synagogue. Published in 1910 by S. Schechter (*Fragments of a Zadokite Work*, Cambridge), they were reprinted with a new Prolegomenon by J. A. Fitzmyer in 1970, re-edited by Chaim Rabin under the title *The Zadokite Documents* (Oxford, 1954) and in the light of the 4Q fragments by M. Broshi, *The Damascus Document Reconsidered*, Jerusalem, 1992. Cf. also J. M. Baumgarten et al. in J. H. Charlesworth et al., eds., *The DSS II: Damascus Document . . .*, 1995, 4–79. For the *editio princeps*, see J. M. Baumgarten, *DJD*, XVIII, 1996.

Dating from the tenth and twelfth centuries respectively, the manuscripts found in Cairo – Manuscript A and Manuscript B – raise a certain number of textual problems in that they present two different versions of the original composition. I have settled the difficulty as satisfactorily as I can by following Manuscript A, to which the 4Q fragments correspond, and by inserting the Manuscript B variants in brackets or footnotes. At a certain point, as the reader will see, Manuscript A comes to an end and we then have to rely entirely on Manuscript B. Furthermore, two of the Cave 4 manuscripts (4Q**266** and **268**) show that page I of the Cairo document was preceded by another section of which both the beginning and the end have survived. Also 4Q**266** and **270** indicate that in antiquity the text corresponding to CD IX, I was preceded by CD XVI. In the translation I have therefore rearranged the order of the pages and placed pages XV and XVI before page IX.

The title 'Damascus Document' derives from the references in the Exhortation to the 'New Covenant' made 'in the land of Damascus'. The significance of this phrase is discussed in Chapter III together with the chronological data included in the manuscript. They suggest that the document was written in about 100 BCE and this hypothesis is indirectly supported by the absence of any mention in the historical passages of the Kittim (Romans) whose invasion of the Orient did not take place until after 70 BCE.

The work is divided into an Exhortation and a list of Statutes. In the Exhortation, the preacher – probably a Guardian of the Community – addresses his 'sons' on the themes of the sect's teaching, many of which appear also in the Community Rule. His aim is to encourage the sectaries to remain faithful, and with this end in view he sets out to demonstrate from the history of Israel and the Community that fidelity is always rewarded and apostasy chastised.

During the course of his argument, the author of the Damascus Document frequently interprets biblical passages in a most unexpected way. I have mentioned one of these commentaries on the marriage laws in Chapter IV (pp. 69–70), but there is another intricate exposition of Amos v, 26–7 on p. 133 which may not be easy to understand.

In the Bible these verses convey a divine threat: the Israelites were to take themselves and their idols into exile: 'You shall take up Sakkuth your king and Kaiwan your star-god, your images which you made for yourselves, for I will take you into exile beyond Damascus.' But the Damascus Document transforms this threat into a promise of salvation; by changing certain words in the biblical text and omitting others its version read: 'I will exile the tabernacle of your king and the bases of your statues from my tent to Damascus.'

In this new text, the three key phrases are interpreted symbolically as follows: 'tabernacle' = 'Books of the Law'; 'king' = 'congregation'; 'bases of statues' = 'Books of the Prophets'. Thus: 'The Books of the Law are the *tabernacle* of the king; as God said, *I will raise up the tabernacle of David which is fallen* (Amos ix, 11). The *king* is the congregation; and the *bases of the statues* are the Books of the Prophets whose sayings Israel despised.'

The omission of any reference to the 'star-god' is made good by introducing a very different 'Star', the messianic 'Interpreter of the Law' with his companion the 'Prince of the congregation'. 'The star is the Interpreter of the Law who shall come to Damascus; as it is written, *A star shall come forth out of Jacob and a sceptre shall rise out of Israel* (Num. xxiv, 17). The sceptre is the Prince of the whole congregation ...'

The second part of the Damascus Document, the Statutes, consists of a collection of laws which mostly reflect a sectarian reinterpretation of the biblical commandments relative to vows and oaths, tribunals, purification, the Sabbath and the distinction between ritual purity and impurity. They are followed by rules concerned with the institutions and organization of the Community. Some of the particular laws of the Damascus Rule appear also in the Temple Scroll (cf. p. 191).

Whereas the Exhortation represents a literary *genre* adopted by both Jewish and Christian religious teachers (e.g. the Letter to the Hebrews), the methodical grouping of the Statutes prefigures that of the Mishnah, the oldest extant Jewish code.

The Statutes as they appear in the Qumran fragments include the form of the ritual for the Feast of the Renewal of the Covenant, so it may be assumed that the entire Damascus Document was originally connected with that festival. 4Q**266**, as will be seen presently, specifies that it occurred in the third month, i.e. that it coincided with the Feast of Weeks, celebrated on the fifteenth day of the third month according to the sect's calendar.

The translation of those Cave 4 fragments which are additional to CD will follow the presentation of the Cairo manuscripts.

## *The Exhortation*

**I** Listen now[1] all you who know righteousness, and consider the works of God; for He has a dispute with all flesh and will condemn all those who despise Him.

For when they were unfaithful and forsook Him, He hid His face from Israel and His Sanctuary and delivered them up to the sword. But remembering the Covenant of the forefathers, He left a remnant to Israel and did not deliver it up to be destroyed. And in the age of wrath, three hundred and ninety years after He had given them into the hand of King Nebuchadnezzar of Babylon, He visited them, and He caused a plant root to spring from Israel and Aaron to inherit His Land and to prosper on the good things of His earth. And they perceived their iniquity and recognized that they were guilty men, yet for twenty years they were like blind men groping for the way.

And God observed their deeds, that they sought Him with a whole heart, and He raised for them a Teacher of Righteousness to guide them in the way of His heart. And he made known to the latter generations that which God had done to the latter generation, the congregation of traitors, to those who departed from the way. This was the time of which it is written, *Like a stubborn heifer thus was Israel stubborn* (Hos. iv. 16), when the Scoffer arose who shed over Israel the waters of lies. He caused them to wander in a pathless wilderness, laying low the everlasting heights, abolishing the ways of righteousness and removing the boundary

1. 4Q**268** adds: to me.

with which the forefathers had marked out their inheritance, that he might call down on them the curses of His Covenant and deliver them up to the avenging sword of the Covenant. For they sought smooth things and preferred illusions (Isa. xxx, 10) and they watched for breaks (Isa. xxx, 13) and chose the fair neck; and they justified the wicked and condemned the just, and they transgressed the Covenant and violated the Precept. They banded together against the life of the righteous (Ps. xciv, 21) and loathed all who walked in perfection; they pursued them with the sword and exulted in the strife of the people. And the anger of God was kindled against **II** their congregation so that He ravaged all their multitude; and their deeds were defilement before Him.

Hear now, all you who enter the Covenant, and I will unstop your ears concerning the ways of the wicked.[2]

God loves knowledge. Wisdom and understanding He has set before Him, and prudence and knowledge serve Him. Patience and much forgiveness are with Him towards those who turn from transgression; but power, might, and great flaming wrath by the hand of all the Angels of Destruction towards those who depart from the way and abhor the Precept. They shall have no remnant or survivor. For from the beginning God chose them not; He knew their deeds before ever they were created and He hated their generations, and He hid His face from the Land until they were consumed. For He knew the years of their coming and the length and exact duration of their times for all ages to come and throughout eternity. He knew the happenings of their times throughout all the everlasting years. And in all of them He raised for Himself men called by name[3] that a remnant might be left to the Land, and that the face of the earth might be filled with their seed. And He made known His Holy Spirit to them by the hand of His anointed ones, and He proclaimed the truth (to them). But those whom He hated He led astray.

Hear now, my sons, and I will uncover your eyes that you may see and understand the works of God, that you may choose that which pleases Him and reject that which He hates, that you may walk perfectly in all His ways and not follow after thoughts of the guilty inclination and after eyes of lust. For through them, great men have gone astray and mighty heroes have stumbled from former times till now. Because they walked

**2**. 4Q**266** fr. 2 ii, 3 adds: so that from all the paths of the sin[ners you shall keep away].
**3**. Or: men called (4Q**266**, fr. 2 ii, 11).

in the stubbornness of their heart the Heavenly Watchers fell; they were caught because they did not keep the commandments of God. And their sons also fell who were tall as cedar trees and whose bodies were like mountains. All flesh on dry land perished; they were as though they had never been because they did their own will and did not keep the commandment of their Maker so that His wrath was kindled against them. **III** Through it, the children of Noah went astray, together with their kin, and were cut off. Abraham did not walk in it, and he was accounted a friend of God because he kept the commandments of God and did not choose his own will. And he handed them down to Isaac and Jacob, who kept them, and were recorded as friends of God and party to the Covenant for ever. The children of Jacob strayed through them and were punished in accordance with their error. And their sons in Egypt walked in the stubbornness of their hearts, conspiring against the commandments of God and each of them doing that which seemed right in his own eyes. They ate blood, and He cut off their males in the wilderness. And at Kadesh He said to them, *Go up and possess the land* (Deut. ix, 23). But they chose their own will and did not heed the voice of their Maker, the commands of their Teacher, but murmured in their tents; and the anger of God was kindled against their congregation. Through it their sons perished, and through it their kings were cut off; through it their mighty heroes perished and through it their land was ravaged. Through it the first members of the Covenant sinned and were delivered up to the sword, because they forsook the Covenant of God and chose their own will and walked in the stubbornness of their hearts, each of them doing his own will.

But with the remnant which held fast to the commandments of God He made His Covenant with Israel for ever, revealing to them the hidden things in which all Israel had gone astray. He unfolded before them His holy Sabbaths and his glorious feasts, the testimonies of His righteousness and the ways of His truth, and the desires of His will which a man must do in order to live. And they dug a well rich in water; and he who despises it shall not live. Yet they wallowed in the sin of man and in ways of uncleanness, and they said, 'This is our (way).' But God, in His wonderful mysteries, forgave them their sin and pardoned their wickedness; and He built them a sure house in Israel whose like has never existed from former times till now. Those who hold fast to it are destined to live for ever and all the glory of Adam shall be theirs. As God ordained for them by the hand of the Prophet Ezekiel, saying, *The*

*Priests, the Levites, and the sons* **IV** *of Zadok who kept the charge of my sanctuary when the children of Israel strayed from me, they shall offer me fat and blood* (Ezek. xliv, 15).

The *Priests* are the converts of Israel who departed from the land of Judah, and (the *Levites* are) those who joined them. The *sons of Zadok* are the elect of Israel, the men called by name who shall stand at the end of days. Behold the exact list of their names according to their generations, and the time when they lived, and the number of their trials, and the years of their sojourn, and the exact list of their deeds . . .

(They were the first men) of holiness whom God forgave, and who justified the righteous and condemned the wicked. And until the age is completed, according to the number of those years, all who enter after them shall do according to that interpretation of the Law in which the first (men) were instructed. According to the Covenant which God made with the forefathers, forgiving their sins, so shall He forgive their sins also. But when the age is completed, according to the number of those years, there shall be no more joining the house of Judah, but each man shall stand on his watch-tower: *The wall is built, the boundary far removed* (Mic. vii, 11).

During all those years Belial shall be unleashed against Israel, as He spoke by the hand of Isaiah, son of Amoz, saying, *Terror and the pit and the snare are upon you, O inhabitant of the land* (Isa. xxiv, 17). Interpreted, these are the three nets of Belial with which Levi son of Jacob said that he catches Israel by setting them up as three kinds of righteousness. The first is fornication, the second is riches, and the third is profanation of the Temple. Whoever escapes the first is caught in the second, and whoever saves himself from the second is caught in the third (Isa. xxiv, 18).

The 'builders of the wall' (Ezek. xiii, 10) who have followed after 'Precept' – 'Precept' was a spouter of whom it is written, *They shall surely spout* (Mic. ii, 6) – shall be caught in fornication twice by taking a second wife while the first is alive, whereas the principle of creation is, *Male and female created He them* (Gen. i, 27). **V** Also, those who entered the Ark went in two by two. And concerning the prince it is written, *He shall not multiply wives to himself* (Deut. xvii, 17); but David had not read the sealed book of the Law which was in the ark (of the Covenant), for it was not opened in Israel from the death of Eleazar and Joshua, and the elders who worshipped Ashtoreth. It was hidden and (was not) revealed until the coming of Zadok. And the deeds of David rose up, except for the murder of Uriah, and God left them to him.

Moreover, they profane the Temple because they do not observe the distinction (between clean and unclean) in accordance with the Law, but lie with a woman who sees her bloody discharge.

And each man marries the daughter of his brother or sister, whereas Moses said, *You shall not approach your mother's sister; she is your mother's near kin* (Lev. xviii, 13). But although the laws against incest are written for men, they also apply to women. When, therefore, a brother's daughter uncovers the nakedness of her father's brother, she is (also his) near kin.

Furthermore, they defile their holy spirit and open their mouth with a blaspheming tongue against the laws of the Covenant of God saying, 'They are not sure.' They speak abominations concerning them; *they are all kindlers of fire and lighters of brands* (Isa. l, 11), *their webs are spiders' webs and their eggs are vipers' eggs* (Isa. lix, 5). No man that approaches them shall be free from guilt; the more he does so, the guiltier shall he be, unless he is pressed. For (already) in ancient times God visited their deeds and His anger was kindled against their works; *for it is a people of no discernment* (Isa. xxvii, 11), *it is a nation void of counsel inasmuch as there is no discernment in them* (Deut. xxxii, 28). For in ancient times, Moses and Aaron arose by the hand of the Prince of Lights and Belial in his cunning raised up Jannes and his brother when Israel was first delivered.[4]

And at the time of the desolation of the land there arose removers of the bound who led Israel astray. And the land was ravaged because they preached rebellion against the commandments of God given by the hand of Moses and **VI** of His holy anointed ones, and because they prophesied lies to turn Israel away from following God. But God remembered the Covenant with the forefathers, and he raised from Aaron men of discernment and from Israel men of wisdom, and He caused them to hear. And they dug the Well:[5] *the well which the princes dug, which the nobles of the people delved with the stave* (Num. xxi, 18).

The *Well* is the Law, and those who dug it were the converts of Israel who went out of the land of Judah to sojourn in the land of Damascus. God called them all *princes* because they sought Him, and their renown was disputed by no man. The *Stave* is the Interpreter of the Law of whom Isaiah said, *He makes a tool for His work* (Isa. liv, 16); and the *nobles of the*

**4**. Or: when he acted wickedly against Israel the first time (4Q**266**, fr. 3 ii, 6–7).

**5**. 4Q**266**, fr. 3 ii, 10 adds: of which Moses said:

*people* are those who come to dig the *Well* with the staves with which the *Stave* ordained that they should walk in all the age of wickedness – and without them they shall find nothing – until he comes who shall teach righteousness at the end of days.

None of those brought into the Covenant shall enter the Temple to light His altar in vain. They shall bar the door, forasmuch as God said, *Who among you will bar its door?* And, *You shall not light my altar in vain* (Mal. i, 10). They shall take care to act according to the exact interpretation of the Law during the age of wickedness. They shall separate from the sons of the Pit, and shall keep away from the unclean riches of wickedness acquired by vow or anathema or from the Temple treasure; they shall not rob the poor of His people, to make of widows their prey and of the fatherless their victim (Isa. x, 2). They shall distinguish between clean and unclean, and shall proclaim the difference between holy and profane. They shall keep the Sabbath day according to its exact interpretation, and the feasts and the Day of Fasting according to the finding of the members of the New Covenant in the land of Damascus. They shall set aside the holy things according to the exact teaching concerning them. They shall love each man his brother as himself; they shall succour the poor, the needy, and the stranger.

A man shall seek his brother's well-being **VII** and shall not sin against his near kin. They shall keep from fornication according to the statute. They shall rebuke each man his brother according to the commandment and shall bear no rancour from one day to the next. They shall keep apart from every uncleanness according to the statutes relating to each one, and no man shall defile his holy spirit since God has set them apart. For all who walk in these (precepts) in perfect holiness, according to all the teaching of God, the Covenant of God shall be an assurance that they shall live for thousands of generations (MS. B: as it is written, *Keeping the Covenant and grace with those who love me and keep my commandments, to a thousand generations*, Deut. vii, 9).

And if they live in camps according to the rule of the Land (MS. B: as it was from ancient times), marrying (MS. B: according to the custom of the Law) and begetting children, they shall walk according to the Law and according to the statute concerning binding vows, according to the rule of the Law which says, *Between a man and his wife and between a father and his son* (Num. xxx, 17). And all those who despise (MS. B: the commandments and the statutes) shall be rewarded with the retribution of the wicked when God shall visit the Land, when the saying shall come to pass which is written[6] among the words of the Prophet Isaiah son of Amoz: *He will bring upon you, and upon your people, and upon your father's house, days such as have not come since the day that Ephraim departed from Judah* (Isa. vii, 17). When the two houses of Israel were divided, Ephraim departed from Judah. And all the apostates were given up to the sword, but those who held fast escaped to the land of the north; as God said, *I will exile the tabernacle of your king and the bases of your statues from my tent to Damascus* (Amos v, 26–7).

The Books of the Law are the *tabernacle* of the king; as God said, *I will raise up the tabernacle of David which is fallen* (Amos ix, 11). The *king* is the congregation; and the *bases of the statues* are the Books of the Prophets whose sayings Israel despised. The *star* is the Interpreter of the Law who shall come to Damascus; as it is written, *A star shall come forth out of Jacob and a sceptre shall rise out of Israel* (Num. xxiv, 17). The *sceptre* is the Prince of the whole congregation, and when he comes *he shall smite all the children of Seth* (Num. xxiv, 17).

At the time of the former Visitation they were saved, whereas the apostates **VIII** were given up to the sword; and so shall it be for all the members of His Covenant who do not hold steadfastly to these (MS. B: to the curse of the precepts). They shall be visited for destruction by the hand of Belial. That shall be the day when God will visit. (MS. B: As He said,) *The princes of Judah have become* (MS. B: *like those who remove the bound*); *wrath shall be poured upon them* (Hos. v, 10). For they shall hope for healing but He will crush them. They are all of them rebels, for they[7] have not turned from the way of traitors but have wallowed in the ways of whoredom and wicked wealth. They have taken revenge and borne malice, every man against his brother, and every man has hated his fellow, and every man has sinned against his near kin, and has approached for unchastity, and has acted arrogantly for the sake of riches and gain. And every man has done that which seemed right in his eyes and has

6. MS. B continues: by the hand of the prophet Zechariah: *Awake, O Sword, against my shepherd, against my companion, says God. Strike the shepherd that the flock may be scattered and I will stretch my hand over the little ones* (Zech. xiii, 7). The humble of the flock are those who watch for Him. They shall be saved at the time of the Visitation whereas the others shall be delivered up to the sword when the Anointed of Aaron and Israel shall come, as it came to pass at the time of the former Visitation concerning which God said by the hand of Ezekiel: *They shall put a mark on the foreheads of those who sigh and groan* (Ezek. ix, 4). But the others were delivered up to the avenging sword of the Covenant.

7. MS. B inserts: they have entered the Covenant of repentance but they have not turned, etc.

chosen the stubbornness of his heart. They have not kept apart from the people (MS. B: and their sin) and have wilfully rebelled by walking in the ways of the wicked of whom God said, *Their wine is the venom of serpents, the cruel poison* (or *head*) *of asps* (Deut. xxxii, 33).

The *serpents* are the kings of the peoples and their *wine* is their ways. And the *head of asps* is the chief of the kings of Greece who came to wreak vengeance upon them. But all these things the *builders of the wall and those who daub it with plaster* (Ezek. xiii, 10) have not understood because a follower of the wind, one who raised storms and rained down lies, had preached to them (Mic. ii, 11), against all of whose assembly the anger of God was kindled.

And as for that which Moses said, *You enter to possess these nations not because of your righteousness or the uprightness of your hearts* (Deut. ix, 5) *but because God loved your fathers and kept the oath* (Deut. vii, 8), thus shall it be with the converts of Israel who depart from the way of the people. Because God loved the first (men) who[8] testified in His favour, so will He love those who come after them, for the Covenant of the fathers is theirs. But He hated the *builders of the wall* and His anger was kindled (MS. B: against them and against all those who followed them); and so shall it be for all who reject the commandments of God and abandon them for the stubbornness of their hearts. This is the word which Jeremiah spoke to Baruch son of Neriah, and which Elisha spoke to his servant Gehazi.

None of the men who enter the New Covenant in the land of Damascus, (B **I**) and who again betray it and depart from the fountain of living waters, shall be reckoned with the Council of the people or inscribed in its Book from the day of the gathering in (B **II**) of the Teacher of the Community until the coming of the Messiah out of Aaron and Israel.

And thus shall it be for every man who enters the congregation of men of perfect holiness but faints in performing the duties of the upright. He is a man who has melted in the furnace (Ezek. xxii, 22); when his deeds are revealed he shall be expelled from the congregation as though his lot had never fallen among the disciples of God. The men of knowledge shall rebuke him in accordance with his sin against the time when he shall stand again before the Assembly of the men of perfect holiness. But when his deeds are revealed, according to the interpretation of the Law in which the men of perfect holiness walk, let no man defer to him with

**8.** MS. B adds: bore witness against the people, so will He love, etc.

regard to money or work, for all the Holy Ones of the Most High have cursed him.

And thus shall it be for all among the first and the last who reject (the precepts), who set idols upon their hearts and walk in the stubbornness of their hearts; they shall have no share in the house of the Law. They shall be judged in the same manner as their companions were judged who deserted to the Scoffer. For they have spoken wrongly against the precepts of righteousness, and have despised the Covenant and the Pact – the New Covenant – which they made in the land of Damascus. Neither they nor their kin shall have any part in the house of the Law.

From the day of the gathering in of the Teacher of the Community until the end of all the men of war who deserted to the Liar there shall pass about forty years (Deut. ii, 14). And during that age the wrath of God shall be kindled against Israel; as He said, *There shall be no king, no prince, no judge, no man to rebuke with justice* (Hos. iii, 4). But those who turn from the sin of Jacob, who keep the Covenant of God, shall then speak each man to his fellow, to justify each man his brother, that their step may take the way of God. And God will heed their words and will hear, and a Book of Reminder shall be written before Him of them that fear God and worship His Name, against the time when salvation and righteousness shall be revealed to them that fear God. *And then shall you distinguish once more between the just and the wicked, between one that serves God and one that serves Him not* (Mal. iii, 18); *and He will show loving-kindness to thousands, to them that love Him and watch for Him, for a thousand generations* (Exod. xx, 6).

And every member of the House of Separation who went out of the Holy City and leaned on God at the time when Israel sinned and defiled the Temple, but returned again to the way of the people in small matters, shall be judged according to his spirit in the Council of Holiness. But when the glory of God is made manifest to Israel, all those members of the Covenant who have breached the bound of the Law shall be cut off from the midst of the camp, and with them all those who condemned Judah in the days of its trials.

But all those who hold fast to these precepts, going and coming in accordance with the Law, who heed the voice of the Teacher and confess before God, (saying), 'Truly we have sinned, we and our fathers, by walking counter to the precepts of the Covenant, Thy judgements upon us are justice and truth'; who do not lift their hand against His holy precepts or His righteous statutes or His true testimonies; who have learned from the former judgements by which the members of the Community were judged; who have listened to the voice of the Teacher of Righteousness and have not despised the precepts of righteousness when they heard them; they shall rejoice and their hearts shall be strong, and they shall prevail over all the sons of the earth. God will forgive them and they shall see His salvation because they took refuge in His holy Name.[9]

## *The Statutes*

... (He shall not) **XV** swear by (the Name), nor by *Aleph* and *Lamed* (Elohim), nor by *Aleph* and *Daleth* (Adonai), but a binding oath by the curses of the Covenant.

He shall not mention the Law of Moses for ... were he to swear and then break (his oath) he would profane the Name.

But if he has sworn an oath by the curses of the Covenant before the judges and has transgressed it, then he is guilty and shall confess and make restitution; but he shall not be burdened with a capital sin.

And all those who have entered the Covenant, granted to all Israel for ever, shall make their children who have reached the age of enrolment, swear with the oath of the Covenant. And thus shall it be during all the age of wickedness for every man who repents of his corrupted way. On the day that he speaks to the Guardian of the congregation, they shall enrol him with the oath of the Covenant which Moses made with Israel, the Covenant to return to the Law of Moses with a whole heart and soul, to whatever is found should be done at that time. No man shall make known the statutes to him until he has stood before the Guardian, lest when examining him the Guardian be deceived by him. But if he transgresses after swearing to return to the Law of Moses with a whole heart and soul, they (the members) shall be innocent should he transgress. And should he err in any matter that is revealed of the Law to the multitude of the camp, the Guardian shall {instruct} (4Q**266**, fr. 8 i, 5) him and shall issue directions concerning him: he should stu[dy] for a full year.[10] And according to his (the Guardian's) knowledge, {no madman, or lunatic shall enter, no simpleton, or fool, no blind man, or maimed, or lame, or

**9**. The end of the Exhortation of CD is followed in 4Q**266**, fr. 4, lines 11–12, by a badly preserved allusion to the Messiah: 'God [will set up] a shep[herd for His people] and he will feed [them] in [pastures] ...'

**10**. 4Q**266**, fr. 8 i, 6 adds: and (then) draw near.

deaf man, and no minor, none of these shall enter into the Community, for the Angels of Holiness are [in their midst]} (4Q**266**, 8 i, 6–9).

(For God made) **XVI** a Covenant with you and all Israel; therefore a man shall bind himself by oath to return to the Law of Moses, for in it all things are strictly defined.

As for the exact determination of their times to which Israel turns a blind eye, behold it is strictly defined in the *Book of the Divisions of the Times into their Jubilees and Weeks*. And on the day that a man swears to return to the Law of Moses, the Angel of Persecution shall cease to follow him provided that he fulfils his word: for this reason Abraham circumcised himself on the day that he knew.

And concerning the saying, *You shall keep your vow by fulfilling it* (Deut. xxiii, 24), let no man, even at the price of death, annul any binding oath by which he has sworn to keep a commandment of the Law.

But even at the price of death, a man shall fulfil no vow by which he has sworn to depart from the Law.

*Concerning the oath of a woman*

Inasmuch as He said, *It is for her husband to cancel her oath* (Num. xxx, 9), no husband shall cancel an oath without knowing whether it should be kept or not. Should it be such as to lead to transgression of the Covenant, he shall cancel it and shall not let it be kept. The rule for her father is likewise.

*Concerning the statute for free-will offerings*

No man shall vow to the altar anything unlawfully acquired. Also, no Priest shall take from Israel anything unlawfully acquired. And no man shall consecrate the food of his house to God, for it is as he said, *Each hunts his brother with a net* (or *votive-offering*: Mic. vii, 2). Let no man consecrate ... And if he has consecrated to God some of his own field ... he who has made the vow shall be punished ... {[with] one sixth of his valuation money} (4Q**266**, fr. 8 ii, 2–3) ...

**IX**[11] Every vow by which a man vows another to destruction (cf. Lev. xxvii, 29) by the laws of the Gentiles shall himself be put to death. And concerning the saying, *You shall not take vengeance on the children of your people, nor bear any rancour against them* (Lev. xix, 18), if any member of

11. 4Q**266**, fr. 8 ii, 8; **270**, fr. 6 iii, 15 add: And that which He said:

the Covenant accuses his companion without first rebuking him before[12] witnesses; if he denounces him in the heat of his anger or reports him to his elders to make him look contemptible, he is one that takes vengeance and bears rancour, although it is expressly written, *He takes vengeance upon His adversaries and bears rancour against His enemies* (Nah. i, 2). If he holds his peace towards him from one day to another[13] and thereafter speaks of him in the heat of his anger, he testifies against himself concerning a capital matter because he has not fulfilled the commandment of God which tells him: *You shall rebuke your companion and not be burdened with sin because of him* (Lev. xix, 17).

*Concerning the oath with reference to that which He said, You shall not take the law into your own hands* (1 Sam. xxv, 26)

Whoever causes another to swear in the field instead of before the Judges, or at their decree, takes the law into his own hands. When anything is lost, and it is not known who has stolen it from the property of the camp in which it was stolen, its owner shall pronounce a curse, and any man who, on hearing (it), knows but does not tell, shall himself be guilty.

When anything is returned which is without an owner, whoever returns it shall confess to the Priest, and apart from the ram of the sin-offering, it shall be his.

And likewise, everything which is found but has no owner shall go to the Priests, for the finder is ignorant of the rule concerning it. If no owners are discovered they shall keep it.

Every sin which a man commits against the Law, and which his companion witnesses, he being alone, if it is a capital matter he shall report it to the Guardian, rebuking him in his presence, and the Guardian shall record it against him in case he should commit it again before one man and he should report it to the Guardian once more. Should he repeat it and be caught in the act before one man, his case shall be complete.

And if there are two (witnesses), each testifying to a different matter, the man shall be excluded from the pure Meal provided that they are trustworthy and that each informs the Guardian on the day that they witnessed (the offence). In matters of property, they shall accept two trustworthy witnesses and shall exclude (the culprit) from the pure Meal on the word of one witness alone.

**12**. Or: through (4Q**270**, fr. 6 iii, 18).

**13**. (4Q**267**, fr. 9 i,1) adds: and from one month to another.

No **X** Judge shall pass sentence of death on the testimony of a witness who has not yet attained the age of enrolment and who is not God-fearing.

No man who has wilfully transgressed any commandment shall be declared a trustworthy witness against his companion until he is purified and able to return.

*And this is the Rule for the Judges of the Congregation*

Ten shall be elected from the congregation for a definite time, four from the tribe of Levi and Aaron, and six from Israel. (They shall be) learned in the Book of Meditation and in the constitutions of the Covenant, and aged between twenty-five and sixty years. No man over the age of sixty shall hold office as Judge of the Congregation, for 'because man sinned his days have been shortened, and in the heat of His anger against the inhabitants of the earth God ordained that their understanding should depart even before their days are completed' (Jubilees, xxiii, 11).

*Concerning purification by water*

No man shall bathe in dirty water or in an amount too shallow to cover a man. He shall not purify himself with water contained in a[14] vessel. And as for the water of every rock-pool too shallow to cover a man, if an unclean man touches it he renders its water as unclean as water contained in a vessel.

*Concerning the Sabbath to observe it according to its law*

No man shall work on the sixth day from the moment when the sun's orb is distant by its own fulness from the gate (wherein it sinks); for this is what He said, *Observe the Sabbath day to keep it holy* (Deut. v, 12). No man shall speak any vain or idle word on the Sabbath day. He shall make no loan to his companion. He shall make no decision in matters of money and gain. He shall say nothing about work or labour to be done on the morrow.

No man shall walk in the field[15] to do business on the Sabbath. He shall not walk more than one thousand cubits beyond his town.

No man shall eat on the Sabbath day except that which is already prepared. He shall eat nothing lying in the fields. He shall not drink except in the camp. **XI** If he is on a journey and goes down to bathe, he shall drink where he stands, but he shall not draw water into a vessel. He

14. Or: in any (4Q270, 6 iv, 21).
15. Or: his field (4Q266).

shall send out no stranger on his business on the Sabbath day. No man shall wear soiled garments, or garments brought to the store, unless they have been washed with water or rubbed with incense. No man shall willingly mingle (with others) on the Sabbath.

No man shall walk more than two thousand cubits after a beast to pasture it outside his town. He shall not raise his hand to strike it with his fist. If it is stubborn he shall not take it out of his house.

No man shall take anything out of the house or bring anything in. And if he is in a booth, let him neither take anything out nor bring anything in. He shall not open a sealed vessel on the Sabbath.

No man shall carry perfumes on himself whilst going and coming on the Sabbath. He shall lift neither stone nor dust in his dwelling.

No man minding a child shall carry it whilst going and coming on the Sabbath.

No man shall chide[16] his manservant or maidservant or labourer on the Sabbath.[17] No man shall assist a beast to give birth on the Sabbath day. And if it should fall into a cistern or pit, he shall not lift it out on the Sabbath.

No man shall spend the Sabbath in a place near to Gentiles on the Sabbath.

No man shall profane the Sabbath for the sake of riches or gain on the Sabbath day. But should any man fall into water or (fire), let him not be pulled out with the aid of a ladder or rope or (some such) utensil.

No man on the Sabbath shall offer anything on the altar except the Sabbath burnt-offering; for it is written thus: *Except your Sabbath offerings* (Lev. xxiii, 38).

No man shall send to the altar any burnt-offering, or cereal offering, or incense, or wood, by the hand of one smitten with any uncleanness, permitting him thus to defile the altar. For it is written, *The sacrifice of the wicked is an abomination, but the prayer of the just is as an agreeable offering* (Prov. xv, 8).

No man entering the house of worship shall come unclean and in need of washing. And at the sounding of the trumpets for assembly, he shall go there before or after (the meeting), and shall not cause the whole service to stop, **XII** for it is a holy service.

No man shall lie with a woman in the city of the Sanctuary, to defile the city of the Sanctuary with their uncleanness.

**16**. Or: show bitterness to (4Q**271**, fr. 5 i, 7).
**17**. 4Q**270**, fr. 6 v, 17 adds: day.

Every man who preaches apostasy under the dominion of the spirits of Belial shall be judged according to the law relating to those possessed by a ghost or familiar spirit (Lev. xx, 27). But no man who strays so as to profane the Sabbath and the feasts shall be put to death; it shall fall to men to keep him in custody. And if he is healed of his error, they shall keep him in custody for seven years and he shall afterwards approach the Assembly.

No man shall stretch out his hand to shed the blood of a Gentile for the sake of riches and gain. Nor shall he carry off anything of theirs, lest they blaspheme, unless so advised by the company of Israel.

No man shall sell clean beasts or birds to the Gentiles lest they offer them in sacrifice. He shall refuse, with all his power, to sell them anything from his granary or wine-press, and he shall not sell them his manservant or maidservant inasmuch as they have been brought by him into the Covenant of Abraham.

No man shall defile himself by eating any live creature or creeping thing, from the larvae of bees to all creatures which creep in water. They shall eat no fish unless split alive and their blood poured out. And as for locusts, according to their various kinds they shall plunge them alive into fire or water, for this is what their nature requires.

All wood and stones and dust defiled by the impurity of a man shall be reckoned like men having defilement of oil on them; whoever touches them shall be defiled by their defilement. And every nail or peg in the wall of a house in which a dead man lies shall become unclean as any working tool becomes unclean (Lev. xi, 32).

The Rule for the assembly of the towns of Israel shall be according to these precepts that they may distinguish between unclean and clean, and discriminate between the holy and the profane.

And these are the precepts in which the Master shall walk in his commerce with all the living in accordance with the statute proper to every age. And in accordance with this statute shall the seed of Israel walk and they shall not be cursed.

*This is the Rule for the assembly of the camps*

Those who follow these statutes in the age of wickedness until the coming of the Messiah of Aaron **XIII** and Israel shall form groups of at least ten men, by *Thousands, Hundreds, Fifties, and Tens* (Exod. xviii, 25). And where the ten are, there shall never be lacking a Priest learned in the Book of Meditation; they shall all be ruled by him.

But should he not be experienced in these matters, whereas one of the

Levites is experienced in them, then it shall be determined that all the members of the camp shall go and come according to the latter's word.

But should there be a case of applying the law of leprosy to a man, then the Priest shall come and shall stand in the camp and the Guardian shall instruct him in the exact interpretation of the Law.

Even if the Priest is a simpleton, it is he who shall lock up (the leper); for theirs is the judgement.

*This is the Rule for the Guardian of the camp*

He shall instruct the Congregation in the works of God. He shall cause them to consider His mighty deeds and shall recount all the happenings of eternity to them [according to] their [ex]planation (4Q**267**, fr. 9 iv, 2). He shall love them as a father loves his children, and shall carry them in all their distress like a shepherd his sheep. He shall loosen all the fetters which bind them that in his Congregation there may be none that are oppressed or broken. He shall examine every man entering his Congregation with regard to his deeds, understanding, strength, ability and possessions, and shall inscribe him in his place according to his rank in the lot of L[ight].

No member of the camp shall have authority to admit a man to the Congregation against the decision of the Guardian of the camp.

No member of the Covenant of God shall give or receive anything from the sons of Dawn (*shahar*) [or: of the Pit (*shahat*)] except for payment.

No man shall form any association for buying and selling without informing the Guardian of the camp and shall act on (his) advice and they shall not go {astray. Likewise he who marri[es]} (4Q**266**, fr. 9 ii, 4) a woma[n] ... advice. Likewise he who divorces (his wife). And he (the Guardian) shall instruct {their sons [and their daughters in a spiri]t} (4Q**266**, fr. 9 ii, 6–7) of humility and in loving-kindness and shall not keep {anger} (4Q**266**, fr. 9 ii, 8) towards them ...

This is the Rule for the assembly of the camps during all [the age of wickedness, and whoever does not hold fast to] these (statutes) shall not be fit to dwell in the Land [when the Messiah of Aaron and Israel shall come at the end of days].

[And] these are the [precepts] in which the Master [shall walk in his commerce with all the living until God shall visit the earth. As He said, *There shall come upon you, and upon your people, and upon your father's house, days*] **XIV** *such as have not come since Ephraim departed from Judah* (Isa. vii, 17); but for whoever shall walk in these (precepts), the Covenant of

God shall stand firm to save him from all the snares of the Pit, whereas the foolish shall be punished.[18]

*The Rule for the assembly of all the camps*

They shall all be enrolled by name: first the Priests, second the Levites, third the Israelites, and fourth the proselytes. And they shall be inscribed by name, one after the other: the Priests first, the Levites second, the Israelites third, and the proselytes fourth. And thus shall they sit and thus be questioned on all matters. And the Priest who is appointed {to head} (4Q267, fr. 9 v, 11) the Congregation shall be from thirty to sixty years old, learned in the Book of Meditation and in all the judgements of the Law so as to pronounce them correctly.

The Guardian of all the camps shall be from thirty to fifty years old, one who has mastered all the secrets of men and the languages of all their clans. Whoever enters the Congregation shall do so according to his word, each in his rank. And whoever has anything to say[19] with regard to any suit or judgement, let him say it to the Guardian.

*This is the Rule for the Congregation by which it shall provide for all its needs*

They shall place the earnings of at least two days out of every month into the hands of the Guardian and the Judges, and from it they shall give to the fatherless, and from it they shall succour the poor and the needy, the aged sick and the man who is stricken (with disease), the captive taken by a foreign people, the virgin with no near kin, and the ma[id for] whom no man cares . . .

And this is the exact statement of the assembly . . .

*This is the exact statement of the statutes in which [they shall walk until the coming of the Messia]h of Aaron and Israel who will pardon their iniquity*

[Whoever] deliberately lies in a matter of property . . . and shall do penance for six days . . .

[Whoever slanders his companion or bears rancour] unjustly [shall do penance for one] year . . .

**18**. Or: transgress (4Q267, fr. 9 v, 5).
**19**. 4Q266, fr. 10 i, 4 adds: to the congregation.

# Damascus Document manuscripts from Cave 4

Three Qumran caves have provided supplementary documentation to the text preserved in the Cairo Genizah. Of these the evidence furnished by Caves 5 (CD IX, 7–10) and 6 (CD IV, 19–21, V, 13–14, V, 18–VI, 2, VI, 20–VII, 1) is negligible, but the fragments discovered in Cave 4 (4Q**266–273**) are of the highest importance. Furthermore 4Q**265** provides a kind of hybrid connecting the Damascus Document and the Community Rule.

The 4Q material represents (1) a prologue missing from CD (4Q**266**, fr. 1a–b; fr. 2 i, 1–6, combined with 4Q**267**, fr. 1 and **268**, fr. 1) and substantial legal sections which follow the broken ending of the Statutes of CD. These laws relate to (2) the admission or dismissal of candidates (4Q**266**, fr. 5); to (3) criteria for disqualifying priests (4Q**266**, fr. 5; **267**, fr. 5 ii; **273**, frs. 2, 4 i); to (4) detailed rulings concerning the diagnosis and quarantining of persons suffering from skin disease (4Q**266**, fr. 6; **272**, fr. 1); to (5) laws pertaining to gleanings (4Q**266**, fr. 6 iii–iv) and to the agricultural priestly dues (4Q**270**, fr. 3 ii–iii; **271**, fr. 2; **269**, fr. 8 i–ii). (6) A penal code partly overlapping with 1QS VII follows (4Q**266**, fr. 10; **270**, fr. 7 i; **269**, fr. 11 i–ii). The two main manuscripts (4Q**266**, fr. 11 and **270**, fr. 7 i–ii) end with the ritual for the dismissal of unworthy members used in the ceremony marking entry into and expulsion from the Covenant. This festival was celebrated in the third month and coincided with the Feast of Weeks or Pentecost. Finally (7) the hybrid S–D (4Q**265**), in which the Community Rule and the Damascus Document merge, allows a glimpse into the interrelationship between the two main constitutional documents of the Community.

For the *editio princeps*, see J. M. Baumgarten, *DJD*, XVIII: Qumran Cave 4–XIII (Oxford, 1996).

# *(1) THE OPENING OF THE DAMASCUS DOCUMENT ACCORDING TO 4QD* (4Q**266–8**)

Three Cave 4 manuscripts of the Damascus Document (4Q**266**, fr. 1a–b; fr. 2 i, 1–6, combined 4Q**267** fr. 1 and **268** fr. 1) have preserved parts of a prologue unattested in the Cairo version. The prologue contains a title vaguely reminiscent of the opening of 4QS$^{d}$. The context is eschatological and alludes to a revelation by God to those 'who search His commandments and walk in the perfection of way'. CD II, 1 follows on directly from the end of the prologue.

## 4Q**266**, fr. 1a–b

[For the Master to instruct the s]ons of Light to keep away from the way[s of wickedness] ... until the completion of the appointed time for the visitation of [the spirit of injustice] ... God [will destro]y all her deeds, bringing destruction on ... the removers of boundaries and He will inflict destruction [on the assembly] of wickedness. [And now listen] to me and I will let you know the awesome des[igns of God] and His marvellous [mighty deeds]. I will recount to you [all that is concealed] from man [all the d]ays of his life ...

## Fr. 2 (4Q**267**, fr. 1; **268**, fr. 1)

**1** flesh and creature ... until it comes to them for they shall not be either early or late from their appointed times ... He decreed an age of wrath for the people who did not know Him, and He established appointed times of goodwill for those who search His commandments and walk in the perfection of way. And He revealed hidden things to their eyes, and opened their ears so that they might hear deep (secrets) and understand all future things before they befall them. Listen now, all you who know righteousness ... (=CD 1, 1).

## *(2) INITIATION RULES*
## 4Q**266**, fr. 5

This fragment contains echoes of the Community Rule's regulations regarding admission and dismissal of candidates and CD's identification of the sons of Zadok as the 'converts of Israel'.

**I** . . .
. . . [that they may bring near] each according to [his] spirit [and deeds] . . . they shall depart by the decision of the Guardian (cf. 1QS VI, 16–17) . . . [And these are the precepts] in which all the converts of Israel [shall wa]lk . . . the sons of Zadok, the Priests (cf. CD IV, 2–3), behold the[y are the converts of Israel . . . [the interpretation of the] last Law. And these are the precepts for the Mas[ter] in which [he shall walk (1QS IX, 12)] in regard to all Israel, for [God] shall not save any of those who are not established] in His ways to walk perfec[tly] . . .

## *(3) RULES RELATING TO THE DISQUALIFICATION OF PRIESTS*
## 4Q**266**, fr. 5 (4Q**267**, fr. 5 ii; **273**, frs. 2, 4 i)

In this section of priestly legislation, the Community specifies (1) that only priests able to speak clearly and distinctly were allowed to read the Bible in public; (2) that priests who had been war prisoners were disqualified from Temple service; and (3) that priests who migrated to Gentile countries were deprived of their leading position and forbidden to partake in holy things.

For a preliminary edition, see J. M. Baumgarten, 'The Disqualification of Priests in the 4Q Fragments of the "Damascus Document", a Specimen of Recovery of pre-Rabbinic Halakha', in *MQC* II, 503–13.

**II** Whoever speaks too fast (or: too quietly, lit. swift or light with his tongue) or with a staccato voice and does not split his words to make [his voice] heard, no one from among these shall read the Book of [the] La[w] that he may not misguide someone in a capital matter. . . . [Any man] from among the sons of Aaron who has been taken prisoner by the nations . . . to defile him with their uncleanness. He shall not come close to the [holy] worship . . . Let him not eat the most holy [things] . . . Any son of Aaron who retreats to ser[ve the nations] ... to teach his people the constitution of the people and also to betray ... [Any son] of Aaron whose name has been rejected from the Truth ... [who has walked] in the stubbornness of his heart, eating from the holy ...

## *(4) DIAGNOSIS OF SKIN DISEASE*
## (4Q**266**,**269**,**272**,**273**)

The rules relating to the diagnosis of a skin disease affecting the scalp and the face (Lev. xiii, 29–37) are missing from the Cairo manuscripts, but can be partially reconstructed from 4Q**272** and **266** and also from 4Q**269** and **273**. The introductory formula prefixed to Lev. xiii, 33, viz., 'And as for that which is said', usually indicative of a repeat citation, suggests that a longer Leviticus quotation preceded it. The skin disease section is followed by laws relating to various sexual discharges causing uncleanness and impurity linked with childbirth.

For the *editio princeps*, see J. M. Baumgarten, *DJD*, XVIII, 50–51, 186–7. For his preliminary reconstruction of the text, see 'The 4Q Zadokite Fragments of Skin Disease', *JJS* 41 (1990), 153–65 and J. H. Charlesworth et al., eds., *The DSS II: Damascus Document*, 1995, 59–75.

### 4Q**272**, fr. I

**I** ... a discoloration or a scab or a bright spot ... And the scab resulting from a blow by wood [or st]one or whatever blow, when the spi[rit] enters [and sei]zes the artery, and the blood recedes up and down, and the artery ... after the blood ...

[And the priest shall observe the skin, the living and] the dead. If the dead (skin) [exceeds] the living (skin), he shall lock him up [until the blood re]turns to the artery until the flesh grows. And the priest shall observe him and shall make a comparison [on] the seventh [d]ay, [and if the spir]it of life is moving up and down, and the flesh grows, [the plague is healed, clean is] the scab. The priest shall not observe the skin on the flesh.

## 4Q266, fr. 6

**I** But if the discoloration or the scab is lower [than the skin ... and the Pr]iest sees it as the appearance of living flesh, it is [a 'leprosy' (skin disease)] which has seized the living skin. And a similar rule concerning ... the Priest shall see on the seventh day. If some living flesh has become dead, the leprosy is malignant. And the law for the scab of the head or the bea[rd, when the Priest shall see] that the spirit has entered the head and the beard seizing the artery, and [the plague] spreads from under the hair and turns its appearance to fine yellow; for it is like a plant which has a worm under it and bites its root and makes its flower wither. And as for that which is said, *And the Priest shall order that they shave his head, but shall not shave the scab* (Lev. xiii, 33). This is in order that the Priest may count the dead and live hair. And he will see whether anything has been added from the live to the dead (hair) during the seven days. If there has, he is unclean. But if nothing has been added from the live (hair) to the dead, and the artery is filled with bl[ood] and the sp[i]rit of life goes up and down in it, this plague [is cured]. And this is the rule of the law of 'leprosy' for the sons of Aaron to set apart ...

And the law concerning a man with a flux. Any man with a [fl]ux issuing from [his] flesh, [o]r one that causes a [lew]d thought to arise or ...

**II** the woma[n] ... [the man who ap]proaches [her] will have [the s]in of menstrual uncleanness on him. And if she sees (blood) a[gain] and this is not [during the uncleanness] of seven days, she shall not eat sacred (food) and shall not en[ter] the Sanctuary until the sun has set on the eighth day. *vacat*

*And a woman who* [*conceiv*]*es and bears a male child* [*shall be unclean*] *for seven* [*days like*] *in her menstrual d*[*ays. On the eighth day the flesh of his*] *foreskin* [*shall be circumcised. She shall continue for thirty-three days in the blood of her purifying. But if she bears a female child, she shall be unclean for a fortnight as in*] *her* [*menstr*]*uation. For* [*sixty-six days she shall continue in her blood of purifying* (Lev. xii, 2–5). And she] shall not eat [sacred (food) and shall not enter the Sanctuary, for] it is a capital crime ... [Let her give the chi]ld to a wet-nurse who is in [(the state of) pur]ity. ... [*And*] *if she cannot afford a lamb, then she shall take a turtledove or a young pigeon* (Lev. xii, 8) and she shall substitute it for the [lamb]. ...

## *(5) RULES CONCERNING GLEANINGS AND AGRICULTURAL PRIESTLY DUES*
## (4Q**266**,**269**,**270**,**271**)

**III** ... [Concer]ning [gleanings (of grain) and the gleanings (of grapes) from the vine]yard. (A cluster is up to ten berries.)

And all the gleanings (of grain) up to a *seah* (measure of capacity=*c.* 12 litres) per *bet seah* (area requiring one *seah* of seed for sowing) ... [And a field] which produces no seed, is not subject to (a levy of) *terumah*-offering or of fallen grapes or of clusters up to ten berries. And for the harvest of olives and the fruit of its produce, if it is complete, isolated olives are one in thirty.

But if the field was ravaged or consumed by burning,

### 4Q**270**, fr. 3

should the amount (remaining) be a *seah* per *bet seah*, it is to be tithed. If one person gleans one *seah* from it one day, the *terumah* will be one *isaron* (=30 per cent of a *seah*). [Concerning the two] loaves of the *terumah*. All the families (lit. houses) of Israel, those who eat the bread of the land, are to offer the *terumah* once a year (cf. Num. xv, 19–20; Lev. xxiii, 17). One (loaf) shall be one *isaron*.

### 4Q**266**, fr. 6

**IV** ... All sacred offerings from the planting of vineyards and all fruit trees (producing) food shall belong to them (the priests), as is decreed for them, in the holy [lan]d and in the land of (their) sojourn. And afterwards they may sell of them to bu[y] ... a man may plant, in the fourth year he may n[ot ea]t (of it) for they sanctified it in [that] y[ear] ...

### 4Q**271**, fr. 2 (4Q**269**, fr. 8 i–ii; **270**, fr. 3 iii)

... he shall take off from (the grain of) the threshing-floor one tenth of a *ho*[*mer* (measure of volume, *c.* 220 litres), that is one *eph*]*ah* [or *bath*

(22 litres), as is established]. The *ephah* and the *bath* are both the same measure. And from [the wheat o]ne sixth of [an *ephah* out of a *homer* and one tenth of a *bath*] for the fruit of trees. Let no one separate himself (from the norm of 1 out of 200, cf. Ezek. xlv, 15) by offering one lamb out of a hundred. Let [no] man eat [from the threshing-floor] and from the garden before [the prie]sts have stretched out their hand [to ble]ss first. ... a house belonging to a man, he may sell and with ... and he shall be innocent. ... Let no man bring ... to his pure food. Neither shall he bring close to his pure food any gold or silver or [copper], or tin or le[ad] from which the nations have made idols, except new (metal) coming straight from the furnace. Let no man bring any leather or garment or any vessel [which is used for] work and which has been defiled by the corpse of a man unless they were sprinkled according to the law [of purity with the water] for uncleanness in the age of wickedness (by) a man pure of all uncleanness who has allowed the sun to set (i.e. one who after bathing himself did not proceed until after sunset). No young man who has not yet reached the age to pass the mu[ster shall sprinkle] ...

## *(6) THE PENAL CODE AND THE RENEWAL OF THE COVENANT RITUAL* (4Q266,270)

CD XIV ends with scrappy relics of a penal code. The Cave 4 manuscripts $D^a$ and $D^e$ include a list of breaches of the rule punished by exclusion and penance of varying lengths. They closely resemble the code contained in the Community Rule (1QS VII). The principal difference consists in the explicit mention of women (*fornication* with one's wife and murmuring against the Mothers) which once again renders the silence of *Serekh* concerning any matter pertaining to the female sex particularly eloquent. The penal code is followed by a Covenant ritual, which ends the Cave 4 version of the Damascus Document and contains the words spoken by the priestly head of the sect, following the expulsion of the unfaithful members of the congregation. The passage includes the reference to the 'third month' as the date of this festive assembly and presents the message of this writing as 'the last interpretation of the Law'.

For a preliminary study with a comparative table of the penalties, cf. J. M. Baumgarten, 'The Cave 4 Versions of the Qumran Penal Code', *JJS* 43 (1992), 268–76.

## 4Q**266**, fr. 10 (4Q**270**, fr. 7 i; **269**, fr. 11 i–ii)

... **II** [He shall be excluded for] two [hundred] days and do penance for one hundred days. But if it was a capital matter and he bears (a grudge), [he] shall not return [again. And whoev]er has in[sulted] his companion without a reason [shall be exc]luded for one year and do pe[nan]ce for s[ix months] (cf. 1QS vii, 4). Whoever has spoken a foolish word, shall do penance for t[wen]ty [days and will be excluded] for three month[s (cf. 1QS vii, 9). And whoever in]terrupts the w[ords of his companion and lets himself go, will do penance for ten] days (1QS vii, 9–10). [And whoever lies do]wn [and] falls asleep at [the mee]t[ing of the Congregation ... shall be excluded] for thirty days [and] do penance for ten days. [And likewise, whoever has] left [without the consent of the Congregation and gratu]itously as many as three ti[mes in] one [session], he [shall do penance for ten] days. But if he has left the session [when they were standing, he shall do penance for thir]ty day[s]. And whoever has walked [naked] before [his] companion, whether he has walked in the house or in the field, he has walked n[aked before the peo]ple; he shall be excluded for six [months] ... (1QS vii, 10–12). And whoever has [d]rawn his hand from under [his] gar[ment and he was so poorly dressed that his nakedness was seen, he shall be separated for thir]ty [day]s and shall do penance for ten (1QS vii, 13–14). And whoever has gu[ffawed foolishly making his voi]c[e heard, shall be excluded for th]irty (days) and shall do penance for fif[teen days. And whoever has drawn out] his le[ft h]and [to gesticu]late with it, shall do penance [for ten days (1QS vii, 14–15). And who]ever has gone [slandering his com]panion, they shall exclude him from the purity for one year.

## 4Q**270**, fr. 7

**I** [and shall do penance for six months. But whoever has slandered the Congregation shall be expelled] and shall not return ag[ain] (1QS vii, 15–16). [If he has murmured against his companion unjustly, he shall do penance for six months (1QS vii, 17–18). And] the m[a]n whose spirit has so trembled [before the authority of the Community that he has betrayed the truth and walked in the stubbornness of his heart, he shall be excluded for two years] and do penance for sixty [days] (1QS vii,

18–19). [When his two years are completed, the Congregation shall consider [his ca]se, [and if he is admitted,] he shall be ins[cribed in his rank and may then question about the law (1QS VII, 20–21). And whoever] has despised the law of the Congregation shall leave and [shall not return again. And whoever has taken] his food (from another person) outside the rules, he shall return it to the man fr[om whom] he has taken it. *vacat* And whoever has approached his wife, not according to the rules, (thus) fornicating, he shall leave and will not return again. [If he has murmured] against the Fathers, he shall leave and shall not return [again (cf. 1QS VII, 17). But if he has murmured] against the Mothers, he shall do penance for ten days. For the Mothers have no *rwqmh* (distinction ?) within [the Congregation. *vacat*

And these are the r]ules in [which they shall walk, all those who have been corrected. Whoever comes to report someone to the Priest [over]seeing

## 4Q266, fr. 11 (4Q270, fr. 7 i–ii)

**II** the Congregation, he shall willingly accept His judgement, as He has ordered by the hand of Moses regarding the soul that sins by inadvertence that he shall bring his sin-offering and his guilt-offering. And concerning Israel it is written, *I will go to the ends* [*of*] *heaven and will not smell the smell of your sweet odour* (Lev. xxvi, 31). And in another passage it is written, *To return to God with crying and fasting* (Joel ii, 13). And in another passage it is written, *Rend your heart and not your garment* (ibid.) and it is written to return to God *with fasting and weeping* (Joel ii, 12). And whoever rejects these rules which follow all the precepts found in the Law of Moses, shall not be counted with all the sons of His truth, for his soul has detested the righteous corrections (cf. 1QS III, 1). As a rebel, he shall be dismissed from the Congregation. The Priest [over]seeing the Congregation shall speak about him. Answering, [he shall] say: 'Blessed art Thou, "Lord" of the universe. Everything is in Thine hands and Thou art the maker of everything. Thou hast founded the [pe]oples according to their families and the languages of their nations. Thou hast made them err in confusion without a way. And Thou hast chosen our Fathers and hast given to their seed the precepts of Thy truth and Thine holy judgements by which a man, if he practises them, shall live. And Thou hast established boundaries for us and cursed those who transgress them.

And we are the people of Thy redemption and the flock of Thy pasture. Thou hast cursed those who transgress it (the boundary?) but we maintain (it).' And the dismissed man shall leave, and whoever eats from what is his, and greets (literally, inquires about the welfare – *shalom* – of) the man who has been dismissed, and agrees with him, his case shall be recorded by the Guardian according to the decree, and his judgement shall be complete. And all [the inhabitants] of the camps shall assemble in the third month and shall curse him who turns aside, to the right [or to the left from the] Law. And this (the foregoing) is the interpretation of the laws which they shall observe in all the age [of visitation] which will be visited on them during al]l the age of wrath and in their marches for all those who dwell in their camps and all their towns. Behold all this is according to the last interpretation of the Law.

## *(7) A HYBRID COMMUNITY RULE – DAMASCUS DOCUMENT TEXT* (4Q265)

Twelve fragments of a manuscript, dating probably to the end of the first century BCE, have preserved remains of a writing dependent both on the Community Rule and on the Damascus Document but also including material which is in neither of these sources. Fr. 1 deals with the initiation into the Community and the penal code in terms recalling 1QS VI–VII, and fr. 7, lines 7–10 contains a description of the Council of the Community which is an abridged version of 1QS VIII, 1–9. It is worth noting that the 'twelve men and three priests' of 1QS VIII, 1 is replaced here by 'fift[een men]'. Elements of the Sabbath laws from CD XI figure on columns I–II of fr. 7, while on one point the borrowing is probably from the Temple Scroll LII, 17–18. As for material alien to 1QS and CD, fr. 2 cites Isaiah liv, 1–2 in full and the last four lines of fr. 7 ii reproduce Lev. xii, 2, 4a, 5, 4b, but omitting xii, 3. This quotation is part of an account of the ages of the world arranged according to weeks, beginning with the garden of Eden.

For a preliminary edition of the concluding section of fr. 7, see J. M. Baumgarten, 'Purification after Childbirth and the Sacred Garden in 4Q265 and Jubilees', in G. J. Brooke, ed., *New Qumran Texts and Studies* (Leiden, 1994), 3–10.

## Fr. 1

**I** ... [and he shall be punished for t]en d[a]ys ... [and he shall be punished] thirty days ... [and he shall be punished during that time with the half of his food for fifte[en days] ... and he shall be punished for three months wi[th half of his food. The man who speaks before] his fellow inscribed before him, shall be excluded ... [and he shall be punished with half of his food.] And the man who insu[lts his fellow ... shall be punished] for thirty days. And the man who know[ingly] deceives [shall be punished for six] months (1QS vii, 3–4) and shall be punished during that time with half of his food. And the man who ... knowingly in any matter shall be punished for thirty days ... know[ingly], they shall exclude him for six months. **II** ... [and falls asle]ep during a session of the Congregation shall be punished for thirt[y days] ... the book, he falls asleep up to three times and if ... And the man who comes to j[oi]n the Council of the [Commu]nity ... the Congregation, if it falls to him he shall instruct him in the study (?) for [one] year ... [and after he shall stand] before the Congregation and they shall deliberate [over h]im (cf. 1QS vi, 15). If he is not found [fit for the discipline (cf. 1QS vi, 14), he shall depart (1QS vi, 16). If he is to enter,] the Guardian shall [teach him the interpretation] of the Law. He shall not [touch the pure Meal of the Congregation until] another full year (1QS vi, 16–17). [And on completing] his year (1QS vi, 18) of ... the Guardian of the Congregation ... [Wh]en he comes ...

## Fr. 2

... as it is written [in the Book of] ... [as] it is written in the B[ook] of Isaiah the prophet: [*Sing, o barren one, who did not bear; break forth in singing and*] *cry aloud you who have not been in travail! For the sons* [*of the desolate one*] *will be more* [*than the children of her who is married, says the Lord*]. *Enlar*[*ge*] *the place of* [*your*] *ten*[*t*] ... (Isa. liv, 1–2)

## Fr. 4

... Why does a ma[n] betray his brother ... [and why] do a young man and a woman eat [anything leavened during the feast] of Passover? ...

## Fr. 7

**I** ... on Sabbath day let no [man wear] soiled [garment]s (CD xi, 3). No man shall be dr[ess]ed in garments on which there is dust or ... on the Sabbath day. No [ma]n shall ta[ke] out of his tent a vessel and foo[d] on the Sabbath day. No man shall lift an animal which has fallen into water on the Sabbath day (CD xi, 13–14). But if a man falls into water on the Sabbath [day], he shall pass to him his garment to lift him out, but he shall not carry an instrument [to lift him out on] the Sabbath [day] (cf. CD xi, 16–17). And if the army ... **II** ... [on] the Sabbath [day]. And let no ... Let [n]o man of the seed of Aaron sprinkle [purifying] w[aters (cf. 1QS iii, 9; iv, 21) on the Sabbath day.] ... And with a beast he shall walk two thousand cubits [on the Sabbath day (CD xi, 5–6). Every beast with a defect in it shall be kept at a distance of(?)] thirty stadia [from the city of the Sanc]tuary (cf. 11QTemple lii, 17–18) ... When there shall be in the Council of the Community fift[een men, perfectly versed in all that is revealed of the Law (1QS viii, 1) and the Pr]ophets, the Council of the Community shall be established [in truth (1QS viii, 5). They shall be witnesses to the truth at the judgement and elect] of Goodwill. They shall be an agreeable offering atoning on behalf of the Land (cf. 1QS viii, 6, 9) for a[ll iniquity ... He shall terminate the ages of injustice (cf. 1QS iv, 18) ...

In the first week [Adam was created ... until] he was not brought to the garden of Eden and a bone [from his bones was taken to become the woman] .... but she (Eve) had [no name (?)] until she was not brought to [him (Adam) ... For holy is a garden of Eden, and every fresh shoot that is in it is holy [as it is written, *If a woman conceives and bears a male child,*] *then she shall be unclean for seven days; as at the time of her menstruation, she shall be unclean* (Lev. xii, 2). *Then* [*she shall continue for*] *thi*[*rty-three days in the blood*] *of her purifying* (Lev. xii, 4). *But if she bears a female child,* [*then she shall be unclean two weeks as in her menstruation. And she shall contin*]*ue in the blood of her purifying* [*for sixty-six days* (Lev. xii, 5). *She shall not touch*] *any hallowed things, nor come into the Sanctuary until the days of her purification are completed*] (Lev. xii, 4).

# The Messianic Rule

## (1QSa=1Q28a)

The Messianic Rule was published in 1955 by D. Barthélemy in *DJD*, I (Oxford, 1955, pp. 107–18). Originally included in the same Scroll as the Community Rule, this short but complete work presents the translator with great difficulties owing to its bad state of preservation and to the carelessness of the scribe.

Barthélemy named the work 'The Rule of the Congregation', but I have given it a new title for the following reasons: (1) it was intended for 'all the congregation in the *last days*'; (2) it is a Rule for a Community adapted to the requirements of the messianic war against the nations; (3) it refers to the presence of the Priest and the Messiah of Israel at the Council, and at the Meal described in column II.

As in the Cave I version of the Community Rule and in the Damascus Document, but contrary to the version preserved in 4QS$^{d}$ (=4Q**258**) and 4QS$^{b}$ (=4Q**256**), 'the sons of Zadok, the Priests' form the chief authority in the sect.

In the main, the precepts and the doctrinal concepts of the Messianic Rule foreshadow those of the War Rule. A mid-first-century BCE date may safely be proposed.

**I** *This is the Rule for all the congregation of Israel in the last days, when they shall join [the Community to wa]lk according to the law of the sons of Zadok the Priests and of the men of their Covenant who have turned aside [from the] way of the people, the men of His Council who keep His Covenant in the midst of iniquity, offering expiation [for the Land]*

When they come, they shall summon them all, the little children and the women also, and they shall read into their [ears a]ll the precepts of the Covenant and shall expound to them all their statutes that they may no longer stray in their [errors].

*And this is the Rule for all the hosts of the congregation, for every man born in Israel*

From [his] youth they shall instruct him in the Book of Meditation and shall teach him, according to his age, the precepts of the Covenant. They [shall be edu]cated in their statutes for ten years . . .

At the age of twenty years [he shall be] enrolled, that he may enter upon his allotted duties in the midst of his family (and) be joined to the holy congregation. He shall not [approach] a woman to know her by lying with her before he is fully twenty years old, when he shall know [good] and evil. And thereafter, he shall be accepted when he calls to witness the judgements of the Law, and shall be (allowed) to assist at the hearing of judgements.

At the age of twenty-five years he may take his place among the foundations (i.e. the officials) of the holy congregation to work in the service of the congregation.

At the age of thirty years he may approach to participate in lawsuits and judgements, and may take his place among the chiefs of the Thousands of Israel, the chiefs of the Hundreds, Fifties, and Tens, the Judges and the officers of their tribes, in all their families, [under the authority] of the sons of [Aar]on the Priests. And every head of family in the congregation who is chosen to hold office, [to go] and come before the congregation, shall strengthen his loins that he may perform his tasks among his brethren in accordance with his understanding and the perfection of his way. According to whether this is great or little, so shall one man be honoured more than another.

When a man is advanced in years, he shall be given a duty in the [ser]vice of the congregation in proportion to his strength.

No simpleton shall be chosen to hold office in the congregation of Israel with regard to lawsuits or judgement, nor carry any responsibility in the congregation. Nor shall he hold any office in the war destined to vanquish the nations; his family shall merely inscribe him in the army register and he shall do his service in task-work in proportion to his capacity.

The sons of Levi shall hold office, each in his place, under the authority of the sons of Aaron. They shall cause all the congregation to go and come, each man in his rank, under the direction of the heads of family of the congregation – the leaders, Judges, and officers, according to the number of all their hosts – under the authority of the sons of Zadok the Priests, [and] (under the direction) [of all the] heads of family of the congregation. And when the whole assembly is summoned for judgement, or for a Council of the Community, or for war, they shall sanctify them for three days that every one of its members may be prepared.

*These are the men who shall be called to the Council of the Community . . .*

All the wi[se men] of the congregation, the learned and the intelligent, men whose way is perfect and men of ability, together with the tribal chiefs and all the Judges and officers, and the chiefs of the Thousands, [Hundreds,] **II** Fifties, and Tens, and the Levites, each man in the [cla]ss of his duty; these are the men of renown, the members of the assembly summoned to the Council of the Community in Israel before the sons of Zadok the Priests.

And no man smitten with any human uncleanness shall enter the assembly of God; no man smitten with any of them shall be confirmed in his office in the congregation. No man smitten in his flesh, or paralysed in his feet or hands, or lame, or blind, or deaf, or dumb, or smitten in his flesh with a visible blemish; no old and tottery man unable to stay still in the midst of the congregation; none of these shall come to hold office among the congregation of the men of renown, for the Angels of Holiness are [with] their [congregation]. Should [one] of them have something to say to the Council of Holiness, let [him] be questioned privately; but let him not enter among [the congregation] for he is smitten.

*[This shall be the ass]embly of the men of renown [called] to the meeting of the Council of the Community*

When God engenders[1] (the Priest-) Messiah, he shall come with them [at] the head of the whole congregation of Israel with all [his brethren, the sons] of Aaron the Priests, [those called] to the assembly, the men of renown; and they shall sit [before him, each man] in the order of his dignity. And then [the Mess]iah of Israel shall [come], and the chiefs of the [clans of Israel] shall sit before him, [each] in the order of his dignity, according to [his place] in their camps and marches. And before them shall sit all the heads of [family of the congreg]ation, and the wise men of [the holy congregation,] each in the order of his dignity.

And [when] they shall gather for the common [tab]le, to eat and [to drink] new wine, when the common table shall be set for eating and the

1. This reading (*yolid*), which has been queried by many, including myself, seems to be confirmed by computer image enhancement.

new wine [poured] for drinking, let no man extend his hand over the firstfruits of bread and wine before the Priest; for [it is he] who shall bless the firstfruits of bread and wine, and shall be the first [to extend] his hand over the bread. Thereafter, the Messiah of Israel shall extend his hand over the bread, [and] all the congregation of the Community [shall utter a] blessing, [each man in the order] of his dignity.

It is according to this statute that they shall proceed at every me[al at which] at least ten men are gathered together.

# The War Scroll

## (1QM, 1Q33, 4Q491–7, 4Q471)

The nineteen badly mutilated columns of this manuscript from Cave 1 first appeared in 1954 in a posthumous work by E. L. Sukenik, and were re-edited in 1955, with an English introduction, under the title *The Dead Sea Scrolls of the Hebrew University* (Jerusalem). A few detached scraps are represented by 1Q**33** and copious fragments of six further manuscripts were discovered in Cave 4, and published in 1982 by M. Baillet in *DJD*, VII (4Q**491–6** or 4QM$^{a-f}$). 4Q**497** represents tiny fragments of a related text, and 4Q**471** or 4QM$^{g}$ a shorter version of 1QM (cf. E. and H. Eshel, '4Q**471** Fragment I and Ma'amadot in the War Scroll', *MQC* II, 611–20). For a new edition of all the War Scroll material except 4Q**471** see J. Duhaime in J. H. Charlesworth et al., eds., *The DSS II, Damascus Document, War Scroll and Related Documents*, 1995, 80–203.

Some of the 4Q fragments basically reflect the Cave 1 text and help to complete its gaps: M$^{a}$, M$^{b}$, M$^{d}$ and M$^{e}$ have been used for this purpose, especially in columns I, XIV and XIX. On the other hand, M$^{a}$ and M$^{c}$ attest different recensions of the War Rule. Representative sections from these manuscripts will be translated separately.

The contents of the War Rule are as follows:
Proclamation of war against the Kittim (I)
Reorganization of Temple worship (II)
Programme of the forty years' war (II)
The trumpets (III)
The standards (III–IV)
Disposition and weapons of the front formations (V)
Movements of the attacking infantry (VI)
Disposition and movements of the cavalry (VI)
Age of the soldiers (VI–VII)
The camp (VII)
Duties of the Priests and Levites

(exhortation, trumpet signals) (VII–IX)
Addresses and prayers of the battle liturgy (X–XII)
Prayer recited at the moment of victory (XIII)
Thanksgiving ceremony (XIV)
Battle against the Kittim (XV–XIX)

Since the five last columns are more or less repetitious, there has been some doubt concerning the unity of the composition as a whole. Those who consider all nineteen columns to be the work of one writer find in column I an introduction, in columns II–XIV general rules, and in columns XV–XIX a 'prophetic' description of the final battle fought according to those rules. Other experts explain that columns XV–XIX are a Rule annexe dependent on the principal Rule (II–XIV).

I am myself inclined to follow the theory first advanced by J. van der Ploeg (*Le Rouleau de la guerre*, Leiden, 1959, 11–22). The primitive work, represented in the present composition by columns I and XV–XIX, draws its inspiration from Daniel xi, 40–xii, 3, and describes the final battle against the Kittim. This account was later combined with the concept of a holy forty years' war against the entire Gentile world, and was extended by the addition of a long series of Rules concerned with the military and religious preparation and with the conduct of the fighting (columns II–XIV). This appears to me to offer a more satisfactory explanation of the literary complexities of the manuscript than do the previous hypotheses. The text of the manuscripts from Cave 4, especially $M^a$ (4Q**491**) and $M^c$ (4Q**493**), indicate that diverse redactions of the War Rule coexisted in the Qumran library.

The only certain pointer to the date of the compilation of the War Rule is that, since the author made use of the Book of Daniel written shortly after 164 BCE, his own work must have been started after that time. But a more accurate dating may be attempted by studying the military strategy and tactics described in the Scroll. Scholars are divided in their opinion as to whether the sons of light modelled them on Greek or Roman custom, or whether they merely drew their ideas from the Bible. Scripture doubtless exercised a definite influence on the author of this Rule, but there is nevertheless a great deal of material completely foreign to it, and he must have possessed, in addition, at least some acquaintance with contemporary warfare.

With Y. Yadin and other archaeologists and historians, I believe that both the weapons and the tactics of the War Rule correspond to the art of war practised by the Roman legion rather than by the Greek phalanx. In particular, the square shield (*scutum*) of the foot-soldier, and the buckler of the horseman (*parma* or *clipeus*), the battle array of three lines (*acies triplex*), the 'gates of war' or openings between the units (*intervalla*), seem to be characteristically Roman. In addition, only the cavalry were to wear greaves – a custom introduced into the Roman army during the time of Julius Caesar in the middle of the first century BCE. This and similar details, as well as the general representation of the Kittim as masters of the world, lead one to conclude that the War Rule was written some time after the middle of the first century BCE, and since the reference to the 'king' of the Kittim points to the Imperial epoch (after 27 BCE), the date of its composition should probably be placed in the last decades of the first century BCE or at the beginning of the first century CE.

This work should not be mistaken for a manual of military warfare pure and simple. It is a theological writing, and the war of which it treats symbolizes the eternal struggle between the spirits of Light and Darkness. The phases of its battle are fixed in advance, its plan established and its duration predetermined. The opposing forces are equally matched and only by the intervention of 'the mighty hand of God' is the balance between them to be disturbed when he deals an 'everlasting blow' to 'Belial and all the host of his kingdom'.

**I** *For the M[aster. The Rule of] War on the unleashing of the attack of the sons of light against the company of the sons of darkness, the army of Belial: against the band of Edom, Moab, and the sons of Ammon, and [against the army of the sons of the East and] the Philistines, and against the bands of the Kittim of Assyria and their allies the ungodly of the Covenant.*

The sons of Levi, Judah, and Benjamin, the exiles in the desert, shall battle against them in ... all their bands when the exiled sons of light return from the Desert of the Peoples to camp in the Desert of Jerusalem; and after the battle they shall go up from there (to Jerusalem?).

[The king] of the Kittim [shall enter] into Egypt, and in his time he shall set out in great wrath to wage war against the kings of the north, that his fury may destroy and cut the horn of [Israel]. This shall be a time of salvation for the people of God, an age of dominion for all the members of His company, and of everlasting destruction for all the company of Belial. The confusion of the sons of Japheth shall be [great] and Assyria shall fall unsuccoured. The dominion of the Kittim shall come to an end and iniquity shall be vanquished, leaving no remnant; [for the sons] of darkness there shall be no escape. [The sons of righteous]ness shall shine over all the ends of the earth; they shall go on shining until all the seasons of darkness are consumed and, at the season appointed by

God, His exalted greatness shall shine eternally to the peace, blessing, glory, joy, and long life of all the sons of light.

On the day when the Kittim fall, there shall be battle and terrible carnage before the God of Israel, for that shall be the day appointed from ancient times for the battle of destruction of the sons of darkness. At that time, the assembly of gods and the hosts of men shall battle, causing great carnage; on the day of calamity, the sons of light shall battle with the company of darkness amid the shouts of a mighty multitude and the clamour of gods and men to (make manifest) the might of God. And it shall be a time of [great] tribulation for the people which God shall redeem; of all its afflictions none shall be as this, from its sudden beginning until its end in eternal redemption.

On the day of their battle against the Kittim [they shall set out for] carnage. In three lots shall the sons of light brace themselves in battle to strike down iniquity, and in three lots shall Belial's host gird itself to thrust back the company [of God. And when the hearts of the detach]ments of foot-soldiers faint, then shall the might of God fortify [the hearts of the sons of light]. And with the seventh lot, the mighty hand of God shall bring down [the army of Belial, and all] the angels of his kingdom, and all the members [of his company in everlasting destruction] ...

{... The priests, the Levites and the heads of [the tribes] ... the priests as well as the Levites and the divisions of} **(4Q464) II** the fifty-two heads of family of the congregation.

They shall rank the chief Priests below the High Priest and his vicar. And the twelve chief Priests shall minister at the daily sacrifice before God, whereas the twenty-six leaders of the priestly divisions shall minister in their divisions.

Below them, in perpetual ministry, shall be the chiefs of the Levites to the number of twelve, one for each tribe. The leaders of their divisions shall minister each in his place.

Below them shall be the chiefs of the tribes together with the heads of family of the congregation. They shall attend daily at the gates of the Sanctuary, whereas the leaders of their divisions, with their numbered men, shall attend at their appointed times, on new moons and on Sabbaths and on all the days of the year, their age being fifty years and over.

These are the men who shall attend at holocausts and sacrifices to prepare sweet-smelling incense for the good pleasure of God, to atone for all His congregation, and to satisfy themselves perpetually before

Him at the table of glory. They shall arrange all these things during the season of the year of Release.

During the remaining thirty-three years of the war, the men of renown, those summoned to the Assembly, together with all the heads of family of the congregation, shall choose for themselves fighting-men for all the lands of the nations. They shall arm for themselves warriors from all the tribes of Israel to enter the army year by year when they are summoned to war. But they shall arm no man for entry into the army during the years of Release, for they are Sabbaths of rest for Israel. In the thirty-five years of service, the war shall be fought during six; the whole congregation shall fight it together. And during the remaining twenty-nine years the war shall be divided. During the first year they shall fight against Aram-Naharaim; during the second, against the sons of Lud; during the third, against the remnant of the sons of Aram, against Uz and Hul and Togar and Mesha beyond the Euphrates; during the fourth and fifth, they shall fight against the sons of Arpachshad; during the sixth and seventh, against all the sons of Assyria and Persia and the East as far as the Great Desert; during the eighth year they shall fight against the sons of Elam; during the ninth, against the sons of Ishmael and Keturah. In the ten years which follow, the war shall be divided against all the sons of Ham according to [their clans and in their ha]bitations; and during the ten years which remain, the war shall be divided against all [the sons of Japheth in] their habitations.

[*The Rule for the trumpets of Summons and the trumpe*]*ts of Alarm according to all their duties*

... [the trumpets of Summons shall sound for disposal in] **III** battle formations and to summon the foot-soldiers to advance when the gates of war shall open; and the trumpets of Alarm shall sound for massacre, and for ambush, and for pursuit when the enemy shall be smitten, and for retreat from battle.

On the trumpets calling the congregation they shall write, *The Called of God.*

On the trumpets calling the chiefs they shall write, *The Princes of God.*

On the trumpets of the levies they shall write, *The Army of God.*

On the trumpets of the men of renown and of the heads of family of the congregation gathered in the house of Assembly they shall write, *Summoned by God to the Council of Holiness.*

On the trumpets of the camps they shall write, *The Peace of God in the Camps of His Saints.*

And on the trumpets for breaking camp they shall write, *The mighty Deeds of God shall Crush the Enemy, Putting to Flight all those who Hate Righteousness and bringing Shame on those who Hate Him.*

On the trumpets for battle formations they shall write, *Formations of the Divisions of God for the Vengeance of His Wrath on the Sons of Darkness.*

On the trumpets summoning the foot-soldiers to advance towards the enemy formations when the gates of war are opened they shall write, *Reminder of Vengeance in God's Appointed Time.*

On the trumpets of massacre they shall write, *The Mighty Hand of God in War shall Cause all the Ungodly Slain to Fall.*

On the trumpets of ambush they shall write, *The Mysteries of God shall Undo Wickedness.*

On the trumpets of pursuit they shall write, *God has Smitten All the Sons of Darkness; His Fury shall not End until They are Utterly Consumed.*

On the trumpets of retreat, when they retreat from battle to the formation, they shall write, *God has Reassembled.*

On the trumpets of return from battle against the enemy when they journey to the congregation in Jerusalem they shall write, *Rejoicings of God in the Peaceful Return.*

*The Rule for the standards of the whole congregation according to their levies*

On the great standard at the head of the people they shall write, *The People of God*, together with the names of Israel and Aaron, and the names of the twelve [tribes of Israel] according to the order of their precedence.

On the standards of the camp columns formed by three tribes they shall write, ... *of God*, together with the name of the leader of the camp ...

On the standard of the tribe they shall write, *Banner of God*, together with the name of the leader of [the tribe and the names of the chiefs of its clans].

[On the standard of the Myriad they shall write, ... *of God*, together with] the name of the chief of the Myriad and the names of the [leaders of its Thousands].

[On the standard of the Thousand they shall write, ... *of God*, together with the name of the chief of the Thousand and the names of the leaders of its Hundreds].

[On the standard of Hundred] ...

**IV** On the standard of Merari they shall write, *The Votive-Offering of God*, together with the name of the chief of Merari and the names of the leaders of its Thousands.

On the standard of the Thousand they shall write, *The Wrath of God is Kindled against Belial and against the Men of his Company, Leaving no Remnant*, together with the name of the chief of the Thousand and the names of the leaders of its Hundreds.

On the standard of the Hundred they shall write, *From God comes the Might of War against All Sinful Flesh*, together with the name of the chief of the Hundred and the names of the leaders of its Fifties.

On the standard of the Fifty they shall write, *The Stand of the Ungodly is Ended by the Power of God*, together with the name of the chief of the Fifty and the names of the leaders of its Tens.

On the standard of the Ten they shall write, *Praised be God on the Ten-stringed Harp*, together with the name of the chief of the Ten and the names of the nine men under his command.

When they march out to battle they shall write on their standards, *Truth of God, Justice of God, Glory of God, Judgement of God*, followed by the whole ordered list of their names.

When they approach for battle they shall write on their standards, *Right Hand of God, Appointed Time of God, Tumult of God, Slain of God*, followed by the whole list of their names.

When they return from battle they shall write on their standards, *Honour of God, Majesty of God, Splendour of God, Glory of God*, together with the whole list of their names.

*The Rule for the standards of the congregation*

When they set out for battle they shall write on the first standard *Congregation of God*, on the second standard *Camps of God*, on the third standard *Tribes of God*, on the fourth standard *Clans of God*, on the fifth standard *Divisions of God*, on the sixth standard *Assembly of God*, on the seventh standard *The Called of God*, on the eighth standard *Hosts of God*; and they shall write the list of their names with all their order.

When they approach for battle they shall write on their standards, *War of God, Vengeance of God, Trial of God, Reward of God, Power of God, Retributions of God, Might of God, Extermination of God for all the Nations of Vanity*; and they shall write on them the whole list of their names.

When they return from battle they shall write on their standards, *Salvation of God, Victory of God, Help of God, Support of God, Joy of God, Thanksgivings of God, Praise of God, Peace of God.*

[The measurements of the standards.] The standard of the whole congregation shall be fourteen cubits long; the standard [of the three tribes,] thirteen cubits long; [the standard of the tribe,] twelve cubits; [the standard of the Myriad], eleven cubits; [the standard of the Thousand, ten cubits; the standard of the Hundred,] nine cubits; [the standard of the Fifty, eight] cubits; the standard of the Ten, s[even cubits] . . .

**V** And on the sh[ield of] the Prince of all the congregation they shall write his name, together with the names of Israel, Levi and Aaron, the the names of the twelve tribes of Israel according to the order of their precedence, with the names of their twelve chiefs.

*The Rule for the ordering of the battle divisions to complete a front formation when their host has reached its full number*

The formation shall consist of one thousand men ranked seven lines deep, each man standing behind the other.

They shall all hold shields of bronze burnished like mirrors. The shield shall be edged with an interlaced border and with inlaid ornament, a work of art in pure gold and silver and bronze and precious stones, a many-coloured design worked by a craftsman. The length of the shield shall be two and a half cubits and its width one and a half cubits.

In their hands they shall hold a spear and a sword. The length of the spear shall be seven cubits, of which the socket and spike shall measure half a cubit. The socket shall be edged with three embossed interlaced rings of pure gold and silver and bronze, a work of art. The inlaid ornaments on both edges of the ring shall be bordered with precious stones – patterned bands worked by a craftsman – and (embossed) with ears of corn. Between the rings, the socket shall be embossed with artistry like a pillar. The spike shall be made of brilliant white iron, the work of a craftsman; in its centre, pointing towards the tip, shall be ears of corn in pure gold.

The swords shall be made of pure iron refined by the smelter and blanched to resemble a mirror, the work of a craftsman; on both sides (of their blades) pointing towards the tip, figured ears of corn shall be embossed in pure gold, and they shall have two straight borders on each side. The length of the sword shall be one and a half cubits and its width four fingers. The width of the scabbard shall be four thumbs. There shall be four palms to the scabbard (from the girdle), and it shall be attached (to the girdle) on both sides for a length of five palms (?). The hilt of the sword shall be of pure horn worked by a craftsman, with patterned bands in gold and silver and precious stones ... *vacat*

When ... shall stand, the ... they shall order the seven battle divisions, division after division ... thirty cubits where the me[n of the division] shall stand ...

**VI** seven times and shall return to their positions.

And after them, three divisions of foot-soldiers shall advance and shall station themselves between the formations, and the first division shall hurl seven javelins of war towards the enemy formation. On the point of the javelins they shall write, *Shining Javelin of the Power of God*; and on the darts of the second division they shall write, *Bloody Spikes to Bring Down the Slain by the Wrath of God*; and on the javelins of the third division they shall write, *Flaming Blade to Devour the Wicked Struck Down by the Judgement of God*. All these shall hurl their javelins seven times and shall afterwards return to their positions.

Then two divisions of foot-soldiers shall advance and shall station themselves between the two formations. The first division shall be armed with a spear and a shield, and the second with a shield and a sword, to bring down the slain by the judgement of God, and to bend the enemy formation by the power of God, to pay the reward of their wickedness to all the nations of vanity. And sovereignty shall be to the God of Israel, and He shall accomplish mighty deeds by the saints of his people.

Seven troops of horsemen shall also station themselves to the right and to the left of the formation; their troops shall stand on this (side) and on that, seven hundred horsemen on one flank and seven hundred horsemen on the other. Two hundred horsemen shall advance with the thousand men of the formation of foot-soldiers; and they shall likewise station themselves on both [flanks] of the camp. Altogether there shall be four thousand six hundred (men), and one thousand cavalrymen with the men of the army formations, fifty to each formation. The horsemen, together with the cavalry of the army, shall number six thousand: five hundred to each tribe.

The horses advancing into battle with the foot-soldiers shall all be stallions; they shall be swift, sensitive of mouth, and sound of wind, and of the required age, trained for war, and accustomed to noise and to every (kind of) sight. Their riders shall be gallant fighting men and skilled horsemen, and their age shall be from thirty to forty-five years. The horsemen of the army shall be from forty to fifty years old. They [and their mounts shall wear breast-plates,] helmets, and greaves; they shall carry in their hands bucklers, and a spear [eight cubits] long. [The horseman advancing with the foot-soldiers shall carry] bows and arrows and javelins of war. They shall all hold themselves prepared ... of God and to spill the blood of the wicked ...

**VII** The men of the army shall be from forty to fifty years old. The inspectors of the camps shall be from fifty to sixty years old. The officers shall be from forty to fifty years old. The despoilers of the slain, the plunderers of booty, the cleansers of the land, the keepers of the baggage, and those who furnish the provisions shall be from twenty-five to thirty years old.

No boy or woman shall enter their camps, from the time they leave Jerusalem and march out to war until they return. No man who is lame, or blind, or crippled, or afflicted with a lasting bodily blemish, or smitten with a bodily impurity, none of these shall march out to war with them. They shall all be freely enlisted for war, perfect in spirit and body and prepared for the Day of Vengeance. And no man shall go down with them on the day of battle who is impure because of his 'fount', for the holy angels shall be with their hosts. And there shall be a space of about two thousand cubits between all their camps for the place serving as a latrine, so that no indecent nakedness may be seen in the surroundings of their camps.

When the battle formations are marshalled facing the enemy, formation facing formation, seven Priests of the sons of Aaron shall advance from the middle gates to the place between the formations. They shall be clothed in vestments of white cloth of flax, in a fine linen tunic and fine linen breeches; and they shall be girdled with fine cloth of flax embroidered with blue, purple, and scarlet thread, a many-coloured design worked by a craftsman. And on their heads they shall wear mitred turbans. These shall be battle raiment; they shall not take them into the Sanctuary.

The first Priest shall advance before the men of the formation to strengthen their hand for battle, and the six other Priests shall hold in their hands the trumpets of Summons, and the trumpets of the Reminder, and the trumpets of Alarm (for massacre), and the trumpets of Pursuit, and the trumpets of Retreat. And when the Priests advance to the place between the formations, seven Levites shall accompany them bearing in their hands seven rams' horns; and three officers of the Levites shall walk before the Priests and Levites. The Priests shall sound the two trumpets of Sum[mons for the gates of] war to open fifty shields (wide) and the foot-soldiers shall advance, fifty from one gate [and fifty from the other. With them shall advance] the officers of the Levites, and they shall advance with every formation according to all this R[ule].

[The Priests shall sound the trumpets, and two divisions of foot-] soldiers [shall advance] from the gate [and shall] station [themselves] between the two [formations] ... **VIII** the trumpets shall sound to direct the slingers until they have cast seven times. Afterwards, the Priests shall sound for them the trumpets of Retreat and they shall return to the flank of the first formation to take up their position.

Then the Priests shall sound the trumpets of Summons and three divisions of foot-soldiers shall advance from the gates and shall station themselves between the formations; the horsemen shall be on their flanks, to the right and to the left. The Priests shall sound a sustained blast on the trumpets for battle array, and the columns shall move to their (battle) array, each man to his place. And when they have taken up their stand in three arrays, the Priests shall sound a second signal, soft and sustained, for them to advance until they are close to the enemy formation. They shall seize their weapons, and the Priests shall then blow a shrill staccato blast on the six trumpets of Massacre to direct the battle, and the Levites and all the blowers of rams' horns shall sound a mighty alarm to terrify the heart of the enemy, and therewith the javelins shall fly out to bring down the slain. Then the sound of the horns shall cease, but the Priests shall continue to blow a shrill staccato blast on the trumpets to direct the battle until they have thrown seven times against the enemy formation. And then they shall sound a soft, a sustained, and a shrill sound on the trumpets of Retreat.

It is according to this Rule that the Priests shall sound the trumpets for the three divisions. With the first throw, the [Priests] shall sound [on the trumpets] a mighty alarm to direct the ba[ttle until they have thrown seven times. Then] the Priests [shall sound] for them on the trumpets [of Retreat a soft, a sustained, and a shrill sound, and they shall return] to their positions in the formation.

[Then the Priests shall blow the trumpets of Summons and the two divisions of foot-soldiers shall advance from the gates] and shall stand [between the formations. And the Priests shall then blow the trumpets of] Massacre, [and the Levites and all the blowers of rams' horns shall sound an alarm, a mighty blast, and therewith] **IX** they shall set about to bring down the slain with their hands. All the people shall cease their clamour but the Priests shall continue to blow the trumpets of Massacre to direct the battle until the enemy is smitten and put to flight; and the Priests shall blow to direct the battle.

And when they are smitten before them, the Priests shall sound the trumpets of Summons and all the foot-soldiers shall rally to them from the midst of the front formations, and the six divisions, together with the fighting division, shall take up their stations. Altogether, they shall be seven formations: twenty-eight thousand fighting men and six thousand horsemen.

All these shall pursue the enemy to destroy him in an everlasting destruction in the battle of God. The Priests shall sound for them the trumpets of Pursuit, and they shall deploy against all the enemy in a pursuit to destruction; and the horsemen shall thrust them back on the flanks of the battle until they are utterly destroyed.

And as the slain men fall, the Priests shall trumpet from afar; they shall not approach the slain lest they be defiled with unclean blood. For they are holy, and they shall not profane the anointing of their priesthood with the blood of nations of vanity.

*The Rule for changes in battle order to form the position of a squa[re with towers], a concave line with towers, a convex line with towers, a shallow convex line obtained by the advance of the centre, or (by the advance of) both flanks to terrify the enemy*

The shields of the towers shall be three cubits long and their spears eight cubits. The tower shall advance from the formation and shall have one hundred shields to each side; in this [manner,] the tower shall be surrounded on three sides by three hundred shields. And it shall also have two gates, [one to the right] and one to the left.

They shall write on all the shields of the towers: on the first, *Michael*, [on the second, *Gabriel*, on the third,] *Sariel*, and on the fourth, *Raphael*. *Michael* and *Gabriel* [shall stand on the right, and *Sariel* and *Raphael* on the left] ... they shall set an ambush to ...

... **X** our camps and to keep us from all that is indecent and evil.

Furthermore, (Moses) taught us, 'Thou art in the midst of us, a mighty God and terrible, causing all our enemies to flee before [us].' He taught our generations in former times saying, *When you draw near to battle, the Priest shall rise and speak to the people saying, Hear, O Israel! You draw near to battle this day against your enemies. Do not fear! Do not let your hearts be afraid! Do not be [terrified], and have no fear! For your God goes with you to fight for you against your enemies that He may deliver you'* (Deut. xx, 2–4).

Our officers shall speak to all those prepared for battle. They shall strengthen by the power of God the freely devoted of heart, and shall make all the fearful of heart withdraw; they shall fortify all the mighty men of war. They shall recount that which Thou [saidst] through Moses: *When you go to war in your land against the oppressor who oppresses you, [you] shall blow the trumpets, and you shall be remembered before your God and shall be saved from your enemies* (Num. x, 9).

O God of Israel, who is like Thee
in heaven or on earth?
Who accomplishes deeds and mighty works like Thine?
Who is like Thy people Israel
which Thou hast chosen for Thyself
from all the peoples of the lands;
the people of the saints of the Covenant,
instructed in the laws
and learned in wisdom ...
who have heard the voice of Majesty
and have seen the Angels of Holiness,
whose ear has been unstopped,
and who have heard profound things?

[Thou, O God, hast created] the expanse of the heavens
and the host of heavenly lights,
the tasks of the spirits
and the dominion of the Holy Ones,
the treasury of glory
[and the canopy of the] clouds.
(Thou art Creator of) the earth
and of the laws dividing it into desert and grassland;

of all that it brings forth
and of all its fruits [according to their kinds;]
of the circle of the seas
and of the gathering-place of the rivers
and of the divisions of the deeps;
of the beasts and birds
and of the shape of Adam
and of the gene[rations of] his [seed];
of the confusion of tongues
and of the scattering of the peoples,
of the dwelling in clans
and of the inheritance of lands;
. . . of the sacred seasons
and of the cycles of the years
and of time everlasting.

**XI** Truly, the battle is Thine! Their bodies are crushed by the might of Thy hand and there is no man to bury them.

Thou didst deliver Goliath of Gath, the mighty warrior, into the hands of David Thy servant, because in place of the sword and in place of the spear he put his trust in Thy great Name; for Thine is the battle. Many times, by Thy great Name, did he triumph over the Philistines. Many times hast Thou also delivered us by the hand of our kings through Thy loving-kindness, and not in accordance with our works by which we have done evil, nor according to our rebellious deeds.

Truly the battle is Thine and the power from Thee! It is not ours. Our strength and the power of our hands accomplish no mighty deeds except by Thy power and by the might of Thy great valour. This Thou hast taught us from ancient times, saying, *A star shall come out of Jacob, and a sceptre shall rise out of Israel. He shall smite the temples of Moab and destroy all the children of Sheth. He shall rule out of Jacob and shall cause the survivors of the city to perish. The enemy shall be his possession and Israel shall accomplish mighty deeds* (Num. xxiv, 17–19).

By the hand of Thine anointed, who discerned Thy testimonies, Thou hast revealed to us the [times] of the battles of Thy hands that Thou mayest glorify Thyself in our enemies by levelling the hordes of Belial, the seven nations of vanity, by the hand of Thy poor whom Thou hast redeemed [by Thy might] and by the fullness of Thy marvellous power. (Thou hast opened) the door of hope to the melting heart: Thou wilt do to them as Thou didst to Pharaoh, and to the captains of his chariots in the Red Sea. Thou wilt kindle the downcast of spirit and they shall be a flaming torch in the straw to consume ungodliness and never to cease till iniquity is destroyed.

From ancient times Thou hast fore[told the hour] when the might of Thy hand (would be raised) against the Kittim, saying, *Assyria shall fall by the sword of no man, the sword of no mere man shall devour him* (Isa. xxxi, 8). For Thou wilt deliver into the hands of the poor the enemies from all the lands, to humble the mighty of the peoples by the hand of those bent to the dust, to bring upon the [head of Thine enemies] the reward of the wicked, and to justify Thy true judgement in the midst of all the sons of men, and to make for Thyself an everlasting Name among the people [whom Thou hast redeemed] ... of battles to be magnified and sanctified in the eyes of the remnant of the peoples, that they may know ... when Thou chastisest Gog and all his assembly gathered about him ...

For Thou wilt fight with them from heaven ... **XII** For the multitude of the Holy Ones [is with Thee] in heaven, and the host of the Angels is in Thy holy abode, praising Thy Name. And Thou hast established in [a community] for Thyself the elect of Thy holy people. [The list] of the names of all their host is with Thee in the abode of Thy holiness; [the reckoning of the saints] is in Thy glorious dwelling-place. Thou hast recorded for them, with the graving-tool of life, the favours of [Thy] blessings and the Covenant of Thy peace, that Thou mayest reign [over them] for ever and ever and throughout all the eternal ages. Thou wilt muster the [hosts of] Thine [el]ect, in their Thousands and Myriads, with Thy Holy Ones [and with all] Thine Angels, that they may be mighty in battle, [and may smite] the rebels of the earth by Thy great judgements, and that [they may triumph] together with the elect of heaven.

For Thou art [terrible], O God, in the glory of Thy kingdom, and the congregation of Thy Holy Ones is among us for everlasting succour. We will despise kings, we will mock and scorn the mighty; for our Lord is holy, and the King of Glory is with us together with the Holy Ones. Valiant [warriors] of the angelic host are among our numbered men, and the Hero of war is with our congregation; the host of His spirits is with our foot-soldiers and horsemen. [They are as] clouds, as clouds of dew (covering) the earth, as a shower of rain shedding judgement on all that grows on the earth.

Rise up, O Hero!
Lead off Thy captives, O Glorious One!
Gather up Thy spoils, O Author of mighty deeds!
Lay Thy hand on the neck of Thine enemies
  and Thy feet on the pile of the slain!
Smite the nations, Thine adversaries,
  and devour the flesh of the sinner with Thy sword!
Fill Thy land with glory
  and Thine inheritance with blessing!
Let there be a multitude of cattle in Thy fields,
  and in Thy palaces silver and gold and precious stones!

O Zion, rejoice greatly!
O Jerusalem, show thyself amidst jubilation!
Rejoice, all you cities of Judah;
keep your gates ever open
  that the hosts of the nations
  may be brought in!

Their kings shall serve you
  and all your oppressors shall bow down before you;
  [they shall lick] the dust [of your feet].
Shout for joy, [O daughters of] my people!
Deck yourselves with glorious jewels
  and rule over [the kingdoms of the nations!
Sovereignty shall be to the Lord]
  and everlasting dominion to Israel.

. . .

. . . **XIII** (The High Priest) shall come, and his brethren the Priests and the Levites, and all the elders of the army shall be with him; and standing, they shall bless the God of Israel and all His works of truth, and shall execrate Belial there and all the spirits of his company. Speaking, they shall say:

Blessed be the God of Israel for all His holy purpose and for His works of truth! Blessed be all those who [serve] Him in righteousness and who know Him by faith!

Cursed be Belial for his sinful purpose and may he be execrated for his wicked rule! Cursed be all the spirits of his company for their ungodly purpose and may they be execrated for all their service of uncleanness!

Truly they are the company of Darkness, but the company of God is one of [eternal] Light.

[Thou art] the God of our fathers; we bless Thy Name for ever. We are the people of Thine [inheritance]; Thou didst make a Covenant with our fathers, and wilt establish it with their children throughout eternal ages. And in all Thy glorious testimonies there has been a reminder of Thy mercies among us to succour the remnant, the survivors of Thy Covenant, that they might [recount] Thy works of truth and the judgements of Thy marvellous mighty deeds.

Thou hast created us for Thyself, [O God], that we may be an everlasting people. Thou hast decreed for us a destiny of Light according to Thy truth. And the Prince of Light Thou hast appointed from ancient times to come to our support; [all the sons of righteousness are in his hand], and all the spirits of truth are under his dominion. But Belial, the Angel of Malevolence, Thou hast created for the Pit; his [rule] is in Darkness and his purpose is to bring about wickedness and iniquity. All the spirits of his company, the Angels of Destruction, walk according to the precepts of Darkness; towards them is their [inclination].

But let us, the company of Thy truth, rejoice in Thy mighty hand and be glad for Thy salvation, and exult because of Thy suc[cour and] peace. O God of Israel, who can compare with Thee in might? Thy mighty hand is with the poor. Which angel or prince can compare with Thy [redeeming] succour? [For Thou hast appointed] the day of battle from ancient times ... [to come to the aid] of truth and to destroy iniquity, to bring Darkness low and to magnify Light ... to stand for ever, and to destroy all the sons of Darkness ...

... **XIV** like the fire of His wrath against the idols of Egypt.

And when they have risen from the slain to return to the camp, they shall all sing the Psalm of Return. And in the morning, they shall wash their garments, and shall cleanse themselves of the blood of the bodies of the ungodly. And they shall return to the positions in which they stood in battle formation before the fall of the enemy slain, and there they shall all bless the God of Israel. Rejoicing together, they shall praise His Name, and speaking they shall say:

Blessed be the God of Israel
who keeps mercy towards His Covenant,
and the appointed times of salvation
with the people He has delivered!

He has called them that staggered
to [marvellous mighty deeds],
and has gathered in the assembly of the nations
to destruction without any remnant.
He has lifted up in judgement the fearful of heart
and has opened the mouth of the dumb
that they might praise {the mighty} (4Q491) works [of God].
He has taught war [to the hand] of the feeble
and steadied the trembling knee;
he has braced the back of the smitten.
Among the poor in spirit [there is power]
over the hard of heart,
and by the perfect of way
all the nations of wickedness have come to an end:
not one of their mighty men stands,
but we are the remnant [of Thy people.]

{Blessed be} (4Q491) Thy Name, O God of mercies,
who hast kept the Covenant with our fathers.
In all our generations Thou hast bestowed
Thy wonderful favours on the remnant [of Thy people]
under the dominion of Belial.
During all the mysteries of his Malevolence
he has not made [us] stray from Thy Covenant;
Thou hast driven his spirits [of destruction]
far from [us],
Thou hast preserved the soul of Thy redeemed
[when the men] of his dominion {acted wickedly} (4Q491).
Thou hast raised the fallen by Thy strength,
but hast cut down the great in height
[and hast brought down the lofty].
There is no rescue for all their mighty men
and no refuge for their swift men;
Thou givest to their honoured men a reward of shame,
all their empty existence [hast Thou turned to nothing].

But we, Thy holy people, will praise Thy Name
because of the works of Thy truth.
We will exalt Thy splendour because of Thy mighty deeds
[in all the] seasons and appointed times for ever,
at the coming of day and at nightfall
and at the departure of evening and morning.
For great {is the design of Thy glory} (4Q**491**)
and of Thy wonderful mysteries on high
that [Thou shouldst raise up] dust before Thee
and lay low the 'gods'.

Rise up, rise up, O God of gods,
raise Thyself in mig{ht, King of Kings} (4Q**491**)!
May all the sons of Darkness [scatter before Thee]!
The light of Thy greatness [shall shine forth]
[on 'go]ds' and men.
[It shall be like a fire bur]ning
in the dark places of perdition;
it shall burn the sinners in the perdition of hell,
in an eternal blaze
... in all the eternal seasons.

They shall recite there [all the] war [hy]mns. Afterwards they shall return to [their] cam[ps] ... **XV** For this shall be a time of distress for Israel, [and of the summons] to war against all the nations. There shall be eternal deliverance for the company of God, but destruction for all the nations of wickedness.

All those [who are ready] for battle shall march out and shall pitch their camp before the king of the Kittim and before all the host of Belial gathered about him for the Day [of Revenge] by the Sword of God.

Then the High Priest shall rise, with the [Priests], his brethren, and the Levites, and all the men of the army, and he shall recite aloud the Prayer in Time of War [written in the Book] of the Rule concerning this time, and also all their Hymns. He shall marshal all the formations there, as is [written in the Book of War], and the priest appointed for the Day of Revenge by the voice of all his brethren shall go forward to strengthen the [hearts of the fighting men]. Speaking, he shall say:

Be strong and valiant; be warriors! Fear not! Do not be [confused and do not let your hearts be afraid!] Do not be fearful; fear them not! Do not fall back ... for they are a congregation of wickedness and all their works are in Darkness; they tend towards Darkness. [They make for themselves] a refuge [in falsehood] and their power shall vanish like smoke. All the multitudes of their community ... shall not be found. Damned as they are, all the substance of their wickedness shall quickly fade, like a flower in [the summer-time].

[Be brave and] strong for the battle of God! For this day is [the time of the battle of] God against all the host of Belial, [and of the judgement of] all flesh. The God of Israel lifts His hand in His marvellous [might] against all the spirits of wickedness. [The hosts of] the warrior 'gods' gird themselves for battle, [and the] formations of the Holy Ones [prepare themselves], for the Day [of Revenge] ... **XVI** ... For the God of Israel has called out the sword against all the nations, and He will do mighty deeds by the saints of His people.

*And they shall obey all this Rule* [*on*] *the* [*day*] *when they stand before the camps of the Kittim*

The Priests shall afterwards sound for them the trumpets of the Reminder, and the gates of war shall open; the foot-soldiers shall advance and the columns shall station themselves between the formations. The Priests shall sound for them the signal, 'Battle Array', and at the sound of the trumpets the columns [shall deploy] until every man is in his place. The Priests shall then sound a second signal [for them to advance], and when they are within throwing distance of the formation of the Kittim, each man shall seize his weapon of war. Then the six [Priests shall blow on] the trumpets of Massacre a shrill staccato blast to direct the battle, and the Levites and all the blowers of rams' horns shall sound [a battle alarm], a mighty clamour; and with this clamour they shall begin to bring down the slain from among the Kittim. All the people shall cease their clamour, [but the Priests shall continue to] sound the trumpets of Massacre, and battle shall be fought against the Kittim (*vacat*). And when [Belial] girds himself to come to the aid of the sons of darkness, and when the slain among the foot-soldiers begin to fall by the mysteries of God, and when all the men appointed for battle are put to ordeal by them, the Priests shall sound the trumpets of Summons for another formation of the reserve to advance into battle; and they shall take up their stand between the formations. And for those engaged [in battle] they shall sound the 'Retreat'.

Then the High Priest shall draw near, and standing before the formation, he shall strengthen by the power of God their hearts [and hands] in

His battle. Speaking he shall say: ... the slain, for you have heard from ancient times through the mysteries of God ...

... **XVII** He will pay their reward with burning [fire by the hand of] those tested in the crucible. He will sharpen His weapons and will not tire until all the wicked nations are destroyed. Remember the judgement [of Nadab and Ab]ihu, sons of Aaron, by whose judgement God showed Himself holy in the eyes [of Israel. But Eleazar] and Ithamar He confirmed in an everlasting [priestly] Covenant.

Be strong and fear not; [for they tend] towards chaos and confusion, and they lean on that which is not and [shall not be. To the God] of Israel belongs all that is and shall be; [He knows] all the happenings of eternity. This is the day appointed by Him for the defeat and overthrow of the Prince of the kingdom of wickedness, and He will send eternal succour to the company of His redeemed by the might of the princely Angel of the kingdom of Michael. With everlasting light He will enlighten with joy [the children] of Israel; peace and blessing shall be with the company of God. He will raise up the kingdom of Michael in the midst of the gods, and the realm of Israel in the midst of all flesh. Righteousness shall rejoice on high, and all the children of His truth shall jubilate in eternal knowledge. And you, the sons of His Covenant, be strong in the ordeal of God! His mysteries shall uphold you until He moves His hand for His trials to come to an end.

After these words, the Priests shall sound to marshal them into the divisions of the formation; and at the sound of the trumpets the columns shall deploy until [every man is] in his place. Then the Priests shall sound a second signal on the trumpets for them to advance, and when the [foot-]soldiers approach throwing distance of the formation of the Kittim, every man shall seize his weapon of war. The Priests shall blow the trumpets of Massacre, [and the Levites and all] the blowers of rams' horns shall sound a battle alarm, and the foot-soldiers shall stretch out their hands against the host of the Kittim; [and at the sound of the alarm] they shall begin to bring down the slain. All the people shall cease their clamour, but the Priests shall continue to blow [the trumpets of Massacre and battle shall be fought against the Kittim.]

... and in the third lot ... that the slain may fall [by the mysteries] of God ... **XVIII** [In the seventh lot] when the great hand of God is raised in an everlasting blow against Belial and all the hosts of his kingdom, and when Assyria is pursued [amidst the shouts of Angels] and the clamour of the Holy Ones, the sons of Japheth shall fall to rise no more.

The Kittim shall be crushed without [remnant, and no man shall be saved from among them].

[At that time, on the day] when the hand of the God of Israel is raised against all the multitude of Belial, the Priests shall blow [the six trumpets] of the Reminder and all the battle formations shall rally to them and shall divide against all the [camps of the] Kittim to destroy them utterly. [And as] the sun speeds to its setting on that day, the High Priest shall stand, together [with the Levites] who are with him and the [tribal] chiefs [and the elders] of the army, and they shall bless the God of Israel there. Speaking they shall say:

Blessed be Thy Name, O God [of gods], for Thou hast worked great marvels [with Thy people]! Thou hast kept Thy Covenant with us from of old, and hast opened to us the gates of salvation many times. For the [sake of Thy Covenant Thou hast removed our misery, in accordance with] Thy [goodness] towards us. Thou hast acted for the sake of Thy Name, O God of righteousness ... [Thou hast worked a marvellous] miracle [for us], and from ancient times there never was anything like it. For Thou didst know the time appointed for us and it has appeared [before us] this day ... [Thou hast shown] us [Thy merciful hand] in everlasting redemption by causing [the dominion of] the enemy to fall back for ever. (Thou hast shown us) Thy mighty hand in [a stroke of destruction in the war against all] our enemies.

And now the day speeds us to the pursuit of their multitude ... Thou hast delivered up the hearts of the brave so that they stand no more. For Thine is the power, and the battle is in Thy hands! ... **XIX** For our Sovereign is holy and the King of Glory is with us; the [host of his spirits is with our foot-soldiers and horsemen. They are as clouds, as clouds of dew] covering the earth, and as a shower of rain shedding righteousness on [all that grows there].

[Rise up, O Hero!
Lead off Thy captives, O Glorious One!
Gather up] Thy spoils, O Author of mighty deeds!
Lay Thy hand on the neck of Thine enemies
and Thy feet [on the pile of the slain!
Smite the nations, Thine adversaries],
and devour flesh with Thy sword!
Fill Thy land with glory
and Thine inheritance with blessing!

[Let there be a multitude of cattle in Thy fields,
and in] Thy palaces
[silver and gold and precious stones]!

O Zion, rejoice greatly!
Rejoice all you cities of Judah!
[Keep your gates ever open
that the] hosts of the nations
[may be brought in]!
Their kings shall serve you
and all your oppressors shall bow down before you;
[they shall lick the dust of your feet.
Shout for joy, O daughters of] my people!
Deck yourselves with glorious jewels
[and rule over the kingdom of the nations!
Sovereignty shall be to the Lord]
and everlasting dominion to Israel.

## (1QM combined with 4QM[b]=4Q492)

{Then they shall gather in} the camp that night to rest until the morning. And in the morning {they shall go to the place where the formation stood before the} warriors of the Kittim fell, as well as the multitudes of Assyria, and the hosts of all the [assembled] nations {to discover whether} the multitude of the stricken are dead {with none to bury them}, those who fell there under the Sword of God. And the High Priest shall draw near, [with his vicar, and the chief Priests] {and the Levites} with the Prince of the battle, and all the chiefs of the formations and their numbered men; [they shall return to the positions which they held before the] slain [began to fall] from among the Kittim, and there they shall praise the God {the Most High} . . .

# The War Scroll from Cave 4

## (4Q491, 493)

Of the two groups of fragments belonging to M$^{a}$ (4Q491), the first echoes sections from columns II, VII, XVI and XVII of 1QM, but it also contains passages without parallels there. The second unit, a poem, entitled by the editor 'The Song of Michael and of the Just', is additional to 1QM.

As for the manuscript designated M$^{c}$ (4Q493), its surviving lines recall 1QM VII, XVI, etc., but do not represent the same recension.

### M$^{a}$ = 4Q491, frs. 1–3

... There shall be one thousand cubits between the [camp and the latrine and] no nakedness [whatever] shall be seen in their surroundings. And when they set out to prepare the battle [to cur]b [the enemy, there shall be] among them some exempted in the lot of each tribe according to their numbered men for [each] day's duty. On that day, some men from all their tribes shall set out from their camps towards the House of Meeting ... the [Priest]s, the Levites, and all the chiefs of the camps shall go out towards them. They will pass there before ... according to the Thousands, Hundreds, Fifties and Tens. Whoever shall not [be clean because of his 'fount' on] that [nig]ht shall not go with them to the battle, for the holy angels shall be with their formations together ... When the formation called up for that day's battle to pass to all ... of the war, three formations shall stand, formations behind formations. They shall set a space between [all] the formations [and they shall go out] to battle in succession. These are the [foot-soldie]rs and beside them the [horse]men. [They shall stand between the forma]tions. And if they set up an ambush for a formation, the three ambushing formations shall be at a distance and shall not ri[se] ... of the war and they [shall he]ar the trumpets of Alarm and the [foot-]soldiers [will begin to bring dow]n the guilty dead. Afterwards the ambush shall rise from its hiding-place arranged in formations. The reassembly: from the right and from the left, from be[hind and from the front, f]our direction[s] ... in the battles of annihilation. And all the formations engaged in combat with the ene[my will be in] one [place. The f]irst formation [will go out to the battle] and the second stand ... on their post. With the completion of their time, the first shall return and rise ... The sec[ond] ... When the battle is joined. And the second formation shall have completed its time and they shall return and st[and on their post]. And the th[ird] ...

And the chief Priest and his brethren, [the Priests, and] the Levites and the m[en of the orde]r [shall stand]. And the Priests shall blow the trumpets continuously ... and a girdle of fine cloth of flax embroidered with blue, purple and scarlet threads, a many-coloured design produced by a craftsman, and a fine linen tunic and fine linen breeches and a mitred turban [on their heads]. They shall not take them to the sanctuary f[or] they are ba[ttle] raiments. According to all this rule ...

## 4Q491, fr. 11

### *The Song of Michael and the Just*

... a throne of strength in the congregation of 'gods' so that not a single king of old shall sit on it, neither shall their noble men ... my glory is incomparable, and apart from me none is exalted. None shall come to me for I dwell in ... in heaven, and there is no ... I am reckoned with the 'gods' and my dwelling-place is in the congregation of holiness. [My] des[ire] is not according to the flesh, [and] all that I value is in the glory of ... [... the pl]ace of holiness. Whom do I count as despicable, and who is comparable to me in my glory? Who is like ... the young (?) like me? Is there a companion who resembles me? I have ..., and no instruction resembles [my instruction] ... Who shall attack me when [I] op[en my mouth]? And who can deal with the issue of my lips? Who shall summon me to be destroyed by my judgement? ... [F]or I am reckoned with the 'gods', and my glory is with the sons of the King. No pure gold or gold of Ophir ...

## $M^c$ = 4Q493

. . . the battle. The Priests, the sons of Aaron, shall stand before [the] formations and shall blow the trumpets of Reminder. After this, they shall open the g[ate]s for the foot-soldiers. The Priests shall blow the battle trumpets to [strike] the formations of the nations. The Priests shall depart from among the slain and stand on either side next to the . . . and they shall not profane the oil of their priesthood [by the blood of the s]lai[n]. They shall not approach any of the formations of the foot-soldiers. They shall sound a shrill blast with the trumpets of Massacre for the wa[rr]iors to go out to fight between the formations. They shall begin to wage war. When their time is completed, the trumpets of Return shall sound for them (summoning them) to come to the gates, and the second formation shall set out. According to this rule, the Le[vites] shall blow for them during (their) times (of action). When they go out, they shall blow for them the tr[umpets of Summons], and when (their time) is complete, the trumpets of Alarm, and when they return, they shall bl[ow for them the trumpets of] Retr[eat]. According to [this] sta[tute] they will blow for a[ll the formations . . .]

# The Rule of War

## (4Q285, 11Q14)

A collection of ten small fragments, designated by J. T. Milik as *Serekh ha-Milḥamah* or Rule of War, are akin to the War Scroll, probably representing its missing end section. Allusions are found to Levites blowing trumpets (fr. 8), to the archangel Michael (fr. 10), to the Prince of the Congregation, identified as the Branch of David (frs. 4–5), as well as to the Kittim and their slain (frs. 2, 4, 5), all familiar from 1QM. The poorly preserved benediction (fr. 1) can be reconstructed with the help of 11Q14 which contains, however, some notable variants. Fragment 4 seems to identify the defeated opponent as the biblical Gog (Ezek. xxxix), the chief foe of the final age, here no doubt equated with the king of the Kittim. Fragment 5, erroneously labelled by some as the 'Pierced Messiah fragment', is based on an interpretation of Isa. x, 34–xi, 1, and should be read in connection with 4Q161, frs. 8–10, an Isaiah Commentary from Cave 4, and the Blessing of the Prince of the Congregation (1QS$^{b}$, v, 20–29), both referring to the triumphant Davidic Messiah, expected to put an opponent, no doubt the king of the Kittim, to death. Only frs. 1, 4, 5 and 10 are suitable for translation.

For preliminary studies, see G. Vermes, 'The Oxford Forum for Qumran Research: Seminar on the Rule of War (4Q285)', *JJS* 43 (1992), 85–90; R. Eisenman and M. Wise, *DSSU*, 24–9; B. Nitzan, 'Benedictions and Instructions for the Eschatological Community', *RQ* 16 (1993), 70–90; M. G. Abegg, 'Messianic Hope and 4Q285: A Reassessment', *JBL* 113 (1994), 81–91.

### 4Q285, fr. 1

[Answering, he shall say] to the sons of [I]srael: May you be blessed in the name of the Most High [God] . . . and may His holy name be blessed for ever and ever. [May all His holy angels be blessed. May] the M[ost High] God [bless] you. [May He shine His face towards you and open for you His] good [treasure] which is in heaven [to bring down on your land] showers of blessing, dew, rain, [early rain] and late rain in His/its time, and to give [you the fruit of the produce of corn, wine and o]il plentiful. And may the land [prod]uce for [you fruits of delight. And you shall eat and grow fa]t. And there shall be no miscarriage [in yo]ur [la]n[d] and no [sickness, blight or mildew] shall be seen in [its] produ[ce. And there shall be no loss of children n]or stumbling in [your] congrega[tion, and wild beasts shall withdraw] from your land and there shall be no pestil[ence in your land.] For God is wi[th you and His holy angels stand in your congregation, and His] holy [name] shall be invoked upon you ... in your midst ...

## 11Q14

And he shall bless them in the name [of the God] of Israel. Answering he shall say, ... to the sons of Israel: May [yo]u be blessed for ever and ever and may His ... be blessed ... and may His holy angels be blessed. May the Most High God bless you. May He shine His face towards you and open to you His good treasure which is in heaven to bring down on your land showers of blessing, dew, rain, early rain and late rain in His/its time to give you the fruit of the produce of corn, wine and oil plentiful. May the land produce for you fruits of delight. And you shall eat and grow fat. And there shall be no miscarriage in your land and no sickness, blight or mildew shall be seen in its produce. There shall be no loss of children, nor stumbling in your congregation and the wild beasts shall withdraw from [your land.] The sword shall not pass through your land. For God is with you and His holy angels shall be present in your congregation, and His holy name shall be invoked upon you.

## 4Q285, fr. 4

... wickedness will be smitten ... [the Prin]ce of the Congregation and all Is[rael] ... [which wa]s written [in the book of Ezekiel the Prophet, *I will strike your bow from your left hand and will make your arrows drop from your right hand.*] *On the mountains of* [*Israel you shall fall*] ... [the king of] the Kittim ... [the Pr]ince of the congregation [will pursue them] as far as the [Great] Sea ... [and they shall fle]e from before Israel. In that time ... he shall stand against them and they shall be stirred against them ...

and they shall return to the dry land. In that time ... and they shall bring 10
him (the king of the Kittim?) before the Prince [of the Congregation] ...

## 4Q285, fr. 5

### *The Messiah, Branch of David*

[As it is written in the book of] Isaiah the Prophet, [*The thickets of the forest*] *will be cut* [*down with an axe and Lebanon by a majestic one will f*]*all. And there shall come forth a shoot from the stump of Jesse* [ ... ] the Branch of David and they will enter into judgement with [ ... ] and the Prince of the Congregation, the Br[anch of David] will kill him [ ... by strok]es and by wounds. And a Priest [of renown(?)] will command [ ... the s]lai[n] of the Kitti[m ... ]

## 4Q285, fr. 10

... because of Thy name and ... Michael, G[abrie]l, [Sariel and Raphael] ... with the elect of ...

# The Temple Scroll

## (11QT=11Q19, 20, 4Q365a)

Discovered in 1956 in Cave 11, the Temple Scroll did not emerge from semi-clandestinity until the Six Day War in June 1967. It is the longest Qumran manuscript, measuring over twenty-eight feet. There are also other fragments pertaining to the same document from Cave 11 (11Q20) and from Cave 4 (4Q365a). Originally it consisted of sixty-seven columns.

The major part of the scroll deals with the Temple (building and furniture) and cultic worship, especially sacrifices on Sabbaths and the many feasts of the year. Most of the legislation depends, directly or indirectly, on Exodus, Leviticus, and more particularly on Deuteronomy, but there are also occasional non-biblical regulations. The beginning of the manuscript is badly mutilated. Column I is missing. Columns III–XII are so fragmented that only a very hypothetical reconstruction, exclusively from biblical texts, is possible (cf. most extensively E. Qimron, *The Temple Scroll*, 1996). I have decided not to translate them but indicate their probable contents in the summary that follows:

1. Covenant between God and Israel (II).
2. Building of the Temple, measurements of the Sanctuary, the Holy of Holies, the chambers and colonnades (III–VII).
3. Description of the mercy seat, the cherubim, the veil, the table, the golden lamp-stand, etc. (VII–XI).
4. Outline of the sacrifices and the altar (XI–XII).
5. Daily, weekly and monthly sacrifices and those offered on festivals (XIII–XXIX).
6. Buildings in the Temple courtyards: the stairhouse, the house of the laver, the house for sacred vessels, the slaughterhouse, etc. (XXX–XXXV).
7. The three courtyards of the Temple, one for the priests, one for Jewish men over twenty years of age, and one for women and children (XXXVI–XLV).
8. Purity regulations concerning the Temple and the city of the Sanctuary (XLVI–XLVIII).

9. Purity regulations concerning the cities of Israel (XLVIII–LI).
10. Judges and officers (LI).
11. Laws relating to idolatry and to sacrificial animals (LI–LIII).
12. Vows and oaths (LIII–LIV).
13. Laws against apostasy (LIV–LV).
14. Laws relating to priests and Levites and detailed statutes of the Jewish king (LVI–LIX).
15. Miscellaneous laws regarding priestly dues, idols, witnesses, the conduct of war, the rebellious son, crimes punishable by 'hanging', and incestuous relations (LX–LXVI).

The sequence of subjects generally follows the Bible, but an obvious effort has been made to systematize, harmonize and reinterpret the laws. Sections complementary to Scripture include the Temple legislation (III–XII, XXX–XLV), festivals (XVII–XXIX), purity material as rules relating to the Temple and the city (XLVI–XLVII), and the statutes of the king (LVI–LIX). The aim of the redactor is to present the message of the scroll not as an interpretation of the Bible, but as an immediate divine revelation. For this purpose, not only does he formulate the supplementary legislation as directly spoken by God, but also frequently substitutes 'I' for 'the Lord = YHWH' of Scripture.

Although the view has been advanced that the Temple Scroll is not a Qumran composition, the contrary thesis has a solid foundation. The relationship between this writing and the Damascus Document is particularly striking in the case of the prohibition of royal polygamy, of marriage between uncle and niece, and of marital relations within the city of the Sanctuary (compare CD IV, 20–V, 11; XII, 1–2 with TS LVII, 16–18; LXVI, 15–17; XLV, 11–12), to name the most significant instances. Note also that the death penalty of 'hanging' (probably crucifixion) reserved for traitors appears both in TS LXIV, 6–13 and in the Nahum Commentary (cf. p. 473). Since the Damascus Document and the Nahum Commentary are more likely to depend on the Temple Scroll than vice versa, the latter may safely be dated to the second century BCE. But it may also have an antecedent history reaching back to the pre-Qumran age.

As noted, Cave 4 has also yielded five fairly mutilated fragments (4Q**365a**), palaeographically dated to the mid-first century BCE, some of which have been used by Yadin. Fragment 1 deals with the festival of Unleavened Bread (11QTS XVII, 11); fragment 2 corresponds to 11QTS XXXVIII, 4–15 while the other three fragments cannot be placed within the known version of the text.

The composition is available in a magisterial edition by Yigael Yadin, who first published it in Hebrew in 1977 and subsequently, shortly before his death, in English under the title, *The Temple Scroll I–III* (Jerusalem, 1983). My translation is often indebted to Yadin's editorial work. Further improvements are due to E. Qimron, *The Temple Scroll: A Critical Edition with Extensive Reconstructions* (Beer-Sheva/Jerusalem, 1996). For 11Q**20** and 4Q**365a** see F. García Martínez, '11QTemple[b]. A Preliminary Publication', in *MQC* II, 363–91 and S. White, '4QTemple?' in *DJD* XIII, 319–33.

**II** [Behold, I will make a covenant.]

[For it is something dreadful that I] will do [to you.] [I myself will expel from before you] the A[morites, the Canaanites, the Hittites, the Girgashit]es, the Pe[rizzites, the Hivites and] the Jebusites. Ta[ke care not to make a cove]nant with the inhabitants of the country [which you are to] enter so that they may not prove a sn[are for you.] You must destroy their [alta]rs, [smash their] pillars [and] cut down their [sacred trees and burn] [their] idols [with fire]. You must not desire silver and gold so [that you may not be ensnared by them; for that would be abominable to me]. You must [not] br[ing any abominable idol] into your house [and come] under the ban together with it. You shall de[test and abominate it], for it is under the ban. You shall not worship [another] go[d, for YHWH, whose name is] [Jealous], is a jealous God. Take care not to make a [covenant with the inhabitants of the country] [so that, when they whore] after [their go]ds [and] sacrifice to [them and invite you,] [you may not eat of their sacrifices and] t[ake their daughters for your sons, and their daughters may not whore after] their [gods] and cau[se your sons to whore after them.] ...[1]

**XIII** [This is what you shall offer on the altar:] t[wo y]ear[ling lambs] without blemish [every day as a perpetual holocaust. You shall offer the first in the morning; and you shall offer the other lamb in the evening; the corresponding grain-offering will be a te]nth of fine flour mixed with [a quarter of a hin of beaten oil; it shall be a perpetual holocaust of soothing odour, an offering by fire] to YHWH; and the corresponding drink-offering shall be a quart[er of a hin of] wine. [The priest who offers the holocaust shall receive the skin of] the burnt-[offering which he has offered. You shall offer the other lamb in the even]ing with the same grain-[offering as in the] morning and with the corresponding drink-offering as an offering by fire, a soothing odour to YHWH ...

On the S[abbath] days you shall offer two [yearling rams without

1. For the contents of the badly damaged columns III–XII, see p. 190.

blemish and two] **XIV** [tenths of an *ephah* of fine flour, mixed with oil, for a grain-offering and the corresponding drink-offering. This is the holocaust of every Sabbath in addition to the perpetual holocaust and the corresponding drink-offering. On the first day of each month you shall offer a holocaust to YHWH: two young bulls, one ram, seven yearling rams without blemish and a grain-offe]ring of fine flour, [three tenths of an *ephah*] mix[ed with half a hin of oil, and a drink-offering, ha]lf a hin for [each young bull and a grain-offering of fine flour mixed with oil, two tenths of an *ephah*] with a third [of a hin, and wine for a drink-offering, one third of a hin for each ram;] ... one tenth [of fine flour for] a grain-[offering, mixed with a quarter of a hin, and wine, a quarter of a hi]n for each lamb ... a soothing [odour] to YHWH on the first day of each month. This is the burnt-offering for each month for the months of the year ... On the first day of the [first] month [the months (of the year) shall start; it shall be the first month] of the year [for you. You shall do no] work. [You shall offer a he-goat for a sin-offering.] It shall be offered by itself to expiate [for you. You shall offer a holocaust: a bullock], a ram, [seven yearli]ng ram lambs [without blemish] ... [ad]di[tional to the bu]r[nt-offering for the new moon, and a grain-offering of three tenths of fine flour mixed with oil], half a hin [for each bullock, and wi]ne for a drink-offering, [half a hin, a soothing odour to YHWH, and two] tenths of fine flour mixed [with oil, one third of a hin. You shall offer wine for a drink-offering,] one th[ird] of a hin for the ram, [an offering by fire, of soothing odour to YHWH; and one tenth of fine flour], a grain-offerin[g mixed with a quarter of a hin of oil. You shall offer wine for a drink-offering, a quarter of a hin] for each [ram] ... lambs and for the he-g[oat] ... **XV** [ea]ch day ... seven [year]ling [lambs] and a he-[goat] ... according to this statute. For the ordination (of the priests), one ram for each [day, and] baskets of bread for all the ra[ms of the ordination, one basket for] each [ram]. They shall divide all the rams and the baskets for the seve[n days of the ordination for each] day; according to [their] division[s, they shall offer to YHWH the right thigh] of the ram as a holocaust and [the fat covering the entrails and the] two kidneys and the fat on them [and on] the loins and the whole fat tail close to the backbone and the appendage of the liver and the corresponding grain-offering and drink-offering according to the sta[tute. They shall take one unleavened cake from the] basket and one cake of bread with oil and [one] wafer, [and they shall put it all on the fat] together with the offering of the right thigh. Those who sacrifice shall wave the rams and the baskets of bread as a wa[ve-offering be]fore YHWH. This is a holocaust, an offering by fire, of soothing odour before YHWH. [They shall burn everything on the altar over] the holocaust, to complete their ordination during the seven days of [ordination].

If the High Priest is to [minister to YHWH, whoever] has been ordained to put on the vestments in place of his father, shall offer [a bull fo]r all the people and another for the priests. He shall offer the one for the priests first. The elders of the priest[s] shall lay [their hands] **XVI** [on] its [hea]d and after them the High Priest and all the [priests. They shall slaughter] the bull [before YHWH]. The elders of the priests shall take from the blood of the bull and [place] it [with their finger on the horns of the altar] and they shall pour [the blood] around the four corners of the [altar] ledge ... [and they shall take from its blood and pl]ace it [on his right ear lobe and on the thumb of his right hand and the big toe of his] right [foot. They shall sprinkle on him and his vestments some of the blood which was on the altar]... [he] shall be [holy] all his days. [He shall not go near any dead body]. He shall [not] render himself unclean [even for his father or mother,] for [he is] hol[y to YHWH, his God] ... [He shall offer on the al]tar and burn [the fat of the first bull] ... [all] the fat on the entrails and [the appendage of the liver and the two kidne]ys and the fat on the[m] and [the fat on] the loins, and the corresponding grain-offering and drink-[offering according to their statute,] he shall bur[n them on the altar.] It shall be [a burnt-]offering, an offering by fire, of soothing odour be[fore YHWH. The flesh of the bull], its skin and offal, they shall burn outside the [sanctuary city on a wood fire] in a place reserved for sin-offerings. There they shall bur[n it with its head and legs] together with all its entrails. They shall burn all of it there except the fat. It is a sin-[offering]. He shall take the second bull, which is for the people, and by it he shall expiate [for all the people of] the assembly, by its blood and fat. As he did with the fir[st] bull, [so he shall do] with the bull of the assembly. He shall place with his finger some of its blood on the horns of the [altar, and the remainder of] its blood, he shall sprinkle o[n the f]our corners of the altar ledge, and [its fat and] the corresponding [grain-] offering and drink-offering, he shall burn on the altar. It is a sin-offering for the assembly. **XVII** ... They shall rejoice because expiation has been made for them ... This day [shall] be a holy gathering for them, [an eternal rule for all their generations] wherever they dwell. They shall rejoice and ...

[Let] them [prepare on the fourtee]nth day of the first month [between dusk and dark the Passover of YHWH]. They shall sacrifice (it) before the evening offering and shall sacrifice ... men from twenty years of age and over shall prepare it. They shall eat it at night in the holy courts. They shall rise early and each shall go to his tent ...

On the fifteenth day of this month (there shall be) a ho[ly] gathering. You shall do no work of labour on it. (It shall be) a seven-day feast of unleavened bread for YHWH. You shall offer on each of the[se] seven days a holocaust to YHWH: two young bulls, a ram, and seven ram lambs without blemish and a he-goat for a sin-offering and the corresponding grain-offering and drink-offering [according to the sta]tute for the young bulls, rams, l[am]bs and the he-goat. On the seventh day [(there shall be) an assembly] for [YHWH]. You shall do no work on it. **XVIII** ... [he-] goat for a sin-offering ... [the corresponding grain-offering and drink-] offering according to the statute; one tenth of fine flour [mixed with a quarter of a hin of oil and] a quarter of a hin of wine for a drink-offering ... [he shall expiate] for all the guilt of the people of the assembly ... This shall be an eternal [ru]le for you [for your generations wherever you dwell.] Then they shall offer the one ram, on[ce], on the day of the waving of the sheaf.

You shall count seven complete Sabbaths from the day of your bringing the sheaf of [the wave-offering. You shall c]ount until the morrow of the seventh Sabbath. You shall count [fifty] days. You shall bring a new grain-offering to YHWH from your homes, [a loaf of fine fl]ou[r], freshly baked with leaven. They are firstfruits to YHWH, wheat bread, twe[lve cakes, two] tenths of fine flour in each cake ... the tribes of Israel. They shall offer **XIX** ... their [grain-offerin]g and dr[ink-offering] according to the statute. The [priests] shall wave ... [wave-offering with the bread of] the firstfruits. They shall b[elong to] the priests and they shall eat them in the [inner] court[yard], [as a ne]w [grain-offering], the bread of the firstfruits. Then ... new bread from freshly ripened ears. [On this] da[y] there shall be [a holy gathering, an eter]nal [rule] for their generations. [They] shall [do] no work. It is the feast of Weeks and the feast of Firstfruits, an eterna[l] memorial.

You [shall count] seven weeks from the day when you bring the new grain-offering to YHW[H], the bread of firstfruits. Seven full Sabbaths [shall elapse un]til you have counted fifty days to the morrow of the seventh Sabbath. [You] shall [bring] new wine for a drink-offering, four hins from all the tribes of Israel, one third of a hin for each tribe.

They shall offer on this day with the wine twelve rams to YHWH; all the chiefs of the clans of Israel **XX** ... [r]ams and the corresponding grain-offering according to the statute: two [tenths of fine flour mixed with oil, one third of a h]in of oil for a ram; with this drink-offering ... seven yearling ram lambs and a he-[goat] ... assembly ... their [grain-offering and drink-offering] (shall be) according to the statute concerning young bulls and the ram ... to YHWH. At the quarter of the day, they shall offer ... [the r]ams and the drink-offering. They shall offer ... fourteen yearling ram lambs ... the burnt-offering. They shall prepare them ... and they shall burn their fat on the altar, [the fat covering the entrails] and the fat that is on them, and [the appendage of the liver with] the kidneys he shall remove and the fat on [them], and that which is on the loins and the fat tail close to the backbone. They shall b[urn all on the altar] together with the corresponding grain-offering and drink-offering, an offering by fire, of soothing odou[r before YHWH]. They shall offer every grain-offering joined to a drink-offering according to [the statute]. They shall take a handful from [eve]ry grain-offering offered either with frankincense or dry, (this being) its [memorial portion], and burn it on the altar. They shall eat the remainder in the [in]n[er] courtyard. The priests shall e[a]t it unleavened. It shall not be eaten with leaven. It shall be ea[ten] on that day [before] sun[se]t. They shall salt all their offerings. You shall never allow the covenant of salt to fail.

They shall offer to YHWH an offering from the rams and the lambs, the right thigh, the breast, [the cheeks, the stomac]h and the foreleg as far as the shoulder bone, and they shall wave them as a wave-offering. **XXI** [The priests'] portions [shall] be the thigh of the offering and the breast ... [the foreleg]s, the cheeks and the stomachs ... [as an eternal rule, from the children of Isra]el and the shoulder remaining of the foreleg [shall be for the Levites] ... an eternal rule for them and for their seed . . the princes of the Thousands ... [from] the rams and from [the lambs, one ram and one ram lamb (shall belong) to the priests; to the Levites], one [ra]m, one lamb; and to every [tribe, on]e [ram], one lamb for all the tri[bes], the [twe]lve tribes of Israel. They shall eat them [on that day, in the out]er [courtyard] before YHWH.

... [the priest]s shall drink there first and the Levites [second] ... the princes of the standards first ... [men of] renown. After them the whole people, from the great to the small, shall begin to drink the new wine. They [shall not e]a[t] any un[ri]pe grapes from the vines, for [on] this [da]y they shall expiate for the *tirosh*. The children of Israel shall rejoice before YHWH, an eternal [rule] for their generations wherever they dwell. They shall rejoice on [this] d[ay for they have begun] to pour out an intoxicating drink-offering, the new wine, on the altar of YHWH, year by year.

[You sha]ll count from that day seven weeks, seven times (seven days), forty-nine days; there shall be seven full Sabbaths; until the morrow of the seventh Sabbath you shall count fifty days. You shall then offer new oil from the homes of [the tr]ibes of the ch[ildren of Is]rael, half a hin from a tribe, new beaten oil ... oil on the altar of the holocaust, first-fruits before YHWH. **XXII** ... [shall expi]ate with it for all the congregation before [YHWH] ... with this oil, half a hin ... [according to the st]atute, a holocaust, an offering by fire, of soothing [odour to YHWH] ... [With] this oil they shall light the lamps ... the princes of the Thousands with ... fourteen [yearling] m[ale lamb]s and the corresponding grain-offering and drink-offering ... [for the lambs and] the rams. The Levites shall slaughter ... [and] the priests, the sons of Aaron, [shall spri]nkle their blood [on the altar all around] ... [and] they shall burn their fat on the altar of the [holocaust] ... [and the corresponding grain-offering] and drink-offering, they shall burn over the fats ... [an offering by fire, of soothing odour to] YHWH. They shall take away fr[om] ... the right thigh and the breast ... the cheeks and the stomach shall be the priests' portion according to the statute concerning them. (They shall give) to the Levites the shoulder. Afterwards they shall bring them (the offerings) out to the children of Israel, and the children of Israel shall give the prie[st]s one ram, one lamb, and to the Levites, one ram, one lamb, and to each tribe, one ram, one lamb. They shall eat them on that day in the outer courtyard before YHWH, an eternal rule for their generations, year by year. Afterwards they shall eat from the olives and anoint themselves with the new oil, for on this day they shall expiate for [al]l [the o]il of the land before YHWH once yearly. They shall rejoice **XXIII** ...

The High Priest shall offer the [holocaust of the Levites] first, and afterwards he shall send up in smoke the holocaust of the tribe of Judah, and w[hen he] is sending it up in smoke, they shall slaughter before him the he-goat first and he shall lift up its blood in a bowl to the altar and with his finger he shall pu[t some] of the blood to the four horns of the alta[r] of the holocaust and to the four corners of the altar ledge, and shall toss the blood towards the bas[e] of the altar ledge all around. He shall burn its fat on the altar, the fat covering the entrails and that over the entrails. The appendage of the liver with the kidneys he shall remove as well as the fat over them and on the loins. He shall send up in smoke all of them on the altar together with the corresponding grain-offering and drink-offering, an offering by fire of soothing odour to YHWH. And **XXIV** ... the flesh, of [soothing] odour; it shall be [an offering by fire to YHWH. Thus they must do to every] young bull, and to every ram and to [every lamb] and its limbs (?) shall remain apart. The corresponding [grain-offering] and drink-offering shall be on it, an [eternal] rule for your generations before YHWH.

After this holocaust he shall offer the holocaust of the tribe of Judah separately. As he has done with the holocaust of the Levites, so shall he do with the holocaust of the children of Judah after the Levites. On the second day he shall first offer the holocaust of Benjamin and after it he shall offer the holocaust of the children of Joseph, Ephraim and Manasseh together. On the third day, he shall offer the holocaust of Reuben separately, and the holocaust of Simeon separately. On the fourth day he shall offer the holocaust of Issachar separately and the holocaust of Zebulun separately. On the fifth day he shall offer the holocaust of Gad separately and the holocaust of Asher separately. On the sixth day **XXV** [he shall offer the holocaust of Dan separately and the holocaust of Naphtali separately] ...

In the [seventh] m[onth, on the first day of the month, you shall have] a sacred rest, a remembrance announced by a trumpet blast, a [holy] ga[thering. You shall offer a holocaust, an offering by fire, of soothing odour be]fore YHWH. You shall o[ffer on]e [young bull,] one ram, seve[n] ye[ar]ling [lamb]s [without blemish and one he-goat for a sin-offering, and] the corresponding grain-offering and drink-offering according to the statute concerning the[m, of soothing odour to YHWH, in addition to] the perpetual [holocaus]t [and the holo]caust of the new moon. Afterwards [you shall offer] this [holocaust] at the third part of the day, an eternal rule for your generation[s wherever you dwell.] You shall rejoice on this day. On it you shall do no work. A sacred rest shall this day be for you.

The tenth of this month is the Day of Atonement. You shall mortify yourselves. For any person who does not mortify himself on this self-same day shall be cut off from his people. You shall offer on it a holocaust to YHWH: one young bull, one ram, seven ram lambs, one he-goat for a sin-offering, in addition to the sin-offering of the atonement and the corresponding grain-offering and drink-offering according to the statute concerning the young bull, the ram, the lambs and the he-goat. For the sin-offering of the atonement you shall offer two rams for holocaust. The High Priest shall offer one for himself and his father's house **XXVI** ... [The High Prie]st [shall cast lots on the two goats,] o[ne] lot for YHWH and one for Azazel. He shall slaughter the goat [on] which [YHWH's lot has fallen and shall lift up] its blood in a golden bowl which is in [his ha]nd, [and do] with its blo[od as he has done with the blood of] his young bull and shall expiate with it for all the people of the assembly. He shall send up in smoke its fat and the corresponding grain- and drink-offering on the altar of the holocaust. Its flesh, skin and dung they shall burn beside his young bull. It is a sin-offering for the whole assembly. He shall expiate with it for all the people of the assembly and it shall be forgiven to them. He shall wash his hands and feet of the blood of the sin-offering and shall come to the living goat and shall confess over its head the iniquities of the children of Israel together with all their guilt, all their sins. He shall put them on the head of the goat and despatch it to Azazel in the desert by the hand of the man who is waiting ready. The goat shall bear all the iniquities of (the children of Israel). **XXVII** ... [and he shall expiate] for all the children of Israel and it shall be forgiven to them ... Afterwards he shall offer the young bull, the r[a]m, and [the lambs, according to] the [sta]tute relating to them, on the altar of the holocaust, and the [ho]locaust will be accepted for the children of Israel, an eternal rule for their generations. Once a year this day shall be for them a memorial. They shall do no work on it, for it shall be [to] them a Sabbath of sacred rest. Whoever shall do work on it or shall not mortify himself on it, shall be cut off from the midst of his people. A Sabbath of sacred rest, a holy gathering shall this day be for you. You shall sanctify it as a memorial wherever you dwell and you shall do no work.

On the fifteenth day of this month **XXVIII** ... [the corresponding] grain-offering [and drink-offering, all on] the altar, an offering by fire, of s[oothing odour to YHWH. On] the second [day:] twelve young bulls, [two rams, four]teen [lambs] and one he-goat [for a sin-offerin]g [and the corresponding gr]ai[n-offering and drink-offering] according to the statute concerning the young bulls, the ram[s], the lambs [and] the he-goat; it is an offering by fire, of soothing odour to YHWH.

On the third day eleven young bulls, two rams, fourteen lambs and one he-goat for a sin-offering and the corresponding grain-offering and drink-offering according to the statute concerning the young bulls, the rams, the lambs and the he-goat.

On the fo[ur]th day ten young bulls, two rams, fourteen yearling ram lambs and one he-goat for a sin-offering and the corresponding grain-offering and drink-offering for the young bulls, **XXIX** [the rams, the lambs and the he-goat . . . On the fifth day . . . and the corresponding grain-offering] and drink-offer[ing] . . . in the house on which I [shall cause] my name to rest . . . holocausts, [each on its] day according to the law of this statute, always from the children of Israel in addition to their freewill-offerings in regard to all that they offer, their drink-offerings and all their gifts that they shall bring to me in order to be acceptable. I shall accept them and they shall be my people and I shall be for them for ever. I will dwell with them for ever and ever and will sanctify my [sa]nctuary by my glory. I will cause my glory to rest on it until the day of creation on which I shall create my sanctuary, establishing it for myself for all time according to the covenant which I have made with Jacob in Bethel.

**XXX** . . . You shall make . . . for stairs, a stair[case] . . . in the house which you shall build . . . You [shall make] a staircase north of the Temple, a square house, twenty cubits from one corner to the other alongside its four corners. Its distance from the wall of the Temple shall be seven cubits on the north-west. You shall make the width of its wall four cubits . . . like the Temple and its inside from corner to corner twelv[e cubits.] (There shall be) a square column in its middle, in the centre; its width four cubits on each side around which the stairs wind . . . **XXXI** In the upper chamber of [this] ho[use you shall make a ga]te opening to the roof of the Temple and a way (shall be) made through this gate towards the entrance . . . of the Temple by which one can reach the upper chamber of the Temple. Overlay with gold [a]ll this stairhouse, its walls, its gates and its roof, from inside [and from] outside, its column and its stairs. [You] shall do everything as I tell you. You shall make a square house for the laver in the south-east, on all its sides, (each) twenty-one cubits; fifty cubits distant from the altar. The width of the wall shall be four cubits, and the height [t]wenty cubits . . . Make gates for it on the east, on the north and on the west. The width of the gates shall be four cubits and the height seven **XXXII** . . . You shall make in the wall of this house, on the inside, recesses, and in them . . . one cubit (in) width and their height four cubits above the ground. They shall be overlaid with gold on which they shall place their clothes which they have worn on arrival. Above the house of the . . . when they come to minister in the sanctuary. You shall make a trench around the laver beside its house and the trench shall go [from the house of] the laver to a cavity. It shall descend [rapid]ly to the ground where the water shall flow and disappear. It shall not be touched by any man for it is mingled with the blood of the holocaust. **XXXIII** They shall sanctify my people in the sacred vestments which ...

You shall make a house east of the house of the [l]av[er] according to the measurement of [the house of the bas]in. Its wall shall be at a distance of seven cubits from the wall of the house of the laver. Its whole building and rafters shall be like (those of) the house of the laver. It shall have two gates on the north and the south, one opposite the other, according to the measurement of the gates of the house of the laver. Inside all the walls of this house shall have apertures, their width (and depth) two cubits each and their height four (?) with which the entrails and the feet are raised to the altar. When they have completed the sending up in smoke **XXXIV** ... They close the wheels and ... and tie the horns of the young bulls to the rings and ... by the rings. Afterwards they shall slaughter them and collect [the blood] in bowls and toss it around the altar base. They shall open the wheels and strip the skin of the young bulls from their flesh and cut them up into pieces, salt the pieces, wash the entrails and the legs, salt them and send them up in smoke on the fire which is on the altar, each young bull with its pieces beside it and the corresponding grain-offering of fine flour on it, the wine of the drink-offering beside it and some of it on it. The priests, the sons of Aaron, shall send everything up in smoke on the altar, an offering by fire, of soothing odour before YHWH. You shall make chains hanging from the rafters of the twelve columns **XXXV** ... whoever is not a priest shall die, and whoever ... [a prie]st who shall come ... and he is not clothed in the [holy] vest[ments in which] he was ordained, they too shall be put to death and shall not pro[fane the san]ctuary of their God, thus incurring the iniquity of mortal guilt. You shall sanctify the environs of the altar, the Temple, the laver and the colonnade and they shall be most holy for ever and ever.

You shall make a place west of the Temple, a colonnade of pillars standing around for the sin-offerings and the guilt-offerings, divided from one another, the sin-offerings of the priests, the he-goats, and the sin-offerings of the people and their guilt-offerings. None of these shall be mingled one with another, for their places shall be divided from one another in order that the priests may not err concerning all the sin-offerings of the people, and all the rams (?) of the guilt-offerings, (thus) incurring the sin of guilt.

The birds for the altar: he shall prepare turtledoves **XXXVI** ... from the corner of ... [to the corne]r of the gat[e, one hundred and twenty cubits.] The gate (shall be) forty [cubits] wide. Each side shall be [according to this measurement. The wid]th of [its wa]ll shall be seven cubits, [and] its [height forty]-five [cubits to the raft]ers of [its] roof. The width of its ch[ambers] (shall be) twenty-six cubits from corner to corner. The gates of entrance and exit: the gate shall be fourteen cubits wide and [tw]enty-eight cubits high from the threshold to the lintel. The height of the rafters above the lintel shall be fourteen cubits. (The gate shall be) roofed with a panelling of cedar wood overlaid with pure gold. Its doors shall be overlaid with fine gold.

From the corner of the gate to the second angle of the courtyard, (there shall be) one hundred and twenty cubits. Thus shall be the measurement of all these gates of the inner courtyard. The gates shall lead inside into the courtyard. **XXXVII** You shall make [in]side the court[yard] seats for the priests, and tables in front of the seats, in the inner colonnade by the outer wall of the courtyard, places made for the priests and their sacrifices, for the firstfruits and the tithes, for their peace-offering sacrifices which they shall sacrifice. The sacrifices of the peace-offerings of the children of Israel shall not be mingled with the sacrifices of the priests.

In the four corners of the courtyard you shall make for them a place for cooking-stoves where they shall seethe their sacrifices [and] sin-offerings. **XXXVIII** ... There they shall eat ... the bird, the turtle-dove and the young pigeons ...

You shall make a second [co]urtyard aro[u]nd [the in]ner [courtyard], one hundred cubits wide, and four hundred and eighty cubits long on the east side, and thus shall be the width and length of all its sides: to the south, to the west and to the north. Its wall shall be [fo]ur cubits wide and twenty-eight cubits high. Chambers shall be made in the wall outside and between each chamber there shall be three-[and-a-half cubits] **XXXIX** ... that all the congregation of the children of Israel may bow down before me ... No woman shall come there, nor a child until the day that he has fulfilled the rule ... [and has paid for] himself [a ransom] to YHWH, half a shekel, an eternal rule, a memorial wherever they dwell. The shekel (consists of) twenty *gerahs*.

When they shall collect from him the half-shekel ... to me. Afterwards they shall enter from the age of twenty ... The na[mes of the g]ates of this [co]urtyard sha[ll b]e according to the nam[es of] the children of Is[ra]el: Simeon, Levi and Judah in the east; Reuben, Joseph and Benjamin in the south; Issachar, Zebulun and Gad in the west; Dan, Naphtali and Asher in the north. Between each gate the measurement (shall be): from the north-eastern corner to the gate of Simeon, ninety-nine cubits, and the gate twenty-eight cubits. From this gate of Simeon to the gate of Levi, ninety-nine cubits, and the gate, twenty-eight cubits. From the gate of Levi to the gate of Judah **XL** ... You shall make a third courtyard ... to their daughters and to the strangers who [were] born ... [wi]de around the middle courtyard ... in length about one thousand six [hundred] cubits from one corner to the next. Each side shall be according to this measurement: on the east, the south, the west and the no[rt]h. The wall shall be seven cubits wide and forty-nine cubits high. Chambers shall be made between its gates along the foundation as far up as its 'crowns' (= crenellations: Yadin). There shall be three gates in the east, three in the south, three in the west and three in the north. The gates shall be fifty cubits wide and their height seventy cubits. Between one gate and another there shall be three hundred and sixty cubits. From the corner to the gate of Simeon, three hundred and sixty cubits. From the gate of Simeon to the gate of Levi, likewise. From the gate of Levi to the gate of Judah, likewise three [hundred and] sixty (cubits). **XLI** ... From the gate of Issachar [to the gate of Zebulun, three] hundred [and sixty] cubits. From the gate of Zebulun to the gate of Gad, three hundred and sixty cubits. From the ga[te of] Gad to the northern corner, three hundred and sixty cubits. From this corner to the gate of Dan: three hundred and sixty cubits. Thus from the gate of Dan to the gate of Naphtali, three hundred and sixty cubits. From the gate of Naphtali to the gate of Asher, three hundred and sixty cubits. From the gate of Asher to the eastern corner, three hundred and sixty cubits. The gates shall jut outwards from the wall of the courtyard seven cubits, and extend inwards from the wall to the courtyard thirty-six cubits. The entrance of the gate shall be fourteen cubits wide and twenty-eight cubits high up to the lintel. The rafters at the doorways (?) shall be of cedar wood and overlaid with gold. The doors shall be overlaid with pure gold. Between each gate inwards you shall make storehouses, **XLII** [rooms and colonnades.]

The room shall be ten cubits wide, twenty cubits long, and four[teen] cubits high ... with cedar wood. The wall shall be two cubits wide. On the outside there shall be storehouses. [The storehouse shall be ten cubits wide and] twenty cubits [long]. The wall shall be two cubits wide [and fourteen cubits high] up to the lintel. Its entrance shall be three cubits wide. [You shall make in this way] all the storehouses and the [corresponding] rooms. The colon[nade] ... shall be ten cubits [wi]de. Between each gate [you shall make eight]een storehouses and the corresponding eight[een] rooms ...

You shall make a staircase next to the walls of the gates towards the colonnade. Winding stairs shall go up to the second and third colonnades and to the roof. You shall build storehouses and corresponding rooms and colonnades as on the ground floor. The second and the third (levels) shall follow the measurement of the lower one. On the roof of the third you shall make pillars roofed with rafters from one pillar to the next (providing) a place for tabernacles. The (pillars) shall be eight cubits high and the tabernacles shall be made on their (roof) each year at the feast of the Tabernacles for the elders of the congregation, for the princes, the heads of the fathers' houses of the children of Israel, the captains of the thousands, the captains of the hundreds, who will ascend and dwell there until the sacrificing of the holocaust on the festival which is the feast of the Tabernacles, each year. Between each gate there shall be **XLIII** ... on the days of the firstfruits of the corn, of the w[ine (*tirosh*) and the oil, and at the festival of the offering of] wood. On these days (the tithe) shall be eaten. They shall not put aside anything from it from one year to another. For they shall eat it in this manner. From the feast of the Firstfruits of the corn of wheat they shall eat the corn until the next year, until the feast of the Firstfruits, and (they shall drink) the wine from the day of the festival of Wine until the next year, until the day of the festival of the Wine, and (they shall eat) the oil from its festival, until the next year, until the festival, the day of offering the new oil on the altar. Whatever is left (to last beyond) their festivals shall be sanctified by being burnt with fire. It shall no longer be eaten for it is holy. Those who live within a distance of three days' walk from the sanctuary shall bring whatever they can bring. If they cannot carry it, they shall sell it for money and buy with it corn, wine, oil, cattle and sheep, and shall eat them on the days of the festivals. On working days they shall not eat from this in their weariness for it is holy. On the holy days it shall be eaten, but it shall not be eaten on working days. **XLIV** ...

You shall allot [the rooms and the corresponding chambers. From the gate of Simeo]n to the gate of Judah shall be for the priests ... All that is to the right and to the left of the gate of Levi, you shall allo[t] to Aaron, your brother, one hundred and eight rooms and corresponding chambers and two tabernacles which are on the roof. (You shall allot) to the sons of Judah (the area) from the gate of Judah to the corner: fifty-four rooms and corresponding chambers and the tabernacle that is over them. (You shall allot) to the sons of Simeon (the area) from the gate of Simeon to the second corner: their rooms, the corresponding chambers and tabernacles. (You shall allot) to the sons of Reuben (the area) from the corner which is beside the sons of Judah to the gate of Reuben: fifty-two rooms and the corresponding chambers and tabernacles. (The area) from the gate of Reuben to the gate of Joseph (you shall allot) to the sons of Joseph, to Ephraim and Manasseh. (The area) from the gate of Joseph to the gate of Benjamin (you shall allot) to the sons of Kohath from the Levites. (The area) from the gate of Benjamin to the western corner (you shall allot) to the sons of Benjamin. (The area) from this corner to the gate of Issachar (you shall allot) to the sons of Issachar. (The area) from the gate (of Issachar) **XLV** ... the second (= incoming) [priestly course] shall enter on the left ... and the first (= outgoing) shall leave on the right. They shall not mingle with one another nor their vessels. [Each] priestly course shall come to its place and they shall stay there. One shall arrive and the other leave on the eighth day. They shall clean the rooms, one after the other, when the first (priestly course) leaves. There shall be no mingling there.

No man who has had a nocturnal emission shall enter the sanctuary at all until three days have elapsed. He shall wash his garments and bathe on the first day and on the third day he shall wash his garments and bathe, and after sunset he shall enter the sanctuary. They shall not enter my sanctuary in their impure uncleanness and render it unclean. No man who has had sexual intercourse with his wife shall enter anywhere into the city of the sanctuary where I cause my name to abide, for three days. No blind man shall enter it in all his days and shall not profane the city where I abide, for I, YHWH, abide amongst the children of Israel for ever and ever.

Whoever is to purify himself of his flux shall count seven days for his purification. He shall wash his garments on the seventh day and bathe his whole body in running water. Afterwards he shall enter the city of the sanctuary. No one unclean through contact with a corpse shall enter there until he has purified himself. No leper nor any man smitten (in his body) shall enter there until he has purified himself and has offered ... **XLVI** ... [No] unclean bird shall fly over [my] sanctua[ry] ... the roofs of the gates ... the outer courtyard ... be in my sanctuary for ever and ever all the time that I [abide] among them.

You shall make a terrace round about, outside the outer courtyard, fourteen cubits wide like the entrances of all the gates. You shall make twelve steps (leading) to it by which the children of Israel shall ascend there to enter my sanctuary.

You shall make a one-hundred-cubits-wide ditch around the sanctuary which shall divide the holy sanctuary from the city so that no one can rush into my sanctuary and defile it. They shall sanctify my sanctuary and hold it in awe because I abide among them.

You shall make for them latrines outside the city where they shall go out, north-west of the city. These shall be roofed houses with holes in them into which the filth shall go down. It shall be far enough not to be visible from the city, (at) three thousand cubits.

You shall make three areas to the east of the city, divided from one another, where the lepers, those suffering from a flux and men who have had a (nocturnal) emission **XLVII** ...

Their cities [shall be] pure ... for ever. The city which I will sanctify, causing my name and [my] sanctuar[y] to abide [in it], shall be holy and pure of all impurity with which they can become impure. Whatever is in it shall be pure. Whatever enters it shall be pure: wine, oil, all food and all moistened (food) shall be clean. No skin of clean animals slaughtered in their cities shall be brought there (to the city of the sanctuary). But in their cities they may use them for any work they need. But they shall not bring them to the city of my sanctuary, for the purity of the skin corresponds to that of the flesh. You shall not profane the city where I cause my name and my sanctuary to abide. For it is in the skins (of animals) slaughtered in the sanctuary that they shall bring their wine and oil and all their food to the city of my sanctuary. They shall not pollute my sanctuary with the skins of animals slaughtered in their country which are tainted (= unfit for the Temple). You cannot render any city among your cities as pure as my city, for the purity of the skin of the animal corresponds to the purity of its flesh. If you slaughter it in my sanctuary, it shall be pure for my sanctuary, but if you slaughter it in your cities, it shall be pure (only) for your cities. Whatever is pure for the sanctuary, shall be brought in skins (fit) for the sanctuary, and you shall not profane my sanctuary and my city where I abide with tainted skins.

**XLVIII** ... [the cormorant, the stork, every ki]nd of [heron,] the hoop[oe and the bat] ...

You may eat [the following] flying [insects]: every kind of great locust, every kind of long-headed locust, every kind of green locust, and every kind of desert locust. These are among the flying insects which you may eat: those which walk on four legs and have legs jointed above their feet to leap with them on the ground and wings to fly with. You shall not eat the carcass of any bird or beast but may sell it to a foreigner. You shall not eat any abominable thing, for you are a holy people to YHWH, your God.

You are the sons of YHWH, your God. You shall not gash yourselves or shave your forelocks in mourning for the dead, nor shall you tattoo yourselves, for you are a holy people to YHWH, your God. You shall not profane your land.

You shall not do as the nations do; they bury their dead everywhere, they bury them even in their houses. Rather you shall set apart areas in the midst of your land where you shall bury your dead. Between four cities you shall designate an area for burial. In every city you shall set aside areas for those stricken with leprosy, with plague and with scab, who shall not enter your cities and profane them, and also for those who suffer from a flux; and for menstruating women, and women after childbirth, so that they may not cause defilement in their midst by their impure uncleanness. The leper suffering from chronic leprosy or scab, who has been pronounced unclean by the priest **XLIX** ... with cedar wood, hyssop and ... your cities with the plague of leprosy and they shall be unclean.

If a man dies in your cities, the house in which the dead man has died shall be unclean for seven days. Whatever is in the house and whoever enters the house shall be unclean for seven days. Any food on which water has been poured shall be unclean, anything moistened shall be unclean. Earthenware vessels shall be unclean and whatever they contain shall be unclean for every clean man. The open (vessels) shall be unclean for every Israelite (with) whatever is moistened in them.

On the day when the body is removed from there, they shall cleanse the house of all pollution of oil, wine and water moisture. They shall rub its (the house's) floor, walls and doors and shall wash with water the bolts, doorposts, thresholds and lintels. On the day when the body is removed from there, they shall purify the house and all its utensils, hand-mills and mortars, all utensils of wood, iron and bronze and all utensils capable of purification. Clothes, sacks and skins shall be washed. As for the people, whoever has been in the house or has entered the house shall bathe in water and shall wash his clothes on the first day. On the third day they shall sprinkle purifying water on them and shall bathe. They shall wash their garments and all the utensils in the house.

On the seventh day they shall sprinkle (them) a second time. They shall bathe, wash their clothes and utensils and shall be clean by the evening of (the impurity contracted) from the dead so as to (be fit to) touch their pure things. As for a man who has not been rendered unclean on account of **L** ... they have been unclean. No longer ... until they have sprinkled (them) the second [time] on the seventh day and shall be clean by the evening at sunset.

Whoever touches the bone of a dead person in the fields, or one slain by the sword, or a dead body or the blood of a dead person, or a tomb, he shall purify himself according to the rule of this statute. But if he does not purify himself according to the statute of this law, he is unclean, his uncleanness being still in him. Whoever touches him must wash his clothes, bathe and he shall be clean by the evening.

If a woman is with child and it dies in her womb, as long as it is dead in her, she shall be unclean like a tomb. Any house that she enters shall be unclean with all its utensils for seven days. Whoever touches it shall be unclean till the evening. If anyone enters the house with her, he shall be unclean for seven days. He shall wash his clothes and bathe in water on the first (day). On the third day he shall sprinkle and wash his clothes and bathe. On the seventh day he shall sprinkle a second time and wash his clothes and bathe. At sunset he shall be clean.

As for all the utensils, clothes, skins and all the materials made of goat's hair, you shall deal with them according to the statute of this law. All earthenware vessels shall be broken for they are unclean and can no more be purified ever.

All creatures that teem on the ground you shall proclaim unclean: the weasel, the mouse, every kind of lizard, the wall gecko, the sand gecko, the great lizard and the chameleon. Whoever touches them dead **LI** ... [and whatever com]es out of the[m] ... [shall be] unclean [to you.] You shall [not] render yourselves unclean by th[em. Whoever touches them] dead shall be unclean un[til the] evening. He shall wash his clothes and bathe [in water and at] sun[set] he shall be clean. Whoever carries any of their bones, their carcass, skin, flesh or claw shall wash his clothes and bathe in water. After sunset he shall be clean. You shall forewarn the children of Israel about all the impurities.

They shall not render themselves unclean by those of which I tell you on this mountain and they shall not be unclean.

For I, YHWH, abide among the children of Israel. You shall sanctify them and they shall be holy. They shall not render themselves abominable by anything that I have separated for them as unclean and they shall be holy.

You shall establish judges and officers in all your towns and they shall judge the people with just judgement. They shall not be partial in (their) judgement. They shall not accept bribes, nor shall they twist judgement, for the bribe twists judgement, overturns the works of justice, blinds the eyes of the wise, produces great guilt, and profanes the house by the iniquity of sin. Justice and justice alone shall you pursue that you may live and come to inherit the land that I give you to inherit for all days. The man who accepts bribes and twists just judgement shall be put to death. You shall not be afraid to execute him.

You shall not do in your land as the nations do. Everywhere they sacrifice, plant sacred trees, erect sacred pillars and set up carved stones to bow down before them and build for them **LII** ... You shall not plant [any tree as a sacred tree beside my altar to be made by you.] You shall not erect a sacred pillar [that is hateful to me.] You shall not make anywhere in your land a carved stone to bow down before it. You shall not sacrifice to me any cattle or sheep with a grave blemish, for they are abominable to me. You shall not sacrifice to me any cattle or sheep or goat that is pregnant, for this would be an abomination to me. You shall not slaughter a cow or a ewe and its young on the same day, neither shall you kill a mother with her young.

Of all the firstlings born to your cattle or sheep, you shall sanctify for me the male animals. You shall not use the firstling of your cattle for work, nor shall you shear the firstling of your small cattle. You shall eat it before me every year in the place that I shall choose. Should it be blemished, being lame or blind or (afflicted with) any grave blemish, you shall not sacrifice it to me. It is within your towns that you shall eat it. The unclean and the clean among you together (may eat it) like a gazelle or a deer. It is the blood alone that you shall not eat. You shall spill it on the ground like water and cover it with dust. You shall not muzzle an ox while it is threshing. You shall not plough with an ox and an ass (harnessed) together. You shall not slaughter clean cattle or sheep or goat in any of your towns, within a distance of three days' journey from my sanctuary. It is rather in my sanctuary that you shall slaughter it, making of it a holocaust or peace-offering. You shall eat and rejoice before me in the place on which I choose to set my name. Every clean animal with a blemish, you shall eat it within your towns, away from my sanctuary at a distance of thirty stadia. You shall not slaughter it close to my sanctuary for its flesh is tainted. You shall not eat in my city, which I sanctify by placing my name in it, the flesh of cattle, sheep or goat which has not entered my sanctuary. They shall sacrifice it there, toss its blood to the base of the altar of holocaust and shall burn its fat. **LIII** [When I extend your frontiers as I have told you, and if the place where I have chosen to set my name is too distan]t, and you say, 'I will eat meat', because you [l]ong for it, [whatever you desire,] you may eat, [and you may slau]gh[ter] any of your small cattle or cattle which I give you according to my blessing. You may eat it within your towns, the clean and the unclean together, like gazelle or deer (meat). But you shall firmly abstain from eating the blood. You shall spill it on the ground like water and cover it with dust. For the blood is the life and you shall not eat the life with the flesh so that it may be well with you and with your sons after you for ever. You shall do that which is correct and good before me, for I am YHWH, your God.

But all your devoted gifts and votive donations you shall bring when you come to the place where I cause my name to abide, and you shall sacrifice (them) there before me as you have devoted and vowed them with your mouth. When you make a vow, you shall not tarry in fulfilling it, for surely I will require it of you and you shall become guilty of a sin. You shall keep the word uttered by your lips, for your mouth has vowed freely to perform your vow.

When a man makes a vow to me or swears an oath to take upon himself a binding obligation, he must not break his word. Whatever has been uttered by his mouth, he shall do it.

When a woman makes a vow to me, or takes upon herself a binding obligation by means of an oath in her father's house, in her youth, if her father hears of her vow or the binding obligation which she has taken upon herself and remains silent, all her vows shall stand, and her binding obligation which she has taken upon herself shall stand. If, however, her father definitely forbids her on the day that he hears of it, none of her vows or binding obligations which she has taken upon herself shall stand, and I will absolve her because (her father) has forbidden her **LIV** [when he] h[eard of them. But if he annuls them after] the da[y that he has] hea[rd of them, he shall bear] her guilt: [her] fa[ther has annulled them. Any vow] or binding oath (made by a woman) [to mortify herself,] her husband may confi[rm it] or annul it on the day that he hears of it, and I will absolve her.

But any vow of a widow or a divorced woman, whatever she has taken upon herself shall stand in conformity with all that her mouth has uttered.

Everything that I command you today, see to it that it is kept. You shall not add to it, nor detract from it.

If a prophet or a dreamer appears among you and presents you with a sign or a portent, even if the sign or the portent comes true, when he says, 'Let us go and worship other gods whom you have not known!', do not listen to the words of that prophet or that dreamer, for I am testing you to discover whether you love YHWH, the God of your fathers, with all your heart and soul. It is YHWH, your God, that you must follow and serve, and it is him that you must fear and his voice that you must obey, and you must hold fast to him. That prophet or dreamer shall be put to death for he has preached rebellion against YHWH, your God, who brought you out of the land of Egypt and redeemed you from the house of bondage, to lead you astray from the path that I have commanded you to follow. You shall rid yourself of this evil.

If your brother, the son of your father or the son of your mother, or your son, or your daughter, or the wife of your bosom, or your friend who is like your own self, (seeks to) entice you secretly, saying, 'Let us go and worship other gods whom you have not known', neither you, **LV** [nor] your [fa]thers, some of the gods [of the peoples that are round about you, whether near you or far off from you], from the one end of the earth to [the other, you shall not yield to him or listen to him, nor shall your eye pity] him, nor shall you spare [him, nor shall you conceal him; but you shall kill him; your hand shall be first against him to put him to death, and afterwards the hand of all the people. You shall stone him to death with stones because he sought to] draw you away [from me who brought you out of the land of Egypt, out of the house of bondage. And all Israel shall hear, and fear, and never again do such an evil thing] among you. If in on[e of your cities in which I] give you to dw[ell] you hear this said: 'Men, [s]ons of [Beli]al have arisen in your midst and have led astray all the inhabitants of their city saying, "Let us go and worship gods whom you have not known!",' you shall inquire, search and investigate carefully. If the matter is proven true that such an abomination has been done in Israel, you shall surely put all the inhabitants of that city to the sword. You shall place it and all who are in it under the ban, and you shall put the beasts to the sword. You shall assemble all the booty in (the city) square and shall burn it with fire, the city and all the booty, as a whole-offering to YHWH, your God. It shall be a ruin for ever and shall never be rebuilt. Nothing from that which has been placed under the ban shall cleave to your hand so that I may turn from my hot anger and show you compassion. I will be compassionate to you and multiply you as I told your fathers, provided that you obey my voice, keeping all my commandments that I command you today, to do that which is correct and good before YHWH, your God.

If among you, in one of your towns that I give you, there is found a man or a woman who does that which is wrong in my eyes by transgressing my covenant, and goes and worships other gods, and bows down before them, or before the sun or the moon, or all the host of heaven, if you are told about it, and you hear about this matter, you shall search and investigate it carefully. If the matter is proven true that such an abomination has been done in Israel, you shall lead out that man or that woman and stone him (to death) with stones.

**LVI** ... [You shall go to the Levitical priests o]r to the [j]u[dges then in office]; you shall seek their guidance and [they] shall pro[nounce on] the matter for which [you have sought their guidance, and they shall procl]aim the(ir) judgement to you. You shall act in conformity with the law that they proclaim to you and the saying that they declare to you from the book of the Law. They shall issue to you a proclamation in truth from the place where I choose to cause my name to abide. Be careful to do all that they teach you and act in conformity with the decision that they communicate to you. Do not stray from the law which they proclaim to you to the right or to the left. The man who does not listen but acts arrogantly without obeying the priest who is posted there to minister before me, or the judge, that man shall die. You shall rid Israel of evil. All the people shall hear of it and shall be awe-stricken, and none shall ever again be arrogant in Israel.

When you enter the land which I give you, take possession of it, dwell in it and say, 'I will appoint a king over me as do all the nations around me!', you may surely appoint over you the king whom I will choose. It is from among your brothers that you shall appoint a king over you. You shall not appoint over you a foreigner who is not your brother. He (the king) shall definitely not acquire many horses, neither shall he lead the people back to Egypt for war to acquire many horses and much silver and gold, for I told you, 'You shall never again go back that way'. He shall not acquire many wives that they may not turn his heart away from me. He shall not acquire very much silver and gold.

When he sits on the throne of his kingdom, they shall write for him this law from the book which is before the priests. **LVII** This is the law [that they shall write for him] ... [They shall count,] on the day that they appoint hi[m] king, the sons of Israel from the age of twenty to sixty years according to their standard (units). He shall install at their head captains of thousands, captains of hundreds, captains of fifties and captains of tens in all their cities. He shall select from among them one thousand by tribe to be with him: twelve thousand warriors who shall not leave him alone to be captured by the nations. All the selected men whom he has selected shall be men of truth, God-fearers, haters of unjust gain and mighty warriors. They shall be with him always, day and night. They shall guard him from anything sinful, and from any foreign nation in order not to be captured by them. The twelve princes of his people shall be with him, and twelve from among the priests, and from among the Levites twelve. They shall sit together with him to (proclaim) judgement and the law so that his heart shall not be lifted above them, and he shall do nothing without them concerning any affair.

He shall not marry as wife any daughter of the nations, but shall take a wife for himself from his father's house, from his father's family. He shall not take another wife in addition to her, for she alone shall be with him all the time of her life. But if she dies, he may marry another from his father's house, from his family. He shall not twist judgement; he shall take no bribe to twist a just judgement and shall not covet a field or a vineyard, any riches or house, or anything desirable in Israel. He shall (not) rob **LVIII** ...

When the king hears of any nation or people intent on plundering whatever belongs to Israel, he shall send for the captains of thousands and the captains of hundreds posted in the cities of Israel. They shall send with him (the captain) one tenth of the people to go with him (the king) to war against their enemies, and they shall go with him. But if a large force enters the land of Israel, they shall send with him one fifth of the warriors. If a king with chariots and horses and a large force (comes), they shall send with him one third of the warriors, and the two (remaining) divisions shall guard their city and their boundaries so that no marauders invade their land. If the war presses him (the king) hard, they shall send to him half of the people, the men of the army, but the (other) half of the people shall not be severed from their cities.

If they triumph over their enemies, smash them, put them to the sword and carry away their booty, they shall give the king his tithe of this, the priests one thousandth and the Levites one hundredth from everything.

They shall halve the rest between the combatants and their brothers whom they have left in their cities.

If he (the king) goes to war against his enemies, one fifth of the people shall go with him, the warriors, all the mighty men of valour. They shall avoid everything unclean, everything shameful, every iniquity and guilt. He shall not go until he has presented himself before the High Priest who shall inquire on his behalf for a decision by the Urim and Tummim. It is at his word that he shall go and at his word that he shall come, he and all the children of Israel who are with him. He shall not go following his heart's counsel until he (the High Priest) has inquired for a decision by the Urim and Tummim. He shall (then) succeed in all his ways on which he has set out according to the decision which **LIX** . . . and they shall disperse them in many lands and they shall become a h[orror], a byword, a mockery. With a heavy yoke and in extreme want, they shall there serve gods made by human hands, of wood and stone, silver and gold. During this time their cities shall become a devastation, a laughing-stock and a wasteland, and their enemies shall devastate them. They shall sigh in the lands of their enemies and scream because of the heavy yoke. They shall cry out but I will not listen; they shall scream but I will not answer them because of their evil doings. I will hide my face from them and they shall become food, plunder and prey. None shall save them because of their wickedness, because they have broken my covenant and their soul has loathed my law until they have incurred every guilt. Afterwards they will return to me with all their heart and all their soul, in conformity with all the words of this law, and I will save them from the hand of their enemies and redeem them from the hand of those who hate them, and I will bring them to the land of their fathers. I will redeem them, and increase them and exult over them. I will be their God and they shall be my people.

The king whose heart and eyes have gone astray from my commandments shall never have one to sit on the throne of his fathers, for I will cut off his posterity for ever so that it shall no more rule over Israel. But if he walk after my rules and keep my commandments and do that which is correct and good before me, no heir to the throne of the kingdom of Israel shall be cut off from among his sons for ever. I will be with him and will save him from the hand of those who hate him and from the hand of those who seek his life. I will place all his enemies before him and he shall rule over them according to his pleasure and they shall not rule over him. I will set him on an upward, not on a downward, course, to be the head and not the tail, that the days of his kingdom may be lengthened greatly for him and his sons after him.

**LX** ... and all their wave-offerings. All their firstling male [bea]sts and all ... of their beasts and all their holy gifts which they shall sanctify to me together with all their holy gifts of praise and a proportion of their offering of birds, wild animals and fish, one thousandth of their catch, and all that they shall devote, and the proportion of the booty and the plunder.

To the Levites shall belong the tithe of the corn, the wine and the oil that they have sanctified to me first; the shoulder from those who slaughter a sacrifice and a proportion of the booty, the plunder and the catch of birds, wild animals and fish, one hundredth; the tithe from the young pigeons and from the honey one fiftieth. To the priests shall belong one hundredth of the young pigeons, for I have chosen them from all your tribes to attend on me and minister (before me) and bless my name, he and his sons always. If a Levite come from any town anywhere in Israel where he sojourns to the place where I will choose to cause my name to abide, (if he come) with an eager soul, he may minister like his brethren the Levites who attend on me there. He shall have the same share of food with them, besides the inheritance from his father's family.

When you enter the land which I give you, do not learn to practise the abominations of those nations. There shall be found among you none who makes his son or daughter pass through fire, nor an augur or a soothsayer, a diviner or a sorcerer, one who casts spells or a medium, or wizards or necromancers. For they are an abomination before me, all who practise such things, and it is because of these abominations that I drive them out before you. You shall be perfect towards YHWH, your God. For these nations that **LXI** ... to ut[ter a word] in [my] n[ame which I have n]ot comman[ded him to] utter, or wh[o speaks in the name of oth]er go[ds], that prophet shall be put to death. If you say in your heart, 'How shall we know the word which YHWH has not uttered?', when the word uttered by the prophet in the name of YHWH is not fulfilled and does not come true, that is not a word that I have uttered. The prophet has spoken arrogantly; do not fear him.

A single witness may not come forward against a man in the matter of any iniquity or sin which he has committed. It is on the evidence of two witnesses or three witnesses that a case can be established. If a malicious witness comes forward against a man to testify against him in a case of a crime, both disputants shall stand before me and before the priests and the Levites and before the judges then in office, and the judges shall inquire, and if the witness is a false witness who has testified falsely against his brother, you shall do to him as he proposed to do to his brother. You shall rid yourselves of evil. The rest shall hear of it and shall be awe-stricken and never again shall such a thing be done in your midst. You shall have no mercy on him: life for life, eye for eye, tooth for tooth, hand for hand, foot for foot.

When you go to war against your enemies, and you see horses and chariots and an army greater than yours, be not afraid of them, for I am with you who brought you out of the land of Egypt. When you approach the battle, the priest shall come forward to speak to the army and say to them, 'Hear, Israel, you approach . . .' . . . **LXII** [and another man shall use its fruit. If any man has betrothed a woman but has not yet married her, he shall return] home. Otherwise he may die in the war and another man may take her. [The] of[ficers shall continue] to address the army and say, 'If any man is afraid and has lost heart, he shall go and return. Otherwise he may render his kinsmen as faint-hearted as himself.'

When the judges have finished addressing the army, they shall appoint army captains at the head of the people.

When you approach a city to fight it, (first) offer it peace. If it seeks peace and opens (its gates) to you, then all the people found in it shall become your forced labourers and shall serve you. If it does not make peace with you, but is ready to fight a war against you, you shall besiege it and I will deliver it into your hands. You shall put all its males to the sword, but the women, the children, the beasts and all that is in the city, all its booty, you may take as spoil for yourselves. You may enjoy the use of the booty of your enemies which I give you. Thus shall you treat the very distant cities, those which are not among the cities of these nations. But in the cities of the peoples which I give you as an inheritance, you shall not leave alive any creature. Indeed you shall utterly exterminate the Hittites, the Amorites, the Canaanites, the Hivites, the Jebusites, the Girgashites and the Perizzites as I have commanded you, that they may not teach you to practise all the abominations that they have performed to their gods.

**LXIII** . . . [a heifer with which] he has not worked, which [has not drawn the yoke. The elders of] that city [shall bring down] the heifer to a ravine with an ever-flowing stream which has never been sown or cultivated, and there they shall break its neck.

The priests, the sons of Levi, shall come forward, for I have chosen them to minister before me and bless my name, and every dispute and every assault shall be decided by their word. All the elders of the city nearest to the body of the murdered man shall wash their hands over the head of the heifer whose neck has been broken in the ravine. They shall declare, 'Our hands did not shed this blood, nor did our eyes see it happen. Accept expiation for thy people Israel whom thou hast redeemed, O YHWH, and do not permit the guilt of innocent blood to rest among thy people, Israel. Let this blood be expiated for them.' You shall rid Israel (of the guilt) of innocent blood, and you shall do that which is correct and good before YHWH, your God. When you go to war against your enemies, and I deliver them into your hands, and you capture some of them, if you see among the captives a pretty woman and desire her, you may take her to be your wife. You shall bring her to your house, you shall shave her head, and cut her nails. You shall discard the clothes of her captivity and she shall dwell in your house, and bewail her father and mother for a full month. Afterwards you may go to her, consummate the marriage with her and she will be your wife. But she shall not touch whatever is pure for you for seven years, neither shall she eat of the sacrifice of peace-offering until seven years have elapsed. Afterwards she may eat. **LXIV** ... [the firstfruits of his virility; he has the right of the first-born.]

If a man has a disobedient and rebellious son who refuses to listen to his father and mother, nor listens to them when they chastise him, his father and mother shall take hold of him and bring him to the elders of his city, to the gate of his place. They shall say to the elders of his town, 'This son of ours is disobedient and rebellious; he does not listen to us; he is a glutton and a drunkard.' All the men of his city shall stone him with stones and he shall die, and you shall rid yourselves of evil. All the children of Israel shall hear of it and be awe-stricken. If a man slanders his people and delivers his people to a foreign nation and does evil to his people, you shall hang him on a tree and he shall die. On the testimony of two witnesses and on the testimony of three witnesses he shall be put to death and they shall hang him on the tree. If a man is guilty of a capital crime and flees (abroad) to the nations, and curses his people, the children of Israel, you shall hang him also on the tree, and he shall die. But his body shall not stay overnight on the tree. Indeed you shall bury him on the same day. For he who is hanged on the tree is accursed of God and men. You shall not pollute the ground which I give you to inherit. If you see your kinsman's ox or sheep or donkey straying, do not neglect them; you shall indeed return them to your kinsman. If your kinsman does not live near you, and you do not know who he is, you shall bring the animal to your house and it shall be with you until he claims (it). **LXV** ...

[Wh]en a bird's nest happens to lie before you by the roadside, on any tree or on the ground, with fledglings or eggs, and the hen is sitting on the fledglings or the eggs, you shall not take the hen with the young. You shall surely let the hen escape and take only the young so that it may be well with you and your days shall be prolonged. When you build a new house, you shall construct a parapet on the roof so that you do not bring blood-guilt on your house if anyone should fall from it.

When a man takes a wife, has sexual intercourse with her and takes a dislike to her, and brings a baseless charge against her, ruining her reputation, and says, 'I have taken this woman, approached her, and did not find the proof of virginity in her', the father or the mother of the girl shall take the girl's proof of virginity and bring it to the elders at the gate. The girl's father shall say to the elders, 'I gave my daughter to be this man's wife; he has taken a dislike to her and has brought a baseless charge against her saying, "I have not found the proof of virginity in your daughter." Here is the proof of my daughter's virginity.' They shall spread out the garment before the elders of that city. The elders of that city shall take that man and chastise him. They shall fine him one hundred pieces of silver which they shall give to the father of the girl, because he (the husband) has tried to ruin the reputation of an Israelite virgin. He shall not **LXVI** ... [When a virgin betrothed to a man is found by another man in the city and he lies with her, they shall bring both of them to the gate] of that city and stone them with stones and they shall be put to death: the girl because she has not shouted (for help, although she was) in the city, and the man because he has dishonoured his neighbour's wife. You shall rid yourselves of evil. If the man has found the woman in the fields in a distant place hidden from the city, and raped her, only he who has lain with her shall be put to death. To the girl they shall do nothing since she has committed no crime worthy of death. For this affair is like that of a man who attacks his neighbour and murders him. For it was in the fields that he found her and the betrothed girl shouted (for help), but none came to her rescue.

When a man seduces a virgin who is not betrothed, but is suitable to him according to the rule, and lies with her, and he is found out, he who has lain with her shall give the girl's father fifty pieces of silver and she shall be his wife. Because he has dishonoured her, he may not divorce her all his days. A man shall not take his father's wife and shall not lift his father's skirt. A man shall not take the wife of his brother and shall not lift the skirt of his brother, the son of his father or the son of his mother, for this is unclean. A man shall not take his sister, the daughter of his father or the daughter of his mother, for this is abominable. A man shall not take his father's sister or his mother's sister, for this is immoral. A man shall not take the daughter of his brother or the daughter of his sister for this is abominable. (A man) shall not take **LXVII** . . .

# MMT (Miqsat Ma'ase Ha-Torah) – Some Observances of the Law

## (4Q394–9)

Mutilated fragments of six Cave 4 manuscripts have acquired international notoriety on account of a lawsuit filed before the Jerusalem district court which found that one of the official editors of this text, Elisha Qimron, owned the copyright of the MMT text as reconstructed by him. Hershel Shanks, of the Biblical Archaeology Society of Washington, was held responsible for breaching this copyright and ordered to pay $43,000 damages. However, an appeal having been lodged with the Israeli Supreme Court, the matter is still *sub judice*.

When the contents of the six copies are assembled into a single account, they amount to 120 lines mostly of a fragmentary nature. The document begins with a sectarian calendar (section A), which may or may not pertain to the original MMT; it continues with a series of special rules (section B), and ends with an exhortation (section C). MMT has been called an epistle, but since it lacks the introductory and concluding formulae of a letter, it is more likely to be a kind of legal tractate. It is addressed to a single leading personality who is compared to King David. The *dramatis personae* consist of a 'we' party, a 'you' party, and a 'they' party. The group responsible for MMT, who refer to themselves as 'we', seek to detach the leader of the 'you' party from the erroneous views propounded by the 'they' party. The editors claim that MMT was written by the Teacher of Righteousness and sent to the Wicked Priest; that the views of the 'we' party are akin to those of the Sadducees; and that the 'they' party are the Pharisees. However, these are no more than hypotheses. In particular, the identification of the author with the Teacher of Righteousness is less likely than that of the leader of the 'you' group with the man who was to become the Wicked Priest, probably Jonathan Maccabaeus.

It has also been advanced that the original nucleus of the Qumran Community, responsible for MMT, consisted of early or proto-Sadducees. However, one should bear in mind that the priests in this writing are never called sons of Zadok or Sadducees, but are referred to as sons of Aaron (cf. $4QS^b$ (=4Q256) and $4QS^d$ (4Q258) above, p. 118). The alleged Sadducee connection relies on three legal rules, out of a list of more than twenty, in MMT which represent opinions identical with the halakhah attributed in rabbinic literature to the Sadducees, and contrasted with the stance taken by the Pharisees (cf. mParah 5:4 and MMT B 13–17; mYad 4:7; mToh 8:9 and MMT B 55–8; mYad 4:6 and MMT B 72–4).

The chief topics of controversy are (1) the calendar (if it is an integral part of the document); (2) ritual purity (acceptability of Gentile offerings, law on slaughter, the 'red heifer' ritual, exclusion of the blind and the deaf, law relating to lepers, purity of running liquids, fourth-year fruit and tithe of cattle, ban on dogs in Jerusalem, the law regulating contact with dead bodies); (3) marriage and intermarriage rules, and (4) decrees regulating entry into the congregation. MMT is particularly important as a source of ancient legal debate. It is unique among the Dead Sea Scrolls and foreshadows the halakhic process developed and practised by later rabbis.

Instead of presenting a composite text, the translation will reflect actual manuscripts and follow their line numbering. If there are overlapping fragments, gaps in the main manuscript will be filled from the parallel text and the borrowing will appear between { }. However, to assist the reader who desires to consult the Qimron–Strugnell edition, the line numbers of their composite text are given in brackets. Unlike the editors, I have been economical with purely conjectural restorations of the many gaps. Obscurities in the translation therefore faithfully reflect the real status of the Hebrew original.

For the *editio princeps*, see E. Qimron and J. Strugnell, *Qumran Cave 4 – V* (*DJD*, X, Clarendon Press, Oxford, 1994). Cf. also F. García Martínez, *The Dead Sea Scrolls Translated*, 77–85, containing the rendering of the Qimron–Strugnell composite text and, separately, the translation of the six individual MMT manuscripts.

## 1. MMT A = A SECTARIAN CALENDAR (4Q**394** 1–2)

(The fragmentary calendar is presented in five parallel columns which originally covered eighteen lines. Hence the end of the calendar at the top of 4Q**394** 3–7 i is listed as lines 19 to 21 by Qimron–Strugnell. Whether this calendar is part of the original MMT or is merely copied on the same scroll is uncertain.)

**I** [On the sixteenth of it (of the second month): sabbath.]
On the twenty-third of it: sabbath.
[On] the thir[tie]th [of it: sabbath.
On the seventh of the third month: sabbath.

On the fourteenth of it: sabbath.
On the fifteenth of it: Feast of Weeks.
On the twenty-] **II** [f]irs[t] of it: sabbath.
[On] the twenty-eighth of it: sabbath.
The first of the sabbath (=Sunday), and the secon[d da]y (=Monday) [and the third are to be added.
And the season is complete: ninety-one days.
The first of the fourth month: Memorial day.
On the fourth] **III** of it: [sabbath.]
On the e[leventh] of it: sabbath.
On the eighteenth of it: sabbath.
On the twenty-fifth of it: sabbath.
On the second of the fift[h] (month): [sa]bb[ath.
On the third of it: Feast of Wine, first of sabbath (Sunday).]
**IV** [On the ninth of it: sabbath.]
On the sixteenth of it: sabbath.
On the twenty-third of it: sabbath.
[On the th]irtieth [of it: sabbath.
On the seventh of the sixth (month): sabbath.
On the fourteenth of it: sabbath.
On the twenty-first] **V** of it: sabbath.
On the twenty-second of it: Feast of Oil, fir[st of sab]bath (Sunday).
Af[terwards]: offe[ring of Wood].

## 4Q**394** 3–7 i

**(19)** [The (twenty)-eighth of it (of the twelfth month)]: sabbath.

The first [of the] s[abbath (=Sunday) and the second day (=Monday) and the third are to be ad]ded to it. **(20)** And the year is complete: three-hundred and si[xty-four] **(21)** days. *vacat*

## 2. MMT B = SPECIAL RULES (4Q**394** 3–7 i conflated with 4Q**395**)

**(1)** These are some of our teachings [ ] which are [ **(2)** the] works which w[e think and a]ll of them concern [ ] **(3)** and the purity of . . .

[And concerning the offering of the wh]eat of the [Gentiles which they ...] **(4)** and they touch it ... and de[file it ... One should not accept anything] **(5)** from the wheat [of the Gen]tiles [and none of it is] to enter the Sanctuary.

[And concerning] {the sacrifice} (4Q**395**) ... **(6)** which they cook in a vessel ... {in it} (4Q**395**) **(7)** the meat of their sacrifices and that they ... in the courtyar[d ...] {it} (4Q**395**) **(8)** with the broth of their sacrifice.

And concerning the sacrifice of the Gentiles ... [we consider that] they {sacrifice} (4Q**395**) **(9)** to [an idol and] that is [like] a woman fornicating with him.

... {the sacrifice} (4Q**395**) **(10)** of peace-off[erings] which they postpone from one day to the next. But [it is written (cf. Lev. 7:15)] **(11)** that the meal-offe[ring] {is eaten} (4Q**395**) with the fat and the meat on the day of [their] being sacrifi[ced. For the sons] **(12)** of the priest[s] {are to take care of this matter} (4Q**395**) so as not to **(13)** burden the people with sin.

{And concerning the purity of the heifer of the sin-offering} (4Q**395**), **(14)** he who slaughters it and he who burns it and he who collects {its ashes and he who sprinkles the} (4Q**395**) [water] **(15)** of purification – all these {are to be pure} (4Q**395**) at sunset **(16)** so that the pure shall sprinkle the impure. For the sons

## (4Q**394** 3–7 ii conflated with 4Q**395**)

**(17)** {of Aaron are to be} (4Q**395**) ...

And furthermore **(18)** concerning the sk]ins of the cattle [and the sheep ... from] **(19)** their [skin]s vessel[s ... [they are] not to **(20)** bring] them to the Sanctua[ry ...

## (4Q**397** 1–2 conflated with 4Q**398** 1–3)

**(21)** ...

And furthermore concerning the skin[s and bones of unclean animals, they shall not make from their bones] and from their s[k]i[ns] **(22)** handles of v[essels and] ...

And furthermore concerning the s]kin of the carcass **(23)** of a clean [animal], he who carries their carcass shall not touch the [sacred] purity.

**(24)** And concerning ... **(25)** ...

## (4Q**394** 3–7 ii conflated with 4Q**397** 3)

[the sons of] **(26)** the pri[es]ts are to [be care]f[ul] regarding {all these matters} (4Q**397** 3) so as not **(27)** to burden the people with sin.

[And concern]ing that which is written, [*If a man slaughters in the camp or* **(28)** *slaughters*] *outside the camp an ox or a lamb or a goat* (Lev. 7:13) for ... {on the northern side of the camp} (4Q**397** 3). **(29)** And we consider the Sanctuary [as the tent of meeting and Je]rusale[m] as **(30)** the {camp and *out*[*side*] *the*} (4Q**397** 3) *camp* [i.e. outside Jerusalem], that is the camp **(31)** of their towns. Outside the camp ... they bring out the ashes [**(32)** of the] altar and they burn ... For Jerusalem] is the place which **(33)** [He has chosen] {from all the tri[bes of Israel]} (4Q**397** 3) ...

## (4Q**396** 1–2 i conflated with 4Q**394** 8 iii and 4Q**397** 5)

**(35)** ... they [do no]t slaughter in the Sanctuary.

**(36)** [And concerning pregnant animals] {we consider} (4Q**397** 5) [that one should not sacrifice] the mother and the unborn young on the same day.

**(37)** [And concerning eating, w]e consider that the unborn young **(38)** may be eaten ... (provided it has been slaughtered) ... [this is] so and the saying is written concerning a pregnant animal. *vacat*

**(39)** [And concerning the Ammon]{ite and the Moabite} (4Q**394** 8 iii) and the {bastard} (4Q**397** 5) [and the man whose testicles] have been crushed [and one] whose penis [has been cut off] who enter **(40)** the congregation, [... and] they [ta]ke [wives so as to be] {one} (4Q**397** 5) bone (with them) ... **(41)** ...

## (4Q**394** 8 iii conflated with 4Q**396** 1–2 i–ii and 4Q**397** 5)

**(42)** {impurities.

And furthermore we consider} (4Q**397** 5) **(43)** [that they should not ... and should not have intercour]se with them. **(44)** [... and they should] {not unite with them} (4Q**397** 5) so as to make them **(45)** [into one bone **(46)** ... that some of the people ... **(47)** ... **(48)** {from all}

(4Q**397** 5) (sexual) mingling **(49)** . . . {and to be fearful of the Sanctuary} (4Q**396** 1–2 ii).

## (4Q**396** 1–2 ii)

[And furthermore concerning] {the blind} (4Q**394** 8 iv) **(50)** who do not see how to beware of all mingl[ings]

## (4Q**394** 8 iv conflated with 4Q**396** 1–2 ii and 4Q**397** 6–13)

**(51)** and do not see the minglings which entail guilt (offering). **(52)** And furthermore concerning the deaf who have not heard the decrees and judgements and purity (rules) and have not **(53)** heard the judgements of Israel – for he who has not seen and has not heard (them) does not **(54)** know how to practise (them); yet they come to the pure food of the Sanctuary. *vacat*

**(55)** And furthermore concerning the pouring (of liquids), we say that it contains no **(56)** purity.

And furthermore the pouring does not separate the impure **(57)** {from the pure} (4Q**397** 6–13) for the poured liquid and that in the receptacle are alike, **(58)** one liquid.

And {dogs} (4Q**397** 6–13) are not to be brought to the sacred camp for **(59)** they may eat some of the bones from the Sanctua[ry] to which meat is still attached. For **(60)** Jerusalem is {the sacred camp} (4Q**397** 6–13) and is the place

## (4Q**396** 1–2 iii conflated with 4Q**394** 8 iv and 4Q**397** 6–13)

**(61)** which He has chosen from all the tribes of Israel, for Jerusalem is the head **(62)** of the camps of Israel.

And furthermore con[cerning the pl]anting of fruit trees planted **(63)** in the land of Israel, they are like {firstfruits} (4Q**397** 6–13) destined for the {priests} (4Q**397** 6–13). {And the tithe} (4Q**394** 8 iv) of the cattle **(64)** and sheep is for the priests.

And furthermore concerning the lepers, we **(65)** s[ay that they shall not c]ome (into contact) with the sacred pure food for {they shall be} (4Q**397** 6–13) separated **(66)** ...

Furthermore it is written that from the time he (the leper) has shaved and washed, he shall stay outside **(67)** ... [for seven] days. And now while their impurity is with them ... [they shall not **(68)** come into contact w]ith the sacred pure food of the house. And you know **(69)** ... and it is concealed from him, he is to bring **(70)** {a sin-offering} (4Q**397** 6–13).

[And concerning the person who does anything with a high hand it is writ]ten that he is one who despises and reviles (God) (cf. Num. xv, 30–31). **(71)** ... {impurities of leprosy} (4Q**397** 6–13), they are not to eat from the holy things

## (4Q**396** 1–2 iv conflated with 4Q**397** 6–13)

**(72)** until the sun has set on the eighth day.

And concerning [the impurities] **(73)** {of a man, we say that every} (4Q**397** 6–13) bone to which **(74)** flesh is or [is not] attached is to be treated according to the law of the dead or slain. *vacat*

**(75)** And concerning fornication practised by the people, they should be s[ons of] holiness, **(76)** as it is written, {*Israel*} (4Q**397** 6–13) *is holy* (Jer. ii, 3).

And concerning [his clea]n ani[mal, **(77)** it is written that it shall not be mated with a different kind.

And concerning [his] clothes], it is written that they shall not **(78)** be of mixed material.

And he shall not sow his field and vine[yard with two kind]s. **(79)** For they are holy and the sons of Aaron are most h[oly]. **(80)** And you know that some of the priests and [the people mingle] **(81)** [and they] unite and defile the [holy] seed and also **(82)** their [seed] with whores f[or] ...

## (4Q**397** 14–21)

...

**(4)** And concerning the wome[n ... violen]ce and betrayal ... **(5)** For in these ... [on account of] the violence and fornication they perish[ed ...] **(6)** places.

[And furthermore] it is written [in the Book of Moses that] *You shall not bring an abominable thing in[to your house* (cf. Deut. vii, 26) for] **(7)** an abominable thing is detestable.

## 3. MMT C = THE EXHORTATION (4Q**397** 14–21 followed by 4Q**398**)

[And you know that] we have separated from the mass of the peo[ple] ... **(8)** and from mingling with them in these matters and from being in contact with them in these (matters). And you k[now that no] treachery or lie or evil **(9)** is found in our hands for we give for [these] th[e ...

And furthermore] **(10)** we [have written] to you (sing.) that you should understand {the Book of Moses} (4Q**398** 14–17 i) and the Book[s of the Pr]ophets and Davi[d and all **(11)** the events] of every age. And in {the Book is written} (4Q**398** 14–17 i) ... not [for] **(12)** you {and the days of old} (4Q**398** 14–17 i).

And furthermore it is written that [you will depart] from the w[a]y and that evil will befall you (cf. Deut. xxxi, 29). {And it is written} (4Q**398** 14–17 i),

### (4Q**398** 14–17 I)

**(13)** *And it* **(14)** [*shall come to pas*]*s when all these* {*things*} (4Q**397** 14–21) [*be*]*fall you in the en*[*d*] *of days, the blessing* **(15)** *and the curse,* [*then you will call them to mind*] *and retu*[*rn to Him with all your heart* **(16)** *and all your soul* (Deut. xxx, 1–2) at the end of days. **(17)** [And it is written in the Book] of Moses and in the Boo[ks of the Prophet]s that there shall come ... **(18)** [and the blessings came]

### (4Q**398** 11–13)

in the days of Solomon the son of David. And the curses **(19)** came from in the days of Jeroboam the son of Nebat **(20)** until Jerusalem and Zedekiah king of Judah were exiled that He will b[rin]g them to ... And we recognize that some of the blessings and curses which are **(21)** written in the B[ook of Mo]ses have come. And this is at the end of days when they will come back to Israel **(22)** for [ever] . . . and shall not turn backwar[ds]. And the wicked shall act **(23)** wickedly and . . .

Remember the kings of Israel and understand their works that each of them who **(24)** feared [the To]rah was saved from troubles, and to those who were seekers of the Law, **(25)** their iniquities

## (4Q398 14–17 ii conflated with 4Q399)

were [par]doned.

Remember David, that he was a man of piety, and that **(26)** he was also saved from many troubles and pardoned.

We have also written to you (sing.) concerning **(27)** some of the observances of the Law (*miqsat ma'ase ha-Torah*), which we think are beneficial to you and your people. For [we have noticed] that **(28)** prudence and knowledge of the Law are with you.

Understand all these (matters) and ask Him to straighten **(29)** your counsel and put you far away from thoughts of evil and the counsel of Belial. **(30)** Consequently, you will rejoice at the end of time when you discover that some of our sayings are true. **(31)** And it will be reckoned for you as righteousness when you perform what is right and good before Him, for your own good **(32)** and for that of Israel. *vacat*

# The Wicked and the Holy

## (4Q181)

The first fragment of a document from Cave 4 (4Q**181**), which its editor has left untitled, describes in a manner similar to Community Rule IV the respective destinies of the damned and the chosen. See J. M. Allegro and A. A. Anderson, *DJD*, V, 79–80; cf. J. Strugnell, *RQ* 7 (1970), 254–5; J. T. Milik, *JJS* 23 (1972), 114–18.

... for guilt with the congregation of his people, for it has wallowed in the sin of the sons of men; (and it was appointed) for great judgements and evil diseases in the flesh according to the mighty deeds of God and in accordance with their wickedness. In conformity with their congregation of uncleanness, (they are to be separated) as a community of wickedness until (wickedness) ends.

In accordance with the mercies of God, according to His goodness and wonderful glory, He caused some of the sons of the world to draw near (Him) ... to be counted with Him in the com[munity of the 'g]ods' as a congregation of holiness in service for eternal life and (sharing) the lot of His holy ones ... each man according to his lot which He has cast for ... for eternal life ...

# 4QTohorot (Purities) A

## (4Q274)

This is the first of ten Cave 4 manuscripts dealing with purity matters. The text translated represents column I of the document and the first word of column II. 4Q274 deals with uncleanness caused by bodily fluxes and issues of blood and with the means of its removal. Parts of fr. 3 are concerned with the uncleanness associated with the juice oozing out of fruit.

For a preliminary edition, see J. M. Baumgarten, 'The Laws about Fluxes in 4QTohora[a] (4Q274)', in D. Dimant and L. H. Schiffman, eds., *Time to Prepare the Way in the Wilderness* (Brill, Leiden, 1985), 1–8; cf. also J. Milgrom, '4QTohora[a]: An Unpublished Qumran Text on Purities', ibid., 59–68. See further J. M. Baumgarten, 'Liquids and Susceptibility to Defilement in New 4Q Texts', *JQR* 85 (1994), 96–9.

**I** ... [Let him not] begin to cast his lot. He shall lie on a bed of sorrow and sit in a seat of sighs. He shall dwell in isolation with all the unclean, and away from (food) purity at a distance of twelve cubit in the wing (assigned) to him (?) on the north-west of every dwelling-house according to this measure. Every man from among the unclean ... he shall bathe in water [on the seven]th d[ay] and wash his clothes, and afterwards he may eat. For this is what he said, *He shall cry, Unclean, unclean* (Lev. xiii, 45), as long as [the pla]gue af[fects him].

A woman with a seven-day issue of blood shall not touch a man with a flux, nor any vessel touched by a man who has a flux, nor anything he has lain or sat on. But if she has touched (them), she shall wash her garments and bathe, and afterwards she may eat. Above all, she shall not mingle (with the pure) [during] her seven days so that she may not pollute the c[amp]s of the Ho[ly] of Israel. Neither shall she touch any woman with a long-term issue of blood. And the person, either male or female, who counts (the seven days: cf. Lev. xv, 13) shall not touch the menstruant during her uncleanness. Only when she has purified herself [from] her

[un]cleanness (may she be touched), for the blood of the menstruant is reckoned as a flux for anyone who touches it. And if he has touched [bodily] f[lux or s]emen, h[e shall] be unclean. [And he who has tou]ched a man from among all these unclean persons during the seven days of [his] cleans[ing] he shall [n]ot eat. If he has become unclean because of a corp[se, he shall bathe in wat]er, wash (his garments) and afterwards **II** he may e[at].

## 4Q274 3 i–ii

**I** . . . and he is unclean . . . [if] (the fruit's) juice [has not oozed out, he shall eat it in purity, but all those] which have been squeezed so that their juice has oozed out, no man should eat them [if] an unclean man [has to]uched them. [And al]so from the greens . . . or ripe cucumber. Whoever has . . .

**II** . . . and any (vessel) which has a seal . . . [shall be unclean] for a cleaner man. Any green [that has no] moisture of dew [on it] may be eaten. And if it is n[ot eaten, let him put it] into the midst of the water. For if a man [were to put it on] the ground, and [water] reached it when the rain [descended] on it, if an [unclean man] touches it, [let him not eat it] in the field by any means until the period [of his purification] . . .

Any earthen vessel which . . . which is in its midst . . . the liquid . . .

# 4QTohorot B–C

## (4Q276–7)

These two fragments deal with the biblical law of the 'red heifer', the ashes of which were used for the preparation of the 'water for (the removal of) uncleanness' necessary for the cleansing of impurity resulting from contact with a dead body. Relevant extracts from Num. xix are freely quoted. The subject is treated also in MMT B 13 (4Q**394** frs. 3–7 i, 16–20).

For a preliminary study, see J. M. Baumgarten, 'The Red Cow Purification Rites in Qumran Texts', *JJS* 46 (1995), 112–19.

### 4Q276

[And the priest wears the garments] in which he is not ministering in the Sanctuary ... renders the garments guilty. And he slaughtered [the] heifer before Him. He shall carry her blood in a clay vessel which is [not brough]t near the altar. And with his finger he shall sprinkle some of her blood seven [times towa]rds the front of the tent of meeting. And he shall cast the cedar wood, [the hyssop and the scarlet ma]terial in the midst of her burning. [And he who burns (it)], a man who is clean of every corpse uncleanness, [shall wash his clothes and gather] up the ashes of the heifer [and shall de]posit them to be kept [by the children of Israel for the water for uncleanness, for the removal of sin. And] the priest

### 4Q277

And the priest who atones with the blood of the heifer shall dress and all ... with [whi]ch they atone with the law of the [red heifer] ... in water [and he shall be un]clean until the evening. And he who carries the cauldron of the water for uncleanness shall be uncl[ean and shall wash himself in water and wash (his clothes). And [the] man [shall sprinkle] the water for uncleanness on those defiled by uncleanness, for a pure priest ... on them, fo[r he shall] atone for the unclean. No wanton man shall sprinkle on the unclean ... the water for uncleanness and he shall bring him to the water and shall purify him from corpse uncleanness. ... [The pri]est shall scatter on them the water for uncleanness to purify [them] ... for they will indeed be purified and their flesh shall be p[ure] and anyone who touches [him] ... his flux ... and [his] h[ands] are not drenched in water. His [b]ed and [his] dwelli[ng] shall be unclean ... they who touch his flux are like one who has touched the uncleanness of one who has touched (a corpse); [he will be unc]lean until the evening. And he who carries his [cl]othes shall wash and shall be unclean until the evening.

# 4QTohorot G [Leqet]

## (4Q284a)

Four fragments of a document, previously designated as *Leqet* (gathering), have survived in a late Hasmonaean–early Herodian script (mid-first century BCE). They deal with matters of uncleanness affecting fruits. Only fr. 1 is translatable. The phrase 'liquids of the Congregation' links this fragment to 1QS VI, 20, VII, 20.

For a preliminary study, see J. M. Baumgarten, 'Liquids and Susceptibility to Defilement in New 4Q Texts', *JQR* 85 (1994), 93–6.

### Fr. 1

... bask[et ... And let him no]t gather them ... may not touch the liquids of the Congregation, for these [render unclean the] basket and the figs [and the pomegranates, if] their [liq]uids if their ju[ice] oozes out wh[en he squee]zes them all and [a man] who has not been brou[ght into the C]ovenant has gathered them. And if they press [olives in the olive press], let him not pollute them in a[ny man]ner by opening them until he pours [them into the press]. ... in purity ...

# Exhortation by the Master addressed to the Sons of Dawn

## (4Q298)

Eight fragments of a manuscript which, apart from its title, is written in a cryptic alphabet, contain an exhortation to a group, designated as 'sons of dawn' by the 'Master' (*maskil*), the title of the teacher in charge of instruction in the Community (cf. Community Rule). The phrase, 'sons of dawn' (*bene ha-shahar*) is possibly attested in the Damascus Document XIII, 14 (cf. M. Broshi, *The Damascus Document Reconsidered*, Jerusalem, 1992, [35]: 'No member of the Covenant shall have any dealings with the sons of dawn except for payment'). The earlier reading was 'sons of the Pit' (*bene ha-shahat*). S. Pfann suggests that 'the sons of dawn' (not yet 'sons of light') are newcomers to the sect at the earliest stages of their initiation. The exhortation recalls the opening pages of the Damascus Document. The square script of the title is said to belong to the second half of the first century BCE. Parts of frs. 1–2 and 3–4 are large enough to be translated.

For a preliminary study, see Stephen Pfann, '4Q**298**: The Maskil's Address to All Sons of Dawn', *JQR* 85 (1994), 203–35. See also M. Kister, 'Commentary to 4Q**298**', ibid., 237–49.

### 4Q**298**, frs. 1–2 i

[Wor]d of the Master which he spoke to all the sons of Dawn. Liste[n to me a]ll men of heart (=intelligence) and understand my word. [And seeke]rs of righteousness, h[ea]r my word in all that proceeds from [my] lips. Those who [k]now have sear[ch]ed [th]ese (matters) and [have] returned [to the path] of life . . .

## Frs. 3–4 ii

. . . And now listen, [O wise men], and hear, O you with knowledge, hear. And men of understanding, in[crease migh]t, and modesty, you who search judgement. [You who] kn[ow the way, increase strength, and men of truth, pursu[e righteousness], and you who love kindness, increase humility . . . appointed time which . . . you will understand the end of the ages and you will gaze at ancient things to know . . .

# Register of Rebukes

## (4Q477)

Fragments of two columns of a document contain a list of Community members rebuked for offences against the rules. This is the only scroll fragment which reveals the names of individual members: Yohanan son of Ar[ ], Hananiah Notos and Hananiah son of Sim[on]. According to Esther Eshel, responsible for the preliminary edition of this work, the rebukes listed here were read out in public by the *mebaqqer* (or Guardian), hence the title given by her, The Rebukes by the Overseer. To be more precise, it is likely that the rebukes originated with witnesses of the offence. They reported it to the Guardian who was to record the infringement (cf. CD IX, 2–4; 16–20). The epithet Notos attached to the name of Hananiah probably means 'Southerner' in line with a parallel Masada inscription (no. 462: Shim'on bar Notos) according to Y. Yadin and J. Naveh, *Masada I* (Jerusalem, 1989), 40. D. Flusser, as reported by Eshel, associates Notos with the Greek nothos (bastard). In col. II, l. 8, Eshel, following M. Broshi, reads *shyr (=sh'r) bsrw* (i.e. near kin); R. Eisenman and M. Wise have *shpk bsrw* (emission of his body) and J. M. Baumgarten (*JJS* 45 (1994), 277 *swd bsrw* (the carnal foundation of man).

Frs. 1, 2 i and 3: the text is too fragmentary for translation. Note the significant phrases '[to] recall their transgression', 'men of the [Community?]', 'to rebuke' and ['c]amps of the Congregation' and 'they rebuked'.

For preliminary studies, see E. Eshel, 'The Rebukes by the Overseer', *JJS* 45 (1994), 111–22; R. Eisenman and M. Wise, *DSSU*, 269–73; C. Hempel, 'Who Rebukes in 4Q477?', *RQ* 16 (1995), 655–6; S. A. Reed, 'Genre, Setting and Title of 4Q477', *JJS* 47 (1996), 147–8.

### Fr. 2

**II** ... who ... [wh]o acted wickedly ... the Congregation ... Yohanan son of Ar ... [they rebuked because] he was short-tempered ... with him ... the iniquity with him and also the spirit of pride was with [him] ...

[blank] They rebuked Hananiah Notos because he ... [to dis]turb the spirit of the Communi[ty ... and] also to mingle the ... they rebu[k]ed because evil ... was with him and also because he was not ... and also because he loved his bodily nature (or: showed preference to his near kin) ... [blank] And [they rebuked] Hananiah son of Sim[on] [because he ... and he also loves the goodness ...

# Remonstrances (before Conversion?)

## (4Q471[a])

This small fragment, written in Herodian script, contains reproofs addressed in the second person plural to a group of wicked Jews. The context is that of a war. It is unlikely to belong to the War Scroll or the Rule of War as neither of these includes speeches to outsiders. According to a conjecture proposed by Esther Eshel and Menahem Kister, the opponents of the sect thus criticized are the ruling class of Judaea (Hasmonaeans and perhaps also Sadducees), but nothing in the surviving text positively supports their cautiously presented surmise. However, the second half of the fragment can be interpreted in a positive sense in which case the scene may be a last-minute mass conversion of unfaithful Jews before the final battle.

For a preliminary study, see Esther Eshel and Menahem Kister, 'A Polemical Qumran Fragment', *JJS* 43 (1992), 277–81.

... time(?) you have commanded not to ... You have been unfaithful to His covenant ... [You] said: Let us fight His wars for He has redeemed us ... Your [mighty men] shall be humbled. And they did not know that He has despised ... you shall show yourselves mighty in war. And you have been reckoned ... by His measuring line(?). You shall seek righteous judgement and the work ... you shall exalt yourselves. And He has chosen t[hem] ... for a cry ... And you will return ... sweet

# B. Hymns and Poems

'Thanksgiving Scroll',
*The Shrine of the Book,*
*Israel Museum, Jerusalem*

# The Thanksgiving Hymns
## (1QH, 1Q36, 4Q427–32)

The Hymns Scroll was published by E. L. Sukenik in 1954–5 (*The Dead Sea Scrolls of the Hebrew University*, Jerusalem). It has suffered a good deal of deterioration and the translator has difficulty, not only in making sense of the poems, but also in determining where one ends and another begins. For a method of restoration of the Hymns, see E. Puech, 'Quelques aspects de la restauration du Rouleau des Hymnes', *JJS* 39 (1988), 38–55. He has convincingly argued that apart from some fragments, the first three columns of the original Hymns Scroll are lost. The missing beginning should be followed by the existing columns in the following order: XVII (sheet 1), XIII–XVI (sheet 2), I–IV (sheet 3), V–VIII (sheet 4) and IX–XII of the *editio princeps*. Four further columns (XXI–XXIV) may be reconstructed with the help of the former col. XVIII and various fragments published by Sukenik. Puech tentatively suggests also two further columns (XXV–XXVI) made up from other fragments.

Our presentation of the Hymns is now rearranged according to Puech's thesis and his reconstruction of the poem in col. VI (formerly XIV) is also adopted (cf. art. cit., 53–4). No translation is offered for the extremely fragmentary cols. XXIV–XXVI, though it should be noted that col. XXV includes the beginning of a new poem, 'For the Master. A s[ong (?)]' from 1QH, fr. 8. Further fragments, occasionally used to improve the reading of 1QH, may be found at 1Q**35** (cf. also 1Q**36** and **37–40**; see *DJD*, I, 136–43) and 4Q**427–32**; see Eileen Schuller, 'The Cave 4 Hodayot Manuscripts: a Preliminary Description', *JQR* 85 (1994), 137–50; 'A Hymn from a Cave Four Hodayot Manuscript: 4Q**427** 7 i + ii', *JBL* 112 (1993), 605–28; 'A Thanksgiving Hymn from 4QHodayot$^{b}$ (4Q**428** 7)', *RQ* 16 (1995), 527–41; 'The Cave 4 *Hodayot* Manuscripts: A Preliminary Description', in H.-J. Fabry et al., *Qumranstudien*, Göttingen, 1996, 78–100.

The poems contained in the Scroll are similar to the biblical Psalms. They are mostly hymns of thanksgiving, individual prayers as opposed to those intended for communal worship, expressing a rich variety of spiritual and doctrinal detail.

But the two fundamental themes running through the whole collection are those of salvation and knowledge. The sectary thanks God continually for having been saved from the 'lot' of the wicked, and for his gift of insight into the divine mysteries. He, a 'creature of clay', has been singled out by his Maker to receive favours of which he feels himself unworthy and he alludes again and again to his frailty and total dependence on God. Whereas some of the Hymns give expression to thoughts and sentiments common to all the members of the sect, others, particularly nos. 1, 2, and 7–11, appear to refer to the experiences of a teacher abandoned by his friends and persecuted by his enemies. Several scholars tend to ascribe the authorship of these to the Teacher of Righteousness, and even consider that he may be responsible for all the Hymns. But although this hypothesis is not impossible, no sure conclusion can yet be reached. Nor are we in a position to date any particular composition. The most we can say is that the collection as such probably attained its final shape during the last pre-Christian century.

Philo's account of the banquet celebrated by the contemplative Essenes, or Therapeutae, on the Feast of Pentecost may indicate the use to which the Hymns were put. He reports that when the President of the meeting had ended his commentary on the Scriptures, he rose and chanted a hymn, either one of his own making or an old one, and after him each of his brethren did likewise (*The Contemplative Life*, § 80). Similarly, it is probable that the psalms of this Scroll were recited by the Guardian and newly initiated members at the Feast of the Renewal of the Covenant. Hymn 4 (formerly 21) expressly refers to the oath of the Covenant, and Hymn 5 (formerly 22) appears to be a poetic commentary on the liturgy marking the entry into the Community. Indeed, the relative poverty of principal themes may be due to the fact that all this poetry was intended for a special occasion and its inspirational scope was thereby limited.

Cols. I–III are missing.

**IV** (formerly **XVII**) . . .

*Hymn 1* (formerly *23*)

. . .
As Thou hast said by the hand of Moses,
  Thou forgivest transgression, iniquity, and sin,
  and pardonest rebellion and unfaithfulness.

For the bases of the mountains shall melt
  and fire shall consume the deep places of Hell,

but Thou wilt deliver
  all those that are corrected by Thy judgements,
that they may serve Thee faithfully
  and that their seed may be before Thee for ever.
  Thou wilt keep Thine oath
  and wilt pardon their transgression;
  Thou wilt cast away all their sins.

Thou wilt cause them to inherit all the glory of Adam
  and abundance of days.

### *Hymn 2* (formerly *24*)

[I give Thee thanks]
  because of the spirits which Thou hast given to me!
I [will bring forth] a reply of the tongue
  to recount Thy righteous deeds,
and the forbearance ...
  and the works of Thy mighty right hand,
  and [the pardon] of the sins of the forefathers.
[I will bow down] and implore Thy mercy
  [on my sins and wicked] deeds,
  and on the perversity of [my heart],
for I have wallowed in uncleanness,
  and have [turned aside] from the counsel [of Thy truth]
and I have not laboured ...
[For] Thine, Thine is righteousness,
  and an everlasting blessing be upon Thy Name!
[According to] Thy righteousness,
  let [Thy servant] be redeemed
  [and] the wicked be brought to an end.

For I have understood that [it is Thou
  who dost establish] the path of whomsoever Thou choosest;
Thou dost hedge him in with [true] discernment
  that he may not sin against Thee,
and that his humility [may bear fruit]
  through Thy chastisement.
[Thou dost purify] his heart in [Thy trials].
[Preserve] Thy servant, [O God], lest he sin against Thee,

or stagger aside from any word of Thy will.
Strengthen the [loins of Thy servant
that he may] resist the spirits [of falsehood,
that] he may walk in all that Thou lovest,
and despise all that Thou loathest,
[that he may do] that which is good in Thine eyes.
[Destroy] their [dominion] in my bowels,
for [within] Thy servant is a spirit of [flesh].

### *Hymn 3* (formerly 25)

[I thank Thee, O Lord,
for] Thou didst shed [Thy] Holy Spirit upon Thy Servant
...

### **V** (formerly **XIII**)

...
All these things [Thou didst establish in Thy wisdom.
Thou didst appoint] all Thy works
before ever creating them:
the host of Thy spirits
and the Congregation [of Thy Holy Ones,
the heavens and all] their hosts
and the earth and all it brings forth.
In the seas and deeps ...
... and an everlasting task;
for Thou hast established them from before eternity.

And the work of ...
and they shall recount Thy glory
throughout all Thy dominion
For Thou hast shown them that
which they had not [seen
by removing all] ancient things
and creating new ones,
by breaking asunder things anciently established,
and raising up the things of eternity.
For [Thou art from the beginning]
and shalt endure for ages without end.
And Thou hast [appointed] all these things

in the mysteries of Thy wisdom
to make known Thy glory [to all].

[But what is] the spirit of flesh
that it should understand all this,
and that it should comprehend
the great [design of Thy wisdom]?
What is he that is born of woman
in the midst of all Thy terrible [works]?
He is but an edifice of dust,
and a thing kneaded with water,
whose beginning [is sinful iniquity],
and shameful nakedness,
[and a fount of uncleanness],
and over whom a spirit of straying rules.
If he is wicked he shall become [a sign for] ever,
and a wonder to (every) generation,
[and an object of horror to all] flesh.

By Thy goodness alone is man righteous,
and with Thy many mercies [Thou strengthenest him].
Thou wilt adorn him with Thy splendour
and wilt [cause him to reign amid] many delights
with everlasting peace and length of days.
[For Thou hast spoken],
and Thou wilt not take back Thy word.

And I, Thy servant,
I know by the spirit which Thou hast given to me
[that Thy words are truth],
and that all Thy works are righteousness,
and that Thou wilt not take back Thy word

. . .

**VI** (formerly **XIV**)

. . .

*Hymn 4* (formerly *21*)

[Blessed art Thou,] O Lord
who hast given understanding
to the heart of [Thy] servant

that he may understand all these things
. . .
   and resist [the works] of wickedness
   and bless justly all those who choose Thy will,
[and that he may love all] that Thou lovest
   and loathe all that Thou [hatest].
Thou shalt instruct Thy servant
   . . . [spi]rits of man
for Thou hast cast their (lot) according to the spirits
   between good and evil
   to accomplish their task.
And I know through the understanding
   which comes from Thee,
that in Thy goodwill towards m[a]n
   [Thou hast] increa[sed his inheritance] in Thy Holy Spirit
   and thus Thou hast drawn me near to understanding of Thee.
And the closer I approach,
   the more am I filled with zeal
   against all the workers of iniquity
   and the men of deceit.

For none of those who approach Thee
   rebels against Thy command,
nor do any of those who know Thee
   alter Thy words;
for Thou art righteous,
   and all Thine elect are truth.
Thou wilt blot out all injustice and wickedness for ever,
   and Thy righteousness shall be revealed
   before the eyes of all Thy creatures.

I know through Thy great goodness;
and with an oath I have undertaken
   never to sin against Thee,
nor to do anything evil in Thine eyes.
And thus do I bring into community
   all the men of my Council.

I will cause each man to draw near
   in accordance with his understanding,

and according to the greatness of his inheritance,
so will I love him.
I will not honour an evil man,
nor consider [the bribes of shame];
I will [not] barter Thy truth for riches,
nor one of Thy precepts for bribes.
But [I will lo]ve [each ma]n
according to his sp[eech](?)
and according as Thou removest him far from Thee,
so will I hate him;
and none of those who have turned [from] Thy [Co]venant
will I bring into the Council [of Thy] t[ruth].

## *Hymn 5* (formerly 22)

[I thank] Thee, O Lord,
as befits the greatness of Thy power
and the multitude of Thy marvels for ever and ever.
[Thou art a merciful God] and rich in [favours],
pardoning those who repent of their sin
and visiting the iniquity of the wicked.
[Thou delightest in] the free-will offering [of the righteous]
but iniquity Thou hatest always.
Thou hast favoured me, Thy servant,
with a spirit of knowledge,
[that I may choose] truth [and goodness]
and loathe all the ways of iniquity.
And I have loved Thee freely
and with all my heart;
[contemplating the mysteries of] Thy wisdom
[I have sought Thee].
For this is from Thy hand
and [nothing is done] without [Thy will].
...

**VII** (formerly **XV**)

...
I have loved Thee freely
and with all my heart and soul
I have purified ...

[that I might not] turn aside from any of Thy commands.
I have clung to the Congregation . . .
that I might not be separated from any of Thy laws.

I know through the understanding which comes from Thee
that righteousness is not in a hand of flesh,
[that] man [is not master of] his way
and that it is not in mortals to direct their step.
I know that the inclination of every spirit
[is in Thy hand];
Thou didst establish [all] its [ways] before ever creating it,
and how can any man change Thy words?
Thou alone didst [create] the just
and establish him from the womb
for the time of goodwill,
that he might hearken to Thy Covenant
and walk in all (Thy ways),
and that [Thou mightest show Thyself great] to him
in the multitude of Thy mercies,
and enlarge his straitened soul to eternal salvation,
to perpetual and unfailing peace.
Thou wilt raise up his glory
from among flesh.

But the wicked Thou didst create
for [the time] of Thy [wrath],
Thou didst vow them from the womb
to the Day of Massacre,
for they walk in the way which is not good.
They have despised [Thy Covenant]
and their souls have loathed Thy [truth];
they have taken no delight in all Thy commandments
and have chosen that which Thou hatest.

[For according to the mysteries] of Thy [wisdom],
Thou hast ordained them for great chastisements
before the eyes of all Thy creatures,
that [for all] eternity
they may serve as a sign [and a wonder],

and that [all men] may know Thy glory
and Thy tremendous power.

But what is flesh
that it should understand [these things]?
And how should [a creature of] dust direct his steps?
It is Thou who didst shape the spirit
and establish its work [from the beginning];
the way of all the living proceeds from Thee.
I know that no riches equal Thy truth,
and [have therefore desired
to enter the Council of] Thy holiness.
I know that Thou hast chosen them before all others
and that they shall serve Thee for ever.
Thou wilt [take no bribe for the deeds of iniquity],
nor ransom for the works of wickedness;
for Thou art a God of truth
and [wilt destroy] all iniquity [for ever,
and] no [wickedness] shall exist before Thee.
...

## **VIII** (formerly **XVI**)

...
Because I know all these things
my tongue shall utter a reply.
Bowing down and [confessing all] my transgressions,
I will seek [Thy] spirit [of knowledge];
cleaving to Thy spirit of [holiness],
I will hold fast to the truth of Thy Covenant,
that [I may serve] Thee in truth and wholeness of heart,
and that I may love [Thy Name].

Blessed art Thou, O Lord,
Maker [of all things and mighty in] deeds:
all things are Thy work!
Behold, Thou art pleased to favour [Thy servant],
and hast graced me with Thy spirit of mercy
and [with the radiance] of Thy glory.

Thine, Thine is righteousness,
for it is Thou who hast done all [these things]!

I know that Thou hast marked the spirit of the just,
and therefore I have chosen to keep my hands clean
in accordance with [Thy] will:
the soul of Thy servant [has loathed]
every work of iniquity.
And I know that man is not righteous
except through Thee,
and therefore I implore Thee
by the spirit which Thou hast given [me]
to perfect Thy [favours] to Thy servant [for ever],
purifying me by Thy Holy Spirit,
and drawing me near to Thee by Thy grace
according to the abundance of Thy mercies
. . .
[Grant me] the place [of Thy loving-kindness]
which [Thou hast] chosen for them that love Thee
and keep [Thy commandments,
that they may stand] in Thy presence [for] ever.
. . .
Let no scourge [come] near him
lest he stagger aside from the laws of Thy Covenant.
. . .
I [know, O Lord,
that Thou art merciful] and compassionate,
[long]-suffering and [rich] in grace and truth,
pardoning transgression [and sin].
Thou repentest of [evil against them that love Thee]
and keep [Thy] commandments,
[that] return to Thee with faith
and wholeness of heart
. . . to serve Thee
[and to do that which is] good in Thine eyes.
Reject not the face of Thy servant

### *Hymn 6* (formerly *1*)

**IX** (formerly **I**)

...

Thou art long-suffering in Thy judgements
   and righteous in all Thy deeds.

By Thy wisdom [all things exist from] eternity,
   and before creating them Thou knewest their works
   for ever and ever.
[Nothing] is done [without Thee]
   and nothing is known unless Thou desire it.

Thou hast created all the spirits
   [and hast established a statute] and law
   for all their works.
Thou hast spread the heavens for Thy glory
   and hast [appointed] all [their hosts]
   according to Thy will;
the mighty winds according to their laws
   before they became angels [of holiness]
   ... and eternal spirits in their dominions;
the heavenly lights to their mysteries,
   the stars to their paths,
[the clouds] to their tasks,
   the thunderbolts and lightnings to their duty,
and the perfect treasuries (of snow and hail)
   to their purposes,
... to their mysteries.

Thou hast created the earth by Thy power
   and the seas and deeps [by Thy might].
Thou hast fashioned [all] their [inhabi]tants
   according to Thy wisdom,
   and hast appointed all that is in them
   according to Thy will.

[And] to the spirit of man
   which Thou hast formed in the world,
[Thou hast given dominion over the works of Thy hands]
   for everlasting days and unending generations.

. . . in their ages
Thou hast allotted to them tasks
  during all their generations,
and judgement in their appointed seasons
  according to the rule [of the two spirits.
For Thou hast established their ways]
  for ever and ever,
[and hast ordained from eternity]
  their visitation for reward and chastisements;
Thou hast allotted it to all their seed
  for eternal generations and everlasting years . . .
In the wisdom of Thy knowledge
  Thou didst establish their destiny before ever they were.
All things [exist] according to [Thy will]
  and without Thee nothing is done.

These things I know
  by the wisdom which comes from Thee,
for Thou hast unstopped my ears
  to marvellous mysteries.

And yet I, a shape of clay
  kneaded in water,
a ground of shame
  and a source of pollution,
a melting-pot of wickedness
  and an edifice of sin,
a straying and perverted spirit
  of no understanding,
  fearful of righteous judgements,
what can I say that is not foreknown,
  and what can I utter that is not foretold?
All things are graven before Thee
  on a written Reminder
  for everlasting ages,
and for the numbered cycles
  of the eternal years
  in all their seasons;
they are not hidden or absent from Thee.

What shall a man say
concerning his sin?
And how shall he plead
concerning his iniquities?
And how shall he reply
to righteous judgement?
For Thine, O God of knowledge,
are all righteous deeds
and the counsel of truth;
but to the sons of men is the work of iniquity
and deeds of deceit.

It is Thou who hast created breath for the tongue
and Thou knowest its words;
Thou didst establish the fruit of the lips
before ever they were.
Thou dost set words to measure
and the flow of breath from the lips to metre.
Thou bringest forth sounds
according to their mysteries,
and the flow of breath from the lips
according to its reckoning,
that they may tell of Thy glory
and recount Thy wonders
in all Thy works of truth
and [in all Thy] righteous [judgements];
and that Thy Name be praised
by the mouth of all men,
and that they may know Thee
according to their understanding
and bless Thee for ever.

By Thy mercies and by Thy great goodness,
Thou hast strengthened the spirit of man
in the face of the scourge,
and hast purified [the erring spirit]
of a multitude of sins,
that it may declare Thy marvels
in the presence of all Thy creatures.
[I will declare to the assembly of the simple]

the judgements by which I was scourged,
and to the sons of men, all Thy wonders
by which Thou hast shown Thyself mighty [in me
in the presence of the sons of Adam].

Hear, O you wise men, and meditate on knowledge;
O you fearful, be steadfast!
Increase in prudence, [O all you simple];
O just men, put away iniquity!
Hold fast [to the Covenant],
O all you perfect of way;
[O all you afflicted with] misery,
be patient and despise no righteous judgement!
. . .
[but the foo]lish of heart
shall not comprehend these things
. . .

**X** (formerly **II**)

. . .
Upon my [uncircumcised] lips
Thou hast laid a reply.
Thou hast upheld my soul,
strengthening my loins and restoring my power;
my foot has stood in the realm of ungodliness.
I have been a snare to those who rebel,
but healing to those of them who repent,
prudence to the simple,
and steadfastness to the fearful of heart.
To traitors Thou hast made of me
a mockery and scorn,
but a counsel of truth and understanding
to the upright of way.
I have been iniquity for the wicked,
ill-repute on the lips of the fierce,
the scoffers have gnashed their teeth.
I have been a byword to traitors,
the assembly of the wicked has raged against me;
they have roared like turbulent seas
and their towering waves have spat out mud and slime.

But to the elect of righteousness
  Thou hast made me a banner,
and a discerning interpreter of wonderful mysteries,
  to try [those who practise] truth
  and to test those who love correction.
To the interpreters of error I have been an opponent,
  [but a man of peace] to all those who see true things.
To all those who seek smooth things
  I have been a spirit of zeal;
like the sound of the roaring of many waters
  so have [all] the deceivers thundered against me;
  [all] their thoughts were devilish [schemings].

They have cast towards the Pit the life of the man
  whose mouth Thou hast confirmed,
and into whose heart
  Thou hast put teaching and understanding,
that he might open a fountain of knowledge
  to all men of insight.
They have exchanged them for lips of uncircumcision,
  and for the foreign tongue
  of a people without understanding,
  that they might come to ruin in their straying.

### *Hymn* 7 (formerly 2)

I thank Thee, O Lord,
  for Thou hast placed my soul
  in the bundle of the living,
and hast hedged me about
  against all the snares of the Pit.

Violent men have sought after my life
  because I have clung to Thy Covenant.
For they, an assembly of deceit,
  and a horde of Belial,
know not that my stand
  is maintained by Thee,
and that in Thy mercy Thou wilt save my soul
  since my steps proceed from Thee.

From Thee it is
  that they assail my life,
that Thou mayest be glorified
  by the judgement of the wicked,
and manifest Thy might through me
  in the presence of the sons of men;
for it is by Thy mercy that I stand.

And I said, Mighty men
  have pitched their camps against me,
and have encompassed me
  with all their weapons of war.
They have let fly arrows
  against which there is no cure,
and the flame of (their) javelins
  is like a consuming fire among trees.
The clamour of their shouting
  is like the bellowing of many waters,
like a storm of destruction
  devouring a multitude of men;
as their waves rear up,
  Naught and Vanity spout upward to the stars.
But although my heart melted like water,
  my soul held fast to Thy Covenant,
and the net which they spread for me
  has taken their own foot;
they have themselves fallen
  into the snares which they laid for my life.
But my foot remains upon level ground;
  apart from their assembly I will bless Thy Name.

### *Hymn 8* (formerly *3*)

I thank Thee, O Lord,
  for Thou hast [fastened] Thine eye upon me.
Thou hast saved me from the zeal
  of lying interpreters,
and from the congregation of those
  who seek smooth things.
Thou hast redeemed the soul of the poor one

whom they planned to destroy
by spilling his blood because he served Thee.

Because [they knew not]
that my steps were directed by Thee,
they made me an object of shame and derision
in the mouth of all the seekers of falsehood.
But Thou, O my God, hast succoured
the soul of the poor and the needy
against one stronger than he;
Thou hast redeemed my soul
from the hand of the mighty.
Thou hast not permitted their insults to dismay me
so that I forsook Thy service
for fear of the wickedness of the [ungodly],
or bartered my steadfast heart for folly
. . .

## *Hymn 9* (formerly *4*)

**XI** (formerly **III**)
. . .
They caused [me] to be
like a ship on the deeps of the [sea],
and like a fortified city
before [the aggressor],
[and] like a woman in travail
with her first-born child,
upon whose belly pangs have come
and grievous pains,
filling with anguish her child-bearing crucible.

For the children have come to the throes of Death,
and she labours in her pains who bears a man.
For amid the throes of Death
she shall bring forth a man-child,
and amid the pains of Hell
there shall spring from her child-bearing crucible
a Marvellous Mighty Counsellor;
and a man shall be delivered from out of the throes.

When he is conceived
all wombs shall quicken,
and the time of their delivery
shall be in grievous pains;
they shall be appalled
who are with child.
And when he is brought forth
every pang shall come upon the child-bearing crucible.

And they, the conceivers of Vanity,
shall be prey to terrible anguish;
the wombs of the Pit
shall be prey to all the works of horror.
The foundations of the wall shall rock
like a ship upon the face of the waters;
the heavens shall roar
with a noise of roaring,
and those who dwell in the dust,
as well as those who sail the seas,
shall be appalled by the roaring of the waters.

All their wise men
shall be like sailors on the deeps,
for all their wisdom shall be swallowed up
in the midst of the howling seas.
As the Abysses boil
above the fountains of the waters,
the towering waves and billows shall rage
with the voice of their roaring;
and as they rage,
[Hell and Abaddon] shall open
[and all] the flying arrows of the Pit.
shall send out their voice to the Abyss.

And the gates [of Hell] shall open
[on all] the works of Vanity;
and the doors of the Pit shall close
on the conceivers of wickedness;
and the everlasting bars shall be bolted
on all the spirits of Naught.

## *Hymn 10* (formerly 5)

I thank Thee, O Lord,
for Thou hast redeemed my soul from the Pit,
and from the hell of Abaddon
Thou hast raised me up to everlasting height.

I walk on limitless level ground,
and I know there is hope for him
whom Thou hast shaped from dust
for the everlasting Council.
Thou hast cleansed a perverse spirit of great sin
that it may stand with the host of the Holy Ones,
and that it may enter into community
with the congregation of the Sons of Heaven.
Thou hast allotted to man an everlasting destiny
amidst the spirits of knowledge,
that he may praise Thy Name in a common rejoicing
and recount Thy marvels before all Thy works.

And yet I, a creature of clay,
what am I?
Kneaded with water,
what is my worth and my might?
For I have stood in the realm of wickedness
and my lot was with the damned;
the soul of the poor one was carried away
in the midst of great tribulation.
Miseries of torment dogged my steps
while all the snares of the Pit were opened
and the lures of wickedness were set up
and the nets of the damned (were spread) on the waters;
while all the arrows of the Pit
flew out without cease,
and, striking, left no hope;
while the rope beat down in judgement
and a destiny of wrath (fell) upon the abandoned
and a venting of fury upon the cunning.
It was a time of the wrath of all Belial
and the bonds of death tightened without any escape.

The torrents of Belial shall reach
  to all sides of the world.
In all their channels
  a consuming fire shall destroy
  every tree, green and barren, on their banks;
unto the end of their courses
  it shall scourge with flames of fire,
and shall consume the foundations of the earth
  and the expanse of dry land.
The bases of the mountains shall blaze
  and the roots of the rocks shall turn
  to torrents of pitch;
it shall devour as far as the great Abyss.

The torrents of Belial shall break into Abaddon,
  and the deeps of the Abyss shall groan
  amid the roar of heaving mud.
The land shall cry out because of the calamity
  fallen upon the world,
  and all its deeps shall howl.
And all those upon it shall rave
  and shall perish amid the great misfortune.
For God shall sound His mighty voice,
  and His holy abode shall thunder
  with the truth of His glory.
The heavenly hosts shall cry out
  and the world's foundations
  shall stagger and sway.
The war of the heavenly warriors shall scourge the earth;
  and it shall not end before the appointed destruction
  which shall be for ever and without compare.

## *Hymn 11* (formerly *6*)

I thank Thee, O Lord,
  for Thou art as a fortified wall to me,
  and as an iron bar against all destroyers
...
Thou hast set my feet upon rock ...
  that I may walk in the way of eternity

and in the paths which Thou hast chosen
. . .

**XII** (formerly **IV**)
. . .

*Hymn 12* (formerly 7)

I thank Thee, O Lord,
for Thou hast illumined my face by Thy Covenant,
. . .
I seek Thee,
and sure as the dawn
Thou appearest as [perfect Light] to me.
Teachers of lies [have smoothed] Thy people [with words],
and [false prophets] have led them astray;
they perish without understanding
for their works are in folly.
For I am despised by them
and they have no esteem for me
that Thou mayest manifest Thy might through me.
They have banished me from my land like a bird from its nest;
all my friends and brethren are driven far from me
and hold me for a broken vessel.

And they, teachers of lies and seers of falsehood,
have schemed against me a devilish scheme,
to exchange the Law engraved on my heart by Thee
for the smooth things (which they speak) to Thy people.
And they withhold from the thirsty the drink of Knowledge,
and assuage their thirst with vinegar,
that they may gaze on their straying,
on their folly concerning their feast-days,
on their fall into their snares.

But Thou, O God,
dost despise all Belial's designs;
it is Thy purpose that shall be done
and the design of Thy heart
that shall be established for ever.

As for them, they dissemble,
  they plan devilish schemes.
They seek Thee with a double heart
  and are not confirmed in Thy truth
A root bearing poisoned and bitter fruit
  is in their designs;
they walk in stubbornness of heart
  and seek Thee among idols,
and they set before themselves
  the stumbling-block of their sin.
They come to inquire of Thee
  from the mouth of lying prophets deceived by error
who speak [with strange] lips to Thy people,
  and an alien tongue,
that they may cunningly turn
  all their works to folly.

For [they hearken] not [to] Thy [voice],
  nor do they give ear to Thy word;
of the vision of knowledge they say, ‘It is unsure’,
  and of the way of Thy heart, ‘It is not (the way)’.
But Thou, O God, wilt reply to them,
chastising them in Thy might
  because of their idols
  and because of the multitude of their sins,
that they who have turned aside from Thy Covenant
  may be caught in their own designs.
Thou wilt destroy in Judgement
  all men of lies,
  and there shall be no more seers of error;
for in Thy works is no folly,
  no guile in the design of Thy heart.
But those who please Thee
  shall stand before Thee for ever;
those who walk in the way of Thy heart
  shall be established for evermore.

Clinging to Thee, I will stand.
I will rise against those who despise me
  and my hand shall be turned

against those who deride me;
for they have no esteem for me
[that Thou mayest] manifest Thy might through me.
Thou hast revealed Thyself to me in Thy power
as perfect Light,
and Thou hast not covered my face with shame.
All those who are gathered in Thy Covenant
inquire of me,
and they hearken to me who walk in the way of Thy heart,
who array themselves for Thee
in the Council of the holy.

Thou wilt cause their law to endure for ever
and truth to go forward unhindered,
and Thou wilt not allow them to be led astray
by the hand of the damned
when they plot against them.
Thou wilt put the fear of them into Thy people
and (wilt make of them) a hammer
to all the peoples of the lands,
that at the Judgement they may cut off
all those who transgress Thy word.

Through me Thou hast illumined
the face of the Congregation
and hast shown Thine infinite power.
For Thou hast given me knowledge
through Thy marvellous mysteries,
and hast shown Thyself mighty within me
in the midst of Thy marvellous Council.
Thou hast done wonders before the Congregation
for the sake of Thy glory,
that they may make known Thy mighty deeds to all the living.

But what is flesh (to be worthy) of this?
What is a creature of clay
for such great marvels to be done,
whereas he is in iniquity from the womb
and in guilty unfaithfulness until his old age?
Righteousness, I know, is not of man,

nor is perfection of way of the son of man:
to the Most High God belong all righteous deeds.
The way of man is not established
except by the spirit which God created for him
to make perfect a way for the children of men,
that all His creatures may know
the might of His power,
and the abundance of His mercies
towards all the sons of His grace.

As for me, shaking and trembling seize me
and all my bones are broken;
my heart dissolves like wax before fire
and my knees are like water
pouring down a steep place.
For I remember my sins
and the unfaithfulness of my fathers.
When the wicked rose against Thy Covenant
and the damned against Thy word,
I said in my sinfulness,
'I am forsaken by Thy Covenant.'
But calling to mind the might of Thy hand
and the greatness of Thy compassion,
I rose and stood,
and my spirit was established
in face of the scourge.

I lean on Thy grace
and on the multitude of Thy mercies,
for Thou wilt pardon iniquity,
and through Thy righteousness
[Thou wilt purify man] of his sin.
Not for his sake wilt Thou do it,
[but for the sake of Thy glory].
For Thou hast created the just and the wicked
...

**XIII** (formerly **V**)

...

### *Hymn 13* (formerly *8*)

I thank Thee, O Lord,
for Thou hast not abandoned me
whilst I sojourned among a people [burdened with sin].

[Thou hast not] judged me
according to my guilt,
nor hast Thou abandoned me
because of the designs of my inclination;
but Thou hast saved my life from the Pit.
Thou hast brought [Thy servant deliverance]
in the midst of lions destined for the guilty,
and of lionesses which crush the bones of the mighty
and drink the blood of the brave.

Thou hast caused me to dwell with the many fishers
who spread a net upon the face of the waters,
and with the hunters of the children of iniquity;
Thou hast established me there for justice.
Thou hast confirmed the counsel of truth in my heart
and the waters of the Covenant for those who seek it.
Thou hast closed up the mouth of the young lions
whose teeth are like a sword,
and whose great teeth are like a pointed spear,
like the venom of dragons.
All their design is for robbery
and they have lain in wait;
but they have not opened their mouth against me.

For Thou, O God, hast sheltered me
from the children of men,
and hast hidden Thy Law [within me]
against the time when Thou shouldst reveal
Thy salvation to me.
For Thou hast not forsaken me
in my soul's distress,
and Thou hast heard my cry
in the bitterness of my soul;
and when I groaned,
Thou didst consider my sorrowful complaint.

Thou hast preserved the soul of the poor one
in the den of lions
which sharpened their tongue like a sword.
Thou hast closed up their teeth, O God,
lest they rend the soul of the poor and needy.
Thou hast made their tongue go back
like a sword to its scabbard
[lest] the soul of Thy servant [be blotted out].

Thou hast dealt wondrously with the poor one
to manifest Thy might within me
in the presence of the sons of men.
Thou hast placed him in the melting-pot,
[like gold] in the fire,
and like silver refined
in the melting-pot of the smelters,
to be purified seven times.
The wicked and fierce have stormed against me
with their afflictions;
they have pounded my soul all day.
But Thou, O my God,
hast changed the tempest to a breeze;
Thou hast delivered the soul of the poor one
like [a bird from the net
and like] prey from the mouth of lions.

### *Hymn 14* (formerly *9*)

I thank Thee (corrected: Blessed art Thou) O Lord,
for Thou hast not abandoned the fatherless
or despised the poor.
For Thy might [is boundless]
and Thy glory beyond measure
and wonderful Heroes minister to Thee;
yet [hast Thou done marvels] among the humble
in the mire underfoot,
and among those eager for righteousness,
causing all the well-loved poor
to rise up together from the trampling.

But I have been [iniquity to] those who contend with me,
dispute and quarrelling to my friends,
wrath to the members of my Covenant
and murmuring and protest to all my companions.

[All who have ea]ten my bread
have lifted their heel against me,
and all those joined to my Council
have mocked me with wicked lips.
The members of my [Covenant] have rebelled
and have murmured round about me;
they have gone as talebearers
before the children of mischief
concerning the mystery which Thou hast hidden in me.
And to show Thy great[ness] through me,
and because of their guilt,
Thou hast hidden the fountain of understanding
and the counsel of truth.

They consider but the mischief of their heart;
[with] devilish [schemings] they unsheathe
a perfidious tongue
from which ever springs the poison of dragons.
And like (serpents) which creep in the dust,
so do they let fly [their poisonous darts],
viper's [venom] against which there is no charm;
and this has brought incurable pain,
a malignant scourge
within the body of Thy servant,
causing [his spirit] to faint
and draining his strength
so that he maintains no firm stand.

They have overtaken me in a narrow pass without escape
and there is no [rest for me in my trial].
They sound my censure upon a harp
and their murmuring and storming upon a zither.
Anguish [seizes me]
like the pangs of a woman in travail,
and my heart is troubled within me.

I am clothed in blackness
  and my tongue cleaves to the roof [of my mouth];
[for I fear the mischief of] their heart
  and their inclination (towards evil)
  appears as bitterness before me.
The light of my face is dimmed to darkness
  and my radiance is turned to decay.

For Thou, O God, didst widen my heart,
  but they straiten it with affliction
  and hedge me about with darkness.
I eat the bread of wailing
  and drink unceasing tears;
truly, my eyes are dimmed by grief,
  and my soul by daily bitterness.
[Groaning] and sorrow encompass me
  and ignominy covers my face.
My bread is turned into an adversary
  and my drink into an accuser;
it has entered into my bones
  causing my spirit to stagger
  and my strength to fail.
According to the mysteries of sin,
  they change the works of God by their transgression.

Truly, I am bound with untearable ropes
  and with unbreakable chains.
A thick wall [fences me in],
  iron bars and gates [of bronze];
my [prison] is counted with the Abyss
  as being without [any escape]
...
[The torrents of Belial] have encompassed my soul
  [leaving me without deliverance]
...

### *Hymn 14* (formerly *10*)

**XIV** (formerly **VI**)

. . .
Thou hast unstopped my ears
[to the correction] of those who reprove with justice
. . .
[Thou hast saved me] from the congregation of [vanity]
and from the assembly of violence;
Thou hast brought me into the Council of . . .
[and hast purified me of] sin.
And I know there is hope
for those who turn from transgression
and for those who abandon sin
. . .
and to walk without wickedness
in the way of Thy heart.
I am consoled for the roaring of the peoples,
and for the tumult of k[ing]doms when they assemble;
[for] in a little while, I know,
Thou wilt raise up survivors among Thy people
and a remnant within Thine inheritance.
Thou wilt purify and cleanse them of their sin
for all their deeds are in Thy truth.
Thou wilt judge them in Thy great loving-kindness
and in the multitude of Thy mercies
and in the abundance of Thy pardon,
teaching them according to Thy word;
and Thou wilt establish them in Thy Council
according to the uprightness of Thy truth.

Thou wilt do these things for Thy glory
and for Thine own sake,
to [magnify] the Law and [the truth
and to enlighten] the members of Thy Council
in the midst of the sons of men,
that they may recount Thy marvels
for everlasting generations
and [meditate] unceasingly upon Thy mighty deeds.

All the nations shall acknowledge Thy truth,
  and all the people Thy glory.

For Thou wilt bring Thy glorious [salvation]
  to all the men of Thy Council,
  to those who share a common lot
  with the Angels of the Face.
And among them shall be no mediator to [invoke Thee],
  and no messenger [to make] reply;
for . . .
They shall reply according to Thy glorious word
  and shall be Thy princes in the company [of the Angels].

They shall send out a bud [for ever]
  like a flower [of the fields],
and shall cause a shoot to grow
  into the boughs of an everlasting Plant.
It shall cover the whole [earth] with its shadow
  [and its crown] (shall reach) to the [clouds];
its roots (shall go down) to the Abyss
  [and all the rivers of Eden shall water its branches].
. . .
A source of light
  shall become an eternal ever-flowing fountain,
and in its bright flames
  all the [sons of iniquity] shall be consumed;
[it shall be] a fire to devour all sinful men
  in utter destruction.

They who bore the yoke of my testimony
  have been led astray [by teachers of lies],
  [and have rebelled] against the service of righteousness.
Whereas Thou, O my God, didst command them
  to mend their ways
[by walking] in the way of [holiness],
  where no man goes who is uncircumcised
  or unclean or violent,
they have staggered aside from the way of Thy heart
  and languish in [great] wretchedness.
A counsel of Belial is in their heart

[and in accordance with] their wicked design
they wallow in sin.

[I am] as a sailor in a ship
amid furious seas;
their waves and all their billows
roar against me.
[There is no] calm in the whirlwind
that I may restore my soul,
no path that I may straighten my way
on the face of the waters.
The deeps resound to my groaning
and [my soul has journeyed] to the gates of death.

But I shall be as one who enters a fortified city,
as one who seeks refuge behind a high wall
until deliverance (comes);
I will [lean on] Thy truth, O my God.
For Thou wilt set the foundation on rock
and the framework by the measuring-cord of justice;
and the tried stones [Thou wilt lay]
by the plumb-line [of truth],
to [build] a mighty [wall] which shall not sway;
and no man entering there shall stagger.

For no enemy shall ever invade [it
since its doors shall be] doors of protection
through which no man shall pass;
and its bars shall be firm
and no man shall break them.
No rabble shall enter in with their weapons of war
until all the [arrows] of the war of wickedness
have come to an end.

And then at the time of Judgement
the Sword of God shall hasten,
and all the sons of His truth shall awake
to [overthrow] wickedness;
all the sons of iniquity shall be no more.
The Hero shall bend his bow;
the fortress shall open on to endless space

and the everlasting gates shall send out weapons of war.
They shall be mighty
   from end to end [of the earth
and there shall be no escape]
   for the guilty of heart [in their battle];
they shall be utterly trampled down
   without any [remnant.
There shall be no] hope
   in the greatness [of their might],
   no refuge for the mighty warriors;
for [the battle shall be] to the Most High God
. . .
Hoist a banner,
   O you who lie in the dust!
O bodies gnawed by worms,
   raise up an ensign for [the destruction of wickedness]!
[The sinful shall] be destroyed
   in the battles against the ungodly.

The scourging flood when it advances
   shall not invade the stronghold
. . .

**XV** (formerly **VII**)

. . .
As for me, I am dumb . . .
[my arm] is torn from its shoulder
   and my foot has sunk into the mire.
My eyes are closed by the spectacle of evil,
   and my ears by the crying of blood.
My heart is dismayed by the mischievous design,
   for Belial is manifest in their (evil) inclination.
All the foundations of my edifice totter
   and my bones are pulled out of joint;
my bowels heave like a ship in a violent tempest
   and my heart is utterly distressed.
A whirlwind engulfs me
   because of the mischief of their sin.

## *Hymn 15* (formerly *11*)

I thank Thee, O Lord,
  for Thou hast upheld me by Thy strength.
Thou hast shed Thy Holy Spirit upon me
  that I may not stumble.

Thou hast strengthened me
  before the battles of wickedness,
and during all their disasters
  Thou hast not permitted that fear
  should cause me to desert Thy Covenant.
Thou hast made me like a strong tower, a high wall,
  and hast established my edifice upon rock;
eternal foundations
  serve for my ground,
and all my ramparts are a tried wall
  which shall not sway.

Thou hast placed me, O my God,
  among the branches of the Council of Holiness;
Thou hast [established my mouth] in Thy Covenant,
  and my tongue is like that of Thy disciples;
  whereas the spirit of disaster is without a mouth
  and all the sons of iniquity without a reply;
  for the lying lips shall be dumb.
For Thou wilt condemn in Judgement
  all those who assail me,
distinguishing through me
  between the just and the wicked.
For Thou knowest the whole intent of a creature,
  Thou discernest every reply,
and Thou hast established my heart
  [on] Thy teaching and truth,
directing my steps into the paths of righteousness
  that I may walk before Thee
  in the land [of the living],
into paths of glory and [infinite] peace
  which shall [never] end.
For Thou knowest the inclination of Thy servant,

that I have not relied [upon the works of my hands]
to raise up [my heart],
nor have I sought refuge
in my own strength.
I have no fleshly refuge,
[and Thy servant has] no righteous deeds
to deliver him from the [Pit of no] forgiveness.
But I lean on the [abundance of Thy mercies]
and hope [for the greatness] of Thy grace,
that Thou wilt bring [salvation] to flower
and the branch to growth,
providing refuge in (Thy) strength
[and raising up my heart].

[For in] Thy righteousness
Thou hast appointed me for Thy Covenant,
and I have clung to Thy truth
and [gone forward in Thy ways].

Thou hast made me a father to the sons of grace,
and as a foster-father to men of marvel;
they have opened their mouths like little babes ...
like a child playing in the lap of its nurse.
Thou hast lifted my horn above those who insult me,
and those who attack me
[sway like the boughs] (of a tree);
my enemies are like chaff before the wind,
and my dominion is over the sons [of iniquity,
For] Thou hast succoured my soul, O my God,
and hast lifted my horn on high.
And I shall shine in a seven-fold light
in [the Council appointed by] Thee for Thy glory;
for Thou art an everlasting heavenly light to me
and wilt establish my feet
[upon level ground for ever].

### *Hymn 16* (formerly *12*)

I [thank Thee, O Lord],
for Thou hast enlightened me through Thy truth.

In Thy marvellous mysteries,
and in Thy loving-kindness to a man [of vanity,
and] in the greatness of Thy mercy to a perverse heart
  Thou hast granted me knowledge.

Who is like Thee among the gods, O Lord,
  and who is according to Thy truth?
Who, when he is judged,
  shall be righteous before Thee?
For no spirit can reply to Thy rebuke
  nor can any withstand Thy wrath.

Yet Thou bringest all the sons of Thy truth
  in forgiveness before Thee,
[to cleanse] them of their faults
  through Thy great goodness,
and to establish them before Thee
  through the multitude of Thy mercies
  for ever and ever.

For Thou art an eternal God;
  all Thy ways are determined for ever [and ever]
  and there is none other beside Thee.
And what is a man of Naught and Vanity
  that he should understand Thy marvellous mighty deeds?

### *Hymn 17* (formerly *13*)

[I thank] Thee, O God,
  for Thou hast not cast my lot
  in the congregation of Vanity,
  nor hast Thou placed {my decree} (4Q**428** 7)
  in the council of the cunning.
[Thou hast] called me to Thy grace
  and to [Thy] forgiveness Thou hast brought me,
and, by the multitude of Thy mercies,
  to all judgements of [righteousness.
As for me, I am an] uncl[ean ma]n,
  and from the womb of her who conceived me
I am an unclean man,
  and from the womb of her who has conceived me

I am in sinful guilt,
  [and from the breast of my mother] in injustice,
  and in the bosom [of my nurse] in great impurity.
And from my youth (I am) in blo[od,
  and until [my old age in the iniquity of the flesh.
But Thou,] O my God,
Thou hast established my feet in the way of Thy heart,
  and hast opened] my ears to [Thy wonderful] tidings,
  and my heart to understand Thy truth

**XVI** (formerly **VIII**)

. . .
for I have closed my ears to Thy teaching
  until . . .
. . . [without] knowledge
hast Thou cut out of me,
  and glor[y] . . .
  [no] more for me a stumbling-block of iniquity.
For Thou dost rev[eal Thy salvation],
  and Thy righteousness is made firm for ever.
For m[an] is not the master of his way,
  f[or] Thou hast done [all this for Thy glory.]

### *Hymn 18* (formerly *14*)

I [thank Thee, O Lord,
  for] Thou hast placed me beside a fountain of streams
  in an arid land,
and close to a spring of waters
  in a dry land,
and beside a watered garden
  [in a wilderness].

[For Thou didst set] a plantation
  of cypress, pine, and cedar for Thy glory,
trees of life beside a mysterious fountain
  hidden among the trees by the water,
and they put out a shoot
  of the everlasting Plant.
But before they did so, they took root

and sent out their roots to the watercourse
that its stem might be open to the living waters
and be one with the everlasting spring.

And all [the beasts] of the forest
fed on its leafy boughs;
its stem was trodden by all who passed on the way
and its branches by all the birds.
And all the [trees] by the water rose above it
for they grew in their plantation;
but they sent out no root to the watercourse.

And the bud of the shoot of holiness
of the Plant of truth
was hidden and was not esteemed;
and being unperceived,
its mystery was sealed.
Thou didst hedge in its fruit, [O God],
with the mystery of mighty Heroes
and of spirits of holiness
and of the whirling flame of fire.
No [man shall approach] the well-spring of life
or drink the waters of holiness
with the everlasting trees,
or bear fruit with [the Plant] of heaven,
who seeing has not discerned,
and considering has not believed
in the fountain of life,
who has turned [his hand against] the everlasting [bud].

And I was despised by tumultuous rivers
for they cast up their slime upon me.

But Thou, O my God, hast put into my mouth
as it were rain for all [those who thirst]
and a fount of living waters which shall not fail.
When they are opened they shall not run dry;
they shall be a torrent [overflowing its banks]
and like the [bottom]less seas.
They shall suddenly gush forth

which were hidden in secret,
[and shall be like the waters of the Flood
to every tree], both the green and the barren;
to every beast and bird [they shall be an abyss.
The trees shall sink like] lead in the mighty waters,
fire [shall burn among them]
and they shall be dried up;
but the fruitful Plant
[by the] everlasting [spring
shall be] an Eden of glory
[bearing] fruits [of life].

By my hand Thou hast opened for them
a well-spring and ditches,
[that all their channels] may be laid out
according to a certain measuring-cord,
and the planting of their trees
according to the plumb-line of the sun,
that [their boughs may become
a beautiful] Branch of glory.
When I lift my hand to dig its ditches
its roots shall run deep into hardest rock
and its stem . . . in the earth;
in the season of heat it shall keep its strength.
But if I take away my hand
it shall be like a thistle [in the wilderness];
its stem shall be like nettles in a salty land,
and thistles and thorns shall grow from its ditches,
and brambles and briars.
Its border [trees] shall be like the wild grapevine
whose foliage withers before the heat,
and its stem shall not be open to [the spring].

[Behold, I am] carried away with the sick;
[I am acquainted] with scourges.
I am forsaken in [my sorrow] . . .
and without any strength.
For my sore breaks out in bitter pains
and in incurable sickness impossible to stay;
[my heart laments] within me

as in those who go down to Hell.
My spirit is imprisoned with the dead
for [my life] has reached the Pit;
my soul languishes [within me]
day and night without rest.

My wound breaks out like burning fire
shut up in [my bones],
whose flames devour me for days on end,
diminishing my strength for times on end
and destroying my flesh for seasons on end.
The pains fly out [towards me]
and my soul within me languishes even to death.
My strength has gone from my body
and my heart runs out like water;
my flesh is dissolved like wax
and the strength of my loins is turned to fear.

My arm is torn from its socket
[and I can] lift my hand [no more];
My [foot] is held by fetters
and my knees slide like water;
I can no longer walk.
I cannot step forward lightly,
[for my legs and arms] are bound by shackles
which cause me to stumble.
The tongue has gone back which Thou didst make
marvellously mighty within my mouth;
it can no longer give voice.
[I have no word] for my disciples
to revive the spirit of those who stumble
and to speak words of support to the weary.
My circumcised lips are dumb.
. . .

**XVII** (formerly **IX**)

. . .
[For] the throes of death [encompass me]
and Hell is upon my bed;
my couch utters a lamentation

[and my pallet] the sound of a complaint.
My eyes are like fire in the furnace
and my tears like rivers of water;
my eyes grow dim with waiting,
[for my salvation] is far from me
and my life is apart from me.

But behold,
from desolation to ruin,
and from the pain to the sore,
and from the travail to the throes,
my soul meditates on Thy marvellous works.
In Thy mercies Thou hast not cast me aside;
season by season, my soul shall delight
in the abundance of mercy.
I will reply to him who slanders me
and I will rebuke my oppressor;
I will declare his sentence unjust
and declare Thy judgement righteous.

For I know by Thy truth,
and I choose Thy judgement upon me:
I delight in my scourges
for I hope for Thy loving-kindness.
Thou hast put a supplication
in the mouth of Thy servant
and Thou hast not threatened my life
nor rejected my peace.
Thou hast not failed my expectation,
but hast upheld my spirit in face of the scourge.

For it is Thou who hast founded my spirit
and Thou knowest my intent;
in my distress Thou hast comforted me.
I delight in forgiveness,
and am consoled for the former transgression;
for I know there is hope in Thy grace
and expectation in Thy great power.
For no man can be just in Thy judgement
or [righteous in] Thy trial.

Though one man be more just than another,
one person [more] wise [than another],
one mortal more glorious
than another creature [of clay],
yet is there no power to compare with Thy might.
There is no [bound] to Thy glory,
and to Thy wisdom, no measure;
[to Thy truth] there is no ...
and all who forsake it ...

...

and my oppressor shall [not] prevail against me.
I will be a stumbling-block to [those who swallow me up,
and a snare to] all those who battle against me;
[I will be for my enemies a] cause of shame,
and a cause of disgrace
to those who murmur against me.
For Thou, O my God ...
Thou wilt plead my cause;
for it is according to the mystery of Thy wisdom
that Thou hast rebuked me.

Thou wilt conceal the truth until [its] time,
[and righteousness] until its appointed moment.
Thy rebuke shall become my joy and gladness,
and my scourges shall turn to [eternal] healing
and everlasting [peace].
The scorn of my enemies shall become a crown of glory,
and my stumbling (shall change) to everlasting might.

For in Thy ...
and my light shall shine forth in Thy glory.
For as a light from out of the darkness,
so wilt Thou enlighten me.
[Thou wilt bring healing to] my wound,
and marvellous might in place of my stumbling,
and everlasting space to my straitened soul.
For Thou art my refuge, my high mountain,
my stout rock and my fortress;
in Thee will I shelter

from all the [designs of ungodliness,
for Thou wilt succour me] with eternal deliverance.

For Thou hast known me from (the time of) my father,
[and hast chosen me] from the womb.
[From the belly of] my mother
Thou hast dealt kindly with me,
and from the breast of her who conceived me
have Thy mercies been with me.
[Thy grace was with me] in the lap of her who reared me,
and from my youth Thou hast illumined me
with the wisdom of Thy judgement.

Thou hast upheld me with certain truth;
Thou hast delighted me with Thy Holy Spirit
and [hast opened my heart] till this day.
Thy just rebuke accompanies my [faults]
and Thy safeguarding peace delivers my soul.
The abundance of (Thy) forgiveness is with my steps
and infinite mercy accompanies Thy judgement of me.
Until I am old Thou wilt care for me;
for my father knew me not
and my mother abandoned me to Thee.
For Thou art a father
to all [the sons] of Thy truth,
and as a woman who tenderly loves her babe,
so dost Thou rejoice in them;
and as a foster-father bearing a child in his lap
so carest Thou for all Thy creatures.

*Hymn 19* (formerly *15*)

[I thank Thee, O Lord]
...

**XVIII** (formerly **X**)
... and nothing exists except by Thy will;
none can consider [Thy deep secrets]
or contemplate Thy [mysteries].

What then is man that is earth,
  that is shaped [from clay] and returns to the dust,
that Thou shouldst give him to understand such marvels
  and make known to him the counsel of [Thy truth]?

Clay and dust that I am,
  what can I devise unless Thou wish it,
  and what contrive unless Thou desire it?
What strength shall I have
  unless Thou keep me upright,
and how shall I understand
  unless by (the spirit) which Thou hast shaped for me?
What can I say unless Thou open my mouth
  and how can I answer unless Thou enlighten me?
Behold, Thou art Prince of gods
  and King of majesties,
Lord of all spirits,
  and Ruler of all creatures;
nothing is done without Thee,
  and nothing is known without Thy will.
Beside Thee there is nothing,
  and nothing can compare with Thee in strength;
in the presence of Thy glory there is nothing,
  and Thy might is without price.

Who among Thy great and marvellous creatures
  can stand in the presence of Thy glory?
  How then can he who returns to his dust?
For Thy glory's sake alone hast Thou made all these things.

## *Hymn 20* (formerly *16*)

Blessed art Thou, O Lord,
  God of mercy [and abundant] grace,
for Thou hast made known [Thy wisdom to me
  that I should recount] Thy marvellous deeds,
  keeping silence neither by day nor [by night]!

[For I have trusted] in Thy grace.
In Thy great goodness,

and in [the multitude of Thy mercies]
...
For I have leaned on Thy truth
...
[And unless] Thou rebuke,
there is no stumbling;
unless Thou foreknow it,
[there is no] scourge;
[nothing is done without] Thy [will].

[I will cling to Thy ways]
according to my knowledge [of Thy] truth;
contemplating Thy glory
I will recount Thy wonderful works,
and understanding [Thy goodness
I will lean on the] multitude of Thy mercies
and hope for Thy forgiveness.

For Thou Thyself hast shaped [my spirit]
and established me [according to Thy will];
and Thou hast not placed my support in gain,
[nor does] my [heart delight in riches];
Thou hast given me no fleshly refuge.
The might of warriors [rests] on abundant delights,
[and on plenty of corn] and wine and oil;
they pride themselves in possessions and wealth.
[But the righteous is like a] green [tree]
beside streams of water,
bringing forth leaves and multiplying its branches;
for [Thou hast chosen them
from among the children of] men
that they may all grow fat from the land.

Thou wilt give to the children of Thy truth
[unending joy and] everlasting [gladness],
and according to the measure of their knowledge,
so shall they be honoured one more than another.

And likewise for the son of man ...
Thou wilt increase his portion
in the knowledge of Thy truth,

and according to the measure of his knowledge,
so shall he be honoured . . .
[For the soul] of Thy servant has loathed [riches] and gain,
and he has not [desired] exquisite delights.
My heart rejoices in Thy Covenant
and Thy truth delights my soul.
I shall flower [like the lily]
and my heart shall be open to the everlasting fountain;
my support shall be in the might from on high.
But . . .
and withers like a flower before [the heat].
My heart is stricken with terror,
and my loins with trembling;
my groaning goes down to the Abyss,
and is shut up in the chambers of Hell.
I am greatly afraid when I hear of Thy judgement
of the mighty Heroes,
and of Thy trial of the host
of Thy Holy Ones
. . .

**XIX** (formerly **XI**)
. . .

### *Hymn 21* (formerly *17*)

I thank Thee, my God,
for Thou hast dealt wondrously to dust,
and mightily towards a creature of clay!
I thank Thee, I thank Thee!

What am I, that Thou shouldst [teach] me
the counsel of Thy truth,
and give me understanding
of Thy marvellous works;
that Thou shouldst lay hymns of thanksgiving
within my mouth
and [praise] upon my tongue,
and that of my circumcised lips
(Thou shouldst make) a seat of rejoicing?

I will sing Thy mercies,
   and on Thy might I will meditate all day long.
I will bless Thy Name evermore.
I will declare Thy glory in the midst of the sons of men
   and my soul shall delight in Thy great goodness.

I know that Thy word is truth,
   and that righteousness is in Thy hand;
that all knowledge is in Thy purpose,
   and that all power is in Thy might,
   and that every glory is Thine.
In Thy wrath are all chastisements,
   but in Thy goodness is much forgiveness
   and Thy mercy is towards the sons of Thy goodwill.
For Thou hast made known to them
   the counsel of Thy truth,
and hast taught them Thy marvellous mysteries.

For the sake of Thy glory
   Thou hast purified man of sin
that he may be made holy for Thee,
   with no abominable uncleanness
   and no guilty wickedness;
that he may be one [with] the children of Thy truth
   and partake of the lot of Thy Holy Ones;
that bodies gnawed by worms may be raised from the dust
   to the counsel [of Thy truth],
and that the perverse spirit (may be lifted)
   to the understanding [which comes from Thee];
that he may stand before Thee
   with the everlasting host
   and with [Thy] spirits [of holiness],
to be renewed together with all the living
   and to rejoice together with them that know.

### *Hymn* 22 (formerly *18*)

I thank Thee, my God!
I praise Thee, my Rock!
. . .

For Thou hast made known to me the counsel of Thy truth
[and hast taught me Thy marvellous mysteries;]

and hast revealed Thy [wonders] to me.
I have beheld {Thy marvels} (4Q**427** fr. 1, 1) [towards the children] of grace,
and I know [that] righteousness is Thine,
that in Thy mercies there is [hope for me],
but without Thy grace [destruction] without end.
But a fountain of bitter mourning opens for me,
[and my tears fall down].
Distress is not hidden from my eyes
when I think of the (evil) inclinations of man,
of his return [to dust],
{I understand and observe} (4Q**427** fr. 1, 3) sin and the sorrow of guilt.
They enter my heart and reach into my bones
to...
and to meditate in sorrowful meditation.
I will groan with the zither of lamentation
in all grief-stricken mourning and bitter complaint
until iniquity and [wickedness] are consumed
and the disease-bringing scourge is no more.
Then will I play on the zither of deliverance
and the harp of joy,
[on the tabors of prayer] and the pipe of praise
without end.

Who among all Thy creatures
is able to recount [Thy wonders]?
May Thy Name be praised
by the mouth of all men!
May they bless Thee for ever
in accordance with [their understanding],
and proclaim Thee with the voice of praise
in the company of [the Sons of Heaven]!
There shall be neither groaning nor complaint
and wickedness [shall be destroyed for ever];
Thy truth shall be revealed in eternal glory
and everlasting peace.

Blessed art [Thou, O my Lord],
who hast given to [Thy servant]
  the knowledge of wisdom
that he may comprehend Thy wonders,
  and recount Thy . . .
  in Thy abundant grace!
Blessed art Thou,
  O God of mercy and compassion,
for the might of Thy [power]
  and the greatness of Thy truth,
and for the multitude of Thy favours
  in all Thy works!
Rejoice the soul of Thy servant with Thy truth
  and cleanse me by Thy righteousness.
Even as I have hoped in Thy goodness,
  and waited for Thy grace,
so hast Thou freed me from my calamities
  in accordance with Thy forgiveness;
and in my distress Thou hast comforted me
  for I have leaned on Thy mercy.

Blessed art Thou, O Lord,
  for it is Thou who hast done these things!
Thou hast set [hymns of praise]
  within the mouth of Thy servant,
and hast established for me a response of the tongue.
. . .

*Hymn 23* (formerly *19*)

**XX** (formerly **XII**)

. . . {with the ever[lasting] spirits} (4Q**427**, fr. 3 ii, l. 4)
securely in a dwelling {of peac[e,} (4Q**427**, fr. 2, ll. 1–2)
in sil]ence and quietness in the tents of security and salvation.

I will praise Thy Name among them that fear Thee.
Bowing down in prayer I will beg Thy favours
  from season to season always:

when light emerges from [its dwelling-place],
and when the day reaches its appointed end
in accordance with the laws
of the Great Light of heaven;
when evening falls and light departs
at the beginning of the dominion of darkness,
at the hour appointed for night,
and at its end when morning returns
and (the shadows) retire to their dwelling-place
before the approach of light;
always;
at the genesis of every period
and at the beginning of every age
and at the end of every season,
according to the statute and signs
appointed to every dominion
by the certain law from the mouth of God,
by the precept which is and shall be
for ever and ever without end.
Without it nothing is nor shall be,
for the God of knowledge established it
and there is no other beside Him.

I, the Master, know Thee O my God,
by the spirit which Thou hast given to me,
and by Thy Holy Spirit I have faithfully hearkened
to Thy marvellous counsel.
In the mystery of Thy wisdom
Thou hast opened knowledge to me,
and in Thy mercies
[Thou hast unlocked for me] the fountain of Thy might.
...

Before Thee no man is just ...
[that he may] understand all Thy mysteries
or give answer [to Thy rebuke.
But the children of Thy grace
shall delight in] Thy correction
and watch for Thy goodness,

for in Thy mercies [Thou wilt show Thyself to them]
  and they shall know Thee;
at the time of Thy glory
  they shall rejoice.
[Thou hast caused them to draw near]
  in accordance [with their knowledge],
and hast admitted them
  in accordance with their understanding,
and in their divisions they shall serve Thee
  throughout their dominion
[without ever turning aside] from Thee
  or transgressing Thy word.

Behold, [I was taken] from dust
  [and] fashioned [out of clay]
as a source of uncleanness,
  and a shameful nakedness,
a heap of dust,
  and a kneading [with water,]
. . .
  and a house of darkness,
  a creature of clay returning to dust,
returning [at the appointed time
  to dwell] in the dust whence it was taken.

How then shall dust reply to its Maker,
  [and how] understand His [works]?
How shall it stand before Him who reproves it?
. . .
  [and the Spring of] Eternity,
the Well of Glory
  and the Fountain of Knowledge.
Not even [the wonderful] Heroes [can] declare all Thy glory
  or stand in face of Thy wrath,
and there is none among them
  that can answer Thy rebuke;
for Thou art just and none can oppose Thee.
How then can (man) who returns to his dust?

I hold my peace;
   what more shall I say than this?
I have spoken in accordance with my knowledge,
   out of the righteousness given to a creature of clay.
And how shall I speak unless Thou open my mouth;
   how understand unless Thou teach me?
How shall I seek Thee unless Thou uncover my heart,
   and how follow the way that is straight
   unless [Thou guide me?
How shall my foot] stay on [the path
   unless Thou] give it strength;
and how shall I rise ...

**XXI** (formerly **XVIII**, 16–33+fr. 3)

*Hymn 24* (formerly *25*)

...
[How] shall I look,
   unless Thou open my eyes?

Or hear,
   [unless Thou unstop my ears]?
My heart is astounded,
for to the uncircumcised ear
   a word has been disclosed,
and a heart [of stone
   has understood the right precepts].

I know it is for Thyself
   that Thou hast done these things, O God;
for what is flesh
   [that Thou shouldst act] marvellously [towards it]?
It is Thy purpose to do mightily
   and to establish all things for Thy glory.
[Thou hast created] the host of knowledge
   to declare (Thy) mighty deeds to flesh,
   and the right precepts to him that is born [of woman].
Thou hast [caused the perverse heart to enter]
   into a Covenant with Thee,

and hast uncovered the heart of dust
that it may be preserved from evil
   and saved from the snares of Judgement
   in accordance with Thy mercies.

And I, a creature [of clay
   kneaded with water,
a heap of dust]
   and a heart of stone,
for what am I reckoned to be worthy of this?
For into an ear of dust [Thou hast put a new word]
   and hast engraved on a heart of [stone] things everlasting.
Thou hast caused [the straying spirit] to return
   that it may enter into a Covenant with Thee,
and stand [before Thee for ever]
   in the everlasting abode,
illumined with perfect Light for ever,
   with [no more] darkness,
   [for un]ending [seasons of joy]
   and un[numbered] ages of peace.

...
And as for me, a creature of dust, ...

## Fr. 3

...
Pile of dust, how shall I stand in front of the tempest?
   ... and He will guard me
   according to the mysteries of His good pleasure. For He
      knows ...

...
And they will hide snares of wickedness, net after net.
   ... every creature of deceit will come to an end ...

...
[wickedness will] turn to nothing
   and the inclination towards iniquity will vanish
   and deeds of deceit [will perish].

. . .
As for me, creature of [clay] . . .
. . . how will it gain strength for Thee?
Thou art the God of [knowledge]
. . .
Thou hast made them [according to Thy design]
and without Thee [nothing exists].
[As for me, creature] of dust, I know
through the spirit which Thou hast put into me
that . . .
injustice and deceit will be awe-struck
and insolence will cease.
. . .
[wo]rks of uncleanness will (turn into) sickness
and judgements (leading to) plague and destruction . . .

**XXII** (formerly **XVIII** ii, 27–29+fr. 1 i+fr. 52 bottom+fr.4+fr. 47)

. . . [hol]iness that are in heaven
. . . and He is wonder.
But they cannot [understand] Thy [marvel]s
and they will not be able to know all [Thy mysteries].
[How then can he who retur]ns to his dust?
As for me, I am a man of sin
who has wallowed [in the ways of uncleanness]
[and been defiled] by the guilt of wickedness.
As for me, in the times of wrath [I have fallen(?)].
How can I rise in view of my wound
and keep myself . . .
For there is hope for man . . .
As for me, creature of clay,
I have leaned [on Thy loving-kindness
and on the multitude of Thy mysteries,] O my God.
And I know that truthful is [Thy mouth,
and that Thy words are not] revoked.
As for me, I will rely in my time [on Thy Covenant
and will rai]se myself to the post
which Thou hast established for me . . .

## Fr. 4

... As for me, I was frightened by Thy judgements
...
Who is found clean in Thy judgement?
  And what is [man before Thee?
Thou bringest] him to judgement
  and he returns to his dust.
  ... [my G]o[d].
Thou hast opened my heart for Thy understanding
  and hast unstopped [my] ear[s] ...
  to lean on Thy goodness.
My heart murmurs ...
  and my heart melts like wax
  because of iniquity and sin. ...
Blessed art Thou, God of knowledge,
  who hast established ...
And Thou hast met Thy servant with this for Thy sake.
For I know Thy [loving-kindness
  and in] Thy [mercies] I hope in all my existence,
  and I bless Thy name always.
...
Do not forsake me in the times [of distress (?)]
...

**XXIII** (formerly **XVIII**, 1–16+fr. 57 i+2 i)
...
they are confirmed in [the ears] of Thy servant for ever
... [to announce] Thy marvellous tidings
...
Withdraw not Thy hand ...
  that he may be confirmed in Thy Covenant
  and stand before Thee [for ever].

[For Thou, O my God,] didst open a [fountain]
  in the mouth of Thy Servant.
Thou didst engrave by the measuring-cord
  [Thy mysteries] upon his tongue,
[that] out of his understanding

[he might] preach to a creature,
and interpret these things
to dust like myself.

Thou didst open [his fountain]
that he might rebuke the creature of clay for his way,
and him who is born of woman
for the guilt of his deeds;
that he might open [the fount of] Thy truth
to a creature whom Thou upholdest by Thy might;
[that he might be], according to Thy truth,
a messenger [in the season] of Thy goodness;
that to the humble he might bring
glad tidings of Thy great mercy,
[proclaiming salvation]
from out of the fountain [of holiness
to the contrite] of spirit,
and everlasting joy to those who mourn.
...

## Fr. 2

...
... [to prai]se Thee
and to recount all Thy glory.
As for me, what am I?
For I was taken from dust.
But Th[ou, O my God],
Thou hast done all these [for] Thy [g]lory.
According to the greatness of Thy loving-kindness
put the guard of Thy righteousness
[in the hand of Th]y [servant] for ever
until deliverance.
May the interpreters of knowledge be with all my steps
and those who decide truth [in all my ways].
For what is dust among al[l] ...
Ashes are in their hand: nothing at all.
...
and Thou hast shed [Thy Holy] Spirit over dust

...
  [to bring him into the company] of the 'gods'
  and unite them with the Sons of Heaven.
...
Thou hast shed Thy [Ho]ly [Spirit] to atone for guilt
...
...
for they are established in Thy truth.
...
[And Thou, my God],
Thou hast acted wondrously for Thy glory
...

## 4Q427 7 i–ii (1QH, frs. 7, 46, 55, 56, 4Q428 15, 4Q431 1)

**I** ...
For I am made to stand with the 'gods',
  and I will not ... [glory or majes]ty for me with fine gold;
gold and purified gold, [I will] not ... in me;
  ... will not be reckoned for me.
Chant, O beloved, sing to the King [of glory.
  Rejoice, in the cong]regation of God.
Exult in the tents of salvation.
  Give thanks in the dwelling
  [of holiness],
  extol together with the eternal host.
Magnify our God and glorify our King.
Sanctify His name with powerful lips.
  and a victorious tongue.
Lift up alone your voice in all ages,
  Let a joyous meditation be heard.
Burst out in eternal rejoicings
  and prostrate incessantly in the common assembly.
Bless the wonderful Maker of exalted things,
  Him who proclaims the power of His hand,
sealing mysteries and revealing secrets,
  lifting up those who stumble and fall,

[rest]oring the progress of those who hope for knowledge
and humbling the meetings of the everlastingly haughty;
[seal]ing the mysteries of sp[lendour]
and establi[shing the won]ders of glory.
O Judge, whose anger is destructive,
... in righteous loving-kindness and great mercy,
be gracious to ...
... mercy to those who bear fruits of His great goodness,
and the source of ...
**II** ... wickedness ends ...
[op]pression [ceases], the tyrant ceases ...
treachery [sto]ps and there are no senseless perversities.
Light shines and joy bursts forth;
mourning [vanishes] and sorrow flees.
Peace is revealed, dread ceases.
A spring has opened up for an [eternal] bles[sing]
and for healing in all the everlasting ages.
Iniquity has stopped, plague has ceased with no more illn[ess].
... has been gathered in and ... will be no more.
Announce and say: Great is God, Ma[ker of marvels].
For He humbles the proud spirit with no remnant
and from the dust He lifts up the poor to [eternal heights].
And He lifts him up to the clouds
to share a common assembly with the 'gods'.
And ...
anger for everlasting destruction.
He raises freely the totterers on earth,
and [His] mi[ght is with] their steps,
and everlasting joy is in their dwellings,
eternal glory without end [for ever].

Let them say: Blessed be God, Author of majestic [w]onders,
who reveals might splendidly,
and justifies with knowledge all His creatures,
so that goodness is on their faces.
They know the multitude of [His] loving [kindness]
and the abundance of His mercies
to all the children of His truth.
We know Thee, O God of righteousness,

and we comprehend [Thy . . . , O King]
of glory.
For we have seen Thy zeal through Thy mighty power
and have observed [Thy] d[eeds
in the abundance] of Thy mercies and wondrous forgiveness.

What is flesh compared to these?
What do [dust and ashes] amoun[t to]
that they recite these things from age to age,
and hold themselves upright [before Thee
and enter into communion with] the Sons of Heaven.
No interpreter can answer according to Thy mouth
and . . . to Thee.
For Thou hast established us according to [Thy] ple[asure]
in the territory [of iniquity] . . .
. . . we have spoken to Thee and not to a medi[ator] . . .
[And Thou hast lent] an ea[r] to the issue of our lips.

Annou[nce and say: Blessed be God,
Creator] of the heavens by His power,
Desig[ner] of all their devices [by] His strength,
of the earth by [His] migh[t] . . .

# Apocryphal Psalms (I)

## (11QPs$^{a}$=11Q5, 4Q**88**)

The incomplete Psalms scroll from Cave 11 (11QPs$^{a}$), published by J. A. Sanders (*DJD*, IV, Oxford, 1965), contains seven non-canonical poems interspersed among the canonical Psalms. One of these figures as Ps. 151 in the Greek Psalter, and four further compositions have been preserved in Syriac translation. Three previously unknown poems and an extract from the Hebrew version of Sirach li also feature in the Scroll.

In Ps. 151A and B or Syriac Ps. i, the story of the election of David, the shepherd boy, as ruler of Israel, and his victory over Goliath, are poetically retold. Ps. 154 or Syr. Ps. ii is a sapiential hymn, the beginning and end of which are extant only in Syriac, but 4Q**448**, column A (lines 8–10) represents a few words in Hebrew corresponding to Ps. 154, 17–20 (cf. E. and H. Eshel and A. Yardeni, 'A Qumran Composition Containing Part of Ps. 154 ... ', *IEJ* 42 (1992), 201–14). Ps. 155 or Syr. Ps. iii is an amalgam of an individual complaint and thanksgiving. Part of it is an alphabet acrostic, i.e. the lines begin with consecutive letters of the Hebrew alphabet. *Plea for Deliverance* is an individual thanksgiving hymn, the beginning of which is lost. The *Zion Psalm*, of which lines 1–3 and 8–15 are also in a fragmentary Psalms scroll from Cave 4 (4Q**88** VII–VIII), is another alphabetic acrostic hymn praising Jerusalem. Finally, the *Psalm of the Creation* is a further sapiential hymn.

A midrashic account of the poetic activities of David is inserted in column XXVII of 11Q**5**, crediting him with 4,050 compositions, subdivided into psalms, songs for the daily holocaust, songs for the Sabbath sacrifice, songs for festivals and songs for exorcism. The mention of fifty-two Sabbaths and the 364 days indicates that the author envisaged the solar year of the Qumran calendar.

The figure of 4,050 should be viewed against the equally prolific literary achievement claimed for Solomon in 1 Kings v, 12 (3,000 proverbs and 1,005 songs according to the Hebrew text; 3,000 proverbs and 5,000 songs according to the Septuagint). As for Josephus, he attributes to Solomon 1,005 *books* of poems and 3,000 *books* of parables (*Antiquities* VIII, 44).

Only this catalogue, written in prose, is definitely sectarian. The psalms themselves probably belong to the second century BCE at the latest, but they may even date to the third century BCE.

## *Psalm 151A*

**XXVIII** Hallelujah. Of David, son of Jesse.
1 I was smaller than my brothers, and younger than the sons of my father.
He made me shepherd of his flock, and a ruler over his kids.
2 My hands have made a pipe and my fingers a lyre.
I have rendered glory to the Lord; I have said so in my soul.
3 The mountains do not testify to him, and the hills do not tell (of him).
The trees praise my words and the flocks my deeds.
4 For who can tell and speak of and recount the works of the Lord?
God has seen all, he has heard all, and he listens to all.
5 He sent his prophet to anoint me, Samuel to magnify me.
My brothers went out to meet him, beautiful of figure, beautiful of appearance.
6 They were tall of stature with beautiful hair, yet the Lord did not choose them.
7 He sent and took me from behind the flock, and anointed me with holy oil.
As a prince of his people, and a ruler among the sons of his Covenant.

## *Psalm 151B*

The first display of David's power after God's prophet had anointed him.
1 Then I saw the Philistine taunting [from the enemy lines] ...

## *Syriac Psalm ii = Psalm 154*

1 **XVIII** [Glorify God with a great voice. Proclaim his majesty in the congregation of the many.
2 Glorify his name amid the multitude of the upright and recount his greatness with the faithful.
3 Join] your souls to the good and to the perfect to glorify the Most High.
4 Assemble together to make known his salvation.

And be not slow in making known his strength, and his majesty to all the simple.
5 For wisdom is given to make known the glory of the Lord and to recount the greatness of his deeds. She is made known to man,
7 to declare his strength to the simple, and to give insight into his greatness to those without understanding,
8 they who are far from her gates, who have strayed from her entrances.
9 For the Most High is the Lord of Jacob, and his majesty is over all his works.
10 And a man who glorifies the Most High is accepted by him as one bringing an offering,
11 as one offering he-goats and calves, as one causing the altar to grow fat on a multitude of burnt-offerings, as an agreeable incense by the hand of the righteous.
12 From the doors of the righteous her voice is heard, and from the congregation of the devout her song.
13 When they eat their fill, she is mentioned, and when they drink in community together.
14 Their meditation is on the Law of the Most High, and their words are for making known his strength.
15 How far from the wicked is her word, and her knowledge from the insolent.
16 Behold the eyes of the Lord have compassion on the good,
17 and his mercy is great over those who glorify him; from an evil time he saves [their] souls.
18 [Bless] the Lord who redeems the humble from the hand of str[angers]
[and deliv]ers [the perfect from the hand of the wicked;]
19 [who lifts up a horn out of Ja]cob, and a judge [out of Israel].
20 [He desires his tabernacle in Zion, and chooses Jerusalem for ever.]

## *Syriac Psalm iii = Psalm 155*

1 **XXIV** O Lord, I have called to Thee, hear me.
2 I have spread out my hands towards Thy holy dwelling-place.
3 Turn Thine ear and grant me my request,
4 and do not withhold my plea from me.
5 Construct my soul and do not cast it away,

6 and do not leave it alone before the wicked.
7 May the true judge turn away from me the rewards of evil.
8 Lord, do not judge me according to my sins,
for no living man is righteous before Thee.
9 Lord, cause me to understand Thy Law and teach me Thy judgements.
10 And the multitude shall hear of Thy deeds, and peoples shall honour Thy glory.
11 Remember me and forget me not, and bring me not to unbearable hardships.
12 Put away from me the sin of my youth, and may my sins not be remembered against me.
13 Lord, cleanse me from the evil plague, and let it not return to me.
14 Dry up its roots within me, and permit not its leaves to flourish in me.
15 Lord, Thou art glory; therefore my plea is fulfilled before Thee.
16 To whom shall I cry so that he will grant it to me? What more can the po[wer] of the sons of men do?
17 From before Thee, O Lord, comes my trust.
I cried to the Lord and he answered me; he healed the brokenness of my heart.
18 I was sleepy [and I] slept; I dreamt and also [I awoke].
19 [Lord, Thou didst support me when my heart was stricken, and I called upon the Lor]d [my saviour].
20 Now I will see their shame; I have relied on Thee, and I will not be ashamed. (Render glory for ever and ever.)
21 Redeem Israel, Thy pious one, O Lord, and the house of Jacob, Thine elect.

### *Prayer for Deliverance*

**XIX** For no worm thanks Thee, nor a maggot recounts Thy loving-kindness.

Only the living thank Thee, all they whose feet totter, thank Thee, when Thou makest known to them Thy loving-kindness, and causest them to understand Thy righteousness.

For the soul of all the living is in Thy hand; Thou hast given breath to all flesh.

O Lord, do towards us according to Thy goodness, according to the greatness of Thy mercies, and according to the greatness of Thy righteous deeds.

The Lord listens to the voice of all who love his name and does not permit his loving-kindness to depart from them.

Blessed be the Lord, doer of righteous deeds, who crowns his pious ones with loving-kindness and mercies.

My soul shouts to praise Thy name, to praise with jubilation Thy mercies,

to announce Thy faithfulness; there is no limit to Thy praises.

I belonged to death because of my sins, and my iniquities had sold me to Sheol.

But Thou didst save me, O Lord, according to the greatness of Thy mercies, according to the greatness of Thy righteous deeds.

I, too, have loved Thy name, and have taken refuge in Thy shadow.

When I remember Thy power, my heart is strengthened and I rely on Thy mercies.

Forgive my sins, O Lord, and purify me of my iniquity.

Grant me a spirit of faithfulness and knowledge; let me not be dishonoured in ruin.

Let not Belial dominate me, nor an unclean spirit; let pain and the evil inclination not possess my bones.

For Thou, O Lord, art my praise, and I hope in Thee every day.

My brethren rejoice with me and the house of my father is astounded by Thy graciousness.

... for ever I will rejoice in Thee.

## *Apostrophe to Zion*

**XXII** I will remember you, O Zion, for a blessing;
with all my might I love you;
your memory is to be blessed for ever.
Your hope is great, O Zion;
Peace and your awaited salvation will come.
Generation after generation shall dwell in you,
and generations of the pious shall be your ornament.
They who desire the day of your salvation
shall rejoice in the greatness of your glory.
They shall be suckled on the fullness of your glory,
and in your beautiful streets they shall make tinkling sounds.
You shall remember the pious deeds of your prophets,
and shall glorify yourself in the deeds of your pious ones.

Cleanse violence from your midst;
lying and iniquity, may they be cut off from you.
Your sons shall rejoice within you,
and your cherished ones shall be joined to you.
How much they have hoped in your salvation,
and how much your perfect ones have mourned for you?
Your hope, O Zion, shall not perish,
and your expectation will not be forgotten.
Is there a just man who has perished?
Is there a man who has escaped his iniquity?
Man is tried according to his way,
each is repaid according to his deeds.
Your oppressors shall be cut off from around you, O Zion,
and all who hate you shall be dispersed.
Your praise is pleasing, O Zion;
it rises up in all the world.
Many times I will remember you for a blessing;
I will bless you with all my heart.
You shall attain to eternal righteousness,
and shall receive blessings from the noble.
Take the vision which speaks of you,
and the dreams of the prophets requested for you.
Be exalted and increase, O Zion;
Praise the Most High, your Redeemer!
May my soul rejoice in your glory!

*Hymn to the Creator*

**XXVI** The Lord is great and holy, the Most Holy for generation after generation.

Majesty goes before him, and after him abundance of many waters.

Loving-kindness and truth are about his face; truth and judgement and righteousness are the pedestal of his throne.

He divides light from obscurity; he establishes the dawn by the knowledge of his heart.

When all his angels saw it, they sang, for he showed them that which they had not known.

He crowns the mountains with fruit, with good food for all the living.

Blessed be the master of the earth with his power, who establishes the world by his wisdom.
By his understanding he stretched out the heaven, and brought forth [wind] from his st[ores].
He made [lightnings for the rai]n, and raised mist from the end [of the earth].

## *An Account of David's Poems*

**XXVII** David son of Jesse was wise and brilliant like the light of the sun; (he was) a scribe, intelligent and perfect in all his ways before God and men.

YHWH gave him an intelligent and brilliant spirit, and he wrote 3,600 psalms and 364 songs to sing before the altar for the daily perpetual sacrifice, for all the days of the year; and 52 songs for the Sabbath offerings; and 30 songs for the New Moons, for Feast-days and for the Day of Atonement.

In all, the songs which he uttered were 446, and 4 songs to make music on behalf of those stricken (by evil spirits).

In all, they were 4,050.

All these he uttered through prophecy which was given him from before the Most High.

# Apocryphal Psalms (II)

## (4Q88)

The last four columns (VII–X) of a fragmentary Psalms manuscript from Cave 4 have preserved three apocryphal poems. The first of these (cols. VII–VIII) is identical with 11Q5 XXII already presented (pp. 305–6). Of the other two, the first (col. IX) focuses on the final judgement and the second (col. X) is a hymn to Judah.

For a preliminary edition, see J. Starcky, 'Psaumes apocryphes de la grotte 4 de Qumrân', *RB* 73 (1966), 353–71.

**IX** . . . Congregation
and they shall praise
the name of the Lord,
for He has come to judge every action,
to remove the wicked from the earth
[so that the sons] of iniquity shall not be found.
The heavens [shall give] their dew
   and there shall be no . . . [within] their [boundarie]s.
And the earth
   shall [give] its fruit in its time
and its [prod]uct shall not fail.
The fruit trees [shall] . . . of its vineyards
and its . . . shall not lie.
The poor shall eat
   and the God-fearers shall be sated.
. . .

**X** . . .
. . .
Then heaven and earth shall exult together.
Let all the stars of the evening twilight exult.
Rejoice, Judah, rejoice!

Rejoice, rejoice and be glad with gladness!
Celebrate your feasts and pay your vows
  for there is no Belial in your midst.
Raise your hand and fortify your right hand!
Behold the enemy shall perish
  and all the workers of iniquity shall be dispersed.
But, Thou, O Lord, art for eve[r].
Thy glory shall be for eve[r and eve]r.
[Ha]ll[eluiah].

# Apocryphal Psalms (III)

## (11QapPs$^{a}$=11Q11)

Badly worn remains of five columns of a Scroll with apocryphal psalms, at least partly devoted to exorcism, have survived in Cave 11. Most of the columns are so poorly preserved that no continuous reading is possible. In col. i, where the name of Solomon implies that this was one of the poems attributed to him, the repeated use of the term 'demons' and mention of 'healing' suggest the genre of the composition. In col. iii a 'powerful angel' is mentioned who seems to be charged with defeating the demon and casting it to the 'great abyss' and the 'nethermost [hell]'. Col. v, 3–13 has been recognized as the canonical Psalm xci, preceded by small remains of the exorcistic poem of col. iv and followed by a liturgical formula, 'And they shall an[swer, Amen, amen.] Selah.' All the lacunae of col. iv have been conjecturally filled by E. Puech in a French rendering. His presentation will be reproduced here in English; it provides a possible general understanding of the text, but with no guarantee that any of the restored details is correct.

For preliminary editions, see J. P. M. van der Ploeg, 'Un petit rouleau de psaumes apocryphes (11QPsAp$^{a}$)', in G. Jeremias et al., eds., *Tradition und Glaube* (K. G. Kuhn Festschrift) (Göttingen, 1971), 128–39; E. Puech, 'Les deux derniers psaumes davidiques du rituel d'exorcisme, 11QPsAp$^{a}$ iv 4–v 14', in D. Dimant and V. Rappaport, eds., *The Dead Sea Scrolls: Forty Years of Research* (Leiden, 1992), 64–89; cf. esp. pp. 68–9.

**IV** ...

To David. O[n words of incanta]tion. [Cry out al]l the time in the name of the Lor[d]
towards heave[n when] Beli[al] comes to you.
[And sa]y to him:
Who are you? [Be afraid of] man and of the seed of the ho[ly ones].
Your face is a face of [nothin]g and your horns are horns of dr[eam].
[You ar]e [d]arkness and not light; [injustic]e and not righteousness.

[The prin]ce of the h[os]t [is against you]; the Lord [will cast] you [to] the nethermost [hell],
[closed by] bronze ga[tes] through [which n]o light [shall pass];
nor [shall shine there the light of the] sun which [will rise] over the righteous to il[lumine his face.
And] you will say:
Is [there not an angel with the ri]ghteous when [judgement] comes [for] S[atan for] he caused him evil?
[And the spirit of t]ruth [will save him] from dar[kness because right]eousness is for him.
... **V** ... for ever [all the] son of Bel[ial. Amen, amen.] Selah.

# Non-canonical Psalms

## (4Q380–81)

Two poorly preserved manuscripts, the first consisting of seven and the second of 110 fragments, contain apocryphal Hebrew religious poetry resembling biblical Psalms more than the Hodayot (1QH) from Qumran. Some of them reuse and combine canonical Psalms (e.g. fr. 15 re-employing Pss. lxxxvi and lxxxix, and fr. 24, Ps. xviii). Not one single line has survived intact and only a few of these largely mediocre poems can be translated. Their editor, Eileen Schuller, assigns the collection to the Persian–Hellenistic era and considers it to be a pre-sectarian composition. No historical allusions are included. Like many of the biblical Psalms, these poems bore titles, three of which have been preserved: 'Psalm of Obadiah' (4Q**380** 1 11, 8); 'Hymn of the Man of God' (4Q**381** 24, 4) and 'Prayer of Manasseh, King of Judah when the King of Assyria imprisoned him' (4Q**381** 33, 8). The attributions are no doubt pseudepigraphic. Whether Obadiah is the minor prophet or the court official mentioned in 1 Kings xviii, 3 cannot be decided.

For a preliminary edition, see Eileen Schuller, *Non-Canonical Psalms from Qumran: A Pseudepigraphic Collection* (Harvard Semitic Studies 28, Scholars Press, Atlanta, 1986).

### 4Q380, fr. 1

**I** ... [Jeru]salem, that is [the city
   chosen by the L]ord from everlasting to [everlasting.]
... the holy ones
[for the na]me of the Lord is called on her,
   [and his glory] is seen on Jerusalem and Zion.
Who will utter the name of the Lord,
   and who makes all his praises heard?
The Lord [remem]bered him in his favour

and visited him
that he might show him the prosperity [of] his [cho]sen ones,
making him re[joice in the gladness of his nation]
(cf. Ps. cvi, 2, 4–5).

**II** [And] he made for you a man w[who ... ]
for he is the one [whose] words they kept
which are for all the sons of Israel ...
... your hand will save you,
for the strength of [your] God does good.
And those (filled with) wicked hatred,
how long will you delight to do evil? ...
*vacat*
Psalm of Obadiah.
God ... truth is in it, and his loving kindness ...

## 4Q381, fr. 1

... [his wisdom] I have declared,
and I will meditate on his marvel,
and it will become my teacher.
Judgement ... of my mouth,
and to the simple and they will understand,
and to the senseless and they will know.
O Lord, how mi[ghty] ... marvels
When (?) he made heaven and earth, and by his word ...
... and ... its lights (?) ...
night and stars and constellations ...
[every] tree and every fru[it of the vineyar]d
and every produce of the field.
And according to his words ... all ...
m[ankind] and by his spirit he established them
to have dominion over all this,
over the ground and all [its produce(?)]
from new moon to new moon, from festival to festival,
from day to day to eat its fruit, fruit of ...
... and birds and all that belongs to them
to eat the best of everything and also ...

... in them and all his hosts and ...
   to serve man and to minister to him ...

## Fr. 15

...
[Turn to me and take pity on me;
   give thy strength to thy servant]
   and save the son of Thy handmaid.
Show me [a sign of thy favour,
   that those who hate me may see and be put to shame
because thou,] my [G]od, hast helped me (Ps. lxxxvi, 16–17)
   and I will prepare (a sacrifice) for Thee, my God.
... [Thou dost rule the rag]ing of the sea;
   Thou stillest its waves.
[Thou didst crush Rahab like a carcass,
Thou didst scatter Thine enemies with Thy mighty arm]
   (Ps. lxxxix, 10–11).
[The world and] all that is in it, Thou hast founded them
   (ibid. 12).
Thou hast a [mighty] arm; strong is Thy hand,
   high Thy right hand (ibid. 14)
[For who in the skies can be compared to thee,] my God?
And who among the sons of 'gods'
   and in all [the council of the holy ones? ...
... For Thou] art the glory of its majesty.
As for me, Thine anointed one, I have understood ...
[I will make] thee [know]n, for Thou hast made me know;
I will have insight, for Thou hast given me insight ...
For on Thy name, my God, we shall call,
   and [we shall wait] for Thy salvation.
And they will put it on like a garment
   and like a dress ...

## Fr. 24

... Psalm of the Man of God.
Lord, God ...
He has redeemed Judah from all distress
and from Ephraim ...
... generation.
Those who have passed his test will praise him
and say, 'Arise [O God'] ...
Thy name is my salvation,
my rock, my fortress and [my] refuge [is my God] (Ps. xviii, 3).
I will call on the Lord and he will answer me,
my help ... those who hate me.
And he will say, ...
[My c]ry be[fore him] comes to his ears (Ps. xviii, 7)
[From his temple he will hear my] voi[ce].
[And] the earth will [re]el [and rock,
and the foundations of the mountains tremble ... for he is angry.
Smoke went up from his nostrils (Ps. xviii, 7–9) ...

## Fr. 31

... [Prayer of ... k]ing of Judah.
Hear o [my] Go[d] ...
I will recount before those who fear Thee ...
Who can understand Thy [th]oughts?
For my oppressors have increased before Thee.
Thou hast known them
and Thou hast subdued the enemies of my soul before Thine e[yes].
For I will live ...
[and] Thou shalt conceal my iniquity to those with understanding.
Thou shalt slay them (the enemies) O God of my salvation.
The days of my existence are treasured up.
What can a man say (but) 'Here I am' ? ...

## Fr. 33

. . . Rise [above the heaven]s, O Lord,
and [my] God . . .
And let us glory in thy might
for [Thy wonders] are inscrutable
. . . Thou shalt place me
and Thy chastisement will be my [joy].
. . . everlasting and to extol thee.
For my sins have become too many for me . . .
But Thou, my God, shalt send Thy spi[rit]
[and Thy mercy]
to the son of Thy handmaid
and Thy loving-kindness to the servant who is near Thee . . .
I will exult and rejoice in Thee before those who fear [Thee],
for [Thou shalt judge] Thy servants in Thy righteousness,
and according to Thy loving-kindness
. . . to save . . . to thee. Selah.
*vacat*
Prayer of Manasseh, King of Judah when the King of Assyria
gaoled him.
. . . [my G]od . . . my salvation is near in Thine eyes . . .
I wait for Thy delivering presence,
and I feel faint before Thee because of my s[in].
For [Thou hast] enlarged [Thy mercies(?)],
and I have multiplied guilt.
And thus . . .
from eternal joy
and my soul shall not see goodness . . .
He has lifted me up on high
above a nation . . .
And I did not remember thee [in Thy plac]e of h[oliness];
I did not serve [thee] . . .

## Fr. 46

Man will not be strong and will not rise
... [and] Thou hast [t]ested all.
And the elect, like offerings, Thou wilt purify before Thee,
but the hated ones Thou wilt reject like impurity.
And a stormy wind ... their [p]ractice.
And those who fear Thee shall be before Thee always.
(Their) horns are horns made of iron to gore many,
and they will gore ...
And Thou wilt make their hoofs of bronze
but sinners like dung shall be trampled upon the ground ...

## Fr. 69

... When he saw that the peoples [of the la]nd behaved abominably,
... all the land (turned) wholly into impure uncleanness,
and from the beginning marvellously ... he consulted his heart
to destroy them from it (the land) and make on it a [holy(?)] people.
... in you and he gave you through his spirit prophets
to instruct and teach you ...
... your [God(?)] descended from heaven and spoke to you
to instruct you and bring you back
from the works of the inhabitants [of the land].
... [pre]cepts, laws and commandments
he established through a covenant by the hand [of Moses].
... dwelt (?) on the land. Then it will be cleansed and ...
... to consider you whether you will be his.
And if [not,] ...
And to breach the covenant which he made with you
and to become a stranger and not ...
... over wickedness and to change the words of his mouth ...

## Frs. 76–7

... Who among you will answer and stand up against his
 rebuke? ...
... For you have many judges and countless (hostile) witnesses.
But ... the Lord will sit in judgement against you,
 judging truly and without injustice ...
... his spirits to pronounce on you true judgements.
Is there understanding for you to learn ... ?
 ... Lord of lords, mighty and marvellous and none is like him.
He has chosen y[ou instead of power]ful [peoples]
 and great nations to be his people to rule over all ...
... [hea]ven and earth
 and as the highest above all the nations of the earth ...

# Lamentations

## (4Q179, 4Q501)

Several fragments of a poem inspired by the biblical Book of Lamentations have been preserved in Cave 4 (4Q179). Only fragment 2 offers a text long enough for intelligible translation. See J. M. Allegro and A. A. Anderson, *DJD*, V, 75–7; cf. J. Strugnell, *RQ* 7 (1970), 250–52. A second work of a similar nature (4Q501) has appeared in M. Baillet, *DJD*, VII, 79–80. Both texts are dated to the second half of the first century BCE.

### 4Q179, fr. 2

...
[How] solitary [lies] the city,
...
the princess of all the peoples is desolate
like a forsaken woman;
and all her [dau]ghters are forsak[en]
[like] a forsaken woman,
like a woman hurt and forsaken
by her [husband].
All her palaces and [her] wal[ls] are
like a barren woman;
and like a sheltered woman,
are all [her] paths;
[all her] ...
like a woman of bitterness,
and all her daughters are like women
mourning for [their] hus[bands];
[all her] ... like women
deprived of their only children.

Weep, weep, Jer[usalem]
...
[her tears flow] upon her cheeks
  because of her sons ...

## 4Q501

Give not our inheritance to strangers,
  nor our (hard-earned) property to foreigners.
Remember that we are [the forsaken] of Thy people
  and the forsaken of Thine inheritance.
Remember the desolate children of Thy Covenant ...
T[hy] freely devoted ...;
they err with no one to bring them back;
  they are broken with none to bind them;
  [they are bent down with none to ra]ise them up.
The damned of Thy people have surrounded me
  with their lying tongues.
They have been turned ...
  and Thy boughs to the progeny of a woman.
Look and see the shame of the sons of [Thy people (?),
  for] our skin [is burning]
and feverish heat has seized us
  because of their reviling tongue.

# Songs for the Holocaust of the Sabbath

## (4Q400–407, 11Q17, Masada 1039–200)

Fragments of a document concerned with heavenly worship were first published by J. Strugnell under the title 'The Angelic Liturgy', *Congress Volume Oxford, Supplements to Vetus Testamentum*, VII (Leiden, 1960), 318–45. The full material, viz. eight manuscripts from Cave 4 (4Q400–407), small fragments from Cave 11 (11Q17) and a large fragment from Masada (1039–200), was subsequently edited by Carol Newsom (*Songs of the Sabbath Sacrifice: A Critical Edition*, Harvard Semitic Studies 27, Atlanta, 1985). The songs contain angelic praises of God assigned to the first thirteen sabbaths, i.e. the first quarter of the solar year. They imply the simultaneity of heavenly and earthly worship. Although often obscure, the poems depict the celestial sanctuary, the throne-chariot, and the various groups participating in the angelic liturgy; they also include the words of the benedictions sung by the seven archangels.

The main source of inspiration is the Book of Ezekiel, especially chapters i and x in connection with the throne-chariot and xl–xlviii for the heavenly sanctuary.

The songs include nothing that can be dated. On the basis of the script and on general grounds the composition is said to belong to the first century BCE.

The *Merkabah*, or divine throne-chariot, was a central subject in ancient and medieval Jewish esotericism and mysticism. Hence this early post-biblical manifestation of the speculation is of considerable historical importance for the study of the so-called *Merkabah* mysticism and of the *Hekhaloth* ('heavenly palaces') literature. It is noteworthy that the Mishnah prohibits the use of Ezekiel's passage about the chariot as a prophetic reading in synagogue (Megillah IV, 10) or even its discussion in private, unless with a sage already familiar with the subject (Hagigah II, 1).

The presence of this Qumran document in the fortress of Masada is best explained by assuming either that a number of Essenes joined the revolutionaries and took with them some of their manuscripts, or that the rebels occupied the Qumran area after its evacuation by the Community and later transferred some Essene manuscripts to their final place of resistance.

## 4Q400

[To the Master. Song of the holocaust of the] first [Sabba]th, on the fourth of the first month.

Praise [the God of ... ] the 'gods' (= *elohim*) of supreme holiness; in [his] divine [kingship, rejoice. For he has established] supreme holiness among the everlastingly holy, to be for him the priests of [the inner Temple in his royal sanctuary], ministers of the Presence in his glorious innermost Temple chamber. In the congregation of all the gods (= *elim*) of [knowledge, and in the councils of all the spirits of] God, he engraved his precepts for all the spiritual works, and [his glorious] judgements [for all who lay the foundations of] knowledge, the people (endowed with) his glorious understanding, the 'gods' who are close to knowledge ... of eternity and from the fountain of holiness to the sanctuary of supreme [holiness] ... prie[sts] of the inner Temple, ministers of the Presence of the [most] holy King ... his glory. They shall grow in strength decree by decree to be seven [eternal councils. For he fo]unded them [for] himself as the most [holy, who minister in the h]oly of holies ... do not endure [those who per]vert the way. There is [n]othing impure in their holy gifts. He engraved for them [precepts relating to ho]ly gifts; by them, all the everlastingly holy shall sanctify themselves. He shall purify the [luminously] pure [to rewar]d all those who render their way crooked. Their expiations shall obtain his goodwill for all those who repent from sin ... knowledge among the priests of the inner Temple, and from their mouth (proceed) the teachings of the holy with the judgements of [his glory] ... his [gra]ces for everlasting merciful forgiveness. In his zealous vengeance ... he has established for himself as priests of the inner Temple, the most holy ... of gods, the priests of the highest heights who are near [to] ...

## 4Q400 2

wonderfully to extol Thy glory among the divine beings of knowledge, and the praises of Thy kingship among the most holy. They are glorified amid all the camps of the 'gods' and feared by companies of men. They recount his royal majesty according to their knowledge and exalt [his glory in all] his royal heavens. In all the highest heights [they shall sing] marvellous psalms according to all [their understanding, and the glorious splendour] of the King of the 'gods' they shall recount on their stations ... for what shall we be counted among them? For what shall our priesthood be counted in their dwellings? [How shall our] ho[liness compare with their supreme] holiness? How does the offering of our tongue of dust compare with the knowledge of the divine [beings] ...

## MASADA FRAGMENT 1, 1–7=4Q402 4, 11–15

... wonderful new works. All these he has done wonder[fully with all the eternally hidden things] ... all the words of knowledge; for from the God of knowledge (comes) all that exists for ever, [and from] his [plan]s (come) all the eternally appointed. He produces the former things in their appointed times, and the latter things in their seasons. None among those who know the [wonderfully] revealed things can comprehend them before he makes them. When he makes them, none of [the doers of righteous]ness can understand his plan, for they are his glorious works. Before they come into being, (they derive) [from] his [pla]n.

[For the Master. So]ng of the holocaust of the sixth Sabbath on the ninth of the [second] month.

[Praise the G]od of gods, you inhabitants of the highest heights... [h]oly of holies and exalt his glory ... [kn]owledge of the everlasting gods ...

## 4Q403 1, i, 1–29=MASADA FRAGMENT 1039–200

[Psalm of exaltation (uttered) by the tongue] of the third of the sovereign Princes, an exaltation ... He shall exalt the God of the angels on high seven times with seven wonderful exaltations.

Psalm of praise (uttered) by the tongue of the four[th] to the Mighty One above all the [gods], seven wonderful mighty deeds. He shall praise the God of mighty deeds seven times with seven words of [marvellous] prais[e].

Psalm of thanksgiving (uttered) by the tongue of the fifth to the [K]in[g] of glory with its seven wonderful thanksgivings. He shall thank the God of glory se[ven times with se]v[en wor]ds of wonderful thanksgivings.

[Psalm of] exultation (uttered) by the tongue of the sixth to [the] God of goodness with its seven [wonderful] exultations. He shall exult before the Ki[ng of] goodness seven times with sev[en words of] wonderful exultation.

Psalm of [singing (uttered) by the t]ongue of the seventh of the [sovereign] Prin[ces], a powerful song [to the Go]d of ho[liness] with its se[ven] marvellous [songs]. He shall sing [to] the Kin[g of ho]liness seven times with [seven w]ords of [wonderful] so[ngs; sev]en psa[lms (singing) his blessings; sev]en [psalm]s of magnification of [his righteousness; seven psalms] of exaltation of [his] kingshi[p; seven] psalms of [praises of his glory; sev]en p[salms of thanksgivings for his marvellous deeds]; [seven psalms of ex]ul[tation of] his power; seven [psalms singin]g his holiness; ... [seven times with seven wonderful words, words of ... ]

In the glo[ri]ous name of God, [the first of] the sov[erei]gn Princes sha[ll bless] all the ... [with seven wonderful words blessing all] their [councils] in [his holy] sanctuary [with sev]en wonderful wo[rd]s, [and he shall bless those who kn]ow the everlasting things.

[In the name of] his truth, [the second of the sovereign Princes shall bless] all [their] sta[tions with] se[ven] wonderful word[s and he shall bless with] seven [wonderful] words. [He shall bless all those who exalt the] King with seven g[lor]iou[s] w[ords of his] marvels, [all the] eternally pure.

[In the name of] his exalted kingship, the third [of the sovereign Princes shall bless all who are lif]ted up [in kn]owledge with se[ven w]ords of exal[ta]tion ... [of his true kn]ow[ledge], he shall bless with seven marvellous words; and he shall bless all [who are destined] for righteousness [with seven] wonderful [w]ords.

In the name of the King's majesty, [the fourth] of the [sovereign] Princes shall bless with seven [majestic] words [all who] walk [up]rightly. He shall bless all the gods [close to] true knowledge [with seve]n righteous words (for gaining) [his gl]o[rious] favours.

In the name of [the majesty] of his marvellous deeds, the fifth [sovereign] Prince shall bless with seven [words] of his exalted truth [all who] ... purity. [He shall bless] all who eagerly do his will with seven [marvellous words. And he shall bless] all who confess him with seven majestic [wor]ds that they may thank [him for ever].

In the name of [the mighty deeds of] the gods the sixth sovereign Prince shall bless with seven words of his marvellous mighty deeds all who are mighty in wisdom. He shall bless all the perfect of way with seven marvellous words to be in attendance for [ever]. He shall bless all who wait for him with seven marvellous words that they may obtain the return of his [gracious] favours.

In the name of his holiness, the seventh of the sovereign Princes shall bless with seven words of his marvellous holiness all the holy founders of kno[wledge. He shall bless] all who exalt his statutes with sev[en] marvellous [wo]rds (which shall be for them) stout shields. He shall bless all [who are destined for] righteousness [and always] forever [pra]ise his glorious kingship with seven [marvellous words] for everlasting peace.

In [the name of his holiness] all the [sovereign] Princes [shall bless together] the God of the divine beings [in] all their sevenfold t[estimonies]. They shall bless those destined for righteousness and all the blessed ... the eter[na]ll[y ble]ssed for them.

Blessed be [the] Lo[r]d, the Kin[g of] all, who is above all blessing and p[raise. He shall bless all the holy] who bless [him and proclaim him righ]te[ous] in the name of his glory. [And he shall b]less all who are blessed for ever.

## 4Q403 1, i, 30–46

For the Master. Song of the holocaust of the seventh Sabbath on the sixteenth of the month.

Praise the most high God, O you high among all the gods of knowledge.

Let the holy ones of the 'gods' sanctify the King of glory, who sanctifies by his holiness all his holy ones.

O Princes of the praises of all the 'gods', praise the God of majestic praises,

For in the splendour of praises is the glory of His kingship.

In it are (contained) the praises of all the 'gods' together with the splendour of all [His] king[ship].

Exalt His exaltation on high, O 'gods', above the gods on high, and His glorious divinity above all the highest heights.

For He [is the God of gods], of all the Princes on high, and the King of king[s] of all the eternal councils.

By a discerning goodwill (expressed by) the words of His mouth a[ll the gods on high] come into being, at the opening of His lips, all the eternal spirits, by His discerning goodwill, all His creatures in their undertakings.

Exult, O you who exult [in his knowledge, with] an exultation among the wonderful 'gods';

utter His glory with the tongue of all who utter knowledge;
may His wonderful exultation be in the mouth of all who utter [His knowledge].
[For He] is the God of all who exult in everlasting knowledge,
and the Judge through His might of all the spirits of understanding.
Celebrate O all celebrating gods, the King of majesty, for all the gods of knowledge celebrate His glory,
and all the spirits of righteousness celebrate His truth, and seek acceptance of their knowledge by the judgements of His mouth,
and of their celebrations when His mighty hand executes (?) judgements of reward.
Sing to the God of power with an offering of the princely spirit, a song of divine joy,
and a jubilation among all the holy, a wonderful song for eter[nal] rejoicing.
With these all the f[oundations of the hol]y of holies shall praise,
the pillars bearing the highest abode, and all the corners of its structure.
Sing to the Go[d who is a]wesome in strength ...
to extol together the splendid firmament, the supreme purity of [His] holy sanctuary.
[Praise] Him, O divine spirits, prai[sing for ever and] ever the firmament of the highest heavens,
all ... and its walls, a[l]l its [struc]ture, its shape.
[The spi]rits of the hol[y] of holies, the living 'gods', [the spir]its of [et]ernal holiness above all the holy [ones];
... marvellous marvel, majesty and beauty and marvel.
[Gl]ory is in the perfect light of knowledge ... in all the marvellous sanctuaries.
The divine spirits surround the dwelling of the King of truth and righteousness; all its walls ...

## 4Q403 1, ii, 18–29

For the Master. Song of the holocaust for the eighth Sabbath on the tw[enty]-third [of the second month].
[Praise the God of all the highest heights, all the holy ones for ever] and ever,

they who are second among the priests of the inner Temple, the second council in the wonderful dwelling, with seven words of ... eternally.

Extol Him, O sovereign Princes, in his marvellous portion, praise [the God of gods, O you seven priesthoods of His inner Temple].

... height, the seven wonderful domains by the precept concerning His sanctuaries.

The sovereign Princes of the [wonderful] priest[hood] ... the seven priest[hoods] in the wonderful sanctuary for seven councils of holiness ... the Prince, the angels of the King in the wonderful dwellings. The knowledge of their understanding is for seven ... Prince from the priest of the inner Temple. The Princes of the congregation of the King in the assembly of ... and praises of exaltation to the King of glory and a tower of ... for the God of gods, the King of purity. The offering of their tongues ... the seven mysteries of knowledge in the wonderful mystery of the seven domains [of] the Ho[ly of holies] ... [The tongue of the first shall be seven times stronger than the tongue of the second; the tongue of the second shall be] seven times [stronger] than that of the third: [the to]ngue of the thi[rd shall be] seven tim[es] stronger [than that of the fourth; the tongue of the fourth shall be seven times stronger than the tongue of the fifth: the tongue of the fifth shall be seven times stronger than the tongue of] the sixth; the tongu[e of the sixth shall be seven times stronger than the] t[ongue of the seventh]; the tongue of the seventh ...

## 4Q405 14–15, i

... tongue of blessing from the likeness [of the gods] issues a [v]oice of blessing for the King of those who exalt, and their wonderful praise is for the God of gods ... their many-coloured ... and they sing ... the vestibules by which they enter, the spirits of the most holy inner Temple ... [And the likene]ss of the living 'gods' is engraved on the vestibules by which the King enters, luminous spiritual figures ... [K]ing, figures of a glorious l[ight, wonderful] spirits; [amo]ng the spirits of splendour there are works of (art of) marvellous colours, figures of the living 'gods' ... [in the] glorious innermost Temple chambers, the structure of [the most ho]ly [sanctuary] in the innermost chambers of the King, design[s of 'go]ds' ... likeness of ... most holy ... [the Temple] chambers of the Ki[ng] ...

## 4Q405 19 ABCD

The figures of the 'gods' shall praise Him, [the most] h[oly] spirits ... of glory; the floor of the marvellous innermost chambers, the spirits of the eternal gods, all ... fi[gures of the innermost] chamber of the King, the spiritual works of the marvellous firmament are purified with salt, [spi]rits of knowledge, truth [and] righteousness in the holy of [ho]lies, [f]orms of the living 'gods', forms of the illuminating spirits. All their [works (of art)] are marvellously linked, many-coloured [spirits], artistic figures of the 'gods', engraved all around their glorious bricks, glorious figures on b[ri]cks of splendour and majes[ty]. All their works (of art) are living 'gods', and their artistic figures are holy angels. From beneath the marvellous inner[most chambers] comes a sound of quiet silence: the 'gods' bless ...

## 4Q405 20 ii, 21–2

For the Mas[ter. Song of the holocaust of] the twelfth [S]abbath [on the twenty-first of the third month.]

[Praise the God of ... w]onder, and exalt Him ... of glory in the te[nt of the God of] knowledge. The [cheru]bim prostrate themselves before Him and bless. As they rise, a whispered divine voice [is heard], and there is a roar of praise. When they drop their wings, there is a [whispere]d divine voice. The cherubim bless the image of the throne-chariot above the firmament, [and] they praise [the majes]ty of the luminous firmament beneath His seat of glory. When the wheels advance, angels of holiness come and go. From between His glorious wheels, there is as it were a fiery vision of most holy spirits. About them, the appearance of rivulets of fire in the likeness of gleaming brass, and a work of ... radiance in many-coloured glory, marvellous pigments, clearly mingled. The spirits of the living 'gods' move perpetually with the glory of the marvellous chariot(s). The whispered voice of blessing accompanies the roar of their advance, and they praise the Holy One on their way of return. When they ascend, they ascend marvellously and when they settle, they stand still. The sound of joyful praise is silenced and there is a whispered blessing of the 'gods' in all the camps of God. And the sound of praise ... from among all their divisions ... and all their numbered ones praise, each in his turn.

## 4Q405 23, i

... his whole-offering. The 'gods' praise Him [when they take] up their station, and all the s[pirits of] the clear firm[am]ent rejoice in His glory. A sound of blessing (is heard) from all His divisions speaking of the firmaments of His glory, and His gates praise with a resounding voice. When the gods of knowledge enter by the doors of glory, and when the holy angels depart towards their realm, the entrance doors and the gates of exit proclaim the glory of the King, blessing and praising all the spirits of God when they depart and enter by the gates. None among them skips over a precept, nor do they ... against the saying of the King ... They run not away from the path, nor slip away from His domain. They are neither too high for His commission nor too lowly. For He shall be compassionate in the realm of His furious, destr[oying ange]r; He will not judge in the provinces of His glorious wrath. The fear of the King of 'gods' is awe-inspiring to [al]l the 'gods', [and they undertake] all His commissions by virtue of His true order, and they go ...

## 4Q405 23, ii

... At their marvellous stations are spirits, many-coloured like the work of a weaver, splendid engraved figures. In the midst of a glorious appearance of scarlet, colours of the most holy spiritual light, they hold to their holy station before [the K]ing, spirits of [pure] colours in the midst of an appearance of whiteness. The likeness of the glorious spirit is like a work (of art) of sparkling fine gold. All their pattern is clearly mingled like the work (of art) of a weaver. These are the Princes of those marvellously clothed for service, the Princes of the kingdom, the kingdom of the holy ones of the King of holiness in all the heights of the sanctuaries of His glorious kingdom. The Princes in charge of offerings have tongues of knowledge, [and] they bless the God of knowledge among all His glorious works ...

## 11Q5–6

... their [mar]vellous marvels by the power of the God of [eter]nity; and they shall exalt the mighty deeds of the G[od] ... From the four foundations of the marvellous firmament they shall pr[oclaim] soundlessly (?) a divine oracle ... wall. They bless and praise the God of gods ...

# Poetic Fragments on Jerusalem and 'King' Jonathan

## (4Q448)

Written in a very difficult semi-cursive script, this text has been brilliantly deciphered by Ada Yardeni and edited by Esther and Hanan Eshel.

The top part of the fragment, or column A, preserving the first two or three words of ten lines, is an unknown Halleluiah psalm. However, the last three lines have been identified by E. Eshel, as well as by M. Kister, as belonging to the last verses of Psalm 154, included in the Psalms Scroll from 11Q, and partly reconstructed from the Syriac (cf. J. A. Sanders, *DJD*, IV, col. XVIII, lines 14–16), and ending with an allusion to God's presence in Zion–Jerusalem (cf. p. 301).

Column B, with its nine lines, is complete. It opens with a reference to the 'Holy City', associated with 'King' Jonathan, but the main theme appears to be a blessing of God's kingdom and name on behalf of the entire people of Israel.

Column C, with the second half of each of its nine lines missing, also mentions Israel, together with God's name and kingdom, as well as what seems to be 'the day of war'. The editors believe that they can read 'Jonathan' in line 8, but this is far from certain.

4Q448 is a unique and significant Qumran text of historical importance. The editors assume that King Jonathan is Alexander Jannaeus or Yannai, i.e. a Hasmonaean ruler who, as a general rule, is presumed by scholars to have been hostile to the Qumran Community. They conjecture, therefore, that 4Q448 is not a sectarian composition. I prefer, by contrast, to identify 'King' Jonathan as Jonathan Maccabaeus at the start of his political-military career, when he was celebrated as the liberator of the Jews and of Jerusalem, and link this text to the statement of the Habakkuk Commentary in VIII, 8–9, concerning the good behaviour 'when he first arose' of the ruler who was to become the Wicked Priest.

For preliminary studies, see Esther Eshel, Hanan Eshel and Ada Yardeni, 'A Qumran Composition containing Part of Ps. 154 and a Prayer for the Welfare of King Jonathan and his Kingdom', *IEJ* 42 (1992), 199–229; G. Vermes, 'The

So-called King Jonathan Fragment (4Q448)', *JJS* 44 (1993), 294–300; P. S. Alexander, 'A Note on the Syntax of 4Q448', *JJS* 44 (1993), 301–2.

**Column A**

Halleluiah. Psal[m ... ] Thou hast loved as ... Thou hast acted as a prince over ... *vacat* And those who ha[te Thee ... ] many. The heav[ens ... ] The deep of the sea ... [Behold the eyes of the Lord have compassion on the good, and His mercy] is [great] over those who glorify Him. [From an evil time He saves their soul. He redeems] the poor from the hand of oppressors, [and delivers the perfect from the hand of the wicked. He desires] his tabernacle in Zion, (and) ch[ooses Jerusalem for ever].

**Column B**

Holy City for King Jonathan and for all the congregation of Thy people Israel, who are in the four corners of heaven. May the peace of them all be on Thy kingdom! May Thy name be blessed.

**Column C**

I will glo[ry in] Thy love ... during the day and until the evening ... to draw near to be ... to visit them for a blessing ... on Thy name which is invoked ... kingdom to be blessed ... [o]n t[he] day war ... to King Jonathan (?) ...

# C. Calendars, Liturgies and Prayers

'Phases of the Moon',
*Israel Antiquities Authority*

# Calendars of Priestly Courses

## (4Q320–30)

Eleven fragmentary manuscripts from Cave 4 present in various forms the peculiar 'solar' calendar – constructed in six-year sequences – of the Qumran Community. Their year consisted of twelve months of thirty days each, plus four extra days added to each of the four seasons (cf. above, pp. 78–9). Some documents from 4Q (**320** and **321**) attempt to combine this calendar with the various priestly courses which served in turn in the Temple for a week at a time from one sabbath to the following Friday. They also combine it with the dates of the full moon given according to the days of the week of duty of the priestly course, the date of the solar month and the equivalent date of the lunar calendar of mainstream Judaism (a year of twelve months of 29 or 30 days = 354 days). E.g. (The full moon falls): 'On the 5th (day) in the week of Jedaiah, corresponding to the 29th day of the lunar month, which falls on the 30th day of the 1st solar month.' 4Q**321** records in addition the occurrence of the New Moon. E.g. 'And the New Moon is on the third day in the week of Mijamin which is on the twelfth day in the eighth month.'

The badly mutilated remains of 4Q**322–4b** record the names of political figures, Jewish and Roman, as well as dated historical events in a calendar of priestly courses. E.g.: '... [in] the seventh [mon]th ... (the week of) Gamul... Aemilius killed ... ' Yet others specify the dates of sabbaths and festivals or list the priestly course on duty in the first week of the year and in the first week of each of the four yearly seasons (4Q**325**, **327** and **328**).

For preliminary editions and studies, see J. T. Milik, 'Le travail d'édition des manuscrits du Désert de Juda', *Suppl. to Vetus Testamentum*, IV (Leiden, 1957), 17–26; B. Z. Wacholder and M. G. Abegg, *A Preliminary Edition of the Unpublished Dead Sea Scrolls*, Fasc. 1 (Washington, 1991), 60–101, especially Appendix B, 103–18, containing a useful layout of the Qumran calendar, the priestly courses, as well as the phases of the moon and the various festivals. Cf. also *DSSU*, 106–34; S. Talmon, 'A Calendrical Document from Qumran Cave 4 (Mishmarot D, 4Q**325**)', in Z. Zevit et al., eds., *Solving Riddles and Untying Knots* (J. C. Greenfield Memorial) (Winona Lake, 1995), 327–44.

The following table will help readers understand the relationship between the priestly courses on weekly duty, the 'solar' dates, the moon's phases and the feast-days falling in the month in question.

*First month of the first year in a six-year cycle*

Sigla: bold number=feast; †=New Moon; ††=full moon

| *Su* | *M* | *T* | *W* | *Th* | *F* | *Sa* | *Course* | *Feasts* |
|---|---|---|---|---|---|---|---|---|
| | | | 1†† | 2 | 3 | 4 | Gamul | |
| 5 | 6 | 7 | 8 | 9 | 10 | 11 | Delaiah | |
| 12 | 13 | **14** | 15 | 16 | 17† | 18 | Maaziah | Passover [eve] |
| 19 | 20 | 21 | 22 | 23 | 24 | 25 | Joiarib | |
| **26** | 27 | 28 | 29 | 30†† | | | Jedaiah | Waving of the Sheaf |

## Mishmarot A (4Q320)

### Fr. 1

**I** . . . to show it from the east. [And] to cause it to shine [in] the middle of heaven, in the foundation [of the firmam]ent, from evening till morning.

(There is full moon)

On the 4th (day) in the week [of the sons of G]amul in the first month of [*the firs*]*t year*.

[On the 5th (day) in (the week of) Jedai]ah, (corresponding) to the 29th (day of the lunar month, which falls) on the 30th (day) of the 1st (solar month).

[On the sabbath in (the week of) Hak]koz, (corresponding) to the 30th (day of the lunar month, which falls) on the 30th of the second (solar month).

[On the 1st (day) in (the week of) Elia]shib, (corresponding) to the 29th (day of the lunar month), (which falls) on the 29th (day) in the third (solar month).

[On the 3rd (day) in (the week of) Bilg]ah, (corresponding) to the 30th (day of the lunar month, which falls) on the 28th day in the fourth (solar month).

[On the 4th (day) in (the week of) Peta]hiah, (corresponding) to the

29th (day of the lunar month which falls) on the 27th day in the fifth (solar month).

On the 6th (day) in (the week of) Delaiah, (corresponding) to the 30th (day of the lunar month which falls) on the 27th (day) in the sixth (solar month).

[On the sabbath in (the week of) Seori]m, (corresponding) to the 29th (day of the lunar month which falls) on the 25th (day) in the seventh (solar month).

[On the 2nd (day) in (the week of) Abiah, (corresponding) to the 3]0th (day of the lunar month which falls) on the 25th (day) in the eighth (solar month).

[On the 3rd (day) in (the week of) Jakim, (corresponding) to the 2]9th (day of the lunar month which falls) on the 24th (day) in the ninth (solar month).

**II** On the 5th (day) in (the week of) Immer, (corresponding) to the 30th (day of the lunar month which falls) on the 23rd (day) in the tenth (solar month).

On the 6th (day) in (the week of) Jehezekel, (corresponding) to the 29th (day of the lunar month which falls) on the 22nd (day) in the eleventh (solar) month.

On the 1st (day) in (the week of) Jeiarib, (corresponding) to the 30th (day of the lunar month which falls) on the 22nd (day) in the twelfth (solar) month.

*The second year.*

On the 2nd (day) in (the week of) Malchiah, (corresponding) to the 29th (day of the lunar month which falls) on the 20th (day) in the first (solar month).

On the 4th (day) in (the week of) Jeshua, (corresponding) to the 30th (day of the lunar month which falls) on the 20th (day) in the second (solar month).

On the 5th (day) in (the week of) Huppah, (corresponding) to the 29th (day of the lunar month which falls) on the 19th [in the third] (month).

On the sabbath in (the week of) Pizzez, (corresponding) to the 30th (day of the lunar month which falls) on the 18th in the f[ourth] (month).

On the 1st (day) in Gamul, (corresponding) to the [29th (day of the lunar month which falls) on the 17th day in the fifth] (solar month).

On the 3rd (day) in (the week of) Jedaiah, (corresponding) to the 30th (day of the lunar month which falls) [on the 17th (day) in the sixth] (solar month).

On the 4th (day) in (the week of) Mijamin, (corresponding) to the 2[9th (day of the lunar month which falls) on the 15th day] in the seventh (solar month).

On the 6th (day) in Shecaniah, (corresponding) to the 3[0th (day of the lunar month which falls) on the 15th (day) in the eighth] (solar month).

On the sabbath in (the week of) Bil[gah, (corresponding) to the 29th (day of the lunar month which falls) on the 14th (day) in the ninth] (solar month).

[On the 2nd (day) in (the week of) Petahiah, (corresponding) to the 30th (day of the lunar month which falls) on the 13th (day) in the tenth] (solar month).

**III** [On the 3rd (day) in (the week of) Delaiah, (corresponding) to the 29th (day of the lunar month which falls) on the 12th (day) in the eleventh] (solar month).

[On the 5th (day) in Harim, (corresponding) to the 30th (day of the lunar month which falls) on the 12th (day) of the twelfth (solar month)].

*(The third year)*

[On the 6th (day) in (the week of) Hakkoz, (corresponding) to the 29th (day of the lunar month which falls) on the 10th (day) in the first] (solar month).

[On the 1st (day) in (the week of) Jakim, (corresponding) to the 30th (day of the lunar month which falls) on the 10th (day) in the second] (solar month).

[On the 2nd (day) in (the week of) Immer, (corresponding) to the 29th (day of the lunar month which falls) on the 9th (day) in the third] (solar month).

[On the 4th (day) in Jehezekel, (corresponding) to the 30th (day of the lunar month which falls) on the 8th (day) of the fourth] (solar month).

[On the 5th (day) in Maaziah, (corresponding) to the 29th (day of the lunar month which falls) on the 7th (day) in the fifth] (solar month).

[On the sabbath in (the week of) Malchiah, (corresponding) to the 30th (day of the lunar month which falls) on the 7th (day) in the sixth] (solar month).

On the 1st (day) in (the week of) Je[shua, (corresponding) to the 29th (day of the lunar month which falls) on the 5th (day) in the seventh] (solar month).

On the 3rd (day) in (the week of) Huppah, (corresponding) to the 30th (day of the lunar month which falls) on the 5th (day) in the eighth (month).

On the 4th (day) in (the week of) Hezir, (corresponding) to the 29th (day of the lunar month which falls) on the 4th (day) in the ninth (solar month).

On the 6th (day) in Jachin, (corresponding) to the 30th (day of the lunar month which falls) on the 3rd (day) in the tenth (solar month).

On the sabbath in (the week of) Jedaiah, (corresponding) to the 29th (day of the lunar month which falls) on the 2nd (day) of the eleventh (solar) month.

On the 2nd (day) [of Mijami]n, (corresponding) to the 30th (day of the lunar month which falls on) the second day in the twelfth (solar) month.

## Fr. 4

**II** ...

the days, the sabbaths [and] the months [for] years and for sabbatical years and for jubilees. On the 4th (day) of the week of the sons of Gamul.

**III** *The first year: its feasts.* On the third (day in the week of) Meoziah: the Passover.

On the 1st (day) [in (the week of) Jeda[iah]: the Waving of the [Sheaf].

On the 5th (day) in (the week of) Seorim: the [Second] Passover. *vacat*

On the 1st (day) in (the week of) Jeshua: the Feast of Weeks.

On the 4th (day) in (the week of) Meoziah: the Day of Memorial.

[On] the 6th (day) in Jeiarib: the Day of Atonement [in the] seventh [month]. *vacat*

[On the 4th (day) in (the week of) Jeda]iah: the Feast of Tabernacles.

*The second (year): its feasts.* [On the 3rd (day)] in (the week of) Seorim: the Passov[er].

[On the 1st (day)] in (the week of) Mijamin: the Waving of the [Sheaf].

[On the 5th (day) in (the week of) Abiah: the Second Passover].

**IV** On the 1st (day) [in (the week of) H]uppah: [the Feast of W]eeks.
On the 4th (day) in (the week of) Seorim: the Day of Mem[orial].
On the 6th (day) in (the week of) Malchia[h]: the Day of Ato[nement].
On [the 4th (day) in (the week of)] Mijamin: the Feast of Tabernacles.
*vacat*

*The third (year): its feasts.* On the 3rd (day) in (the week of) Abiah: the Passover.
On the 21st (day) in (the week of) Shecaniah: the Waving of the Sheaf.
On the 5th (day) in (the week of) Jakim: the [Second] Passover.
On the 1st (day) in (the week of) Hezir: [the Feast of Weeks].
On the 4th (day) in (the week of) Abiah: the Day of Memorial.
On the 6th (day) in (the week of) Jeshua: the Day of Atonement.
On the 4th (day) in (the week of) Shecaniah: the Feast of Tabernacles.

*The fourth (year): its feasts.*]
**V** [On the 3rd (day) in (the week of) Jaki]m: the Passover.
On the 1st (day) [in (the week of) Jeshebeab: the Waving of the Sheaf.
On [the 5th (day) in (the week of) Im]mer: the Second Passover.
[On the 1st (day) in (the week of) Piz]zez: [the Feast] of Weeks.
[On] the 4th (day) in (the week of) Jakim: the Day of Memorial.
[On] the 6th (day) in (the week of) Huppah: the Day of Atonement.
[On the 4th] (day) in (the week of) Jeshebeab: the Feast of Tabernacles.
*vacat*

[*The fifth (year): its feasts.*]
On the 3rd (day) in (the week of) Immer: the Passover.
On the 1st (day) in (the week of) Pizzez: the Waving of the Sheaf.
[On the 5th (day)] in (the week of) Jehezekel: the Second Passover.
[On the 1st (day) in (the week of) Joiari]b: the Feast of [Weeks].
[On the 4th (day) in (the week of) Immer: the Day of Memorial].

**VI** On the 6th (day) in (the week of) Hezir: the Day of Atonement.
On the 4th (day) in (the week of) Pizzez: the Feast of Tabernacles.
*vacat*

*The sixth (year): its feasts.*
On the 3rd (day) in (the week of) Jehezekel: the Passov[er].
On the 1st (day) in (the week of) Gamul: the Waving of the Sheaf.
[On the 3rd (day)] in (the week of) Maaziah: the [Second] Passover.

On the 1st (day) in (the week of) Malchiah: the Feast of [Weeks].
[On] the 4th (day) in (the week of) Jehezeke[l: the Day of Memorial].
[On] the 6th (day) in (the week of) Jachin: [the Day of Atonement.
On the 4th (day) in (the week of) Gamul: the Feast of Tabernacles] . . .

## Mishmarot B (4Q**321**, fr. 1)

(There is full moon)

. . .

**I** [And the New Moon is on the 1st (day) in (the week of) Jedaiah which is on the twel]fth (day) in it (=the seventh month).

On the second (day) in (the week of) Abia[h which is on the] twe[nty-fifth (day) in the eighth (month).

And the New Moon is on the third (day) in (the week of) Mijamin which is on the twelfth (day)] in (the eighth month).

On the third (day) in (the week of) Jakim which is on the [twenty]-fou[rth (day) in the ninth (month).

And the New Moon is on the fourth (day) in Shecaniah which is on the eleve]nth (day) in (the ninth month).

On the fifth (day) in (the week of) Immer which is on the thirteenth (day) in the ten[th (month).

And the New Moon is on the sixth (day) in (the week of) Je]shabeab [which is on the tenth (day) in (the tenth month)].

On [the s]ixth (day) in (the week of) Jehezekel which is on the twenty-second (day) in the eleventh (month).

And [the New Moon is on sabbath in (the week of)] Petahiah which is [on the ninth (day) in (the eleventh month)].

On the first (day) in (the week of) Joiarib which is on the twenty-second (day) in the twelfth month.

And [the New Moon is on the secon]d (day) in (the week of) Delaiah [which is on the ninth (day) in (the twelfth month)]. *vacat*

*[The] second (year), the first (month).*
On the second (day) in (the week of) Malchiah which is on the twen[tieth (day) in the first (month).

And] the New Moon [is on the third (day) in (the week of) Harim which is on the se]venth (day) in (the first month).

On the fourth (day) in (the week of) Jeshua which is [on] the twentieth (day) in the second (month).

And [the New Moon is on the fifth (day) in (the week of)] Hakkoz which is on the ninth (day) [in (the second month).

On the fifth (day) in (the week of) Huppah which is on the nine]teenth (day) in the third (month).

And the New Mo[on] is on the sixth (day) [in (the week of) E]l[iashib] which is on the sixth (day) [in (the third month).

On the sabba]th in (the week of) Pizzez

**II** [which is on the eighteenth (day) in the fourth (month).

And the New Moon is on the first (day) in (the week of) Immer which is on the fifth (day)] in (the fourth month).

On the first (day) in (the week of) [Gamul, which is on the seventeenth (day) in the fifth (month).

And the New Moon is on the second (day) in (the week of) Je[hezek]el which is on the fourth (day) in (the fifth month).

On the third (day) in (the week of) Jed]aiah which is on [the seventeenth (day) in the sixth (month).

And the New Moon is on the fourth (day)] in (the week of) Maoziah which is on the fourth (day) in (the sixth month).

On the fourt[h (day) in (the week of) Mijamin which is on the fifteenth (day)] in the seventh (month).

And the New Moon is on the f[ifth (day)] in (the week of) Seorim which is on the second in (the seventh month).

On the sixth (day) in (the week of) Shecaniah which is on the fif[teenth (day) in the eighth (month).

And the New] Moon is on the sabbath in Abiah which is on the second (day) in (the eighth month). [On the sabbath in (the week of) Bilgah] which is on the fourteenth (day) of the ninth (month).

And the New Moon is [on the first (day)] in the ninth month.

And the second [New Moo]n is on the third (day) in [(the week of) Hezir, which is on the thirty]-first in [(the ninth month).

On] the second (day) in (the week of) Petahiah which is on the thir[teenth (day) in the tenth (month)].

And the New Moon is on the fourt[h (day) in (the week of) Ja]chin which is on the twenty-nin[th (day) in (the tenth month)].

On [the third (day) in (the week of) Delai]ah which is on the twelfth (day) in the ele[venth month.

And the New] Moon is on the sixth (day) in (the week of) Joiar]ib which is on the tw]enty-ninth (day) in [(the eleventh month)].

On the fifth (day) in (the week of) Harim which is on the twelfth (day) of the twelfth month. And the New Moo[n] is on the sabbath [in (the week of)] Mijamin which is on the twenty-eighth (day) in (the twelfth month).

*The third* (*year*). The [first] (month).

**III** [On the sixth (day) in (the week of) Hakkoz which is on the tenth (day) in the first (month).

And the New Moon is on the second (day) in (the week of) Shecaniah which is on the twenty-seventh (day) in (the first month).

On the first (day) in (the week of) Jakim which is on the tenth (day) in the second (month).

And the New Moon is on the third (day) in (the week of) Jeshebeab which is on the twenty-sixth (day) in (the second month).

On the second (day) in (the week of) Immer which is on the ninth (day) in the third (month).

And the New Moon is on the fifth (day) in (the week of) Pizzez which is on the twenty-sixth (day) in (the third month).

On the fourth (day) in (the week of) Jehezekel which is on the eighth (day) in the fourth (month).

And the New Moon is on the sixth (day) in (the week of) Gamul which is on the twenty-fourth (day) in (the fourth month).

On the fifth (day) in (the week of) Meoziah which is on the seventh (day) in the fifth (month).

And the New Moo]n is on the first (day) in (the week of) Har[im which is on the twenty-fourt]h (day) in (the fifth month).

On the sabbath in (the week of) Mal[chiah which is on the seventh (day) of the sixth (month).

And the New Moon is on the second (day) in (the week of) Hakkoz which is on the twenty-third (day) in (the sixth month).

On the first (day) in (the week of) Jeshua which is on the fifth (day)] in the seventh (month).

And the New Moon on the fourth (day) in (the week of) Eliashib which is on the [twenty-]second (day) [in (the seventh month).

On the third (day) in (the week of) Huppah which is on the fifth (day) in the eighth (month).

And the New Moon is in the fifth (day) in (the week of) Bilgah which is on the twenty-first (day) in] (the eighth month).

On the fourth (day) in (the week of) Hezir which is on the fourth (day) in the ninth (month).

And the New Moon is on the sabbath in (the week of) J[ehezekel which is on the twenty-first (day) in (the ninth month).

On the sixth (day) in (the week of) Jachin which is on the third (day) in the tenth (month).

And the New Moon is on the first (day) in (the week of) Maaziah which is on the nine]teenth in (the tenth month).

On the sabbath in (the week of) Jedaiah which is on the second (day) in the eleventh month.

And the New Moon is [on the third (day) in Seorim which is on the nineteenth (day) in (the eleventh month).

On the second (day) in (the week of) Mijamin which is on the second (day) in the twelfth month.

And the New] Moon is on the fourth (day) in (the week of) Abiah which is on the eighteenth (day) in (the twelfth month).

*The fourth (year).*

On the fourth (day) in (the week of) Shecan[iah which is on the first (day) in the first month].

And the New Moon is on the sixth (day) in (the week of) Jakim which is on the seventeenth (day) in (the first month).

[On the fifth (day) in (the week of) Pizzez which is on the thirtieth (day) in] the first (month).

On the sabbath [in (the week of)] Petahiah which is on the thirtieth of the second month.

And the New Moon is on the first (day) in (the week of) Hez[ir]

## Fr. 2

*(Seventh year)*

**I** [which is on the seventh (day) in the fifth (month).

And the N]ew Moon is on the first (day) in [(the week of) Bilg]ah which is on the twe[nty-f]ou[r]th (day) in (the fifth month).

On the sabbath in (the week of) Hezir which is on the sevent[h (day) in the sixth (month).

And the New Moon is on the second (day) in (the week of) Petahiah] which is on the twenty-third (day) in (the sixth month).

On the first (day) in (the week of) Jachin which is on the fifth (day) in the seventh (month).

And the New Moon is on the fourth (day) [in (the week of) Delaiah which is on the twenty-second (day)] in (the seventh month).

On the third (day) in (the week of) Joiarib which is on the fifth (day) in the eighth (month).

And the New Moon is on the fifth (day) in (the week of) Harim [which is on the twenty-first (day) in the eighth month.

On the fou]rth (day) in (the week of) Malchiah which is on the fourth (day) in the ninth (month).

And the New Moon is on the sabbath in (the week of) Abiah which is on the [twenty-]first (day) in ([the ninth month).

On the sixth (day) in (the week of) Je]shua which is [on] the third (day) in the tenth (month).

And the New Moon is on the first (day) in (the week of) Jakim which is on the nineteenth (day) in [(the tenth month).

On the sabbath in (the week of) Jeshebeab which is on the second (day) of the elev]enth month.

And the New Moon is on the thi[rd (day) in (the week of) Immer] which is on the nineteenth (day) in (the eleventh month).

[On the second (day) in (the week of) Pizzez which is on the second (day) in the twel]fth month.

And the New Moon is on the four[th (day) in (the week of) Jehezek]el which is on the eighteenth (day) [in the twelfth month.] *vacat* . . .

(*First year*)

**II** in Jeshua: the Feast of Week[s] is in it.

[The fou]r[th (month begins) in (the week of) E]liashib.

The fifth (month begins) in [(the week of) Bilgah.

The sixth (month begins) in (the week of) J]ehezekel.

The seve[nth (month begins) in (the week of) Maoziah]. In Maoziah is the Day of Memorial. In Joiarib is the Day of Atonement. In Jedaiah is [the Feast of] Tabernacles.

The eighth (month begins) [in (the week of) Seorim].

The ninth (month begins) in (the week of) Jeshua.

The tenth (month begins) in (the week of) Huppah.

The eleventh (month begins) in (the week of) Hezir.

The twelfth (month begins) in (the week of) Gamul. *vacat*

*The second (year).*

The first (month begins) in (the week of) Jedaia[h]. In (the week of) Seorim is the Passover. In (the week of) Mijamin is the Waving of the Sheaf.

The second (month begins) in (the week of) M[ijamin. In (the week of) Abiah] is the Second Passover.

The [third (month begins) in (the week of) E]l[iashib] and in (the week of) Hu[ppah] is the Feast of Weeks.

[The] fourth (month begins) [in (the week of) B]ilgah.

The fifth (month begins) in (the week of) Petahiah.

[The sixth (month begins) in (the week of) Maaziah.

The seventh (month begins) in (the week of) Seorim. In (the week of) Seorim is the Da]y of Memorial. In (the week of) Malchiah [is the Day of] Atonement. In (the week of) Mijamin [is the Feast] of Tabernacles.

[The eighth (month begins) in (the week of) Abiah.

The ninth (month begins) in (the week of)] Huppah.

The tenth (month begins) in (the week of) Hezir.

The e[leventh] (month begins) in (the week of) Jachin.

[The twel]fth mo[nt]h (begins) [in (the week of) Jedaiah]. *vacat*

*The third (year).*

The first (month begins) in (the week of) M[ijam]in. In (the week of) Abiah is the Passover. In (the week of) Shecaniah is the Waving of the Sheaf.

The se[cond] (month begins) in (the week of) Shecaniah and in (the week of) Jakim is the Second Passover.

The third (month begins) in (the week of) Bilgah. In [(the week of) Hez]ir

**III** [is the Feast] of Week[s.

The fourt]h (month begins) in [(the week of) Petahiah.

The fifth (month begins) in (the week of) Delaiah.

The sixth (month begins) in (the week of) Seorim.

In the seventh (month), in (the week of) Abiah is the D]ay [of Memorial. In (the week of) Jeshua] is the D[ay of Atonement. In (the week of) Shecania]h is the Feast of Tabernacles.

The ei[ghth (month begins) in (the week of) Jakim.

The ninth (month begins) in (the week of) Hezir.

The tenth] (month begins) in (the week of) Jachin.

The ele[venth month begins] in (the week of) Joiarib.
[The twel]fth month (begins) in (the week of) Mij]amin.

*The fourth (year).*

The first (month begins) in (the week of) Shecaniah. In (the week of) Jakim is the Passover. In (the week of) Jeshebeab is the Waving of the Sheaf.

The second (month begins) in (the week of) Jeshebeab. In (the week of) Im[mer is the Second Passover. In (the week of) Jachin is the Fe]ast of [Weeks.

The fourth (month begins) in (the week of) Delaiah.
The fifth] (month begins) in (the week of) Harim.
The sixth (month begins) in [(the week of) Abiah.

The se]venth (month begins) [in (the week of) Jakim]. In (the week of) Jaki[m is the Da]y [of Memorial]. In (the week of) Huppah [is the Day of Atonement. In (the week of) Jeshebeab is the Feast of Tabernacle]s.

The eighth (month begins) in (the week of) Immer.
The ninth (month begins) in [(the week of) Jachin.
The tenth (month begins) in (the week of) Joiari]b.
The ele[vent]h [month (begins)] in (the week of) Ma[lchiah.
The twelfth month (begins) in (the week of) Shecaniah]. *vacat*

*The fifth (year).*

The f[irst] (month begins) in [(the week of) Jeshebeab. In (the week of) Immer] is the Passover. In (the week of) Pi[zzez i]s the Waving of the Sheaf.

The se[cond (month begins) in (the week of) Pizze]z. In Jehezekel is the Second Passover.

The third (month begins) in [(the week of) Delaiah. In (the week of) Joiarib is the Feast of W]eeks.

The f[ourth] (month begins) in (the week of) Harim.
The fifth (month begins) in (the week of) Hakk[o]z.
[The si]xth (month begins) in (the week of) Jakim.

The seventh (month begins) in (the week of) Immer. In (the week of) Immer is the Day of Memori[al. In (the week of) Hezir is the Day of Atonement. In (the week of) Pi]zzez is the Feast of Tabernacles.

The eighth (month begins) in (the week of) Jehezekel.

The ninth (month begins) in (the week of) Joiar[ib] and the tenth (month begins)

**IV** [in (the week of) Malchiah.
The eleventh month (begins) in (the week of) Jeshua.
The twelfth month (begins) in (the week of) Jeshebeab.

[*The sixth* (*year*).
The first (month begins) in (the week of) Pizzez. In (the week of) Jehezekel is the Passover. In (the week of) Gamul is the Waving of the Sheaf.

The second (month begins) in (the week of) Gamul. In (the week of) Maaziah is the Second Passover.

The third month (begins) in (the week of) Harim. In (the week of) Malchiah is the Feast of Weeks.

The fourth (month begins) in (the week of) Hakkoz.

The fifth (month begins) in (the week of) Eliashib. The sixth (month begins) in (the week of) Immer.

The seventh (month begins) in (the week of) Jehezekel. In (the week of) Jehezekel is the Day of Memorial. In (the week of) Jachin is the Day of Atonement. In (the week of) Gamul i]s the Feast [of Tabernacles.

The eighth (month begins) in (the week of) Maaziah.
The ninth (month begins) in (the week of) Malchiah.
The tenth (month begins) in (the week of) Jeshua].
The eleven[th] month (begins) in (the week of) Huppah.
[The twelfth month (begins) in (the week of) Pizzez].

## Mishmarot C$^{a}$ (4Q322)

### Fr. 2

... [to] give him honour with prudenc[e] ... [on the n]inth of Shebat – that is ... which is the twentieth (day) of the month ... Shelamzion came ...... to seek to visit ... Hyrcanus, King of ... to seek to visit ...

### Fr. 3

... [of the Kit]tim killed ... [on the] fifth [day] in (the week of) Jedaiah – this is ...

## Mishmarot $C^b$ (4Q**324a**)

### Fr. 2

... [in (the week of) Je]hezekel which is ... Aemilius killed ...... [in] the seventh [mon]th ... (the week of) Gamul ... Aemilius killed ...

## Mishmarot $C^e$ (4Q**324b**)

### Fr. 1

... Shelamzion ...

### Fr. 2

...
h[igh] priest ... Johanan to bring to ...

## Mishmarot D (4Q**325**)

### Fr. 1

**I** [The first ye]ar. On the eighteenth (day) in (the first month) is the sabbath of [(the week of) Joiarib] ... in the evening.

On the twenty-fifth (day) in (the first month) is the sabbath of (the week of) Jedaiah. During the same week is [the Feast] of Barley on the twenty-sixth (day) in (the first month), after the sabbath.

The beginning of the [second] month [is on the s]ixth [day] of (the week of) Jedaiah.

On the second (day) in (the second month) is the sabbath of Harim.

On the ninth (day) in (the second month) is the sabbath [of Seorim].

On the sixteenth (day) in (the second month) is the sabbath of Malchiah.

On the twenty-third (day) in (the second month) [is the sabbath of M]ijamin.

On the thirtieth (day) in (the second month) is the sabbath of Hakkoz. *vacat* The beginning of the third month after the sabbath

**II** ...

**III** [On the sixth (day) in (the week of) Bilgah. On the second (day) in (the fifth month) is the sabbath of I]mmer. On the thi[r]d (day) i[n (the fifth month) is the Feast of the New Wine after the sabbath of Immer.

On] the ninth (day) in (the fifth month) is the sabbath of Hezir. [On the sixteenth (day) in (the fifth month) is the sabbath of Aphses. On the twenty-]third (day) in (the fifth month) is the sabbath [of Petahiah.

On the thirtieth (day) in (the fifth month) is the sabbath of Jehezekel. The beginni]ng of the sixth month is after the sabbath (=Sunday) of Jehezekel. On the seventh (day) in (the sixth month) is the sabbath of Jachin. On the fou]rteenth (day) [in (the sixth month) is the sabbath of Gamul. On the twenty-first (day) in (the sixth month) is the sabbath of Delaiah. On the twenty-]second (day) in (the sixth month) is the Feast of New Oil. After the Feast of New Oil is the Feast of the Offering of Wo]od.

## Mishmarot E$^{b}$ (4Q327)

### Fr. 1

**I** ... [in it a sabbath.]
On the sixteenth (day) in (the fifth month) is a sabbath.
On the twenty-third (day) in (the fifth month) is a sabbath.
[On the th]irtieth [in (the fifth month) is a sabbath] ...

**II** [On the twenty-firs]t (day) in (the fifth month) is a sabbath.
On the twenty-second (day) in (the fifth month) is the Festival of Oil.
Af[ter the sab]bath ... is the Offeri[ng of wood].

## Mishmarot F$^{a}$ (4Q328)

... [In the fifth (year): Jeshabe]ab. In the sixth: Hapizzez.
These are the beginnings of the years.
[In the first [year]: Gamul, Eliash[ib], Moazia[h, Huppah.

In] the second: Jedaiah, Bilgah, Se[or]im, He[zir].
[In the third]: Mij[amin], Petahiah, Ab[iah, Jachin].
[In the fourth: Shecaniah, De]laiah, Jakim, Joia[rib.
In the fifth: Jeshabeab, Harim, Immer, Malchiah.
In the s[ixth: Hapizzez, Hakkoz] ...

# Calendric Signs (*Otot*)

## (4Q319)

The so-called *Otot* or 'Signs' document was copied as the continuation of 4QS[e] (4Q259). Whether it was part of the original composition is as debatable as the attachment of a calendar to MMT at 4Q394 1–2 (cf. above, p. 220).

4Q319 represents a calendrical system based on the weekly rotation of the twenty-four priestly courses during a six-year period and constructed into six consecutive Jubilees, i.e. 294 years. The 'sign' which recurs in every three years probably identifies the years in which the shorter lunar year of 354 days is supplemented by means of the intercalation of an extra month of 30 days (3×354+30=1,092) to equal the length of three 'solar' years of 364 days each (3×364=1,092).

For preliminary studies, see B. Z. Wacholder and M. G. Abegg, *A Preliminary Edition of the Unpublished Dead Sea Scrolls*, Fasc. 1 (Washington, 1991), 96–101; U. Glessmer, 'The Otot-texts (4Q3129) and the Problem of Intercalations in the Context of the 364-day Calendar', *'Qumran Studies': Schriften des Institutum Judaicum Delietzschianum* III (Göttingen, 1995), 125–64.

**I** . . . its light on the fourth (day) of the wee[k] of the creation (in the first year) in (the week of) G[amul.
The sign of Shecaniah: in the fourth (year).
The sign of Gamul: in the (year) of Release (i.e. the first sabbatical year).

(Second sabbatical cycle):
The si]gn [of Shecaniah: in the thi]rd (year).
The sign of [G]amul: in the sixth (year).

(Third sabbatical cycle):
The sign [of Shecaniah: in the second (year).
The sign of G]amul: [in the fifth (year).

(Fourth sabbatical cycle):
The sig]n of Shecaniah: after the (year of) Release.
The sign of Gamu[l: in the fourth (year).
The sign of Shec]an[i]ah:
[in the (year of) Release.

(Fifth sabbatical cycle):
The sig]n of Gamul: in the third (year).
The sign of Shecaniah: [in the sixth (year).

(Sixth sabbatical cycle):
The sign of Gam]ul: [in the second (year).
The si]gn of She[caniah]: in the fifth (year).

(Seventh sabbatical cycle):
The sign of Gam[ul: after the (year of) Release.
The sign of Shecaniah: in the fou]rth (year).
The sign of Gamul: in the (year of) Release
(which is) the sign of the en[d of the Jubilee.
The signs of [the second J]ubilee: 17 signs.
Of this in the (year of) Release: [2] signs.

... of the creation ...
[The si]gn of Shecaniah:
in the second (year).
[The sign of Ga]mul: in the fifth (year).
The sign of Shecaniah: after the (year of) Release.

[The sign of Ga]mul: **II** [in the fourth (year).
The sign of Shecaniah: in the (year of) Release.

The sign of Gamul: in the third (year).
The sign of Shecaniah: in the sixth (year).

The sign of Gamul: in the second (year).
The sign of Shecaniah: in the fifth (year).
The sign of Gamul: after the (year of) Releas]e.

The sign of Shecaniah: in the fo[urth (year).
The sign of Gamul: in the (year of) Release.

The sign of Shecaniah: in the thi]rd (year).
The sign of Gamul: in the si[xth (year)

(which is) the sign] of the end
of the Jubilee.

The signs of the third Jubilee: 16 signs].
Of this in the (year of) Release: 2 signs.

[The sign] of Shecaniah: in the second year.
[The sign of Gam]ul: in the fifth (year).
The sign of Shecaniah: after the (year of) Release.

The sig[n of Gamul: in the fourth (year).
The sig]n of Shecaniah: in the (year of) Release.

The sign of Gamul: in the third (year).
The sign [of Shecaniah: in the sixth (year).

The sign of G]amul: in the second (year).
The sign of Shecaniah: in the fifth (year).
The sign [of Gamul: after the (year of)] Release.

The sign of Shecaniah:
in the fourth (year).
The sign of Gamul: [in the (year of) Release.

The sign] of Shecaniah: in the third (year).
The sign of Gamul: in the sixth (year).

The sign of Shec[aniah: in the second (year).
The sign] of Gamul: in the fifth (year).
The sign of Shecaniah: after the (year of) Release
[(which is) the sign of the end of the Jubilee.

The signs of the] fourth [Jubi]lee: 17 signs.
Of this in the (year of) Release: 3 signs.

[The sign of Gamul]: in the fourth year.
The sign of Shecaniah: [in the (year of) Rel]ease.

The sign of Gamul: in [the third (year).
The sign of Shecaniah: in the sixth (year).

The sign of Gamul]:
in the second (year).
The sign of Shecaniah: in the fi[fth (year).
The sign of Gamul: after the (year of) Release.

The sign of Shecaniah]: in the fourth (year).
The sign of Gamul]: in the sixth (year).

The sign of She[caniah: in the second (year).
The sign of Gamul: in the fifth (year).
The sign of Shecaniah: after the [(year of)] Release.

The sign of Ga[mul: in the fourth (year).
The sign of Shecaniah: in the (year of) Release
(which is) the sign of the end of the Jubilee.

The signs of the fifth Jubilee: 16 signs.
Of this in the (year of) Release: **III** 2 signs.

[The sign of Gamul: in the third year.
The sign of Shecaniah: in the sixth (year).

The sign of Gamul: in] the second (year).
The sign of Shecaniah: in [the fifth year].
The sign of Gamul: after the (year of) Rel]ease.

[The si]gn of Shecaniah: in the fourth (year).
The sign of Ga[mul: in the (year of) Release.

The sign of Shecaniah]: in the third (year).
The sign of Gamul: in the sixth (year).

The sign of Shecaniah: [in the second (year).
The sign] of Gamul: in the f[if]th (year).
The sign of Shecaniah: after [the (year of) Release.

The si]gn of Gamul: in [the four]th (year).
The sign of Shecaniah: in the (year of) Relea[se.

The sign of Gamul: in] the third (year).
The si[gn of Shecaniah: in the s]ixth (year)
(which is) the sign of the end of the Ju[bilee.

The signs of the sixth] Jubilee: 1[6 signs.
Of this in [the (year of) Release]: 2 signs.
...
and for the Jubi[lee].

[The sign of Gamul: in the second (year).
The sign of Shecaniah: in the fifth (year).
The sign of Gamul: after] the (year of) Relea]se.

The sign of Shecaniah: in the four]th (year).
The sign of Gamu[l: in] the (year of) Relea[se.

The sign of Shecaniah: in the third (year).
The sign] of Gamul: in the sixth (year).

The sig[n of Shecaniah: in] the second (year).
The si[gn of Gamul]: in the fifth (year).
The sign of Shecaniah: [after] the (year of) Relea[se.

The sign of G]amul: in the fourth (year).
The sign of Shecaniah: in the (year of) Re[lease.

The sign]
of Gamul: [in the thir]d (year).
The sign of Shecaniah: in the sixth (year).

The sign [of Gamul]: in the sec[ond (year).
The sign of Shecaniah]: in the fifth (year)
(which is) the sign of the end of the Jubi[lee.

The signs of the] seventh [Jubilee] 16 signs.
Of this in the (year of) Release: [3 signs].

# 'Horoscopes' or Astrological Physiognomies
## (4Q186, 4Q534, 4Q561)

Three documents from Cave 4, one in Hebrew and two in Aramaic, all dating probably to the end of the first century BCE, contain fragments of 'horoscopes' or, more precisely, astrological physiognomies claiming a correspondence between the features and destiny of a person and the configuration of the stars at the time of his birth.

The Hebrew text, published by J. M. Allegro (**4Q186**), is written in a childish cipher. The text runs from left to right instead of the normal right to left and uses, in addition to the current 'square' Hebrew alphabet, letters borrowed from the archaic Hebrew (or Phoenician) and Greek scripts. The spiritual qualities of three individuals described in the work are reflected in their share of Light and Darkness. The first man is very wicked: eight parts of Darkness to a single part of Light. The second man is largely good: six parts of Light against three parts of Darkness. The last is almost perfect: eight portions of Light and only one of Darkness.

As far as physical characteristics are concerned, shortness, fatness and irregularity of features are associated with wickedness, their opposites reflect virtue.

In the astrological terminology of the document, the 'second Column' doubtless means the 'second House'; and a birthday 'in the foot of the Bull' should probably be interpreted as the presence, at that moment, of the sun in the lower part of the constellation Taurus.

The first Aramaic 'horoscope' (**4Q534**) is, according to J. Starcky, that of the final Prince of the Congregation, or Royal Messiah. It is just as likely, however, that the text alludes to the miraculous birth of Noah and it has therefore been placed together with the other remains of Noah literature (cf. pp. 521–2 below). **4Q561**, also in Aramaic, is too short to allow an identification but it is unlikely to refer to Noah as the qualities seem to be in some middle position between good and evil.

Whether the sectaries forecast the future by means of astrology, or merely used horoscope-like compositions as literary devices, is impossible to decide at present, though I am inclined towards the latter alternative. That such texts are found among the Scrolls should not, however, surprise anyone. For if many Jews frowned on astrology, others, such as the Hellenistic Jewish writer Eupolemus, credited its invention to Abraham! (Cf. G. Vermes, *Scripture and Tradition in Judaism*, Leiden, 1973, 80–82.)

For the texts see J. M. Allegro and A. A. Anderson, *DJD*, V, 88–91; J. Strugnell, *RQ* 7 (1970), 274–6; J. Starcky, 'Un texte messianique araméen de la grotte 4 de Qumrân', *Mémorial du Cinquantenaire 1914–1964 de l'École des Langues Orientales Anciennes de l'Institut Catholique de Paris*, Paris, 1964, 51–66; P. S. Alexander, in E. Schürer, G. Vermes, F. Millar and M. Goodman, *The History of the Jewish People in the Age of Jesus Christ*, III, Edinburgh, 1986, 364–6.

## 4Q**186**, fr. 1

**II** . . . and his thighs are long and lean, and his toes are thin and long. He is of the second Column. His spirit consists of six (parts) in the House of Light and three in the Pit of Darkness. And this is his birthday on which he (is to be/was?) born: in the foot of the Bull. He will be meek. And his animal is the bull.

**III** . . . and his head . . . [and his cheeks are] fat. His teeth are of uneven length (?). His fingers are thick, and his thighs are thick and very hairy, each one. His toes are thick and short. His spirit consists of eight (parts) in the House of Darkness and one from the House of Light . . .

## Fr. 2

**I** . . . order. His eyes are black and glowing. His beard is . . . and it is . . . His voice is gentle. His teeth are fine and well aligned. He is neither tall, nor short. And he . . . And his fingers are thin and long. And his thighs are smooth. And the soles of his feet . . . [And his toes] are well aligned. His spirit consists of eight (parts) [in the House of Light, of] the second Column, and one [in the House of Darkness. And this is] his birthday on which he (is to be/was) born: . . . And his animal is . . .

## 4Q561

... mixed but not too much. His eyes will be between white and black. His nose will be long and beautiful. His teeth will be even. His beard will be thin but not too much so. His limbs will be smoot[h and] be[tween re]duced and thick ...

# Phases of the Moon

## (4Q317)

Seventy-six fragments of an astronomical text written in a cryptic alphabet record the phases of the moon, divided into 1/14ths of the full size of the moon, over the consecutive days of a 364-day solar calendar. J. T. Milik has reconstructed a fourteen-line section, based on fr. 1 ii, 2–14 and supplemented with other smaller fragments.

For a preliminary edition, see J. T. Milik, *The Aramaic Books of Enoch* (Oxford, 1976), 68–9.

**II** . . . [On the f]ifth (day) of it (the month), [tw]elve (fourteenths of the moon's surface) are covered and thus it [enters the day. On the sixth (day) of it] thir[teen (fourteenths of its surface) are covered and thus it enters the day. On the seventh (day) of it [fourteen (fourteenths of its surface)] are covered and thus] it enters the day. *vacat* On the eighth (day) of it . . . the firmament above . . . its light is to be covered . . . on the first of the Sabbath (Sunday). *vacat* [On the ninth (day) of it one (fourteenth) portion (of its surface) [is revealed [and thus it enters the night]. On the tenth (day) of it [two (fourteenths of its surface)] are [revealed and it enters] the night. *vacat* On the ele[venth (day) of it three (fourteenths of its surface) are revealed] and thus it enters the night. *vacat*

# A Zodiacal Calendar with a Brontologion

## (4Q318)

A fascinating, but unfortunately fragmentary, calendar indicates the passage of the moon through the various Zodiacal signs during the successive months of the year from Nisan to Adar. The fragment begins with the month of Tevet, continues with Tishri and ends with Adar. The last four lines of col. VIII have preserved a *brontologion*, i.e. prediction of prodigies or ill-omens by means of an interpretation of the sound of thunder on certain specified days of the month. The actual prediction of woe survives only at the end of the text in lines 8–9. It takes the form of a famine and the invasion of the country by a conquering foreign army.

For preliminary studies, see J. C. Greenfield and M. Sokoloff (with Appendices by D. Pingree and A. Yardeni), 'An Astrological Text from Qumran (4Q**318**) and Reflections on some Zodiacal Names', *RQ* 16 (1995), 507–25.

**IV** ... ... and on 13 and [1]4 [Pisces; on 15 and 16 Aries; on 17 and 18 Taurus; on 1]9 and 20 and 2[1 Gemini; on 22 and 23 Cancer; on 24 and 25 Leo; on 26 and] 27 and 28 [Virgo; on 29 and 30 Libra] *vacat* [*Tishri*. On 1 and 2 Scorpio; on 3 and 4 Sagittarius; on 5 and 6 and 7] Capricorn; on 8 **VII** and on 13 and 14 Cancer; on 15 and 16 Leo; on 17 and 18 Virgo; on 19 and 20 and 21 Libra; on 22 [and 23] Scorpio; on 24 and 25 Sagit[tarius]; on 26 and 27 and 28 [Capricorn]; on 29 and 30 Aquari[us]. *vacat Shevat*. On 1 and 2 [Pisce]s; on 3 and 4 [Aries; on] 5 and [6 and] 7 Taurus; on 8 [and 9 Gemini]; on 10 [and 11] Cancer; on 12 [and] 13 and 14 Leo; [on 15 and 16 Virgo]; on 17 and 18 Libra; on 19 [and 20 and 21 S]corpio; on 22 [and] 23 [Sagit]tarius; on 24 and 25 Capricorn; on [26 and] 27 and 28 Aquarius; on 29 and 30 Pisces *vacat*

**VIII** *Adar*. On 1 and 2 Aries; on 3 and 4 Taurus; on 5 [and 6 and 7 Gemini]; on 8 and 9 [Cancer; on 10 and 11 L]eo; on 12 and 13 [and 14] Virg[o]; on 15 and [16 Libra; on] 17 and on 18 [Scorpio]; [on] 19 and 20 (and 21) Sag[ittarius]; on 22 and 23 [Cap]ricorn; [on 24 and 25]

Aquarius; on 26 and 27 [and 28] Pi[sces; on 29 and 30] Aries. *vacat* [If in Taurus] it thunders ... [and] hard labour for the country and sword [in the cour]t of the king and in the country of ... to the Arabs (?) [ ... ] starvation and they will pillage one anoth[er ... ]. *vacat* If in Gemini it thunders, terror and affliction (will be brought) by strangers and by ...

# Order of Divine Office

## (4Q334)

Cave 4 has yielded five fragments of a liturgical work, listing the number of songs and words of praise to be sung during the night and during the day on consecutive days of the month. Only fr. 2 can be built up into a coherent text.

For a preliminary edition, see *UDSS* III, 124.

### Fr. 2

[And on the eighth of it (of the month) at night: e]ight [so]ngs and forty- . . . [w]ords of prai[se, and during the day: . . . songs and] sixtee[n wor]ds [of praise. And on the nint]h of it at night: [eight songs and] fort[y-t]wo [words of praise, and during the d]ay: . . . songs [and . . . words of praise]. And on the tenth of i[t] at night: eight songs [and . . . words of praise, and during the day: . . . songs] and twenty words of p]raise] . . .

# The Words of the Heavenly Lights

## (4Q504–6)

Surviving in three fragmentary manuscripts from Cave 4 (4Q504–6), 'The Words of the Heavenly Lights' are collective prayers for the days of the week which are full of biblical reminiscences. In the best-preserved of them (4Q504), the Sabbath and the fourth day are expressly mentioned in the surviving text. The editor of the document, M. Baillet (*DJD*, VII (1982), 137–75), attributes to it an exaggeratedly early date, the mid-second century BCE.

### 4Q504

**I** ... Amen! Amen!

... **II** ... We pray Thee, O Lord, do in accordance with Thyself, in accordance with the greatness of Thy might, Thou who didst pardon our fathers when they rebelled against Thy saying. Thou wert angry with them so as to wish to destroy them, but because of Thy love for them and for the sake of Thy Covenant – for Moses had atoned for their sin – and in order that Thy great might and the abundance of Thy mercy might be known to everlasting generations, Thou didst take pity on them. So let Thine anger and wrath against all [their] sin turn away from Thy people Israel. Remember Thy marvels which Thou didst for the poor of the nations. For we were called by Thy Name ... to [cause] us [to repent] with all (our) heart and soul and to plant Thy Law in our heart [that we might never depart from it, straying neither] to right nor to left. For Thou wilt heal us of foolishness and of blindness and confusion [of heart ... Behold] we were sold because of our iniquities but despite our offences Thou didst call us ... Thou wilt save us from sinning against Thee ... and to make us understand the testimonies ...

**III** ... Behold, all the nations are as nothing beside Thee, they are counted as void and naught before Thee. We have called on Thy Name alone. Thou hast created us for Thy glory and made us Thy children in the sight of all the nations. For Thou hast named Israel 'My son, my first-born', and hast chastised us as a man chastises his son. Thou hast brought us up throughout the years of our generations [by means of] evil diseases, famine, thirst, pestilence, and the sword ... of Thy Covenant. Because Thou hast chosen us [from all] the earth [to be Thy people,] therefore hast Thou poured out Thine anger [and jealousy] upon us in all the fury of Thy wrath. Thou hast caused [the scourge] of Thy [plagues] to cleave to us of which Moses wrote, and Thy servants the Prophets, that Thou wouldst send evil against us in the last days ...

**IV** ... Thy dwelling-place ... a resting-place in Jerus[alem, the city which] Thou hast [chosen] from all the earth that Thy [Name] might remain there for ever. For Thou hast loved Israel above all the peoples. Thou hast chosen the tribe of Judah and hast established Thy Covenant with David that he might be as a princely shepherd over Thy people and sit before Thee on the throne of Israel for ever. All the nations have seen Thy glory, Thou who hast sanctified Thyself in the midst of Thy people Israel. They brought their offering to Thy great Name, silver and gold and precious stones together with all the treasures of their lands, that they might glorify Thy people, and Zion Thy holy city, and the House of Thy majesty. And there was neither adversary nor misfortune, but peace and blessing ... and they ate and were satisfied and grew fat ...

**V** ... [they forsook] the fount of living waters ... and served a strange god in their land. Also, their land was ravaged by their enemies; for Thy fury and the heat of Thy wrath overflowed, in the fire of Thy jealousy, making of it a desert where no man could go and return. Yet notwithstanding all this, Thou didst not reject the seed of Jacob, neither didst Thou cast away Israel to destruction, breaking Thy Covenant with them. For Thou alone art a living God and there is none beside Thee. Thou didst remember Thy Covenant, Thou who didst rescue us in the presence of all the nations, and didst not forsake us amid the nations. Thou wert gracious towards Thy people Israel in all the lands to which Thou didst banish them, that they might remember to return to Thee and to hearken to Thy voice [according to] all Thou hadst commanded by the hand of Moses Thy servant.

For Thou hast shed Thy Holy Spirit upon us, bringing upon us Thy blessings, that we might seek Thee in our distress [and whis]per (prayers) in the ordeal of Thy chastisement. We have entered into distress, have been [stri]cken and tried by the fury of the oppressor. For we also have tired God with our iniquity, we have wearied the Rock with [our] sins. [But] in order that we may profit, Thou hast not wearied us who leadest [us] in the way in [which we must walk. But] we have not heeded ...

**VI** ... [Thou hast taken away] all our transgressions and hast purified us of our sin for Thine own sake. Thine, Thine is righteousness, O Lord, for it is Thou who hast done all this! Now, on the day when our heart is humbled, we expiate our iniquity and the iniquity of our fathers, together with our unfaithfulness and rebellion. We have not rejected Thy trials and scourges; our soul has not despised them to the point of breaking Thy Covenant despite all the distress of our soul. For Thou, who hast sent our enemies against us, strengthenest our heart that we may recount Thy mighty deeds to everlasting generations. We pray Thee, O Lord, since Thou workest marvels from everlasting to everlasting, to let Thine anger and wrath retreat from us. Look on [our affliction] and trouble and distress, and deliver Thy people Israel [from all] the lands, near and far, [to which Thou hast banished them], every man who is inscribed in the Book of Life ... serve Thee and give thanks to [Thy holy Name] ... from those who vex them ... **VII** ... who deliverest us from all distress. Amen! [Amen!]

### *Hymns for the Sabbath Day*

Give thanks ...
[Bless] His holy Name always
... all the angels of the holy firmament
... [above] the heavens,
the earth and all its deep places,
the great [Abyss] and Abaddon
and the waters and all that is [in them.]
[Let] all His creatures [bless Him] always
for everlasting [ages. Amen! Amen!]
... bless His holy Name.
Sing to God ...

## Fr. 3

**II** ... Blessed be the God who has given us rest. [Amen], amen. [Prayer on the] fourth [da]y. Remember, O Lord ...

## Fr. 4

**II** ... We know these through Thy Ho[ly] Spirit which Thou hast granted us. [Have mercy on us] and remember us not for the iniquities of the men of old in all their evi[l] dealings, [nor] their stiff necks. Thou redeem us and, [pray,] forgive our iniquities and [our] s[ins].

## Fr. 6

**II** ... Remember, pray, that we are Thy people and that Thou hast carried us marvellously [on the wings of] eagles and hast brought us towards Thee. And like an eagle which rouses its nestlings and hovers over [its young], spreads out its wings, takes one and carries it on [its pinions], so we dwell apart and are not reckoned among the nations and ... Thou art in our midst in the pillar of fire and the cloud [of] Thy [holi]ness walking before us, and as it were Thy glory in our mid[st] ...

## Fr. 8 recto

**II** ... [Rememb]er, O Lo[r]d that ... Thou hast fashioned A[dam], our [f]ather, in the likeness of [Thy] glory; Thou didst breathe [a breath of life] into his nostrils and, with understanding, knowledge [Thou didst give him] ... Thou didst make [him] to rule [over the Gar]den of Eden which Thou didst plant ... and to walk in the land of glory ... he guarded. And Thou didst enjoin him not to st[ray ... ] ... he is flesh and to dust [he will return (?)] ... And Thou, Thou knowest ... for everlasting generations ... a living God and Thy hand ... man in the ways of ... [to fill the] earth with [vi]olence and to shed [innocent blood] ...

# Liturgical Prayer

## (1Q34 and $34^{\text{bis}}$)

The following fragments, published by J. T. Milik (*DJD*, I, 152–5), belong to a collection of prayers for Jewish festivals. The title of the present section is lost, but reference to the renewal of the Covenant seems to indicate that we have here another part of the sect's Pentecostal liturgy.

**I** ... Thou wilt cause the wicked to be our ransom and the unfaithful to be our redemption. [Thou wilt] blot out all our oppressors and we shall praise Thy Name for ever [and ever]. For this hast Thou created us and [to say to Thee] this: Blessed art Thou ...

**II** ... the Great Light (of heaven) for the [day]time, [and the Little Light (of heaven) for the night] ... without transgressing their laws, ... and their dominion is over all the world.

But the seed of man did not understand all that Thou caused them to inherit; they did not discern Thee in all Thy words and wickedly turned aside from every one. They heeded not Thy great power and therefore Thou didst reject them. For wickedness pleases Thee not, and the ungodly shall not be established before Thee.

But in the time of Thy goodwill Thou didst choose for Thyself a people. Thou didst remember Thy Covenant and [granted] that they should be set apart for Thyself from among all the peoples as a holy thing. And Thou didst renew for them Thy Covenant (founded) on a glorious vision and the words of Thy Holy [Spirit], on the works of Thy hands and the writing of Thy Right Hand, that they might know the foundations of glory and the steps towards eternity ... [Thou didst raise up] for them a faithful shepherd ...

# Prayers for Festivals

## (4Q507–9)

Three badly worn manuscripts from Cave 4 (4Q507–9) partly correspond to the foregoing fragments from Cave 1 (1Q34 and $34^{\text{bis}}$). They have preserved prayers for festivals, two of which are explicitly associated with the Day of Atonement and the Day of Firstfruits. The editor, M. Baillet (*DJD*, VII, 175–215), dates them to the beginning of the first century CE.

### 4Q507, fr. 1

We are (encompassed) by iniquity since the womb, and since the breast by guilt. While we live, we walk in iniquity . . .

### 4Q508, fr. 1 (cf. 1Q$34^{\text{bis}}$)

[And the righteous . . . to grow fat thanks to the clouds of heaven and the produce of the land, to distingui]sh the righteous from the wicked. And Thou shalt make of the wicked our expiation, and by the upright Thou shalt destroy all our oppressors. And we will praise Thy na[m]e for ever and ever. For [Thou hast created us for this] and we answer Thee with this: Blessed be . . .

### Fr. 2 (cf. 1Q$34^{\text{bis}}$)

. . . Prayer for the Day of Atonement. Remember O Lord, the feast of mercies and the time of return (?) . . . Thou hast established it for us as a feast of fasting, and an everlas[ting] precept . . . Thou knowest the hidden things and the things reveal[ed] . . .

## Fr. 3

... Thou didst establish [Thy Covenant] with Noah ...

## 4Q509, fr. 3 (cf. 1Q34bis)

For Thou hast caused us to rejoice, removing our grief, and hast assembled our banished ones for a feast of ... Thou shalt gather our dispersed women for the season of ... Thy [me]rcies on our congregation like ra[in-drops on the earth in the season of sowing ... and like showers on the gr]ass in the seasons of sprouting and ... We shall recount Thy marvels from generation to generation. Blessed be the Lord who has caused us to rejoice ...

## Fr. 132

**II** [Prayer for the Day of] Firstfruits. Remember, O Lord, the feast of ... and the pleasing free-will offerings which Thou hast commanded ... [to br]ing before Thee the firstfruits of [Thy] works ...

# Daily Prayers

## (4Q503)

A manuscript from Cave 4 (4Q503) consisting of 225 papyrus fragments, edited by M. Baillet (*DJD*, VII, 105–36), lists evening and morning benedictions for each day of the month. The calendar followed appears to be lunar since evening precedes morning. The editor places the writing in the first quarter of the first century BCE.

**III** And when the sun rises ... the firmament of heaven, they shall bless. Answer[ing they shall say:] Blessed be the Go[d of Israel ... ] Today ... in the fourt[h of the gates of light ... ] On the fifth [of the month in the eve]ning, they shall bless. Answering, they shall say: Blessed be the God [of Israel] who hides ... before him in every division of his glory ... today the fourte[enth] ... light of the day. Peace be on you, Israel ... [When the sun] rise[s] to illumine the earth, they shall bless, and again the numbe[r shall be] ele[ven days] to the feasts of joy and the appointed times of g[lory,] for [this d]ay is in the fifteenth of the gate[s of light] ... [Peace be on you,] Israel. On the sixth of the month in the evening, they shall bless. Answering, they shall [say]: Bles[sed be the God] of Israel ... And when [the sun rises to illumine the earth, they shall bless. Answering, they shall say]

### Frs. 7–9

**IV** ... Peace [be on you, Israel] ... On the seventh of [the month in the evening, they shall bless. Answering, they shall say:] Blessed be the God of Is[rael] ...

## Fr. 11

[On the t]welfth of the month in the evening [they shall bless] ... (This probably continues up to the 26th of the month.)

# Prayer or Hymn Celebrating the Morning and the Evening

## (4Q408)

One medium sized and fifteen or sixteen small fragments represent a collection of liturgical prayers of which only one can be partly translated. Palaeographically the document is placed in the Hasmonaean era (c. 100 BCE).

For a preliminary study, see Annette Steudel, '4Q408: A Liturgy on Morning and Evening Prayer – Preliminary Edition', *RQ* (1994), 313–34.

### Fr. 1

... [Bl]essed art Thou, O Lord, who art righteous in all Thy ways. Be mighty in strength ... [in Thy judge]ments. Thou who art faithful ... Thou art understanding [with all in]telligence ... might. Thou who art ... to bring out ... who hast created the morning as a sign to reveal the dominion of the light as the boundary of the daytime ... for their work. To bless Thy holy name Thou hast created them. For the light is good ... ... [Thou art ... ] who hast created the evening as a sign to reveal the dominion [of darkness ... from labour. Thou hast [c]reated them to bless [Thy holy name] ...

# Blessings

## (1QSb=1Q28b)

These fragments from a collection of blessings were originally attached to the Scroll containing the Community Rule and the Messianic Rule. They have been skilfully pieced together by J. T. Milik (*DJD*, I, 118–29), who dates them to around 100 BCE.

The Blessings were to be recited by the Master or Guardian, and were, as it seems, intended for the messianic age, and perhaps for the ceremony of the institution of the new Community. It is, however, possible that they were actually used during the course of some liturgy anticipating and symbolizing the coming of the messianic era. All the members of the Covenant are blessed first, followed by someone who seems to be the priestly head of the Community, the Messiah of Aaron. The next blessing is addressed to the sons of Zadok, the Priests (and Levites?), and finally the Prince of the Congregation, the Messiah of Israel, is blessed. The rest of the document is lost.

For an additional fragment, see G. J. Brooke and J. M. Robinson, 'A Further Fragment of 1QSb: The Schøyen Collection MS 1909', *JJS* 46 (1995), 120–33.

### *The Blessing of the Faithful*

**I** Words of blessing. The Master shall bless them that fear [God and do] His will, that keep His commandments, and hold fast to His holy [Covenant], and walk perfectly [in all the ways of] His [truth], whom He has chosen for an eternal Covenant which shall endure for ever.

May the [Lord bless you from the Abode of His holiness]; may He open
for you from heaven an eternal fountain which [shall not fail]!

. . .

May He [favour] you with every [heavenly] blessing; [may He teach you]
the knowledge of the Holy Ones!

[May He unlock for you the] everlasting [fountain; may He not withhold the waters of life from] them that thirst!

. . .

### *The Blessing of the High Priest*

**II** . . .

**III** May the Lord lift His countenance towards you; [may He delight in the] sweet odour [of your sacrifices]!

May He choose [all] them that sit in your pries[tly college]; may He store up all your sacred offerings, and in the [season of] . . . all your seed!

May He [lift] His countenance towards all your congregation!

May He place upon your head [a diadem] . . . in [everlasting] glory; may He sanctify your seed in glory without end!

May He grant you everlasting [peace] . . .

May He fight [at the head of] your Thousands [until the generation of falsehood is ended] . . . [to bend] many peoples before you . . . all the riches of the world . . .

For God has established all the foundations of . . . may He lay the foundation of your peace for ever!

. . .

### *The Blessing of the Priests*

Words of blessing. The M[aster shall bless] the sons of Zadok the Priests, whom God has chosen to confirm His Covenant for [ever, and to inquire] into all His precepts in the midst of His people, and to instruct them as He commanded; who have established [His Covenant] on truth and watched over all His laws with righteousness and walked according to the way of His choice.

May the Lord bless you from His holy [Abode]; may He set you as a splendid jewel in the midst of the congregation of the saints!

May He [renew] for you the Covenant of the [everlasting] priesthood; may He sanctify you [for the House] of Holiness!

May He [judge all] the leaders by your works, and all [the princes] of the peoples by the words from out of your lips!

May He give you as your portion the firstfruits of [all delectable things]; may He bless by your hand the counsel of all flesh!

**IV** . . . may everlasting blessings be the crown upon your head!

. . .

[For] He has chosen you [to] . . . and to number the saints and to [bless] your people . . . the men of the Council of God by your hand, and not by the hand of a prince . . .

. . . May you be as an Angel of the Presence in the Abode of Holiness to the glory of the God of [hosts] . . .

May you attend upon the service in the Temple of the Kingdom and decree destiny in company with the Angels of the Presence, in common council [with the Holy Ones] for everlasting ages and time without end; for [all] His judgements are [truth]!

May He make you holy among His people, and an [eternal] light [to illumine] the world with knowledge and to enlighten the face of the Congregation [with wisdom]!

[May He] consecrate you to the Holy of Holies! For [you are made] holy for Him and you shall glorify His Name and His holiness . . .

**V** . . .

*The Blessing of the Prince of the Congregation*

The Master shall bless the Prince of the Congregation . . . and shall renew for him the Covenant of the Community that he may establish the kingdom of His people for ever, [that he may judge the poor with righteousness and] dispense justice with {equity to the oppressed} (Schøyen) of the land, and that he may walk perfectly before Him in all the ways [of truth], and that he may establish His holy Covenant at the time of the affliction of those who seek God.

May the Lord raise you up to everlasting heights, and as a fortified tower upon a high wall!

[May you smite the peoples] with the might of your hand and ravage the earth with your sceptre; may you bring death to the ungodly with the breath of your lips!

[May He shed upon you the spirit of counsel] and everlasting might, the spirit of knowledge and of the fear of God; may righteousness be the girdle [of your loins] and may your reins be girdled [with faithfulness]!

May He make your horns of iron and your hooves of bronze; may you toss like a young bull [and trample the peoples] like the mire of the streets!

For God has established you as the sceptre. The rulers ... [and all the kings of the] nations shall serve you. He shall strengthen you with His holy Name and you shall be as a [lion; and you shall not lie down until you have devoured the] prey which naught shall deliver ...

# Benedictions

## (4Q280, 286–90)

Five fragmentary copies of a text containing liturgical blessings and curses have survived in Cave 4. Of these 4QBerakhot$^a$ (4Q**286**), preserved on three photographic plates (PAM 43.311–13), provides continuous passages. They parallel Community Rule II and War Rule XIII, and the style of 4Q**286** 1 also recalls the Songs of the Holocaust for the Sabbath (4Q400–407). I agree with Bilhah Nitzan that 4QBerakhot is probably an independent version of part of the ceremony of the renewal of the covenant included in 1QS II, 3–17. Part of the curses figuring in 4Q**286** 2 were first edited by J. T. Milik. The remaining Benedictions are too fragmentary for translation.

Cf. B. Nitzan, '4QBerakhot (4Q**286–90**): A Preliminary Report', in G. J. Brooke (ed.), *New Qumran Texts and Studies* (E. J. Brill, Leiden, 1994), 53–71 and pl. 3; J. T. Milik, 'Milki-sedeq et Milki-resha' dans les anciens écrits juifs et chrétiens', *JJS* 23 (1972), 130–35 and pl. II.

### 4Q**286**=4QBerakhot$^a$

*Blessings*

Fr. 1

**II** The seat of Thy splendour and the footstool of Thy glory in the [h]eights of Thy standing and Thy holy stepping-place. And Thy glorious chariots, their cherubim and their wheels and all [their] companies; foundations of fire and flames of brightness and shinings of majesty and str[eam]s of fire and wonderful luminaries; [majes]ty and splendour and glorious height, holy foundation and sou[rce of] majesty and height of glory, ma[rvel of than]ksgivings and reservoir of might, splendour of praises and great in wonderful things and healing[s] and miraculous deeds, foundation of wisdom and pattern of knowledge and source of understanding, source of prudence and holy counsel and true foundation, treasure-house of intelligence, building of righteousness and place of upright[ness, great] in loving-kindness and in good answers and true loving-kindness and everlasting mercies and mysteries of mar[vels] in [the]ir reve[lations] and holy weeks in their appointed time and squads of months ... [... of ye]ars in their circuits and glorious festive seasons in [their] ... fixed moments ... and the sabbatical years of the land in [their] divi[sions, ap]pointed times for libe[rty ... eternity ... [l]ight and dar[kness ... ]

## Fr. 2

... [thei]r ... in the strength of Thy majesty and all the [sp]irits of those who bring to the Sanctua[ry] ... in [their] comp[anies and in] their [do]minions, the mighty of the 'gods' with power. *vacat* ... zeal for judgement with strength. *vacat* ... [they shall] all [bless in com]munity Thy holy name.... [Ho]ly of Holies and light ... knowledge ... *vacat* ... mystery

# 4Q**286** (4Q**287**, fr. 6)=4Q Berakhot$^{b}$

## *Curses of Belial*

## Fr. 7

...

**II** council of the Community shall all say together, Amen, amen. Afterwards [they] shall damn Belial and all his guilty lot. They shall answer and say, Cursed be [B]elial in his hostile design, and damned in his guilty dominion. Cursed be all the spirits of his [lo]t in their wicked design, and damned in their thoughts of unclean impurity. For they are the lot of darkness and their visitation is for eternal destruction. Amen, amen.

Cursed be the Wicke[d One in all ... ] of his dominions, and may all the sons of Belial be damned in all the works of their service until their annihilation [for ever, Amen, amen.]

And [they shall continue to say: Be cursed, Ang]el of Perdition and

Spir[it of Dest]ruction, in all the thoughts of your g[uilty] inclination [and all your abomina]ble [plots] and [your] wicked design, [and] may you be [da]mned ... Amen, am[en].

[Cursed be a]ll those who practi[se] their [wicked designs] and establish [in their heart] your (evil) devices, [plotting against Go]d'[s Covenant] ... to exchange the judgemen[ts of truth for folly.]

## 4Q280=4QBenedictions[f]

### *Curses of Melkiresha'*

**4Q280** depends mainly on Community Rule II, but reveals Satan's specific name, *Melkiresha'* (My king is wickedness), the counterpart of *Melkizedek* (My king is justice), chief of the Army of Light (cf. below, pp. 500, 534). See Milik, *JJS* 23 (1972), 126–35.

[May God set him apart] for evil from the midst of the Sons of Li[ght because he has turned away from following Him.

And they shall continue saying: Be cur]sed, Melkiresha', in all the thou[ghts of your guilty inclination. May] God [deliver you up] for torture at the hands of the vengeful Avengers. May God not heed [when] you call on Him. [May He raise His angry face] towards you. May there be no (greeting of) 'Peace' for you in the mouth of all those who hold fast to the Father[s. May you be cursed] with no remnant, and damned without escape.

Cursed be those who practi[se their wicked designs] and [es]tablish in their heart your (evil) devices, plotting against the Covenant of God ..., seers of [His] truth.

[Who]ever refuses to enter [His Covenant, walking in the stubbornness of his heart] ...

# Confession Ritual

## (4Q393)

Fragmentary remains of a communal confession of sins, spoken in the first person plural, recall the language of Psalm li, Jeremiah and Deuteronomy, and resemble confession prayers in Ezra ix, 5–15; Daniel ix, 4–19, 1QS I, 24–II, 1. In the latter text, the parallel confession is part of the ceremony of the renewal of the Covenant.

For a preliminary study, see Daniel Falk, '4Q393: A Communal Confession', *JJS* 45 (1994), 184–207.

I ... in order that Thou be justified by Thy wor[ds] ... in our iniquities ... they [stiff]ened the neck. Our God, hide Thy face from [our] si[ns and] blot out [al]l our iniquities and create in us a new spirit, O Lord.... [do not] withhold faithfulness and to rebels ... and bring back sinners to Thee. And [do not] reject from Thee the broken [spir]it, O God. According to Thy people in order to ... and always on ... nations and kingdoms ... their word[s] ... to Thy peoples in order to ...

**II** ... our God who keeps [the] covenant and loving-kindness to those who love Him ... to Moses. Do not forsake Thy people [and] Thine [in]heritance. And let no man walk in the stubbornness of his [evil] heart. O God, in Thy goodwill ... Thy people and Thine inheritance shall not be forsa[k]en and let no man walk in the stubbornness of his evil heart. And where is Strength? And on whom shalt Thou cause Thy face to shine without his being purified? And they shall be sanctified and exalted above everything. It is Thou O Lord who hast chosen our fathers from of old. Thou hast caused us to stand for them as a remnant to give us (the covenant) which Thou hast established with Abraham for Israel that they might possess the proud ... mighty men, the hosts of those who are powerful began to give us houses filled with ... water, vineyards and olive trees [and] an inheritance of the people.

# Purification Ritual

## (4Q512)

Badly worn papyrus fragments from Cave 4 (4Q512) contain prayers: to be recited to obtain purification from various kinds of ritual uncleanness. M. Baillet (*DJD*, VII, 263–86) suggests an early first-century BCE date for the script.

### Frs. 29–32

**VII** And he will bless there [the God of Israel. Answering, he will say: Blessed art Thou, God of Israel. And I stand] before Thee on the feas[t] ... Thou hast ... me for purity ... and his burnt-offering and he will bless. Answering he will say: Blessed art Thou, [God of Israel, who hast delivered me from al]l my sins and purified me from impure indecency and hast atoned so that I come ... purification and the blood of the burnt-offering of Thy goodwill and the pleasing memorial ...

### Fr. 11

**X** [*And on completin*]g [*his*] *seven days of puri*[*fication*] ... *and he shall wash his clothes with w*[*ater and cleanse his body*] *and he shall put on his garments and shall bless ag*[*ain*] ... *the God of* Isra[e]l ...

# A Liturgical Work

## (4Q392)

This is a religious text, possibly liturgical, but strongly reminiscent of the language of the Thanksgiving Hymns.

For a preliminary edition, see *UDSS* II, 38.

... [G]od and not to depart from ... and their soul will cling to His Covenant and ... the words of the mouth of ... The Go[d] ... the heaven above and to search out the ways of the sons of man (leaving) no secret [in their heart(?)]. He created darkness [and l]ight is His, and in His dwelling is the most perfect light, and all gloominess ceases before Him. It is not for Himself the distinction between light and darkness, for He has distinguished them for the sons of man: light during the day by means of the sun; (and during the) night (by means of ) moon and stars. The inscrutable light is with Him, and His knowledge is without [end, f]or all the works of God are multiple (?). We who are flesh, should we not consider this? With us ... for countless signs and wonders ... [wi]nds and lightnings ... [s]ervants of the most holy pla[ce]. From before the couches ...

# D. Apocalyptic Works

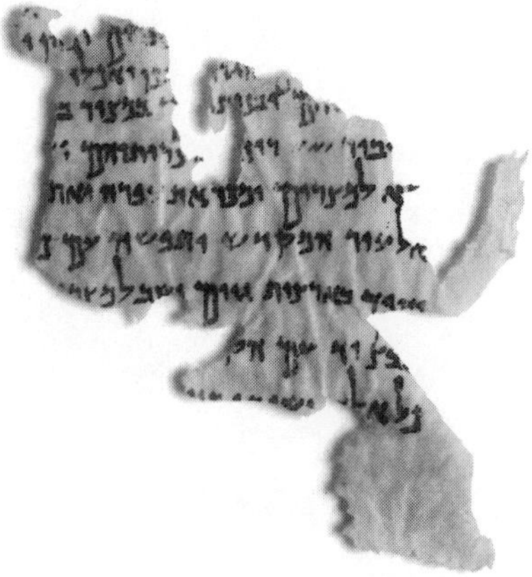

'Conquest of Egypt and Jerusalem
or Acts of a Greek King',
*Israel Antiquities Authority*

# Apocalyptic Chronology or Apocryphal Weeks

## (4Q247)

A fragment consisting of seven mutilated lines, and palaeographically dated to the last decades of the first century BCE, appears to belong to an apocalyptic account of world history, divided into weeks of years and possibly centred on the Temple of Jerusalem. Despite the lack of continuous narration, the significant details justify the inclusion of this text in the volume.

For a preliminary study, see J. T. Milik, *The Aramaic Books of Enoch* (Oxford, 1976), 256.

... [de]termined [end] ... [And afterwards will co]me the fif[th] week ...

four-hundred [and thirty years (after the exodus from Egypt)] Solo[mon] (built the Temple) ... (It was destroyed in the time) [of Zede]kiah king of Judah ...

(It was restored by) the Levites and the people of the Lan[d] ... (Final stage) ... kin[g] of the Kittim ...

# Conquest of Egypt and Jerusalem or Acts of a Greek King

## (4Q**248**)

The story told in this ten-line fragment, which contains only broken lines, resembles the account of Daniel xi concerning the 'King of the North' (Antiochus IV Epiphanes) who invades Egypt and ill-treats Jerusalem.

For a preliminary edition, see M. Broshi and E. Eshel, 'The Greek King is Antiochus IV' (4Q**248**), *JJS* 48/1 (1997).

... in Egypt and Zion and ... Therefore they shall eat ... their [s]ons and their daughters in a siege in ...

[And] .... (the Lord) shall cause [His] wind to pass [through] their courtyards and ... he shall come to Egypt and sell her dust and ... to the city of the Temple and shall capture her with all [her ... ] And he shall turn against the lands of the nations and shall return to Egyp[t] ... [And] ... When all these [come into being] the children [of Israel] shall return ...

# The Triumph of Righteousness or Mysteries

## (1Q27, 4Q299–301)

Originally entitled *The Book of Mysteries* by J. T. Milik (*DJD*, I, 102–5), these fragments expound the familiar theme of the struggle between good and evil, but their nature is difficult to determine. Perhaps they derive from a sermon, or from an apocalyptical writing. Three further manuscripts (4Q299–301) yield badly damaged fragments belonging to the same writing. 4Q300 3 and 4Q299 partly overlap with 1Q27. An earlier passage may be reconstructed from 4Q300 and 4Q299.

For a preliminary edition of the Cave 4 fragments, see L. H. Schiffman, '4QMysteries[b], A Preliminary Edition', *RQ* 16 (1993), 203–23; '4QMysteries[a]: A Preliminary Edition and Translation', in Z. Zevit et al., eds., *Solving Riddles* . . . (J. C. Greenfield Memorial) (Winona Lake, 1995), 207–60.

## 1Q27 combined with 4Q300, fr. 3

**I** . . . all {so that they might know the difference between g[ood and evil] . . . } (4Q300) the mysteries of sin . . . {all their wisdom} (4Q300).

They know not the mystery to come, nor do they understand the things of the past. They know not that which shall befall them, nor do they save their soul from the mystery to come.

And this shall be the sign for you that these things shall come to pass.

When the breed of iniquity is shut up, wickedness shall then be banished by righteousness as darkness is banished by the light. As smoke clears and is no more, so shall wickedness perish for ever and righteousness be revealed like a sun governing the world. All who cleave to the mysteries of sin shall be no more; knowledge shall fill the world and folly shall exist no longer.

This word shall surely come to pass; this prophecy is true. And by this may it be known to you that it shall not be taken back.

Do not all the peoples loathe iniquity? And yet it is spread by them all. Does not the fame of truth issue from the mouth of all the nations? Yet is there a lip or tongue which holds to it? Which nation likes to be oppressed by another stronger than itself, or likes its wealth to be wickedly seized? And yet which nation has not oppressed another, and where is there a people which has not seized [another]'s wealth? . . .

## 4Q300 1 ii 4=4Q299 2 i 14

. . . [the sorc]erers, experts in sin, have uttered the parable and proclaimed the riddle in advance. And then you will know if you have considered . . . and the attestations of heave[n] . . . your foolishness for the [s]eal of the vision is sealed away from you. And you have not considered the mysteries of eternity and have not comprehended understanding. Th[en] you will say . . . for you have not considered the root of wisdom. And if you open the vision, it will remain shut from you . . . all your wisdom for the . . . is for you . . . his name for [wh]at is the hidden wisdom . . .

## Fr. 5

. . . And what shall man be called . . . wise and righteous, for man has no . . . , nor concealed wisdom save the wisdom of wicked cunning and the de[sign of] . . . a deed that shall not be done again except . . . the word of his Maker. And what shall a m[an] do . . . who rebels against the word of his Maker, his name shall be expunged from the mouth of all . . . Listen, you who hold up [truth (?)] . . .

# A Messianic Apocalypse

## (4Q521)

Commonly referred to as the 'Resurrection fragment', this writing consists of eleven fragments, and possibly six further tiny pieces. Fragment 2 is the largest and contains the remains of three columns of which the second, translated here, is the best preserved. The script is dated to the beginning of the first century BCE. Whether the designation 'apocalypse' is fully justified is a moot point: the writing comes across as a composition in verse akin to the poetry of the late biblical period. The surviving fragments do not appear to include anything patently sectarian. The term 'Messiah', probably in the singular, is used without the addition of Aaron or Israel, and the noun '*hasidim*', absent from the big scrolls and little attested elsewhere, figures in lines 5 and 7. The divine name 'Lord' represents, not the Tetragram, but *Adonai* (four times). The poem incorporates Ps. cxlvi, 6–7 and Isa. lxi, 1, the latter cited also in the New Testament (Lk. iv, 18). As in the Gospels, healing and resurrection are linked to the idea of the Kingdom of God. Line 12 furnishes the most explicit evidence concerning the raising of the dead. Fragment 7, line 6, repeats the same idea, referring to God as 'He who revives the dead of His people'.

For preliminary publications, see E. Puech, 'Une apocalypse messianique (4Q521)', *RQ* 15 (1991–2), 475–522; G. Vermes, 'Qumran Forum Miscellanea I', *JJS* 43 (1992), 303–4.

### Fr. 2

**II** … [the hea]vens and the earth will listen to His Messiah, and none therein will stray from the commandments of the holy ones.

Seekers of the Lord, strengthen yourselves in His service!

All you hopeful in (your) heart, will you not find the Lord in this?

For the Lord will consider the pious (*hasidim*) and call the righteous by name.

Over the poor His spirit will hover and will renew the faithful with His power.

And He will glorify the pious on the throne of the eternal Kingdom.

He who liberates the captives, restores sight to the blind, straightens the b[ent] (Ps. cxlvi, 7–8).

And f[or] ever I will clea[ve to the h]opeful and in His mercy . . .

And the fr[uit . . . ] will not be delayed for anyone

And the Lord will accomplish glorious things which have never been as [He . . . ]

For He will heal the wounded, and revive the dead and bring good news to the poor (Isa. lxi, 1).

. . . He will lead the uprooted and knowledge . . . and smoke (?)

. . .

# E. Wisdom Literature

'The Seductress',
*Israel Antiquities Authority*

# The Seductress

## (4Q184)

A long and relatively well-preserved Wisdom poem from Cave 4 (4Q184) depicts, by means of the metaphor of the harlot, the dangers and attraction of false doctrine. See J. M. Allegro and A. A. Anderson, *DJD*, V, 82–5; J. Strugnell, *RQ* 7 (1970), 263–8. Palaeographically, the text is dated to the first century BCE, but the work may be much older, possibly antedating the Qumran sect.

. . . speaks vanity
  and . . . errors.
She is ever prompt to oil her words,
  and she flatters with irony,
  deriding with iniquitous l[ips].
Her heart is set up as a snare,
  and her kidneys (affections) as a fowler's nets.
Her eyes are defiled with iniquity,
  her hands have seized hold of the Pit.
Her legs go down to work wickedness,
  and to walk in wrong-doings.
Her. . . are foundations of darkness,
  and a multitude of sins is in her skirts.
Her. . . are darkness of night,
  and her garments. . .
Her clothes are shades of twilight,
  and her ornaments plagues of corruption.
Her couches are beds of corruption,
  and her . . . depths of the pit.
Her inns are couches of darkness,
  and her dominions in the midst of the night.
She pitches her dwelling on the foundations of darkness
  she abides in the tents of silence.

Amid everlasting fire is her inheritance,
   not among those who shine brightly.
She is the beginning of all the ways of iniquity.
Woe (and) disaster to all who possess her!
   And desolation to all who hold her!
For her ways are ways of death,
   and her paths are roads of sin,
   and her tracks are pathways to iniquity,
   and her by-ways are rebellious wrong-doings.
Her gates are gates of death,
and from the entrance of the house
   she sets out towards the underworld.
None of those who enter there will ever return,
   and all who possess her will descend to the Pit.
She lies in wait in secret places,
. . .
In the city's squares she veils herself,
   and she stands at the gates of towns.
She will never re[st] from wh[orin]g,
   her eyes glance hither and thither.
She lifts her eyelids naughtily
   to stare at a virtuous man and join him,
   and an important man to trip him up,
   at upright men to pervert their way,
   and the righteous elect to keep them from the
      commandment,
   at the firmly established to bring them down wantonly,
   and those who walk in uprightness to alter the statute;
to cause the humble to rebel against God,
   and turn their steps away from the ways of justice,
   to bring insolence to their heart,
   so that they march no more in the paths of uprightness;
   to lead men astray to the ways of the Pit,
   and seduce with flatteries every son of man.

# Exhortation to Seek Wisdom

## (4Q185)

Large fragments of a Wisdom poem in which a teacher encourages his 'people', his 'sons', the 'Simple', to search for Wisdom have been preserved in Cave 4 (4Q185). The script is believed to be late Hasmonaean, i.e. from the first half of the first century BCE. As is often the case in Wisdom literature, events of the patriarchal and Mosaic past are used for didactic purposes. See J. M. Allegro and A. A. Anderson, *DJD*, V, 85–7; cf. J. Strugnell, *RQ* 7 (1970), 269–73.

**I** ...
And you, sons of men, woe to you!
For he (man) sprouts from his ground like grass,
and his grace blossoms like a flower.
His [gl]ory blows away and his grass dries up,
and the wind carries away its flower
...
so that it is found no more ...
They shall seek him but shall not find him,
and there is no hope (for him);
and his days are like a shadow over the ea[rth].
Now pray hearken to me, my people;
heed me, O you Simple;
become wise through the might of God.
Remember His miracles which He did in Egypt,
and His marvels in the land of Ham.
Let your heart shake because of His fear,
**II** and do His will ...
... your souls according to His good graces,
and search for yourself a way towards life,
a highway [towards ... ]
a remnant for your sons after you.

And why have you given up your soul to vanity,
  ... judgement?
Hearken to me, O my sons,
  and do not rebel against the words of YHWH.
Do not walk ...
  [but in the way He established] for Jacob,
  and in the path which He decreed for Isaac.
Is one day not better ...
... His fear,
  and not to be afflicted (?) by dread and the fowler's net.
... to be set apart from His angels,
  for there is no darkness, nor gloom ...
And you, what do you understand ...
  before Him evil shall go towards every people.
Happy is the man to whom it (Wisdom) has been given thus,
  ... the evil,
  nor let the wicked boast, saying:
It has not been given me, nor ...
  [For God gave it] to Israel,
  and with a good measure He measures it;
  and He will redeem all His people,
  and He will put to death those who hate His Wisdom.

Seek her and find her, grasp her and possess her!
With her is length of days and fatness of bone,
  the joy of the heart and ...
Happy is the man who works it
...
  who does not seek it ... of deceit,
  nor holds to it with flatteries.
As it has belonged to his fathers,
  so will he inherit it,
  and hold fast to it with all the strength of his might,
  and all his immeasurable ...
  and he shall cause his offspring to inherit it.

I know how to labour for good ...

**III** . . .

. . .
[God inspects] all the chambers of the womb
and He tries all its inward parts.
[God shapes] the tongue
and knows its words.
God makes the hand
[and understands their deeds (?)] . . .

# Parable of the Tree

## (4Q302$^{a}$)

This text comprises a badly damaged fragment of which only the opening lines provide any coherent sense. The topic seems to be the giant 'good' tree which produces thorns.

For a preliminary edition, see *UDSS* II, 229.

**II** Sages, reflect on this.
If a man has a good tree
[which grows] as far as heaven
[and its branches reach (?)]
to the ex[tremitie]s of the lands,
yet it [pr]oduces thorny fruits (?)
... former rain and latter rain ...
and in thirst ...
...

# A Sapiential Work (i)

## (4Q413)

Two fragments have preserved the first four lines of a column from a Wisdom composition.

For a preliminary study, see E. Qimron, 'A Work concerning Divine Providence: 4Q413', in Z. Zevit et al., eds., *Solving Riddles* ... (J. C. Greenfield Memorial) (Winona Lake, 1995), 191–202.

... I will teach you [knowledge(?)] and wisdom.
And understand the ways of man
and the works of the sons of ma[n].
[According to] God's [loving-kindness] towards man,
He has enlarged his inheritance in the knowledge of His truth,
and according to His rejection of every ev[il man,]
no-one who [walks after] his ears and his eyes shall live.
And now [His] loving-kindness ... the ancient,
they will consider the years of all the generations
as God has revealed ...

# A Sapiential Work (ii)

## (4Q**415–18**, **423**, 1Q**26**)

A substantial Wisdom composition, probably dating to the second century BCE, has survived in six fragmentary manuscripts, one from Cave 1 (1Q**26**) and five partly overlapping scrolls from Cave 4 (4Q**415**, **416**, **417**, **418a** and **b** and **423**). Apart from the last-mentioned manuscript, dated to the first half of the first century CE, all are said to be early Herodian (30–1 BCE). The work is unquestionably sectarian and displays a terminology akin to the Community Rule, the Damascus Document and the Thanksgiving Hymns. T. Elgvin has attempted to reconstruct the original work and he sums up its contents as follows: argument with a neighbour; relationship of the elect to God and man; God as provider for all his creatures; business ethics; a modest life; deposit to be returned in full; the hope of the just man; divine mysteries to be studied and the praise of God's name; attitude to parents, wife, children; the elect and the sage's escape from God's anger; God as permanent judge of wickedness; God as creator of the heavenly beings and luminaries; God as future judge; mankind's submission to God; the fate of the just and the wicked; religious life; first-born sons of God in praise of him; the use of insight; God's eternal plant: the saints; God's providence; the distribution of the portions of the elect; the farmer and the garden of Eden; Warning: God is to try man. Cf. T. Elgvin, 'The Reconstruction of Sapiential Work A', *RQ* 16 (1995), 559–80.

### 4Q**416**, fr. 1 (=4Q**418**, fr. 2)

In heaven He judges the work of wickedness
and all the sons of truth will be pleased with . . .
. . . [until] his end
and all those who have wallowed in it
shall be frightened and scream.
For heaven . . .

The waters and abysses shall be frightened,
and all the spirits of flesh shall be laid bare.
And the sons of heaven ... its [jud]gement.
And all injustice will yet come to an end
and the age of trut[h] will be completed ...
... in all the everlasting ages.
For He is the God of truth, and from the beginning of years ...
to establish righteousness between good and ev[il].
...
[For] his is a fleshly [in]clination
and his foundation ...

## 4Q417, fr. 1 i (=4Q416, fr. 2 i)

And you shall not swallow up his spirit,
for you have spoken in whisper ...
And he has recited quickly his rebuke ...
Do not overlook your sin ...
for he is as righteous as you are.
For he is a prince among pr[inces]
... he will do.
For how unique is he in all activity with[out] ...
Do not reckon an unjust man as a help,
nor one filled with hatred apart from the wickedness of his deeds.
At his visitation he will know them.
Walk with him ...
Let [instr]uction not depart from your heart
and God will be for you, yourself.
Widen ... in your head,
for who is more insignificant than a poor man.
Do not be jolly while in mourning
lest you labour all your life.
Look at the approaching mystery
and grasp the sources (or: begetters) of salvation,
and know who is to inherit glory or injustice.
Will they not ...

and for their mourning everlasting joy.
...
Be an advocate for your business ... all your sins.
Pronounce your judgement like a righteous ruler.
Do not ...
and do not overlook your sin.
...
Then God will see and His anger will cease,
and He will forgive your sins ...
[Before His greatness (?)] no one can stand,
And who is righteous in His judgement?
And without pardon, how can the poor [stand firm]?
And as for you, if you are in need of food,
your need and your plenty ... you will make abundant.
Be led to the sustenance of His delight,
and take from Him your inheritance ...
... [by the word] of his mouth everything is
and whatever He feeds you with, eat it.
...
If in your need you borrow money from people
do not ... day and night
and do not cease ...
Do not lie to him/me.
Why should you bear guilt?
...

## Fr. 1 ii (=4Q**416**, fr. 2 i–ii)

... Do not ask for your nourishment,
for He opens His mercies ...
...
and to give nourishment to all the living.
...
If he keeps his hand tight,
the spirit of all flesh is gathered in.
Do not take ...
...
and the debtor ... let him quickly repay (his debt).

As for you, settle with him,
for you must keep an eye on your money purse.
At[tend] your creditor on behalf of your friend
and . . . all your life in him(?).
Give quickly that he may not take your purse.
Let your spirit not diminish because of your words;
do not exchange your holy spirit for any wealth,
for no price equals it . . .
For a man in favour does not thrust Thee away.
Seek His face and speak according to His tongue
and you will then find your pleasure
. . . your . . .
Do not abandon your precepts
and take care of your mysteries.
If he assigns you some work to do,
do not rest or sleep until it is done.
. . . and look, for it is great.
Man's zeal circumvents the heart.
. . .
And also by His goodwill you will hold fast to His service
and His gentle wisdom . . .
. . . you will consult with me.
And you will be His first-born son
and (He will) have compassion on you
like a man on his only son;
for you . . .
Do not trust your likeness
and do not keep awake because of the storm.
. . .
And also do not humble yourself
to one who is not your equal.

Then you will be . . .
Do not strike him who is without your strength
lest you stumble and your shame increase greatly.
Do not increase your appetite for wealth;
it is better for you to be a slave in spirit.
Serve your master freely
and do not sell your glory for a price.

Do not give money in pledge for your inheritance
lest it impoverish your body.
Do not satiate yourself with bread
while there is no clothing.
Do not drink wine
while there is no food.
Do not seek luxury
when you lack bread.

Do not glorify yourself in your need if you are poor
lest you degrade your life.
Also do not treat with contempt
your ordained instrument
...

## 4Q416 2 iii

...
and remember that you are poor ...
What you lack, you will not find ...
[If someone has left] a deposit with you,
do not put your hand on it lest it be burnt
and your body be devoured by its flame.
As you have received it, so return it
and you will rejoice if you have no responsibility for it.
Accept no goods from someone whom you do not know
lest he increase your poverty.
But if he has thrust it on you, let it be a deposit until death,
but do not let your spirit be destroyed for it.
Then you will lie with the truth
and your memory will flower ... when you die,
and your posterity will inherit joy.

[If] you are poor, do not desire anything save your inheritance,
and do not be devoured by it lest you change your boundary.
But if He brings you back to glory, walk in it,
and in the approaching mystery search its beginnings.

Then you will know
His inheritance and you will walk in righteousness
For God will . . . in all your ways.
Honour Him who glorifies you and praise His name always.
For your head is above the summit of the mountains
and He has given you a seat among the nobles
and has made you to rule over an inheritance of glory.
Seek diligently His pleasure.

You are a poor man. Do not say:
Since I am poor, I will not seek knowledge.
Shoulder every discipline and with every . . . refine
  your heart,
and your thoughts with a multitude of understanding.
Search the approaching mystery
and consider all the ways of truth,
and behold the roots of injustice.
Then you will know what is bitter for a man
and what is sweet for a human being.
Honour your father in your poverty
and your mother in your steps.
For his father is like God to a man
and his mother like a ruler to a human being.
For they are the crucible from which you were born
and as He placed them over you as rulers
and a frame for the spirit (?), so serve them,
and as He has revealed to you the approaching mystery,
honour them for your honour's sake
and in . . . the splendour of their face
for your life's sake and for the length of your days.
And if you are as poor as . . .
without precept.
You have taken a wife in your poverty,
take the offspring . . .
from the approaching mystery
when you are joined together.
Walk with the helpmate of your flesh . . .

## 4Q**416** iv

his father and his mother . . .
did not make him (her father) rule over her
and He separated her from her mother
and towards you [will be her longing] . . .
[and she will be] one flesh for you.
He will separate your daughter for one
and your sons . . .
And you will become one with the wife of your bosom,
for she is the flesh of your na[kedness]
and whoever rules over her apart from you
has changed
the boundary of his life.
He has made you to rule over her spirit
so that she may walk according to your pleasure.
Let her not increase vows and free-will offerings . . .
Bring back (her?) spirit to your good pleasure,
and annul by a word of your mouth
every binding oath of hers by which to vow a vow.
And by your will, stop her . . .
of your lips . . .

## Fr. 2 i (=4Q**418**, fr. 43)

. . .
[day and] night he meditates on the approaching mystery
and studies (it) always.
Then you will know truth and injustice,
wisdom [and folly . . . ]
. . . in all their ways
together with their visitation
for all the eternal ages and everlasting visitation.
Then you will know the difference
between good and evil relating to their deeds.
For the God of knowledge is the foundation of truth,
and through the approaching mystery

He set apart its foundation,
the work of [His hands] . . .
and in pure understanding were revealed
. . . the secrets of his thought
with his perfect conduct in all his deeds.
Always seek these eagerly,
and understand all their results.
And then you will know everlasting glory
and His marvellous mysteries, and the might of His deeds.
And you will understand the beginning of your reward
at the memorial of the time that has come.
Engraved is the decree and all the visitation is determined.
For God's ordinance is engraved
over all the in[iquities] of the sons of Seth.
And a book of memorial is written before Him
for those who keep His word.
And this is the vision issuing from the meditation
on the book of memorial.
And He gave it as a heritage
to mankind and to the people of the spirit.
For his (man's) shape is modelled on the holy ones,
but meditation belongs no more to the fleshly spirit,
for it cannot distinguish between g[ood] and evil
according to the judgement of its spirit.
And you, son, look . . . at the approaching mystery
and know the heritage of all the living.
And his conduct and his visitation . . .
. . . whether large or small . . .

## 4Q418, fr. 69

**II** . . .
[What] is silence if no one is there (?),
and what is judgement if it has no foundation?
Why do the dead groan over their j[udgement]. . .
. . . their creation (?)
and your return is to eternal destruction.

Darkness will roar at your multitude and all those who
have for ever existed.
Those who search truth will be aroused for judgement
[and] . . . all the foolish hearts will be destroyed,
and the sons of injustice will be found no more,
[and a]ll the supporters of wickedness will be put to shame.
The foundations of the firmament scream at your judgement
and all the . . . will thunder.
. . .
And you, elect of truth
and pursuers of [righteousness and] jud[gement]
. . . guardians of all knowledge,
how will you say:
We labour for understanding
and keep awake to pursue knowledge
. . . and be not weary in all the years of eternity.
Will he not delight in truth for ever
and knowledge . . .
The s[ons of] heaven whose inheritance is eternal life,
Will they indeed say:
We have laboured in the works of truth
and we exhausted ourselves in all the ages.
Will they not walk in eternal light
[and inherit g]lory and great splendour.
. . .

## 4Q418, fr. 81

Your lips are the opening of a spring to bless the holy,
and in the eternal spring you have praised . . .
The [Hol]y . . . has separated you from every spirit (bound to)
flesh.
As for you, separate from all that He hates,
and keep away from all the abomination of the soul.
For He has made all,
and caused them to inherit each his heritage.
He is your portion and your heritage among the sons of man,
[and] He has made you ruler [in] his [her]itage.

And in this you glorify Him, in consecrating yourself to Him.
When He made of you the holy of holies . . .
And in all these
He cast your lot.
And He has much increased your glory
and has made you the first-born among . . .
. . . and I give you my goodness.
As for you, is not His goodness for you?
In His faithfulness He has walked always.
. . . your deeds.
And as for you, search His judgements with the help
of everyone . . .
. . . I will love Him, and with eternal loving-kindness,
and with mercy towards all who keep His word.
And . . .
And as for you, He has opened understanding to you
and has made you the ruler over His treasury
and appointed [you] a receptacle of truth . . .
. . . them with you,
and to revoke anger from the men of goodwill by your hand.
And to visit . . . with you,
and before you take your heritage from His hand,
glorify(?) His holy ones;
and bef[ore] . . .
. . . He has opened the [spr]ing of all the holy ones,
and everyone called holy by His name . . .
. . . with all the ages,
his beauty and splendour to become an ever[lasting] plant.
. . .
For God has assigned a heritage to all the [living]
and all those wise in heart will understand . . .

## Fr. 103 ii

. . .
Why should it be a mixture like a mule,
and you should be like one dres[sed in mixed materials],
in wool and in linen,

and you should labour with an ox and an ass (yoked) together.
Your produce also would be like that of one who sows mixed seeds.
Let the seed and the crop and the produce of the [vineyard] be holy
...

## 4Q423, fr. 5

...
He has unstopped your ear ...
He has divided the inheritance of all the rulers
and the formation of every deed is in His hand.
He [knows] the reward of [their works
and] j[udges] them all in truth.
He visits the sons for (the sins of ) the fathers,
... with all the natives.
...
inspect the seasons of the summer
and gather in your produce in its time,
and the period of ...
Observe your produce and your work,
... the good with the bad,
the intelligent man with the fool
...

# A Sapiential Work (iii): Ways of Righteousness

## (4Q420–21)

Two badly fragmented copies of a Wisdom composition portray the behaviour of the righteous man in universal terms. However, since the vocabulary of 4Q421 1 i echoes the terminology of the Community Rule, the whole work may be classified as sectarian.

For a preliminary edition, see *UDSS* II, 159–62.

### 4Q420, fr. 1 (4Q421, fr. 1 ii)

**II** to practise righteousness in the ways of God (4Q421 1 ii).
... he shall not reply before he has heard,
nor shall he speak before he has gained understanding.
He shall patiently respond and ... shall issue words.
He shall seek truth (and) judgement
and by searching righteousness he shall find its outcome.
A humble and modest man shall not turn back
until ...
A faithful man shall not depart from the ways of righteousness
and he shall set his heart to ...
and the bones (of) his hands to ...
He shall be redeemed through righteousness;
through understanding ... his fields.
His territory ...
to [practise ri]ghteousness ...

# A Sapiential Work (iv)

## (4Q424)

The main theme of this poetic composition is to instruct the just man how to ensure the progress of wisdom by not entrusting its propagation to the unworthy.

For a preliminary study, see *UDSS* II, 174–5.

### Fr. 1

... and he will choose to build it,
and will spread plaster on its wall.
He too ... will become loose because of the rain.
Do not learn a precept in the company of hypocrites
nor come to the furnace with a totterer,
for he will melt away like lead,
and will not stand up to the fire ...
and do not entrust a sleepy man with something delicate,
for he will not treat your work gently ...
Do not send ... learning (?),
for he will not smooth down your paths.
Do not [send ... ] a grumbler to procure money for your need,
nor put your trust in a man with twisted lips,
[for] he will surely twist your judgement by his lips.
His desire will not follow the truth,
... by the fruit of his lips.
Do not put a stingy man in charge of mone[y],
... mete out your food according to your desire ...
... those who bring abundance ...
but at the time of gathering he will be found ungodly.

The short-tempered . . . the simple,
for he will surely swallow them up . . .

## Fr. 3

. . . and he will not do his deed by weighing it.
A man who judges before inquiry,
and one who believes before . . . ,
do not put him in charge of those who pursue knowledge,
for he will not understand their manner
so as to justify the just and declare the wicked [wicked];
he too will be for contempt.
Do not send a blind man to bring a vision to the upright;
li[kewise] do not send a man who is hard of hearing to inquire
into judgement,
for he will not smooth out a quarrel between people.
Like one who scatters into the wind . . .
. . . who does not test,
so is he who speaks to an ear which does not listen,
and talks to a man deep asleep through a spirit . . .
Do not send a 'fat-hearted' (dense) man to acquire thoughts,
for the wisdom of his heart is hidden,
and he will not be in charge o[f his heart],
and will not find wisdom for his hands.
An intelligent man gains un[derstanding],
a knowing man will bring forth wisdom . . .
an upright man delights in justice,
a man . . .
a mighty man is zealous for . . .
He is an adversary to all changers of boundaries,
. . . righteousness for the poor of . . .

# Bless, My Soul

## (Barki nafshi[a], 4Q**434**–**7**)

Cave 4 has yielded five manuscripts (4Q**434**–**8**) of a poetic composition designated by the opening words of the first section as *Barki nafshi* or 'Bless, my soul'. A sixth manuscript (4Q**439**) is said to be akin to it. 4Q**434**, fr. 1 is not unlike some of the Thanksgiving Hymns, but includes no sectarian features.

For a preliminary study, see *UDSS* III, 310, 314–17.

### 4Q**434**, fr. 1

Bless, my soul, the Lord
for all His marvels for ever,
and may His name be blessed.
For He has delivered the soul of the poor,
and has not despised the humble,
and has not forgotten the misery of the deprived.
He has opened His eyes towards the distressed,
and has heard the cry of the fatherless,
and has turned His ears towards their crying.
He has been gracious to the humble by His great kindness,
and has opened their eyes to see His ways,
and [thei]r e[ar]s to hear His teaching.
He has circumcised the foreskin of their heart,
and has delivered them because of His kindness,
and has directed their feet towards the way.
He has not forsaken them amid the multitude of their misery,
neither has He handed them over to the violent,
nor has He judged them together with the wicked.
[He has] not [directed] His anger against them,

neither did he annihilate them in His wrath.
While all His furious wrath was not growing weary,
He has not judged them in the fire of His ardour,
but He has judged them in the greatness of His mercy.
The judgements of His eyes were to try them,
and He has brought His many mercies among the nations,
[and from the hand of] men He has delivered them.
He has not judged them (amid) the mass of nations,
and in the midst of peoples He has not judged [them].
But He hid them in [His] ...
He has turned darkness into light before them,
and crooked places into level ground,
He has revealed to them abundance of peace and truth.
He has made their spirit by measure,
and has established their words by weight,
and has caused them to sing(?) like flutes.
He has given them a [perfect] heart,
and they have walked in the w[ay of His heart],
He has also caused them to draw near to the w[ay of his heart].
For they have pledged their spirit (?).
And He has surrounded them with a hedge
and has commanded that no blow should smite them.
He has placed His angels around them to protect them [from Belia]l
lest he destroy them by the hand of their enemies.

## 4Q436 (combined with 4Q435 i)

**I** understanding to strengthen the contrite heart and the spirit (which is) in it for ever; to comfort the weak in the time of their distress and the hands of the fallen so that they may rise; to make instruments of knowledge; to give knowledge to the wise so that the upright may increase understanding; so that they may understand Thy deeds which Thou hast done in the years of old, in the years of all generations. Eternal understanding which ... before me, and Thou keepest Thy law before me and Thou hast entrusted Thy covenant to me. And Thou dost strengthen the heart ... to walk in Thy ways. Thou has visited my heart and Thou hast sharpened my kidneys (affections) that they may not forget Thy precepts ... Thou hast ... Thy law. Thou hast opened my kidneys and hast strengthened me to pursue Thy ways ... Thy ... Thou hast made my mouth into a sharp sword and opened my tongue for words of holiness. And Thou hast set ... discipline that they may not meditate on man's actions, on the talk of his lips. Thou hast strengthened my feet ... and with Thy hand Thou hast strengthened my right hand and Thou hast sent me ...

... Thou hast chased away from me. And Thou hast placed a pure heart in its stead; Thou hast chased away the evil inclination [from my] ...

**II** And Thou hast placed [the spirit of holine]ss into my heart and hast taken away from me the eyes of fornication. And Thou hast looked ... Thy [wa]ys; Thou hast removed from me the stiff neck and replaced it with humility. Thou hast taken away [from me] the rage of anger and hast placed in me the spirit of patience [4Q**435**, fr. 1]. A haughty heart and lofty eyes Thou hast cleansed away (?) from me ... to me. Thou hast blotted out the spirit of lies [4Q**435** i] ... hast given me ...

## 4Q**437**, fr. 2 i

...
They have hidden a net to catch me and have pursued
  [my] sou[l] ...
[Let] their sword enter their heart and may their bows
  be smashed ...
[For all] this I will bless Thy name while I live,
for Thou hast delivered me from the lure of the nations.
And Thy loving-kindness is a shield around (me)
and Thou guardest my soul among the nations.
... Thou hast put to shame my ...
I have not forgotten Thy precepts in the distress of my soul.
Thou hast not hidden Thy face from my supplications
and Thou hast seen my sorrow.
And my iniquities ... covers my spirit,
In my distress Thou hast heard my voice.
[Thou hast] concealed me in Thy quiver
and hast turned me into a polished arrow (Isa. xlix, 2).

Thou hast sheltered me in Thy protective hand.
Thou hast delivered me [from the mire] lest I sink
and from the stream of the nations lest I ...
And [Thou hast] brought [me up] from Sheol
(the underworld) ...
Thou hast comforted me with children of righteousness.
Thou wilt [jud]ge [me] by the measuring-cord.
Thou hast rejoiced ...

I will bless the Lord with a[ll my soul] ...
I remember Thee, O Lord, and my heart braces itself
be[fore] Thee
... I remember. My heart exults in Thee.
Thou hast raised ... in thirst ...
I will sing Thy deeds.
I remember Thee on my couch during the watches
[of the night].

# Songs of the Sage

## (4Q510–11)

Scraps of two manuscripts from Cave 4 (4Q510–11) represent a mixture of sapiential psalms and poems of exorcism. Their editor, M. Baillet (*DJD*, VII, 215–62), assigns the script to the end of the first century BCE, or the turning of the era. The first fragment preserves an interesting list of names of demons.

### 4Q510

... praises. Ben[edictions for the K]ing of glory. Words of thanksgiving in psalms of ... to the God of knowledge, the Splendour of power, the God of gods, Lord of all the holy. [His] domini[on] is over all the powerful mighty ones and by the power of his might all shall be terrified and shall scatter and be put to flight by the splendour of the dwel[ling] of his kingly glory. And I, the Master, proclaim the majesty of his beauty to frighten and ter[rify] all the spirits of the destroying angels and the spirits of the bastards, the demons, Lilith, the howlers (?) and [the yelpers ...] they who strike suddenly to lead astray the spirit of understanding and to appal their heart and their ... in the age of the domination of wickedness and the appointed times for the humiliation of the sons of ligh[t], in the guilt of the ages of those smitten by iniquity, not for eternal destruction but for the humiliation of sin. Exalt, O just, the God of marvels. My psalms are for the upright ... May all whose way is perfect exalt him.

### 4Q511, fr. 1

... [on the ea]rth and in all the spirits of his dominion always. Let the seas b[le]ss him in their turn and all the creatures living in them. May they proclaim the ... of beauty all of them. Let them rejoice before the

God of justice with shouts of salvation, for there shall be no destroyer in their territories, and no spirit of wickedness shall walk in there. For the glory of the God of knowledge has shone forth in his words, and none of the sons of iniquity shall endure.

## Fr. 2

**I** For the Master. [First] Song. Praise the name of his holiness; all who know [justice], exalt him ... He put an end to the chief of the dominations without ... eternal [joy] and everlasting life, to cause light to shine ... his [l]ot is the best of Jacob and the inheritance of G[o]d ... of Israel ... they who guard the way of God and the pat[h] of his [hol]iness for the saints of his people. By the discerning knowledge [of Go]d, he placed Israel in twelve camps ... the lot of God with the ange[ls] of the luminaries of his glory. In his name the praises ... he has established for the feast of the year and for a common government that they may walk [in] the lot of [God] according to [his] glory [and] serve him in the lot of the people of his throne. For the God of ...

## Fr. 8

[For the Master]. Second [S]ong to frighten those who terrify him ...

## Fr. 18

**II** I have hated all the works of impurity. For God has caused the knowledge of understanding to shine in my heart. Just chastisers (deal) with my perversity, and faithful judges with all my sinful guilt. For God is my judge and by the hand of a stranger [He] shall not ...

## Frs. 28–9

... [they shall] rejoice in God with jubilation. And I [will thank Th]ee for, because of Thy glory, Thou hast [s]et knowledge on my foundations of dust to pr[aise Thee]. ... out of a shape [of clay] was I moulded and from darkness was I kneaded ... and iniquity is in the limbs of my flesh ...

## Fr. 30

Thou hast sealed ... the [e]arth ... and they are deep. [The heavens and the heavens of the] heavens, and the abysses and the dar[k places of the earth] ... Thou, O my God, hast sealed them all and there is none to open (them) ... Does one measure by the hollow of a human hand the waters of the great (ocean)? Are [the heavens estimated by the span (of fingers)? In one third (of a measure)] can any contain the dust of the earth, and weigh the mountains in a balance, or the hills in scal[es]? Man did not make these. How can he measure the spirit of [God]?

## Fr. 35

... God in all flesh, and an avenging judgement to destroy wickedness, and for the raging anger of God towards those seven times refined. God shall sancti[fy] (some) of the holy as an everlasting sanctuary for himself, and purity shall endure among the cleansed. They shall be priests, his righteous people, his host, servants, the angels of his glory. They shall praise him with marvellous prodigies. I, I spread the fear of God in the ages of my generations to exalt the name ... [to terrify] by his might al[l] the spirits of the 'bastards', subduing them by [his] fear ...

## Frs. 63–4

**II** ... I will bless Thy name and in my appointed periods I will recount Thy marvels and I will engrave them as precepts of Thy glory's praises. At the beginning of every thought of a knowing heart and (with) the offering of that which flows from the righteous lips when ready for all true worship and with all ...

## Fr. 63

**III** As for me, my tongue shall extol Thy righteousness, for Thou hast released it. Thou hast placed on my lips a fount of praise and in my heart the secret of the commencement of all human actions and the completion of the deeds of the perfect of way and the judgements regarding all the service done by them, justifying the just by Thy truth and condemning the wicked for their guilt. To announce peace to all the men of the Covenant and to utter a dreadful cry of woe for all those who breach it ...**IV** May they bless all Thy works always and blessed be Thy name for ever and ever. Amen, amen.

# Beatitudes

## (4Q525)

The title given to this piece of Wisdom poetry derives from the repeated use of 'Blessed' ('*ashre*), modelled on Ps. i, 1, and recalling the Beatitudes of the New Testament (Matth. v, 3–11). The main structural difference between Matthew and 4Q525 lies in that the former each time lists the reward of the virtue for which people are blessed, whereas the Cave 4 text provides ordinary, mostly antithetic, parallelisms instead.

For preliminary studies, see E. Puech, 'Un hymne essénien en partie retrouvé et les béatitudes', *RQ* 13 (1988), 59–88; '4Q525 et les péricopes des béatitudes en Ben Sira et Matthieu', *RB* 98 (1991), 80–106.

### Fr. 2

**II** [Blessed is] . . . with a pure heart
and does not slander with his tongue.
Blessed are those who hold to her (Wisdom's) precepts
and do not hold to the ways of iniquity.
Blessed are those who rejoice in her,
and do not burst forth in ways of folly.
Blessed are those who seek her with pure hands,
and do not pursue her with a treacherous heart.
Blessed is the man who has attained Wisdom,
and walks in the Law of the Most High.
He directs his heart towards her ways,
and restrains himself by her corrections,
and always takes delight in her chastisements.
He does not forsake her when he sees distress,
nor abandon her in time of strain.
He will not forget her [on the day of] fear,

and will not despise [her] when his soul is afflicted.
For always he will meditate on her,
and in his distress he will consider [her?]
. . .
[He will place her] before his eyes,
so as not to walk in the ways of [folly].
. . .

## Fr. 4

. . .
[Do not] forsake your [inheri]tance [to the nations]
nor your portion to strangers
. . .
Those who [f]ear God observe her (Wisdom's) ways
and walk in [all] her precepts
and do not reject her corrections.
The intelligent will bring out . . .
[and all] those who walk in perfection
will turn aside injustice,
but they will not reject her admonitions
and will carry [her] . . .
The sensible will recognize her ways
[and meditate on (?)] her depths.
. . .

# F. Bible Interpretation

'The Targum of Job',
*Israel Antiquities Authority*

# *Introductory Note*

Five types of biblical commentary have been recovered from the Qumran caves.

The first and least developed form of exegesis is contained in the so-called 'Reworked Pentateuch' texts, consisting of a quasi-traditional text of the Bible, occasionally rearranged and supplemented. To this category belong 4Q**158**, **364–7**, **422**, **382**, etc. The Temple Scroll (11Q**19–20**) may also be assigned to this group, as well as the fairly, though not strictly, literal Aramaic translations or Targums of the Hebrew Scriptures (4Q**156–7**; 11Q**10**), to which should be added some small fragments of the Greek Bible from Caves 4 and 7.

The second type, represented by the Genesis Apocryphon, sets out to render the Bible story more intelligible and attractive by giving it more substance, by reconciling conflicting statements, and by reinterpreting in the light of contemporary standards and beliefs any passages which might seem to give offence. In a somewhat similar manner, a Commentary on Genesis from Cave 4 (4Q**252**) attempts to adjust the chronology of the Flood to the specific sectarian calendar of the Qumran Community.

The third type of commentary departs from the biblical text and, relying on one or several passages, creates a new story. Among others, the Admonition associated with the Flood (4Q**370**, **185**), the Words of Moses (1Q**22**), the New Jerusalem texts (4Q**554–5**, 5Q**15**, etc.) and the Prayer of Nabonidus (4Q**242**), inspired by Genesis, Deuteronomy, Ezekiel and Daniel respectively, come into this category.

The fourth and most characteristic form of exegesis applies prophetic texts to the past, present and future of the sect. Normally the commentator expounds a biblical book verse by verse, e.g. Isaiah (4Q**161–4**); Nahum (4Q**169**); Habakkuk (1QpHab); the Psalms (4Q**171**, **173**), etc., but some works – A Midrash on the Last Days (4Q**174**), The Heavenly Prince Melchizedek (11Q**13**), etc. – follow the traditional Jewish example and assemble passages from different parts of Scripture in order to develop a common theme.

Finally, a substantial amount of free compositions modelled on the Bible, e.g. Jubilees (4Q**216–28**), Enoch and the Giants (4Q**201–12**, **530–33**), or circulating together with the Bible, e.g. the Para-Danielic fragments (4Q**243–5**), and works attributed to Noah (1Q**19**, etc.), the Patriarchs Levi (4Q**213–14**, **537–41**), Moses (4Q**374–7**, **390**), and many others constitute a fifth category of exegesis. In one way, the Aramaic and Hebrew manuscripts of one of the Apocrypha, the Book of Tobit (4Q**196–200**), pertain to this class.

# Aramaic Bible Translations (Targums)

Two books of the Hebrew Bible have survived in Aramaic translation in the Qumran caves. A small scroll, found in Cave 11 and measuring 109 cm, has preserved in Aramaic a large portion of the last seven chapters of the Book of Job. Twenty-seven smaller fragments cover parts of Job xvii, 14 to xxxvi, 33. This text, together with small remains from Cave 4 of Leviticus (4Q**156**=xvi, 12–21, see below) and of another manuscript of Job (4Q**157**=iii, 5–9; iv, 16–v, 4), represent the oldest extant Aramaic renderings of the Hebrew Bible. The translation of Job frequently differs from the customary text of the Hebrew Bible, but it is unclear whether the divergences are due merely to the difficulty of translating poetry, or to a Hebrew original not identical with the traditional Scripture.

| *Hebrew Job xl, 12* | *11QarJob* |
|---|---|
| Look on every one that is proud<br>and bring him low;<br>and tread down the wicked<br>where they stand. | And every proud spirit<br>you will smash;<br>and extinguish the wicked<br>below them. |

It is clear, on the other hand, that the prose narrative of xlii, 9–11 displays notable departures from the text known to us, as may be seen from the following parallel translations:

| *Hebrew Job xlii* | *11QarJob* |
|---|---|
| (9) So Eliphaz the Temanite and<br>Bildad the Shuhite and Zophar the<br>Naamathite went and did what the<br>Lord had told them; and the Lord<br>accepted Job's prayer.<br>(10) And the Lord restored the | (9) . . .<br>. . . . . .<br>God. God heard the voice of<br>Job and forgave the (his<br>friends') sins because of him.<br>(10) And the Lord returned |

| | |
|---|---|
| fortunes of Job, when he had prayed for his friends; and the Lord gave Job twice as much as he had before. | to Job with mercy and doubled all that he had owned. |
| (11) Then came to him all his brothers and sisters and all who had known him before, and ate bread with him in his house; and they showed him sympathy and comforted him for all the evil that the Lord had brought upon him; and each of them gave him a piece of money (or: sheep) and a ring of gold. | (11) All his friends, brothers and acquaintances came to Job and they ate bread with him in his house; and they comforted him for all the evil that God had brought upon him; and each of them gave him a lamb and a ring of gold. |

The English version provided below (Job xxxvii, 11 to xlii, 11) should therefore be read side by side with the translation of the canonical Job. It will be noticed that Job xxxix, 24 is missing from the Aramaic and xlii, 3 is replaced by xl, 5. Furthermore, in Job xxxviii, 7 the phrase 'angels' is substituted for 'sons of God', a doctrinally suspect expression since Jews rejected the idea of God having children. The same substitution is found in the Greek Septuagint and the Targum of Job used in rabbinic Judaism. Similarly the Targum to Lev. xvi, 14 and xvi, 20 (4Q**156**) specifies, as do the later Targums, that 'the Holy' designates 'the House of Holiness' or 'Sanctuary'. In short, the Qumran Targums prefigure to some extent the style of the later Targums without attesting, however, the exegetical expansions which characterize the Palestinian Targums to the Pentateuch.

For the *editio princeps* of 11Q**18**, see J. P. M. van der Ploeg et al., *Le Targum de Job de la grotte XI de Qumrân* (Leiden, 1971); cf. also M. Sokoloff, *The Targum to Job from Qumran Cave XI* (Ramat Gan, 1974). For the Targums of Leviticus and Job (4Q**156**, **157**), see J. T. Milik, *DJD* VI, 85–91.

# The Targum of Job

## (11Q10, 4Q157)

**XXIX** (*Job xxxvii*)
(11) With it (water) He wipes the cloud[s],
and brings fire out of the cloud.
(12) He speaks and they listen to Him
and proceed with their works.
He appoints them over all
that He has created on earth:
(13) either for striking or for (benefiting) the earth;
either for famine or shortage;
or for something good to be on it.
(14) Listen to this, Job, and arise!
Observe the might of God.
(15) [Do you] know what God has put on them
and how He has made light to shine from the cloud?
(16) [Do you k]now how to robe the cloud with mi[ght]?
(17) Because your robe ...
For He possesses knowledge ...
(18) [Do you know how to] beat the cloud
[to] compress [it into a mir]ror?
(19) He knows ...

**XXX** (*Job xxxviii*)
(3) Please gird [your] lo[ins] like a man,
[and I will que]stion you and you will answer me.
(4) Where were you when I made the earth?
Explain it to me if you possess wisdom.

(5) Do you know who fixed its measures?
Who stretched a line over it?
(6) Or to what were its foundations joined
or who set its cut stone
(7) when the morning stars were shining together
and all the angels of God exclaimed together?
(8) Can you shut in the sea with gates
when it bursts forward from the womb of the abyss,
(9) when the clouds were made into its robe
and the haze its swaddling-clothes.
(10) Can you set boundaries to it . . . ?
(11) Did you say, Up to here!
And you must not go beyond . . . [your wa]ves.
(12) In your days did you order [the morning]
. . .
(13) . . . the win[gs] of the ear[th] . . .

**XXXI** (23) . . .
for the day of battle and revolt.
(24) . . . from where will (the wind) go out
and will it blow before Him on the earth?
(25) Who fixed a time for the rain
and a path for the quick clouds
(26) to bring it (the rain) down to a land of wilderness
with no man on it,
(27) to satiate the low-lying and isolated (places)
to produce sprouting grass.
(28) Has the rain a father
and who begets the mist of dew?
(29) And from whose womb did ice come out
. . .
(30) The waters contracted like a st[one] because of
Him,
and the face of the ab[yss?] . . .
(31) . . . Pleiades or the fence of Orion . . .

**XXXXII** (*Job xxxix*)
(1) the mountain goats, and the birth p[angs] . . .
(2) . . . their months are completed,
and do you know when they give birth,

(3) delivering their young and ejecting them,
and do you send away their birth pangs?
(4) They raise their young and make them go;
they depart and do not come back to them.
(5) Who has set the wild ass free
and who has loosed the onager's rope,
(6) to whom I gave the desert for his home
and made the salty land his dwelling.
(7) He laughs at the great commotion of the city
and his master's urging he does not hear.
(8) He chooses for himself mountains for [pasture]
and he goes after everything green.
(9) Does the wild ox wish to serve you
or will he lodge in your stable?
(10) Will you tie [the wild ox] with a yoke
and will he plough(?) in the valley [aft]er you?
And will you ...
Will you depend on hi[m because] great is
[his strength]?

## XXXIII

(20) Will you frighten him (the horse) with a strong ...
his ... is fear and dread.
(21) He searches out the valley, he trembles and
rejoices,
and mightily advances towards the sword.
(22) He laughs at fear and does not shudder,
and does not turn back from the sword.
(23) Upon him hangs a lance,
a javelin and a sharp sword,
(25) and at the sound of the trumpet, he says, Aha,
and from afar he smells the battle,
and he enjoys the rattle of the weapons and the war
cries.
(26) Does the hawk get excited because of your wisdom
and spread his wings towards the winds?
(27) Or does [the eagle] rise at your order
and the bird of prey build [its] nest on high?
(28) It dwells on the rock and nests ...

## XXXIV (*Job xl*)

...

(6) [From ...] and from the cloud
God answered Job and said to him:
(7) Like a man, please gird your loins;
I will question you, and you will answer me.
(8) Would you indeed tear up the judgement
and declare me guilty so that you may be innocent?
(9) Or do you have an arm like God
or thunder with a voice like his?
(10) Throw away, please, pride and haughtiness
and you will put on splendour, glory and honour.
(11) Throw away, please, the heat of your wrath
and observe every proud man and humble him.
(12) And every proud spirit you will smash
and you will extinguish the wicked [in] their [pl]aces.
(13) And hide them all in the dust
[and] cover [with a]shes ...

## XXXV

...

(23) ... the Jordan its banks,
he (the hippopotamus) trusts that he will get it.
(24) When he lifts his eyes, who will restrain him,
... his nose with a hook.
(25) Will you pull a crocodile with a hook
or tie up its tongue with a rope?
(26) Will you put a muzzle on his nose
and will you pierce his cheek with your chisel?
(27) Will he speak gently with you
or will he speak with you pleadingly?
(28) Will he make a covenant with you
or will you handle him as a slave for ever?
(29) Will you play with him like a b[ird,
and] will you bind him with a string for your daughters?

...

## XXXVI (*Job xli*)

...
(8) They cling to one another
and no breath passes between them.
(9) One holds to another,
and they do not separate.
(10) His sneezing lights fire between his eyes
like the shine of dawn (?).
(11) Torches come forth out of his mouth;
they leap like tongues of fire.
(12) From his nostrils smoke goes forth
like burning thorn and incense.
(13) His breath spews out coals
and sparks come out of his mouth.
(14) His strength dwells in his neck
and vigour springs before him.
(15) The folds of his flesh are clinging,
mould[ed over him] like iron.
(16) [His] heart ... like stone
...

## XXXVII (*Job xli–xlii*)

(26) ...
and he is king over all the reptiles.
(1) Job answered and said before God:
(2) I know that Thou canst do all things
and dost not lack in strength and wisdom.
(xl, 5) I have spoken once and will not revoke it,
a second time, and I will not add to it.
(xlii, 4) Listen, please, and I will speak;
I will question you and you must answer me.
(5) I had heard of you by the hearing of the ear
and now my eyes see you.
(6) Therefore I am melting and dissolve
and become dust and ashes ...

## XXXVIII

(9) ... God. God heard the voice of Job and forgave them their sins because of him. (10) And God returned to Job with mercy and doubled all that he had owned. (11) All his friends, brothers and acquaintances came to Job and they ate bread with him in his house, and they comforted him for all the misery that God had brought on him and each gave him a ewe-lamb and a ring of gold.

# The Targum of Leviticus

## (4Q156)

### Fr. 1

. . .

And he (Aaron) shall take some [of the blood of the bull and sprinkle it with his finger o]n the mercy seat. And before the mercy seat – to the east – [he shall sprinkle fr]om the blood with his finger [seven times] (Lev. xvi, 14). . . .

### Fr. 2

. . . Whe[n he has made an end of atoning] for the House of Holiness [and for] the tent of meeting and [for the altar, he shall offer] a live goat (Lev. xvi, 20). . . .

# Appendix

## (A) GREEK BIBLE TRANSLATIONS (4Q119–22; 7Q1–2)

Compared to the quantity of Hebrew and Aramaic manuscripts, the Greek documents found in two of the Qumran caves, Caves 4 and 7, are remarkably few, and this scarcity is significant in itself as regards the cultural identity of the Qumran Community. Those which have been identified with certainty belong to the Greek translation of the Bible, mostly the Pentateuch. Cave 4 has yielded remains of two scrolls of Leviticus, one of leather (**4Q119**) and one of papyrus (**4Q120**), as well as one of Numbers (**4Q121**) and of Deuteronomy (**4Q122**), all dating to the second or the first century BCE. On the whole, they represent the traditional text of the Septuagint with minor variations such as a word being replaced by its synonym (harvesting by threshing, for example, or nation by people), but 4QLXX Numbers (**4Q121**) testifies to an effort to bring the LXX closer to the Hebrew Pentateuch. Since the translation scarcely differs from the original, there is no purpose in reproducing it. However, it is worth noting that in Lev. iv, 27 (**4Q120**, fr. 20, 4) the Tetragram (the divine name YHWH) is rendered semi-phonetically as *Iao*, and is not replaced, as was customary later, by the Greek *Kurios* (Lord).

Among the nineteen minute fragments found in Cave 7 – which contained only Greek texts – two have been identified as relics of Exodus xxviii, 4–7 (**7Q1**) and the Letter of Jeremiah, verses 43–4 (**7Q2**). The former is said to be closer to the traditional Hebrew text than to the LXX. Both are dated to about 100 BCE.

## (B) OTHER GREEK FRAGMENTS (4Q126–7; 7Q3–19)

The remaining two Greek texts in Cave 4 date roughly to the turn of the era. One (**4Q126**) cannot be identified and the other (**4Q127**) is either a paraphrase of Exodus, mentioning among others Pharaoh, Moses and Egypt, or possibly an apocryphal account of Israel in Egypt.

Seventeen out of the nineteen minute Greek papyrus fragments from Cave 7 have been declared by the editors to be unidentifiable. Yet against all verisimilitude, several of them have generated sensational and even revolutionary claims, especially that they represented the earliest textual examples of the Greek New Testament.

The contention originated with a Spanish Jesuit, José O'Callaghan, who in 1972 persuaded himself that these hardly legible scraps derived from six books of the New Testament: the Gospel of Mark iv, 28 (7Q**6** 1), vi, 48 (7Q**15**), vi, 52–3 (7Q**5**), xii, 17 (7Q**7**); the Acts of the Apostles xxviii, 38 (7Q**6** 2); 1 Timothy iii, **16**, iv, 1, 3 (7Q**4**); James i, 23–4 (7Q**8**) and even one of the latest New Testament writings, 2 Peter i, 15 (7Q**10**). Of these, the case for Mark vi, 52–3 is purported to be the 'strongest'. The real facts are the following. We are dealing with a fragment on which the written area measures 3.3 × 2.3 cm. Letters appear on four lines; these are of unknown length since both the beginning and the end of each line are missing. An unrecognizable trace of another letter is observed at the top of the fragment. In the *editio princeps* seventeen letters are identified of which only nine are certain. A single complete word has survived: the Greek *kai* = and!

The leading experts in the field, the late C. H. Roberts of Oxford and the German Kurt Aland, unhesitatingly discarded O'Callaghan's theory. Roberts jokingly told me that if he wanted to waste his time, he was sure he would be able to 'demonstrate' that 7Q**5** belonged to any ancient Greek text, biblical or non-biblical. Yet this unlikely and clearly unprovable hypothesis was revived in the 1980s by C. P. Thiede and others, only to encounter the same fate of summary dismissal as Father O'Callaghan's a decade or so earlier.

For the *editio princeps* of the 4Q and 7Q material, see P. W. Skehan and E. Ulrich, *DJD* IX (Oxford, 1992), 161–97, 219–42; M. Baillet et al., *DJD* III (Oxford, 1962), 142–6. For the theory that 7Q contains New Testament texts, see J. O'Callaghan, *Los papipros griegos de la cueva 7 de Qumrân* (Madrid, 1974), and C. P. Thiede, *The Earliest Gospel Manuscripts* (London, 1992); *Re-Kindling the Word* (Valley Forge, Pa, 1996). For views for and against expressed at a symposium, see B. Mayer, ed., *Christen und Christliches in Qumran?* (Regensburg, 1992). Against the theory, see C. H. Roberts, 'On Some Presumed Papyrus Fragments of the New Testament from Qumran', *Journal of Theological Studies* 23 (1972), 446–7; K. Aland, 'Neue neutestamentlische Papyri III', *New Testament Study* 20 (1973–4), 357–81. For the latest authoritative views, see G. Stanton, *Gospel Truth?* (London, 1995); E. Puech, 'Des fragments grecs de la grotte 7 et le Nouveau Testament?', *RB* 102 (1995), 570–84; M.-E. Boismard (the first decipherer of the fragment), 'A propos de 7Q5 et Mc. 6, 52–53', ibid., 102–4.

# The Reworked Pentateuch

## (4Q158, 4Q364–7)

Five badly preserved manuscripts have been classified as reworkings of the Pentateuch, i.e. copies of the Torah partly entailing rearrangements of biblical passages and partly incorporating interpretative supplements inserted into the text. The length of the supplement varies from a few words to seven or eight lines, the most significant example being the long, but broken, addition to the Song of Miriam in 4Q**365** 6a ii, c. Judging from the surviving passages, the original Reworked Pentateuch must have been a very substantial document, probably the longest of all the Qumran Scrolls. All the manuscripts may be dated on palaeographical grounds to the first century BCE. Only those texts which contain more or less intelligible supplements (printed in italics) are included.

For the official edition of the Reworked Pentateuch, see J. M. Allegro in *DJD*, V, 1–6 (4Q**158**) and E. Tov and S. White in *DJD*, XIII, 187–351 (4Q**364–7**). Cf. also E. Tov, 'The Textual Status of 4Q**364–367** (4QPP)' in *MQC* 1, 43–82.

### 4Q**158**, frs. 1–2
### (Gen. xxxii,24–32; Exod. iv,27–28+Supplement)

... And [J]ac[ob] w[as left a]lone there. And [a man] wrestl[ed with him. When the man did not prevail against Jacob, he touched his thigh; and Jacob's thigh was put out of joint] as he wrestled with him and he seized him. And he said to hi[m, What is your name? ... And he said to him, Jacob. And he said, Your name shall be Israel, for you have striven with God and with] men and have prevailed. And Jacob asked [and] sai[d, Tell me, pray, wh[at is your name. And he said, Why it is that you ask my name, and he bless]ed him there. And he said to him, 'May the Lo[rd] make you fruitful [and multiply] you. May he grant you kn]owledge and understanding and may he save you from all violence and ... until this day and until everlasting generations. And he went on his way after he has blessed him there. And he ... And] the sun [rose] upon him as he passed Penuel, limping because of his thigh. ... on this day. And he said, You shall not e[at the sinew of the hip which is] upon the two hollows of the thigh until [this day. (Exod. iv) And the Lord said] to Aaron, Go to me[et Moses in the wilderness. So he went and met him at the mountain of God and kissed him. And Moses told Aaron all] the words of the Lord with which he had s[ent] him and all [the signs which he had charged him to do. And] *the Lord [spoke] to me saying, When you bring out the [people of Israel]* ... *to go as slaves and behold these are [four hundred and] thirty [years]* ...

## **4Q364**, fr. 3
## (Supplement+Gen. xxviii,6)

**II** you shall see him ... you shall see in peace ... your death. And upon [your] eyes ... *[Why should I be bereft of] both of you?* (Gen. xxvii, 45) And [Isaac] called [Rebecca his wife and told] her all [these] wor[ds] ... after Jacob her son ... And Esau saw that [Isaac had blessed Jacob and sent him away to] Pa[dan] Aram to take [a wife] from [there] ...

## **4Q365**, fr. 6b, 6a ii, 6c
## (Exod. xv, 16–21+Supplement+xv, 22–6)

### Fr. 6b

...
till [Thy people, O Lord], p[ass by,
till the people pass by whom thou hast purchased.
Thou wilt bring them in, and plant them] on thine own mountain,
the place, [O Lord, which thou hast made] for thine abode,
the sanctuary which thy hands have established].
The Lord will reign for ever and ever.
For when [the horses of Pharaoh with his chariots and his horsemen]
went [into the sea, the Lo]rd [brought back] the waters of the sea
upon them; but the people of Israel walked on dry ground in the midst of the sea.
[And the water]s were a wall to them on their right and on their left

(cf. Exod. xiv, 22, 29). [And Miriam the prophetess, sister of Aaron], took
[a timbrel in her hand; and al]l the women went out after her with
[timbrels and dancing. And Miriam sang to them,
Sing to the Lord, for he has triumphed gloriously;
the horse and his rider he has thrown into the sea].

## Fr. 6a ii, 6c

*... thou hast despised ...*
*For pride ...*
*Thou art great, a saviour ...*
*The hope of the enemy has perished*
*and ... has stopped ...*
*They have perished in the mighty waters,*
*the enemy ... and lifts up to their height.*
[*Thou hast given a ransom*] ...
... [*he who ac*]*ts proudly.*

And Moses led [Israe]l onward from the sea, and they went to the wilderness of Sh[ur; they went three days and found no water. They came to Marah, but [they] could [not] drink the water of Marah because [it was] bit[ter; therefore it was named Marah].
And the people murmured ag[ainst Moses] saying, What shall we drink? And Moses cried to [the Lord who showed him] a tree, and he threw it into [the wate]r, and the water became sweet. There he made for them a statute and [an ordinance and there he proved them. And he said], If [you will lis]ten di[li]gent]ly [to the v]oice of the Lord your God and do that which is right in his eyes and [give heed to his commandments and judgements, and keep] all his statutes, [I will put none] of the diseases [upon you] which I put on the E[gyptians. For I am the Lord, your [heale]r.

## Fr. 23
### (Lev. xxii, 42–xxiv, 2+Supplement)

You shall dwell [in bo]oths for seven days; all that are native in Israel shall dwell in booths, tha[t your] gen[erations may kno]w that I made your fathers dwell in booths when I brought them out of the land of

Egypt; I am the Lord you[r] God. *vacat* And Moses declared to the people of Israel the appointed feasts of the Lord. *vacat* And the Lord said to Moses, Command the children of Israel, *saying, When you enter the land which I am giving to you as an inheritance, and you dwell upon it securely, you shall bring wood for a burnt-offering and for all the service of* [*the H*]*ouse which you shall build for me in the land, to lay it on the altar of burnt-offering,* [*and*] *the calves ... for Passover sacrifices and peace-offerings and thank-offerings and free-will offerings and burnt-offerings daily ... and for the doors and for all the service of the House you shall offer ... the festival of Oil, the twel*[*ve tribes*] *they shall offer wood ... Those who offer on the first day shall be Levi and ...* [*on the third day, Reu*]*ben and Simeon,* [*and on*] *the fou*[*rth*] *day ...*

# A Paraphrase of Genesis and Exodus

## (4Q422)

Nine fragments of a manuscript written in Hasmonaean characters contain a paraphrase of Gen. i–iv, vi–ix, judging from disconnected expressions relating to the creation of the world by God's word, to various living creatures, the establishment of man as ruler over the rest of beings, the prohibition against eating from the tree of knowledge and the rebellion against God which led to the flood. Fr. 10 refers to the throwing of Israelite boys into the Nile, the commissioning of Moses, his vision of the burning bush, Moses's and Aaron's encounter with Pharaoh and the plagues which afflicted Egypt. The text can be arranged in three columns. Further unidentified fragments, which are not included here, are numbered from A to T. If the word *ywsr* in col. 1, line 12 actually means 'inclination', the phrase 'evil inclination' could be the earliest attestation of the rabbinic concept. Cf. T. Elgvin and E. Tov, *DJD*, XIII, 417–41.

**I** ...

... [The heavens and the earth and all] their host He made by [His] word. [And God rested on the seventh day from all the work whi]ch He had made. And [His] holy spirit ... [all th]e living and creeping [creatu]res ... [He put man on the ear]th to rule over it and to eat the frui[ts of the ground] ...... w[ith]out eating from the tree of kn[owledge of good and evil] ... He rose against Him and they forgot ... with an evil inclination and for deed[s of] ... peace/payment ...

**II** ... the Flood

... God [cl]osed behind them ... the windows of heave[n] op[en]ed under all the heav[en ... for] the waters to rise on the ear[th forty] days and for[ty] nights was [rain] ov[er] the earth ... and in order to know the glory of the Most Hi[gh] ... to reach to Him, He enlightened the heaven ... sign for generatio[ns] of eternity ... [and never more] will a flood [destroy the earth] ... the periods of day and night ... to shine [o]n heaven and earth ... **III** ... their [s]ons into the rive[r] ... [And] He sent to them Moses ... in the vision ... in the signs and marvels ... And He sent them to Pharaoh ... plagues ... marvels for Egypt ... and they carried His word to Pharaoh to send away [their people]. But He hardened [his] (Pharaoh's) heart [to] sin so that the m[en of Isra]el might know for eternal gene[rations]. And He changed their [wate]rs to blood. Frogs were in all their land and lice in all their territories, gnats in their houses and they struck all their ... And He smote with pestile[nce all] their flock and their beasts He delivered to de[at]h. He pu[t dark]ness into their land and obscurity into their [hou]ses so that they could not see one another. [And He smote] their land with hail and [their] soil [with] frost to cause [al]l the fruit of nourishment [to perish]. And He brought locust to cover the face of the ea[rth], heavy locust in all their territory to eat everything green in [their] la[nd] ... And God hardened Ph[araoh's] heart so that he should not [dis]miss [them] ... and in order to increase wonders. [And He smote their first-born], the beginning of al[l their strength] ...

# The Genesis Apocryphon

## (1Q20)

Found in Cave 1, and partly published by N. Avigad and Y. Yadin (*A Genesis Apocryphon*, Jerusalem, 1956), 1QapGen is an incomplete manuscript with twenty-two surviving columns of Aramaic text (cf. also 1Q20). Remains of a further column, 'The Genesis Apocryphon Col. XII', have since been edited by J. C. Greenfield and E. Qimron (*Studies in Qumran Aramaic, Abr-Nahrain*, Suppl. 3 (1992), 70–77). A preliminary transcription and translation of the rest of the unpublished material, deciphered with the help of advanced infra-red technology, has been issued by M. Morgenstern, E. Qimron and D. Sinan in 'The Hitherto Unpublished Volumes of the Genesis Apocryphon', *Abr-Nahrain* 33 (1995), 30–52.

The beginning of the manuscript is missing. But since the sheet starting with col. v is numbered by the Hebrew letter *pe*, col. x by *'ayin*, and col. xvii by *sade*, i.e. the seventeenth, eighteenth and nineteenth letters of the Hebrew alphabet, it would seem that the surviving section was preceded by sixteen sheets of which only the end of the last one has been preserved (cf. M. Morgenstern, 'A New Clue to the Original Length of the Genesis Apocryphon', *JJS* 47/2 (1996), 345–7). If so, the story of Noah which begins the existing portion of the scroll must have been preceded by an extensive account of the creation, Adam and Eve, and the Genesis story up to Enoch and Noah. Columns ii–v narrate the miraculous birth of Noah (on Noah see also the minute fragments from 1Q19 and **19b**), whose father, Lamech, suspects that his wife has conceived by one of the fallen angels. Her denials fail to convince him and he asks his father, Methuselah, to travel to Paradise and obtain reassurance from his own father, Enoch. Columns vi–xv contain Noah's first-person account of the Flood and of his journeys. Col. x describes Noah's sacrifice after the Flood. Col. xi deals with the covenant between God and Noah with a mention of a ban on eating blood. Col. xii recounts the planting of a vineyard by Noah and his tasting of wine. The badly damaged cols. xiii–xv contain a vision concerning trees and its interpretation. Two further columns (xvi–xvii) deal with the division of the earth among the sons of Noah. Col. XVIII is completely lost. Cols. XIX–XXII, corresponding to Gen. xii–xv, deal with Abraham's journey to Egypt, his return to Canaan, the war against the invading Mesopotamian kings, and the renewal to him of a divine promise of a son. This lively and delightful narrative, largely devoid of sectarian bias, throws valuable light on inter-Testamental Bible interpretation. It is a mixture of Targum, Midrash, rewritten Bible and autobiography. Most scholars assign the manuscript to the late first century BCE or the first half of the first century CE. The composition itself is generally thought to originate from the second century BCE. Its relationship to the mid-second-century Book of Jubilees is generally accepted, but views differ on whether it depends on Jubilees or vice versa. I slightly prefer the theory that in its pre-Qumran version the Genesis Apocryphon precedes Jubilees, which would postulate for the former a date at least as early as the first half of the second century BCE.

... **II** Behold, I thought then within my heart that conception was (due) to the Watchers and the Holy Ones ... and to the Giants ... and my heart was troubled within me because of this child. Then I, Lamech, approached Bathenosh [my] wife in haste and said to her, '... by the Most High, the Great Lord, the King of all the worlds and Ruler of the Sons of Heaven, until you tell me all things truthfully, if ... Tell me [this truthfully] and not falsely ... by the King of all the worlds until you tell me truthfully and not falsely.'

Then Bathenosh my wife spoke to me with much heat [and] ... said, 'O my brother, O my lord, remember my pleasure ... the lying together and my soul within its body. [And I tell you] all things truthfully.'

My heart was then greatly troubled within me, and when Bathenosh my wife saw that my countenance had changed ... Then she mastered her anger and spoke to me saying, 'O my lord, O my [brother, remember] my pleasure! I swear to you by the Holy Great One, the King of [the heavens] ... that this seed is yours and that [this] conception is from you. This fruit was planted by you ... and by no stranger or Watcher or Son of Heaven ... [Why] is your countenance thus changed and dismayed, and why is your spirit thus distressed ... I speak to you truthfully.'

Then I, Lamech, ran to Methuselah my father, and [I told] him all these things. [And I asked him to go to Enoch] his father for he would surely learn all things from him. For he was beloved, and he shared the lot [of the angels], who taught him all things. And when Methuselah heard [my words ... he went to] Enoch his father to learn all things truthfully from him ... his will.

He went at once to Parwain and he found him there ... [and] he said to Enoch his father, 'O my father, O my lord, to whom I ... And I say to you, lest you be angry with me because I come here ...

**VI** [I abstained] from injustice and in the womb of her who conceived me I searched for truth. And when I emerged from my mother's womb, I was planted for truth and I lived all my days in truth and walked in the paths of eternal truth. And the Holy One (was) with me ... on my pathways truth sped to warn me off the ... of lie which led to darkness ... and I girded my loins with the vision of truth and wisdom ... paths of violence. *vacat* Then I, Noah, became a man and clung to truth and seized ... and I took Amzara, his daughter as my wife. She conceived and bore me three sons [and daughters]. Then I took wives for my sons from among my brother's daughters, and I gave my daughters to my brother's sons according to the law of the eternal precept which the Most High [ordained] to the sons of man. *vacat* And in my days, when according to my reckoning ... ten jubilees had been completed, the (moment) came for my sons to take wives for themselves ... heaven, I saw in a vision and was explained and made known the action of the sons of heaven and ... the heavens. Then I hid this mystery in my heart and explained it to no man. *vacat* ... to me and a great and ... and in a message of the Holy One ... and he spoke to me in a vision and he stood before me ...

... and the message of the great Holy One called out to me: 'To you they say, O Noah, ... ' and I reckoned the whole conduct of the sons of the earth. I knew and explained all ... two weeks. Then the blood which the Giants had spilled. ... I was at ease and waited until ... the holy ones with the daughters of man ... [Then] I, Noah, found grace, greatness and truth ...

... till the gates of heaven ... to men and cattle, and wild beasts and birds ...

**VII** ... on them; the earth and all that is on it, in the seas and on the mountains ... all the constellations of heaven, the sun, the moon and the stars and the Watchers ...

... I shall reward you ... *vacat* the great Holy One. And I rejoiced in the words of the Lord of heaven and I shouted ...

it ... you all to your Master ... the King of all the world for ever and ever until all eternity. *vacat* ... [until] the ark rested on one of the mountains of Ararat (HWRRT). And eternal fire ... And I atoned for the whole earth, all of it. And the beginning of ... and I burned the fat on the fire. Secondly, ... I poured out their blood on the base of the altar and I burned all their flesh on the altar. And thirdly the turtledoves ... on the altar as an offering. ... I put on it fine flour mixed with oil and with incense as a meal offering... . I put salt on all of them. And the smell of my offering rose up to heaven. *vacat* ...

**XI** ... the mountains and the deserts ...

... four ... *vacat* [Then] I, Noah, went out and walked on the earth, through its length and breadth ... delight on her in their leaves and in their fruit. And all the land was filled with grass and herbs and grain. Then I blessed the Lord of heaven who made splendid things. He is for ever and praise is his. And I repeated the blessing on account of his grace for the earth and on account of his removing and causing to perish from it all those who do violence and wickedness and lies and on account of his rescuing the righteous man ... *vacat* [God] was revealed to me and [the Lord] of heaven spoke to me and said to me: 'Do not fear, Noah. I shall be with you and with your sons who will be like you for ever ... of the earth and rule over them ... and over its deserts and its mountains and all that are on them. And behold, I give all of it to you and to your sons to eat the green things and the grass of the earth. But you shall not eat any blood. Your fear and awe ... for ever.' ...

**XII** ... in the mountains of Ararat (HWRRT). And afterwards I descended ... I and my sons and the sons [of my sons] ... for the destruction was great on the earth ... after the Flood. To my first son [Shem] was born, to begin with, a son, Arpachshad, two years after the Flood. [And] all the sons of Shem, all of them, [were Ela]m, and Ashur, Arpachshad, Lud and Aram, and five daughters. [And the sons of Ham: Kush and Misrai]n and Put and Canaan, and seven daughters. And the sons of Japhet: Gomer and Magog and Madai and Yavan [and Tu]bal and Mashok and Tiras, and four daughters. [And] I began, I and all my sons, to fill the land and I planted a big vineyard on Mount Lubar and in the fourth year it produced wine for me ... [And] when the first festival c[ame], on the first day of the first festival in the ... month ... I opened this jar (?) and I began to drink on the first day of the fifth year ... On this day I summoned my sons, my grandsons and all our wives and their daughters, and we assembled together and we went ... and I blessed the Lord of heaven, the Most High God, the Great Holy One who saved us from perdition ...

**XIII** ... they were cutting gold and silver and stones and clay and taking part of them for themselves. I saw the gold and the silver ... iron, and they cut down every tree and took some for themselves. I saw the sun and the moon and the stars cutting and taking some for themselves. ... I turned to see the olive tree and behold, the olive tree was rising upwards and for many hours ... many leaves ... appeared in them. I observed this olive tree and behold the abundance of its leaves ... they tied to it. And I was greatly amazed by this olive tree and its leaves. I was amazed ... the four winds of heaven were blowing powerfully and they damaged this olive tree, breaking off its branches and smashing them. First [came] the westerly [wind] and struck it, and shook off its leaves and fruit, and scattered them in every direction. Then ...

**XIV** ... listen and hear! You are the great cedar ... standing before you in a dream on the top of mountains ...

... truth. The willow that springs from it and rises towards the heights (these are) three sons ... And that which you did see, (namely that) the first willow caught the stump of the cedar ... and the wood from it ... will not separate from you all its days. And among its posterity ... will be called ... will spring a righteous plant ... will stand for ever. And that which you did see, (namely that) the willow caught the stump [of the cedar] ...

... the last willow ... *vacat* ... part of their branch entered (got entangled with?) the branch of the first (willow), two sons ... And that which you did see, (namely that) part of their branch entered the branch of the first ... I explained to him the mystery ...

**XV** ... And that you did see all of them ... they will go around, the majority of them will be wicked. And that which you did see, (namely that) a man came from the south of the land, with a sickle in his hand, and fire with him ... who will come from the south of the land ... And they will cast wickedness on the fire, all ... And he shall come between ... Four angels ... between all the nations. And all of them will worship and be confounded ... I will explain to you all, in truth. And thus it is written concerning you. And I, Noah, awoke from my sleep and the sun ...

**XVI** ... until the river Tina ... and all the land of the north, all of it, until it reaches ... And this boundary passes by the waters of the Great Sea as far as ... divided by lot to Japhet and his sons to inherit as an eternal inheritance. *vacat* The second lot came to Shem to inherit, he and his sons, as an eternal inheritance ... the waters of the river Tina ... as far as the river Tina ... to the great Sea of Salt. And this boundary goes as a spring from this bay ... to the east

**XVII** ... And Shem, my son, divided (his inheritance) among his sons. And the first (lot) fell to Elam in the north, by the waters of the river Tigris as far as the Red Sea, whose source is in the north, and it turns to the west to Assyria as far as the Tigris ... And after it to Aram, the land between the two rivers, as far as the top of the mountain of Ashur ... [To] ... fell this Mount of the Ox and the portion stretched and went westwards as far as Magog ... east in the north ... this bay which is at the head of three portions by this sea to Arpachshad to the boundary that turns towards the south, all the land watered by the Euphrates, and all ... all the valleys and plains that are between them, and the island that is in the middle of the bay ... to the sons of Gomer ... and Amana as far as the Euphrates ... the portion that his father Noah divided and gave him. *vacat* Japhet divided (his inheritance) between his sons. He gave the first (lot) to Gomer in the north as far as the river Tina, and afterwards to Magog, and afterwards to Media, and afterwards to Yavan (the Greeks), all the islands that are by Lydia. And (the lot) which is between the bay of Lydia and the second bay, (he gave) to Tubal ... in the land. And to Meshek the sea ... to Tiras ... which is by the portion of the sons of Ham ... *vacat* ...

**XVIII** ...

**XIX** ... And I said, 'Thou art ... ' ... ' ... until now you have not come to the Holy Mountain.'

And I (Abram) departed ... and I travelled towards the south ... until I came to Hebron [at the time when Hebron] was being built; and I dwelt there [two years].

Now there was famine in all this land, and hearing that there was prosperity in Egypt I went ... to the land of Egypt ... I [came to] the river Karmon, one of the branches of the River (Nile) ... and I crossed the seven branches of the River ... We passed through our land and entered the land of the sons of Ham, the land of Egypt.

And on the night of our entry into Egypt, I, Abram, dreamt a dream; [and behold], I saw in my dream a cedar tree and a palm tree ... men came and they sought to cut down the cedar tree and to pull up its roots, leaving the palm tree (standing) alone. But the palm tree cried out saying, 'Do not cut down this cedar tree, for cursed be he who shall fell [it].' And the cedar tree was spared because of the palm tree and [was] not felled.

And during the night I woke from my dream, and I said to Sarai my wife, 'I have dreamt a dream ... [and I am] fearful [because of] this dream.' She said to me, 'Tell me your dream that I may know it.' So I began to tell her this dream ... [the interpretation] of the dream ... '... that they will seek to kill me, but will spare you ... [Say to them] of me, "He is my brother", and because of you I shall live, and because of you my life shall be saved ... '

And Sarai wept that night on account of my words ...

Then we journeyed towards Zoan, I and Sarai ... by her life that none should see her ...

And when those five years had passed, three men from among the princes of Egypt [came at the command] of Pharaoh of Zoan to inquire after [my] business and after my wife and they gave ... goodness, wisdom, and truth. And I exclaimed before them ... because of the famine ... And they came to ascertain ... with much food and drink ... the wine ...

(During the party, the Egyptians must have seen Sarai, and on their return they praised her to the king.)

**XX** ... '... and beautiful is her face! How ... fine are the hairs of her head! How lovely are her eyes! How desirable her nose and all the radiance of her countenance ... How fair are her breasts and how beautiful all her whiteness! How pleasing are her arms and how perfect her hands, and how [desirable] all the appearance of her hands! How fair are her palms and how long and slender are her fingers! How comely are her feet, how perfect her thighs! No virgin or bride led into the marriage chamber is more beautiful than she; she is fairer than all other women. Truly, her beauty is greater than theirs. Yet together with all this grace she possesses abundant wisdom, so that whatever she does is perfect (?).' When the king heard the words of Harkenosh and his two companions, for all three spoke as with one voice, he desired her greatly and sent out at once to take her. And seeing her, he was amazed by all her beauty and took her to be his wife, but me he sought to kill. Sarai said to the king, 'He is my brother,' that I might benefit from her, and I, Abram, was spared because of her and I was not slain.

And I, Abram, wept aloud that night, I and my nephew Lot, because Sarai had been taken from me by force. I prayed that night and I begged and implored, and I said in my sorrow while my tears ran down: 'Blessed art Thou, O Most High God, Lord of all the worlds, Thou who art Lord and king of all things and who rulest over all the kings of the earth and judgest them all! I cry now before Thee, my Lord, against Pharaoh of Zoan the king of Egypt, because of my wife who has been taken from me by force. Judge him for me that I may see Thy mighty hand raised against him and against all his household, and that he may not be able to defile my wife this night (separating her) from me, and that they may know Thee, my Lord, that Thou art Lord of all the kings of the earth.' And I wept and was sorrowful.

And during that night the Most High God sent a spirit to scourge him, an evil spirit to all his household; and it scourged him and all his household. And he was unable to approach her, and although he was with her for two years, he knew her not.

At the end of those two years the scourges and afflictions grew greater and more grievous upon him and all his household, so he sent for all [the sages] of Egypt, for all the magicians, together with all the healers of Egypt, that they might heal him and all his household of this scourge. But not one healer or magician or sage could stay to cure him, for the spirit scourged them all and they fled.

Then Harkenosh came to me, beseeching me to go to the king and to pray for him and to lay my hands upon him that he might live, for the king had dreamt a dream ... But Lot said to him, 'Abram my uncle cannot pray for the king while Sarai his wife is with him. Go, therefore, and tell the king to restore his wife to her husband; then he will pray for him and he shall live.'

When Harkenosh had heard the words of Lot, he went to the king and said, 'All these scourges and afflictions with which my lord the king is scourged and afflicted are because of Sarai the wife of Abram. Let Sarai be restored to Abram her husband, and this scourge and the spirit of festering shall vanish from you.'

And he called me and said, 'What have you done to me with regard to [Sarai]? You said to me, She is my sister, whereas she is your wife; and I took her to be my wife. Behold your wife who is with me; depart and go hence from all the land of Egypt! And now pray for me and my house that this evil spirit may be expelled from it.'

So I prayed [for him] ... and I laid my hands on his [head]; and the scourge departed from him and the evil [spirit] was expelled [from him], and he lived. And the king rose to tell me ... and the king swore an oath to me that ... and the king gave her much [silver and gold] and much raiment of fine linen and purple ... And Hagar also ... and he appointed men to lead [me] out [of all the land of Egypt]. And I, Abram, departed with very great flocks and with silver and gold, and I went up from [Egypt] together with my nephew [Lot]. Lot had great flocks also, and he took a wife for himself from among [the daughters of Egypt.

I pitched my camp] **XXI** [in] every place in which I had formerly camped until I came to Bethel, the place where I had built an altar. And I built a second altar and laid on it a sacrifice, and an offering to the Most High God. And there I called on the name of the Lord of worlds and praised the Name of God and blessed God, and I gave thanks before God for all the riches and favours which He had bestowed on me. For He had dealt kindly towards me and had led me back in peace into this land. After that day, Lot departed from me on account of the deeds of our shepherds. He went away and settled in the valley of the Jordan, together with all his flocks; and I myself added more to them. He kept his sheep and journeyed as far as Sodom, and he bought a house for himself in Sodom and dwelt in it. But I dwelt on the mountain of Bethel and it grieved me that my nephew Lot had departed from me. And God appeared to me in a vision at night and said to me, 'Go to Ramath Hazor which is north of Bethel, the place where you dwell, and lift up your eyes and look to the east and to the west and to the south and to the north; and behold all this land which I give to you and your seed for ever.'

The next morning, I went up to Ramath Hazor and from that high place I beheld the land from the River of Egypt to Lebanon and Senir, and from the Great Sea to Hauran, and all the land of Gebal as far as Kadesh, and all the Great Desert to the east of Hauran and Senir as far as the Euphrates. And He said to me, 'I will give all this land to your seed and they shall possess it for ever. And I will multiply your seed like the dust of the earth which no man can number; neither shall any man number your seed. Rise and go! Behold the length and breadth of the land, for it is yours; and after you, I will give it to your seed for ever.'

And I, Abram, departed to travel about and see the land. I began my journey at the river Gihon and travelled along the coast of the Sea until I came to the Mountain of the Bull (Taurus). Then I travelled from the coast of the Great Salt Sea and journeyed towards the east by the Mountain of the Bull, across the breadth of the land, until I came to the river Euphrates. I journeyed along the Euphrates until I came to the Red Sea (Persian Gulf) in the east, and I travelled along the coast of the Red Sea until I came to the tongue of the Sea of Reeds (the modern Red Sea) which flows out from the Red Sea. Then I pursued my way in the south until I came to the river Gihon, and returning, I came to my house in peace and found all things prosperous there. I went to dwell at the Oaks of Mamre, which is at Hebron, north-east of Hebron; and I built an altar there, and laid on it a sacrifice and an oblation to the Most

High God. I ate and drank there, I and all the men of my household, and I sent for Mamre, Ornam and Eshkol, the three Amorite brothers, my friends, and they ate and drank with me.

Before these days, Kedorlaomer king of Elam had set out with Amrafel king of Babylon, Ariok king of Kaptok, and Tidal king of the nations which lie between the rivers; and they had waged war against Bera king of Sodom, Birsha king of Gomorrah, Shinab king of Admah, Shemiabad king of Zeboim, and against the king of Bela. All these had made ready for battle in the valley of Siddim, and the king of Elam and the other kings with him had prevailed over the king of Sodom and his companions and had imposed a tribute upon them.

For twelve years they had paid their tribute to the king of Elam, but in the thirteenth year they rebelled against him. And in the fourteenth year, the king of Elam placed himself at the head of all his allies and went up by the Way of the Wilderness; and they smote and pillaged from the river Euphrates onward. They smote the Refaim who were at Ashteroth Karnaim, the Zumzamim who were at Ammon, the Emim [who were at] Shaveh ha-Keriyyoth, and the Horites who were in the mountains of Gebal, until they came to El Paran which is in the Wilderness. And they returned . . . at Hazazon Tamar.

The king of Sodom went out to meet them, together with the king [of Gomorrah], the king of Admah, the king of Zeboim, and the king of Bela, [and they fought] a battle in the valley [of Siddim] against Kedorlaomer [king of Elam and the kings] who were with him. But the king of Sodom was vanquished and fled, and the king of Gomorrah fell into the pits . . . [And] the king of Elam [carried off] all the riches of Sodom and [Gomorrah] . . . and they took Lot the nephew **XXII** of Abram who dwelt with them in Sodom, together with all his possessions.

Now one of the shepherds of the flocks which Abram had given to Lot escaped from captivity and came to Abram; at that time Abram dwelt in Hebron. He told him that Lot his nephew had been taken, together with all his possessions, but that he had not been slain and that the kings had gone by the Way of the Great Valley (of the Jordan) in the direction of their land, taking captives and plundering and smiting and slaying, and that they were journeying towards the land of Damascus.

Abram wept because of Lot his nephew. Then he braced himself; he rose up and chose from among his servants three hundred and eighteen fighting men trained for war, and Ornam and Eshkol and Mamre went with him also. He pursued them until he came to Dan, and came on them while they were camped in the valley of Dan. He fell on them at night from four sides and during the night he slew them; he crushed them and put them to flight, and all of them fled before him until they came to Helbon which is north of Damascus. He rescued from them all their captives, and all their booty and possessions. He also delivered Lot his nephew, together with all his possessions, and he brought back all the captives which they had taken.

When the king of Sodom learned that Abram had brought back all the captives and all the booty, he came out to meet him; and he went to Salem, which is Jerusalem.

Abram camped in the valley of Shaveh, which is the valley of the king, the valley of Beth-ha-Kerem; and Melchizedek king of Salem brought out food and drink to Abram and to all the men who were with him. He was the Priest of the Most High God. And he blessed Abram and said, 'Blessed be Abram by the Most High God, Lord of heaven and earth! And blessed be the Most High God who has delivered your enemies into your hand!' And Abram gave him the tithe of all the possessions of the king of Elam and his companions.

Then the king of Sodom approached and said to Abram, 'My lord Abram, give me the souls which are mine, which you have delivered from the king of Elam and taken captive, and you may have all the possessions.'

Then said Abram to the king of Sodom, 'I raise my hand this day to the Most High God, Lord of heaven and earth! I will take nothing of yours, not even a shoe-lace or shoe-strap, lest you say, Abram's riches come from my possessions! I will take nothing but that which the young men with me have eaten already, and the portion of the three men who have come with me. They shall decide whether they will give you their portion.' And Abram returned all the possessions and all the captives and gave them to the king of Sodom; he freed all the captives from this land who were with him, and sent them all back.

After these things, God appeared to Abram in a vision and said to him, 'Behold, ten years have passed since you departed from Haran. For two years you dwelt here and you spent seven years in Egypt, and one year has passed since you returned from Egypt. And now examine and count all you have, and see how it has grown to be double that which came out with you from Haran. And now do not fear, I am with you; I am your help and your strength. I am a shield above you and a mighty safeguard round about you. Your wealth and possessions shall multiply greatly.' But Abram said, 'My Lord God, I have great wealth and possessions but what good shall they do to me? I shall die naked; childless shall I go hence. A child from my household shall inherit from me. Eliezer son ... shall inherit from me.' And He said to him, 'He shall not be your heir, but one who shall spring [from your body shall inherit from you].' ...

# Genesis Commentaries

## (4Q252–4)

From this non-continuous paraphrase of Genesis, four sections are reproduced here, two of which are of sectarian inspiration. The composition on the first fragment attempts to adapt the chronology of the biblical Flood story to the solar calendar of the Qumran Community. Along more general lines, it seeks also to explain certain peculiarities of the scriptural text, e.g., why, despite Ham's disrespect to his father, it was not he, but his son Canaan, who was cursed by Noah. The exegesis attested in this section is distinct from the *pesher*, and resembles partly the style of the 'rewritten Bible' such as the Genesis Apocryphon, and partly the 'plain', or *peshat*, interpretation of the rabbis.

The subject of the second excerpt is the blessing of Judah, i.e. the tribe in which David originated. The sectarian commentator (see the mention of the 'men of the Community' in line 5) emphasizes that the royal power will belong for ever to the descendants of David, thereby implying that all non-Davidic rulers, such as the contemporary Hasmonaean priest-kings, unlawfully occupy the throne. If so, the composition best fits to the first half of the first century BCE. Only four tiny fragments of 4Q253 are extant. Fr. 1 mentions the ark. Fr. 3, col. 1 contains a citation from Mal. iii, 16–18. This is the only translatable excerpt. Fifteen mostly insignificant scraps of 4Q254 correspond partly to the Noah story and partly to the blessings of the Patriarchs. Only frs. 1 and 5 can be translated. Fr. 1, lines 2–4 overlap with 4Q252 ii, l.6.

For preliminary editions see Timothy H. Lim, 'The Chronology of the Flood Story in a Qumran Text (4Q252)', *JJS* 43 (1992), 288–98; 'Notes on 4Q252 fr. 1, cols. i–ii', *JJS* 44 (1993), 121–6; J. M. Allegro, 'Further Messianic References in Qumran Literature', *JBL* 75 (1956), 174–6; G. J. Brooke, 'The Thematic Content of 4Q252', *JQR* 85 (1994), 33–59; '4Q253: A Preliminary Edition', *JSS* 40 (1995), 227–39.

## 4Q252, fr. 1 (Gen. vi, 3–xv, 17)

**I** [In the] four hundred and eightieth year of the life of Noah came their end (that of antidiluvian mankind). And God said, *My spirit shall not abide in man for ever and their days shall be determined to be one hundred and twenty years* (Gen. vi, 3) – until the end of the Flood. *And the waters of the Flood arrived on the earth in the six hundredth year of the life of Noah, in the second month* – on the first day of the week – *on the seventeenth* (of the month). *On that day all the fountains of the great deep burst forth and the windows of the heavens were opened. And rain fell on the earth forty days and forty nights* (vii, 11–12) until the twenty-sixth day of the third month, the fifth day of the week. *And the waters prevailed upon the [ea]rth a hundred and fifty days* (vii, 24) – until the fourteenth day *of the seventh month*, the third day of the week. *And* at the end of *a hundred and fifty days, the waters had abated* – two days, the fourth and the fifth day, and on the sixth day – *the ark came to rest on the mountains of* Hurarat (or: Turarat), *on the seventeenth day of the seventh month* (viii, 3–4). *And the waters [con]tinued to abate until the [ten]th month, the first day* of (the month) – the fourth day of the week – *and the tops of the mountains appeared* (viii, 5). *At the end of forty days* – after the tops of the mountains had been seen – *Noah [op]ened the window of the ark* (viii, 6) – on the tenth day of the ele[venth] month. *And he sent forth the dove to see if the waters had subsided* (viii, 8), *but she did not find a resting-place and returned to him to the ark* (viii, 9). *He waited an[other] seven days and again sent her forth* (viii, 10). *She came back to him with a plucked olive leaf in her beak* (viii, 10–11) – [this is the twenty-] fourth [day] of the eleventh month, the first day of the wee[k. *And Noah knew that the waters had subsided*] *from the earth* (viii, 11). At the end of *another [seven days, he sent forth the dove and it did not] return again* (viii, 12) – this is the f[irst] day [of the twelfth] month, [the first day] of the week. At the end of three [weeks after Noah had sent forth the dov]e which *did not return to him any more, the wa[ters] dried up [from the earth and] Noah removed the covering of the ark and looked, and behold, the face of the ground was dry* (viii, 13). This was the *first day of the first month*. [And it happened] **II** *in the six hundred and first year of the life of Noah*, on the seventeenth day of *the second month that the earth was dry* (viii, 14) – on the first day of the week. On that day *Noah went forth* from the ark (viii, 18) at the end of a full year of three hundred and sixty-four days, on the first day of the week, on the seven[teenth] of the second month] *vacat* on and six *vacat* Noah from the ark at the appointed time of a full year *vacat And Noah awoke from his wine and knew what his youngest son had done to him. And he said, Cursed be Canaan; a slave of slaves shall he be to* [*his*] *bro*[*thers*] (ix, 24–5). But he did not curse Ham but only his son, for *God had blessed the sons of Noah. And let him dwell in the tents of Shem* (ix, 27). He gave the land to Abram, his beloved. [Terah] was one hundred and for[t]y-five years old when he *went forth from Ur of the Chaldees and came to Haran* (xi, 31). Now Ab[ram was se]venty years old and for five years Abram dwelt in Haran. And afterwards Abram went forth to the land of Canaan. Six[ty-five years] ... *the heifer and the ram and the go*[*at*] (xv, 9) ... [the torch of] *fire when it pass*[*ed over*] (xv, 17) ...

## (Gen. xxxvi, 12)

**IV** *Timna was the concubine of Eliphaz son of Esau and she bore* to him *Amalek* (xxxvi, 12), whom Saul smo[te] as He said to Moses, In the last days *you will wipe out the memory of Amalek from under the heaven* (Deut. xxv, 19).

## Blessings of Jacob (Gen. xlix, 3)

**V** *Reuben, you are my first-born, the firstfruit of my strength, pre-eminent in pride and pre-eminent in power. Unstable as water, you shall not have pre-eminence; you went up to your father's bed; you have defiled his couch* ... (xlix, 3) Its interpretation is that he rebuked him because he slept with Bilhah, his concubine, and he said, '[*My*] *first-*[*born*] ... (ibid.) Reuben is the firstfruit ...'

## (Gen. xlix, 10)

**VI** *The sceptre* [*shall not*] *depart from the tribe of Judah* ... [xlix, 10]. Whenever Israel rules, *there shall* [*not*] *fail to be a descendant of David upon the throne* (Jer. xxxiii, 17). For the ruler's staff (xlix, 10) is the Covenant of kingship, [and the clans] of Israel are the divisions,[1] until the Messiah of Righteousness comes, the Branch of David. For to him and his seed is granted the Covenant of kingship over his people for everlasting generations which he is to keep ... the Law with the men of the Community, for ... it is the assembly of the men of ...

1. Reading *dglyw* (standards = divisions) with the Samaritan Pentateuch against the traditional *rglyw* (feet). Computer enhancement, initiated by George Brooke, has made this reading certain.

# Genesis Commentary B

## (4Q253)

### Fr. 31

[*Then those fearing the Lord spoke with one another;*] *and he heeded* [*and heard them and a book of memorial was written before him of those who feared the Lord and thought of his name.*] *They shall be mine,* [*says the Lord of hosts, my special possession on the day when I act, and I will spare*] *them as* [*a man spares his son who serves him. Then once more you shall distinguish*] *between the righteous and the wicked,* [*between one who serves God and one who does not serve him* (Mal. iii, 16–18). Its interpretation] . . . the righteousness and over . . .

# Genesis Commentary C

## (4Q254)

### Fr. 1 (Gen. ix, 24–5)

...

which he says ... on the doors and ... [*And Noah awoke from his wine*] *and knew what* [*his youngest son had done to him. And he said, Cursed be Canaan;*] *a slave of slaves* [*shall he be to his*] *brothers*] (Gen. ix, 24–5).

### Fr. 5 (Gen. xlix, 15–17)

*And he bowed* [*his shoulder to bear and became*] *a slave* [*at forced labour*] (Gen. xlxi, 15). Its interpretation ... [*Dan shall judge*] *his* [*peo*]*ple as on*[*e*] *of the tr*[*ibes of Israel.*] *Dan shall be a ser*[*pent in the way, a vip*]*er by the pa*[*th that bites*] *the horse's hee*[*ls*] (Gen. xlix, 15–17) ...

# Commentaries on Isaiah

## (4Q161–5, 3Q4)

Translatable fragments of four commentaries on Isaiah were discovered in Cave 4 (4QpIsa$^{a-d}$ = 4Q161–4). A fifth (4QpIsa$^{f}$ = 4Q165) is too mutilated to be rendered into English. The first document alludes to the defeat of the Kittim and expounds the renowned messianic prophecy of Isa. xi. It is related to 4Q285 (cf. p. 187). The second and the third deal with the Jewish opponents of the sect. The fourth, relying on Isa. liv, identifies the Community as the New Jerusalem. They may all be assigned to the first century BCE. (Cf. *DJD*, V, 11–30.) A small fragment from Cave 3 (3Q4) represents a commentary on Isa. i, 1, but with no continuous text.

### 4Q161, frs. 5–6

... when they return from the desert of the peo[ples] ... the Prince of the Congregation and afterwards ... will depart from them ... *He has come to Aiath; he has passed through* [*Migron*]. *At Mikhmash* [*he has left his baggage; they have passed by*] *Maabarah; Geba is their night camp;* [*Ramah*] *trem*[*bles; Gibea of Saul has fled*]; *Bath Gallim,* [*cry out a shrill*] *note;* [*Laish,*] *hear it;* [*answer her, Anathoth;*] *Madmenah* [*flees*]; *the inhabitants of Gebim take refuge.* [*Today he is to stop in Nob. He shakes*] *his hand towards the mountain of the daughter of Zion, the hills of Jerusalem* (x, 28–32).

[The interpretation of the] decree concerns the coming end of days ... [trem]bles when he ascends from the Vale of Acco to wage war against ... and none is like him and in all the cities of ... and as far as the frontier of Jerusalem ...

## Frs. 8–10

... *[and the tallest tre]es [shall be cut down and] the lofty [shall be felled] with the axe, and Lebanon through a powerful one shall fall* (x, 33–4).

[Its interpretation concerns the Kit]tim who shall crush the house of Israel and the humble ... all the nations and the valiant shall be dismayed and [their] he[arts] shall melt. [And that which he said, *The tallest*] *trees shall be cut down*, these are the valiant of the Kit[tim] ... [And that which he sa]id. *The heart of the forest shall be felled with the axe*, th[ey] ... for the war of the Kittim. *And Lebanon through a po[werful one shall fall* (x, 34). Its interpretation concerns the] Kittim who will be given into the hand of his great one ... when he flees from be[fore Is]rael ...

(*vacat*)

*[And there shall come forth a rod from the stem of Jesse and a Branch shall grow out of its roots. And the spirit of the Lord shall rest upon him, the spirit of wisdom and understanding, the spirit of counsel and might, the spirit of knowledge and of the fear of the Lord. And his delight shall be in the fear of the Lord. He shall not judge by what his eyes see, or pass sentence by what his ears hear; he shall judge the poor righteously and shall pass sentence justly on the humble of the earth*] (xi, 1–3).

[Interpreted, this concerns the Branch] of David who shall arise at the end [of days] ... God will uphold him with [the spirit of might, and will give him] a throne of glory and a crown of [holiness] and many-coloured garments ... [He will put a sceptre] in his hand and he shall rule over all the [nations]. And Magog ... and his sword shall judge [all] the peoples.

And as for that which he said, *He shall not [judge by what his eyes see] or pass sentence by what his ears hear*: interpreted, this means that ... [the Priests] ... As they teach him, so will he judge; and as they order, [so will he pass sentence]. One of the Priests of renown shall go out, and garments of ... shall be in his hands ...

## 4Q162

*[For ten acres of vineyard shall produce only one* bath, *and an* omer *of seed shall yield but one* ephah] (v, 10).

Interpreted, this saying concerns the last days, the devastation of the land by sword and famine. At the time of the Visitation of the land there shall be *Woe to those who rise early in the morning to run after strong drink, to those who linger in the evening until wine inflames them. They have zither and harp and timbrel and flute and wine at their feasts, but they do not regard the work of the Lord or see the deeds of His hand. Therefore my people go into exile for want of knowledge, and their noblemen die of hunger and their multitude is parched with thirst. Therefore Hell has widened its gullet and opened its mouth beyond measure, and the nobility of Jerusalem and her multitude go down, her tumult and he who rejoices in her* (v, 11–14).

These are the Scoffers in Jerusalem who have *despised the Law of the Lord and scorned the word of the Holy One of Israel. Therefore the wrath of the Lord was kindled against His people. He stretched out His hand against them and smote them; the mountains trembled and their corpses were like sweepings in the middle of the streets. And [His wrath] has not relented for all these things [and His hand is stretched out still]* (v, 24–5).

This is the congregation of Scoffers in Jerusalem ...

## 4Q163

*Thus said the Lord, the Holy One of Israel, 'You shall be saved by returning and resting; your strength shall be in silence and trust.' But you would not. You [said], 'No. We will flee upon horses and will ride on swift steeds.' Therefore your pursuers shall be speedy also. A thousand shall flee at the threat of one; at the threat of five you shall flee [till] you are left like a flagstaff on top of a mountain and like a signal on top of a hill. Therefore the Lord waits to be [gracious to] you; therefore He exalts Himself to have mercy on you. For the Lord is a God of justice. How blessed are all those who wait for him!* (xxx, 15–18).

This saying, referring to the last days, concerns the congregation of those who seek smooth things in Jerusalem ... [who despise the] Law and do not [trust in God] ... As robbers lie in wait for a man ... they have despised [the words of] the Law ...

*O people of Zion [who live in Jerusalem, you shall weep no more. At the sound of] your crying [He will be gracious to you; He will answer you] when He [hears it. Although the Lord gives you bread of oppression and water of distress, your Teacher] shall be hidden [no more and your eyes shall see your Teacher] ...* (xxx, 19–20).

## 4Q164

*Behold, I will set your stones in antimony* (liv, 11b).

[Interpreted, this saying concerns] ... all Israel is like antimony surrounding the eye.

*And I will lay your foundations with sapphires* (liv, 11c).

Interpreted, this concerns the Priests and the people who laid the foundations of the Council of the Community ... the congregation of His elect (shall sparkle) like a sapphire among stones.

[*And I will make*] *all your pinnacles* [*of agate*] (liv, 12a).

Interpreted, this concerns the twelve [chief Priests] who shall enlighten by judgement of the Urim and Tummim ... which are absent from them, like the sun with all its light, and like the moon ...

[*And all your gates of carbuncles*] (liv, 12b).

Interpreted, this concerns the chiefs of the tribes of Israel ...

# Commentaries on Hosea

## (4Q166–7)

Two fragmentary manuscripts (4Q166–7) include exegeses of Hosea. In the first, the unfaithful wife is the Jewish people led astray by her lovers, the Gentiles. The second refers cryptically to 'the furious young lion', mentioned also in the Commentary on Nahum, and to 'the last Priest who shall ... strike Ephraim' (cf. *DJD*, V, 31–2).

## 4Q166

**II** [*She knew not that*] *it was I who gave her* [*the new wine and oil*], *who lavished* [*upon her silver*] *and gold which they* [*used for Baal*] (ii, 8).

Interpreted, this means that [they ate and] were filled, but they forgot God who ... They cast His commandments behind them which He had sent [by the hand of] His servants the Prophets, and they listened to those who led them astray. They revered them, and in their blindness they feared them as though they were gods.

*Therefore I will take back my corn in its time and my wine* [*in its season*]. *I will take away my wool and my flax lest they cover* [*her nakedness*]. *I will uncover her shame before the eyes of* [*her*] *lovers* [*and*] *no man shall deliver her from out of my hand* (ii, 9–10).

Interpreted, this means that He smote them with hunger and nakedness that they might be shamed and disgraced in the sight of the nations on which they relied. They will not deliver them from their miseries.

*I will put an end to her rejoicing,* [*her feasts*], *her* [*new*] *moons, her Sabbaths, and all her festivals* (ii, 11).

Interpreted, this means that [they have rejected the ruling of the Law, and have] followed the festivals of the nations. But [their rejoicing shall come to an end and] shall be changed into mourning. *I will ravage* [*her vines and her fig trees*], *of which she said, 'They are my wage* [*which my lovers have given me'.*] *I will make of them a thicket and the* [*wild beasts*] *shall eat them* ... (ii, 12).

## 4Q167, fr. 2

... *and your wound shall not be healed* (v, 13).

[Its] in[terpretation concerns] ... the furious young lion ...

*For I will be like a lion* [*to E*]*ph*[*ra*]*im* [*and like a young lion to the house of Judah*] (v, 14a).

[Its interpretation con]cerns the last Priest who shall stretch out his hand to strike Ephraim ...

[*I will go and come back to my place un*]*til they* [*will*] *feel guilty and seek my face; in their distress they will seek me eagerly* (v, 15).

Its interpretation is that God [has hid]den His face from ... and they did not listen ...

## Frs. 7–9

[*But they, like Adam, have b*]*roken the Covenant* (vi, 7).

[Its] interpretation ... they have forsaken God and walked according to the decrees [of the Gentiles] ...

# Commentary on Micah

## (1Q14, 4Q168)

Tiny fragments from Cave 1 (1Q**14**) represent an exposition of Micah (*DJD*, I, 77–80). Although the prophet's words are intended to castigate both Samaria and Jerusalem, the Qumran commentator interprets Samaria as alluding to the 'Spouter of Lies', the enemy of the sect, but relates Judah and Jerusalem to the Teacher of Righteousness and his Community. Further fragments of Micah iv, 8–12 are given the title 'Commentary on Micah (?)', in 4Q**168** (*DJD*, V, 36), but since neither the word *pesher*, nor any interpretative material is extant, the manuscript may be biblical.

*[All this is] for the transgression [of Jacob and for the sins of the House of Israel. What is the transgression of Jacob?] Is it not [Samaria? And what is the high place of Judah? Is it not Jerusalem? I will make of Samaria a ruin in the fields, and of Jerusalem a plantation of vines]* (i, 5–6).

Interpreted, this concerns the Spouter of Lies [who led the] Simple [astray].

*And what is the high place of Judah? [Is it not Jerusalem?]* (i, 5).

[Interpreted, this concerns] the Teacher of Righteousness who [expounded the law to] his [Council] and to all who freely pledged themselves to join the elect of [God to keep the Law] in the Council of the Community, who shall be saved on the Day [of Judgement] . . .

# Commentary on Nahum
## (4Q169)

Substantial remains of a Nahum Commentary were retrieved from Cave 4 (4Q169) and published in *DJD*, V, 37–42. They cover parts of chapters i and ii of the biblical book, and the first fourteen verses of chapter iii. Their historical significance has been discussed in Chapter III (pp. 55–62). It is worthy of note that the commentator employs not only cryptograms (Kittim, furious young lion, etc.), but the actual names of two Greek kings (Demetrius and Antiochus). Reference to 'the furious young lion' as one who 'hangs men alive' shows that 'hanging', probably a synonym for crucifixion, was practised as a form of execution. It is also legislated for in the Temple Scroll (LXIV, 6–13), where it is the capital punishment reserved for traitors. In biblical law, by contrast, only the dead body of an executed criminal is to be hanged, that is, displayed in public as an example (Deut. xxi, 21).

On palaeographical grounds the manuscript is dated to the second half of the first century BCE.

### Frs. 1–2

*[In whirlwind and storm is his way and] cloud is the d[ust of his feet* (i, 3).
Its interpretation] ... The [whirlwinds and the storm]s are (from) the fir[mam]ents of his heaven and of his earth which he has cre[ated].

*He rebu[kes] the sea and dri[es it up]* (i, 4a).
Its [int]erpretation: the sea is all the K[ittim who are] ... to execut[e] judgement against them and destroy them from the face [of the earth,] together with [all] their [com]manders whose dominion shall be finished.

*[Bashan and] Carmel have withered and the sprout of Lebanon withers* (i, 4b).
Its interpretation ... [will per]ish in it, the summit of wickedness for the ... Carmel and to his commanders. Lebanon and the sprout of

Lebanon are [the priests, the sons of Zadok and the men of] their [counc]il and they shall perish from before ... the elect ... [a]ll the inhabitants of the world.

*The mo[untains quake before him] and the hills heave and the earth [is lifted up] before him, and [the world and all that dwell in it. Who can stand before his wrath? And who can arise] against his furious anger?* (i, 5–6a).

[Its] in[terpretation] ...

**I** *[Where is the lions' den and the cave of the young lions?]* (ii, 11).

[Interpreted, this concerns] ... a dwelling-place for the ungodly of the nations.

*Whither the lion goes, there is the lion's cub, [with none to disturb it]* (ii, 11b).

[Interpreted, this concerns Deme]trius king of Greece who sought, on the counsel of those who seek smooth things, to enter Jerusalem. [But God did not permit the city to be delivered] into the hands of the kings of Greece, from the time of Antiochus until the coming of the rulers of the Kittim. But then she shall be trampled under their feet ...

*The lion tears enough for its cubs and it chokes prey for its lionesses* (ii, 12a).

[Interpreted, this] concerns the furious young lion who strikes by means of his great men, and by means of the men of his council.

*[And chokes prey for its lionesses; and it fills] its caves [with prey] and its dens with victims* (ii, 12a–b).

Interpreted, this concerns the furious young lion [who executes revenge] on those who seek smooth things and hangs men alive, ... formerly in Israel. Because of a man hanged alive on [the] tree, He proclaims, '*Behold I am against [you, says the Lord of Hosts*'].

*[I will burn up your multitude in smoke], and the sword shall devour your young lions. I will [cut off] your prey [from the earth]* (ii, 13).

[Interpreted] ... *your multitude* is the bands of his army ... and his *young lions* are ... his *prey* is the wealth which [the priests] of Jerusalem have [amassed], which ... Israel shall be delivered ...

[*And the voice of your messengers shall no more be heard*] (ii, 13b).

[Interpreted] **II** ... his *messengers* are his envoys whose voice shall no more be heard among the nations.

*Woe to the city of blood; it is full of lies and rapine* (iii, 1a–b).

Interpreted, this is the city of Ephraim, those who seek smooth things during the last days, who walk in lies and falsehood.

*The prowler is not wanting, noise of whip and noise of rattling wheel, prancing horse and jolting chariot, charging horsemen, flame and glittering spear, a multitude of the slain and a heap of carcasses. There is no end to the corpses; they stumble upon their corpses* (iii, 1c–3).

Interpreted, this concerns the dominion of those who seek smooth things, from the midst of whose assembly the sword of the nations shall never be wanting. Captivity, looting, and burning shall be among them, and exile out of dread for the enemy. A multitude of guilty corpses shall fall in their days; there shall be no end to the sum of their slain. They shall also stumble upon their body of flesh because of their guilty counsel.

*Because of the many harlotries of the well-favoured harlot, the mistress of seduction, she who sells nations through her harlotries and families through her seductions* (iii, 4).

Interpreted, this concerns those who lead Ephraim astray, who lead many astray through their false teaching, their lying tongue, and deceitful lips – kings, princes, priests, and people, together with the stranger who joins them. Cities and families shall perish through their counsel; honourable men and rulers shall fall through their tongue's [decision].

*Behold, I am against you – oracle of the Lord of Hosts – and you will lift up your skirts to your face and expose your nakedness to the nations and your shame to the kingdoms* (iii, 5).

Interpreted ... cities of the east. For the *skirts* are ... **III** and the nations shall ... among them their filthy idols.

*I will cast filth upon you and treat you with contempt and render you despicable, so that all who look upon you shall flee from you* (iii, 6–7a).

Interpreted, this concerns those who seek smooth things, whose evil deeds shall be uncovered to all Israel at the end of time. Many shall understand their iniquity and treat them with contempt because of their guilty presumption. When the glory of Judah shall arise, the simple of Ephraim shall flee from their assembly; they shall abandon those who lead them astray and shall join Israel.

*They shall say, Niniveh is laid waste; who shall grieve over her? Whence shall I seek comforters for you?* (iii, 7b).

Interpreted, this concerns those who seek smooth things, whose council shall perish and whose congregation shall be dispersed. They shall lead the assembly astray no more, and the simple shall support their council no more.

*Are you better than Amon which lay among the rivers?* (iii, 8a).

Interpreted, *Amon* is Manasseh, and the *rivers* are the great men of Manasseh, the honourable men of . . .

*Which was surrounded by waters, whose rampart was the sea and whose walls were waters?* (iii, 8b).

Interpreted, these are her valiant men, her almighty warriors.

*Ethiopia* [*and Egypt*] *were her* [*limitless*] strength (iii, 9a).

[Interpreted] . . .

[*Put and the Libyans were your helpers*] (iii, 9b).

**IV** Interpreted, these are the wicked of [Judah], the House of Separation, who joined Manasseh.

*Yet she was exiled; she went into captivity. Her children were crushed at the top of all the streets. They cast lots for her honourable men, and all her great men were bound with chains* (iii, 10).

Interpreted, this concerns Manasseh in the final age, whose kingdom shall be brought low by [Israel . . . ] his wives, his children, and his little ones shall go into captivity. His mighty men and honourable men [shall perish] by the sword.

[*You shall be drunk*] *and shall be stupefied* (iii, 11a).

Interpreted, this concerns the wicked of E[phraim . . . ] whose cup shall come after Manasseh . . .

[*You shall also seek*] *refuge in the city because of the enemy* (iii, 11b). Inter[preted, this concerns . . . ] their enemies in the city . . .

[*All your strongholds shall be*] *like fig trees with newly ripe figs* (iii, 12a).

# Commentary on Habakkuk

## (1QpHab)

This well-preserved and detailed exposition of the first two chapters of the Book of Habakkuk comes from Cave 1 and was published in 1950 (M. Burrows, *The Dead Sea Scrolls of St Mark's Monastery*, I, New Haven, 1950, pls. LV–LXI).

The palaeographical dating of the manuscript (30–1 BCE) has been confirmed by radiocarbon tests (120–5 BCE; cf. above, pp. 12–13). The Habakkuk Commentary is one of the main sources for the study of Qumran origins, as well as Essene Bible exegesis and the sect's theology regarding prophecy. The historical and doctrinal aspects of the document are analysed in Chapters III and IV.

**I** [*Oracle of Habakkuk the prophet. How long, O Lord, shall I cry*] *for help and Thou wilt not* [*hear*]? (i, 1–2).

[Interpreted, this concerns the beginning] of the [final] generation ...

[*Or shout to Thee 'Violence', and Thou wilt not deliver?*] (i, 2b) ...

[*Why dost Thou cause me to see iniquity and to look upon trouble? Desolation and violence are before me*] (i, 3).

... God with oppression and unfaithfulness ... they rob riches.

[*There is quarrelling and contention*] (i, 3b).

...

*So the law is weak* [*and justice never goes forth*] (i, 4a–b).

[Interpreted] this concerns those who have despised the Law of God ...

[*For the wicked encompasses*] *the righteous* (i, 4c).

[*The wicked* is the Wicked Priest, and *the righteous*] is the Teacher of Righteousness ...

*[So] justice goes forth [perverted]* (i, 4d).

. . .

*[Behold the nations and see, marvel and be astonished; for I accomplish a deed in your days, but you will not believe it when]* **II** *told* (i, 5).

[Interpreted, this concerns] those who were unfaithful together with the Liar, in that they [did] not [listen to the word received by] the Teacher of Righteousness from the mouth of God. And it concerns the unfaithful of the New [Covenant] in that they have not believed in the Covenant of God [and have profaned] His holy Name. And likewise, this saying is to be interpreted [as concerning those who] will be unfaithful at the end of days. They, the men of violence and the breakers of the Covenant, will not believe when they hear all that [is to happen to] the final generation from the Priest [in whose heart] God set [understanding] that he might interpret all the words of His servants the Prophets, through whom He foretold all that would happen to His people and [His land].

*For behold, I rouse the Chaldeans, that [bitter and hasty] nation* (i, 6a).

Interpreted, this concerns the Kittim [who are] quick and valiant in war, causing many to perish. [All the world shall fall] under the dominion of the Kittim, and the [wicked . . . ] they shall not believe in the laws of [God . . . ]

*[Who march through the breadth of the earth to take possession of dwellings which are not their own]* (i, 6b).

. . . **III** they shall march across the plain, smiting and plundering the cities of the earth. For it is as He said, *To take possession of dwellings which are not their own.*

*They are fearsome and terrible; their justice and grandeur proceed from themselves* (i, 7).

Interpreted, this concerns the Kittim who inspire all the nations with fear [and dread]. All their evil plotting is done with intention and they deal with all the nations in cunning and guile.

*Their horses are swifter than leopards and fleeter than evening wolves. Their horses step forward proudly and spread their wings; they fly from afar like an eagle avid to devour. All of them come for violence; the look on their faces is like the east wind* (i, 8–9a).

[Interpreted, this] concerns the Kittim who trample the earth with their horses and beasts. They come *from afar*, from the islands of the sea, to devour all the peoples *like an eagle* which cannot be satisfied, and they address [all the peoples] with anger and [wrath and fury] and indignation. For it is as He said, *The look on their faces is like the east wind.*

*[They heap up] captives [like sand]* (i, 9b).

...

**IV** *They scoff [at kings], and princes are their laughing-stock* (i, 10a).

Interpreted, this means that they mock the great and despise the venerable; they ridicule kings and princes and scoff at the mighty host.

*They laugh at every fortress; they pile up earth and take it* (i, 10b).

Interpreted, this concerns the commanders of the Kittim who despise the fortresses of the peoples and laugh at them in derision. To capture them, they encircle them with a mighty host, and out of fear and terror they deliver themselves into their hands. They destroy them because of the sins of their inhabitants.

*The wind then sweeps on and passes; and they make of their strength their god* (i, 11).

Interpreted, [this concerns] the commanders of the Kittim who, on the counsel of [the] House of Guilt, pass one in front of the other; one after another [their] commanders come to lay waste the earth. *[And they make of their strength their god]*: interpreted, this concerns [ ... all] the peoples ...

*[Art Thou not from everlasting, O Lord, my God, my Holy One? We shall not die.] Thou hast ordained them, [O Lord],* **V** *for judgement; Thou hast established them, O Rock, for chastisement. Their eyes are too pure to behold evil; and Thou canst not look on distress* (i, 12–13a).

Interpreted, this saying means that God will not destroy His people by the hand of the nations; God will execute the judgement of the nations by the hand of His elect. And through their chastisement all the wicked of His people shall expiate their guilt who keep His commandments in their distress. For it is as he said, *Too pure of eyes to behold evil*: interpreted, this means that they have not lusted after their eyes during the age of wickedness.

*O traitors, why do you stare and stay silent when the wicked swallows up one more righteous than he?* (i, 13b).

Interpreted, this concerns the House of Absalom and the members of its council who were silent at the time of the chastisement of the Teacher of Righteousness and gave him no help against the Liar who flouted the Law in the midst of their whole [congregation].

*Thou dealest with men like the fish of the sea, like creeping things, to rule over them. They draw [them all up with a fish-hook], and drag them out with their net, and gather them in [their seine. Therefore they sacrifice] to their net. Therefore they rejoice [and exult and burn incense to their seine; for by them] their portion is fat [and their sustenance rich]* (i, 14–16).

... **VI** the Kittim. And they shall gather in their riches, together with all their booty, *like the fish of the sea*. And as for that which He said, *Therefore they sacrifice to their net and burn incense to their seine*: interpreted, this means that they sacrifice to their standards and worship their weapons of war. *For through them their portion is fat and their sustenance rich*: interpreted, this means that they divide their yoke and their tribute – *their sustenance* – over all the peoples year by year, ravaging many lands.

*Therefore their sword is ever drawn to massacre nations mercilessly* (i, 17).

Interpreted, this concerns the Kittim who cause many to perish by the sword – youths, grown men, the aged, women and children – and who even take no pity on the fruit of the womb.

*I will take my stand to watch and will station myself upon my fortress. I will watch to see what He will say to me and how [He will answer] my complaint. And the Lord answered [and said to me, 'Write down the vision and make it plain] upon the tablets, that [he who reads] may read it speedily* (ii, 1–2).

... **VII** and God told Habakkuk to write down that which would happen to the final generation, but He did not make known to him when time would come to an end. And as for that which He said, *That he who reads may read it speedily*: interpreted this concerns the Teacher of Righteousness, to whom God made known all the mysteries of the words of His servants the Prophets.

*For there shall be yet another vision concerning the appointed time. It shall tell of the end and shall not lie* (ii, 3a).

Interpreted, this means that the final age shall be prolonged, and shall exceed all that the Prophets have said; for the mysteries of God are astounding.

*If it tarries, wait for it, for it shall surely come and shall not be late* (ii, 3b).

Interpreted, this concerns the men of truth who keep the Law, whose hands shall not slacken in the service of truth when the final age is prolonged. For all the ages of God reach their appointed end as he determines for them in the mysteries of His wisdom.

*Behold, [his soul] is puffed up and is not upright* (ii, 4a).

Interpreted, this means that [the wicked] shall double their guilt upon themselves [and it shall not be forgiven] when they are judged . . .

*[But the righteous shall live by his faith]* (ii, 4b).

**VIII** Interpreted, this concerns all those who observe the Law in the House of Judah, whom God will deliver from the House of Judgement because of their suffering and because of their faith in the Teacher of Righteousness.

*Moreover, the arrogant man seizes wealth without halting. He widens his gullet like Hell and like Death he has never enough. All the nations are gathered to him and all the peoples are assembled to him. Will they not all of them taunt him and jeer at him saying, 'Woe to him who amasses that which is not his! How long will he load himself up with pledges?'* (ii, 5–6).

Interpreted, this concerns the Wicked Priest who was called by the name of truth when he first arose. But when he ruled over Israel his heart became proud, and he forsook God and betrayed the precepts for the sake of riches. He robbed and amassed the riches of the men of violence who rebelled against God, and he took the wealth of the peoples, heaping sinful iniquity upon himself. And he lived in the ways of abominations amidst every unclean defilement.

*Shall not your oppressors suddenly arise and your torturers awaken; and shall you not become their prey? Because you have plundered many nations, all the remnant of the peoples shall plunder you* (ii, 7–8a).

[Interpreted, this concerns] the Priest who rebelled [and violated] the precepts [of God . . . to command] **IX** his chastisement by means of the judgements of wickedness. And they inflicted horrors of evil diseases and took vengeance upon his body of flesh. And as for that which He said, *Because you have plundered many nations, all the remnant of the peoples shall plunder you*: interpreted this concerns the last Priests of Jerusalem, who shall amass money and wealth by plundering the peoples. But in the last days, their riches and booty shall be delivered into the hands of the army of the Kittim, for it is they who shall be the *remnant of the peoples.*

*Because of the blood of men and the violence done to the land, to the city, and to all its inhabitants* (ii, 8b).

Interpreted, this concerns the Wicked Priest whom God delivered into the hands of his enemies because of the iniquity committed against the Teacher of Righteousness and the men of his Council, that he might be humbled by means of a destroying scourge, in bitterness of soul, because he had done wickedly to His elect.

*Woe to him who gets evil profit for his house; who perches his nest high to be safe from the hand of evil! You have devised shame to your house: by cutting off many peoples you have forfeited your own soul. For the* [*stone*] *cries out* [*from*] *the wall* [*and*] *the beam from the woodwork replies* (ii, 9–11).

[Interpreted, this] concerns the [Priest] who . . . **X** that its stones might be laid in oppression and the beam of its woodwork in robbery. And as for that which He said, *By cutting off many peoples you have forfeited your own soul*: interpreted this concerns the condemned House whose judgement God will pronounce in the midst of many peoples. He will bring him thence for judgement and will declare him guilty in the midst of them, and will chastise him with fire of brimstone.

*Woe to him who builds a city with blood and founds a town upon falsehood! Behold, is it not from the Lord of Hosts that the peoples shall labour for fire and the nations shall strive for naught?* (ii, 12–13).

Interpreted, this concerns the Spouter of Lies who led many astray that he might build his city of vanity with blood and raise a congregation on deceit, causing many thereby to perform a service of vanity for the sake of its glory, and to be pregnant with [works] of deceit, that their labour might be for nothing and that they might be punished with fire who vilified and outraged the elect of God.

*For as the waters cover the sea, so shall the earth be filled with the knowledge of the glory of the Lord* (ii, 14).

Interpreted, [this means that] when they return ... **XI** the lies. And afterwards, knowledge shall be revealed to them abundantly, like the waters of the sea.

*Woe to him who causes his neighbours to drink; who pours out his venom to make them drunk that he may gaze on their feasts* (ii, 15).

Interpreted, this concerns the Wicked Priest who pursued the Teacher of Righteousness to the house of his exile that he might confuse him with his venomous fury. And at the time appointed for rest, for the Day of Atonement, he appeared before them to confuse them, and to cause them to stumble on the Day of Fasting, their Sabbath of repose.

*You have filled yourself with ignominy more than with glory. Drink also, and stagger! The cup of the Lord's right hand shall come round to you and shame shall come on your glory* (ii, 16).

Interpreted, this concerns the Priest whose ignominy was greater than his glory. For he did not circumcise the foreskin of his heart, and he walked in the ways of drunkenness that he might quench his thirst. But the cup of the wrath of God shall confuse him, multiplying his ... and the pain of ...

[*For the violence done to Lebanon shall overwhelm you, and the destruction of the beasts*] **XII** *shall terrify you, because of the blood of men and the violence done to the land, the city, and all its inhabitants* (ii, 17).

Interpreted, this saying concerns the Wicked Priest, inasmuch as he shall be paid the reward which he himself tendered to the Poor. For *Lebanon* is the Council of the Community; and the *beasts* are the simple of Judah who keep the Law. As he himself plotted the destruction of the Poor, so will God condemn him to destruction. And as for that which He said, *Because of the blood of the city and the violence done to the land*: interpreted, *the city* is Jerusalem where the Wicked Priest committed abominable deeds and defiled the Temple of God. *The violence done to the land*: these are the cities of Judah where he robbed the Poor of their possessions.

*Of what use is an idol that its maker should shape it, a molten image, a fatling of lies? For the craftsman puts his trust in his own creation when he makes dumb idols* (ii, 18).

Interpreted, this saying concerns all the idols of the nations which they make so that they may serve and worship them. But they shall not deliver them on the Day of Judgement.

*Woe* [*to him who says*] *to wood, 'Awake', and to dumb* [*stone, 'Arise'! Can such a thing give guidance? Behold, it is covered with gold and silver but there is no spirit within it. But the Lord is in His holy Temple*]: **XIII** *let all the earth be silent before Him!* (lii, 19–20).

Interpreted, this concerns all the nations which serve stone and wood. But on the Day of Judgement, God will destroy from the earth all idolatrous and wicked men.

# Commentary on Zephaniah

## (1Q15, 4Q170)

The relics of a Zephaniah Commentary from Cave 1, covering Zeph. i, 18–ii, 2 and using palaeo-Hebrew letters for the divine name, are badly mutilated. A lengthy quotation is followed by the word *pesher* (interpretation), and the expression 'land of Judah' implies that the divine anger spoken of by the prophet was understood to be directed against the Judaeans. Two small fragments from Cave 4 represent two broken lines of Zephaniah i, 12–13; a couple of words which are not biblical precede the introductory formula, *pishro* (its interpretation), but the actual commentary is lost. The two excerpts are presented in the order of the biblical text.

Cf. D. Barthélemy and J. T. Milik, *DJD*, I, 80; J. M. Allegro, *DJD*, V, 42.

### 4Q170

*The Lord* [*will not do goo*]*d, nor will He do ill. And* [*their goods shall be pl*]*undered and* [*their houses laid waste.*] ... cannot ... (Zeph. i, 12–13).

Its interpretation [concerns] ...

### 1Q15

... [*in the fire of His*] *jealous* [*wrath, all the earth*] *shall be consumed;* [*for a full, yea, sudden end He will make of all the inha*]*bitants of the earth* (Zeph. i, 18). *Come together* [*and hold an assembly, O shameless nation, before you are driven away; like*] *chaff, a day has passed away* [*before there comes upon you*] *the fierce anger of the Lord* (ii, 1–2). The interpretation [of this saying concerns all the inhabitants] of the land of Judah ...

# Commentary on Psalms
## (1Q16, 4Q171, 4Q173)

Cave 1 has preserved a few scraps of a commentary on Psalms lvii and lxviii. Most of them are too small for a coherent translation, but frs. 9–10 mention the Kittim (Romans), the name of the final enemy (*DJD*, I, 81–2). More importantly, two manuscripts with Herodian script from Cave 4 (4Q171, 4Q173) include interpretations of Psalms (*DJD*, V, 42–53). The bulk of the text is devoted to Psalm xxxvii, in which the destiny of the just and the wicked is expounded in connection with the story of the sect and its opponents, and in particular, the struggle between the Teacher of Righteousness and the Wicked Priest. Recognizable remains of Psalms xlv and cxxvii also survive.

### 4Q171

**I** ... *[Be sil]ent before [the Lord and] long for him, and be not heated against the successful, the man who [achi]eves his plans* (xxxvii, 7a).

Its interpretation concerns the Liar who has led astray many by his lying words so that they chose frivolous things and heeded not the interpreter of knowledge in order to ... **II** they shall perish by the sword and famine and plague.

*Relent from anger and abandon wrath. Do not be angry; it tends only to evil, for the wicked shall be cut off* (8–9a).

Interpreted, this concerns all those who return to the Law, to those who do not refuse to turn away from their evil. For all those who are stubborn in turning away from their iniquity shall be cut off.

*But those who wait for the Lord shall possess the land* (9b).

Interpreted, this is the congregation of His elect who do His will.

*A little while and the wicked shall be no more; I will look towards his place but he shall not be there* (10).

Interpreted, this concerns all the wicked. At the end of the forty years they shall be blotted out and no [evil] man shall be found on the earth.

*But the humble shall possess the land and delight in abundant peace* (11).

Interpreted, this concerns [the congregation of the] Poor who shall accept the season of penance and shall be delivered from all the snares of Belial. Afterwards, all who possess the earth shall delight and prosper on exquisite food.

*The wicked plots against the righteous and gnashes [his teeth a]t him. [The Lo]rd laughs at him, for He sees that his day is coming* (12–13).

Interpreted, this concerns the violent of the Covenant who are in the House of Judah, who have plotted to destroy those who practise the law, who are in the Council of the Community. And God will not forsake them to their hands.

*The wicked draw the sword and bend their bow to bring down the poor and needy and to slay the upright of way. Their sword shall enter their own heart and their bows shall be broken* (14–15).

Interpreted, this concerns the wicked of Ephraim and Manasseh, who shall seek to lay hands on the Priest and the men of his Council at the time of trial which shall come upon them. But God will redeem them from out of their hand. And afterwards, they shall be delivered into the hand of the violent among the nations for judgement.

*vacat Better is the little which the righteous has than the abundance of many wicked people* (16).

[Interpreted, this concerns ... those who practise the law ... *For the ar[ms of the wicked shall be broken, but] the Lor[d upholds the righteous]* (17).

*[The Lord knows the days of the perfect and their portion shall be for ever. In evil times they shall not be shamed]* (18–19a).

**III** ... to the penitents of the desert who, saved, shall live for a thousand generations and to whom all the glory of Adam shall belong, as also to their seed for ever.

*And in the days of famine they shall be [satisfi]ed, but the wicked shall perish* (19b–20a).

Interpreted, this [means that] He will keep them alive during the famine and the time of humiliation, whereas many shall perish from famine and plague, all those who have not departed [from there] to be with the Congregation of His elect.

*And those who love the Lord shall be like the pride of pastures* (20b).

Interpreted, [this concerns] the congregation of His elect, who shall be leaders and princes . . . of the flock among their herds.

*Like smoke they shall all of them vanish away* (20c).

Interpreted, [this] concerns the princes [of wickedness] who have oppressed His holy people, and who shall perish like smoke [blown away by the wind].

*The wicked borrows and does not repay, but the righteous is generous and gives. Truly, those whom He [blesses shall possess] the land, but those whom He curses [shall be cut off]* (21–2).

Interpreted, this concerns the congregation of the Poor, who [shall possess] the whole world as an inheritance. They shall possess the High Mountain of Israel [for ever], and shall enjoy [everlasting] delights in His Sanctuary. [But those who] shall be *cut off*, they are the violent [of the nations and] the wicked of Israel; they shall be cut off and blotted out for ever.

*The steps of the man are confirmed by the Lord and He delights in all his ways; though [he stumble, he shall not fall, for the Lord shall support his hand]* (23–4).

Interpreted, this concerns the Priest, the Teacher of [Righteousness whom] God chose to stand before Him, for He established him to build for Himself the congregation of . . .

*I [have been young] and now am old, yet [I have] not [seen the righteous] forsaken, or his children begging bread. He is [ever] giving liberally and lending and [his] children become a blessing* (25–6).

Interpreted, this concerns . . .

**IV** *The unjust shall be destroyed for ever and the children of the wi[cked shall be cut off]* (28).

These are the violent . . .

*The righteou[s shall possess the land and dwell] upon it for ever* (29).

[Interpreted, this concerns] ...

*[The mouth of the righteous utters] wisdom and his tongue speaks [justice. The law of God is in his heart, his steps will not slip* (30–31).

Interpreted, it concerns ... ] ...

*The wicked watches out for the righteous and seeks [to slay him. The Lord will not abandon him into his hand or] let him be condemned when he is tried* (32–3).

Interpreted, this concerns the Wicked [Priest] who [watched the Teacher of Righteousness] that he might put him to death [because of the ordinance] and the law which he sent to him. But God will not *aban[don him and will not let him be condemned when he is] tried.* And [God] will pay him his reward by delivering him into the hand of the violent of the nations, that they may execute upon him [judgement].

*[Wait for the Lo]rd and keep to His way, and [He] will exalt you to possess the land; you will lo[ok] on the destruction of the wicked* (34).

[Interpreted, it concerns ... ] who will see the judgement of wickedness and with his elect will rejoice in the heritage of truth.

*I [have seen] a wicked man overbearing ... [like a cedar of Lebanon]. I passed before [him, and], lo, he was [no more], though I [sought him,] he could not [be found* (35–6).

Interpreted, it concerns] the Liar who ... against the e[lec]t of God, [and sought] to bring to an end ...

*[Mark the blameless man and behold] the upright, [for there is posterity for the ma]n of peace* (37).

Its interpretation con[cerns ... ] peac[e].

*But the transgressors shall be altogether destroyed; the post[erity of the wicked shall be cut off* (38).

Interpreted, it concerns ... ] will perish and be cut off from the midst of the congregation of the Community ...

*... he delivers them from the wicked [and saves them, because they take refuge in him* (40).

Interpreted, it concerns ... ] God will save them and deliver them from the w[icked ... ]

*For the choirmaster: according to [the lili]es. [For the sons of Korah. Maskil. A song of love* (Ps. xlv, 1).

Its interpretation is that th]ey are the seven divisions of the penitents of Is[rael ... ].

*My he[art] is astir with a good word. I speak of my work to the King* (xlv, 1). [Its interpretation ... spir]it of holiness for ... books of ...

*And my tongue is the pen of [a speedy scribe* (xlv, 1).

Its interpretation] concerns the Teacher of [Righteousness] ... God with an answering tongue ...

## 4Q173

[... *Vai]n is it for you to rise early and lie down late. You shall eat the bread of toil; [he shall feed those who love him in their] sleep* (cxxvii, 2).

[Its interpretation is th]at they shall seek ... Teacher of Righteousness ... [pri]est at the end of the a[ge] ...

# Commentary on an Unidentifiable Text

## (4Q183)

Three fragments of a biblical commentary, indicated by the introductory formula, 'And that which he said', which is common in *pesher* literature, have been published by J. M. Allegro (*DJD*, V, 81–2). None of the quotations has been preserved, but the phraseology and the historical allusions recall the Habakkuk Commentary and other *pesharim*. The divine names 'God' (*el*) and 'the Lord' (*Yhwh*) are written in palaeo-Hebrew script. Only fr. 2 is suitable for translation. 4Q172 (*DJD*, V, 50–1) is also an amalgam of commentaries on unidentified texts, but the fragments are so small as to preclude altogether any translation.

**II** their enemies. And they profaned their sanctuary ... from them. And they rose for battles one [with another] against his covenant. God saved and delivered ... goodwill. And he gave them a single heart to wal[k in the way of his truth. And they despised] all the wealth of wickedness and kept apart from the wa[y of wickedness] ... the erring spirit and with a tongue of truth ... And they atoned for their iniquity through [their] strokes ... their iniquity. *vacat* And that which he said, ...

# Florilegium or Midrash on the Last Days

## (4Q174)

This collection of texts assembled from 2 Samuel and the Psalter, and combined with other scriptural passages, serves to present the sectarian doctrine identifying the Community with the Temple, and to announce the coming of the two Messiahs, the 'Branch of David' and the 'Interpreter of the Law'. Originating from Cave 4 (4Q174) and known also as 'Florilegium', the composition was edited by J. M. Allegro (*DJD*, V, 53–7); it probably belongs to the late first century BCE.

**I** ... [*I will appoint a place for my people Israel and will plant them that they may dwell there and be troubled no more by their*] *enemies. No son of iniquity* [*shall afflict them again*] *as formerly, from the day that* [*I set judges*] *over my people Israel* (2 Sam. vii, 10).

This is the House which [He will build for them in the] last days, as it is written in the book of Moses, *In the sanctuary which Thy hands have established, O Lord, the Lord shall reign for ever and ever* (Exod. xv, 17–18). This is the House into which [the unclean shall] never [enter, nor the uncircumcised,] nor the Ammonite, nor the Moabite, nor the half-breed, nor the foreigner, nor the stranger, ever; for there shall My Holy Ones be. [Its glory shall endure] for ever; it shall appear above it perpetually. And strangers shall lay it waste no more, as they formerly laid waste the Sanctuary of Israel because of its sin. He has commanded that a Sanctuary of men be built for Himself, that there they may send up, like the smoke of incense, the works of the Law.

And concerning His words to David, *And I* [*will give*] *you* [*rest*] *from all your enemies* (2 Sam. vii, 11), this means that He will give them rest from all the children of Belial who cause them to stumble so that they may be destroyed [by their errors,] just as they came with a [devilish] plan to cause the [sons] of light to stumble and to devise against them a wicked plot, that [they might become subject] to Belial in their [wicked] straying.

*The Lord declares to you that He will build you a House* (2 Sam. vii, 11c). *I will raise up your seed after you* (2 Sam. vii, 12). *I will establish the throne of his kingdom* [*for ever*] (2 Sam. vii, 13). [*I will be*] *his father and he shall be my son* (2 Sam. vii, 14). He is the Branch of David who shall arise with the Interpreter of the Law [to rule] in Zion [at the end] of time. As it is written, *I will raise up the tent of David that is fallen* (Amos ix, 11). That is to say, the fallen *tent of David* is he who shall arise to save Israel.

Explanation of *How blessed is the man who does not walk in the counsel of the wicked* (Ps. i, 1). Interpreted, this saying [concerns] those who turn aside from the way [of the people] as it is written in the book of Isaiah the Prophet concerning the last days, *It came to pass that* [*the Lord turned me aside, as with a mighty hand, from walking in the way of*] *this people* (Isa. viii, 11). They are those of whom it is written in the book of Ezekiel the Prophet, *The Levites* [*strayed far from me, following*] *their idols* (Ezek. xliv, 10). They are the sons of Zadok who [seek their own] counsel and follow [their own inclination] apart from the Council of the Community.

[*Why*] *do the nations* [*rage*] *and the peoples meditate* [*vanity? Why do the kings of the earth*] *rise up,* [*and the*] *princes take counsel together against the Lord and against* [*His Messiah*]*?* (Ps. ii, 1). Interpreted, this saying concerns [the kings of the nations] who shall [rage against] the elect of Israel in the last days. **II** This shall be the time of the trial to co[me concerning the house of J]udah so as to perfect . . . Belial, and a remnant of the people shall be left according to the lot (assigned to them), and they shall practise the whole Law . . . Moses. This is the time of which it is written in the book of Daniel the Prophet: *But the wicked shall do wickedly and shall not understand, but the righteous shall purify themselves and make themselves white* (Dan. xii, 10). The people who know God shall be strong. They are the masters who understand . . .

# Testimonia or Messianic Anthology

## (4Q175)

This short document from Cave 4 (4Q175), dating to the early first century BCE and similar in literary style to the Christian *Testimonia* or collections of messianic proof-texts, includes five quotations arranged in four groups. Only the last of them is followed by an interpretation.

The first group consists of two texts from Deuteronomy referring to the prophet similar to Moses; the second is an extract from a prophecy of Balaam about the Royal Messiah; the third is a blessing of the Levites and, implicitly, of the Priest-Messiah.

The last group opens with a verse from Joshua, which is then expounded by means of a quotation from the sectarian Psalms of Joshua (cf. 4Q379 below, p. 547). Most experts hold that the commentator, bearing in mind the biblical passage, is alluding to three characters: a father ('an accursed man') and his two sons. However, the verb 'arose' in the second sentence is in the singular, and it would seem correct to interpret this text as referring to the two brothers only.

For the *editio princeps*, see J. M. Allegro, *DJD*, V, 57–60.

The Lord spoke to Moses saying:

*You have heard the words which this people have spoken to you; all they have said is right. O that their heart were always like this, to fear me and to keep my commandments always, that it might be well with them and their children for ever!* (Deut. v, 28–9). *I will raise up for them a Prophet like you from among their brethren. I will put my words into his mouth and he shall tell them all that I command him. And I will require a reckoning of whoever will not listen to the words which the Prophet shall speak in my Name* (Deut. xviii, 18–19).

He took up his discourse and said:

*Oracle of Balaam son of Beor. Oracle of the man whose eye is penetrating. Oracle of him who has heard the words of God, who knows the wisdom of the Most High and sees the vision of the Almighty, who falls and his eyes are opened. I see him but not now. I behold him but not near. A star shall come out of Jacob and a sceptre shall rise out of Israel; he shall crush the temples of Moab and destroy all the children of Sheth* (Num. xxiv, 15–17).

And of Levi he said:

*Give Thy Tummim to Levi, and Thy Urim to Thy pious one whom Thou didst test at Massah, and with whom Thou didst quarrel at the waters of Meribah; who said to his father and mother, 'I know you not', and who did not acknowledge his brother, or know his sons. For they observed Thy word and kept Thy Covenant. They shall cause Thy precepts to shine before Jacob and Thy Law before Israel. They shall send up incense towards Thy nostrils and place a burnt-offering upon Thine altar. Bless his power, O Lord, and delight in the work of his hands. Smite the loins of his adversaries and let his enemies rise no more* (Deut. xxxiii, 8–11).

When Joshua had finished offering praise and thanksgiving, he said:

*Cursed be the man who rebuilds this city! May he lay its foundation on his first-born, and set its gate upon his youngest son* (Josh. vi, 26). Behold, an accursed man, a man of Belial, has risen to become a fowler's net to his people, and a cause of destruction to all his neighbours. And [his brother] arose [and ruled in li]es, both being instruments of violence. They have rebuilt [this city and have set up for it] a wall and towers to make of it a stronghold of ungodliness in Israel, and a horror in Ephraim and in Judah ... They have committed an abomination in the land, and a great blasphemy among the children [of Jacob. They have shed blood] like water upon the ramparts of the daughter of Zion and within the precincts of Jerusalem.

# Ordinances or Commentaries on Biblical Law

## (4Q159, 4Q513–14)

Three manuscripts from Cave 4 (**4Q159**, **4Q513–14**), published respectively in *DJD*, V, 6–9, and VII, 287–98, and probably belonging to the turn of the era, include reinterpretations of various biblical laws.

In the first statute, the interpreter deduces from Deut. xxiii, 25–6 that a poor man may eat ears of corn in the field of another person, but is not allowed to take any home. On a threshing-floor, however, he may both eat and gather provisions for his family.

Next follows a statute referring to the half-shekel tax contributed by every Israelite aged twenty to the upkeep of the place of worship. Later Jewish tradition interpreted this passage as instituting a yearly tax to be paid by every male Israelite (cf. Neh. x, 32; Matth. xvii, 24–7; see also the treatise *Shekalim* or *Shekel Dues* in the Mishnah). The Qumran ordinance, however, insists on one single payment, thereby complying with the scriptural rule and at the same time withholding regular support from the Temple in Jerusalem. Here **4Q159** and **4Q513**, frs. 1–2, partly overlap.

The third statute (**4Q159**, frs. 2–4) deals with the prohibition against selling an Israelite as a slave (cf. Lev. xxv, 39–46); with cases to be judged by a court of twelve magistrates; with the forbidden interchange of garments between men and women (cf. Deut. xxii, 5); and with the charge laid by a husband against his wife that she was not a virgin when he married her (Deut. xxii, 13–21).

Finally, **4Q513**, frs. 2–4, and **4Q514** legislate on purity rules.

## 4Q159

**II** ... [And] anyone who has made of it a threshing-floor or a winepress, any destitute [Israelite] who goes into a threshing-floor may eat there and gather for himself and for [his] hou[sehold. But should he walk among corn standing in] the field, he may eat but may not bring it to his house to store it.

Concerning ... the money of valuation that a man gives as ransom for his life, it shall be half [a shekel ... ] He shall give it only once in his life. Twenty *gerahs* make one shekel according to [the shekel of the sanctuary (cf. Exod. xxx, 12–13) ... ] For the 600,000, one hundred talents; for the 3,000, half a talent (=30 *minahs*); [for the 500, five *minahs*;] and for the 50, half a *minah*, (which is) twenty-five shekels (cf. Exod. xxxviii, 25–6) ...

## 4Q159, frs. 2–4

... before Isra[el]. They shall [n]ot serve Gentiles among foreign[ers, for He has brought them out from the land of] Egypt, and He has commanded concerning them that none shall be sold as a slave ... ... [t]en men and two priests, and they shall be judged before these twelve ... spoke in Israel against a person, they shall inquire in accordance with them. Whosoever shall rebel ..., shall be put to death for he has acted wilfully.

Let no man's garment be worn by a woman all [the days of her life]. Let him [not] be covered with a woman's mantle, nor wear a woman's tunic, for this is an abomination.

If a man accuses a virgin of Israel (that she is not a virgin), if this is when he marries her, let him say so and they shall examine her [concerning her] trustworthiness. If he has not lied concerning her, she shall be put to death. But if he has humiliated her [false]ly, he shall be fined two *minahs*, [and] shall [not] divorce her all his life. ...

## 4Q513

... [Tw]enty [*gerahs*] make a shekel according to the she[kel of the sanctuary ...] The half-[shekel consists of twe]lv[e *me*]*ahs*, [two] *zuzim* ... also sources of uncleanness. The *ephah* and the *bath*, also sources of uncleanness, have the same capacity, (viz.) ten *'issarons* (=tenths). A *bath* of wine corresponds to an *ephah* of corn. The *seah* consists of three and one-third *'issarons*, sources of uncleanness, and the tithe of the *ephah* [is the *'issaron*].

# 4Q514

**I** He shall not eat . . . for all the unclean . . . to count for [him seven days of wa]shing and he shall wash and cleanse on the d[a]y of [his] purification. Whoever has not begun his purification from his 'fo[un]t' [shall not eat]. [Neither shall he eat] in his first (degree of) uncleanness. All those temporarily unclean shall wash on the day of their [pu]rification, and cleanse (their garments) with water and shall become clean. Afterwards they may eat their bread according to the law of purity. Whoever has not begun his purification from his 'fount' shall not eat (again?) in his first (degree of) uncleanness. Whoever is still in his first (degree of) uncleanness shall not eat. All those temporarily [un]clean shall on the day of their pu[rification] wash and cleanse (their garments) with water and they shall be clean. Afterwards they may eat their bread according to the l[aw. None] shall e[at] or drink with whomsoev[er] prepares . . .

# The Heavenly Prince Melchizedek

## (11Q13)

A striking first-century BCE document, composed of thirteen fragments from Cave 11 and centred on the mysterious figure of Melchizedek, was first published by A. S. van der Woude in 1965. It takes the form of an eschatological midrash in which the proclamation of liberty to the captives at the end of days (Isa. lxi, 1) is understood as being part of the general restoration of property during the year of Jubilee (Lev. xxv, 13), seen in the Bible (Deut. xv, 2) as a remission of debts.

The heavenly deliverer is Melchizedek. Identical with the archangel Michael, he is the head of the 'sons of Heaven' or 'gods of Justice' and is referred to as *elohim* and *el*. The same terminology occurs in the Songs for the Holocaust of the Sabbath. These Hebrew words normally mean 'God', but in certain specific contexts Jewish tradition also explains *elohim* as primarily designating a 'judge'. Here Melchizedek is portrayed as presiding over the final Judgement and condemnation of his demonic counterpart, Belial/Satan, the Prince of Darkness, elsewhere also called Melkiresha' (cf. pp. 380, 534). The great act of deliverance is expected to occur on the Day of Atonement at the end of the tenth Jubilee cycle.

This manuscript sheds valuable light not only on the Melchizedek figure in the Epistle to the Hebrews vii, but also on the development of the messianic concept in the New Testament and early Christianity.

For the text, see A. S. van der Woude, 'Melchizedek als himmlische Erlösergestalt ...', *Oudtestamentische Studien*, Leiden, 1965, 354–73; M. de Jonge and A. S. van der Woude, '11Q Melchizedek and the New Testament', *NTS* 12 (1966), 301–26; J. T. Milik, *JJS* 23 (1972), 96–109; E. Puech, 'Notes sur le manuscrit de 11Q Melkisédeq', *RQ* 12 (1987), 483–513.

... And concerning that which He said, *In* [*this*] *year of Jubilee* [*each of you shall return to his property* (Lev. xxv, 13); and likewise, *And this is the manner of release:*] *every creditor shall release that which he has lent* [*to his neighbour.*

*He shall not exact it of his neighbour and his brother*], *for God's release* [*has been proclaimed*] (Deut. xv, 2). [And it will be proclaimed at] the end of days concerning the captives as [He said, *To proclaim liberty to the captives* (Isa. lxi, 1). Its interpretation is that He] will assign them to the Sons of Heaven and to the inheritance of Melchizedek; f[or He will cast] their [lot] amid the po[rtions of Melchize]dek, who will return them there and will proclaim to them liberty, forgiving them [the wrong-doings] of all their iniquities.

And this thing will [occur] in the first week of the Jubilee that follows the nine Jubilees. And the Day of Atonement is the e[nd of the] tenth [Ju]bilee, when all the Sons of [Light] and the men of the lot of Mel[chi]zedek will be atoned for. [And] a statue concerns them [to prov]ide them with their rewards. For this is the moment of the Year of Grace for Melchizedek. [And h]e will, by his strength, judge the holy ones of God, executing judgement as it is written concerning him in the Songs of David, who said, ELOHIM *has taken his place in the divine council; in the midst of the gods he holds judgement* (Psalms lxxxii, 1). And it was concerning him that he said, (Let the assembly of the peoples) *return to the height above them*; EL (*god*) *will judge the peoples* (Psalms vii, 7–8). As for that which he s[aid, *How long will you*] *judge unjustly and show partiality to the wicked? Selah* (Psalms lxxxii, 2), its interpretation concerns Belial and the spirits of his lot [who] rebelled by turning away from the precepts of God to ... And Melchizedek will avenge the vengeance of the judgements of God ... and he will drag [them from the hand of] Belial and from the hand of all the sp[irits of] his [lot]. And all the 'gods [of Justice'] will come to his aid [to] attend to the de[struction] of Belial. And *the height* is ... all the sons of God ... this ... This is the day of [Peace/Salvation] concerning which [God] spoke [through Isa]iah the prophet, who said, [*How*] *beautiful upon the mountains are the feet of the messenger who proclaims peace, who brings good news, who proclaims salvation, who says to Zion: Your* ELOHIM [*reigns*] (Isa. lii, 7). Its interpretation; *the mountains* are the prophets ... and *the messenger* is the Anointed one of the spirit, concerning whom Dan[iel] said, [*Until an anointed one, a prince* (Dan. ix, 25)] ... [And he *who brings*] *good* [*news*], *who proclaims* [*salvation*]: it is concerning him that it is written ... [*To comfort all who mourn, to grant to those who mourn in Zion*] (Isa. lxi, 2–3). *To comfort* [*those who mourn*: its interpretation], to make them understand all the ages of t[ime] ... In truth ... will turn away from Belial ... by the judgement[s] of God, as it is written concerning him, [*who says to Zion*]; *your* ELOHIM *reigns. Zion is* ..., those who uphold the Covenant, who turn from walking [in] the way of the people. And *your* ELOHIM is [Melchizedek, who will save them from] the hand of Belial.

As for that which He said, *Then you shall send abroad the trump*[*et in*] *all the land* (Lev. xxv, 9) . . .

# Consolations or Tanhumim

## (4Q176)

A large number of small fragments from a Cave 4 manuscript (4Q**176**), edited by J. M. Allegro in 1968 (*DJD*, V, 60–67), represent a scriptural anthology centred on the theme of divine consolation. Originally, each citation was accompanied by a sectarian exegesis, but only a few examples of the latter survive. The majority of the extant remains belong to Isaiah xl–lv (Ps. lxxix, 2–3; Isa. xl, 1–5; xli, 8–9; xlix, 13–17; xliii, 1–2, 4–6; li, 22–3; lii, 1–3; liv, 4–10; lii, 1–2; Zech. xiii, 9). The translated passage is based on Psalm lxxix, 2–3, and is followed by a new title – From the Book of Isaiah: Consolations – and the quotation of the opening verses of Isa. xl. The four asterisks symbolize the Tetragram indicated in the manuscript simply by dots.

**I** And he shall accomplish Thy miracles and Thy righteousness among Thy people. And they shall . . . Thy sanctuary, and shall dispute with the kingdoms over the blood of . . . Jerusalem and shall see the bodies of Thy priests . . . *and none to bury them* (Ps. lxxix, 3). From the Book of Isaiah: Consolations [*Comfort, comfort, my people*] – *says your God* – *speak to the heart of Jerusalem and c*[*ry to her that*] *her* [*bondage is completed*], *that her punishment is accepted, that she has received from the hand of* **** *double for all her sins* . . . (Isa. xl, 1–3).

# Catenae or Interpretation of Biblical Texts on the Last Days

## (4Q177, 4Q182)

These two documents consist of over thirty fragments, none of which amounts to units of coherent text (*DJD*, V, 67–74, 80–81; cf. J. Strugnell, *RQ* 7 (1970), 236–46, 256). The connecting theme is eschatology, with the phrase 'at the end of days' appearing half a dozen times. The majority of the biblical quotations are from the Psalms (Ps. vi, xi, xii, xiii, xvi, but explicit mentions are also made of 'the Book of the Law' (or possibly 'the Second Law' (4Q177, frs. 1–4, l. 14), 'the Book of Ezekiel, the prophet' (4Q177, fr. 7, l. 3), and 'the Book of Jerem[iah the prophet?]' (4Q182, fr. 1, l. 4). The citations are introduced by 'as it is written', and the expository sections start with *pesher*. The following typically sectarian expressions are attested: 'party of light' (fr. 1–4, l. 8), 'men of his council' (ibid., l. 16), 'congregation of seekers of smooth things' (fr. 9, l. 4), 'men of Belial' (fr. 10–11, l. 4), 'Interpreter of the Law' (ibid., l. 5), 'sons of light' (fr. 12–13 i, l. 7, 11), 'council of the Community' (fr. 14, l. 5).

### 4Q177 frs. 10–11, 7, 9, 20, 26 (as reconstructed by Strugnell)

... The interpretation of the saying concerns the purifying of the heart of the men ... to try them and refine them ... by the spirit and the pure and the purified ... [As for that which] he said, *Lest the enemy say, [I have prevailed over him]* (Ps. xiii, 5) ... They are the congregation of the seekers of smooth things who ... [unt]il they seek to destroy ... by their jealousy and hostilit[y] ... The int[erpretation of this word concerns] ... [whi]ch is written in the Book of Ezekiel the pr[ophet] ...

[The interpretation of the saying concerns the end] of days when there will be gathered against them ...

# G. Biblically Based Apocryphal Works

'Jubilees',
*Israel Antiquities Authority*

# Jubilees

## (4Q216–28, 1Q17–18, 2Q19–20, 3Q5, 4Q482(?), 11Q12)

The pseudepigraphon, known prior to Qumran from a complete Ethiopic and partial Greek, Latin and Syriac translations, has for the first time surfaced in a large number of mostly small fragments in its Hebrew original in five Qumran caves. The work itself is a midrashic retelling of the story of Genesis (and the beginning of Exodus) in the form of a revelation conveyed by angels to Moses. Apart from some 4Q relics, the texts from 1–3Q and 11Q are too mutilated to provide the basis for an English translation and their chief significance lies in their attestation of a Hebrew original generally close to the account preserved in the ancient versions.

The 4Q material includes some larger fragments suitable for rendering into English, and **4Q225**, surnamed pseudo-Jubilees by the editors, but which could just as well be accepted simply as an alternative account, reveals supplementary material of some importance not only for Jubilees in general, but also for the study of the Akedah or story of the sacrifice of Isaac, certain features of which receive here their first pre-Christian attestation.

**4Q216**, which in part may be the earliest Jubilees manuscript and should be dated palaeographically to the last quarter of the second century BCE, testifies in the form of small fragments to the beginning of the book (between I, 1 and II, 24 of the Ethiopic version). It contains the Hebrew title of the work, Book of the Divisions of the Times, repeated also in other 4Q fragments, a title already known from the Damascus Document (XVI, 3). **4Q217** and **218**, the first consisting of eleven tiny papyrus fragments and the second of a single small leather fragment, both probably derive from the opening chapters of Jubilees. **4Q219**, also poorly preserved, has preserved tit-bits from chapters XXI, 1 to XXII, 1. Its only noteworthy contribution is that in col. II, lines 35–6, it dates the death of Abraham correctly to the forty-third jubilee counted from the creation, and not to the forty-fourth, as the Ethiopic version does. Erroneously 4QJub[e] supplies a single largish, hence translatable, fragment of Jub. XXI, 5–10 written in an early Herodian script (last three decades of the first century BCE). It occasionally overlaps with 4Q**219**, thus permitting the filling in of two gaps. The remaining four 4Q Jub manuscripts are once again so fragmentary that no translation is possible. 4Q**221** consists of thirty-seven tiny fragments, covering small identified portions of Jub. XXI, 22 to XXXIX, 9. The six fragments of 4Q**222** echo Jub. XXV, 9–12; XXVII, 6–7 and XLIX, 5(?) and the badly worn papyrus manuscripts of 4Q**223–4**, where identifiable, reflect Jub. XXXII, 18 to XLI, 10.

Remains of three Hebrew manuscripts (4Q**225–7**) have preserved a writing akin to Jubilees or representing a discrepant version of it. In either case, 'Pseudo-Jubilees', the title chosen by the editors, is no doubt a misnomer. Palaeographically, 4Q**225** is dated to the turn of the era; 4Q**226** to the second half, and 4Q**227** to the final decades, of the first century BCE. Of the three fragments, the first and the third are very damaged, but substantial parts of fragment 2 are extant. The author recounts the sacrifice of Isaac with details which differ from the Genesis story and display close parallels to the post-biblical representation of the Akedah or, Binding of Isaac, anticipating features known from the Palestinian Targums (Ps. Jonathan and Neofiti on Gen. xxii, 10 in col. II.4; Ps. Jon. on Gen. xxii, 11, and Pirqe de-Rabbi Eliezer 105c on the same passage in col. II.1). The presence of angels at the sacrifice is repeatedly attested in the Targums. 4Q**225** provides the earliest (pre-Christian) evidence for the rabbinic story of Isaac's voluntary self-sacrifice which is thought to have supplied a model for the formulation by New Testament writers of the teaching on the sacrificial death of Jesus. Cf. G. Vermes, *Scripture and Tradition in Judaism* (Brill, 1961), 193–227. Cf. also G. Vermes, 'New Light on the Akedah from 4Q**225**', *JJS* 47 (1996), 140–46.

4Q**226** or psJub[b] is made up of fourteen fragments, half of them unidentifiable. The first six mention Egypt, the wilderness, Joshua's crossing (of the Jordan) and the land of Canaan. Fr. 7, the largest, returns to the aftermath of the sacrifice of Isaac and furnishes a text closely resembling 4Q**225** 2, ii. The badly damaged fr. 2 of 4Q**227** is centred on the figure of Enoch, instructed by angels, testifying against his contemporaries and the angels called Watchers. Allusion is made to his writing activity, including astronomical knowledge which was to stop the righteous from going astray. The two small fragments of 4Q**227** contain references to Moses and to Enoch (cf. Jub. IV, 17–24) and 4Q**228** consists of one large and eight tiny fragments, one of which (fr. 1, l. 9) displays the phrase, 'For thus is written in the Divisions [of times]'. Hence it is identified as an unknown work quoting the Book of Jubilees.

For the *editio princeps* of 4Q**216–28**, see J. C. VanderKam and J. T. Milik, *DJD*, XIII, 1–185.

## 4Q220

[And do not go a]fter idols and after ... and do not [eat any bl]ood of a wild or domestic animal or a bird which [flies] ... [And if you sac]rifice a peace-offering as a burnt-offering, sacrifice it for (God's) pleasure. And sprinkle their blood on the alt[ar. And all] the flesh of the burnt-offering you will offer on the alt[ar] together with the flour mixed with [o]i[l] of its meal-offering. ... [You] will offer all on the altar as a fire-offering, a pleasant odour before God. [And the ... of peace-offerin]gs you will offer on the fire which is on the altar. And the fat [which is on ... and] the [f]at which is on the innets and the kidneys [and] the [fat which is on them (cf. 4Q219)] ... and the lobes of the liver with the kidneys you shall remove [and you shall offer (cf. 4Q219)] ... with its offering and its libation ...

... [on] that [day] and on the morrow ...

## 4Q225 (4Q226)

**I** ... that so[ul] will be cut off ... [he dwel]t in Haran for twenty [yea]rs (not seventeen as in Jub. xii, 12, 28). [And A]braham [said] to God, 'Behold, I am naked (childless) and it is Eli[ezer, the son] of my household, who will inherit from me.' *vacat*

[And the Lo]rd [said] to A[b]raham, 'Lift up (your eyes) and gaze at the stars and see and count the sand that is on the sea shore and the dust of the earth as to whether [they can be coun]ted. And Abraham bel[ieved in] G[o]d and this was reckoned for him as righteousness. And a son was born af[ter]wards [to Abraha]m and he called his name Isaac. And the prince Ma[s]temah came [to G]od and accused Abraham on account of Isaac. And [G]od said [to Abra]ham, 'Take your son, Isaac, [your] only (son) [whom] you [love] and offer him to me as a burnt-offering on one of the ... mountains [which I will tell] you.' And he ro[se and he we]n[t] from the wells to Mo[unt Moriah] ... And Ab[raham] lifted up **II** his [ey]es [and behold there was] a fire. And he placed [the wood on Isaac, his son, and they went together]. And Isaac said to Abraham, [his father, 'Behold there is the fire and the wood, but where is the lamb] for the burnt-offering?' And Abraham said to [Isaac, his son, 'God will provide a lamb] for himself.' Isaac said to his father, 'T[ie me well' (PsJ,N on xxii, 10)

... the holy angels standing and weeping over [the altar] ... his sons from the earth. And the angels of M[astemah] ... were rejoicing and saying, 'Now he (Isaac) will be destroyed ... [we shall see] whether he will be found weak and whether A[braham] will be found unfaithful [to God.' And he (God) called,] 'Abraham, Abraham.' And he said. 'Here am I.' And he said, 'N[ow I know that (it was a lie that?)] he (Abraham) will no longer be loving.' And the Lord God blessed Is[aac all the days of his life (cf. 4Q**226** 7.3) and he begot] Jacob, and Jacob begot Levi (in the) [third (cf. 4Q**226** 7.4)] genera[tion. And all] the days of Abraham and Isaac and Jacob and Lev[i were ... years]. And the prince Ma[s]temah was bound [and the holy angels (cf. 4Q**226** 7.6)] ... the prince Ma[s]temah, and Belial listened to ...

## 4Q**226**, fr. 7

Abraham was found faithful to [G]o[d and] ... for pleasure. And the Lord blessed [Isaac all the days] of his life. And he begot J[acob and Jacob begot] Levi in the thi[rd] generation. [And all the days] of Abraham, Isaac and Ja[cob and Levi were ... years]. And the holy angels ... Fast here ...

## 4Q**227**

... [E]noch after they/we taught him ... six jubilees of years ... [e]arth towards the children of men. And he testified against all of them ... and against the Watchers. And he wrote all the ... heaven and the ways of its host and the [mon]ths ... [th]at the ri[ghteous] may not stray ...

# The Prayer of Enosh and Enoch

## (4Q369)

Ten fragments, including three large ones, have survived of a manuscript written with Herodian characters, apparently recording prayers. There is no direct reference to the persons in whose mouths the words are placed, but the context seems to indicate that the first fragment is associated with Enosh, who according to Gen. iv, 26, was the first human to call on the name of the Lord. Since line 10 in fr. 1, col. I mentions Enoch, the editors have made a reasonable inference in attributing to him the prayer in fr. 1, col. II. Fr. 2 alludes to a war against the lands without any context and frs. 3–9 contain nothing intelligible.

For full details cf. H. Attridge and J. Strugnell, *DJD*, XIII, 353–62.

### Fr. 1

**I** ... all their fe[stiv]als in their ages ... of Thy marvels, for from old times Thou hast ordered for them his judgement until the age of determined judgement through all everlasting commandments. *vacat* [Kenan was from the fourth generation and Mehalalel] his [son] was the fifth generation. [ ... and Jared his son. And Jared his son was sixth generation and Enoch] his son. Enoch was seven[th] generation ...

**II** Thou hast imparted Thy name as his inheritance to make Thy name dwell there ... She (Jerusalem?) is the glory of the territory of Thy land and on her [Thou] ... Thine eyes on her and Thy glory shall be seen there for ... to his seed for their generations an everlasting possession and al[l] ... Thy good judgements Thou hast purified him for ... in everlasting light and Thou hast established him for Thee as a first-bor[n] son ... like his, as a prince and ruler for all the territory of Thy land ... [the] c[rown] of the heavens and the glory of the clouds Thou hast set [on him] ... and the angel of Thy peace in his congregation and ... [given] him righteous rules like a father to his son ... Thy soul clings to his love ... for through them Thou [hast established] Thy glory ...

# The Book of Enoch

## (4Q201–2, 204–12)

# and the Book of Giants

## (1Q23–4, 2Q26, 4Q203, 530–33, 6Q8)

Various Qumran caves have yielded for the first time the original Aramaic text of one of the major Pseudepigrapha, the Book of Enoch, which was previously known from a complete Ethiopic translation and from a Greek rendering of chapters I–XXXII and XCVII–CI, CVI–CVII, as well as from a number of Greek quotations from chapters VI to XV transmitted by the Byzantine writer George Syncellus. Qumran Cave 4 has yielded seven copies of the writing attested by, but not strictly identical to, the Ethiopic, and four further copies of the related Book of Giants, dependent on chapter VI of Enoch, fragments of which have been discovered also in 1Q and 6Q. Palaeographically, all of them are dated to between 200 BCE and the end of the pre-Christian era. The differences they display concern partly the structure of the work, e.g. the astronomical section is more developed in parts than the text from which the Ethiopic Enoch LXXII–LXXXII was made, while the Book of Parables (chaps. XXXVII–LXXI) with its Son of Man speculation is completely lacking at Qumran. There are also noticeable stylistic divergences which may be attributable more to the absence of a unified text of Enoch than to the work of the Ethiopic translator.

The bulk of the fragments is too small for translation. It would be wholly meaningless to render into English the retranslation into Aramaic of the Ethiopic and/or Greek text supplied by their editor, J. T. Milik, who has conjecturally filled the many gaps in the Qumran manuscripts. The passages included in this volume are those which make sense in themselves. The first excerpt (4Q201) supplies the Aramaic names of the twenty chiefs of the fallen angels. The second (4Q204) relates the miraculous birth of Noah, which should be compared to the parallel accounts in the Genesis Apocryphon col. II and in the fragments of the Book of Noah (1Q19, 4Q534). The third and fourth extracts (4Q206) testify to a recension noticeably different from the corresponding Ethiopic version. The fifth (4Q209), the Astronomical Book, is – as has been noted – considerably longer than the Ethiopic. As for the Book of Giants, they are missing from the

Ethiopic, though it circulated in Manichaean, Talmudic and medieval Jewish literature (cf. J. T. Milik, 298–339).

For a preliminary edition, see J. T. Milik, *The Aramaic Books of Enoch of Qumran Cave 4*, Oxford, 1976. Cf. F. García Martínez, *Qumran and Apocalyptic* (Contribution of the Aramaic Enoch Fragments to our understanding of the Books of Enoch), Leiden, 1992, 45–115. For the Ethiopic, see M. A. Knibb with the assistance of Edward Ullendorff, *The Ethiopic Book of Enoch* I–II, Oxford, 1978. For a general introduction, cf. *HJP* III, 250–68.

## 4Q201 1=En$^{a}$ (1En. vi, 7–vii, 1)

**III**

... And these are [the names of their chiefs]. Shemihazah wh[o was their head, Arataqo]ph (cf. En$^{b}$), his second; Ramta[el, third] to him; Kokabe[l, fourth to him; ... el, fif]th to him; Ramae[l, sixth to him;] Daniel, seve[nth to him; Ziqiel (cf. En$^{a,c}$), eigh]th to him; Baraqel, nin[th to him]; Asael, tenth [to him; Hermoni (En$^{c}$), eleven]th to him; Matarel, twelf[th to him]; Ananel, thirteenth [to him]; Stawel, [fo]urteenth to him; Shamshi[el, fif]teenth to him; Shahriel, [s]ixteenth to him; Tummiel, seven[teenth to him]; Turiel, eighteenth to him; Yomiel, nine[teenth] to him; [Yehaddiel, twentieth to him.] These are the chiefs of the chiefs of tens. The[se and] their [ch]iefs [took for themselves] wives from all those whom they chose and [they began (En$^{b}$) to go in to them and defile themselves with them and to teach them sorcery and (magic (En$^{b}$)] ... And they became pregnant by them and bo[re giants] ...

## 4Q204=En$^{c}$ (1En. cvi, 19–cvii, 2)

**II**

... [And af]ter [these shall co]me a greater wicked[ness than that which will have been accomplished] in [their] d[ays. For] I know the mysteries [of the Lord which] the holy ones have explained and showed me and which I read [in] the heavenly [tablets. And I saw written in them that one generation after another will do evil in this way, and evil will last [until] generations of righteousness [arise] and evil and wickedness shall end and violence shall cease from the earth and un[til good shall come on the earth] on them. *vacat* And now, please go to your [son], Lamech, [and explain to him] that this child is his son in truth and without lie ...

## **4Q206** 1 xxii (1En. xxii, 3–7)

... [the soul] of all the sons of man. And behold, these are the pits for their prison. They were made thus until the day of their judgement, until the final day of the great judgement which will be imposed on them. *vacat* There I saw the spirit of a dead man complaining and his moaning rising to heaven and crying and complaining ...

## **4Q206** 1 xxvi (1En. xxxii, 1–3)

... [And beyond] those [mountains] roughly northwards, on their eastern side, I was shown other mountains n]ard, [full of] excellent [n]ard, and pepperwort, and cinnamon, [and pe]pper. *vacat* And from there I was led [to the east of all those mountains, far from them, to the east of the earth and I was taken over the Red S[ea] and greatly distanced myself from it and crossed over the darkness far from it. And I passed to the Paradise of righteousness ...

## The Astronomical Book of Enoch
## **4Q209** 7 (cf. 1En. lxxiii, 1–lxxiv, 90)

... **II** ... [And it (the moon) shines in the remainder of this night with three seventh (parts); and it grows during this day to four sevenths and a half; and then it sets and enters (its gate) and is covered for the remainder] of this day to [two] sevenths [and a half. And in the night of the twent]y [fourth it is covered four sevenths and a half and [four sevenths and a half] are cut off from its light. [And th]en it comes out (from its gate) and shines in the remainder of this night two sevenths and a half. And it grows [in] this [d]ay five sevenths and then it sets and enters (its gate) and is covered for the remainder of this day [two] sev[enths. *vacat* And in the night, on the twenty-fifth, it is covered five sevenths, (and) five sevenths are cut off from its light. And then it comes out and shines for the remainder of this night two sevenths. And it grows in this day to five sevenths and a half. And then it sets [and] enters the second gate and is covered for the remainder of this day one seventh and a half. *vacat* And in the night of the twenty-sixth it is covered five sevenths and a half and five sevenths and a half are cut off from its light.

And then it comes out of the second gate and shines for the remainder of this night one seventh and a half. And it grows in this day six sevenths. And then it sets and enters and is covered for the remainder of this day one seventh. *vacat* And in the night of the [twe]nty-seventh it is covered six sevenths and [six] sev[enths] are cut off from its light. [And then it comes out and shines for the remain]der of this night one seventh. And it grows in this day [six sevenths and a half. And then it sets and enters] ...

**III** [and shines in the night of the eight]h four [s]ev[enths]. And then it sets and enters. In this night the sun comple[tes] the passage through all the sections (?) of the first gate and recommences to go in and come out through its sections. [And then the moon] sets and enters. And it darkens during the remainder of this night three sevenths. And it grows in this day four sevenths and [a half. And then it comes out and dominates in the remainder of this day two sevenths and a h[al]f. *vacat* And it shines in the night of the ninth four [sevenths] and a half. And then it sets and enters. In this night the sun recommences to go through [its] section[s and to set] in them. And then [the mo]on sets and enters the fifth gate and darkens in the remainder of this night [two] sevenths and a half. And it grows in th[is] day five [sevenths] and in it the ligh[t] equals five sevenths ... equals in full. [And then it comes out] of the [f]if[th] gate ...

## The Book of Giants
## 4Q530

... the giants searched (for one) to explain to th[em the dream ... to Enoch], the interpreter scribe that he might interpret to us the dream *vacat*

Then Ohiyah, his brother, confessed and said before the giants, I, too, saw a wonder in my dream this night. Behold the Ruler of heaven descended to earth ...

... Here is the end of the dream. [Then all the giants ... ] were terrified [and] c[al]led Mahawai and he came to th[em]. And the giants as[ked him] and sent him to Enoch, [the interprete]r [scribe] and said to him, Go ... listen to his voice and say to him that he should expl[ain to you and] inter[p]ret the dreams ...

## 4Q531

... [I showed myself] mighty and by the power of my strong arm and by the vigour of my might [I have ... a]ll flesh and have made war on them. But I ... not ... [fi]nd ... to strengthen (me), for my adversaries dwell [in heave]n (?) and they abide in the holy places and [I will] not ... [for the]y are more powerful than I. *vacat*

... of wild beasts came and a wild horde cried ... And Ohiyah spoke to him thus. My dream has depressed [me] ... [the sl]eep of my eyes on seeing [the dr]eam. For I know that ...

# An Admonition Associated with the Flood

## (4Q370, 4Q185)

4Q370 is a rewritten account of the Noah story based on Genesis vi–ix; two fragmentary columns have survived, only the first of which is suitable for translation. Palaeographically, it is said to be late Hasmonaean, i.e. from the first half of the first century BCE, but the composition itself is pre-Qumran. Both the Tetragram and the divine name *'el* are used. The badly damaged column II switches from narrative to ethics and exhortation. Part of it can be reconstructed with the help of 4Q185.

For the *editio princeps* of 4Q370, see Carol A. Newsom, *DJD*, XIX, 85–97.

### 4Q370 (4Q185)

**I** [And] He crowned the mountains with pro[duce] and poured food on them, and he satisfied every soul with good fruit. 'Whoever does my will, let him eat and be satisfied', says [the Lo]rd. 'And let them bless [my holy] name. But, behold, they have done what is wicked in my eyes,' said the Lord. They rebelled (?) against God through their ac[tio]ns, and the Lord judged them according to all their ways, and according to the thoughts of the inclination of their [evil] hearts. And He thundered at them in [His] power, and all the foundations of the earth [tr]embled, [and the wa]ters burst forth from the abysses. All the windows of heaven opened, and all the abyss[es] overflowed [with] mighty waters. And the windows of heaven [emptied out] rain and He destroyed them by the Flood ... Therefore everything [perished] on the dry land; and men, beasts, birds and winged creatures [died]. And the g[iant]s did not escape ... And God made [a sign ... and] set His bow [in the cloud] that He might remember the covenant ... [that there might no more be on earth] waters of flood ... and that the mass of waters [might not be let loo]se ...

**II** (combined with **4Q185**) ... their wickedness when they know (how to distinguish) bet[ween good and evil ... For behold], they sprout forth [like grass], but a shadow are their days o[n the earth. And now pray hearken to me, my people; heed me, O you Simple for from everlasting] to everlasting he will have mercy ... the might of the Lord. Remember the mira[cles which he did in Egypt and his marvels in the land of Ham. Let your heart shake] because of fear of him, and [your] soul will rejoice according to his good graces ...

# The Ages of the Creation
## (4Q180)

A badly worn manuscript from Cave 4 (4Q180) has been published under this title by J. M. Allegro. Its decipherment and interpretation have been further improved by J. Strugnell and J. T. Milik. The only section yielding coherent sense deals with the myth of the fallen angels and the daughters of men, which is based on Genesis vi, 1–4, and fully developed in 1 Enoch. If Milik's reconstruction is correct, the work presents human history as divided into seventy weeks of years (70 × 7 years), the first ten of which cover the period from Noah to Abraham. The manuscript is claimed by Strugnell to belong to the first century CE. See J. M. Allegro and A. A. Anderson, *DJD*, V, 77–9; cf. J. Strugnell, *RQ* 7 (1970,) 252–4; J. T. Milik, *JJS* 23 (1972), 110–24.

Interpretation concerning the ages made by God, all the ages for the accomplishment [of all the events, past] and future. Before ever He created them, He determined the works of ... age by age. And it was engraved on [heavenly] tablets ... the ages of their domination. This is the order of the cre[ation of man from Noah to Abraham, un]til he begot Isaac; ten [weeks (of years)].

And the interpretation concerns Azazel and the angels who [came to the daughters of men; and] they bore to them giants. And concerning Azazel ... and iniquity, and to cause them all to inherit wickedness ... judgements and judgement of the congregation.

# The Book of Noah

## (1Q**19**, 1Q**19**bis, 4Q**534–6**, 6Q**8**,**19**)

Several groups of small fragments from Qumran Caves 1, 4 and 6 appear to be the relics of a Book of Noah mentioned in Jubilees x, 13 and xxi, 10 and reproduced in an abbreviated form in Aramaic in the Genesis Apocryphon 11ff. and in Enoch cvi (cf. J. T. Milik, *DJD*, I, 84–6; 152; *DJD*, III, 116–19, 136). 1Q**19** and **19**$^{\text{bis}}$ are remains of a Hebrew version; 6Q**8** and **19** belong to an Aramaic Noah narrative.

1Q**19**, 6Q**8** and 1QapGen deal with the miraculous birth of Noah, as does also 4Q**534**, which was originally understood by scholars as describing the birth of the Royal Messiah (cf. p. 357 above). In 1Q**19** fr. 1 the subject is the miserable state of mankind before the Flood; frs. 3 and 13–14 (as well as 6Q**8**) allude to the birth of Noah, accompanied by miraculous signs.

For a preliminary edition of 4Q**534**, see J. Starcky, 'Un texte messianique araméen de la grotte 4 de Qumrân', in *Mémorial du Cinquantenaire 1914–1964 de l'École des Langues Orientales Anciennes de l'Institut Catholique de Paris* (Paris, 1964), 51–66; for 4Q**536**, see K. Beyer, *Die aramäischen Texte vom Toten Meer. Ergänzungsband* (Göttingen, 1994), 126–7.

### 1Q**19**, fr. 3

... [to] his father. And when Lamech (Noah's father) saw the ... [the child made] the rooms of the house [shine] like the rays of the sun ... to frighten the ...

### Frs. 13–14

... for the glory of your splendour ... for the glory of God ... [will be] lifted in glorious majesty ... will be glorified amidst [the sons of h]eaven and ...

## 4Q534

**I** … of his hand: two … a birthmark. And the hair will be red. And there will be lentils on … and small birthmarks on his thigh. [And after t]wo years he will know (how to distinguish) one thing from another. In his youth, he will be like … [like a m]an who knows nothing until the time when he knows the three Books.

And then he will acquire wisdom and learn und[erstanding] … vision to come to him on his knees. And with his father and his ancestors … life and old age. Counsel and prudence will be with him, and he will know the secrets of man. His wisdom will reach all the peoples, and he will know the secrets of all the living. And all their designs against him will come to nothing, and (his) rule over all the living will be great. His designs [will succeed], for he is the Elect of God. His birth and the breath of his spirit … and his designs shall be for ever …

## 4Q536

… Blessed be he! … and he will not die in the days of wickedness. Woe to you, O fool, for your mouth will deceive you by … (incurring) the death penalty. Who will write these words of mine in a book that will not decay, and keep this word of mine [in a scroll (?) which will not] fade away? Behold … and the pleasure of the wicked will cease for ever …

# Words of the Archangel Michael

## (4Q529, 6Q23)

In this poorly preserved Aramaic fragment the speaker, Michael, addresses the angels in general and the archangel Gabriel in line 4 about a vision. The subject is unclear, but since he refers to the sons of Noah, Shem and Ham, and to the construction of a city filled with wickedness, it is possible that the author alludes to the building of the tower of Babel.

For a preliminary edition, see K. Beyer, *Die aramäischen Texte vom Toten Meer. Ergänzungsband* (Göttingen, 1994), 127–8.

**I** Words of the book which Michael spoke to the angels ... He said: I found there divisions of fire [and I saw there] nine mountains: two to the eas[t, and two to the west, and two to the north and two to the so]uth. I saw there the angel Gabriel ... [Then] I showed him the vision. And he said to me: ... in the books of my Master, the Lord of the world, it is written: Behold, ... [between] the sons of Ham and the sons of Shem. And behold my Master, the Lord of the world ... when they ... the tear from ... And behold a city was built to the name of my Master, [the Lord of the world, and there] everything that is evil will be done before my Master, the Lor[d of the world ... And my Master, the Lord of the world, will remember his creation ... [and] my Master, the Lord of the world, [will be] merciful to him and to him ... the man will be in the far-away province ... he, and he will say to him: Behold this ... for me silver and gold ... And he will say: ... [and] the righteous man ...

# The Testament of Levi (i)

## (4Q213–14, 1Q21)

Among the numerous small fragments representing the Aramaic Testament of Levi, a damaged portion of two columns of **4Q213a** contains parts of a prayer of Levi. As the best part of the same text survives also in Greek in a manuscript from Mt Athos (Monastery of Koutloumous, Codex 39, dating to the eleventh century), it is possible to complete most of the missing sections of this prayer. Other small Aramaic fragments of the Testament of Levi, mentioning among other matters the 'kingdom of the high priesthood', are listed under **1Q21** (cf. J. T. Milik, *DJD*, I, 87–91.

For a preliminary edition of **4Q213a**, see M. E. Stone and J. C. Greenfield, 'The Prayer of Levi', *JBL* 112 (1993), 247–66; cf. also K. Beyer, *Die aramäischen Texte vom Toten Meer* (Göttingen, 1984), 183–4. For the Testament of Levi in the Testaments of the Twelve Patriarchs, see *HJP* III, 767–81.

### 4Q213a

**I** [Then] I raised [my eyes and face] towards heaven [and opened my mouth and spoke. And I stretched out] the fingers of my hands and my hands ... for truth towards the holy ones and I prayed and said, Lord, Thou [knowest every heart, and T]hou alone knowest all the thoughts of [the heart. And now my sons are with me. Give me all] the paths of truth, and distance [from me, O Lord, the evil spirit and the e[vil inclination] and fornication and repulse [pride from me. And give me counsel, and w]isdom and knowledge and might so as to do that which pleases Thee] and find favour before Thee [and give thanks for Thy dealings with me, O Lord, in order to do] that which is splendid and good before Thee. [And let n]o adversary have dominion over me [to lead me astray from Thy way. And be merciful t]o me, O Lord, and draw me near that I may be Thy **II** [servant and minister well to Thee] ...

[Thou], O Lord, [hast blessed Abraham my father and Sarah my mother and Thou didst say that Thou wouldst give them a righ[teous] seed [which would be blessed for ever. Listen therefore to] the prayer of [Thy] ser[vant Le]vi ... [to practise] righteous judgement for a[ll eternity ... [And do not remove] the son of Thy servant from be[fore Thee] ... Then I went along ... to my father Jacob. And when ... from Abel-Mayin. Then I lay down and dwelled ...

# Testaments of the Patriarchs: the Testament of Levi (ii)

## (4Q537–41)

An Aramaic work of which numerous fragments are extant in Cave 4 resembles the Testament of Levi from among the Testaments of the Twelve Patriarchs. The central figure is Levi, but the testament is probably that of his father, Jacob. Hence **4Q537** is referred to also as the Jacob Apocryphon (4QAJa ar). Palaeographically, its proposed date is the end of the second century BCE. The text alludes to an eschatological priestly figure (recalling the pseudepigraphic Testament of Levi XVII–XVIII) whose mission encounters opposition due to the wickedness of the men of his generation. **4Q537** probably represents Jacob's dream at Bethel. Minute fragments (**4Q538–9**), unsuitable for translation, are conjecturally identified as belonging to a Testament of Judah and a Testament of Joseph by J. T. Milik, 'Écrits pré-esséniens de Qumrân: d'Hénoch à Amram', in *Qumrân: Sa piété, sa théologie et son milieu*, ed. M. Delcor (Gembloux, 1978), 91–106.

For a preliminary edition of the Testament of Levi, see Emile Puech, 'Fragments d'un apocryphe de Lévi et le personnage eschatologique 4QTestLévi$^{c-d(?)}$ et 4QAJ$^{a}$', in *MQC*, II, 449–501.

## 4Q537

... and how will be the buildin[g] ... [and how will the prie]sts be dressed and [their hands] be purified, and how will they] offer sacrifices on the altar, and ho[w] ... [on the who]le earth they shall eat part of their sacrifices [and how they shall drink the water] which will come out of the city under the walls ...

## 4Q541, fr. 9

... w]isdom. He will atone for all the sons of his generation and will be sent to all the sons of his [peo]ple. His word is like a word of heaven, and his teaching is according to the will of God. His eternal sun will shine, and his fire will spring forth to all the ends of the earth, and will shine over darkness. The darkness will pass away [fr]om the earth, and deep darkness from the dry land. They will utter many words against him and many [ ... ]s. They will invent stories about him, and will utter everything dishonourable against him. Evil will overturn his generation [because ... ] will be, and because lies and violence will (fill) his existence, and the people will go astray in his days and will become perplexed.

## 4Q541, fr. 24 ii

... Search and seek and know what is sought by the dove and do not smite one who is exhausted with consumption and troubles ... And you will make a joyous name for your father and a tried foundation for your brothers. And you will see and rejoice in the everlasting light ...

# The Testament of Naphtali

## (4Q215)

Two reasonably intact fragments, dating to the turn of the era, represent the Hebrew text of the Testament of Naphtali, with occasional similarities to the version which survives in Greek. Fr. 1 partly overlaps with TNaphtali 1, 9, 11–12, without being identical with it. Fr. 2 depicts the blessedness of the end of time and may belong to a separate sectarian document.

For a preliminary study, see M. E. Stone, 'Testament of Naphtali', *JJS* 47 (1996), 311–21.

### Fr. 1

... with the sisters(?) of the father of Bilhah, ... Deborah, who suckled Reb[eccah]. And he went into captivity and Laban sent out and rescued him and gave him Hannah, one of [his] maidservants. [And she conceived and bore] a first [daughter], Zilphah, and gave her the name Zilphah after the name of the town whe[re] he was taken into captivity. She conceived and bore Bilhah, my mother, and Hannah called her name Bilhah, for when she was born, [she was in] a hurry to suck. And she said, 'What? Is my daughter in a hurry?' And she called her again Bilhah. *vacat* When my father Jacob came to Laban, fleeing from Esau, his brother, and after ... the father of Bilhah my mother. And Laban led Hannah, the mother of my mother and her two daughters, [and he gave one to Lea]h and one to Rachel. And when it came to pass that Rachel did not bear sons, ... [Jaco]b my father, and he gave him Bilhah my mother and she bore Dan [my] brother ...

## Fr. 2

... and the stressful constraint and the ordeal of the pit and they shall be refined by them to become the elect of righteousness ... because of His loving-kindness. For the age of wickedness is complete and all injustice has [passed] away. [For] the time of righteousness has come and the earth is full with knowledge and the praise of God. In the day[s of] ... has come the age of peace and the precepts of truth and the testimony of righteousness to make one understand the ways of God and the might of His deeds for ever and ever. Every ... shall bless Him and every man shall prostrate himself before Him. [And they shall have] one [he]art. For He knows their recompense before they were created and had assigned the service of righteousness as their boundaries ... in their generations. For the dominion of righteousness/of goodness has come and He shall raise up the throne of the [kingdom], and intelligence is greatly exalted; prudence and soundness are tried by [His] h[o]ly desi[gn] ...

# A Joseph Apocryphon

## (4Q371–2)

4Q372 is a very fragmentary Hebrew narrative, the script of which is dated to the second half of the first century BCE. Another earlier (mid-Hasmonaean) manuscript (4Q371), even worse for wear, partly overlaps with the present text, as has been shown by the official editor, Eileen Schuller. She sees in 4Q372 a relic of an anti-Samaritan polemical work, antedating the destruction of the Temple on Mount Gerizim under John Hyrcanus I (134–104 BCE). No sectarian features are apparent in this writing. It should be noted that the joint reference to the tribes of Levi, Judah and Benjamin (line 14) is paralleled in 1QM 1, 2.

For a preliminary study, see Eileen Schuller, '4Q372 1: A Text about Joseph', *RQ* 14 (1989–90), 348–76; M. A. Knibb, 'A Note on 4Q372 and 4Q390', in F. García Martínez, ed., *Scripture and the Scrolls*, 1992, 164–77.

## 4Q372, fr. 1

... the precepts of God. Judah was also with him and he stood at the crossroads to ... to be together with his two brothers. And for all this, Joseph was thrown to un[known] lands, to a strange nation and they (the northern Israelites) were dispersed in the whole world. All their mountains were horrified on their account ... and fools ... They made for themselves a high place on an elevated mountain to excite the jealousy of Israel. They spoke wor[ds of ... ] of the sons of Jacob and caused disgust with the words of their mouth, blaspheming against the Tent of Zion. They spoke [words of falsehood and all the] words of lies to enrage Levi, Judah and Benjamin by their words. And for all this, Joseph [was put] into the hands of strangers to consume his strength and break his bones until the time of his end ... cried to the mighty God that He should save him from their hands. He said, 'My Father and my God, do not abandon me to the hands of the nations. Execute judgement for me so that the humble and the poor may not perish. Thou hast no need of any nation or people to help Thee. [Thy] fing[er] is greater and more powerful than anything in the world. For Thou optest for the truth, and in Thy hand there is no violence whatever. Also Thy mercies are many and Thy loving-kindness is great for all those who seek Thee. They are stronger than I and all my brothers who have joined me' . . .

## Fr. 3

. . . the Lord has opened my mouth
and the words of my tongue are from Him
and they speak to me to proclaim . . .
. . . His mercies.
He will not give His precepts to another nation,
nor will He crown them for every stranger,
for . . .
. . . of Abraham which He made with Jacob,
that they should be His people for all eternity.
. . .
destruction [for I]srael
to exterminate them by the hand of the nations.
All the plagues in the inheritan[ce of] . . .
and He will seek their blood from their hands.
And He inflicted dread on Midian,
. . . one – he was Zimri the son of Salu (Num. xxv, 14) –
and the five kings of Midian were killed . . .

# The Testament of Qahat

## (4Q542)

The Testament of Qahat is an Aramaic work of which two columns, one complete and one damaged, have survived. It is a typical example of moralizing death-bed literature, similar to the Testaments of the Twelve Patriarchs, but characterized, like the Testaments of Levi and Amram, by its priestly perspective. The script has been palaeographically dated to the end of the second century BCE, but the carbon 14 test, performed in 1990, places it considerably earlier, possibly to 388–353 BCE, or more probably to 303–235 BCE. It is not a sectarian composition. Only the undamaged part of the text is translated here.

Two further small fragments have survived without providing anything continuous and meaningful. Fr. 2 alludes to darkness and light, and fr. 3 mentions precious stones extant in large numbers apparently on account of *zenuta* (fornication, whoredom).

For a preliminary study, see Emile Puech, 'Le Testament de Qahat en araméen de la grotte 4 (4QTQahat)', *RQ* 15 (1991–2), 23–54.

... **I** and the God of gods for all eternity. And He will shine light on you and will let you know His great Name. And you will know Him, that He is the God of eternity, and the Lord of all the deeds, and the Ruler of all, dealing with them according to His good pleasure. And He will make for you rejoicing and for your sons joy for the generations of truth, for ever. Now, my sons, be careful with the heritage that is handed over to you, which your fathers have given you. Do not give your heritage to strangers, and your inheritance to knaves so that you become humiliated and foolish in their eyes and they despise you, for, although sojourners among you, they will be your chiefs. So hold to the word of Jacob, your father, and seize the laws of Abraham and the righteousness of Levi and mine. And be holy and pure of all fornication in the community. And hold the truth and walk straight, and not with a double heart, but with a pure heart and a true and good spirit. And you will give me a good name among you, and a rejoicing to Levi, and joy to Jacob, delight to Isaac, and glory to Abraham, because you will keep and walk (in) the herit[age] which your fathers will have left you: truth and righteousness and uprightness and perfection and pur[ity and ho]liness and the priesthood according to all that you have been commanded (?), and according to all that **II** I will have taught you in truth from now until all [the age] ... ... every word of truth will come upon yo[u ... eternal blessing will reside on you and will be[come for you] ... stay for all the eternal generations and will no more ... from your correction and you will establish yourselves to pronounce judgement ov[er ... ] and to see the faults of all the sinners of the ages ... [to be cast] into the fire and the oceans and into all the cavities for ... in the generations of truth. And all the sons of wickedne[ss ... ] And now Amram, my son, I instruct you ... and your sons to their sons. I instruct [you ... ] and they have given to Levi my father, and Levi my father g[ave (it/them) to me ... all my books in testimony that through them you should beware ... [and that there should be] for you through them much merit when you walk in conformity with them. *vacat*

# The Testament of Amram

## (4Q543–8)

An Aramaic document surviving in five or six (?) fragmentary copies from Cave 4 contains an admonition by Amram, the father of Moses, to his children. The context is that of the Book of Exodus, but the visions and teachings are the author's free compositions. Amram's age at his death (137 years) is borrowed from Exod. vi, 20, but its dating to the 152nd year of the captivity reflects the tradition according to which the Israelites remained in Egypt, not for 430 years (Exod. xii, 40), nor 400 years (Gen. xv, 13), but 210 years. Cf. J. Heinemann, '210 Years of Egyptian Exile', *JJS* 22 (1971), 19–30.

In the gravely damaged text of the vision, Amram sees the chief Angel of Darkness, Melkiresha‘, already mentioned in the *Curses of Belial* and the *Curses of Melkiresha‘* (pp. 379–80). He also addresses the leader of the Army of Light, whose name has disappeared in one of the many lacunae. But it is highly probable that one of his 'three names' is Melchizedek, as appears from the reading of the Melchizedek document from Cave 11 (p. 500 above). See J. T. Milik, '4Q visions de Amram et une citation d'Origène', *RB* 79 (1972), 77–97; *DSSU*, 151–6.

### 4Q545 (=4Q543, fr. 1)

**I** Copy of the book of the words of the vision of Amram, son of Kehat, son of Levi, al[l that] he explained to his sons and enjoined on them on the day of [his] death, in his one-hundred-and-thirty-seventh year, which was the year of his death, [in] the one-hundred-and-fifty-second year of Israel's exile in Egypt ... to call Uzziel, his youngest brother, and he ma[rried] to him Miriam, [his] daughter, and said (to her), 'You are thirty years old.' And he gave a banquet lasting seven days. And he ate and drank and made merry during the banquet. Then, when the days of the banquet were completed, he sent to call Aaron, his son, and he was ... years old ...

## 4Q544, fr. 1

(I saw Watchers) in my vision, a dream vision, and behold two (of them) argued about me and said ... and they were engaged in a great quarrel concerning me. I asked them: 'You, what are you ... thus ... [about me?'] They answered and [said to me: 'We have been made m]asters and rule over all the sons of men.' And they said to me: 'Which of us do you [choose ...']

I raised my eyes and saw one of them. His looks were frightening [like those of a vi]per, and his [ga]rm[en]ts were multi-coloured and he was extremely dark ...

And afterwards I looked and behold ... by his appearance and his face was like that of an adder, and he was covered with ... together, and his eyes ...

## Fr. 2

... this [Watcher]: 'Who is he?' He said to me: 'This Wa[tcher] ... [and his three names are ... ] and Melkiresha'.' ...

And I said: 'My Lord, what ...' [And he said to me] ... [and all his paths are dark]ness, and all his work is darkness, and he is ... in darkness ... you see. And he rules over all darkness and I [rule over all light] ...

... [the order] of the Most High as far as 'the Lands' (beyond the Ocean). I rule over all Light, and over al[l that is God's], and I rule over the men of His grace and p[eace. And I] rule [over all the Sons of Lig]ht.'

... And I asked and said to him: 'What are [your names?'] ... [He answered and sa]id to me: '[My] three names are ...'

## 4Q548

... I an[nou]nce (this) to you [and al]so I will indeed inform y[ou ... For all the Sons of Light] will shine, [and all the Sons] of Darkness will be dark. [For all the Sons of Light] ... and by all their knowledge they will ... and the Sons of Darkness will be burnt ... For all folly and wicked[ness are dar]k, and all [pea]ce and truth are brigh[t. For all the

Sons of Light g]o towards the light, towards [eternal] jo[y and rej]oicin[g], and all the Sons of Dar[kness go towards death] and perdition ... The people shall have brightness ... and they will cause them to live ...

And now to you, Amram my son, [I] enjo[in] ... and [to] your [son]s, and to their sons I enjoin ..., and they gave them to Levi my father, and Levi my father [gave them] to me ... and my books in testimony that they might be warned by them ...

# The Words of Moses

## (1Q22)

Fragments of four very mutilated columns of a manuscript from Cave 1 have been skilfully reconstructed by J. T. Milik (*DJD*, I, 91–7). They form a farewell discourse of Moses which takes its inspiration from various passages of Deuteronomy and is chiefly remarkable for the emphasis laid on the appointment of special teachers, or interpreters, of the Law (Levites and Priests). The last two columns are so mutilated as to be untranslatable. Another document, consisting of two insignificant fragments, tentatively entitled 'A Moses Apocryphon' (2Q21) and including a prayer attributed to Moses, has been published by J. T. Milik (*DJD*, III, 79–81).

**I** [God spoke] to Moses in the [fortieth] year after [the children of] Israel had come [out of the land of] Egypt, in the eleventh month, on the first day of the month, saying:

'[Gather together] all the congregation and go up to [Mount Nebo] and stand [there], you and Eleazar son of Aaron. Inter[pret to the heads] of family of the Levites and to all the [Priests], and proclaim to the children of Israel the words of the law which I proclaimed [to you] on Mount Sinai. Proclaim care[fully] into their ears all that I [require] of them. And [call] heaven and [earth to witness against] them; for they will not love what I have commanded [them to do], neither [they] nor their children, [during all] the days they shall [live upon the earth].

[For] I say that they will abandon [Me, and will choose the abominations of the nations,] their horrors [and their idols. They will serve] false gods which shall be for them a snare and a pitfall. [They will sin against the] holy [days], and against the Sabbath and the Covenant, [and against the commandments] which I command you to keep this day.

[Therefore I will smite] them with a mighty [blow] in the midst of the land [which they] cross the Jordan [to possess]. And when all the curses come upon them and catch up with them to destroy them and [blot] them out, then shall they know that the truth has been [fulfilled] with regard to them.'

Then Moses called Eleazar son of [Aaron] and Joshua [son of Nun and said to them,] 'Speak [all these words to the people] ... :

[Be still,] **II** O Israel, and hear! This [day shall you become the people] of God, your [God. You shall keep My laws] and My testimonies [and My commandments which I] command you to [keep this] day. [And when you] cross the [Jordan so that I may give] you great [and good cities], and houses filled with all [pleasant things, and vines and olives] which [you have not planted, and] wells which you have not dug, [beware,] when you have eaten and are full, that your hearts be not lifted up, and that [you do not forget what I have commanded you to do this day. For] it is this that will bring you life and length of [days].'

And Moses [spoke to the children] of Israel [and said to them]:

'[Behold,] forty [years have passed since] the day we came out of the land [of Egypt, and today has God], our God, [uttered these words] from out of His mouth: [all] His [precepts and] all [His] precepts.

'[But how shall I carry] your loads [and burdens and disputes alone]? When I have [established] the Covenant and commanded [the way] in which you shall walk, [appoint wise men whose] work it shall be to expound [to you and your children] all these words of the Law. [Watch carefully] for your own sakes [that you keep them, lest] the wrath [of your God] kindle and burn against you, and He stop the heavens above from shedding rain [upon you], and [the water beneath the earth from] giving you [harvest].'

And Moses [spoke further] to the children of Israel. 'Behold the commandments [which God has] commanded you to keep ...'

# Sermon on the Exodus and the Conquest of Canaan

## (4Q374)

Only one of the sixteen surviving fragments of a writing, palaeographically dated to the last third of the first century BCE, which deals with the exodus from Egypt and the occupation of Canaan, is large enough to provide an intelligible account. The speaker remains anonymous but may conceivably be Joshua.

For the *editio princeps*, see Carol Newsom, *DJD*, XIX, 99–110.

### Fr. 2

**II** ... And the nations rose up in anger ... in their actions and in the uncleanness of the deeds of ... and there was no remnant for [them] and none who escaped and for their posterity ...

And he made a plantation for u[s] his elect in the land that is the most desirable of all the lands ... And he made him as a god over the mighty and as a cause of dread for Pharaoh ... they melted and their heart trembled and their entrails dissolved. And he had mercy ... And when he made his face shine on them for healing, they strengthened [their] heart once more and knowledge ... None having known you, they melted and trembled ...

# A Moses Apocryphon$^{a}$
## (4Q375)

In a style imitating the Pentateuch, and recalling the Sayings of Moses from Cave 1 (1Q22), 4Q375, fr. 1, col. i lays down instructions regarding the treatment of a person who claims to be a prophet. Should he exhort people to commit apostasy, he is to be executed. However, his tribe may come to his rescue and lodge an appeal with the anointed priest in the city of the sanctuary. The very damaged col. ii contains a sacrificial ritual employing the terminology of the Day of Atonement from Lev. xvi.

For the *editio princeps*, see John Strugnell, *DJD*, XIX, 111–19.

### Fr. 1

**I** ... [You will do all that] your God has commanded you from the mouth of the prophet. You will keep [all] these [pre]cepts and you will return to the Lord your God with all [your heart and al]l your soul. And your God will desist from the wrath of his great anger [to save you] from your misery. And the prophet who will arise and speak defection in your midst, turning you away from your God, shall be put to death. But if the tribe from which he originates stands up (for him) and says, 'Let him not be put to death, for he is righteous; he is a [trus]tworthy prophet', you, your elders and your judges will come with that tribe [t]o the place which your God will choose within one of your tribes (to appear) before [the] anointed priest on whose head the oil of anointing has been poured.

# A Moses Apocryphon[b]

## (4Q376, 1Q29)

This mid-first-century BCE text, which partly overlaps with 1Q29, is a reworking of Exod. xxviii, 9–12, dealing with the two engraved stones set in the shoulder pieces of the high priest's liturgical garment (the ephod). Another fragment introduces the secular head of the community, the 'Prince of the whole congregation' (cf. 1QM v,1; CD vii, 20, etc.) in his military role, confronting the enemies of Israel or attacking one of their towns.

For the *editio princeps*, see John Strugnell, *DJD*, XIX, 121–36.

### Fr. 1

**II** they shall shed light on you. And he shall go out with it with tongues of fire. The left-hand stone on his left side will show itself to the eyes of all the assembly until the priest has completed his speech. And afterwards the ... has gone up ... And you shall keep and d[o al]l [that] he shall speak to you. And the prophe[t] ... ... preaches rebellion ...

**III** according to all this judgement. And if the Prince of the whole congregation shall be in the camp and ... his enemy and Israel is with him, or if they go against a city to besiege it or any matter which ... to the Prince ... the distant field ...

# A Moses Apocryphon$^{c}$
## (4Q377)

This is part of an apocryphal account introducing an elder called Eliab, cursing the Jews who fail to observe the Law mediated by Moses during the latter's stay with God on the mountain.

For a preliminary edition, see *UDSS* III, 164–6.

**II** ... they will understand the precepts of Moses. And Eliab(?) answered and said: Hearken, congregation of the Lord, and listen, all the assembly! ... to al[l His] wor[ds] and judgements. Cursed be the man who does not stand by, keep and prac[tise] all the comman]dments of the L[ord (issued) by the mouth of Moses, His anointed, and follow the Lord, the God of our fathers, He who commanded us from the mountains of Sinai. And He spoke to the people of Israel face to face as a man speaks to his friend ... He made us look at a consuming fire from under the heaven. And on the earth, He stood on the mountain to make it known that there is no god beside Him and no rock like Him. [And all] the assembly ... and trembling seized them because of the glory of God and the marvellous voices ... and they stood at a distance. And Moses the man of God (was) with God in the cloud and the cloud covered him. For ... when he was hallowed and out of His mouth he spoke like an angel. For who is a messenger like him? ... a man of grace who was not created from everlasting to everlasting ...

# Pseudo-Moses$^{e}$

## (4Q390)

In this apocryphal narrative, purporting to be a divine speech, no doubt addressed to Moses (hence the suggested title), the future of Israel is foretold in a framework of jubilees. Consequently, the kinship with the Book of Jubilees is undeniable. The account is also reminiscent of the opening paragraph of the Damascus Document. Two largish fragments form the basis of the translation. The script is considered Herodian, but on the basis of historical allusions contained in other fragments pertaining to the same composition, Devorah Dimant tentatively suggests a second century BCE date, not later than the rule of John Hyrcanus I (134–104 BCE).

For a preliminary study, see Devorah Dimant, 'New Light from Qumran on the Jewish Pseudepigrapha' in *MQC* II, 405–47; M. A. Knibb, 'Note on 4Q**372** and 4Q**390**', in F. García Martínez, *Scripture and the Scrolls*, Leiden, 1992, 164–77.

### Fr. 1

into the hands of the sons of Aa[ron] ... seventy years. The sons of Aaron will rule over them and they will not walk [in] My [wa]ys which I command you (Moses?) that you may testify against them. They will also do what is evil in My eyes just as Israel did in the earlier times of her kingdom, apart from those who will first come up from the land of their captivity to build the Sanctuary. I will speak in their midst, and will send them a commandment, and they will understand all that they and their fathers have forsaken. And from the completion of that generation in the seventh jubilee of the devastation of the land they will forget the precept, and the appointed time, and the sabbath, and the Covenant. They will break all of them and will do what is evil in My eyes. I will hide My face from them and will give them into the hands of their enemies, and will deliver [them] to the sword. But I will cause a remnant to remain so that they will not be des[tr]oyed [by My fury] and by My hiding My face from them. The angels of Per[se]cution will rule over them ... [an]d [they] will come [back] and will do [what is] evil in [My] eyes. They will walk in the stub[bornness of their heart] ...

## Fr. 2

... and the dominion of Belial will be on them to hand them over to the sword for a week of yea[rs ... And in] that jubilee, they will break all My precepts and all My commandments which I will have commanded th[em ... by the hand of] My servants the prophets, [and they will ... ] to contend one with another for seventy years from the day of breaking the [Law and the] Covenant which they will break. I will give them [into the hand of the an]gels of Persecution, and they will rule over them, and they will not know and understand that I am furious with them because of their transgressions [by which they will have for]saken Me and will have done that which is evil in My eyes, and will have chosen that which I do not desire, striving for wealth and gain [and ... , on]e stealing that which is his fellow's, and one oppressing another. They will pollute My Sanctuary and profane My sabbaths ...

# A Moses (or David) Apocryphon

## (4Q**373**, 2Q**22**)

Three small Cave 4 fragments which partly overlap with 2Q**22** published by M. Baillet (*DJD*, III, 81–2) represent a historical narrative of an unnamed speaker in the first person, and with the single actual name of Og, king of Bashan (cf. Num. xxi, 33–5; Deut. iii, 4–5, 11). Baillet and the editor of 4Q**373**, Eileen Schuller, wonder whether the narrator is David and the subject is his fight with Goliath, a theory based on a few verbal similarities to 1 Samuel xvii, which cannot, however, easily account for the mention of Og, apart from his height (see Deut. iii,11) which was comparable to that of the giant Goliath (cf. 1 Sam. xvii, 4). S. Talmon, on the other hand, has argued that the topic of the fragment is more likely to be the defeat of Og by Moses, richly elaborated by Targum, Midrash and Talmud (cf. L. Ginzberg, *The Legends of the Jews* I, 160; III, 340–47; V, n. 181; VI, 667–8, 684–700). On the whole, the second alternative seems slightly preferable.

For a preliminary edition, see Eileen Schuller, 'A Preliminary Study of 4Q**373** and Some Related (?) Fragments', *MQC* II, 515–30. The 'related' (?) fragments are 4Q**372** 2 with a mention of Bashan (whose king was Og) and 4Q**371** 3 which may possibly refer to the Philistines, Goliath's nation.

### 4Q**373** 1–2 (2Q**22**)

... all his servants Og ... his height was ... and a half cubits and two [cubits were his breadth ... ] a spear like a cedar tree ... a shield like a tower. The nimble-footed ... he who removed them seven stadia. [I] did not stand ... and I did not change. The Lord our God broke him. I prepared wounding slings together with bows and not ... for war to conquer fortified cities and to rout ...

# Divine Plan for the Conquest of the Holy Land

## (4Q522, 5Q9)

Two mutilated columns, as well as several further small fragments, of a narrative appear to describe the future conquest and/or division of the Holy Land. It appears to be related to the extremely fragmentary 5Q9, published by J. T. Milik in *DJD*, III, 179–80, which mentions the name of Joshua. Col. i of 4Q522 consists of a list of localities, of which a number appear in Joshua xv–xxi (e.g. Beer Sheba, Bealoth, Keilah, Adullam, etc.) and Judges i (Ashkelon, Kitron). Col. ii predicts the conquest of Zion by David and the building of the Temple. In col. ii, 4 and 7 God is referred to in the third person, but in lines 9–10 he seems to be the speaker.

For a preliminary treatment of 4Q522, see *DSSU*, 89–92.

**II** . . . For behold a son is born to Jesse, son of Perez, son of Ju[dah] . . . [He is to take] the Rock of Zion and from there he is to possess the Amorites . . . to build a house for the Lord, the God of Israel. Gold and silver . . . cedars and cypress trees will he br[ing from] Lebanon to build it. And the sons of . . . and David. The Lor[d] will make (him) dwell in security . . . [The Lord of h]eaven will reside with him [for] ever. But now the Amorites are there and the Canaan[ites] . . . inhabitant whom I consider guilty, whom I have not sought . . . from you. And the Shilonite and the . . . I have made him a slave . . . And now . . . to a distance from . . . Eleazar . . .

# A Joshua Apocryphon (i) or Psalms of Joshua

## (4Q378–9)

Usually designated by the misnomer 'Psalms of Joshua', this badly mutilated composition represents a rewritten account of the story of Joshua. 4Q378, written in Herodian formal script, consists of twenty-seven mostly tiny fragments, while the late Hasmonaean 4Q379 comprises forty-one. The majority of the fragments are too small for meaningful translation. According to Carol Newsom, the overall form of the composition is a farewell speech by Joshua. It contains admonitions, curses and prayers (e.g. 'prayer for our sins', 4Q378 6 i, l.4), a prayer listing the twelve tribes of Israel – Levi, Reuben, Gad, and Dan are legible, 4Q379 1, songs ('songs of praise', 4Q379 22 ii, 7, and a praise mentioning Abraham, Isaac, Jacob, Moses, Eleazar and Ithamar, 4Q379 17). The biblical text used recalls the Septuagint and the Samaritan Pentateuch. The numbering of the fragments appears to be arbitrary, as it does not correspond to the sequence of the biblical story. 4Q379 22 ii is quoted in 4QTestimonia (4Q175).

For a preliminary study, see Carol Newsom, 'The "Psalms of Joshua" from Qumran Cave 4', *JJS* 39 (1988), 56–73; Timothy H. Lim, 'The "Psalms of Joshua" (4Q379, fr. 22, col. 2): A Reconsideration of its Text', *JJS* 44 (1993), 309–12.

## 4Q378 14

... And the children [of Israel] wept [for Moses in the plains of Moab (Deut. xxxiv, 8) [by the Jordan at] Jericho at Bethjeshimoth [as far as Abel-shittim (Num. xxxiii, 48–9) for thirty days and (then) the days of weeping and] mourning for Moses were ended (Deut. xxxiv, 8). And the children of Israel ... [the covenant wh]ich the Lord made for ...

... [Thy [dr]ead and fear ...

## 4Q378 11

... for the Lord yo[ur God] ... [to es]tablish his words which he spoke ... [the oath] which he swore to Abraham to give [him] a good and broad [land], a land of brooks of water, [of fountains and springs, flowing forth in val]leys and hills, a land of wheat and barley, [of vines and fig trees and pomegranates, a land of olive trees and] honey (Deut. viii, 7–8). For [this is] a land flowing with milk and honey; [ ... a land] who[se sto]nes are iron and out of whose hi[ll]s [you can dig] copper (Deut. viii, 9) ...

## 4Q378 22 i

... Moses, O my God. And he did not annihilate them because of their sins ... thy people by the hand of Joshua, minister of thy servant Moses thy ... by the hand of Moses(?) to Joshua for the sake of thy people ... [the covenant] which thou hast made with Abraham

... loving-kindness to thousands

## 4Q379 12

... they [cr]ossed (the Jordan) on dry grounds (cf. Josh. iv, 22) in [the fi]rst month of the forty-f[irst] year of their exodus from the lan[d] of Egypt (cf. Josh. iv, 19). That was a jubilee year at the beginning of their entry into the land of Canaan. And the Jordan overflows its banks from the f[our]th (?) month until the wheat harvest ...

## 4Q379 22 ii (combined with 4Q175, lines 21–30)

Blessed be the Lord, the God of I[srael] ...

When Josh[ua] fini[sh]ed off[ering prai]se in [his] thanksgivings, [he said]: C[ursed be the m]an who rebui[l]ds [this cit]y! [May he lay its foundations on [his] first-born, and [s]et its gate on [his y]oungest son (Josh. vi, 26). Behold, an [accur]sed [man of Belial] [has risen] to be[com]e a fowler's net to his people and a cause of destruction to all his neighbour[s]. And [his brother] arose [and ruled in li]es, both of them being instruments of violence. They have rebuilt [th]is [city] and have set up for it a wall and towers to make it a stronghold of ungodliness in Israel and a horror in Ephraim and in Judah and a great evil among the children of Jacob. [And they have com]mitted an abomination in the land and a great blasphemy and sh[ed] blood] like wa[ters on the ramparts of the daughter] of Zion and in the precincts of Jerusalem ...

# A Joshua Apocryphon (ii)

(Masada 1039–211)

Two fragments detached from an apocryphal account of the end of the Book of Joshua are thought by their editor, S. Talmon, to have originated at Qumran. The composition belongs to the genre of 'rewritten Bible' and testifies to a freedom in retelling scriptural stories. The handwriting places the manuscript towards the turn of the era.

For a preliminary edition, see Shemaryahu Talmon, 'Fragments of a Joshua Apocryphon – Masada 1039–211 (final photo 5254)', *JJS* 47 (1996), 128–39.

## Fr. A

... they were afraid ... [they were praising] the name of the Most High for they saw th[at ... God] was fighting for His people against their enemies [and they were not afraid ... ] because of them for God was with them and blessed them and sa[ve]d them. [And whatever] he said about them happened to them and no word [fe]ll to the ground, and He multiplied their [seed greatly].

# The Samuel Apocryphon
## (4Q160)

Fragments of an account of the story of Samuel from Cave 4 (4Q160), said to pertain to the second century BCE, were published by J. M. Allegro and A. A. Anderson, *DJD*, V, 9–11. They follow the first book of Samuel and include a narrative passage, a dialogue between Samuel and Eli, a prayer and an autobiographical discourse.

### Fr. 1

[F]or [I have s]worn [to] the house [of Eli that the iniquity of the house of Eli relating to sacrifices and offerings shall never be expiated. And] Samue[l] heard the words of the Lord ... [and] Samuel lay down before Eli. And he rose and opened the ga[tes of the house of the Lord. And Samuel was afraid] to report to Eli the oracle. Answering, Eli said [to Samuel: Samuel, my son, let] me know the vision of God. Do not [hide it from me, pray! May God do to you thus and may He add to it] if you hide from me anything of the words that He spoke to you. [And] Samuel [reported all and hid nothing] ...

### Frs. 3–5

... Thy servant. I have not restrained my strength until this (moment), for ... [let them] be gathered, O my God, to Thy people and be a help to it and raise it ... [and deliver] their [fe]e[t] from muddy clay [and] establish for them a rock from of old, for Thy praise [is over all the peo]ples. Thy people shall take refuge [in Thy house] ... Amid the rage of the enemies of Thy people, Thou shalt verify Thy glory [and] over the lands and seas ... and Thy fear is over [al]l ... and kingdom. And all the peoples of Thy lands shall know [that] Thou hast created them … and the multitudes shall understand that this is Thy people … Thy holy ones whom Thou hast sanctified.

# A Paraphrase on Kings

## (4Q382)

154 papyrus fragments, palaeographically dated to the first half of the first century BCE, belong to a kind of paraphrase of the Books of Kings as various personal names (Jezebel, Ahab, Obadiah, Elijah, Elisha) clearly indicate. Only one fragment is extensive enough to allow intelligible translation. An unidentified speaker recounts events pertaining to the history of Israel in the form of an address to God. Cf. S. Olyan, *DJD*, XIII, 363–416.

### Fr. 104

... from Thy word and to rely on Thy covenant and their heart be ... to sanctify Him/it ... hands so that they might be Thine, and Thou theirs and Thou be righteous ... For Thou wilt be a giver of an inheritance ... and lord over them and Thou wilt be a father to them and not ... Thou hast forsaken them to the hand of their kings and hast made them stumble among the people[s] ... not ... Thy life. Didst Thou give them [the Law?] by the hand of Moses ... Thy judgements and lifting the iniquity of Thy people to the heights ... Thy patience and the multitude [of mercies?] ...

# An Elisha Apocryphon

## (4Q481A)

Three minute fragments reproduce the Hebrew text of 2 Kings ii, 14–16 with paraphrastic supplements. Only fr. 2 can be partly reconstructed and translated. The opening words '[And] Elisha went up' are without biblical parallel.

For a preliminary edition, see J. Trebolle, 'Histoire du texte des livres historiques et histoire de la composition et de la rédaction deutéronomistes avec une publication préliminaire de 4Q481A', *Suppl. VT* LXI, *Congress Volume Paris 1992*, ed. J. A. Emerton, Leiden, 1995, 330–34.

### Fr. 2

... [And] Elisha went up. [When the sons of the prophets who were over at Jericho] saw [him over against them, they said, The spirit of Elijah rests over Elish]a. And they came to meet Elisha, [and bowed to the ground before him. And they said to him, Behold now, there are with your servants] fifty [strong] men; [pray, let them go, and seek your master; it may be that the spirit of the Lord has caught him up and cast him upon some mou]nta[in or into some valley].

# A Zedekiah Apocryphon

## (4Q470)

Three badly damaged fragments of an early Herodian manuscript speak in favourable terms of the last Judaean king Zedekiah. He is depicted as conversing with the archangel Michael who promises to make a covenant with him. The Bible is less kind towards this evil-doer (2 Kgs xxiv, 19, etc.), but 4Q470 prefigures Josephus, who praises Zedekiah's 'goodness and sense of justice' (*Antiquities* X, 120), and the Talmud (bShab. 149b; bSanh. 103a; bArak. 17a).

For the *editio princeps* of 4Q470, see Erik Larson, Lawrence H. Schiffman and John Strugnell, *DJD*, XIX, 235–44.

### Fr. 1

... Michael ... Zedekiah [shall en]ter into a covenant on [th]at day ... to practise and to cause all the Torah to be practised. [At] that time M[ich]ael shall say to Zedekiah. ... I will make with you [a cov]e[nant] before the assembly [to p]ractise ...

### Fr. 3

... their [c]ry towards heaven ... [to] restore them to health and help them by the spirit of [his] m[ight] ...

... and by the pillar of fire [many] times ... And Moses wrote when he spoke according to a[ll] ... Kadesh B[arnea] ...

# A Historico-theological Narrative based on Genesis and Exodus

## (4Q462–4)

Palaeographically dated to the mid-first century BCE, the two joined fragments of 4Q**462** represent the only meaningful part of a historical narrative told from a theological point of view. Both the beginning and the end of each of the nineteen lines are missing, but the general tenor of the story can be guessed: after repeated oppression and humiliation, God is to remember Jerusalem. The Tetragram is twice replaced by four dots as in the Community Rule (1QS) VIII, 15. There are six further small fragments.

For the edition of 4Q**462**, see M. S. Smith, *DJD*, XIX, 195–209. 4Q**463**, or Narrative D, contains only a few broken lines, starting with 'And God remembered his word which he said', followed by the quotation of Lev. xxvi, 44. Apparently the fragment has vanished and the text edited by M. Smith (ibid., 211–14) is based on J. Strugnell's transcription. The poorly preserved 4Q**464** (ibid., 215–32) refers to Abraham, Isaac, Jacob and apparently to Joseph. Fr. 3 ii, 7 contains the word *pesher* (interpretation), suggesting that an exegetical comment followed in the lacuna.

## 4Q**462**

... [Shem and] Ham and Japhet ... for Jacob ... for Israe[l] ... ... And he will give (the land?) to the multitude as a heritage. **....** (=the Lord) who rules ... his glory which ... will fill the waters and the earth ... They seized his people. The light was with them and [darkness] was on us ...

The [per]iod of darkness [passed away] and the period of light came and they were to rule for ever. Therefore he will say, ... to Israel, for in our midst was the people of the beloved, (of) Jac[ob] ... And they slaved, and they were safeguarded and they cried to **....** (=the Lord) ... And behold they were handed over to Egypt for the second time in the period of the kingship, and [they] were safeguarded ... [and the inha]bitants of Philistia and Egypt will become a booty and a ruin. And he will make it stand ...

... the fierceness of her face will be changed to brightness and her soiled garments [to] ... And he will remember Jerusalem ...

# Tobit

## (4Q196–200)

Prior to the Qumran finds, the Book of Tobit existed among the Apocrypha in two, a long and a short, Greek recensions and in various secondary ancient versions. Cave 4 has revealed remains of four Aramaic (4Q**196–9**) and one Hebrew (4Q**200**) manuscripts, of which two scrolls, the papyrus Tob[a] (**196**) and the leather Tob[b] (**197**), have yielded copious extracts. They all basically represent the Semitic original from which the longer Greek recension, attested by the fourth-century CE Codex Sinaiticus, and the Old Latin version were made.

Tob[a], Tob[c] and Tob[d] are palaeographically dated to the first century BCE and Tob[b], as well as the Hebrew Tob[e], to the turn of the era (30 BCE–20 CE). The translation of a composite Aramaic text is followed separately by that of the Hebrew fragments. The Aramaic and the Hebrew overlap only in Tob. xiv, 1–2. Of the two, the Aramaic, represented by older and more numerous manuscripts, is likely to be the original language of the composition.

The following illustrate some of the differences between the Aramaic (A), and the Greek (G) Tobit:

i, 22 (A) He was the son of my brother, of my father's house and of my family.
(G) He was my brother's son and of my kindred.

ii, 1 (A) On the day of the Festival of Weeks
(G) At the feast of Pentecost which is the sacred festival of the seven weeks.

vi, 6 (A) Also he salted the rest for the journey. Both of them were going together
(G) and left part of it salted. And they journeyed both of them together

vi, 12 (A) and her father loves her
(G) and her father is an honourable man

xiv, 2 (A) He was fifty-eight years old when he lost his sight and afterward he lived fifty-four years

(G) He was sixty-two years old when he was maimed in his eyes (Sinaiticus)
He was fifty-eight years old when he lost his sight and after eight years he regained it (Vaticanus)

For the *editio princeps* of 4Q**196–200**, see J. A. Fitzmyer, *DJD*, XIX, 1–79.

## 4Q**196**, Fr. 2
## Tob. i, 19–ii, 2

...

(i, 19) [one o]f the men of Niniveh, and he informed the kin[g about me, th]at I was bury[ing them (the murdered Jews) and] I hid myself. When I learned that he knew of me [and sought to kil]l [me], I was frightened and fled. (20) ... [al]l that I possessed and nothing was left to me ... a[part from Hanna]h my wife and Tobiah my son. (21) But not f[orty] days passed [before two of] his (Sennacherib's) [sons killed him] and they fled to the mountains of Ararat. Then [Esarhaddo]n became king [and he] appointed Ahikar, the son of my brother Anael, over all the ac[count]s [of the kingdom. And he was in ch]arge of all the royal treasury accounts. (22) And Ahikar intervened for me ... [And Ahi]kar my brother was the cupbearer, the guardian of the signet ring and the accountant under Sennacherib, king of Assyria, and Esarhaddon reappointed him. Now he was the son of my brother, of my father's house and of my family.

(ii, 1) And in the days of [ki]ng Esarhaddon, when I returned to my home and Hannah my wife and Tobiah my son were restored to me, on the day of the Festival of Wee[ks, I] had an excellent meal and I reclined to [ea]t. (2) And they put a table in front of me and I saw the many delicacies placed on it, [and I] said [to Tob]iah my son, My son, go and bring all those among our brot[hers whom you] can find ... my son, go and bring (them). Let him be brought (here) and eat [together] with me. And behold I ...

## Fr. 6
## Tob. iii, 9–15

(iii, 9) ... [Go] after them (after her seven deceased husbands) and let us n[ot] see a son [or a daughter] of yours [ever.] (10) ... [and she cried and went] up to the upper room of [her father's] house ... [may I not hear] again [such a dis]graceful thing in my life. And ... (11) against ... [May] thy holy [and glo]rious name [be blessed] for all et[ernity. And] may [all thy works] bless [thee]. (12) [And now I have turned] my face [to]wards thee and I have [li]fted my eyes. (13) Say that I should depart from [the earth] ... (14) [Thou, O Lord, kn]owest that I myself am pure o[f a]ll impurity [of man.

(15) And I have not de]filed [my] nam[e and the name of] my [father] in all the land of our captivity. I am [the on]ly child [of my father [and] he has no other son who would inherit from him. Nei[ther has he a brother or a relation [for whom I] should [keep my]self, or a son f[or whom I should b]e a wife. Already seve[n] of my [husbands] have per[ished] ...

## 4Q**197**, fr. 4 + 4Q**196**, fr. 13 Tob. v, 19–vi, 12 [vi, 6–8]

**I** (v, 19) ... Let my son not cleave [to mone]y and like ... (21) [And] he said to her, Do not be afraid. My son will go in peace ... [in pea]ce. Do not be afraid. And do not worry about him, my sister. (22) ... [his] jour[ney] ...

(vi, 1) Once again [she fell silen]t and cried no more. *vacat*

(2) ... [and the ang]el was with him and ... [and they went] together. And [night] came [and they reached] the Tigris. (3) And the young man went down ... [and] a big [fis]h [jumped] out of [the water to swall]ow the foot of the young man ... (4) ... [C]atch the f[ish! And] the young man [se]ized [the fish and brou]ght it to the dry land. And [the angel] s[aid to him, (5) Cut] it open and remove [its gall and] its [heart and its liver. Keep] them, but [throw away its] entrails. [Its gall], its [heart] and its liver are [medicament]. (6) And [he cut out its gall and] its [h]eart and [its liver ... the f]ish and he ate (it). Also {he sa[lted the re]st for the journey} (4Q**196**). Both of them were going [to]gether [until they rea]ched Media. *vacat* (7) {The young man [as]ked the ang[el]} (4Q**196**) [and s]aid to him, Azariah my brother, what kind of medicament is in the heart of the fish and in its liv[er and in its gall? (8) [If you] smoke it in front of a man or a woman smitten by a demon or an [evil] spirit ... they will [n]ever come by again. (9) The gall is for applying to the ey[es of a man] ... white film and he will recover. (10) And when they entered Media and he was already ne[aring Ecbatana, (11) Raphael said to the young] man, T[o]biah my brother. And he said to him, Here am I. And he said

to him, In the house [of Raguel we shall stay. And the m]an is from the house of our father. And he has a beautiful daughter . . . (12) [And] he has [no other (children) except Sarah a]l[one]. And you are re[lat]ed to her . . . And this young girl]

## 4Q**197**, fr. 4 + 4Q**196**, fr. 14 i
## Tob. vi, 12–18 [vi, 13–18]

**II** [wise, stron]g and very beautiful, and her father loves [her] . . . her father. And a just decision has been made concerning you (13) to m[arry her] . . . You will speak about this young girl tonight. You will retain her and take her to be your wif[e . . . And {when we return from [Rages]} (4Q**196**), we shall make for her] a wedding-feast. And I know that Raguel cannot refuse her to you for he knows . . . and to marry his daughter than any (other) ma[n. For h]e kno[ws] that if he were to give her to [another] man [this would be against the law in the Book] of Moses. And now [let us speak about] this [young] gir[l] tonight and let us retain her [for you . . . (14) Then Tobiah replied and said to Rapha]el, Azariah my brother, I have heard . . . (that she had seven husbands who all died) when they went in to her. . . . (15) And now I am [af]raid of this demon who {loves her . . . the demon kills them} (4Q**196**)

. . . (bring) my [fath]er and my mother [to the grave . . . They have] no other son [to bury them.] (16) {[Do you not remember the com]mands of your father} (4Q**196**) who commanded you . . . {[And no]w listen to me, my brother. Do not (be afraid of) this [de]mon and marry (her) {tonight . . . (17) [t]ake from the heart [of the fish] . . . (18) . . . the demon [will sme]ll it and will [flee]} (4Q**196**)

. . . (When you go in) [to be wi]th her, ri[se up] . . . [And do n]ot be afraid [for] she has been allotted to you and for you . . . you will save [her. And] I suppose that you will have [children by her and . . . And when] Tobiah [h]eard the words of Raphae[l that she was her sister and of

## 4Q**197**, fr. 4 + 4Q**196**, fr. 14 ii Tob. vi, 18–vii, 10 [vi, 18–vii, 6]

**III** [the house of his father's family] he fell in love with her [gr]eatly and his heart (was much attached) to her. (vii, 1) And when they entered Ecbat[ana], Tobiạh [said] to him, Aza[riah my brother, l[ead] me straight away to the house of Raguel our brother. He led him there and [they] went [to the house] of Raguel and [they] found Rague[l s]itting in front of the gate of his home. And first they greeted him and he said to them, In peace you have come. Enter in peace, my brothers. And he brought them into his house. (2) Then he said to Edna his wife, How much this young man resembles Tobit, the son of my uncle. (3) And Edna asked them and said to them, Where are you from, my brothers? and they said to her, From among the children of Naphtali [who] are captives in Niniveh. And she said to them, Do you know Tobit our brother? And they said to her, We know him. Is he well? (5) And they said, He is wel[l. And To]biah [sa]id, He is my father. (6) And Raguel jumped to his feet and kissed him and crie[d]. (7) ... A blessing on [you my son. You are the s[on] of a just man ... the neck of Tobiah ... (9) he slaugh[tered] a ram from the flock ... to eat and to drink. ... my sister. (10) And [Raguel] heard ...

## 4Q197, fr. 5
## Tob. viii, 21–ix, 2

(21) ... my son. I am your father and Edna is [your] m[other] ... [Do not be] afraid, my son. *vacat* (ix, 1) [Then Tobiah called Raphael and said to] him, (2) Azariah my brother, take with you from here fo[ur slaves] ... ... [and] you will come to the house of Gab[ae]l and give him the document and take [the money] ...

## 4Q196, fr. 17
## Tob. xiii, 6–12

... [with all]
**II** your heart and [with all] your [s]oul to [do righteousness.
Then [he] will turn to you,
and will no l[onger hide] his [face] from you.
[Give] him [thanks] with all your mouth
and ble[ss the Lord] of righteousness and ex[alt him].
[In the land] of captivity I give him thanks
and I dec[lare] his [m]ight and [his] greatne[ss
before [a people of s]in.
According to your heart

[do] righ[teousness] before him.
[Who] kno[ws if there will be f]orgiveness [for you].
(7) And I exalt my God and] my [so]ul the ki[ng of heaven].
... all the day[s of my life].
... [and let them al]l [pr[aise his greatness.
(8) Let them speak with psalm[s] ...
(9) [Jerusalem] the holy city,
he will [aff]lic[t you] concerning ...
(10) ... [with righ]teousness give thanks ...
... from generation to generation they will give ...
[and his] great name [will be for] everlasting [gene]rations.
(12) Cur[sed] be [a]ll [who] despise (you)
and all who are against [you].
And cursed be al[l who hate] you
and all [who spe]ak [a]gainst you.
Cursed be ...

## 4Q**196**, fr. 18 + 4Q**198**, fr. 1
## Tob. xiii, 12–xiv, 3

...
(18) ... [will] s[a]y, Halle[luiah] ...
[Blessed be for ever] and ever
for in you they will bless [his holy] n[ame] ...

(xiv, 1) [The words of thanksgivings of To]bit [ended] and he died in peace at the a[ge of one hundred and twelve years and he was buried]. (2) [He was] fifty-ei[ght] years [old] ... his [e]yes. He lived a good life and in all ... {[and he gave] alms and continued to fear God and to pr[aise his greatness. (3) And he called Tobiah his son and] his [seven]} (4Q**198**) sons and commanded him and said to [him] ...

## 4Q**200**, fr. 2
## Tob. iv, 3–9

... (4) ... and she carried you in [her] womb ... *vacat* (5) My son, [re]member] God in all your days ... his word. *vacat* [Do] what is true [a]ll the days of [your] l[ife, and do not walk in the way]s of lies. (6) For when you do what is t[rue ... will] be with you. (7) ... My son, with a generous hand [give] alms, and do not hi[de your face from any p]oor. Then [the face of Go]d will not be hid]den [from you. (8) If you have much, [my] son, ... [giv]e al[m]s from it. If you have little, according to the little (you will give). ...

## Fr. 4
## Tob. x, 7–9

[And when] the fourteen days of the [wedding] were completed for them which Raguel had sworn to make for Sarah his daughter, To[b]iah came [to him] and said to him, Send me away (for) I already know that [my father does not believe, n]or does my mother believe that she will see m[e] again. And now I request [y]ou, my father, that you send me away that I may go to my father. Already I have recounted to you how I left them. (8) And Raguel said to Tobiah, My son, remain with me and I will send messengers to Tobit y[o]ur father and the[y] ...

## Fr. 6
## Tob. xii, 20–xiii, 4

... [Record in writing all] this story. And he (Raphael) ascended. (21) ... [and they saw] him [no more]. (22) And they were blessing and extolling God and giving him thanks for] his great d[ee]d and wondered how [an angel of God] had appeared [to them]. (xiii, 1) Then Tobit spoke and wrote a psalm of praise, and s[aid,

Blessed be] the living [God] whose kingdom is for all eternity:
(2) He who [strikes and wh]o is merciful;
He who causes to descend to the nethermost hell,
and he who brings up from the [g]rea[t] abyss.
And who is there who can escape from his hand?
(3) Give him thanks, children of Isra[el, in front of the nations],
you who are exiled among them.
(4) Recite there [his greatness and extol him before al]l the living.
For he is your Lord, and he is [your] God
... [for al]l [eternity].

## Fr. 7
## Tob. xiii, 18–xiv, 2

**II** ... (xiv, 1) And [Tobit's words of praise were] completed, [and he di]ed in peace aged [one hundred and twelve years]. He was fifty-eight years old (when he lost) his [s]ight [and] afterward [he lived fifty]-fo[ur years].

# A Jeremiah Apocryphon

## (4Q384–5$^{B}$)

Originally considered as part of an Ezekiel apocryphon, the remains of these two columns, written in a well-imitated biblical Hebrew, have been identified by Devorah Dimant as pertaining to an apocryphal account of the life of Jeremiah in Babylon and in Egypt. The script probably dates to the end of the first century BCE. The related papyrus fragments of **4Q384** (Jeremiah Apocryphon B) are too small for connected translation.

For a preliminary study, see D. Dimant, 'An Apocryphon of Jeremiah from Cave 4 (4Q**385**$^{B}$ = 4Q**385** 16)', in G. J. Brooke, ed., *New Qumran Texts and Studies* (Brill, Leiden, 1994), 11–30. For 4Q**384**, see M. Smith, *DJD*, XIX, 136–52.

**I** *vacat* ... Jeremiah the Prophet [departed] from before the Lord (YHWH) ... [to accompany the] captives who were taken captive from the land of Jerusalem and came [to ... Nebuchadnezzar,] king of Babel, when Nabuzaradan, the chief of the bodyguard, smote ... and took the vessels of the house of God, the priests ... and the sons of Israel and led them to Babel. And Jeremiah the Prophet went ... the river and he commanded them what they were to do in the land of [their] captivity ... [to obey] the voice of Jeremiah in regard to the words which God commanded him ... and they were to keep the covenant of the God of their fathers in the land [of their captivity ... and they were not to d]o as they had done and their kings and priests [and ... and they] profaned [the na]me of God ...

**II** In Tahpanes wh[ich is in the land of Egypt ... ] and they said to him, Inquire [of G]od for us. ... Inquire] for them, Jeremiah, of me, inquire for them of Go[d ... an exclamation and prayer. And Jeremiah lamented ... lamentations ov]er Jerusalem ... *vacat* [And the word of the Lord was addressed to] Jeremiah in the land of Tahpanes which was in the land of

Eg[ypt . . . Go to] the sons of Israel and the sons of Judah and Benjamin [. . . and speak to them saying,] Day by day seek my decrees and ke[ep] my commandments . . . and do not follow] the i[d]ols of the gentiles [after] which wa[lked . . . for] they will not sa[ve y]ou . . . nor . . .

# The New Jerusalem

## (4Q554–5, 5Q15, 1Q32, 2Q24, 4Q232, 11Q18)

Fragments belonging to an Aramaic writing describing the Jerusalem of the eschatological age have been identified in Caves 1 (1Q32), 2 (2Q24), 4 (4Q554–5), 5 (5Q15) and 11 (11Q18). There are also Hebrew fragments listed under 4Q232. They are all inspired by Ezekiel xl–xlviii (cf. also Revelation xxi). Among the edited manuscripts, only the text found in Cave 5, completed by J. T. Milik with the help of two large unpublished parallel fragments from Cave 4, provides an intelligible portion. On palaeographical considerations, 5Q15 is thought to date to around the turn of the era.

The visionary responsible for this work accompanies an angelic 'surveyor' who measures everything in the New Jerusalem, from the size of the blocks of houses, the avenues and the streets, to the detailed dimensions of rooms, stairs and windows.

The dimensions are given in 'reeds', each of which consists of seven 'cubits'. But there seem to have been two cubits in use as ancient Jewish measurements, one approximately 20 inches (521 mm), the other 18 inches (446 mm) long.

The translation is based on Milik's edition and interpretation of 5Q15 in *DJD*, III, 184–93. (For smaller fragments, see Milik, *DJD*, I, 134–5; M. Baillet, *DJD*, III, 84–90; B. Jongeling, 'Publication provisoire d'un fragment provenant de la grotte 11 de Qumrân (11 Q Jér nouv ar)', *JSJ* (1970), 58–64; J. A. Fitzmyer and D. J. Harrington, *A Manual of Palestinian Aramaic Texts*, Rome, 1978, 46–55; K. Beyer, *Die aramäischen Texte vom Toten Meer*, Göttingen, 1984, 214–22; F. García Martínez, *Qumran and Apocalyptic*, 1992, 180–213.)

### 4Q554, fr. 1

**I** ... [And they call this gate Gate of] Simeon ...
... [And they call this gate] Gate of Joseph ...
... [And they call this gate] Gate of Reuben ...

**II** . . .

. . . [And they] c[al]l [the name of] this (one) [Gate] of Naphtali. And from this gate he measured to the [eastern] gate 25 [s]tadia. And they call this gate Gate of Asher. And he measu[red from] this [ga]te to the eastern corner 25 stadia. *vacat* And he led me into the city, and he measured each block of houses for its length and width, fifty-one reeds by fifty-one, in a square a[ll]

## 5Q15

**I** [round] = 357 cubits to each side. A passage surrounds the block of houses, a street gallery, three reeds = 21 cubits, (wide).

[He] then [showed me the di]mensions of [all] the blo[cks of houses. Between each block there is a street], six reeds = 42 cubits, wide. And the width of the avenues running from east to west: two of them are ten reeds = 70 cubits, wide. And the third, that to the [lef]t (i.e. north) of the Temple, measures eighteen reeds = 126 cubits in width. And the wid[th of the streets] running from south [to north: t]wo of [them] have nine reeds and four cubits = 67 cubits, each street.

[And the] mid[dle street passing through the mid]dle of the city, its [width measures] thirt[een] ree[ds] and one cubit = 92 cubits. And all [the streets of the city] are paved with white stone . . . marble and jasper.

[And he showed me the dimensions of the ei]ghty [side-doors]. The wid[th of the] side-doors is two reeds, [= 14 cubits, . . . Each door has tw]o wings of stone. The width of the w[ing] is [one] reed [= 7 cubits.]

And he showed me [the dimensions] of the twelve [entranc]es. The width of their doors are three reeds [= 21] cubits. [Each door has tw]o [wings]. The width of the wing is one reed and a half = 10½ cubits . . . [And beside each door there are two tow]ers, one to [the r]ight and one to the l[ef]t. Its width [is of the same dimension as] its length, [five reeds by five = 35 cubits. The stairs beside] the inside door, on the [righ]t side of the towers, [rise] to the top of the to[wers. Their width is five cubits. The towers and the stairs are five reeds by five and] five cubits = 40 [cubits], on each side of the door.

[And he showed me the dimensions of the doors of the blocks of houses. Their width] is two reeds = 14 cub[its. And the wi]d[th] . . . [And he measured] the wid[th of each th]reshold: two reeds = 14 cubits, [and the lintel: one cubit. And he measured above each] threshold i[ts win]gs.

And he measured beyond the threshold. Its length is [thirteen] cubits [and its width ten cubits.]

[And he] le[d m]e [be]yond the threshold. [And behold] another threshold, and a door next to the inner wall [on the right side, of the same dimensions as the outer door. Its width] is four [cu]bits, [its] height seven [cubits], and it has two wings. And in front of this door there is [an entrance threshold. Its width is one reed] = 7 **II** [cubits]. And the l[eng]th of the entrance is two reeds = 14 cubits, and its height is two reeds = 14 cubits. [And the door] fa[cing the other do]or opening into the block of houses has the same dimensions as the outer door. On the left of this entrance, he showed [me] a round [staircase]. Its length is of the same dimension as its width: two reeds by two = 14 cubits. The do[ors (of the staircase) facing] the other doors are of the same dimensions. And a pillar is inside the staircase around which the stairs ri[se]; its width and d[epth are six cubits by six], a square. And the stairs which rise beside it, their width is four cubits, and they rise in a spiral [to] a height of [two] r[eeds] to [the roof].

And he led me [into] the block of houses, and he showed me the houses there. From one door to the oth[er, there are fifteen: eigh]t on one side as far as the corner, and seven from the corner to the other door. The length of the house[s is three reed]s = 2[1 cubits, and their width], two [reed]s = 14 cubits. Likewise, for all the chambers; [and their height is t]wo [reeds] = 1[4] cu[bit]s, [and their doors are in the middle.] (Their) width is t[w]o reeds = 1[4] cubits. [And he measured the width (of the rooms) in the middle] of the house, and inside the upper floor: four [cubits]. Length and height: one reed = 7 cubits.

[And he showed] me the dimensions of the dining-[halls]. Each has [a length] of ninete[en] cubits [and a width] of twelve [cubits]. Each contains twenty-two couche[s and ele]ven windows of lattice-work (?) above [the couches]. And next to the hall is an outer conduit. [And he measured] the ... of the window: its height, two cubits; [its width: ... cubits;] and its depth is that of the width of the wall. [The height of the inner (aspect of the window) is ... cubits, and that of the outer (aspect), ... cubits.]

[And he measured the l]im[it]s of the ... [Their length] is nineteen [cubits] and [their] width, [twelve cubits] ...

# Second Ezekiel[a]

## (4Q385–91)

An apocryphal work, modelled on the Book of Ezekiel, has survived in five, or possibly six, Cave 4 manuscripts (4Q**385–9** and **390**), as well as in seventy-eight minute papyrus fragments (4Q**391**). It consists of exchanges between God and the prophet, who is several times named. The translated sections (frs. 2–3) include, among others, Ezekiel's vision of the dry bones. The more damaged fr. 5 retells the Chariot passage. On the basis of its script, 4Q**385** is dated to the late Hasmonaean or early Herodian era, i.e. roughly to mid-first century BCE. There is nothing obviously sectarian in the document.

For a preliminary study, see John Strugnell and Devorah Dimant, '4Q Second Ezekiel', *RQ* 13 (1988), 45–58; M. Kister and E. Qimron, 'Observations on 4Q Second Ezekiel (4Q385 2–3)', *RQ* 15 (1991–2), 595–602. For 4Q**391**, unsuitable for translation, see M. Smith, *DJD*, XIX, 152–93.

### 4Q**385**, fr. 2 (=4Q**386**, fr. 1 i)

['And they will know that I am the Lord] who redeem My people, giving them the Covenant.' *vacat* [And I said, 'Lord,] I have seen many from Israel who have loved Thy name and walked [in] the ways [of righteousness (?), and] when will [these] things come to pass? And how will their piety be rewarded?' And the Lord said to me, 'I will make the sons of Israel see and they will know that I am the Lord.' *vacat* [And He said,] 'Son of man, Prophesy concerning the bones, and say, ["Come together, a bone to its bone, and a bit [to its bit." ' And] s[o it came to pas]s. And He said a second time, 'Prophesy, and let sinews come on them, and let skin spread over them above.' [And] s[o it came to pas]s. And He said again, 'Prophesy concerning the four winds of heaven and let the win[ds of heaven] blow [on them and they shall live]. And a great crowd of men shall stand and they will bless the Lord of hosts wh[o revived them.']

And I said, 'Lord, when will these things come to pass?' And the Lord said to me, '... a tree will bend and stand up ...'

## Fr. 3

... instead of my grief [give me joy, and] rejoice my soul. And the days will hasten quickly until [all the sons of] men will say, 'Are not the days quickening so that the sons of Israel may inherit [their land]?' And the Lord said to me, 'I will not tur[n aw]ay your face, Ezekiel. Be[hold,] I will shorten the days and the year[s] ... a little, as you have said to [Me] ... [For] the mouth of the Lord has spoken these (words).' ...

## 4Q**386**, fr. 1

**II** ... and they will know that I am the Lord. *vacat* And He said to me: Consider, son of man, the land of Israel. And I said: I have seen it, Lord, and behold it is dry. When wilt Thou gather them? The Lord said: A son of Belial is planning to oppress my people but I will not permit him. His dominion will not persist; (his) crowd is unclean (?). No seed will survive. From the press no wine will come nor will the bee (?) make any honey. And I will slay the wicked in Memphis and I will bring my sons out of Memphis and turn favourably towards their remnant. As they say: There is peace and (righteousness?); they also say: The earth is established as it was in the days of ... [in the days] of old. Then let us sing [s]ongs ... [in the fo]ur directions of heaven ... devouring fire ...

**III** he will have no mercy on the poor and he will bring them to Babylon. Babylon is like a cup in the hand of the Lord, like muck He will cast it away. ...

# The Prayer of Nabonidus

## (4Q242)

While the Book of Daniel (iv) writes of the miraculous recovery of Nebuchadnezzar after an illness which lasted seven years, this interesting Aramaic composition tells a similar story about the last king of Babylon, Nabonidus. The principal difference between the two is that Nebuchadnezzar was cured by God Himself when he recognized His sovereignty, whereas a Jewish exorcist healed Nabonidus by teaching him the truth and forgiving his sins. J. T. Milik considers the work to be older than Daniel, but a late second or early first-century BCE dating seems to be less adventurous (cf. 'Prière de Nabonide et autres écrits d'un cycle de Daniel', *RB* 63 (1956), 407–11). Cf. also G. Vermes, *Jesus the Jew*, London, 1973, 67–8.

The words of the prayer uttered by Nabunai king of the l[and of Ba]bylon, [the great] king, [when he was afflicted] with an evil ulcer in Teiman by decree of the [Most High God].

I was afflicted [with an evil ulcer] for seven years ... and an exorcist pardoned my sins. He was a Jew from [among the children of the exile of Judah, and he said], 'Recount this in writing to [glorify and exalt] the name of the [Most High God'. And I wrote this]:

'I was afflicted with an [evil] ulcer in Teiman [by decree of the Most High God]. For seven years [I] prayed to the gods of silver and gold, [bronze and iron], wood and stone and clay, because [I believed] that they were gods ... '

# Para-Danielic Writings
## (4Q243–5)

In addition to the Prayer of Nabonidus, Cave 4 has revealed further Aramaic remains of a composition akin to the biblical Book of Daniel, with three explicit mentions of the name Daniel, who appears to be the narrator of the story. Another personality, Balakros, figures in 4Q243. J. T. Milik tentatively identified him with the Seleucid ruler Alexander Balas, the patron of Jonathan Maccabaeus. With one exception, the fragments are too small for meaningful translation.

For a preliminary study, see J. T. Milik, 'Prière de Nabonide et autres écrits d'un cycle de Daniel', *RB* 63 (1956), 411–15; cf. F. García Martínez, *Qumran and Apocalyptic: Studies on the Aramaic Texts from Qumran* (Leiden, 1992), 137–49.

### 4Q243, fr. 3 combined with 4Q244

... The children of Israel chose themselves rather than [God and they sacri]ficed their sons to the demons of idolatry. God was enraged against them and determined to surrender them to Nebu[chadnezzar, king of Ba]bel and to devastate their land ...

# The Four Kingdoms

## (4Q552–3)

Partly overlapping remains of two manuscripts of an Aramaic work further testify to the existence of a rich para-Danielic literature. These poorly preserved documents allude to the story of the four empires (Dan. vii–viii) in the form of a metaphor of four trees.

For a preliminary edition, see K. Beyer, *Die aramäischen Texte vom Toten Meer. Ergänzungsband* (Göttingen, 1994), 108–9.

### 4Q552

... [I saw an angel] **II** standing on whom light (shone) and four trees [stood by] him. And the trees rose and moved away from him. And he said to [me: Do you see] this shape? And I said: Yes. I see it and consider it. And I saw the tree ... placed.

And I asked it: What is your name? And it said to me: Babel. And I said to it: Are you the one who rules over Persia? And I saw another tree ... and I asked it: What is your name? [And it said to me: ... And I said to it: Are you the one w[ho rules over a]ll the powers of the sea and over the ports [and over] ... ? [And I saw] the third tree [and] I said to [it: What is your name and why] is your appearance ...
**III** ... God Most High ...

# An Aramaic Apocalypse

## (4Q**246**)

Surnamed the 'Son of God fragment' since J. T. Milik's 1972 lecture at Harvard University, reported by J. A. Fitzmyer ('The Contribution of Qumran Aramaic to the Study of the New Testament', *NTS* 20 (1973–4), 391–4), 4Q**246**, with its intriguing phrases 'son of God' and 'son of the Most High', recalling Luke i, 32, 35, has been in the centre of learned and popular speculation for the last twenty years. Four competing interpretations of the 'son of God' figure were proposed before the photograph of the document reached the public. Milik advanced a historical theory, associating the title with the Seleucid ruler, Alexander Balas. Fitzmyer, in turn, considered him to be a Jewish, possibly Hasmonaean, king, but allowed for a 'messianic undertone' in the use of 'son of God'. On the other hand, David Flusser opted for a strictly apocalyptic meaning, and claimed that the idioms referred to the Antichrist. Still apocalyptically, but in a positive sense, F. García Martínez argued in favour of an angelic identity, the 'son of God' being either the heavenly Melchizedek or Michael, the Prince of Light. E. Puech in a recent essay has decided to sit on the fence and recognize in the holder of the titles in question either the future Davidic Messiah or a historical Seleucid pretender.

The overall message of the fragment recalls the apocalyptic section of the Book of Daniel. A Daniel-like person, referred to in column 1, is to explain to a king seated on a throne a vision or dream alluding to wars involving Assyria and Egypt, and the arrival of a final ruler, served by all, and called by them, or designating himself, 'son of God'. But the triumph of peace is not attributed to him – his reign is rather characterized by internecine struggle between nations and provinces – but to the Great God, helping 'the people of God' (cf. Dan. vii, 22, 29), whose dominion over mankind is declared eternal (cf. Dan. vii, 14) and free from the sword.

Relying mainly on the evidence of the existing text, rather than on hypothetical reconstructions of missing passages, I see in the 'son of God' of 4Q**246** neither Flusser's Antichrist, nor the straight historical individual of the Milik–Puech variety, but the last historico-apocalyptic sovereign of the ultimate world empire who, like his model, Antiochus Epiphanes in Dan. xi, 36–7, is expected to proclaim himself and be worshipped as a god.

For preliminary publications, see J. A. Fitzmyer, *A Wandering Aramean*, Missoula, 1979, 90–94; D. Flusser, *Judaism and the Origins of Christianity*, Montana, 1988, 207–13; F. García Martínez, *Qumran and Apocalyptic*, Leiden, 1992, 162–79; E. Puech, 'Fragment d'une apocalypse en araméen (4Q246=pseudo-Dan$^{d}$) et le "royaume de Dieu"', *RB* 99 (1992), 98–131; G. Vermes, 'Qumran Forum Miscellanea I', *JJS* 43 (1992), 301–3.

**I** ... [the spirit of God] dwelt on him, he fell down before the throne ... O [K]ing, you are angry for ever and your years ... your vision and all. For ever you ... [the gre]at ones. An oppression will come to the earth ... a great massacre in the provinces ... the king of Assyria [and E]gypt ... he will be great on earth ... will make and all will serve ... he will be called (or: call himself) [gran]d ... and by his name he will be designated (or: designate himself). **II** The son of God he will be proclaimed (or: proclaim himself) and the son of the Most High they will call him. Like the sparks of the vision, so will be their kingdom. They will reign for years on the earth and they will trample all. People will trample people (cf. Dan. vii, 23) and one province another province *vacat* until the people of God will arise and all will rest from the sword. Their (the people of God's) kingdom will be an eternal kingdom (cf. Dan. vii, 27) and all their path will be in truth. They will jud[ge] the earth in truth and all will make peace. The sword will cease from the earth, and all the provinces will pay homage to them. The Great God (cf. Dan. ii, 45) is their helper. He will wage war for them. He will give peoples into their hands and all of them (the peoples) He will cast before them (the people of God). Their dominion will be an eternal dominion (Dan. vii, 14) and all the boundaries of ...

# Proto-Esther (?)

## (4Q550)

A number of badly damaged fragments of an Aramaic writing report events said to have occurred in the Persian court, thus recalling the biblical story of Esther. The script is dated to the second half of the first century BCE. J. T. Milik, in a very learned, but equally conjectural, manner, has reconstructed the background of the narrative, even restoring the name of Esther from an incomplete word beginning with the letters *aleph* and *samekh*. He has thus discovered an Aramaic *model* of Esther at Qumran, although no remains of the canonical Book of Esther have so far been found there. K. Beyer entitles the writing as Documents of Darius and classifies it as a legendary account relating to Darius I and Xerxes, kings of Persia, who apparently worshipped the God of the Jews.

For a preliminary edition, see J. T. Milik, 'Les modèles araméens du livre d'Esther dans la grotte 4 de Qumrân', *RQ* 15 (1992), 321–406; K. Beyer, *Die aramäischen Texte vom Toten Meer. Ergänzungsband* (Göttingen, 1994), 113–17.

### 4QProto-Esther[a]

... [and they li]sten to Patireza, your father ... and amid the officials of the royal apparel ... to work in the service of the king in accordance with all that you have received ... In that hour the king could not go to sleep (literally, his spirit was stretched) [and he commanded that the b]ooks of his father be read before him. And among the books there was a scroll [the mou]th, of which [was] s[ealed] with seven seals by the signet-ring of his father Darius the heading of which ... [Dar]ius the king to the officials of the kingdom, Peace. It was opened and read and in it was found: Darius the King [to the kings who will reign after me and to the officials of the kingdom, Pe[ac]e. It should be known to you that every tormentor and liar ...

## Proto-Esther[d]

**III** The Most High whom you (Jews) fear and worship rules o[ver the whole e]arth. Everyone whom He wishes (comes) near. Bagasro ... Whoever speaks an evil word against Bagasro [will be] put to death for there is no -o[ne to destroy h]is good for [e]ver. ...

# H. Miscellanea

A cut segment from *The Copper Scroll*

# The Copper Scroll
## (3Q15)

The Copper Scroll (3Q15), which has stimulated much curiosity and speculation, was found by archaeologists in Cave 3 during the excavations of 1952, but the metal had become so badly oxidized during the course of the centuries that the scroll could not be unfolded. It was therefore sent to Professor H. Wright Baker of the Manchester College of Science and Technology who, in 1956, carefully divided it into longitudinal strips and, in the same year, returned it to Jordan. The Hebrew text, representing twelve columns of script, was published by J. T. Milik in *DJD*, III, 199–302. It was preceded by a less trustworthy edition by J. M. Allegro, *The Treasure of the Copper Scroll*, London, 1960.

The inscription lists sixty-four hiding-places, in Jerusalem and in various districts of Palestine, where gold, silver, Temple offerings, scrolls, etc., are said to have been deposited. Allegro reckons that the treasure must have amounted to over three thousand talents of silver, nearly one thousand three hundred talents of gold, sixty-five bars of gold, six hundred and eight pitchers containing silver, and six hundred and nineteen gold and silver vessels. In other words, using the post-biblical value of the talent as a yard-stick, the total weight of precious metal must have added up to sixty-five tons of silver and twenty-six tons of gold.

Who could have possessed such a fortune? Was there ever any truth in it?

J. T. Milik thinks not. He believes that the exaggerated sums indicate that the scroll is a work of fiction and that its chief interest to scholars lies in the fields of linguistics and topography. He dates it from about 100 CE, thus ruling out any connection with the rest of the Qumran writings since the latter were placed in the caves not later than 68 CE.

The treasure was a real one according to other scholars, representing the fortune of the Essenes (A. Dupont-Sommer, S. Goranson) or the Temple treasure (J. M. Allegro, N. Golb). According to Allegro, the Zealots were responsible for the concealment of the gold and silver and for the writing of the scroll. It has also been suggested that we are dealing here with funds collected for the rebuilding of the Temple after 70 CE, or with the hidden treasure of Bar Kokhba, leader of the second Jewish revolution against Rome in 132–5 CE.

Milik's argument would certainly seem to account for the vast quantities of treasure mentioned. It does not, however, explain two of the document's most striking characteristics, namely, the dry realism of its style, very different from that of ancient legends, and the fact that it is recorded on copper instead of on the less expensive leather or papyrus. For if it is, in fact, a sort of fairy-story, the present text can only represent the outline of such a tale, and who in their senses would have engraved their literary notes on valuable metal?

The contention that the treasure was a real one is supported by the very arguments which undermine Milik's. From the business-like approach, and the enduring material on which the catalogue is inscribed, it might sensibly be supposed that the writer was not indulging some frivolous dream. Again, in view of the fact that the Copper Scroll was found among writings known to come from Qumran, Dupont-Sommer and Goranson would appear justified in allocating the fortune to the Essenes. It requires, by comparison, a strong feat of the imagination to accept that all this wealth belonged originally to the treasure chambers of the Temple, and that it was placed in hiding, in a hostile environment, in 68 CE, before, that is to say, there was any immediate danger to the capital city of Jerusalem. Allegro bypassed this objection by presuming that, as Qumran was by then in the hands of the Zealots, it was no longer unfriendly to the Jerusalem authorities. But it has not yet been explained why the sack of the Temple and city should have been foreseen, and provided for, so early. In favour of the Temple treasure hypothesis, it is nevertheless possible to envisage that the Jerusalem sanctuary possessed such riches as these, whereas, despite Dupont-Sommer's undoubtedly true remarks concerning the apparent compatibility of religious poverty and fat revenues, it is still hard to accept that the Essenes, a relatively small community, should have amassed such disproportionate wealth.

This is all that can safely be said of the Copper Scroll at the present time. Study of the original, housed in Amman in Jordan, will allow scholars to improve many of the readings. Meanwhile we are all considerably in J. T. Milik's debt for his pioneering decipherment of an extremely difficult text. See also A. Wolters, 'The Copper Scroll and the Vocabulary of Mishnaic Hebrew', *RQ* 14 (1989–90), 483–95.

Further works to consult: A. Dupont-Sommer, *The Essene Writings from Qumran*, Oxford, 1961, 379–93; N. Golb, 'The Problem of Origin and Identification of the Dead Sea Scrolls', *Proceedings of the American Philosophical Society* 124 (1980), 1–24; A. Wolters, 'Literary Analysis of the Copper Scroll', in Z. J. Kapera, ed., *Intertestamental Essays in Honour of J. T. Milik*, Cracow, 1992,

239–54; S. Goranson, 'Sectarianism, Geography and the Copper Scroll', *JJS* 43 (1992), 282–7.

## Col. I

1. A Horebbah which is in the Vale of Achor under the stairs which go eastwards forty cubits: a box (filled with) silver weighing in all seventeen talents. **KEN**.
2. In the tomb of . . . the third: 100 gold bars.
3. In the great cistern which is in the courtyard of the little colonnade, at its very bottom, closed with sediment towards the upper opening: nine hundred talents.
4. At the hill of Kohlit, containers, sandalwood and ephods (priestly garments). The total of the offering and of the treasure: seven (talents?) and second tithe rendered unclean. At the exit of the canal on the northern side, six cubits towards the cavity of immersion. **XAΓ**
5. In the hole of the waterproofed refuge, in going down towards the left, three cubits above the bottom: forty talents of silver.

## Col. II

6. In the cistern of the esplanade which is under the stairs; forty-two talents. **HN**
7. In the cave of the old Washer's House, on the third platform: sixty-five gold bars. **ΘE**
8. In the underground cavity which is in the courtyard of the House of Logs, where there is a cistern: vessels and silver, seventy talents.
9. In the cistern which is against the eastern gate, which is fifteen cubits away, there are vessels in it.
10. And in the canal which (ends) in it: ten talents. **ΔI**
11. In the cistern which is under the wall on the eastern side, at the sharp edge of the rock: six silver bars; its entrance is under the large paving-stone.
12. In the pond which is east of Kohlit, at a northern angle, dig four cubits: twenty-two talents.

## Col. III

13. In the courty[ard of] . . . in southerly direction [at] nine cubits: silver and gold vessels of offering, bowls, cups, tubes, libation vessels. In all, six hundred and nine.
14. In the other, easterly direction dig sixteen cubits: 40 tal. of silver. **TP**

15. In the underground cavity of the esplanade on its northern side: vessels of offering, garments. Its entrance is in the westerly direction.

16. In the tomb on the north-east of the esplanade three cubits under the trap(?): 13 tal.

**Col. IV**

17. In the great cistern which is in the ..., in the pillar on its northern side: 14 tal[ents]. ◦**K**

18. In the canal which goes [towards ... ] when you enter for[ty-o]ne cubits: 55 tal. of silver.

19. Between the two tamarisk trees in the Vale of Akhon, in their midst dig three cubits. There there are two pots full of silver.

20. In the red underground cavity at the mouth of the 'Aslah: 200 tal. of silver.

21. In the eastern underground cavity at the north of Kokhlit: 70 tal. of silver.

22. In the heap of stones of the valley of Sekhakha dig (...) cubits: 12 tal. of silver.

**Col. V**

23. At the head of the water conduit ... [at] Sekhakha, on the northern side under the large ... dig [thr]ee cub[its]: 7 tal. of silver.

24. In the split which is in Sekhakha in the east of the reservoir of Solomon; vessels of offering.

25. Quite close to them above the canal of Solomon sixty cubits towards the great stone dig three cubits: 23 tal. of silver.

26. In the tomb which is in the wady of Kippah (going) from Jericho to Sekhakha, at its entry from Jericho to Sekhakha, dig seven cubits: 32 tal.

**Col. VI**

27. [In] the eastward-looking cave of the Pillar with two entrances, dig at the northern entrance three [c]ubits; there is a pitcher there, in it a book, under it 22 tal.

28. In the eastward-looking cave of the base of the Stone dig nine cubits at the entrance: 21 tal.

29. In the Dwelling of the Queen on the western side dig twelve cubits: 27 tal.

30. In the heap of stones which is at the Ford of the High Priest

## Col. VII

dig nine [cubits]: 22 ... tal.

31. In the water conduit of Q ... [the grea]ter northern reservoir, in the four direc[tions] measure out twenty-[fo]ur cubits: four hundred talents.
32. In the nearby cave in the proximity of Bet ha-Qos dig six cubits: six silver bars.
33. At Doq under the eastern corner of the guard-post dig seven cubits: 22 tal.
34. At the mouth of the water exit of Koziba dig three cubits towards the rock: 60 tal., two talents of gold.

## Col. VIII

35. [In the wa]ter conduit on the road east of Bet Ahsor, which is east of Ahzor, vessels of offering and books and a bar of sil[ver].
36. In the outside valley ... at the stone dig seventeen cubits underneath: 17 tal. of gold and silver.
37. In the heap of stones at the mouth of the Pottery ravine dig three cubits: 4 tal.
38. In the westward-looking stubble-field of ha–Sho, on the south side, at the underground chamber looking northwards dig twenty-four cubits: 66 tal.
39. In the irrigation of ha-Sho, at the stone sign in it, dig eleven cubits: 70 tal. of silver.

## Col. IX

40. At the 'dovecot' (small opening?) at the exit of ha-Notef, measure out from its exit thirteen cubits, two tusks and, on seven smooth stones, bars (corresponding to) four staters.
41. At 'Violet-scarlet' over (past?) the eastward-looking underground chamber dig eight cubits ... (?): $23\frac{1}{2}$.
42. In the underground chambers of Horon, in the seaward-looking underground chamber in the narrow part (?) dig sixteen cubits: 22 tal.
43. At Qob'ah a large amount of money offerings (?).
44. At the 'sound of waters' (waterfall) close to the edge of the gutter on the east side of the exit dig seven cubits: 9 tal.
45. In the underground cavity on the north side of the mouth of the gorge of Bet Tamar in the parched land of ... (?), all that is in it is *herem* (= devoted to the Temple).

46. At the 'dovecot' which is at Mesad, at the [water] conduit,

**Col. X**

southward at the second stair descending from the top: 9 tal.

47. In the cistern next to the canals fed by the Great Wady, at the bottom; 12 tal.

48. At the reservoir which is in Bet Kerem going to the left of ten notches: sixty-two talents of silver.

49. At the pond of the valley of 'YK (?) on its western side is a ma'ah coin coupled with two ma'ahs. This is the entrance: three hundred talents of gold and twenty pitched vessels.

50. Under the 'Hand' (= Monument) of Absalom on the western side dig twelve notches: 80 tal.

51. At the pond of the privy of Siloa under the watering-trough: 17 tal.

52. [At ... ] in the four

**Col. XI**

angles: gold and vessels of offering.

53. Next to them under the corner of the southern portico at the tomb of Zadok under the pillar of the covered hall: vessels of offering of resin and offering of senna.

54. Next to them at the ... (?) at the top of the westward-looking rock towards the garden of Zadok under the great closing stone which is at the conduit: devoted things.

55. In the tomb which is under the galleries (?): 40 tal.

56. In the tomb of the Sons of ... (?) the Yerahite, in it: vessels of offering of cedar, offering of resin.

57. Next to them, at Bet-Eshdatain (Bethesda), in the reservoir where you enter the small pool: vessels of offering of aloes, offering of ... (?)

58. Next to them, at the western entrance of the tomb is a channel over ... nine hundred [tal. of silver]

**Col. XII**

5 tal. of gold.

59. Sixty talents at its entrance from the west under the black stone.

60. Near to them under the threshold of the sepulchral chamber: 42 tal.

61. On Mount Gerizim under the stairs of the higher underground cavity a box and its contents and 60 tal. of silver.

62. At the mouth of the spring of Bet-Sham vessels of silver and vessels of gold of offering and silver. In all, six hundred talents.
63. In the great underground duct of the sepulchral chamber towards the house of the sepulchral chamber. The whole weighing 71 talents and twenty minas.
64. In the underground cavity which is in the smooth rock north of Kohlit whose opening is towards the north with tombs at its mouth there is a copy of this writing and its explanation and the measurements and the details of each item.

# List of False Prophets

## (4Q339)

This is a brief list of false prophets, recorded in Aramaic and palaeographically Herodian in date. The first six names come from the Bible. The last two lines are completed by the editor as '[Hananiah son of Az]ur' (Jer. xxviii, 1) and '[a prophet from Gib]eon', interpreted as the continuation of the description of Hananiah (see ibid.). One may object to this reconstruction that all the previous names occupy a single line. The name of Yohanan ben Shim'on, i.e. John Hyrcanus I, son of Simon Maccabaeus, has been suggested by A. Rofe and E. Qimron. Hyrcanus I was thought to have been endowed with prophetic gifts (cf. Josephus, *Jewish War* I, 68–9; *Antiquities* XIII, 300), but the anti-Hasmonaean Qumran sect would have condemned him as a false prophet. This identification is distinctly possible, but owing to the fragmentary state of the line the reading is purely conjectural.

For the *editio princeps* of 4Q**339** see M. Broshi and A. Yardeni, *DJD*, XIX, 77–9.

The lying prophets who arose in [Israel: Balaam [son] of Beor (Num. xxii–xxiv); [the] elder from Bethel (1 Kgs xiii, 11–31); [Zed]ekiah son of Ke[n]aanah (1 Kgs xxii, 11); [Aha]b son of K[o]liah (Jer. xxix, 21); [Zed]ekiah son of Ma[a]seiah (ibid.); [Shemaiah the Ne]hlemite (Jer. xxix, 24); . . . ur; . . . 'on.

# List of *Netinim*

## (4Q340)

A badly mutilated fragment, dated to the first half of the first century BCE, lists the Temple servants or *netinim* referred to in the biblical Books of 1 Chronicles, Ezra and Nehemiah. The text is too broken to make good reading, but it proves that such lists were in circulation in late Second Temple times.

For the *editio princeps*, see M. Broshi and A. Yardeni, *DJD*, XIX, 81–4.

These are the *netin*[*im*] who have been identified by [their] na[mes]: Ithra and ... To[biah].

# Entry into the Covenant

## (4Q275)

Previously called 4QTohorot B[a], this tiny fragment represents a document describing the entry into the Covenant, known from the Community Rule (1QS), and alludes to a festival in the third month, i.e. the Feast of Weeks of Pentecost, when according to one of the Cave 4 manuscripts of the Damascus Document (4Q**266**) the Qumran Covenant renewal took place.

For a preliminary edition see *UDSS*, III, 83.

[And the Guardian will come] and the elders with him until ... and they will be introduced into the genealogy ... And the Guardian will [curse (the unrepentant), saying 'Be damned without] mercy. [Let him be cur]sed ...' And he will remove him] from his inheritance for ev[er] ...

# Four Classes of the Community

## (4Q279)

Formerly known as 4QTohorot D[a], this small scrap has partly preserved the division of the Community into four lots or classes, already known from CD XIV, 5–6, viz. Priests, Levites, Israelites and Proselytes.

For a preliminary edition, see *USDD*, III, 89.

... [The first] lot belongs [to the Pries]ts, the sons of Aaron [and the second lot to the Levites ranked in order] each according to his spirit. And the [third] lo[t will belong to the children of Israel in order each according to his spirit. And] the fourth lot will belong to the Prosely[tes] ...

# The Two Ways

## (4Q473)

Inspired by Deuteronomy xi, 26–28, this fragmentary text is akin to the Instruction on the Two Spirits in the Community Rule (1QS III, 13–IV, 25).

For a preliminary edition, see *UDSS*, III, 361.

... and He has placed [before you] t[wo] ways one which is goo[d and one which is evil. If you choose the good way], He will bless you. But if you walk in the [evil] way, [He will curse you] ... and in your [te]nts, and He will destroy you with ... and mildew, snow, ice and hai[l] ... with all.

# Hymnic Fragment

## (4Q255 recto)

The verso side of this papyrus contains the beginning of the Community Rule (4QS[a]). The recto carries a poem similar to the Qumran Hymns or Hodayot, and elaborating the familiar image of the Community as a plant in God's garden.

For a preliminary edition, see *UDSS*, III, 369.

... For the Master ...
a plant of delight, a plant in His garden and in His vineyard.
Its branches will bear fruit and will increase ...
and its branches which are supporting the high heavens.
And ... its splendour for everlasting generations.
And in order to produce frui[t ...] for all who taste it.
Among its fruits none will be bad.
It will have foliage and leaves and blossoms.
Its roots will not be pulled up from its pleasant bed.
For ...

# Two Qumran Ostraca

The inclusion of these documents has been made possible by the kindness of Professor F. M. Cross and Esther Eshel who have generously put at my disposal the following note in advance of their publication of the two inscribed potsherds:

In the spring of 1996 two Hebrew ostraca were found by Professor James F. Strange of the University of South Florida. The ostraca were discovered in the base of the eastern face of the wall separating the community centre from the cemetery. The script is dated to the first century CE.

**Ostracon no. 1**

1. In year two of the [
2. in Jericho, Honi son of [ ] gave
3. to 'El'azar son of Nahmani [ ]
4. Hisday from Holon [ ]
5. from this day to perpetui[ty]
6. the boundaries of the house and [ ]
7. and the fig trees, the ol[ive tree (?), and ]
8. when he fulfilled (his oath) to the Community [
9. and Honi [ ]
10. to him His[day (?) ]
11. and the [ ]
12. And into the hand of [ ]
13. Hisday servant of H[oni (?) ]
15. Holon

The text documents a gift of a slave, together with an estate and produce. Reference is made to fulfilling an oath, or a period of time as a neophyte, to the *Yahad* in line 8, using the term KML(')WTW LYHD 'when he fulfilled (his oath) to the Community'. This terminology resembles that of the Community Rule

(1QS VI), and as such may hint that this ostracon is a draft of an accounting (*heshbon*) of the Overseer.[1]

## Ostracon no. 2

A second ostracon, written by a different hand of the same period, reads:

1. (?)
2. (?)
3. Jose]ph son of Nathna[
4. his [s]ons from ‘En Gedi(?)

1. Line 8 may also be understood as alluding to the completion of a year of initiation in the Community at the end of which the novice had to hand over his property to the Bursar of the sect according to Community Rule (1QS VI, 18–20): ‘And if it be his destiny, according to the judgement of the Priests and the multitude of the men of their Covenant, to enter the company of the Community, his property and earnings shall be handed over to the Bursar of the Congregation who shall register it to his account and shall not spend it for the Congregation.’ ’El‘azar son of Nahmani, mentioned in line 2, may have been the Bursar (or the Overseer/Guardian) of the Community in the first century CE. [GV]

# I. Appendix

# *Scroll Catalogue*

Perhaps the greatest disservice rendered to scholarship by Roland de Vaux and his successors resulted from their obstinate refusal to release the list of the unpublished texts from Caves 4 and 11. 'Outsiders' were not only denied access to them but were not even allowed to know what exactly they were not permitted to see! We had to wait until the spring of 1992 for Emanuel Tov, editor-in-chief of the Dead Sea Scrolls Publication Project since 1990, to correct this injustice by releasing the long-awaited 'secrets' and publishing them, at my invitation, in the *Journal of Jewish Studies*.[1] Here follows a complete inventory of the manuscripts and fragments discovered in the eleven Qumran caves together with source references for all the published texts.[2] For a fuller list, see S. A. Reed et al. (eds.), *The Dead Sea Scrolls Catalogue: Documents, Photographs and Museum Inventory Numbers* (Scholars Press, Atlanta, 1994) and E. Tov with S. A. Pfann (eds.), *Companion Volume to the Dead Sea Scrolls Microfiche Edition* (Brill, Leiden, 1995).

NB. A list of the abbreviations used appears on pp. 91–2.

1. 'The Unpublished Qumran Texts from Caves 4 and 11', *JJS* 43 (1992), 101–36. For a slightly updated version, see *Biblical Archaeologist*, June 1992, 94–104, under the same title.
2. The siglum *DJD* designates the series *Discoveries in the Judaean Desert* published by Clarendon Press, Oxford. The following volumes have appeared so far.

I. D. Barthélemy and J. T. Milik, *Qumran Cave I* (1955).
II. P. Benoit, J. T. Milik and R. de Vaux, *Les grottes de Murabba'at* (1961).
III. M. Baillet, J. T. Milik and R. de Vaux, *Les petites grottes de Qumrân* (1962).
IV. J. A. Sanders, *The Psalm Scroll of Qumran Cave 11* (1965).
V. J. M. Allegro and A. A. Anderson, *Qumran Cave 4, I (4Q158–4Q186)* (1968).
VI. R. de Vaux and J. T. Milik, *Qumrân Grotte 4, II:I. Archéologie. II. Tefillin, Mezuzot et Targum (4Q128–4Q157)* (1977).
VII. M. Baillet, *Qumrân Grotte 4, III (4Q482–4Q520)* (1982).
VIII. E. Tov, *The Greek Minor Prophets from Nahal Hever* (1990).
IX. P. W. Skehan, E. Ulrich and J. E. Sanderson, *Qumran Cave 4, IV: Palaeo-Hebrew*

# CAVE 1

## *Scrolls*

| | |
|---|---|
| **1QIsa[a]** | Complete Isaiah in Millar Burrows et al., *The Dead Sea Scrolls of St Mark's Monastery*, I, New Haven, 1950 |
| **1QIsa[b]** | Incomplete Isaiah in E. L. Sukenik, *The Dead Sea Scrolls of the Hebrew University*, Jerusalem, 1954 (Hebrew), 1955 (English) |
| **1QapGen** | Genesis Apocryphon in N. Avigad and Y. Yadin, *A Genesis Apocryphon*, Jerusalem, 1956 |
| **1QpHab** | Commentary on Habakkuk in Millar Burrows et al., op. cit. |
| **1QS** | Community Rule in Millar Burrows, *The Dead Sea Scrolls of St Mark's Monastery*, II, fasc. 2, New Haven, 1951 |
| **1QH** | Thanksgiving Hymns in E. L. Sukenik, op. cit. |
| **1QM** | War Scroll in E. L. Sukenik, op. cit. |

## *Fragments*

**DJD, I**

**1Q**

| | |
|---|---|
| 1=1QGen | Genesis |
| 2=1QEx | Exodus |
| 3=1QpaleoLev | Leviticus in palaeo-Hebrew script |
| 4–5=1QDeut[a–b] | Deuteronomy |
| 6=1QJudg | Judges |
| 7=1QSam | 1 and 2 Samuel |

*Footnote 2 continued*

*and Greek Biblical Manuscripts* (1992).

X. E. Qimron and J. Strugnell, *Qumran Cave 4, V: Miqsat Ma'ase Ha-Torah* (1994).

XII. Eugene Ulrich, F. M. Cross et al., *Qumran Cave 4, VII: Genesis to Numbers* (1994).

XIII. H. Attridge et al., *Qumran Cave 4, VIII: Parabiblical Texts, Part I* (1994; in fact 1995).

XIV. Eugene Ulrich and F. M. Cross, *Qumran Cave 4, IX: Deuteronomy, Joshua, Judges, Kings* (1996).

XVIII. J. M. Baumgarten, *Qumran Cave IV, XIII* (1996).

XIX. M. Broshi et al., *Qumran Cave 4, XIV: Parabiblical Texts, Part II* (1995).

XXII. G. Brooke et al, *Qumran Cave 4, XVII: Parabiblical Texts, Part III* (1996).

A less up-to-date list, containing, however, a fuller description of the documents and more bibliographical detail, is included in Joseph A. Fitzmyer, *The Dead Sea Scrolls: Major Publications and Tools for Study*, rev. edn, Atlanta, 1990. For the latest, see F. García Martínez and D. W. Parry, *A Bibliography of the Finds in the Desert of Judah 1970–95* (Leiden, 1996).

| | |
|---|---|
| **8**=1QIsa$^{b}$ | Frs. belonging to the incomplete Isaiah Scroll |
| **9**=1QEzek | Ezekiel |
| **10–12**=1QPs$^{a-c}$ | Psalms |
| **13**=1Qphyl | Phylactery |
| **14**=1QpMic | Commentary on Micah |
| **15**=1QpZeph | Commentary on Zephaniah |
| **16**=1QpPs | Commentary on Psalms |
| **17–18**=1QJub$^{a-b}$ | Jubilees |
| **19–19bis**=1QNoah | Book of Noah |
| **20**=1QapGen | Genesis Apocryphon |
| **21**=1QTLevi ar | Aramaic Testament of Levi |
| **22**=1QDM | *Divre Mosheh* (Sayings of Moses) |
| **23–4**=1QEnGiants | Book of Giants (Enoch) |
| **25** | Apocryphal prophecy |
| **26** | Wisdom text |
| **27**=1QMyst | Book of mysteries |
| **28a**=1QSa | Rule of the Congregation (Annex to Community Rule) |
| **28b**=1QSb | Benedictions (Annex to Community Rule) |
| **29** | Liturgical text |
| **30–31** | Liturgical texts |
| **32**=1QJNar | Aramaic New Jerusalem |
| **33**=1QMfrs | War Scroll |
| **34–34bis**=1QLitPr$^{a-b}$ | Liturgical prayers |
| **35**=1QHfrs | Thanksgiving Hymns (1QH) |
| **36–40** | Hymns |
| **41–62** | Unidentified Hebrew fragments |
| **63–8** | Unidentified Aramaic fragments |
| **69** | Unidentified Hebrew fragments |
| **70–70bis** | Unidentified papyrus fragments |
| **71–2**=1QDan$^{a-b}$ | Daniel |

## CAVE 2

### *DJD*, III

### 2Q

| | |
|---|---|
| **1**=2QGen | Genesis |
| **2–4**=2QEx$^{a-c}$ | Exodus |
| **5**=2QpaleoLev | Leviticus in palaeo-Hebrew script |
| **6–9**=2QNum$^{a-d}$ | Numbers |
| **10–12**=2QDeut$^{a-c}$ | Deuteronomy |
| **13**=2QJer | Jeremiah |

| | |
|---|---|
| **14**=2QPs | Psalms |
| **15**=2QJob | Job |
| **16–17**=2QRuth$^{a-b}$ | Ruth |
| **18**=2QSir | Ben Sira |
| **19–20**=2QJub$^{a-b}$ | Jubilees |
| **21**=2QapMoses | Moses Apocryphon |
| **22**=2QapDavid | David Apocryphon |
| **23**=2QapProph | Apocryphal prophecy |
| **24**=2QJNar | Aramaic text on the New Jerusalem |
| **25** | Legal document |
| **26**=2QEnGiants | Book of Giants (Enoch) |
| **27–33** | Unidentified small fragments |

## CAVE 3

### *DJD*, III

### 3Q

| | |
|---|---|
| **1**=3QEzek | Ezekiel |
| **2**=3QPs | Psalms |
| **3**=3QLam | Lamentations |
| **4**=3QpIsa | Commentary on Isaiah |
| **5**=3QJub | Jubilees |
| **6**=3QHym | Hymn |
| **7**=3QTJud? | Testament of Judah? |
| **8** | A text mentioning the Angel of Peace |
| **9** | Sectarian text? |
| **10–11** | Small unidentified Hebrew fragments |
| **12–13** | Small unidentified Aramaic fragments |
| **14** | Unidentified fragments |
| **15**=3QTreasure | Copper Scroll |

## CAVE 4

### *DJD*, XII

| | |
|---|---|
| **1**=Gen–Ex$^{a}$ | Genesis–Exodus |
| **2–8**=Gen$^{b-h1}$ | Genesis |
| **8$^{a}$**–Gen$^{h2}$ | Genesis |
| **8$^{b}$**=Gen$^{h}$para | Parabiblical Genesis |
| **8$^{c}$**=Gen$^{h}$tag | Title tag of Genesis |
| **9–10**=Gen$^{j-k}$ | Genesis |

| | | |
|---|---|---|
| **12**=paleoGen$^{m}$ | Genesis | |
| **13–21**=Ex$^{b–k}$ | Exodus | |
| **23**=Lev–Num$^{a}$ | Leviticus–Numbers | |
| **24–6**=Lev$^{b–d}$ | Leviticus | |
| **27**=Num$^{b}$ | Numbers | |

## 4Q

| | | |
|---|---|---|
| **28**=Deut$^{a}$ | Deuteronomy | White[3] |
| **29**=Deut$^{b}$ | ditto | Duncan[4] |
| **30–31**=Deut$^{c–d}$ | ditto | White (op. cit.) |
| **32**=Deut$^{e}$ | ditto | Duncan (op. cit.) |
| **33–4**=Deut$^{f–g}$ | ditto | White (op. cit.) |
| **35**=Deut$^{h}$ | ditto | Duncan (op. cit.) |
| **36**=Deut$^{i}$ | ditto | White (op. cit.) |
| **37–40**=Deut$^{j–m}$ | ditto | Duncan (op. cit.) |
| **41**=Deut$^{n}$ | ditto | White (op. cit.) |
| **42–3**=Deut$^{o–p}$ | ditto | Duncan (op. cit.) |
| **44**=Deut$^{q}$ | ditto | Skehan[5] |
| **47**=Josh$^{a}$ | Joshua | |
| **48**=Josh$^{b}$ | ditto | Tov[6] |
| **49–50**=Judg$^{a–b}$ | Judges | Trebolle[7] |
| **51–2**=Sam$^{a–b}$ | Samuel | |
| **53**=Sam$^{c}$ | ditto | |
| **54**=Kgs | Kings | Trebolle[8] |
| **55**=Isa$^{a}$ | Isaiah | Muilenburg[9] |
| **56–69**$^{b}$=Isa$^{b–r}$ | ditto | |
| **70**=Jer$^{a}$ | Jeremiah | Janzen, Tov[10] |
| **71–71**$^{a–b}$=Jer$^{b,d–e}$ | ditto | Tov[11] |
| **72**=Jer$^{b}$ | ditto | Tov[12] |

**3**. S. A. White, 'A Critical Edition of Seven Manuscripts of Deuteronomy' (Harvard diss., 1988).
**4**. Duncan, 'A Critical Edition of Deuteronomy Manuscripts from Qumran Cave IV' (Harvard diss., 1989).
**5**. P. W. Skehan, *BASOR* 136 (1954), 12–15.
**6**. E. Tov, 4QJosh$^{b}$, Milik Festschrift 1992, 205–12.
**7**. J. Trebolle Barrera, *RQ* 14 (1989–90), 229–45.
**8**. J. Trebolle Barrera, 'A Preliminary Edition of 4QKings', in J. Trebolle Barrera and L. Vegas Montaner, *The Madrid Qumran Congress* [*MQC*], I, Leiden, 1992, 229–46.
**9**. J. Muilenburg, *BASOR* 135 (1954), 28–32.
**10**. J. G. Janzen, *Studies in the Text of Jeremiah* (1973); E. Tov, *RQ* 14 (1989–90), 189–206.
**11**. E. Tov, *RQ* 15 (1991–2), 531–41.
**12**. E. Tov, '4QJer$^{c}$(4Q72)', in G. Norton and S. Pisano, *Tradition of the Text*, Göttingen, 1991, 248–76.

| | | |
|---|---|---|
| **73–4**=Ezek$^{a-b}$ | Ezekiel | Lust[13] |
| **75**=Ezek$^{c}$ | ditto | |
| **76–81**=XII$^{a-f}$ | Minor prophets | Fuller[14] |
| **82**=XII$^{g}$ | ditto | |
| **83**=Ps$^{a}$ | Psalms | |
| **84**=Ps$^{b}$ | ditto | Skehan[15] |
| **85–7**=Ps$^{c-e}$ | ditto | |
| **88**=Ps$^{f}$ | ditto | Starcky[16] |
| **89–97**=Ps$^{g-p}$ | ditto | |
| **98**=Ps$^{q}$ | ditto | Milik[17] |
| **98a**=Ps$^{r}$ | ditto | |
| **98b**=Ps$^{s}$ | ditto | Skehan[18] |
| **98c–d**=Psfr 1–2 | ditto | |
| **99–100**=Job$^{a-b}$ | Job | |
| **102–3**=Prov$^{a-b}$ | Proverbs | |
| **104–5**=Ruth$^{a-b}$ | Ruth | |
| **106–8**=Cant$^{a-c}$ | Song of Songs | |
| **109**=Qoh$^{a}$ | Ecclesiastes | Muilenburg[19] |
| **110**=Qoh$^{b}$ | ditto | |
| **111**=Lam | Lamentations | Cross[20] |
| **112**=Dan$^{a}$ | Daniel | Ulrich[21] |
| **113–4**=Dan$^{b-c}$ | ditto | Ulrich[22] |
| **115–6**=Dan$^{d-e}$ | ditto | |
| **117**=Ezra | | |
| **118**=Chr | Chronicles | Trebolle[23] |

**13**. J. Lust, *Ezekiel and His Book*, Leuven, 1986, 90–100.
**14**. R. E. Fuller, 'The Minor Prophets Manuscripts from Qumran, Cave IV' (Harvard diss., 1988).
**15**. P. W. Skehan, *CBQ* 26 (1964), 313–22.
**16**. J. Starcky, *RB* 73 (1966), 353–71.
**17**. J. T. Milik, *Biblica* 38 (1957), 245–68.
**18**. P. W. Skehan, in Cazelles Festschrift 1981, 439–52.
**19**. J. Muilenburg, *BASOR* 135 (1954), 20–28.
**20**. F. M. Cross, in Freedman Festschrift 1983, 129–55.
**21**. E. Ulrich, *BASOR* 268 (1987), 17–37.
**22**. E. Ulrich, *BASOR* 274 (1989), 3–26.
**23**. J. Trebolle Barrera, *RQ* 15 (1991–2), 523–9.

## *DJD*, IX

### 4Q

| | |
|---|---|
| **11**=paleoGen–Ex$^{l}$ | Genesis–Exodus |
| **22**=paleoEx$^{m}$ | Exodus |
| **45–6**=paleoDeut$^{r-s}$ | Deuteronomy |
| **101**=paleoJob$^{c}$ | Job |
| **119**=LXXLev$^{a}$ | Greek Leviticus |
| **120**=papLXXLev$^{b}$ | ditto |
| **121**=LXXNum | Greek Numbers |
| **122**=LXXDeut | Greek Deuteronomy |
| **123**=paleoParaJosh | Parabiblical Joshua frs. |
| **124–5**=paleoUnid1–2 | Unidentified frs. |
| **126**=Unid gr | Unidentified Greek frs. |
| **127**=papPara Ex gr | Greek parabibl. Exodus frs. |

## *DJD*, IV

### 4Q

| | |
|---|---|
| **128–48**=phyl$^{a-u}$ | Phylacteries |
| **149–55**=Mez$^{a-g}$ | Mezuzot |
| **156**=tgLev | Targum of Leviticus |
| **157**=tgJob | Targum of Job |

## *DJD*, V

### 4Q

| | |
|---|---|
| **158**=BibPar | Biblical paraphrases |
| **159**=Ord$^{a}$ | Ordinances |
| **160**=VisSam | Vision of Samuel |
| **161–5**=pIsa$^{a-e}$ | Commentaries on Isaiah |
| **166–7**=pHos$^{a-b}$ | Commentaries on Hosea |
| **168**=pMic | Commentary on Micah |
| **169**=pNah | Commentary on Nahum |
| **170**=pZeph | Commentary on Zephaniah |
| **171**=pPs$^{a}$ | Commentary on Psalms |
| **172**=pUnid | Commentary on unidentified texts |
| **173**=pPs$^{b}$ | Commentary on Psalms |
| **174**=Flor | Florilegium |
| **175**=Testim | Testimonia |

| | |
|---|---|
| **176**=Tanh | Tanhumim[24] |
| **177**=Cat$^{a}$ | Catena A |
| **178** | Unnamed |
| **179**=apLam$^{a}$ | Apocryphal lamentations |
| **180**=AgesCreat | Ages of the creation |
| **181** | Unnamed |
| **182**=Cat$^{b}$ | Catena B |
| **183** | Unnamed |
| **184**=Wiles | Wiles of the wicked woman |
| **185** | Unnamed |
| **186**=Cryptic | Cryptic texts[25] |

## 4Q

| | | |
|---|---|---|
| **196–9**=Tob ar$^{a-d}$ | Tobit in Aramaic | *DJD*, XIX, 1–62 |
| **200**=Tob heb | Tobit in Hebrew | Ditto, 63–76 |
| **201–2**=En$^{a-b}$ | Enoch | Milik[26] |
| **203**=EnGiants$^{a}$ | ditto (Giants) | ibid. |
| **204–7**=En$^{c-f}$ | ditto | ibid. |
| **208–11**=Enastr$^{a-d}$ | Astrological Enoch | ibid. |
| **212**=En$^{g}$+Letter | Enoch and his Letter | ibid. |
| **213**=TLevi ar$^{a}$ | Aram. Test. of Levi | Stone–Greenfield[27] |
| **214**=TLevi ar$^{b}$ | ditto | |
| **215**=TNaph | Test. of Naphtali | Stone[28] |
| **216**=Jub$^{a}$ | Jubilees | *DJD*, XIII, 1–22 |
| **217–18**=Jub$^{b-c}$ | ditto 23–38 | |
| **219**=Jub$^{d}$ | ditto 38–53 | |
| **220**=Jub$^{e}$ | ditto 55–61 | |
| **221**=Jub$^{f}$ | ditto 63–85 | |
| **222**=Jub$^{g}$ | ditto 87–94 | |
| **223–4**=papJub$^{h}$ | ditto 95–140 | |
| **225–7**=psJub$^{a-c}$ | ditto 141–75 | |
| **228**=citofJub | ditto 177–85 | |
| **229**=pseudep | Pseudepigraphic work in Mishnaic Hebrew | |
| **230–31**=CatSpir$^{a-b}$ | Catalogue of Spirits | |

**24**. Frs. 19–21 have been identified as belonging to Jubilees by M. Kister, *RQ* 12 (1985–7), 529–36.

**25**. The numbers **187–95** are vacant.

**26**. J. T. Milik, *The Books of Enoch*, Oxford, 1976.

**27**. *JBL* 112 (1993), 247–66.

**28**. M. E. Stone, *JJS* 47 (1996), 311–21.

| | | |
|---|---|---|
| **232**=JNhebr | New Jerusalem in Hebrew | |
| **233**=Toponyms | Frs. with place-names | |
| **234**=Gen27:20f | Scribal exercise | |
| **235**=frs of Kings | Book of Kings | |
| **236**=Psalm 89 | Psalm 89 | |
| **237**=Psalter | Psalter | |
| **238**=Hab3&songs | Habakkuk 3 and Songs | |
| **239**=Pesh | Pesharim on the true Israel | |
| **240**=CommCant? | Commentary on the Song of Songs? | |
| **241**=Lamcit | Frs. citing Lamentations | |
| **242**=prNab | Prayer of Nabonidus | Milik[29] |
| **243–5**=psDan ar$^{a-c}$ | Pseudo-Daniel in Aramaic | ibid. |
| **246**=arApocal | Aramaic apocalypse | Puech[30] |
| **247**=ApocWeeks | Apocalypse of Weeks | Milik[31] |
| **248**=ActsGrKing | Acts of a Greek King | Wacholder–Abegg[32] |
| **249**=papMSM cryp A | Midrash Sefer Mosheh A | |
| **250**=versoMSM | Text written on verso of **249** | |
| **251**=legComm | Legal commentary on Torah | Baumgarten[33] |
| **252–4**=pGen$^{a-c}$ | Commentary on Genesis | Brooke[34] |
| **255–64**S$^{a-j}$ | Serekh$^{a-j}$ | E. Qimron[35] |
| **265**=SD | Serekh-Damascus | Baumgarten[36] |
| **266–73**=D$^{a-h}$ | Damascus$^{a-h}$ | *DJD*, XVIII |
| **274**=TohA | Tohorot A | Baumgarten[37] |
| **275**=TohB$^{a}$ | Tohorot B$^{a}$ | Milik[38] |
| **276–9**=TohB$^{b-c}$–C–D$^{a}$ | Tohorot B$^{b-c}$–C?–D$^{a}$? | Eisenman[39] |
| **280**=TohD$^{b}$? | Tohorot D$^{b}$? | ibid. |
| **281–3**=TohE$^{a-b}$?–F | ditto | |
| **284**=Nidd | Serekh ha-Niddot | |

**29.** J. T. Milik, *RB* 63 (1956), 407–15.
**30.** E. Puech, *RB* 99 (1992), 98–138.
**31.** J. T. Milik, *The Books of Enoch*, 256.
**32.** B. Z. Wacholder–M. G. Abegg, *UDSS* III, xvi, 33.
**33.** J. M. Baumgarten, *JJS* 27 (1976), 36–46.
**34.** G. J. Brooke, *JQR* 85 (1994), 33–59; *JSS* 40 (1995), 227–39.
**35.** J. H. Charlesworth, *DSS* 1, 53–103.
**36.** J. M. Baumgarten, *JJS* 43 (1992), 268–76.
**37.** J. M. Baumgarten, *JQR* 85 (1994), 91–101.
**38.** J. T. Milik, *JJS* 23 (1972), 130–31.
**39.** *DSSU*, 211 (only 276–7).

| | | |
|---|---|---|
| **284a**=Leq | Leqet | Baumgarten[40] |
| **285**=SMilh | Serekh ha-Milhamah | Vermes[41] |
| **286–90**=Ber$^{a-e}$ | Berakhot | Nitzan[42] |
| **291–3**=Prayers | Work containing prayers | |
| **294–7**=Rules | Rules and Euchologies? | |
| **298**=Words of Sage | Words of a Sage to sons of Dawn | Pfann[43] |
| **299–300**=Myst$^{a-b}$ | Mysteries A–B | Schiffman[44] |
| **301**=Myst$^{c}$ | Mysteries C | |
| **302**=papPraise | Praise of God | |
| **302a**=Parable | Parable of the Tree | |
| **303–5**=CreatA$^{a-b}$B | Meditation on Creation A–B | |
| **306**=Wisd | Frs. concerning people who err | |
| **307–8**=Sap | Sapiential frs. | |
| **309**=Arwork | Aramaic work in cursive script | |
| **310**=Arpap | Aramaic work on papyrus | |
| **311**=Hebrpap | Hebrew text on papyrus | |
| **312**=Hebr | Hebrew text in Phoenician cursive | |
| **313**=Crypfr | Cryptic text A | |
| **314–15**=parcels | Four parcels of uninscribed leather | |
| **316**=Hebrfr | Frs. in Hebrew | |
| **317**=Moon crypt | Frs. on the phases of the Moon (cryptic) | Milik[45] |
| **318**=Zod & Bront | Zodiology and Brontology | Greenfield–Sokoloff[46] |
| **319**=Otot | Otot | Glessmer[47] |
| **320–30**=Cal | Calendar | Wacholder–Abegg, Talmon[48] |

**40**. J. M. Baumgarten, *JQR* 85 (1994), 91–101.

**41**. G. Vermes, *JJS* 43 (1992), 85–90.

**42**. Nitzan, in G. J. Brooke, ed., *New Qumran Texts and Studies* (1995), 53–71.

**43**. S. Pfann, *JQR* 85 (1994), 203–35.

**44**. L. H. Schiffman, *RQ* 16 (1993), 203–23; in Z. Zevit et al., eds., *Solving Riddles* ..., 207–60.

**45**. J. T. Milik, *Enoch*, 68–9.

**46**. J. C. Greenfield–M. Sokoloff, *RQ* 16 (1995), 507–25.

**47**. U. Glessmer, *Schriften des Institutum Judaicum Delietzschianum* III (1995), 125–64.

**48**. *UDSS*, 60–101; S. Talmon, in Z. Zevit, 327–44.

| | | |
|---|---|---|
| **331**=papHist[a] | Historical work on papyrus A | |
| **332–3**=Hist[b–c] | ditto B–C | |
| **334**=Ordo | Ordo | |
| **335**–6=Astr? | Astronomical works | |
| **337**=frCal | Calendar | |
| **338**=Geneal | Genealogical list | |
| **339**=FalseProphs | List of False Prophets | *DJD*, XIX, 77–9 |
| **340**=Netin | List of Netinim | ditto, 81–4 |
| **341**=Names | List of proper names | Naveh[49] |
| **342**=Letterar | Letter in Judaeo-Aramaic[50] | |
| **343**=Letternab | Letter in Nabataean | |
| **344**=Debt | Acknowledgement of debt | |
| **345–6**=Salear | Sale of land in Aramaic | |
| **347**=papDocar | Aramaic deed on papyrus | |
| **348**=Deedhebr | Ownership document in Hebrew | |
| **349**=Salehebr | Hebrew sale of property | |
| **350**-Cereal gr | Account of cereal in Greek | |
| **351–4**=Cereal | Accounts of cereal | |
| **355–8**=Money | Accounts of money | |
| **359**=List | List of persons | |
| **360**=Exercise | Scribal exercise | |
| **361**=papDoodles | Doodles on papyrus | |
| **362–3**=CryptB | Undeciphered Cryptic B | |
| **364–5**=ReworkPent[b–e] | Reworked Pentateuch | *DJD*, XIII, 187–318 |
| **365a**=4QTemple? | Reworked Pentateuch | ditto 319–33 |
| **366–7**=ReworkPent[d–e] | Prayer of Enosh | ditto 335–51 |
| **368**=PentAp | Pentateuch Apocryphon | |
| **369**=PrEnosh | | *DJD*, XIII, 353–62 |
| **370**=FloodAp | Flood Apocryphon | *DJD*, XIX, 85–97 |
| **371**=JosAp[a] | Joseph Apocryphon[a] | |
| **372**=JosAp[b] | ditto[b] | Schuller[51] |
| **373**=JosAp[c] | ditto[c] | Schuller[52] |
| **374**=MosApA | Moses Apocryphon A | *DJD*, XIX, 111–19 |
| **375–6**=MosApA–B | Moses Apocryphon B | *DJD*, XIX, 121–36 |
| **377**=MosApC | Moses Apocryphon C | |

49. J. Naveh, *IEJ* 36 (1986), 52–5.
50. Nos. 342–61 probably belong to other (non-Qumran) caves from the Judaean Desert. They have been mistakenly catalogued with 4Q.
51. E. M. Schuller, *RQ* 14 (1989–90), 349–76.
52. E. M. Schuller, in *MQC*, II, 515–30.

| | | |
|---|---|---|
| **378–9**=PsJosh[a–b] | Psalms of Joshua[a–b] | Newsom[53] |
| **380–81**=ApPs | Apocryphal Psalms | Schuller[54] |
| **382**=papparaKings | Para-Kings | *DJD*, XIII 363–416 |
| **383**=apJerA | Apocryphal Jeremiah A? | |
| **384**=papapJerB | ditto B? on papyrus | |
| **385**=psEzek[a] | Pseudo-Ezekiel[a] | Strugnell–Dimant[55] |
| **385a**=psMos[a] | Pseudo-Moses[a] | |
| **385b**=apJer[c] | Apocryphal Jeremiah[c] | Dimant[56] |
| **386–7**=psEzek[b–c] | Pseudo-Ezekiel[b–c] | |
| **387a**=psMos[b] | Pseudo-Moses[b] | |
| **387b**=apJer[d] | Apocryphal Jeremiah[d] | |
| **388**=psEzek[d] | Pseudo-Ezekiel[d] | |
| **388a–9**=psMos[c–d] | Pseudo-Moses[c–d] | |
| **389a**=apJer[e] | Apocryphal Jeremiah[e] | |
| **390**=psMos[e] | Pseudo-Moses[e] | Dimant[57] |
| **391**=pappsEzek[e] | | *DJD*, XIX, 153–93 |
| **392–3**=Lit | Liturgical works | Falk[58] |
| **394–9**=MMT[a–f] | | *DJD*, X |
| **400–407**=Shir Shab[a–h] | Songs of Sabbath Sacrifice[a–h] | Newsom[59] |
| **408**=Wisd | Sapiential work | Steudel[60] |
| **409**=Lit | Liturgy | Qimron[61] |
| **410–13**=Wisd | Sapiential work | |
| **414**=Bapt | Baptismal liturgy | Eisenman[62] |
| **415**=WisdB[a–b] | Sapiential work B[a–b] | |
| **416–18**=WisdA[a–c] | ditto A[a–c] | Eisenman[63] |
| **419**=WisdA[d] | ditto A[d] | |
| **420–1**=Right[a–b] | Ways of Righteousness[a–b] | |
| **422**=ParaphGen&Ex | Commentary on Genesis and Exodus | *DJD*, XIII, 417–41 |
| **423**=Farmer | Rule for the Farmer | |

**53**. C. Newsom in H.-J. Fabry et al., *Qumranstudien* (1996), 35–85.
**54**. E. M. Schuller, *Non-Canonical Psalms from Qumran* (1986); in Dimant and Rappaport, *The DSS* (1992), 90–99.
**55**. J. Strugnell and D. Dimant, *RQ* 13 (1988), 45–58.
**56**. D. Dimant, in G. J. Brooke, ed., *New Qumran Texts and Studies* (1995), 11–30.
**57**. D. Dimant in *MQC* II, 405–47.
**58**. D. Falk, *JJS* 45 (1994), 184–207.
**59**. C. Newsom, *Songs of the Sabbath Sacrifice*, Atlanta, 1985.
**60**. A. Steudel, *RQ* 16 (1994), 313–34.
**61**. E. Qimron, *JQR* 80 (1990), 341–7.
**62**. *DSSU*, 226–8.
**63**. *DSSU*, 244–9 (**416** and **418** only).

| | | |
|---|---|---|
| **423a**=WisdE | Sapiential work E | |
| **424**=Wisd | Sapiential work | Eisenman[64] |
| **425**=WisdC | Sapiential work C | |
| **426**=Wisd | Sapiential work | |
| **427–32**=Hod[a–f] | Thanksgiving hymns[a–f] | |
| **433**=Hod-like | Hodayot-like fr. | |
| **434–8**=Barki[a–e] | Barki nafshi[a–e] | Eisenman[65] |
| **439**=Barki-like | Work similar to Barki nafshi | |
| **440**=Hod-like | Work similar to Hodayot | |
| **441–4**=Pr | Prayers | |
| **445–7**=Poet frs | Poetic fragments | |
| **448**=apPs & Jon | Apocryphal Psalm & King Jonathan | Eshel–Yardeni[66] |
| **449–56**=Prs | Prayers | |
| **457**=Narrs | Narratives | |
| **458**=Narr | Narrative | Eisenman[67] |
| **459–60**=Pseudep | Pseudepigraphic work | |
| **461–3**=Narr | Narrative | *DJD*, XIX, 195–214 |
| **464**=Apoc[b] | Apocryphon[b] | |
| **465**=unid | Unidentified text | |
| **466–9**=Apoc? | Apocryphon | |
| **470**=Zedkfr | Fr. mentioning Zedekiah | *DJD*, XIX, 235–44 |
| **471**=M[g] | War[g] | Eshel[68] |
| **471a**=Polem. fr | Polemical fr. | Eshel–Kister[69] |
| **471b**=PrMich | Prayer of Michael | |
| **472**=Wisd | Sapiential work | |
| **473**=2 ways | Sapiential work: Two Ways | |
| **474–6**=Wisd | Sapiential work | |
| **477**=Sect decr | Decrees of the sect | Eshel[70] |
| **478**=papTob? | Tobit? fr. on papyrus | |
| **479–81**=Unid frs | Unidentified frs. | |
| **481a**=Elisha fr | Fr. mentioning Elisha | Trebolle[71] |

64. *DSSU*, 166–7.
65. *DSSU*, 238–9 (**434** and **436** only).
66. E. and H. Eshel and A. Yardeni, *IEJ* 42 (1992), 199–229.
67. *DSSU*, 48.
68. E. and H. Eshel, in *MQC*, II, 611–20.
69. E. Eshel and M. Kister, *JJS* 43 (1992), 277–81.
70. Eshel, *JJS* 45 (1994), 111–22.
71. J. Trebolle, *Suppl. VT* LXI, *Congress Volume Paris 1992*, 330–34.

| | | |
|---|---|---|
| **481b–e**=Unid frs | Unidentified frs. | |
| **481f**=Misc | Miscellaneous frs. | |

## *DJD*, VII

## 4Q

| | | |
|---|---|---|
| **482–3**=papJub? | Jubilees? on papyrus | |
| **484**=TJudah? | Testament of Judah? | |
| **485**=Proph | Prophetic or sapiential text | |
| **486–7**=Sap$^{a-b}$ | Sapiential work$^{a-b}$ | |
| **488**=Apar | Aramaic apocryphon | |
| **489**=papApocar | Aramaic apocalypse | |
| **490** | Related frs.? | |
| **491–7**=M$^{a-g}$ | War$^{a-g}$ | |
| **498**=HymSap | Hymns or sapiential work | |
| **499**=papHymPr | Fragments of hymns and prayers | |
| **500**=papBen | Benediction | |
| **501**=Lam$^{b}$ | Lamentation$^{b}$ | |
| **502**=papRitMar | Marriage ritual | |
| **503**=papPrQuot | Daily prayers | |
| **504–6**=DivHam$^{a-c}$ | Words of the Heavenly Lights$^{a-c}$ | |
| **507–9**=PrFest$^{a-c}$ | Prayers for Festivals$^{a-c}$ | |
| **510–11**=Shir$^{a-b}$ | Canticle of the Sage$^{a-b}$ | |
| **512**=papRitPur | Ritual of Purification | |
| **513–14**=Ord$^{b-c}$ | Ordinances$^{b-c}$ | |
| **515–20**=pap | Undeciphered papyrus fragments | |
| **521**=MessApoc | Messianic Apocalypse | Puech[72] |
| **522**=Toponyms | Work with place-names | Puech[73] |
| **523**=HebrB | Hebrew fragment B | |
| **524**=Halakh | Halakhic text | |
| **525**=Beat | Sapiential text with beatitudes | Puech[74] |
| **526–8**=HebrC–E | Hebrew fragments C–E | |
| **529**=Mich | Words of Michael | Eisenman[75] |

**72**. E. Puech, *RQ* 15 (1991–2), 479–522.
**73**. E. Puech, *RQ* 9 (1977–8), 547–54.
**74**. E. Puech, *RQ* 13 (1988), 59–88.
**75**. *DSSU*, 38.

| | | |
|---|---|---|
| **530–31**=Giants$^{b–c}$ | Book of Giants (Enoch)$^{b–c}$ | Milik[76] |
| **532**=Giants$^{e}$ | ditto$^{e}$ | Eisenman[77] |
| **533**=psEn | Book of Giants or Pseudo-Enoch | |
| **534**=Elect | Elect of God | Starcky[78] |
| **535–6**=ArNC | Aramaic texts N and C | Eisenman[79] |
| **537**=AJa | Aramaic Jacob | Puech[80] |
| **538**=AJu | Aramaic Judah | Milik[81] |
| **539**=AJo | Aramaic Joseph | Milik[82] |
| **540–41**=TLevi$^{c–d}$? | Testament of Levi?$^{c–d}$ | Puech[83] |
| **542**=TQahat | Testament of Qahat | Puech[84] |
| **543–8**=Amram$^{a–f}$ | Visions of Amram$^{a–f}$ | Milik[85] |
| **549**=HurMir | Work mentioning Hur and Miriam | |
| **550**=PrEsth | Proto-Esther$^{a–e+f}$ | Milik[86] |
| **551**=DanSus? | Susannah episode in Daniel? | Milik[87] |
| **552–3**=4Kg$^{a–b}$ | Four Kingdoms$^{a–b}$ | Beyer[88] |
| **554–5**=JN$^{a}$ | New Jerusalem$^{a}$ | Eisenman[89] |
| **556–7**=Vis$^{a–c}$ | Visions$^{a–c}$ | |
| **559**=papChronol | Biblical chronology | Eisenman[90] |
| **560**=Provs | Proverbs? | ibid.[91] |
| **561**=Physiogn | Physiognomic horoscope | ibid.[92] |
| **562–75**=ArD–Z | Aramaic fragments | D–Z |

**76**. J. T. Milik, *The Books of Enoch*, 304–8.
**77**. *DSSU*, 95.
**78**. J. Starcky, in *Mémorial du Cinquantenaire 1914–1964 de l'École des Langues Orientales Anciennes de l'Institut Catholique de Paris*, Paris, 1964, 51–66.
**79**. *DSSU*, 35–6.
**80**. E. Puech, in *MQC*, II, 449–501.
**81**. J. T. Milik, in M. Delcor, *Qumran*, 1978, 91–106.
**82**. ibid.
**83**. E. Puech, cf. n. 95.
**84**. E. Puech, *RQ* 15 (1991–2), 23–54.
**85**. J. T. Milik, *RB* 79 (1972), 77–97.
**86**. J. T. Milik, *RQ* 15 (1991–2), 321–406.
**87**. J. T. Milik, Cazelles Festschrift, Paris, 1981, 337–59.
**88**. K. Beyer, *Ergänzungsband*, 108–9.
**89**. *DSSU*, 41–3.
**90**. ibid., 92–3.
**91**. ibid., 266.
**92**. ibid., 264.

## CAVE 5

### *DJD*, III

### 5Q

| | |
|---|---|
| **1**=Deut | Deuteronomy |
| **2**=Kgs | Kings |
| **3**=Isa | Isaiah |
| **4**=Am | Amos |
| **5**=Ps | Psalms |
| **6–7**=Lam[a–b] | Lamentations[a–b] |
| **8**=Phyl | Phylactery |
| **9**=Toponyms | Place-names |
| **10**=apMal | Apocryphal Malachi |
| **11**=S | Serekh |
| **12**=D | Damascus |
| **13**=S-like | Fragment similar to S |
| **14**=Curses | Liturgical curses |
| **15**=JNar | Aramaic New Jerusalem |
| **16–25**=Unid | Small unidentified and unclassified fragments |

## CAVE 6

### *DJD*, III

### 6Q

| | |
|---|---|
| **1**=paleoGen | Genesis in palaeo-Hebrew |
| **2**=paleoLev | Leviticus ditto |
| **3**=Deut | Deuteronomy |
| **4**=Kgs | Kings |
| **5**=Ps | Psalms |
| **6**=Cant | Song of Songs |
| **7**=papDan | Daniel on papyrus |
| **8**=papEnGiants | Book of Giants (Enoch) |
| **9**=papSam/Kgs | Samuel–Kings apocryphon on papyrus |
| **10**=apProph | Apocryphal prophecy |
| **11**=Vine | Allegory of the Vine |
| **12**=apProph | Apocryphal prophecy |
| **13**=PriestProph | Priestly prophecy |
| **14**=Apoc ar | Aramaic Apocalypse |
| **15**=D | Damascus |

| | |
|---|---|
| **16**=papBen | Benedictions on papyrus |
| **17**=Cal | Calendar |
| **18**=papHym | Hymns on papyrus |
| **19**=Gen?ar | Aramaic text related to Genesis? |
| **20**=Deut? | Deuteronomy? |
| **21**=frProph | Prophetic fragment |
| **22**=Unid hebr | Unidentified Hebrew text |
| **23**=Unidar | Unidentified Aramaic texts |
| **24–31**=misc | Diverse fragments |

## CAVE 7

### *DJD*, III

### 7Q

| | |
|---|---|
| **1**=papLXXEx | Greek Exodus |
| **2**=papLXXEpJer | Greek Epistle of Jeremiah |
| **3–5**=papGrBibfrs? | Unidentified Greek biblical fragments?[93] |
| **6–18**=papUnid | Unidentified tiny fragments[94] |
| **19**=Grimpr | Imprints of Greek papyrus on plaster |

## CAVE 8

### *DJD*, III

### 8Q

| | |
|---|---|
| **1**=Gen | Genesis |
| **2**=Ps | Psalms |
| **3**=Phyl | Phylactery |
| **4**=Mez | Mezuzah |
| **5**=Hym | Liturgical poem |

**93**. Cf. pp. 440–41 above.
**94**. ibid.

## CAVE 9

### *DJD*, III

**9Q1** Papyrus fragment

## CAVE 10

### *DJD*, III

**10Q1** Ostracon

## CAVE 11

### 11Q

| | | |
|---|---|---|
| **1**=paleoLev | Leviticus in palaeo-Hebrew | Freedman[95] |
| **2**=Lev | Leviticus | Ploeg[96] |
| **3**=Deut | Deuteronomy | ibid.[97] |
| **4**=Ezek | Ezekiel | Brownlee[98] |
| **5**=Ps[a] | Psalms[a] | Sanders[99] |
| **6**=Ps[b] | ditto[b] | Ploeg[100] |
| **7**=Ps[c] | ditto[c] | Ploeg[101] |
| **8–9**=Ps[d–e] | ditto | |
| **10**=tgJob | Targum of Job | Ploeg[102] |
| **11**=apPsa | Apocryphal Psalms | Ploeg[103] |
| **12**=Jub | Jubilees | Woude[104] |

**95**. D. N. Freedman and K. A. Matthews, *The Paleo-Hebrew Leviticus Scroll*, Winona Lake, 1985.
**96**. J. van der Ploeg, *RQ* 12 (1985), 3–15.
**97**. ibid.
**98**. W. H. Brownlee, *RQ* 4 (1963), 11–28.
**99**. J. A. Sanders, *DJD*, IV.
**100**. J. van der Ploeg, *RB* 74 (1967), 408–12.
**101**. J. van der Ploeg, in M. Beek, *Symbolae biblicae et Mesopotamicae* (1973), 307–9.
**102**. J. van der Ploeg and A. S. van der Woude, *Le Targum de Job de la grotte XI de Qumran*, Leiden, 1971.
**103**. J. van der Ploeg, in K. G. Kuhn Festschrift, Göttingen, 1971.
**104**. ibid., 128–46.

| | | |
|---|---|---|
| **13**=Melch | Melchizedek | Woude[105]Puech[106] |
| **14**=Ber | Berakhah | Woude[107] |
| **15–16**=Hym$^{a–b}$ | Hymns$^{a–b}$ | Ploeg[108] |
| **17**=ShirShab | Songs of the Sabbath Sacrifice | Newsom[109] |
| **18**=JN | New Jerusalem | Jongeling[110] |
| **19**=Temple$^{a}$ | Temple Scroll | Yadin[111] |
| **20**=Temple$^{b}$ | Temple Scroll fragments | Yadin[112] |
| **21**=paleoUnid | Unidentified fragments | |
| **22–3**=Unid | ditto | |

## GENERAL OBSERVATIONS

If my calculation, including all the subdivisions of items, is correct, the total number of documents discovered in the eleven caves amounts to 813.[113] The Qumran manuscripts include twelve scrolls: eleven of leather and one of copper. They are all published. Of the 801 (or 783) texts surviving in fragments, 401 have appeared in the various volumes of *DJD*, which means that 400 (or 382) still await 'official' publication. Compared with the pre-1991 situation, the editorial process has been considerably speeded up. Contrary to the fears of some members of the original editorial team, the 'liberation' of the Scrolls has turned out to be a blessing both for the experts and for the interested public at large.

**105**. A. S. van der Woude, *Oudtest. Studien* 14 (1965), 354–73.
**106**. E. Puech, *RQ* 12 (1985–7), 483–513.
**107**. A. S. van der Woude, in H. Bardtke Festschrift (1968), 253–8.
**108**. A. S. van der Woude, in H. Bardtke Festschrift (1968), 253–8.
**109**. C. A. Newsom, *Songs of the Sabbath Sacrifice*, Atlanta, 1985.
**110**. B. Jongeling, *JSJ*, I (1970), 58–64.
**111**. Y. Yadin, *The Temple Scroll* I–III (1983); E. Qimron, *The Temple Scroll: A Critical Edition with Extensive Reconstructions* (1996).
**112**. ibid.; A. S. van der Woude, *RQ* 13 (1988), 89–92; F. García Martínez, in *MQC*, II, 363–91.
**113**. From this sum one may have to deduct 20 if 4Q**342** to **361** are definitely established as unconnected to the Qumran finds.

# *Index of Qumran Texts*

Figures in bold indicate the classification of fragments; other figures are page numbers.

# *Major Editions of Qumran Manuscripts*

## *Microfiche Edition*

E. Tov, ed., *The Dead Sea Scrolls on Microfiche*, Leiden, 1992; *A Companion Volume to the Dead Sea Scrolls Microfiche Edition*, Leiden, 1995.[1]

## *Photographic Edition*

Robert H. Eisenman and James M. Robinson, eds., *A Facsimile Edition of the Dead Sea Scrolls*, I–II, Washington, 1991.

## *Computer Reconstructed Edition*

B. Z. Wacholder and M. G. Abegg, *A Preliminary Edition of the Unpublished Dead Sea Scrolls* I–III, Washington, 1991–5.

## *Cave 1*

M. Burrows, J. C. Trever and W. H. Brownlee, *The Dead Sea Scrolls of St Mark's Monastery*, I, New Haven, 1950 (contains Isaiah[a], Habakkuk Commentary); II/2, New Haven, 1951 (Manual of Discipline = 1QS). There is no II/1.

E. L. Sukenik, *The Dead Sea Scrolls of the Hebrew University*, Jerusalem, 1954–5 (contains Isaiah[b], War Rule, Thanksgiving Hymns).

D. Barthélemy and J. T. Milik, *Discoveries in the Judaean Desert, I: Qumran Cave 1*, Oxford, 1955 (contains all the fragments from 1Q).

N. Avigad and Y. Yadin, *A Genesis Apocryphon*, Jerusalem, 1956.

## *Caves 2–3 and 5–10*

M. Baillet, J. T. Milik and R. de Vaux, *Discoveries in the Judaean Desert of Jordan, III: Les petites grottes de Qumrân*, Oxford, 1963 (contains fragments and the Copper Scroll).

1. The Electronic Publishing division of the Oxford University Press is in the process of producing a CD ROM edition of all the Qumran manuscripts and fragments.

## *Cave 4*

J. M. Allegro and A. A. Anderson, *Discoveries in the Judaean Desert of Jordan, V: I (4Q158–4Q186)*, Oxford, 1968 (contains mostly exegetical fragments). For editorial improvements, see J. Strugnell, 'Notes en marge du volume V des *Discoveries in the Judaean Desert of Jordan*', *RQ* 7 (1970), 163–276.

J. T. Milik, *The Books of Enoch: Aramaic Fragments of Qumran Cave 4*, Oxford, 1976.

R. de Vaux and J. T. Milik, *Discoveries in the Judaean Desert, VI: Qumrân Grotte 4, II: I. Archéologie. II. Tefillin, Mezuzot et Targum (4Q128–4Q157)*, Oxford, 1977.

M. Baillet, *Discoveries in the Judaean Desert, VII: Qumrân Grotte 4, III (4Q482–4Q520)*, Oxford, 1982 (contains fragments of the War Rule and remains of liturgical and sapiential compositions).

Carol Newsom, *Songs of the Sabbath Sacrifice: A Critical Edition*, Atlanta, 1985.

Judith E. Sanderson, *An Exodus Scroll from Qumran: 4QpaleoExod*$^{m}$ *and the Samaritan Tradition*, Atlanta 1986.

Eileen M. Schuller, *Non-Canonical Psalms from Qumran: A Pseudepigraphic Collection*, Atlanta, 1986.

P. W. Skehan, E. Ulrich and Judith E. Sanderson, *Discoveries in the Judaean Desert, IX: Qumran Cave 4, IV, Palaeo-Hebrew and Greek Biblical Manuscripts*, Oxford, 1992.

R. H. Eisenman and M. Wise, *The Dead Sea Scrolls Uncovered*, Shaftesbury/Rockport, Mass., 1992; London, 1993.

X. E. Qimron and J. Strugnell, *Discoveries in the Judaean Desert, X: Qumran Cave 4, V, Miqsat Ma'ase Ha-Torah* (1994).

XII. Eugene Ulrich, F. M. Cross et al., *Discoveries in the Judaean Desert, XII: Qumran Cave 4, VII, Genesis to Numbers* (1994).

XIII. H. Attridge et al., *Discoveries in the Judaean Desert, XIII: Qumran Cave 4, VIII, Parabiblical Texts, Part I* (1994; in fact 1995).

XV. E. Ulrich et al., *Discoveries in the Judaean Desert, XV: Qumran Cave 4, X, The Prophets* (forthcoming).

XVIII. J. M. Baumgarten, *Discoveries in the Judaean Desert, XVIII: Qumran Cave 4, XIII, The Damascus Document (4Q266–4Q273)*, 1996.

XIX. M. Broshi et al., *Discoveries in the Judaean Desert, XIII: Qumran Cave 4, XIV, Parabiblical Texts, Part II* (1995).

XX. B. Nitzan et al., *Discoveries in the Judaean Desert, XX: Qumran Cave 4, XX, Sapiential Texts, Part 1* (forthcoming).

XXII. G. Brooke et al., *Discoveries in the Judaean Desert XXII: Qumran Cave 4, XVII, Parabiblical Texts, Part III* (1996).

## *Cave 11*

J. A. Sanders, *Discoveries in the Judaean Desert of Jordan, IV: The Psalm Scroll of Qumran Cave 11 (11QPsa)*, Oxford, 1965.

J. P. M. van de Ploeg, A. S. van der Woude and B. Jongeling, *Le Targum de Job de la grotte XI de Qumrân*, Leiden, 1971.

Y. Yadin, *Megillat ha-Miqdash* I–III, Jerusalem, 1977 (English edition, *The Temple Scroll* I–III, Jerusalem, 1983).

D. N. Freedman and K. A. Matthews, *The Paleo-Hebrew Leviticus Scroll (11QpaleoLev)*, Winona Lake, 1985.

E. Qimron, *The Temple Scroll: A Critical Edition with Extensive Reconstructions* (Beer-Sheva/Jerusalem, 1996).

XXIII. J. B. Humbert et al., *Discoveries in the Judaean Desert, XXIII: Qumran Cave 11* (forthcoming).

## *Unidentified Cave*

Y. Yadin, *Tefillin from Qumran (XQPhyl 1–4)*, Jerusalem, 1969.

## *Damascus Document*

M. Broshi, *The Damascus Document Reconsidered*, Jerusalem, 1992.

# *General Bibliography*

## 1. *Qumran Bibliographies*

B. Jongeling, *A Classified Bibliography of the Finds in the Desert of Judah: 1958–1969*, Leiden, 1971.

J. A. Fitzmyer, *The Dead Sea Scrolls: Major Publications and Tools for Study*, Missoula, Montana, 1975; 2nd edn, 1977; Atlanta, 1990.

F. García Martínez and D. W. Parry, *A Bibliography of the Finds in the Desert of Judah 1970–1975*, Leiden, 1996.

## 2. *General Studies and Monographs*

M. Burrows, *The Dead Sea Scrolls*, New York, 1955.

T. H. Gaster, *The Dead Sea Scriptures in English Translation*, Garden City, New York, 1956; 3rd edn, 1976.

G. Vermes, *Discovery in the Judean Desert*, New York, 1956.

M. Burrows, *More Light on the Dead Sea Scrolls*, New York, 1958.

F. M. Cross, *The Ancient Library of Qumran and Modern Biblical Studies*, New York, 1958; Grand Rapids, 2nd edn, 1980; 3rd ed Sheffield, 1996.

J. T. Milik, *Ten Years of Discovery in the Wilderness of Judaea*, London, 1959.

A. Dupont-Sommer, *The Essene Writings from Qumran*, Oxford, 1961.

G. Vermes, *The Dead Sea Scrolls in English*, London, 1962; 2nd edn, 1975; 3rd edn, 1987; 4th edn, 1995.

G. R. Driver, *The Judaean Scrolls*, Oxford, 1965.

Edmund Wilson, *The Dead Sea Scrolls 1947–1969*, London, 1969.

R. de Vaux, *The Archaeology of the Dead Sea Scrolls*, London, 1973.

G. Vermes, *The Dead Sea Scrolls: Qumran in Perspective*, London, 1977; Philadelphia, 1981; 2nd edn, London, 1982; 3rd edn, London, 1994.

G. W. E. Nickelsburg, *Jewish Literature Between the Bible and the Mishnah*, Philadelphia and London, 1981.

P. R. Davies, *Qumran*, Guildford, 1982.

B. Z. Wacholder, *The Dawn of Qumran: The Sectarian Torah and the Teacher of Righteousness*, Cincinnati, 1983.

D. Dimant, 'Qumran Sectarian Literature' in M. Stone, ed., *Jewish Writings of the Second Temple Period*, Assen and Philadelphia, 1984.

M. A. Knibb, *The Qumran Community*, Cambridge, 1987.

P. R. Davies, *Behind the Essenes: History and Ideology in the Dead Sea Scrolls*. Atlanta, 1987.

P. R. Callaway, *The History of the Qumran Community*, Sheffield, 1988.

S. Talmon, *The World of Qumran from Within*, Jerusalem/Leiden, 1989.

G. J. Brooke, ed., *Temple Scroll Studies*, Sheffield, 1989.

L. H. Schiffman, ed., *Archaeology and History in the Dead Sea Scrolls*, Sheffield, 1990.

M. O. Wise, *A Critical Study of the Temple Scroll from Qumran Cave 11*, Chicago, 1990.

H. Shanks, ed., *Understanding the Dead Sea Scrolls*, Washington, 1992.

F. García Martínez, *Qumran and Apocalyptic: Studies on the Aramaic Texts from Qumran*, Leiden, 1992.

D. Dimant and U. Rappaport, eds., *The Dead Sea Scrolls: Forty Years of Research*, Leiden, 1992.

J. Trebolle Barrera and L. Vegas Montaner, eds., *The Madrid Qumran Congress 1991*, Vols. I–II, Leiden, 1992.

J. A. Fitzmyer, *Responses to 101 Questions on the Dead Sea Scrolls*, London, 1992.

H. Stegemann, *Die Essener, Qumran, Johannes der Täufer and Jesus*, Freiburg, 1993.

E. Ulrich and J. C. VanderKam, eds., *The Community of the Renewed Covenant*, Notre Dame, 1994.

J. C. VanderKam, *The Dead Sea Scrolls Today*, Grand Rapids/London, 1994.

B. Nitzan, *Qumran Prayer and Religious Poetry*, Leiden, 1994.

A. Steudel, *Der Midrasch zur Eschatologie aus der Qumrangemeinde (4QMidrEschat$^{a,b}$)*, Leiden, 1994.

L. H. Schiffman, *Reclaiming the Dead Sea Scrolls*, Philadelphia, 1994.

F. García Martínez, *The Dead Sea Scrolls Translated: The Qumran Texts in English*, Leiden, 1994.

J.-P. Humbert et al., *Fouilles de Khirbet Qumrân et de Aïn Feshkha* I, *Album de photographies – Répertoire du fonds photographique – Synthèse des notes de chantier du Père Roland de Vaux OP*, Fribourg/Göttingen, 1994.

D. D. Swanson, *The Temple Scroll and the Bible: The Methodology of 11QT*, Leiden, 1995.

G. J. Brooke, ed., *New Qumran Texts and Studies*, Leiden, 1995.

J. Maier, *Die Qumran-Essener: Die Texte vom Toten Meer* I–II, Munich, 1995.

N. Golb, *Who Wrote the Dead Sea Scrolls?* London, 1995.

F. García Martínez and J. Trebolle Barrera, *The People of the Dead Sea Scrolls*, Leiden, 1995.

J. G. Campbell, *The Use of Scripture in the Damascus Document 1–8, 19–20*, Berlin, 1995.

P. R. Davies, *Sects and Scrolls: Essays on Qumran and Related Topics*, Atlanta, 1996.

S. Metso, *The Textual Development of the Qumran Community Rule*, Helsinki, 1996.

H.-J. Fabry et al., *Qumranstudien*, Göttingen, 1996.

J. G. Campbell, *Deciphering the Dead Sea Scrolls*, London, 1996.

D. W. Parry and S. D. Ricks (eds.), *Current Research and Technological Developments on the Dead Sea Scrolls*, Leiden, 1996.

D. J. Harrington, *Wisdom Texts from Qumran*, London/New York, 1996.

M. Wise, M. Abegg and E. Cook, *The Dead Sea Scrolls: A New Translation*, London/San Francisco, 1996.

J. Kampen and M. J. Bernstein (eds.), *Reading 4 QMMT*, Atlanta, 1996.

### *3. Bilingual Edition, Vocalized Hebrew Text and Qumran Hebrew*

J. H. Charlesworth et al., eds., *The Dead Sea Scrolls: 1. Rule of the Community and Related Documents; 2. Damascus Document, War Scroll and Related Documents*, Tübingen/Louisville, 1994–5.

E. Lohse, *Die Texte aus Qumran, Hebräisch und Deutsch*, Munich, 1971.

E. Qimron, *The Hebrew of the Dead Sea Scrolls*, Atlanta, 1986.

### *4. Aramaic Texts and Qumran Aramic*

K. Beyer, *Die aramäischen Texte vom Toten Meer*, Göttingen, 1984; *Ergänzungsband*, 1994.

T. Muraoka, ed., *Studies in Qumran Aramaic, Abr-Nahrain*, Suppl. 3, Leiden, 1992.

### *5. Advanced Introduction*

E. Schürer, G. Vermes, F. Millar and M. Goodman, *The History of the Jewish People in the Age of Jesus Christ*, III, parts 1–2, Edinburgh, 1986.

### *6. The Scrolls and the New Testament*

K. Stendahl, ed., *The Scrolls and the New Testament*, London, 1958.

M. Black, *The Scrolls and Christian Origins*, London, 1961.

J. Murphy-O'Connor, ed., *Paul and Qumran*, London, 1968; New York, 1990.

M. Black, ed., *The Scrolls and Christianity*, London, 1969.

J. H. Charlesworth, ed., *John and Qumran*, London, 1972; New York, 1990.

G. Vermes, *Jesus and the World of Judaism*, London, 1983; Philadelphia, 1984.

R. Eisenman, *Maccabees, Zadokites, Christians and Qumran*, Leiden, 1983.

M. Newton, *The Concept of Purity at Qumran and in the Letters of Paul*, Cambridge, 1985.

N. S. Fujita, *A Crack in the Jar: What Ancient Jewish Documents Tell Us about the New Testament*, New York, 1986.

R. Eisenman, *James the Just in the Habbakuk Pesher*, Leiden, 1986.

J. H. Charlesworth, ed., *Jesus and the Dead Sea Scrolls*, New York/London, 1992.

# *General Index*